# Foundations of Perception

# Foundations of Perception

**George Mather**
*University of Sussex, UK*

Psychology Press
Taylor & Francis Group

HOVE AND NEW YORK

First published 2006
by Psychology Press Ltd
27 Church Road, Hove, East Sussex, BN3 2FA

Simultaneously published in the USA and Canada
by Taylor & Francis Inc.
270 Madison Ave, New York, NY 10016

http://www.psypress.co.uk

*Psychology Press is part of the Taylor & Francis Group*

*British Library Cataloguing in Publication Data*
A catalogue record for this book is available from the British Library

*Library of Congress Cataloging-in-Publication Data*
Mather, George.
    Foundations of perception / George Mather. – 1st ed.
       p. cm.
    Includes bibliographical references and index.
    ISBN 0-86377-834-8 (hardback) – ISBN 0-86377-835-6 (pbk.)
    1. Perception. I. Title.
    BF311.M4255 2005
    152.1–dc22                                                    2004024506

ISBN: 0-86377-834-8 (hbk)
ISBN: 0-86377-835-6 (pbk)
ISBN13: 9-78-0-86377-834-8 (hbk)
ISBN13: 9-78-0-86377-835-6 (pbk)

Cover design by Sandra Heath
Typeset by Newgen Imaging Systems (P) Ltd, Chennai, India
Printed and bound in the UK by Ashford Colour Press Ltd, Gosport, Hampshire

# CONTENTS

# PREFACE

My primary aim in writing this book has been to provide a coherent, up-to-date introduction to the basic facts and theories concerning human sensory perception. A full appreciation of perception requires some understanding of relevant physical stimuli and a basic grasp of sensory physiology. Therefore, the physical and physiological aspects of each sensory modality are considered before its perceptual characteristics. Emphasis is placed on how perceptual experience relates to the physical properties of the world and to physiological constraints in the brain.

The first chapter introduces some of the techniques used to study perception, and some important general principles that apply equally to all the sensory systems. These principles are first applied to the minor senses in the following two chapters: smell and taste (Chapter 2), and touch and balance (Chapter 3). More space is devoted to hearing (Chapters 4 and 5), and yet more to vision (Chapters 7 to 12), reflecting the relative importance of the senses to humans. The final chapter considers individual differences in perception relating to age, sex, culture, and expertise.

The bulk of each chapter is devoted to fundamental material that all students should read. Each chapter also contains a Tutorial section covering more advanced or controversial material, or newly developing areas, to offer an opportunity for further study and a bridge to more advanced texts. For example, tutorials in Chapters 4 and 8 introduce Fourier analysis; tutorials in Chapter 9 discuss Bayesian inference as well as the debate about active versus passive processing; a tutorial in Chapter 13 surveys recent research on sensory integration.

The manuscript has been improved significantly as a result of the critical comments offered by a number of people including Chris Darwin, Graham Hole, Ian Howard, Linda Murdoch, Romi Nijhawan, Daniel Osorio, and several anonymous reviewers. I am very grateful to them all for their valuable contributions, but any remaining errors are of course down to me. I would also like to thank Mike Forster, Ruben Hale, Mandy Collison, and everyone else at Psychology Press for all their encouragement during the protracted period of writing.

Finally I would like to dedicate the book to Anne, Laura, and Luke for their patience and support during the preparation of the manuscript and associated material. Laura was particularly helpful in the preparation of the indexes.

# CHAPTER 1

## CONTENTS

# General principles

## INTRODUCTION

From a subjective standpoint, there seems to be little to explain about perception. Our perception of the world is direct, immediate, and effortless, and there is no hint of any intervening operations taking place in the brain. The apparent simplicity of perception is reinforced by the fact that our perceptions are almost always accurate. We rarely make mistakes when identifying people by their face or voice, or in judging how hot a cup of tea is, or in navigating a flight of steps. Moreover, our own perceptions nearly always agree with those of other people. Sounds, sights, and smells seem to be "out there" in the world, not constructed in our head.

Yet our perceptual world is constructed in the brain, by a huge mass of neurons performing complex, but hidden operations. Three observations hint at the complexity of the brain processes involved in perception. First, a large proportion of the brain's most highly developed structure, the cerebral cortex, is devoted entirely to perception. Vision alone consumes over half of the neurons in the cortex. Second, despite the complexity and power of modern computer technology, computer scientists have not yet succeeded in building general-purpose systems with the perceptual proficiency of even an infant. Relatively confined problems, such as detecting abnormalities in medical images, or identifying a face or a voice, have proven to be formidable problems to solve by computer. Third, as a result of brain damage through injury or disease, a small number of unfortunate individuals suffer deficits in their perceptual capabilities. These deficits can be very specific and debilitating, but also dramatic and perplexing to other people. It seems difficult to believe that someone can fail to recognise their own face reflected in a mirror (**prosopagnosia**), or cannot judge the position of their limbs without looking directly at them. Such cases remind us of the sophisticated brain processes serving perceptual abilities that most of us take for granted.

Spectator sports provide a very clear example of the reliability, and occasional fallibility of the information extracted by our perceptual systems. Everyone involved—participants, referees/umpires, and spectators—must make perceptual judgements in order to interpret events on the sports field, and to decide what should happen next. Did the tennis ball bounce out of court? Did the football enter the goal net? All those involved nearly always agree on what happened, because their perceptual systems arrive at the same decisions. Sporting activities would not be viable either for participants or for spectators without reliable perceptual systems.

**KEY TERM**
**Prosopagnosia**: A clinical condition resulting from brain damage, in which a patient is unable to recognise familiar faces.

**FIG. 1.1**   Fine sensory discriminations during sporting activities probe the limits of our perceptual abilities. Disagreements can arise from the inherent variability of sensory signals. Copyright © Giampiero Sposito/Reuters/Corbis.

Certain critical judgements do require special skills and observation conditions. For instance, the judge who decides whether a tennis ball strikes the top edge of the net during a serve often uses a combination of three senses—sight (deflection of the ball in flight), sound (the impact of the ball on the net), and touch (vibration of the net). As a result, the net judge can detect the slightest contacts between ball and net that are missed by most or all of the spectators. Disagreements between participants or observers can and do arise, and can offer hints about the nature of the underlying perceptual processes (as well as providing additional entertainment; see Figure 1.1).

Common sources of disagreement involve decisions about whether a ball crossed a line on the sports field, such as whether a tennis ball bounced inside a court line, or whether a football crossed a goal line. Participants often reach opposite decisions in "close" calls. This disagreement is not simply a reflection of differences in skill or concentration level, but a natural consequence of the inherent variability in our perceptual decisions. In optimal conditions, perceptual responses are highly reliable, both within and between observers. When a ball bounces some distance on one side of a line, there is no disagreement as to where it bounced. However, **psychophysical** research has taught us that in marginal conditions when stimuli are very close together or indistinct, perceptual responses are probabilistic. When a ball bounces slightly to the left of a line, the response of the perceptual system itself will sometimes lead to a "left" response, and other times lead to a "right" response. As a result, different observers are likely to disagree a certain proportion of the time. Perceptual research aims to estimate the precise degree of uncertainty attached to perceptual judgements, and to identify its likely causes.

*Think of other reasons for disagreements between spectators about the same sporting incident.*

## CLASSIFICATION OF THE SENSES

The senses can be divided into five major groups, as shown in Table 1.1, on the basis of the particular form of environmental stimulation they detect.

**Key Term**
**Psychophysics**: The scientific study of the relationship between physical stimulation and perceptual experience.

| TABLE 1.1 CLASSIFICATION OF THE SENSES | | | | |
|---|---|---|---|---|
| **Sense** | **Stimulus** | **Receptor** | **Sensory structure** | **Cortex** |
| Vision | Electromagnetic energy | Photoreceptors | Eye | Primary visual cortex |
| Hearing | Air pressure waves | Mechanoreceptors | Ear | Auditory cortex |
| Touch | Tissue distortion | Mechanoreceptors, thermoreceptors | Skin, muscle, etc. | Somatosensory cortex |
| Balance | Gravity, acceleration | Mechanoreceptors | Vestibular organs | Temporal cortex |
| Taste/smell | Chemical composition | Chemoreceptors | Nose, mouth | Primary taste cortex, olfactory cortex |

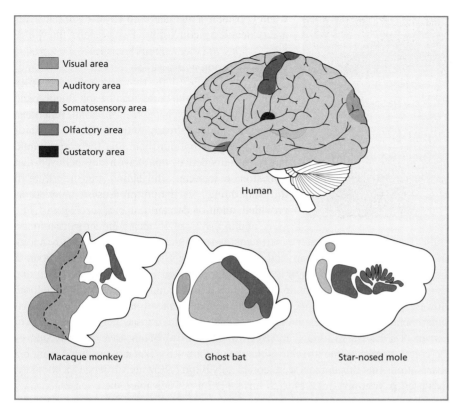

FIG. 1.2 Cortical representation of the senses. Top: Cortical receiving areas in the human brain. Bottom: Total cortical area devoted to three senses in three different animals (re-drawn from Krubitzer, 1995). The broken line identifies the cortical receiving area in macaque monkey. Copyright © 1995 Elsevier. Reproduced with permission.

Receptor cells convert environmental energy into electrical nerve impulses. A variety of methods are used to achieve this **transduction**, including molecular changes in photoreceptors triggered by light absorption, and mechanical deflection of tiny hairs by fluid currents in the inner ear. Receptors in each sense are connected to cells in different specialised areas of the **cerebral cortex** of the brain, as shown in the right hand column of the table. The cortex is a crumpled sheet of cells 2.5 mm thick and 1000 cm$^2$ in surface area (Braitenberg & Schuz, 1991). It contains approximately 20,000,000,000 cells. Figure 1.2 (top) shows a drawing of the human brain, identifying the receiving area for each sense. Activity of cells in these cortical areas is thought to lead to conscious perceptual experience. It is important to note that Figure 1.2 shows only the *receiving* areas. Many other cortical areas are also devoted to the senses, by virtue of connections between cortical cells. There are interesting species differences in the total extent of cortical surface devoted to different senses. In primates, including humans, the visual cortex is the largest sensory area in the brain. Figure 1.2 (bottom) shows the relative area of cortex devoted to vision, hearing, and touch in two other species as well as in primates. Auditory cortex is dominant in bats, and somatosensory cortex is dominant in moles. The relative area of cortex devoted to different senses is indicative of their relative importance to the survival of each animal.

*Think of other reasons for differences in brain area devoted to different senses.*

**KEY TERMS**
**Transduction**: The process by which sensory receptor cells convert environmental energy (e.g. light, sound) into electrical neural signals.
**Cerebral cortex**: The outer layer of the human brain; approximately 2.5 mm thick, it contains the millions of neurons thought to underlie conscious perceptual experience.

## METHODS USED TO STUDY PERCEPTION

A number of techniques have been used to study perception over the last 200 years. Each technique has particular advantages and limitations, but no one technique is to be preferred over the others. Different techniques complement each other, so that

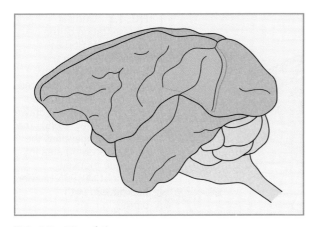

**FIG. 1.3** Site of the lesion in Ferrier's monkeys (re-drawn from Glickstein, 1985). Copyright © 1985 Elsevier. Reproduced with permission.

*How well could you infer the function of a car's components using "lesions" (disconnecting or removing components)?*

when considered together they allow us to construct a very detailed picture of how we perceive the world.

## LESION EXPERIMENTS

We now know that the cortex can be sub-divided into many areas that are specialised for certain functions, as Figure 1.2 has already shown. But in the mid-1800s, scientific opinion held that the cortex could not be sub-divided in this way. Many believed that sensation, perception, and action were represented diffusely throughout the cortex. **Lesion** experiments provided some of the earliest evidence against this view, and in favour of localisation of function in the brain. The procedure in such experiments is to surgically remove or destroy a specific area of an animal's brain, and then observe the consequences for behaviour. If a specific behavioural function is impaired or removed following surgery, then one may infer that the relevant brain area is crucial for the maintenance of that function. However, care is needed if one is to avoid drawing erroneous conclusions from lesion experiments. For example, one of the earliest experiments was performed by David Ferrier (1876). He examined monkeys after removal of an area on each side of the cortex known as the angular gyrus (see Figure 1.3). Ferrier concluded from his observations that the animals were completely blind following surgery. One monkey, for instance, was very fond of tea. Ferrier (1876, p. 166) noted that:

> *On placing a cup of tea close to its lips it began to drink eagerly. The cup was then removed from immediate contact, and the animal though intensely eager to drink further, as indicated by its gestures, was unable to find the cup, though its eyes were looking straight towards it.*

Later experiments, some of which are described below, indicate that Ferrier was mistaken in concluding from his observations that the monkeys were blinded by the lesion. Blindness is associated with damage to the occipital cortex, not the angular gyrus (occipital cortex is at the very back of the brain). According to Glickstein (1985), Ferrier's lesions had disrupted visually guided action, not vision itself. The monkey he described could probably see the cup, but could not perform the actions needed to drink from it. Despite such early mistakes, lesion studies have played an important part in establishing **localisation of function** as a basic principle of cortical organisation.

## CLINICAL STUDIES

Research on localisation of function in humans has relied largely on clinical investigation into the consequences of accidental damage or disease to specific brain areas. The usefulness of these studies is very similar to that of lesion experiments, in that they allow inferences to be drawn about localisation of function. Some of the earliest work to establish the importance of the occipital cortex for vision was undertaken by Tatsuji Inouye in the early 1900s. Inouye was a Japanese army physician, who studied soldiers wounded during combat in the Russo-Japanese war. His job was to assess their degree of blindness following bullet wounds to the head, as this determined the size of their pension (see Glickstein & Whitteridge, 1987).

Inouye devised an instrument to locate precisely in three-dimensions the position of entry and exit wounds (see Figure 1.4).

Assuming a straight path for the bullet, he was then able to identify the brain areas damaged, and relate them to the impairments observed in the soldiers. Inouye was among the first to show that the visual field is mapped in a highly ordered way on the surface of human occipital cortex (see below).

Clinical studies of the consequences of brain damage are necessarily more untidy than lesion studies, since the researcher has no control over the location and extent of the damage. As a result, the inferences that can be drawn from clinical studies are limited. However, clinical studies have led to many important discoveries concerning localisation of function.

## SINGLE-UNIT RECORDINGS

Although a great deal was known about anatomy and about localisation of function prior to the 1950s, nothing was known for certain about how individual nerve cells contributed to sensory processing. As David Hubel (1988, p. 4) remarked:

> I can well remember, in the 1950s, looking at a microscopic slide of visual cortex, showing the millions of cells packed like eggs in a crate, and wondering what they all could conceivably be doing.

Theories of perception were inspired largely by anatomy. The brain was known to contain huge numbers of cells, massively interconnected (but only over short distances) in circuits that are similar over the whole cortex. As we have seen, studies of localised brain damage showed that the visual cortex was mapped **topographically**. These facts inspired the Electrical Field Theory of perception. Visual patterns were thought to set up corresponding fields of electrical activity across the surface of the cortex. Perceptual organisation in complex displays was said to be governed by interactions between fields of current extending across the cortical surface. Experimental tests of the theory included attempts to short-circuit the electrical fields by pinning metallic strips across the surface of the cortex in rhesus monkeys, and then performing tests of visual functioning (e.g. Lashley, Chow, & Semmes, 1951).

In the early 1950s, Stephen Kuffler was among the first to use a new **microelectrode recording** technique to monitor the activity of single sensory cells. He inserted electrodes (very fine insulated wires) through the white of the eye in an awake, anaesthesised cat, and was able to record activity generated in individual retinal ganglion cells by simple visual stimuli placed in front of the animal. Kuffler's

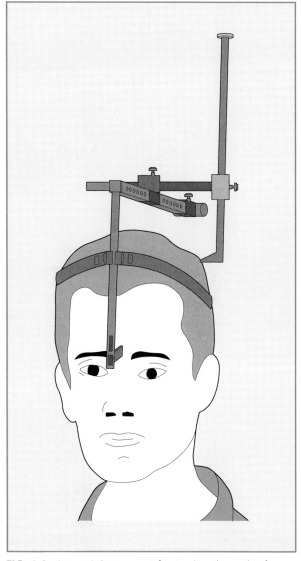

**FIG. 1.4** Inouye's instrument for tracing the path of a bullet in head wounds suffered by Japanese soldiers (re-drawn from Glickstein & Witteridge, 1987).

**KEY TERMS**
**Topographic map**: A spatial arrangement of neurons in a neural structure (e.g. the cortex) in which nearby cells respond to nearby locations in the visual field of view.
**Microelectrode recording**: A technique in which electrical activity is recorded from single cells in a live animal using fine insulated wires.

**FIG. 1.5** Single-unit recording. A stimulus is presented to the animal (in this case a visual stimulus) while a fine electrode registers activity from cells in the sensory system. The activity is recorded and analysed by special-purpose equipment, in this case a computer equipped with appropriate hardware and software.

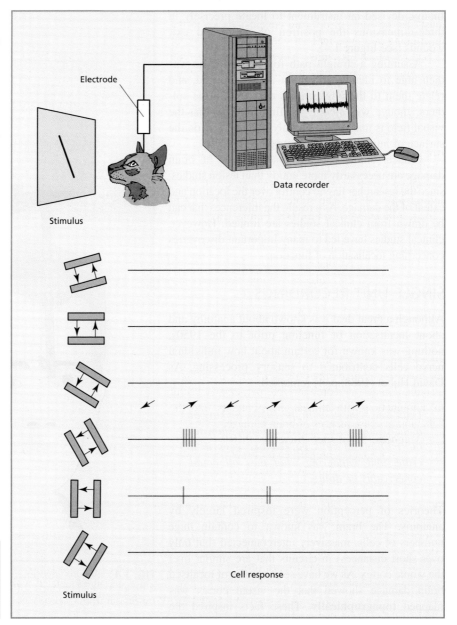

In partnership with Torsten Wiesel, David Hubel performed a series of ground-breaking experiments based on single-cell recordings from cells in the visual system of the cat. They were later awarded a Nobel prize for these discoveries.

(1953) work on the cat retina, along with work by Barlow (1953) on the frog retina, and by Hubel and Wiesel (1959) on the cat visual cortex, provided the first detailed information on the stimulus preferences of individual sensory cells. We now know that, despite anatomical uniformity, functional properties vary hugely from cell to cell. For example, some retinal cells prefer small, bright spots of light, while others prefer large, dark spots. In the cortex, individual cells are highly selective for line orientation, movement direction, colour, size, and so on (see Figure 1.5).

The key word is specialisation rather than uniformity of function. These discoveries led to theories of pattern recognition based on neural "feature detectors". As we shall see in later chapters, this view of single cells as **feature detectors** is rather too simple. One must also be wary of drawing conclusions about the functioning of a huge mass of neurons on the basis of responses in single units. Nevertheless, single-cell recording data have had a profound influence on theories of perception.

## BRAIN IMAGING

Brain-imaging techniques were developed in the 1970s, primarily for use in medicine. The earliest technique to be developed was **computerised tomography** (CT). The subject is placed bodily in a long, thin, cylindrical tube (see Figure 1.6).

X-ray emitters and detectors are positioned around the circumference of the tube. A highly focused X-ray beam is emitted from one side of the cylinder so that it passes through the subject's body before being collected by detectors at the opposite side. X-rays are passed through the head from many directions around the tube. From the resulting pattern of X-ray transmission, sophisticated data analysis procedures can build up a detailed picture of the different structures inside the head, as shown in Figure 1.6. CT scans reveal areas of brain damage, and are therefore particularly useful in combination with clinical investigations into the behavioural consequences of brain damage.

**Magnetic resonance imaging** (MRI) scanners detect the magnetic properties of brain molecules, revealed by passing radio waves through the head in all directions. Functional MRI (fMRI) scanning techniques use MRI scanners to detect minute magnetic changes in haemoglobin induced by variation in blood oxygen concentration. Since variation in blood oxygen concentration is related to neural activity (activity consumes energy) fMRI scans can inform us about brain *function*. The primary inferences from brain scanning data concern localisation of function. Studies using fMRI scans often compare scans obtained while the subject is performing different tasks, in order to identify the brain areas that are associated with those tasks. Brain imaging is expensive and technically complex, and the data obtained require careful interpretation. However, the technique is likely to grow in importance as its use becomes more widespread, and data analysis techniques become more sophisticated still.

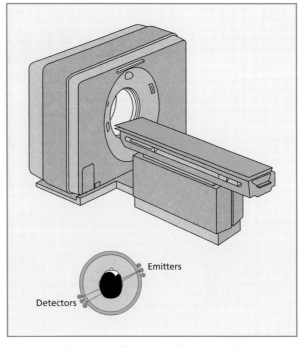

**FIG. 1.6**   CT scanner. The patient lies on a table that can be slid inside the scanner (left). The walls of the scanner are lined with X-ray emitters and detectors. X-rays are emitted from one side of the scanning tube so that they pass through the patient's body before being registered by detectors on the opposite side. A detailed image of the brain can be constructed from the pattern of X-ray transmission in all directions around the head.

## PSYCHOPHYSICS

Psychophysics is the scientific study of relationships between physical stimuli and perceptual phenomena. A typical psychophysical experiment involves carefully controlled stimuli, usually presented by a computer, and highly constrained responses from adult human observers. Figure 1.7 shows a typical psychophysical stimulus, presented on a computer monitor.

In this example, the stimulus is designed to study the subject's ability to discriminate small differences in stimulus contrast (the difference in intensity

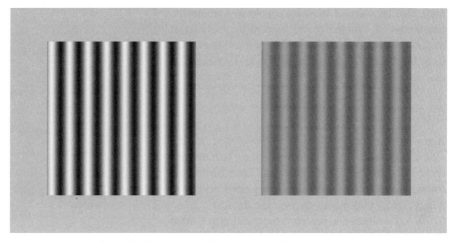

**FIG. 1.7**   A typical psychophysical stimulus, generated by a computer. The subject must select the grating that appears to have the higher contrast between its bright and dark bars. In this case the observer should select the left-hand grating. Responses are usually made by pressing one of two response buttons. The computer records each response before selecting the next stimulus to be displayed. The position of the higher contrast grating varies randomly between left and right from presentation to presentation.

*Why are special experimental techniques required to study perception?*

between bright and dark bars). The subject is given a response pad containing two buttons, labelled "left" and "right". He or she is instructed to press the button corresponding to the stimulus that appears to have higher contrast. The contrast difference between the stimuli is manipulated to find the difference at which the subject achieves the required level of accuracy. A number of experimental techniques have been developed over the last 100 years to ensure that data obtained in psychophysical experiments are not contaminated by uncontrolled variables such as subject expectations or desires. In the example, the position of the higher contrast stimulus would be varied randomly between left and right from trial to trial, and the contrast difference may also vary randomly, without the subject's knowledge. The tutorial at the end of this chapter provides an introduction to the major psychophysical techniques, and their theoretical background. Psychophysical experiments are particularly useful for testing predictions from theories of perception. However, inferences about the neural structures mediating performance must be treated with some caution, and require cross-referencing against physiological data.

## ARTIFICIAL INTELLIGENCE (AI)

In the 1930s the mathematician Alan Turing developed the notion of universal **computation**, according to which all sufficiently powerful computing devices are essentially identical. Any one device can emulate the operation of any other device. If we accept that the brain is a form of computational device, then it follows that it can be emulated by other such devices, namely computers. This is the conceptual basis for AI approaches to brain function. But what does it mean to say that the brain is a computational device? The senses send information about the external world to the brain. The sensory stimulus can be measured and specified very precisely in mathematical terms, for example patterns of light and dark in optical images, or

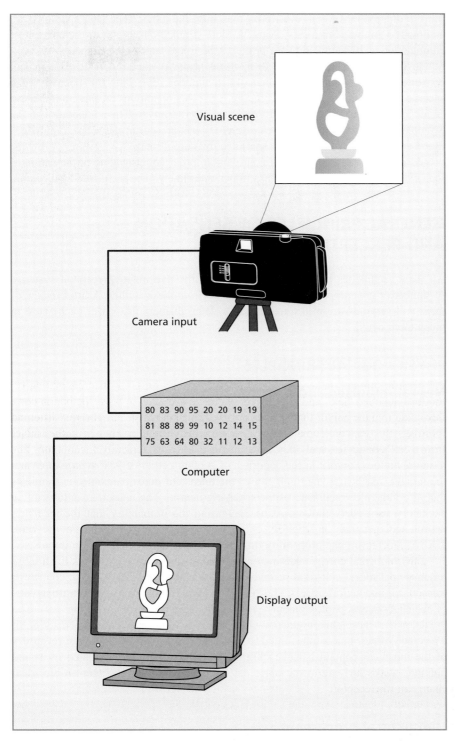

Visual scene

Camera input

80 83 90 95 20 20 19 19
81 88 89 99 10 12 14 15
75 63 64 80 32 11 12 13

Computer

Display output

**FIG. 1.8** Schematic illustration of a computer vision system. A visual scene is captured by a camera and fed into a computer. The scene is converted into a matrix of numbers. Each number represents the intensity of the light at a specific location in the scene. The computer performs computations on the matrix of numbers to create a new output matrix. The output matrix can be converted back into an image, again assuming that the magnitude of each number codes the intensity of light in the output image. In this example the computation has attempted to isolate all the edges of objects in the scene. Values in the output image that depart significantly from mid-grey represent the edges found.

sound-pressure waves entering the ear. The response of the brain can also be described in mathematical terms, for example patterns of neural activity, or consistent patterns of behaviour. Since both the input to the brain and its output can be expressed mathematically, AI researchers attempt to develop formal mathematical

*In what sense, if any, can one regard the brain as a computer?*

rules (computations) that transform one into the other. The computations are assumed to emulate brain processing. A more detailed discussion of the concept of computation as it is applied to the brain can be found later in the chapter.

In the example in Figure 1.8, a visual scene is captured by a camera and converted into a matrix of numbers. Each number represents the intensity of a specific point in the image. The computer performs operations on these numbers to create an output matrix that is converted back into an image. The computation in the example attempts to find the edges of any objects present in the scene. Any edges found appear as very light or dark marks in the output image.

AI research has made a major contribution to our understanding of the nature of sensory information, and of the kinds of operations likely to be performed by the brain.

# GENERAL PRINCIPLES OF SENSATION AND PERCEPTION

All these techniques have been used to study the five major perceptual systems. A number of general principles have emerged from these studies. A brief review of them will serve as a useful introduction to later chapters that cover each sense in much more detail.

## PHYSIOLOGICAL PRINCIPLES

### Neural impulses and transduction

Information in the nervous system is conveyed by trains of electrical signals (**neural impulses**) passed from one cell to another through the system. These impulses travel from a cell's **dendrites** and body to its **terminal buttons**, typically via an **axon**. The terminal buttons connect to the dendrites of another cell or cells at **synapses**. When the impulse reaches a synapse, it causes the release of **neurotransmitter** chemicals that affect the electrical state of the receiving neuron. The neurotransmitter can be excitatory (e.g. acetylcholine, ACh), increasing the probability that the receiving neuron will generate an impulse, or inhibitory (e.g. gamma amino butyric acid, GABA), decreasing the probability that the receiving neuron will fire an impulse.

Environmental energy takes a number of forms, as Table 1.1 showed. Each sense requires specialised cells that receive one particular form of energy and convert or transduce it into neural signals. The eye, for example, contains **photoreceptors**, each of which contains photopigments (two examples are shown in Figure 1.9). The breakdown of these photopigments when struck by light results in the generation of a receptor voltage that is transmitted to neurons in the retina. The **mechanoreceptors** of the inner ear contain hairlike outgrowths (cilia). Vibrations initiated by sound pressure waves arriving at the outer ear deflect the cilia and trigger an electrical change in the receptor.

### Hierarchical processing

Neural signals generated during transduction are transmitted to several structures in the brain. A common feature of all the senses is that ultimately at least some of the signals arrive at a receiving area in the cortex of the brain, as described earlier and pictured in Figure 1.2.

> **KEY TERMS**
> **Neural impulse**: A brief, discrete electrical signal (also known as an action potential) that travels rapidly along a cell's axon.
> **Dendrite**: The branched treelike structure projecting from a neuron's cell body, which makes contact with the terminal buttons of other cells.
> **Terminal button**: A bud at the branched end of an axon, which makes contact with the dendrites of another neuron.
> **Axon**: The long, thin wire-like structure that conveys neural impulses from a neuron's cell body to its terminal buttons.
> **Synapse**: The junction between the terminal button of one neuron and the dendrite of another neuron.
> **Neurotransmitter**: A chemical secreted across a synapse to pass on electrical signals from one cell to another.
> **Photoreceptor**: A specialised nerve cell that produces electrical signals when struck by light.
> **Mechanoreceptor**: A specialised nerve cell that produces electrical signals when subjected to mechanical deformation.

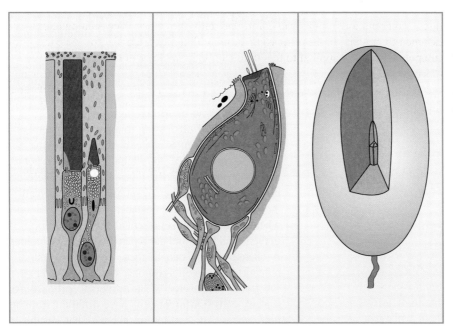

**FIG. 1.9** Sensory receptors. Left: Visual photoreceptors (a rod on the left, and cone on the right). Middle: Auditory inner hair cell. Right: Somatosensory Pacinian corpuscle.

In between transduction and arrival at the cortex, signals from each sense organ pass through a series of synapses at successively higher levels of neural processing. In the case of hearing, for example, there are five synapses on the route from hair cells to cortex. In the case of vision there are three levels of synapse between photoreceptors and brain. In all the senses except olfaction, one of the synapses on the route from sense organ to brain is located in the **thalamus** (olfactory signals are an exception because they pass directly from olfactory bulb to cortex). After the sensory signals arrive at a **receiving area** in the cortex, they are passed on to other cortical areas, often called **association areas**. Figure 1.10 summarises the successive hierarchical stages characteristic of sensory processing.

Arrows in Figure 1.10 identify the direction of flow of neural signals through the system. Signal flow is unidirectional up to the thalamus (at least in mammals), and bi-directional thereafter. Each stage of processing (each box in Figure 1.10) contains a large population of cells, often extensively interconnected. The input signal that arrives at each stage is modified by interactions that take place between the cells in that stage. As a result, the output signal that is passed on to the next stage differs in some way from the input signal—it has undergone a transformation during its passage through the processing stage. The successive transformations that occur as the sensory signal progresses through the hierarchy of processing serve to refine the information it contains. For example, useful information is selectively retained and elaborated, while less useful information is lost.

*Why are there so many processing stages in the sensory systems?*

## Selectivity

Each sensory system responds only to a particular range of stimuli. The human auditory system, for example, responds to sound pressure wave frequencies between 20 **Hz** and 16,000 Hz. Sounds outside this range are not detectable (though they may be detectable to other organisms; dogs, for example, can detect frequencies higher than 16,000 Hz). The range of effective stimuli for a particular system can be

**KEY TERMS**
**Thalamus**: A large dual-lobed mass of neurons lying in the middle of the brain at the top of the brainstem and below each cerebral cortex, which relays information to the cortex from diverse brain regions.
**Cortical receiving area**: An area of the cortex where afferent (incoming) fibres from a sense organ terminate; also known as primary sensory cortex.
**Cortical association area**: An area of the cortex that receives information from neurons in a cortical receiving area; also known as secondary sensory cortex.
**Hz**: The abbreviation of hertz, the unit of frequency in a repetitive, time-varying waveform such as a musical sound; each repetition of the waveform is a single cycle.

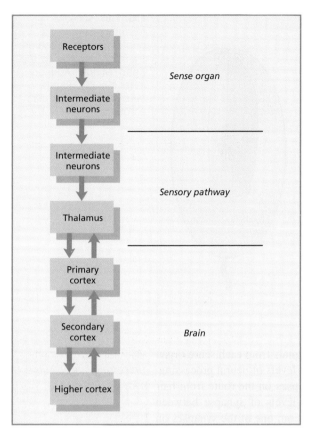

**FIG. 1.10**  Hierarchical stages of sensory processing. Neural signals originate in sensory receptors and pass through a series of processing stages. Each stage consists of a large population of interconnected neurons. Arrows denote the direction of flow of the signals.

described as its sensory space. Within this sensory space, stimuli can vary along many different dimensions. A single spot of visible light can vary in, for example, its horizontal position in the visual field, its vertical position, its size, its intensity, and its wavelength characteristics. Single-unit recording techniques allow us to take an individual neuron at any one level of processing in a sensory system, and examine the particular range of stimuli within the system's sensory space to which that cell responds. Single-unit recording data reveal that sensory cells are highly selective in their response. A specific cell in the visual system, for instance, may respond only when a spot of light is presented at a specific location in the visual field, and has a particular size and colour. A change in any one of these parameters causes a reduction in the cell's response (see Figure 1.11).

Such selectivity is a universal property of sensory cells. Different cells have different stimulus preferences, so a stimulus change that results in a reduction in one cell's response is likely to result in an increase in another cell's response. The limited spatial area of a cell's response (e.g. an area of the visual field for a cell in the visual system, or an area of the body surface for a cell in the somatosensory system) is usually called the cell's **receptive field**.

## Organisation

Each neuron at a particular level of sensory processing, whether in the sense organ, the thalamus, or the cortex, has its own specific stimulus preferences. The physical location of cells at each processing level is highly organised with respect to their stimulus preferences. In general, cells that prefer similar stimuli tend to be located near to each other in the brain. The most dramatic examples of organisation are so-called topographic maps. Figure 1.12 shows an example from vision.

The upper bull's-eye pattern was presented to a monkey so that the area outlined by the rectangle appeared in the animal's right visual field (i.e. fixation at the centre of the pattern). The lower image is a map of the left hemisphere of the monkey's cortex, showing only a portion at the rear of the hemisphere (the area where visual signals arrive—striate cortex). Tootell, Silverman, Switkes, and De Valois (1982) used a physiological **staining** technique to identify which cells in this area of cortex were active while the animal viewed the bull's-eye. Regions containing active cells are drawn in grey. Neurons with receptive fields at nearby retinal positions are clearly located near to each other in the cortex, since the active regions are grouped together. The pattern of activity is so well ordered that it constitutes a map of the pattern of retinal stimulation (often called a topographical map). Notice that the cortical map is distorted. The small region of the image near to fixation (innermost ring of the bull's-eye) occupies a relatively large proportion of the cortical surface (left-hand third of the cortical map). This property of organisation is called **cortical magnification**, and is a common feature across the senses.

## Specific nerve energy

All sense organs generate the same kind of electrical signals, as we have seen. After transduction, there is no feature of the neural signals that marks them as belonging to one of the senses rather than any of the others. How, then, can they evoke different experiences? Differences between the senses are not reflected in the nature of the sensory signals themselves, but in their destination in the brain. As Table 1.1 and Figure 1.2 showed, signals in different sensory systems arrive at different cortical receiving areas. It is the destination that marks a particular signal as arising from a specific sense, giving the signal a characteristic sensory quality. Johannes Muller introduced this idea in 1838, and described it as the law of specific nerve energy.

Dramatic and direct support for the idea of specific nerve energy can be drawn from observations made during neurosurgery. The neurosurgeon removes a section of skull to expose an area of the cortex. In order to navigate the dense folds of the cortical surface safely (avoiding damage to important functions),

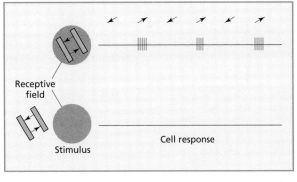

**FIG. 1.11**  Selectivity in neural responses. The visual stimulus was a tilted bar that oscillated back and forth repeatedly (left). The upper trace on the right shows the neural impulses (short vertical lines) recorded from a cat cortical cell by Hubel and Wiesel. Time is plotted horizontally, and arrows represent the two phases in the bar's movement. The cell responded only when the bar moved up and to the right. When it moved out of the cell's receptive field (lower trace), then no response at all was recorded.

> **KEY TERM**
> **Specific nerve energy**: The idea that neural signals in the senses are differentiated by their pathways in the nervous system, rather than by differences in the nature of the signals themselves.

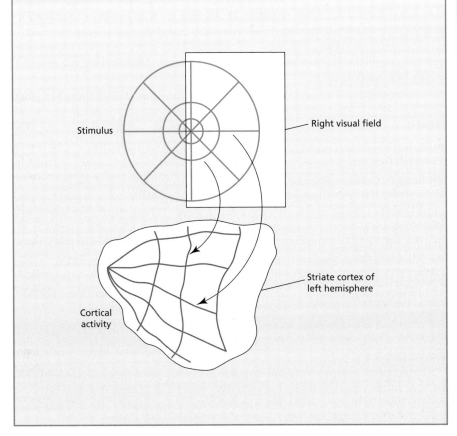

**FIG. 1.12**  Topographic map in the visual system. The bull's-eye pattern in the upper part of the figure was presented to a monkey so that the area enclosed by the rectangle appeared in its right-hand visual field. The lower part of the figure is a flattened view of the animal's left cerebral hemisphere. A physiological staining technique highlights any cells that were active while the pattern was being viewed (grey areas). The pattern of activity is highly organised, and demonstrates how the animal's visual field is laid out topographically across the surface of the cortex. Re-drawn from Tootell, Silverman, Switckes, and De Valois (1982).

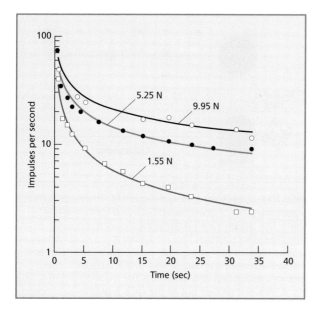

**FIG. 1.13**  Time-course of the response of a pressure receptor to stimuli at three different intensities. Response rate is initially high, but declines steadily over a period of 40 seconds. Re-drawn from Schmidt (1981, p. 88).

*Is adaptation just a by-product of depleted resources?*

small electrical signals are often applied directly to the cortex while the patient is awake but anaesthetised. This stimulation evokes sensations associated with the particular sense organ connected to that part of the cortex, such as visual or tactile sensations (see Chapter 3).

## Plasticity

The neural mechanisms that acquire and process sensory information are modifiable during development and during adulthood. As a human infant grows, the dimensions of his or her body change progressively. Limbs become longer and heavier, the eyes move apart. Sensory systems must be capable of adapting to these changes. Over much shorter time periods, each sensory system is also able to adapt itself to the specific sensory environment that the individual finds him or herself in. For example, as the sun sets the visual system's sensitivity changes progressively to match the prevailing illumination level. If one dresses in the morning with a particularly coarse-textured shirt, the initial feeling of itchiness conveyed by touch receptors in the skin soon subsides as the receptors adapt to their new environment.

The graph in Figure 1.13 shows the change in response of touch receptors to a steadily applied stimulus over a period of 40 seconds. **Adaptability** is a universal feature of sensory systems.

## Noise

The activity level of a neuron can be measured in terms of the frequency with which it generates electrical impulses. Activity level can vary between zero (no impulses at all) to approximately 800 impulses per second, though the typical rate for a very active cell is 100–200 impulses per second. In the example shown in Figure 1.13, the initial activity level of the touch receptor was about 100 impulses/s. Neural signals show a certain degree of variability, even in the absence of adaptation or short-term plasticity. The response to repeated presentation of identical stimuli differs randomly from presentation to presentation. This kind of variability is usually called "noise" because it bears no systematic relation to the incoming stimulation, or signal. There are two sources of variability (White, Rubinstein, & Kay, 2000). First, there are fluctuations in the electrical excitability of neurons, caused mainly by random opening and closing of **ion channels**. Second, there are fluctuations in synaptic transmission caused by, among other factors, the random nature of diffusion and chemical reaction across synapses.

Detection of changes in neural response is crucial, since they reflect changes in the state of the outside world. However, any measure of change in neural response must be made in the face of the inherent variability in the sensory signal. Theories of sensory coding must, as we shall see, accommodate neural noise.

**KEY TERMS**
**Adaptability**: The ability of a sensory system to vary its response characteristics to match prevailing stimulation.
**Ion channel**: A specialised protein molecule that allows certain ions (e.g. sodium, potassium) to enter or leave a cell, so altering its electrical state.

# PERCEPTUAL PRINCIPLES

## Sensation

All the senses share one fundamental property—stimulation of the sense organ causes a conscious mental state. For example, we may sense "sour" when a mild acid is in contact with the tongue; we may sense "sound" when air pressure waves enter the ear; and we may sense "light" when electromagnetic radiation enters the eye. These mental states have particular qualitative, experiential, or felt properties such as loudness, pain, or colour (sometimes called sensations or **qualia**). By their very nature, sensations are private, and accessible only to the person who has them. Most researchers believe that sensations can be regarded as identical to specific brain states or functions of brain states. For example, there is a specific brain state associated with the sensation of the colour red. If one's sensation of colour changed to, say, green, there would be a corresponding change in brain state. The assumed link between sensations and brain states lies at the very foundation of modern theories of perception, as will become clear below. However, an "explanatory gap" (Levine, 1983, 1999) remains between the physical world (brain states) and the mental world (sensations). No one has been able to explain precisely how the qualitative nature of sensation can be explained by reference to neural activity.

## Detectability

There is a very reliable relationship between the intensity of an environmental stimulus and the probability that it will evoke a sensory experience. A graph of the relation between stimulus level and the probability of detection by an observer (a so-called **psychometric function**) always shows a smooth transition between no-detection and detection as stimulus level increases (see Figure 1.14)—detection is probabilistic.

This property of perceptual experience is almost certainly related to the "noisy" nature of neural signals mentioned earlier, although there has been some debate as to the precise explanation (see the tutorial on psychophysical methods later in the chapter).

## Sensory magnitude

Variation in intensity affects not only the detectability of a stimulus, but also its perceived magnitude. For example, the brightness of a light, the loudness of a sound, or the heaviness of a weight increases as stimulus magnitude increases. An experimental technique called **magnitude estimation** allows us to establish the precise relationship between physical stimulus magnitude and sensory magnitude. The subject is initially presented with a standard stimulus at moderate intensity, and asked to assign an arbitrary number to it, such as 100. Other stimuli are then presented one at a time, and the subject is asked to estimate the magnitude of each relative to the standard stimulus using the same numerical scale. If, for example, a stimulus appears twice as intense as

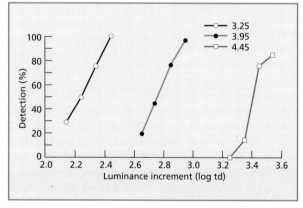

**FIG. 1.14** Psychometric function plotting the probability of a "yes" response to the presentation of a small light increment against a uniform background. The horizontal axis represents the magnitude of the light increment, and the three curves represent data obtained at three different background intensities. Re-plotted from Mueller (1951).

**FIG. 1.15**   The relationship between stimulus intensity and sensory magnitude. The left-hand graphs are plotted using linear axes—sensory magnitude increases non-linearly at different rates in different senses. The right-hand graph shows the same data plotted on logarithmic axes—sensory magnitude now increases linearly, showing the power-law relationship between stimulus intensity and sensory magnitude. Exponents of the plots were taken from Stevens (1961).

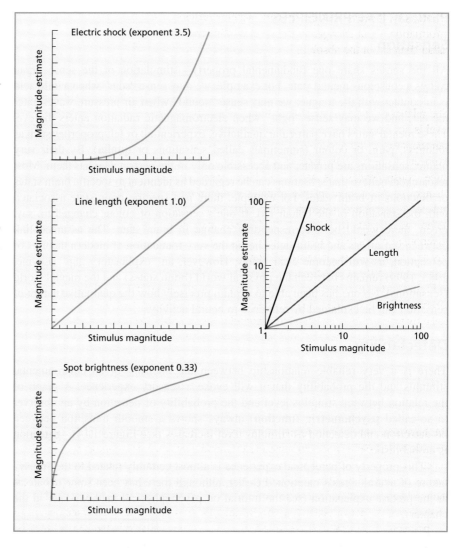

the standard (twice as bright or twice as loud), then the subject should assign the number 200 to it. The technique has been applied to a wide range of sensory stimuli. Representative data are shown on the left of Figure 1.15. The relationship between stimulus intensity and sensory magnitude is not linear.

In some sensory judgements, such as brightness, sensory magnitude increases rapidly at low stimulus intensities, but flattens off or saturates at higher intensities. In others, sensory magnitude shows the opposite pattern. If the data are plotted on logarithmic axes rather than linear axes, they fall along straight lines in the graph (right of Figure 1.15). This means that sensory magnitude data conform to a power law, in which sensory magnitude grows in proportion to stimulus intensity raised to a power (the slope of the each line in the logarithmic graph corresponds to the power to which intensity must be raised for that sensation). This property of sensory magnitude data is known as "**Stevens's power law**" (e.g. Stevens, 1961). The power-law relation between stimulus intensity and sensory magnitude means that equal ratios of intensity correspond to equal ratios of sensory magnitude. For example, each time light intensity increases by a factor of six, brightness increases by a factor of two, at all levels of intensity. It seems that the sensory systems provide information about *changes* in the level of stimulation rather than about the absolute level of stimulation.

## Adaptation

The relation between sensory magnitude and stimulus level is not fixed, but varies so that all sensory systems can adapt to prevailing stimulus conditions. Continuous exposure to a relatively intense stimulus usually has three consequences for sensation. First, sensitivity changes so that a more intense stimulus is required to induce a perceptual response after adaptation than before adaptation. In Figure 1.14, for example, the psychometric function shifts rightward along the intensity axis as background intensity increases. Second, the apparent intensity of the stimulus diminishes, as shown in Figure 1.16. Third, the rate at which sensory magnitude increases with stimulus level steepens. Given that the response capacity of each sensory system is limited, in that it can only respond to a certain range of stimulus levels at any one time, adaptation ensures that this restricted response is well matched to the prevailing stimulation.

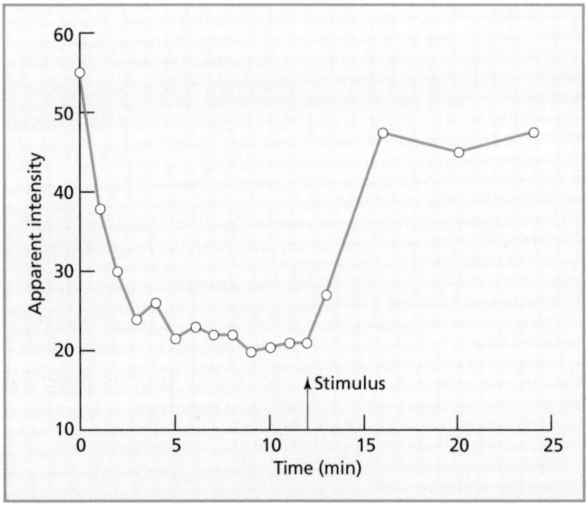

FIG. 1.16 Adaptation to an odour. Sensory magnitude of an odour sensation was measured at regular intervals during a 12-minute exposure, showing adaptation to a constant stimulus. Once the stimulus was removed, sensory magnitude gradually recovered to former levels. Re-plotted from Eckman, Berglund, Berglund, and Lindvall (1967).

## THEORETICAL PRINCIPLES

## Representation

We have seen that certain forms of environmental stimulation cause activation along specific neural pathways from sense organ to brain. At some point in this process, if we accept that there is a causal link between neural activity and consciousness, the activity evokes perceptual experience—we see, hear, feel, taste, or smell something. Although the world appears to be "out there", it is in fact a pattern of neural activity evoked in our head during the act of perceiving. As Boring (1950) noted: "The immediate objects of the perception of our senses are merely particular states induced in the nerves" (p. 82).

A specific internal state of the brain, in the form of a particular pattern of neural activity in some sense *represents* the state of the outside world. Perception must involve the formation of these representations in the brain. Most modern theories of perception are in essence theories about how the brain builds and uses representations of the world. Earlier in the chapter we discussed the idea that neural signals in sensory systems pass through a series of processing stages. According to the notion of representation, each of these stages must contain a representation of the state of the world. The transition through a series of neural processing stages can be viewed as a transition through a series of internal representations.

### The concept of representation

The idea that the state of one physical system (e.g. the brain) can in some sense represent the state of another system (e.g. the world) is very general, and can be applied to many systems. For example, the reading on a thermometer represents the current temperature; the display on a wristwatch represents the current time. As time moves on, the watch's display changes accordingly.

KEY TERM
**Representation**: The idea that the state of one physical system can correspond to the state of another physical system; each state in one system has a corresponding state in the other.

## Analogue and symbolic representations

The analogy with wristwatches is worth pursuing further, because it illustrates a distinction between two basic forms of representation, analogue and symbolic. There are two representational styles available in wristwatches, analogue and digital. In analogue watches the current time is represented in graphical form using a clock-face. The pattern displayed on the clock-face (the positions of the hands relative to hour and minute markers) provides a *pictorial* representation of the time. Marks around the clock face represent the division of each day into hours, and each hour into minutes, and so on. The continuous movement of the second hand is analogous to the passage of time, and the circular design of the display is analogous to the periodic nature of measured time. Digital watches, on the other hand, represent the current time in purely *symbolic* form using a sequence of digits. The digits 0 to 9 are used to represent the current hour, minute, and second. There is no continuous change to represent the passage of time. Instead there is a discrete change from one digit to another every second or every minute. The difference between analogue and digital forms of representation becomes clearer when one considers how to extract time information from them. To establish the time displayed on an analogue clock-face, one must know how to interpret the spatial pattern. For example, the angle between the minute hand and the 12 o'clock mark represents the number of minutes left in the hour. To understand the time displayed on a digital watch, one must be able to understand and manipulate symbols. For example, to obtain the number of minutes left in the hour, one must subtract the minute digits from 60. Digital watches therefore use a discrete, symbolic representation of time.

As a second example of the distinction between analogue and symbolic representation, consider how a bird-spotter's handbook might represent a specific species of bird. The entry for that species may contain a still image of the bird, and a text list of its attributes, as illustrated in Figure 1.17. A multimedia text may also contain an audio clip of the bird's call, and a movie clip of the bird's flight. The image, audio clip, and movie clip are clearly analogue representations, since they

**FIG. 1.17** Entry for a goldfinch in a bird-spotter's handbook. The pictorial image of the bird constitutes an analogue representation, while the list of attributes on the right constitutes a symbolic representation.

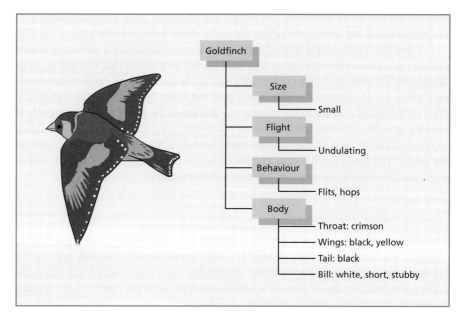

represent the bird in terms of its visual or audible pattern. The text list of attributes is an abstract symbolic representation of the bird.

*Think of another example of how the same information can be represented in both analogue and symbolic form.*

### Representation in the brain

There are two contrasting views about the nature of perceptual representation in the brain, which relate quite closely to the distinction between analogue and symbolic representations in the bird-spotter's handbook. According to one view, perceptual representations are "analogue" representations, in which the pattern of internal activity reflects in a very direct sense the pattern of external stimulation. For instance, the pattern of activity in the sheet of photoreceptors in the retina of the eye can be said to represent the pattern of light and dark in the image. The matrix of numbers in Figure 1.8 depicts the pattern of activity generated by a small region of the image. Intensity at a specific point in the image is represented in terms of a numerical quantity varying between 0 and 255. The numerical quantity is equivalent to the level of activity in a specific sensory cell. Morgan (2003) provides a detailed account of how analogue spatial representations (maps) in the brain are the basis of our perception of space.

According to the alternative view, perception involves "symbolic" representations, in which the state of the world is described using a limited set of abstract symbols. Each symbol would represent a perceptual object or a property of an object, in the same way that words themselves symbolise objects and properties of objects. For example, there may be a perceptual symbol for "creature" that can be set to equal one of a restricted number of types such as biped, quadruped, bird, fish, and so on. This symbol itself may posses a number of symbolic properties such as "size" (small, medium, large), and "flight" (undulating, direct, flitting, gliding), as shown in Figure 1.17. The nature of the representation adopted by a sensory system determines what kind of computations the system can perform on the representation.

## Computation

The concept of computation lies alongside the concept of representation at the heart of most present-day theories of perception. In an abstract sense, computation can be defined as the manipulation of quantities or symbols according to a set of formal rules. It follows from this abstract definition of computation that a neural process that produces a perceptual quantity such as brightness, or a perceptual symbol such as an object property, can be described as a computational process. The formal rules used in computations are sometimes called **algorithms**. The idea that neural processing is a form of computation originated from the work of the mathematician Alan Turing in the 1930s, as mentioned earlier. According to Turing, the brain can be considered as a computing device, in the sense that it manipulates quantities and symbols according to sets of rules.

How exactly does the concept of computation apply to perception? We have seen that perceptual systems can be considered as *representational* systems—internal brain states represent the state of the outside world. Perceptual analysis proceeds through a series of representations, reflecting a series of neural processing stages. The representation at each level is transformed into a new representation at the next level by a computational operation, as depicted in Figure 1.18 (a modification of Figure 1.10).

The nature of the computation that transforms one representation into the next depends on what form the two representations take, analogue or symbolic. Computations performed on analogue representations involve the creation and

> **KEY TERM**
> **Algorithm**: A specific computational procedure used to transform one representation into another.

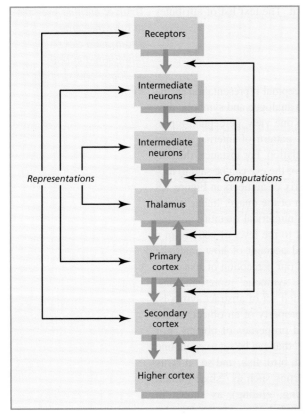

**FIG. 1.18** Representation and computation in relation to the hierarchical processing scheme depicted in Figure 1.10. Each processing stage contains its own representation of the sensory stimulus. The modification that takes place at the transition from one processing stage to the next can be considered as a computational operation that transforms one representation into another.

manipulation of *quantities* according to a set of rules, sometimes called signal processing. The computations involve mathematical manipulations of the values stored in the original representation. For example, given the analogue representation of the sculpture in Figure 1.8, containing many different lightness levels, one might wish to produce a more economical representation that contains only the sharp edges present in the image. Appropriate computations can find the edges, as shown in Figure 1.8. As we shall see in later chapters, this kind of computation captures the essential properties of many cortical cells.

Computations performed on symbolic representations involve the creation and manipulation of *symbols* according to a set of rules. The computations involve comparisons between symbols to test for equality, and the combination of symbols to create new symbol structures. For example, the first representation may contain the symbols illustrated in Figure 1.17 (Size = Small; Flight = Undulating; etc.). The perceptual system may contain a rule that states that (IF Size = Small AND Flight = Undulating AND…THEN Bird = Goldfinch). An instance of the symbol for "goldfinch" would be created at the next level of representation in the processing hierarchy.

Symbolic representations and computations have traditionally been associated with human cognition, such as problem solving (Newell & Simon, 1972), and seem a natural choice for high-level perceptual representations relating to object identity. Early perceptual representations, such as those in sense organs and cortical receiving areas, are probably best considered to be analogue in form. It is not yet clear where and how perceptual representations shift from analogue to symbolic. Some theorists have proposed that symbolic perceptual representations are used even at the earliest levels of analysis (Marr, 1980).

## Linking propositions

Contemporary theories of perception attempt to describe the relationship between the physical state of the brain (patterns of activity in certain groups of neurons) and the mental state of the perceiver (sensations or perceptions). Brindley (1960) recognised that any rigorous theory should express this relationship in terms of explicit propositions that he called psychophysical linking hypotheses. More recently, Teller (1984) defined a **linking proposition** as "a claim that a particular mapping occurs, or a particular mapping principle applies, between perceptual and physiological states" (Teller, 1984, p. 1235).

Rigorous theories of perception usually contain at least one linking proposition of this kind. An example of such a proposition is that the loudness of a sound is coded by the rate of firing of certain cells in the auditory system. Linking propositions provide a bridge between the quantities and symbols that are computed by neural processes, and the perceptual experiences they evoke. Many perceptual theories do not spell out explicitly their linking propositions, but it is important to be aware that such propositions must form part of any theory that attempts to relate neural events to perceptual events.

## Decision rules

Perceptual judgements usually involve a decision of some kind. For example: Is the cup within reach? Did I hear the telephone ring? Many of these decisions must be made in the face of unreliable, incomplete, or inconsistent information. Judgements of distance, for example, can make use of a range of cues including perspective, stereo vision, and relative movement. Each cue may supply a different estimate, but the perceptual judgement must combine them in some way to arrive at a single estimate. To take a second example, a high level of ambient background noise in the environment may mask the sound of the telephone. In addition to such external factors, we have already seen that the internal neural signals mediating perception are subject to fluctuation, so the computations performed during sensory processing must accommodate this variability. The most complete theories of perception therefore incorporate rules governing how decisions are made in the presence of ambiguity, noise, and multiple sources of information. These rules are often based on the mathematics of probability and statistics.

# CHAPTER SUMMARY

Perception involves highly complex neural processes that consume a substantial proportion of the brain's cerebral cortex.

## CLASSIFICATION OF THE SENSES

There are five major groups of senses:

- Vision
- Hearing
- Touch
- Balance
- Taste/Smell.

Senses differ in terms of the environmental stimuli that excite them, and the neural structures involved in transduction and sensory analysis. In humans, a much greater area of cortex is devoted to vision than to the other senses.

## METHODS USED TO STUDY PERCEPTION

Methods include:

- Lesion experiments
- Clinical studies
- Single-unit recordings

- Brain imaging
- Psychophysics
- Artificial intelligence.

Each method has advantages and drawbacks. The different techniques complement each other, so a full understanding of perception requires some acquaintance with all the techniques.

## GENERAL PRINCIPLES OF SENSATION AND PERCEPTION

A number of unifying principles have emerged from studies of sensory systems.
   Physiological principles include:

- Neural impulses and transduction
- Hierarchical processing
- Selectivity
- Organisation
- Specific nerve energy
- Plasticity
- Noise.

Perceptual principles include:

- Sensation
- Detectability
- Sensory magnitude
- Adaptation.

Theoretical principles include:

- Representation
- Computation
- Linking propositions
- Decision rules.

An appreciation of these principles will promote better understanding of the similarities and differences between the sensory modalities.

# TUTORIALS

## PSYCHOPHYSICAL METHODS

As we saw earlier in the chapter, certain physical stimuli evoke perceptual experiences ranging from simple sensations such as "redness" or "loudness" to complex perceptions such as face recognition. How can we study the relationship between physical stimuli and perceptual experience? The simplest method is to use verbal reports, such as "it looks red" or "that is my grandmother". This phenomenological approach is severely limited, for several reasons. First, it obviously requires subjects who can describe their experiences in words, so excludes infants and animals. Second, even when restricted to subjects who can talk, it is contaminated by differences in the way different people use words. Third, it is open to bias introduced by individual expectations and desires. We need precise, accurate measures of perception that can be used to establish the limits of perceptual ability, to monitor how these limits change with stimulus conditions, and to test the predictions of perceptual theories. Ideally these measurement methods should be immune to the effects of verbal ability, expectation, and attitude. Over the last 100 years or so a body of experimental techniques has been developed to provide the required measurements. Since these techniques provide quantitative, physical measures of psychological phenomena, they are called *psychophysical* methods.

## Psychometric functions

Any plot relating a quantifiable response to a physical stimulus measure is known as a psychometric function. One might plot, for example, sound intensity against the probability that the subject will detect the presence of the sound. What is the typical shape of a psychometric function in a detection experiment? One might expect that below a certain stimulus level the sound is never heard, and above it, the sound is always heard—a step function. Real psychometric functions always show a gradual shift from no-detection to detection as stimulus level increases, rather than a sudden shift (as shown earlier in the chapter in Figure 1.14). Why?

## Classical psychophysical theory and the psychometric function

The concept of the threshold is crucial to classical psychophysical theory. A threshold marks a transition from one perceptual experience to another, usually as a result of a simple change in the physical stimulus. For example: How intense must a sound be for us to detect it? How fast must something move for us to see the movement? How different in distance must two objects be for us to tell that one is nearer? There are two kinds of threshold, the **absolute threshold** and the **differential threshold**. The absolute threshold marks the smallest amount of stimulus energy required for an observer to just detect its presence (e.g. the minimum sound intensity or movement velocity required for detection). The differential threshold marks the minimum change in stimulus energy that can be detected by an observer. This threshold is also known as the "just noticeable difference", or JND (e.g. the small change in sound intensity required for the observer to notice a change in loudness). Classical psychophysical methods were basically developed to measure thresholds accurately and reliably.

Classical psychophysical theory explains smooth real-world psychometric functions (as in Figure 1.14) with the following three assumptions. First, there is an ideal threshold function that relates the internal response of the sensory system ("sensory magnitude") to stimulus level. This function is a step function with two levels, "low", and "high". Second, when the internal response is "high", the observer always reports detection of the stimulus, and when the internal response is "low", the observer never reports detection of the stimulus. Third, the exact position of the threshold in relation to stimulus level is subject to some random fluctuation, due to momentary variations in neural sensitivity, arousal level, and so on. Although the threshold tends, on average, to cluster around a specific stimulus level, it occasionally falls below or above this level, so that the probability that the threshold will fall at a particular stimulus level conforms to a bell-shaped curve or **normal distribution**, as in Figure 1.19 (left).

In the figure, at a low stimulus level (top-left graph), the probability that the threshold will be lower than this level is small (arrowed area), so detection rates are low. As the stimulus level increases, the likelihood of detection improves because there is a much greater probability that the threshold will be lower than the stimulus level (lower-left graph). Consequently, if we plot probability of detection against stimulus level, a typical psychometric function is obtained (right-hand graph). At what stimulus level is threshold reached? According to classical theory, the "true" threshold coincides with the mean of the probability distribution in Figure 1.19. Since, by definition, 50% of the distribution lies below the mean, and 50% lies above it, the most logical place on the psychometric function to locate the threshold is at

**FIG. 1.19** Explanation of the empirical psychometric function, according to classical psychophysical theory. The stimulus level at which sensory response reaches threshold is subject to some degree of random variation (left-hand graphs). A low intensity stimulus (e.g. 1.0 in the upper-left graph) is unlikely to be detected (probability 0.1), because only rarely does the threshold drop to such a low stimulus level. A high intensity stimulus (e.g. 4.0 in the lower-left graph) is very likely to be detected (probability 0.9), because most of the time the threshold is lower than this level. As a result detection rates improve gradually with stimulus level (right-hand graph).

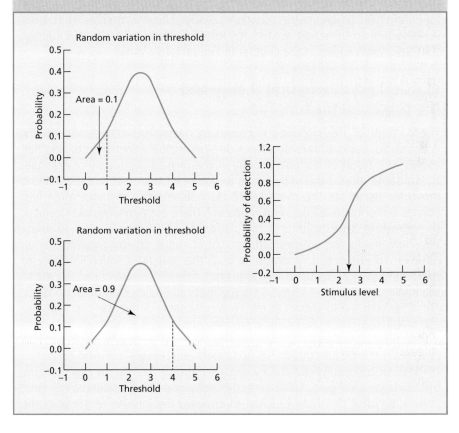

the 50% point. This account of thresholds applies to both absolute and differential thresholds.

## Classical psychophysical methods

All classical methods aim to measure the observer's threshold. Some methods provide an estimate of the whole psychometric function. Others provide an estimate of just one point on the function, usually the 50% point. A number of classical methods were developed at the turn of the 19th century, but this tutorial will describe the only two methods that are still in use, the method of adjustment and the method of constant stimuli.

### Method of adjustment

In this procedure, the observer is given control of the stimulus (e.g. a dial that controls stimulus intensity), and asked to adjust it until it is just detectable. This method is quick and easy to use, but rather unreliable. The observers have direct control of the stimulus, so are free to apply some degree of bias to their settings. Some observers may try to impress with their high sensitivity, and tend to bias dial settings toward low stimulus levels. Other observers may prefer to be cautious and careful, tending to bias their settings toward high stimulus levels.

### Method of constant stimuli

The experimenter selects a range of stimulus levels at the start of the experiment. These different levels are presented to the subject repeatedly in random order, in a series of experimental trials. After each presentation, the subject is required to respond "yes" if the stimulus (or a difference between stimuli) was detected in that trial, or "no" if it was not detected. This method is more trustworthy than adjustment, since the subject has no direct knowledge of the stimulus level presented. It constructs the full psychometric function, so is reliable but more labour-intensive than the method of adjustment. Computers can be used to take care of stimulus selection, increasing the efficiency of the method.

## The problem of bias in classical methods

In classical psychophysics, the subject's response to the stimulus is assumed to depend only on their sensitivity, the stimulus level at which the internal response shifts from low to high. However, responses are also likely to reflect uncontrolled bias effects. The problem is most severe using the method of adjustment, but may also intrude in the method of constant stimuli. Since a stimulus is presented in every trial, the observers are free to apply some degree of bias to their responses. They may, for example, be feeling uncooperative or lacking in confidence, and so unwilling to respond "yes" unless they are very confident of being correct. As a result, the measured threshold will not be a pure estimate of the subject's sensitivity to the stimulus, but will reflect some unknown combination of sensitivity and bias. Signal detection theory was developed specifically to address the problem of bias effects.

## Signal detection theory (SDT)

SDT acknowledges the importance of bias effects by assuming that stimulus detection is a two-stage process (Figure 1.20, top). The first stage is a purely sensory process in which a specific stimulus level produces an internal sensory response that depends on the intensity of the stimulus and the sensitivity of the sensory system. This internal response is subject to random internal "noise" of the kind described earlier in the chapter. The second stage is a decision process in which the sensory response magnitude is compared to an internally set criterion. If the response magnitude exceeds this criterion, the decision process decides that a stimulus was present. If the internal

**FIG. 1.20**  Signal detection theory (SDT). Top: Two hypothetical stages in detection, according to SDT. Middle: According to SDT, both stimulus-absent ("noise only") and stimulus-present ("noise + signal") trials generate a response in the sensory process of the detection system. Each response is subject to some random variation due to internal noise, shown by the two distributions. The observer's sensitivity to the stimulus is characterised by the difference between the means of the two distributions. Bottom: The decision process receives a response from the sensory process, and must decide whether the response came from the noise only distribution or from the noise + signal distribution. A specific response level is selected ("criterion"), above which the decision is that the response came from the noise + signal distribution.

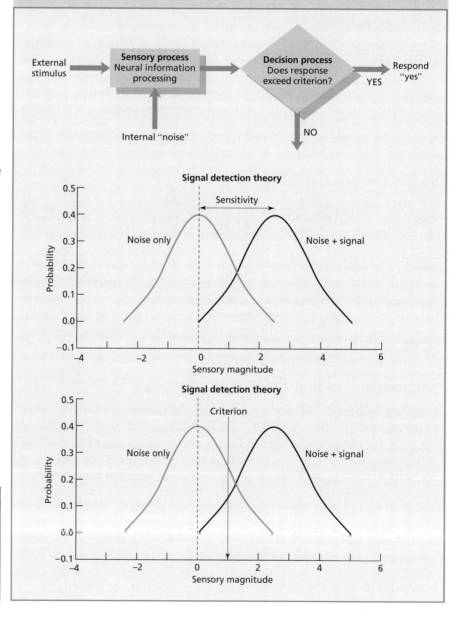

**KEY TERM**

**Signal detection theory**: A theory of performance in psychophysical experiments in which subjects' decisions are determined jointly by their sensory response and by a tendency to respond in a certain way.

response falls below the criterion, then the decision process decides that no stimulus was present. The position of the criterion is influenced by all the factors described earlier that affect bias. Highly motivated subjects may adopt a low criterion, reflecting a bias in favour of accepting rather weak stimuli. Subjects who lack confidence in their judgements may adopt a high criterion, because they are biased toward accepting only relatively intense stimuli. The experimenter is interested primarily in the sensitivity of the sensory system, rather than the subject's bias, but SDT provides methods of estimating both sensitivity and bias.

## SDT methodology: Yes/no and forced-choice tasks

In classical psychophysical methods, every stimulus presentation in the experiment contains a stimulus. In SDT methods only *half* of the presentations contain stimuli, randomly selected. For example, if the subject is required to detect the presence of a visual pattern against a uniform background, then only half of the presentations contain the pattern and background, while the other half contain only the background. Presentations containing a stimulus are called *noise + signal* presentations, for reasons that will become obvious, and presentations not containing a stimulus are called *noise* presentations. The subject must discriminate between noise + signal presentations and noise presentations. Two kinds of task are commonly used. In a **yes/no task**, the subject is presented with a single stimulus event in each experimental trial, which may or may not contain a signal. The subject must respond "yes" if he or she decides that a stimulus was presented in that trial, and "no" otherwise. In a **forced-choice task**, the subject is usually presented with two stimulus events in each trial, side by side or one after the other. In a vision experiment, for example, two stimulus patches may be presented side by side. In a hearing experiment, two sounds may be presented sequentially. Only one event contains the stimulus to be detected. The subject must decide which of the two events contained the stimulus, and respond "left" or "right", or "one" or "two" as appropriate. Tasks of this kind are commonly called two-alternative forced choice or 2AFC tasks.

Notice that in SDT tasks the subject has no direct knowledge of which event contains the required stimulus. This reduces the possibility of bias, because when the stimulus is not detectable the subject is forced to guess as to which event contained the stimulus. However, in yes/no tasks there is a possibility of some bias in favour of "yes" responses, because of a social aversion to saying "no". Many researchers prefer to use forced-choice tasks wherever possible, because the alternative responses are fairly neutral (Green & Swets, 1966).

## SDT measures of sensitivity and bias

This brief description of SDT measures is based on a yes/no task, but also applies (with appropriate modifications) to forced-choice tasks. SDT theory assumes that both noise + signal and noise events generate an internal response in the sensory process of the detection system, because this process is subject to internal noise (Figure 1.20). Noise events reflect only the contribution of internal noise to the response. Noise + signal events reflect contributions from both internal noise and external stimulation. The probability distribution of the response to each event can be plotted, as shown in Figure 1.20. Each distribution simply plots the relative probability of that event generating a specific response magnitude. The noise distribution reflects only the variable level of internal noise, which tends to cluster around a mean value (the peak of the distribution). The noise + signal distribution contains contributions from both internal noise and external stimulation. The effect of the external stimulus is to add a constant value to the noise distribution, displacing it towards higher response magnitudes. The distance over which noise + signal distribution is shifted relative to the noise distribution depends on the system's sensitivity to the stimulation. The difference between the means of the two distributions is taken as a measure of the sensitivity of the system to the stimulus, and is known as **d' (d-prime)**.

In any one trial of a yes/no task, the decision process receives a response at a particular magnitude, and must decide whether that response was drawn from the noise distribution or from the noise + signal distribution. SDT assumes that the decision process selects a specific criterion level of response, shown by the arrow in Figure 1.20. Response levels below this value are deemed to belong to the noise distribution, so are assigned a "no" response. Response levels above this value are deemed to belong to the noise + signal distribution, and are assigned a "yes" response. The level at which the criterion is set depends on biasing factors. It may be "unbiased", or midway between the two distributions, or biased in one direction or the other.

SDT provides various methods for making precise estimates of sensitivity or d' independent of criterion level or **bias** (also known as β). However, for unbiased experiments such as those employing 2AFC tasks, a simple measure of sensitivity is given by the proportion of correct responses recorded by the subject. Readers interested in the mathematical details of SDT measures are referred to Stanislaw and Todorov (1999), who provide formulae and procedures for performing the calculations using general-purpose software such as spreadsheets.

## Evaluation

SDT was first applied to psychophysical problems by Tanner and Swets in the mid-1950s and, as we have seen, it discards the classical notion of the threshold in favour of d'. Fifty years later, despite the widespread acceptance in the scientific community of many of the ideas in SDT, much contemporary research still measures performance in terms of thresholds rather than d' (Gordon, 1997). Why should this be so? Thresholds are still a very useful, and intuitively meaningful way of summarising the performance of a subject, reflecting the stimulus level that is just detectable by the subject. By contrast, d' is a more abstract measure of sensitivity to a specific stimulus level, and is meaningful only if one appreciates the statistical concepts that underlie it. Despite the continuing attachment to thresholds, many researchers measure them using percentage correct responses in 2AFC tasks, having taken on board the concerns about bias effects raised by advocates of SDT.

# THEORETICAL APPROACHES TO PERCEPTION.

The previous tutorial on psychophysical methods introduced some of the techniques that have been developed for collecting perceptual data, and the rationale behind them. This tutorial discusses the major theoretical movements that have motivated psychophysical experiments over the last 150 years. We must first define the essential properties of a theory, and discuss how the adequacy of different theories can be assessed. At the very least, any scientific theory worthy of the name must have three properties (Popper, 1963). First, it must provide a framework for organising and understanding the known facts in an economical manner. Second, it must attempt to provide explanations for the facts, or at least suggest causal links between them. Third, it must be capable of generating predictions that can be tested experimentally. If there are two competing theories to account for a particular set of facts, how can one select the theory that is to be preferred? Several criteria can be applied:

1. *Empirical consistency* One can compare the two theories according to their ability to explain the known facts. A theory is not much use if it cannot account for the data.
2. *Logical consistency or computability* If both theories pass the first test, one can judge their relative merits on the basis of logical consistency. Is the reasoning behind each theory tight and logically consistent? If a theory involves computational operations, can these operations be performed successfully? The inclusion of arbitrary (ad hoc) propositions, or computations that are difficult or impossible to implement, diminishes a theory's attractiveness.
3. *Occam's Razor* If both theories pass the first two tests, then one can apply the principle of Occam's Razor, which states that "Entities must not be multiplied beyond necessity". What this means is that the more parsimonious theory of the two is to be preferred. If a simple theory can explain the data as convincingly as a more complex theory then, other things being equal, the additional complexity is superfluous.
4. *Generality* A final test of two competing theories concerns their generality. Some theories appear to exist in a vacuum, successfully accommodating the data they were devised to explain, but with no obvious connection to other phenomena or theories. Other theories attempt to place themselves in a wider context by, for example, making connections with other theories. In these circumstances, the better-connected theory is to be preferred. This criterion selects theories on the basis of higher order logical consistency. Are different theories invented ad hoc to explain phenomena in isolation, or is there some higher order rationale or structure that links different theories together? Examples of such higher order links would include energy efficiency, ecological validity.

If two competing theories cannot be separated on the basis of *any* of the four criteria, the only course of action is to return to the first criterion, empirical consistency. New predictions must be generated from each theory concerning the outcome of an experiment, formulated in such a way that (ideally) the results are bound to falsify one of the theories. In principle, the aim of any new theory is to provide the only true explanation for a particular phenomenon. However, it is worth remembering that few theories stand the test of time. Most new theories are ultimately discarded either because of empirical inconsistency, or because they prove to be unsatisfactory on the basis of one of the other criteria. Most theorists accept that the best they can hope for a particular theory is that it will provide a closer approximation to the truth than other available theories. Once a new theory appears that offers a better way of understanding the facts, then the old theory must be discarded. This does not mean that theorising is futile and doomed to failure, for two reasons. First, it would be extremely difficult or impossible to arrive at the truth without having first absorbed the insights offered by previous theories. As Isaac Newton remarked: "If I have seen farther, it is by standing on the shoulders of giants" (letter to Hooke, 5 February 1675; see Turnbull, 1959, p. 416). Although Newton's own theories provided the foundation stones for most of the sciences, he acknowledged the debt he owed to predecessors such as Galileo and Kepler. Second, much empirical research would be aimless and trivial unless it was motivated by the need to test the predictions of new theories.

It should now be clear why it is important to understand some of the major theoretical movements in the scientific study of perception. As we shall see, each movement has made a valuable contribution to our understanding of perception. The major theoretical movements were developed in the context of vision, but the ideas can be taken to apply to all the senses. Modern theories of perception began with Structuralism 150 years ago.

## Structuralist approach

Structuralism drew inspiration from the chemical decomposition of complex substances into elements. It proposed that each complex perceptual experience could be decomposed into a large collection of elementary sensations. Structuralists used introspection to break down a particular perceptual experience into its sensory components. For example, Titchener (1902) decomposed the taste of lemonade thus: "The taste of lemonade is made up of a sweet taste, an acid taste, a scent (the fragrance of lemon), a sensation of temperature, and a pricking (cutaneous) sensation" (p. 62).

Introspection proved to be an unsatisfactory basis for theories of perception for reasons that, in retrospect, appear obvious. First, introspective data are inherently qualitative rather than quantitative. Second, observers frequently disagree in their introspections. Third, many important perceptual processes cannot be studied by introspection.

## Gestalt approach

Gestalt psychologists rejected the basic principles of Structuralism, and proposed instead that when a collection of elementary sensations is combined together a new perceptual entity emerges—a Gestalt. The major exponents of Gestaltism (Wertheimer, Kohler, and Koffka) were German, and the German word "gestalt" means form, figure, or configuration. According to **Gestalt psychology**, perceptual systems are not passive recipients of isolated, elementary sensations, but dynamically organise these sensations into meaningful "wholes" or Gestalts. Gestaltism emphasised the importance of structure and organisation in perception. It identified a number of organising principles or laws to describe the variety of ways that perceptual systems achieve organisation. The general theme of these laws is that isolated elements that share some property in common, such as spots of the same colour, or shapes that move in the same direction, or notes of similar pitch, tend to be grouped together perceptually. Elements that form a "good figure" (*pragnanz*), such as dots falling along a smooth curve or forming an enclosed regular shape, also tend to group together perceptually.

The main weakness of Gestalt psychology was that its laws tended to be descriptive rather than explanatory. Its arguments tended to be circular. For example, Gestalt psychologists would explain why certain pattern elements group together by invoking the principle of good figure or *pragnanz*. But what is the principle of *pragnanz*? It is the tendency of elements forming a good figure to group together. Despite its limitations, Gestalt psychology made a valuable contribution to perceptual theory by emphasising the way that entirely new perceptual entities can emerge from the organisation of simpler elements. Gestaltism is no longer at the forefront of perceptual theorising, but is still influential, particularly in European psychology, and is relevant to present-day computational theories.

## Constructivist approach

The German scientist Hermann von Helmholtz introduced the idea of "unconscious conclusion" in his monumental, three-volume *Treatise on Physiological Optics* published between 1856 and 1866:

> The psychic activities that lead us to infer that there in front of us at a certain place there is a certain object of a certain character, are generally not conscious activities, but unconscious ones. In their result they are equivalent to a conclusion, . . . it may be permissible to speak of the psychic acts of ordinary perception as unconscious conclusions.
>
> *(1962 translation of Vol. III, p. 4)*

To expand on this idea, Helmholtz used the example of an astronomer "who computes the positions of the stars in space, their distances, etc." from his conscious knowledge of the laws of optics. He argued that "there can be no doubt" that perception involves the same kind of computation as that used by the astronomer, but at an unconscious level. Helmholtz went further, stating confidently that:

> Our ideas of things cannot be anything but symbols, natural signs for things which we learn how to use in order to regulate our movements and actions.
>
> *(1962 translation of Vol. III, p. 19)*

Helmholtz therefore advocated the view that sensory systems construct some kind of internal representation of the world, and that this representation mediates perceptual experience. Related views on the indirect and inferential nature of perception have been promoted by, among others, Gregory (1980), and Rock (1983).

It is fair to say that constructivism has had a profound impact on theories of perception. Most modern theoretical approaches rely heavily on the notions of representation and computation. Helmholtz's ideas on symbolic representation were remarkably prescient, since they appeared 100 years before Turing laid the foundations of artificial intelligence.

## Ecological approach

Perception begins with physical stimulation and ends with perceptual experience. In between the two, according to the Gestalt psychologists and constructivists, are sophisticated processes that construct internal representations from the sensory information. Perceptual experience has only an indirect relationship to the sensory data. James J. Gibson took the opposite view, in rejecting entirely the need for internal representation. He argued instead that there is sufficient information available in the visual image for unambiguous perception to be derived directly, without the need for intervening processes. He suggested that the brain as a whole "picks up" the relevant information by some kind of "resonance". Gibson used an analogy with a radio set to explain this idea. Your immediate surroundings are almost certainly filled with low-energy electromagnetic radiation broadcast by TV and radio transmitters. A radio, properly tuned, will be able to pick up some of this information and produce intelligible sounds. Gibson would argue that in this situation all the components of the radio resonate with the information available in the electromagnetic radiation. There is no need to assume that some internal representation is constructed by the radio.

Gibson's ideas were inspired by his work in aircraft pilot training during the Second World War. He noticed that conventional treatments of depth cues were of little practical value, and became convinced that the highly structured patterns of movement pilots view from the cockpit were critical for aircraft control. As a plane comes in to land, surface details in the environment, such as markings on the runway, stream across the image projected into the pilot's eyes. They radiate out from the point in the image toward which the aircraft is heading, creating an **optic flow field**. Gibson correctly deduced that this flow field contains sufficient information to specify precisely where and when the aircraft would make contact with the ground. He argued that this information is somehow picked up directly by the sensory system. Gibson identified other properties of natural images, such as texture gradients, that can be used to specify surface depth, slant, and size. Due to its emphasis on natural images, Gibson's perspective became known as the ecological approach to perception. Its denial of the relevance of mediating processes also led to the label "direct perception".

Direct perception performed a valuable service in identifying some powerful sources of information in visual images, but it drastically underestimated the difficulty of the problem posed by picking up this information. Research on artificial intelligence has shown that the

**KEY TERM**
**Optic flow field**: The highly structured movement in the spatial pattern of light reaching the observer, caused by relative movement between the observer and the environment.

information available in visual images is usually not sufficient by itself to recover unambiguous information about the surfaces and objects that created the image.

## Computational approach

The computational approach was anticipated by Helmholtz, in his analogy between astronomical calculations and perceptual conclusions. As mentioned earlier, firm foundations for the computational approach to perception were later laid by Turing. His notion of universal computation led to the idea that the brain was an information-processing device that could be emulated by other such devices, namely computers. An information-processing device receives input data and performs some processing operation on the data to produce an output. An electronic calculator is a good example of an information-processing device. It receives input data in the form of a sequence of numbers and symbols, and processes this data to produce an output, usually the result of a calculation. In the case of perception, the input is environmental data such as a visual image. The output is perceptual data. Intervening processes transform one into the other. Computational theorists attempt to discover the nature of the intervening processes given only the input to the system, and the output it produces. To continue the analogy with an electronic calculator, the task is similar to trying to discover the rules of arithmetic given only the sequence of numbers and symbols providing the input, and the numbers produced by the calculator as output.

Modern computational theories of human cognition began with Newell and Simon's information-processing model of problem solving (e.g. Newell & Simon, 1972). Marr (1980) accepted the notion that vision is "exactly and precisely an information-processing problem". He emphasised the need to define at a very abstract level the nature of the computations performed by the system. Computational theorists such as Marr test their theories by attempting to implement them using computer programs. In a typical test, the computer is given an image and attempts to produce the required output. Experience has shown that many natural images are inherently ambiguous, in that they do not allow the computer to arrive at a single unique and correct output using only the information available in the image. Instead, a range of possible outputs is consistent with the input information. In this situation it becomes necessary to apply some kind of constraint on the output. The constraint may involve restricting the use of the program to certain types of image. Alternatively, it may take the form of additional information that allows the computer to eliminate most of the possible outputs. The additional information may reflect an assumption based on the properties of real-world scenes.

The computational approach has introduced a high degree of rigour into theories of perception. The emphasis on constraints is both a strength and a weakness of the approach. On the one hand, the need for constraints confirms the validity of the constructivist and Gestalt perspectives, since it reinforces the need for mediating processes that bring in their own sources of information. On the other hand, constraints can limit the generality of a computational theory. If the constraint requires the use of artificial images, or of only a sub-set of natural images, then it limits the range of situations in which the theory can operate. If the constraint involves a specific set of assumptions about the properties of natural scenes, there is a danger that they will be arbitrary and ad hoc.

An important limitation of the computational approach is that it provides no account of consciousness. There is an explanatory gap between neural computations and conscious perceptual states, as mentioned earlier in the chapter under Sensation (Levine, 1983, 1999).

## Phenomenology

Phenomenology lies on the opposite side of the explanatory gap from computational theories. It is the study of consciousness from the first-person perspective—how the world appears to me. There is a long tradition of phenomenology in European philosophy and psychology, but it is sometimes dismissed as a legitimate approach to the study of perception, because it is inherently subjective. Scientific approaches are usually considered to require objective methods. However, phenomenological studies can be performed using a variant of standard empirical scientific methods, including hypothesis generation and observation. There are several key differences between conventional psychophysical observations and phenomenological observations. The convention in psychophysics is to keep subjects naïve as to the purpose of the experiment, and give them a well-defined task with highly constrained responses such as "yes" versus "no" (see the previous tutorial). In phenomenological experiments subjects are often fully informed about the purpose of the experiment, and their task is kept relatively open with loosely constrained responses. Response classification may occur only after the data have been examined. A key check on validity in phenomenological experiments is *intersubjectivity*, or agreement among individuals about the nature of their perceptual experience.

Many important discoveries about perception have been made using phenomenological experiments. The Gestalt school discussed earlier was founded on phenomenological observations. Prominent figures in phenomenological studies of perception include the Belgian psychologist Albert Michotte (1881–1965; perception of causality, discussed in Chapter 11), and eminent Italian psychologists such as Vittorio Benussi (1878–1927; lightness), Cesare Musatti (1897–1989; depth from motion), Fabio Metelli (1907–1987; transparency), and Gaetano Kanizsa (1913–1993; subjective figures).

Phenomenological aspects of perception are often underplayed in psychophysical research, but modern studies would make little sense without assuming the existence of a perceptual experience in the subject that could lead to a phenomenological report. Standard psychophysical techniques typically embed phenomenological experience in an artificial task requiring simple, constrained responses. So phenomenological observation frequently underlies the subject's responses. Indeed, initial interest in a research issue is often triggered by phenomenological observations made by the experimenter.

## Neurophysiological approach

The results of single-cell recording experiments have revealed a great deal about the response properties of individual cortical cells, as mentioned earlier in this chapter. Lennie (1998) remarked: "Single-unit recording on its own is a weak instrument for discovering what visual cortex really does, but when harnessed to a theory it is immensely valuable" (p. 924).

Early data from cells in the retina of the frog (Barlow, 1953; Lettvin, Maturana, McCulloch, & Pitts, 1959) quickly led to the idea that these cells were "bug" detectors—their job was to detect the presence of small, dark spots moving across the image, as would be created by bugs for the frog to eat. Barlow (1972) developed this idea into a lucid theoretical position now commonly known as the Neuron Doctrine. He argued that each individual neuron is tuned to detect the presence of a particular stimulus that looks like a particular object (such as a bug) or attribute of an object. He also proposed that activity in such neurons "directly and simply causes the elements of our perception". Recent research on cells in the cortex of monkeys has also been interpreted in terms of feature detection by individual sensory cells.

However, it has become clear that the response of an individual cell is not driven uniquely by a single stimulus feature, but by a constellation of features. As a result there has been much dispute about the correct theoretical interpretation of single-cell data. Lennie (1998) argues that the neural representation of a stimulus property is distributed among the responses of a whole group of cells rather than assigned to just one cell. Although progress in relating cortical physiology to perception has been slow, the basic facts about cortical cell responses have exerted a profound influence on theories of perception. The causal link between cell activity and perception is a basic theoretical assumption accepted by most sensory scientists.

## Evaluation

In its emphasis on a specific set of issues and ideas, each theoretical movement has made its own particular contribution to our understanding of human perception. The modern theoretical approach, as represented in this text, recognises the limitations of each movement in isolation, and attempts to draw elements from all of the movements. The origins of the four theoretical principles outlined earlier in the chapter should now be clear. The emphasis on representation and computation has its origins in Helmholtz's constructivist approach. Linking propositions are central to Barlow's neuron doctrine. Decision rules are an important feature of signal detection theory, originally applied to perception by Tanner and Swets. Yantis (2001) has collected together many of the key papers described in this tutorial, as well as other classic papers in visual perception, and offers an excellent opportunity to study the primary sources that laid the foundations of modern perceptual theories.

The modern amalgam of several theoretical traditions has evolved into a distinctive approach of its own that falls within the realm of neuroscience. The most appropriate description of this modern approach to perception is "sensory neuroscience".

# CHAPTER 2

# 2

# The chemical senses

## INTRODUCTION

The senses of smell and taste are called chemical senses because they extract information from the environment by means of direct chemical interactions. Molecules from external substances interact with receptor molecules in the nose or mouth, resulting in the generation of neural signals. Smell is a distance sense. Chemical molecules are wafted to olfactory chemoreceptors in the nose by atmospheric currents, so the stimulating substance itself can be quite remote from the perceiver. Taste, on the other hand, is a contact sense. Chemical molecules have to be in a solution that makes direct contact with the chemoreceptors. In this chapter each sense will be considered first in terms of its anatomy and physiology, and second in terms of its perceptual properties. Clear relationships between the two perspectives often emerge.

## SMELL

Odours are crucial for many animals. They are used to detect prey and predators, identify potential mates or competitors, and judge the palatability of food. In humans, smell is often thought to be important only for judging food, but it is surprisingly effective in other ways. We can distinguish gender on the basis of breath or hand smell (Doty, Green, Ram, & Yankell, 1982). Doctors once used the smell of a patient to help in the diagnosis of illnesses (Schiffman, 1983). Women who share accommodation have been found to synchronise their menstrual cycles as a result of chemical signals picked up by the sense of smell (see Wilson, 1992).

Odours are also very effective at evoking powerful emotional responses and memories. In many people, the smell of popcorn or hotdogs evokes vivid memories of fairgrounds or cinema theatres, while the smell of disinfectants and medicines brings back painful or fearful memories of spells in hospital. The size of the perfumery industry, and the volume of body perfumes and "air fresheners" manufactured, are a testament to the huge emotional impact of smell.

**FIG. 2.1** Smells can evoke powerful memories of childhood experiences. Copyright © Chuck Savage/Corbis.

Our sense of smell is blunted when we have a cold because of the build up of mucus in the nasal cavity that prevents odour molecules reaching the receptor cilia.

## THE ANATOMY AND PHYSIOLOGY OF SMELL

### Receptors

**Olfactory receptors** are found in the roof of the nasal cavity, on a patch of tissue called the **olfactory epithelium** (see Figure 2.2). In humans this tissue area covers 2–4 square centimetres, and contains about 6 million receptors (Kratskin, 1995). Olfactory receptors are constantly renewed, since each receptor cell lasts approximately 60 days. The actual receptor sites are located on hairs (cilia) that project from each receptor cell into the olfactory mucosa. Each cell possesses about 10–20 cilia. Molecules given off by volatile substances must dissolve in the olfactory mucus in order to arrive at the receptor sites on the olfactory cilia (see Smith, 2000).

As discussed in Chapter 1, the task of receptor cells is to encode information about the chemical composition of odour molecules in neural signals. The exact mechanism of transduction is still not certain, but there are thought to be 500–1000 different types of receptor in humans, each activated by different odour molecules (Ressler, Sullivan, & Buck, 1994). The olfactory mucosa also contains some **free nerve endings** that do not possess receptor processes (these are thought to

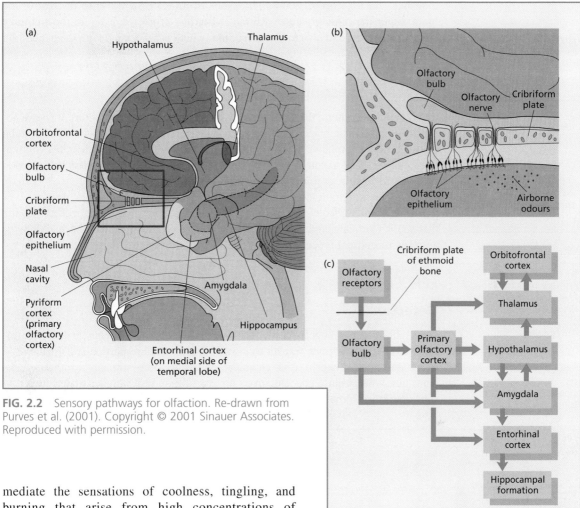

**FIG. 2.2** Sensory pathways for olfaction. Re-drawn from Purves et al. (2001). Copyright © 2001 Sinauer Associates. Reproduced with permission.

mediate the sensations of coolness, tingling, and burning that arise from high concentrations of chemicals). Malnic et al. (1999) measured the response profiles of olfactory receptors and discovered that a single receptor responds to multiple odorants, and that a single odorant excites multiple receptors.

## Sensory pathways

The axon of each receptor cell passes through a perforated bony plate in the skull (the cribriform plate) to project to a specific **mitral cell** in the **olfactory bulb**. There are about 50,000 mitral cells, and each receives approximately 200 axons, all from only one of the 500–1000 different types of receptor cell (Kratskin, 1995). The synapses between receptor cell axons and mitral cell dendrites bundle together to form **olfactory glomeruli** (Carlson, 2004; see Figure 2.2). The different receptor cell types appear to be distributed randomly about the olfactory epithelium. On the other hand, the anatomical positions of the glomeruli to which they project are identical in different animals of

*Why is the emotional impact of smell so great?*

the same species (Smith, 2000). The axons of mitral cells travel to the rest of the brain along the olfactory tract. Mitral cell axons project directly to the **primary olfactory cortex**, and also to the **amygdala**, which is associated with the generation of emotional responses.

## Cortical processing

Smell is unique among the senses in that projections from the olfactory tract are not relayed via the thalamus on the way to the cortex. This arrangement is thought to be a reflection of the relatively early appearance of olfaction during vertebrate evolution (Delcomyn, 1998). Another unusual feature of olfaction is that cortical activation is bilateral following stimulation of only one nostril, whereas lateralised cortical responses are common in other senses. Conscious perception of smell also involves a pathway running from primary olfactory cortex to the orbitofrontal cortex (via the thalamus). Cortical activity seems to be modulated by breathing (see Lorig, 2002, for a review of cortical processing).

Severe blows to the head can result in a loss of the sense of smell, if the shearing force is sufficient to damage the receptor cell axons where they pass through the cribriform plate.

**KEY TERMS**
**Primary olfactory cortex**:
The cortical destination of mitral cell fibres, thought to mediate perception of smell.
**Amygdala**: A nucleus (dense group of neurons) lying deep in the brain, forming part of the limbic system; involved in emotional, sexual, and autonomic responses.

## PERCEPTION

## Detection

Detectability varies hugely with odour. Some chemicals are detectable at concentrations thousands of times weaker than others. Humans are particularly sensitive to musk and to mercaptan (the chemical added to domestic gas to make leaks detectable), but require concentrations up to a million times higher to detect methyl salicylate (the aromatic ingredient in the wintergreen plant).

## Identification

At detection threshold, the ability of a subject to actually identify an odour is usually poor. Identification rates improve as the concentration of the substance increases. Humans can recognise up to 10,000 different smells (Shepherd, 1994). Women perform better than men. Cain (1982) tested the ability of men and women to identify 80 different odours. Men out-performed women in only 15 of the 80 odours. Figure 2.3 plots identification rates for the three odours that men identified best (ammonia, Brut *after-shave, and sherry), and the four odours that* women identified best (coconut, band-aid, fruit gum, and cat food).

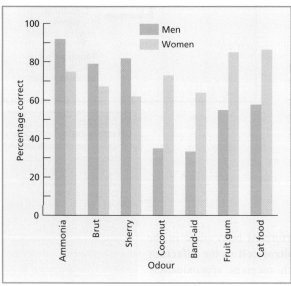

**FIG. 2.3** Odours identified most reliably by men compared with women, and vice versa, from the data set in Cain (1982).

### Theories of odour identification

Any theory to explain odour identification must include a linking proposition to map physiological states (receptor activity) onto mental states (recognition), as discussed in Chapter 1. The simplest possible linking proposition is that each recognisable smell maps onto a specific kind of receptor. When a given receptor is activated, we perceive the smell associated with it.

However, we can we recognise 10,000 different odours with only 500–1000 different kinds of olfactory receptor and mitral cell. There are clearly too few receptors for each recognisable smell to be uniquely associated with a specific kind of mitral cell. In fact most odour-producing substances contain a cocktail of different chemicals that will excite more than one receptor/mitral cell type, but will excite some cell types more than others. Sicard and Holley (1984) measured the responses of 60 different olfactory neurons in the presence of 20 different substances. Figure 2.4 shows a small sample of their data.

Each recognisable substance has its own particular "signature", written in the pattern of activity across odour receptors. A more sophisticated theory of odour recognition is that each smell is identified by matching its signature against stored signatures of known substances. This theory is based on coding stimulus identity in the responses of a whole population of cells. Linking propositions based on **population coding** are very common in theories of perception (Malnic et al., 1999).

Although different receptor types appear to be distributed randomly across the olfactory epithelium, the mitral cells to which they project selectively are distributed in a consistent manner. Consequently, recognition of a particular substance amounts to recognition of a certain spatial pattern of activity across the 50,000 different mitral cells in the olfactory bulb.

## Adaptation

The perceived intensity of a smell drops by 30% or more after continuous exposure. Figure 2.5 illustrates the results of an experiment by Eckman, Berglund, Berglund, and Lindvall (1967) in which subjects rated the intensity of a smell over a 12-minute period of continuous exposure (this graph was also used on Chapter 1 to illustrate the basic principles of adaptation; see Figure 1.16). By the 12th minute, the apparent intensity of the smell had dropped to less than half its initial level. Once the smell was removed, and then *presented only briefly over the next 12 minutes, its* apparent intensity quickly climbed back to pre-adaptation levels. Both adaptation and recovery rates were exponential. In other words, the rate at which adaptation (or recovery) proceeded was proportional to time: as time progressed after the start of adaptation (or recovery), the rate of adaptation (or recovery) declined.

The world is never completely free of odour, so the olfactory system is never completely free of adaptation. We are continuously exposed to the odour of

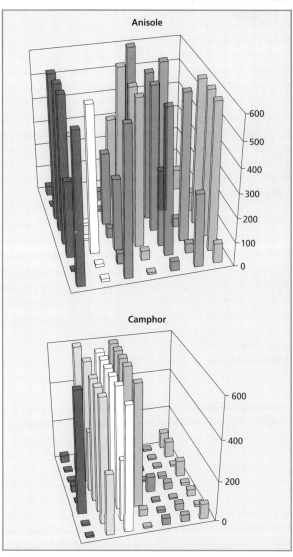

**FIG. 2.4** Spatial coding in olfaction. Each plot represents the response of a set of 56 receptor cells to a specific chemical. The height of each bar represents the response of a single cell to that chemical. The cells involved are actually spatially distributed across the olfactory epithelium, so the differing responses to the chemicals amount to differing spatial patterns of activation, as illustrated in the 3-D plot (the specific spatial layout in the figure is arbitrary). Data taken from Sicard and Holley (1984), Figure 4.

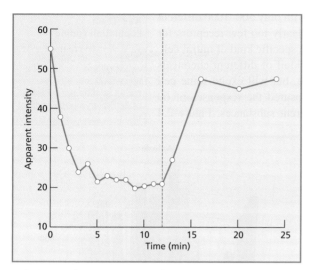

**FIG. 2.5** Adaptation to an odour. Sensory magnitude of an odour sensation was measured at regular intervals during a 12-minute exposure, showing adaptation to a constant stimulus. Once the stimulus was removed, sensory magnitude gradually recovered to former levels. Re-plotted from Eckman et al. (1967).

our own body, and often spend prolonged periods in a specific environment, such as our home. It would serve little purpose to be continually reminded of such constant odours, so adaptation ensures that they become undetectable. It is therefore not surprising that many individuals appear to be insensitive to the smell of their own body or their own house, even when those smells might appear unpleasant to others. Cigarette smokers, for example, are usually unaware of the smell of smoke on themselves or their surroundings, until they give up smoking.

Odour adaptation is selective. Moncrieff (1956) found that exposure to a specific odorant raised thresholds only for odorants with similar smells. For example, thresholds for detecting acetone were raised nearly two hundredfold by prior exposure to acetone, but were raised by a factor of two by exposure to iso-propanol. Berglund and Engen (1993) also found much larger effects for self-adaptation (adapt and test on the same substance) than for **cross-adaptation** (adapt and test on different substances).

## Anosmia

*Think of some everyday consequences of total anosmia.*

Odour blindness or **anosmia** can arise from a variety of sources. Partial anosmia is an inability to detect a specific odour. One person in ten in the general population is insensitive to the smell of cyanide, and one in a thousand is insensitive to butyl mer-captan. Several dozen such partial anosmias are known to exist. They are genetically transmitted, and probably reflect a deficiency in a specific type of olfactory receptor molecule (Smith, 2000).

> **KEY TERMS**
> **Cross-adaptation**: An experimental technique in which subjects are adapted to one stimulus for a period of time before their response to a different stimulus is measured.
> **Anosmia**: Lack of sensitivity to odour.
> **Taste receptor**: A chemoreceptor cell found on taste buds in the mouth, tongue, and throat; there are 50–150 receptors on each bud.
> **Taste bud**: A cluster of cells embedded in the skin of the tongue and mouth, housing taste receptors. The human tongue, contains approximately 5000 taste buds.
> **Gustatory papilla**: A small elevation on the tongue, visible to the naked eye, containing up to several hundred taste buds.

## TASTE

In modern human society, taste (also known as gustation) is used mainly to define our preferences for specific foods. However, gustation is universal in the animal kingdom, and is vital for establishing whether a specific substance is edible and nutritious, or poisonous.

## ANATOMY AND PHYSIOLOGY OF TASTE

### Receptors

Chemoreceptors are found on the tongue, and in the mouth and throat. They are grouped into about 10,000 **taste buds** that are located on small projections known as **papillae** (see Figure 2.6). Each taste bud contains 50–150 receptor cells arranged like the segments of an orange (Smith, 2000). The receptors in each bud form synapses with the dendrites of sensory neurons of the VIIth, IXth, and Xth cranial nerves that convey their responses to the brain.

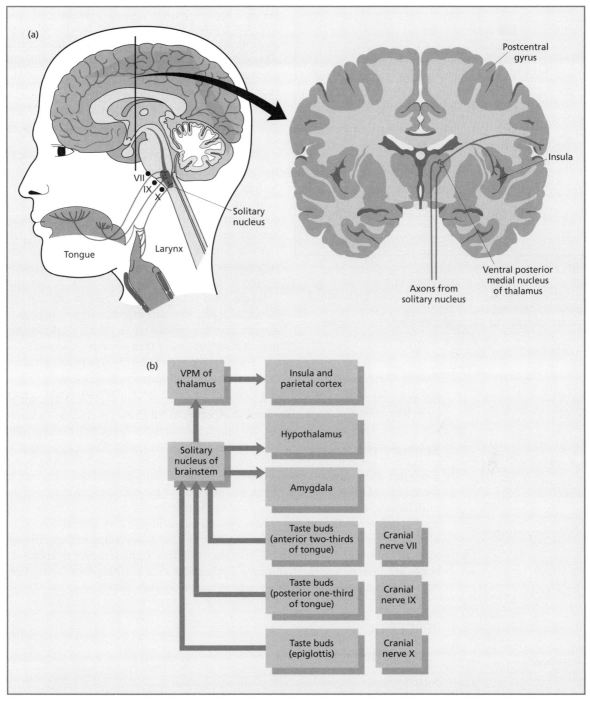

**FIG. 2.6** Sensory pathways for gustation. Re-drawn from Purves et al. (2001). Copyright © 2001 Sinauer Associates. Reproduced with permission.

Taste bud cells have a very short life span of no more than about 10 days. This makes it difficult for investigators to establish their function. During transduction, molecules from a substance placed in the mouth dissolve in saliva and bind to molecules on receptor cells. The resultant change in membrane permeability causes

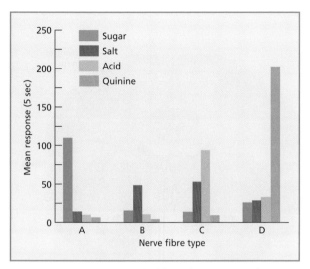

**FIG. 2.7**   Responses recorded from four classes of rat sensory nerve fibre (A–D) during the first 5 seconds of application of each of the four substances. Each class of gustatory fibre responds most strongly to one of the substances, but also responds a little to the other substances. Re-drawn from data in Nowlis and Frank (1977), Figure 4.

receptor potentials. Different substances bind with different types of receptor. The mechanisms of transduction are complex and only partly understood. They also vary from one species to another. Some substances have a more direct chemical effect on the receptor than others (for more details, see Delcomyn, 1998). Recordings from the sensory neurons to which receptors connect have imposed some degree of order on the complex variety of transduction mechanisms. These neurons appear to fall into one of four categories depending on their relative response to four different kinds of substance: sugars, salts, acids, and plant alkaloids.

Figure 2.7 illustrates the four categories of sensory neuron found in the cranial nerve of rats (Nowlis & Frank, 1977). We can infer that each sensory neuron connects mainly with receptors sensitive to one of the four types of substance. Notice that although each nerve responds best to one kind of substance it also responds to some extent to other substances. This may reflect the fact that a single sensory neuron innervates more than one type of receptor.

Some papillae contain free nerve endings that are thought to signal the spiciness of foods such as chilli peppers. Recall that free nerve endings also exist in the olfactory epithelium, and are thought to signal certain "chemical" qualities of smells such as tingle and coolness.

## Sensory pathways

The VIIth, IXth, and Xth cranial nerves carrying gustatory information terminate in the nucleus of the solitary tract in the medulla (part of the brainstem). Neurons in the medulla send axons to the amygdala and to the thalamus. Projections from the thalamus terminate in the primary gustatory cortex (see Figure 2.6). Recordings in the rat have revealed that the separation of gustatory signals according to four different kinds of substance is preserved in brainstem neurons. Cells sensitive to each substance are grouped together in the rat's parabrachial nucleus (Delcomyn, 1998). Very little is known about cortical processing of taste (see Rolls, 2002).

## PERCEPTION

### Taste dimensions

Attempts to decompose taste sensations into a small number of distinct categories or qualities date from the late 1500s, long before anything was known about the anatomy and physiology of taste. Boring (1942) noted that only five qualities appeared in all attempts at classification up to the late 1700s, namely sweetness, saltiness, sourness, bitterness, and sharpness. In the early 1900s, Henning's widely adopted classification dropped sharpness, leaving the four basic sensory qualities or "primaries" of sweet, salt, sour, and bitter. According to Boring (1942), Henning's classification allowed for intermediate qualities that combine pairs of primaries, such as the salty-bitter taste of potassium iodide. Henning devised the **taste tetrahedron** (Figure 2.8), with primary qualities lying at the corners and intermediate qualities lying along the edges.

The four taste primaries map on to the four kinds of substance to which sensory neurons respond, illustrated in Figure 2.7. Sweetness is clearly linked to sugars and saltiness to salts. Sourness is linked to acids such as the citric acid of citrus fruits, and bitterness is linked to plant alkaloids such as quinine.

In addition to these four basic taste primaries, recent evidence suggests that humans perceive a fifth primary quality, known as **umami**. Umami is a Japanese word meaning "good taste" or "yummy", and is used by researchers to refer to the taste evoked by glutamic acid. This substance is present in foods such as parmesan cheese, tomatoes, mushrooms, peas, and monosodium glutamate (MSG). Many snack manufacturers add MSG to their products to enhance their attractiveness, and it is traditionally used as a flavour enhancer in Asian cuisine. Chaudhari, Landin, and Roper (2000) recently provided evidence for the existence of a taste receptor molecule that mediates the detection of glutamate.

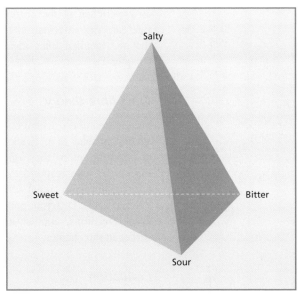

**FIG. 2.8**   Henning's taste tetrahedron.

## Taste adaptation

Prior exposure to one taste can affect perception of a later taste, either by diminishing that taste or by enhancing it (McBurney, 1969). For instance, adaptation to one sour taste, such as citric acid, reduces the apparent intensity of other sour tastes such as acetic acid as well as the intensity of some bitter tastes such as quinine. On the other hand, adaptation to sour compounds will cause water to taste sweet, and adaptation to sweet compounds will cause water to taste sour (McBurney, 1969). Cross-adaptation was mentioned earlier in the discussion of smell adaptation. As we shall see, cross-adaptation techniques are commonly used in perceptual research, because they allow us to draw some inferences about the nature of the neural mechanisms coding different sensory qualities.

## Theories of taste coding

### Taste-primaries theory

Henning's classification of four primary taste qualities has become associated with a strict interpretation of **taste primaries**, according to which any taste can be decomposed perceptually into the contributions from each of the primaries, with no intermediate qualities. For example, the taste of lemonade can be decomposed into contributions from sweetness, sourness, and bitterness sensations. This *taste-primaries* view of gustation is still prevalent (e.g. Bartoshuk and Beauchamp, 1994). Advocates of the taste-primaries theory argue that the four different classes of neuron illustrated in Figure 2.7 are so-called "labelled lines". What they mean by this is that when activity is present in one of the classes of neuron, that activity leads directly to an experience of the corresponding taste quality, because that class is a labelled line carrying information to the brain about a specific kind of substance (notice that the labelled lines idea is an example of a linking proposition, discussed in Chapter 1).

## Cross-fibre theory

Some researchers disagree with this view of neural coding, and favour a **cross-fibre theory** instead (e.g. Erickson, 1982). They point out that each class of neuron responds to more than one type of substance (for example, "sour" neurons in Figure 2.7 also respond to salt), so that "relative amounts of activity in parallel afferent fibres do signal sensory quality for taste" (Erickson, Doetsch, & Marshall, 1965, p. 248). Different patterns of neural activity are presumed to mediate different taste sensations, another example of the population-coding principle introduced earlier in the chapter.

## Evaluation

*Try to relate the two theories of taste coding to the different theoretical movements outlined in Chapter 1.*

Which view of gustatory coding is correct, the taste-primaries theory or the cross-fibre theory? Empirical evidence is equivocal. Data obtained from single sensory nerve fibres (Figure 2.7) are generally interpreted to favour the basic-tastes model, since neurons in each class respond much more strongly to one substance than to any of the others. On the other hand, cross-adaptation described above is not consistent with labelled lines, since responses in one "line" should not affect the signals carried by a different line. Cross-adaptation favours the cross-fibre theory because it implies that perception depends on some kind of interaction between the signals provided by each class of neuron. From a functional point of view, it seems sensible to categorise perceptual responses into four primary tastes, as advocated by the taste-primaries theory, because each taste signifies a specific useful property of a substance.

1. Sweetness clearly relates to sugar content, useful for identifying a substance as a food source.
2. Saltiness relates to the presence of sodium chloride, essential for normal neural function but liable to be depleted due to sweating or bleeding.
3. Sourness is associated with acidity, which tends to be produced by unripe food and by bacteria in spoilt food.
4. Bitterness is associated with plant alkaloids that are toxic, such as strychnine, quinine, morphine, and tubocurarine (alkaloid names generally end in the -ine suffix).

**KEY TERM**
**Cross-fibre theory**: A theory of taste coding based on the idea that perceived taste is based on the pattern of activity across different classes of sensory fibre.

In order to seek out sugars and salts, and to avoid acids and alkaloids, it is clearly useful to be able to detect them as distinct taste qualities, as suggested by the taste-primaries theory. However, the presence of such perceptual categorisation does not, in itself, invalidate the cross-fibre theory. The process of categorisation may actually involve some form of comparison across neurons responsive to different classes of substance. As discussed in Chapter 1, early levels of perceptual analysis are usually thought to involve analogue representations (quantitative variation in firing level across neurons, as in the cross-fibre theory). Later levels may involve more abstract representations (perceptual categories, as in the basic-tastes theory). So the two theories of gustatory coding may apply at different levels of analysis.

## Conditioned taste aversion

If a food induces illness, many animals later show an aversion to consuming that food again (Garcia & Koelling, 1966). The effect is very powerful, and requires only a single learning episode. There have been many experimental demonstrations of the effect in animals given food laced with nausea-inducing chemicals, including experiments on rats, mice, monkeys, ferrets, birds, fish, and reptiles. "Bait-shyness" in rodents can be attributed to conditioned taste aversion. Humans also show conditioned taste aversion. Many people have experienced an aversion to a particular food following a bout of sickness at the time they ate it. Excessive alcohol consumption often leads to a (temporary) aversion to alcohol afterwards. The aversion apparently requires no conscious awareness, and may even develop when a particular food is consumed just before a bout of sickness unconnected with consumption of the food. This is a particular problem for patients undergoing radiotherapy or chemotherapy for the treatment of cancer. Food aversion and loss of appetite are well known, so patients are advised not to eat within a couple of hours of treatment, and to eat non-preferred foods (Schiffman, 1983).

# FLAVOUR

The sensation of eating, or flavour, transcends both smell and taste. It involves an interaction between several perceptual sensations including taste, smell, temperature, touch, sight, sound, and pain. These different sensations appear to interact to determine flavour, so we cannot view flavour as a simple summation of disparate sensations. However, smell and taste seem to be pre-eminent, in that a sensation complex that excludes them does not create a flavour. There are many examples of how the sensory components of flavour interact. For example, certain visual colours are associated with particular flavours, and when colour is altered there is a change in flavour. The rated flavour intensity of foods such as yoghurt, cakes, and sucrose solutions increases with the degree of food colouration. Increases in the amount of gelling agent in a food increase its viscosity and texture thickness, but also reduce its flavour intensity, and it is difficult to relate the flavour change to the chemical effects of the gelling agent. For a review of recent research on flavour, see Delwiche (2004).

# EVALUATION

At this point it is worthwhile pausing to reflect on the general principles introduced in this chapter, and how they relate specifically to the chemical senses.

## PHYSIOLOGICAL PRINCIPLES

Both smell and taste exhibit a clear hierarchy of processing that begins at the receptors in the nose, mouth, and throat and ends with activity in the sensory cortex, passing through intermediate stages on the way (compare Figure 1.10 with Figures 2.2 and 2.6).

Receptors show a high degree of specificity to particular odorants (Figure 2.4) or tastes (Figure 2.7).

## SENSORY PRINCIPLES

The smells and tastes detected by the receptors generate powerful sensory states, or qualia: the clean smell of limes, yumminess in foods containing MSG, the disgusting odour of faeces.

The detectability of olfactory and gustatory stimuli varies markedly over time (Figure 2.5), and helps us to adapt to specific environments.

## THEORETICAL PRINCIPLES

Linda Buck was jointly awarded, with Richard Axel, the 2004 Nobel prize in physiology or medicine for their research on the olfactory system. Their pioneering work has given us a detailed understanding of how the nose is able to distinguish more than 10,000 smells, as well as defining the genes and proteins that control the olfactory response.

Representation is a core principle in sensory neuroscience, and very good examples of it are offered by the chemical senses. In the case of smell, recall that any one receptor responds to multiple odorants, and any one odorant excites multiple receptors. It follows that different odorants excite different combinations of receptors. We can therefore view the pattern of activity across the population of receptor types as representing the unique chemical composition of the odorant. If the odorant composition changes, the pattern of activity (representational state) in the receptors also changes. The pattern of activity actually forms a spatial, analogue representation of the odorant by virtue of the spatial arrangement of glomeruli in the olfactory bulb. Malnic, Hirono, Sato, and Buck (1999) proposed that the pattern of activity constitutes a "combinatorial code" for odour. There are roughly 1000 different receptor types. Even if we assume that just three types respond to each odour, the code would be able to discriminate nearly a billion different odours (Malnic et al., 1999). In other words, it would have nearly a billion different representational states.

In the case of taste, receptors fall into just four classes responding optimally to sugars, salts, acids (sour), and plant alkaloids (bitter). Two representational schemes have been proposed. In the taste-primaries theory, activity in each receptor class uniquely represents the presence of the corresponding substance. In the cross-fibre theory, the pattern of activity across all receptor types represents the presence of the corresponding substance. In both theories a specific state in the sensory system is assumed to map onto a specific state in the outside world (a particular taste stimulus). By now you should be able to identify the linking propositions implicit in the above theories about smell and taste: Our sensation of a specific odour is linked to a specific pattern of activity in the population of odorant receptors; the sensations of saltiness, sweetness, sourness, and bitterness are linked to the pattern of activity in gustatory receptors.

## CHAPTER SUMMARY

The senses of smell and taste are known as chemical senses because they extract information by means of chemical interactions.

### SMELL

● The sense of smell is mediated by 500–1000 different types of sensory receptor in the olfactory epithelium of the nose.
● Each mitral cell in the olfactory bulb of the brain is connected to just one type of receptor. Different environmental substances create different

patterns of activity across the mitral cells. The ability of humans to recognise thousands of different odours must depend on the ability of the olfactory sensory system to distinguish different patterns of activity in mitral cells.

- The large number of partial anosmias found in humans is a reflection of the relatively large number of different olfactory receptors present in the sensory system.

## TASTE

- Gustatory receptors fall into four categories on the basis of dominant responses to one of four types of substance, namely sugars, salts, acids, and plant alkaloids.
- Research on taste perception has concluded that all tastes can be decomposed into contributions from four primary qualities—sweetness, saltiness, sourness, and bitterness. These four qualities map precisely onto the four types of substance to which taste receptors respond.
- In humans, a fifth taste quality has also been identified, umami, that maps onto receptors sensitive to the presence of glutamic acid.
- The taste-primaries theory of taste coding argues that the four receptor types are labelled lines coding the presence of specific substances.
- The cross-fibre theory of taste coding argues that taste coding depends on the pattern of activity across the receptor types.
- Both theories may be correct, but apply to different levels of taste analysis.

## FLAVOUR

- Food flavour during eating involves an interaction between several perceptual sensations including taste, smell, temperature, touch, sight, sound, and pain.

# TUTORIALS

## SMELL AND EMOTION

The hedonic (pleasantness–unpleasantness) aspect of smell has long been regarded as its most important quality (Engen, 1982). Smells do evoke powerful emotional responses ranging from intense pleasure to extreme revulsion. In the Middle Ages it was believed that unpleasant odours actually caused diseases such as the Black Death. Doctors visiting plague victims took elaborate precautions to shield themselves from the unpleasant odour thought to cause the disease. They wore an elaborate mask shaped like a duck's head, with windows made of glass and a beak filled with herbs and petals (see Figure 2.9). They also carried a torch burning a pot-pourri of fragrant herbs.

**FIG. 2.9** Dress worn by doctors during the plague in 18th-century France. The leather coat was covered in honey-scented beeswax, and the beak-like mask with glass eye holes was filled with fresh herbs and dried flower petals (this may be the origin of the slang word for doctors—quacks). A pot-pourri of herbs was burnt in the torch. Based on drawings in Stoddart (1990).

The use of perfume to enhance attractiveness dates back to the beginning of recorded history. The ancient cultures of the Middle and Far East manufactured and traded perfumes on a large scale (Stoddart, 1990). Perfumes became synonymous with, and a substitute for, personal hygiene. Standards of personal hygiene are obviously much higher in modern society than in the Middle Ages, but washing and personal hygiene products are still sold primarily on the basis of their aromatic qualities. The continual search for clean, pleasing smells may reflect the fact that odour perception seems to be dominated by displeasure. Engen (1982) cited a Japanese study which found that only 20% of 400,000 different odours tested were judged to be pleasant. Engen and Ross (1973) reported a tendency for unfamiliar odours to be disliked by naïve subjects. They used 110 different odours and found that only 11% of unfamiliar odours were liked, whereas 46% of familiar odours were liked.

Whether a smell is pleasant or unpleasant, its emotional impact wanes with exposure. There are anecdotal reports that people who work in strong-smelling environments, such as confectionery factories, glue factories, or animal rendering plants become adapted so that the pleasant smell of, for example, chocolate, or the unpleasant smell of animal carcasses becomes less intense. Cain and Johnson (1978) found experimental support for these anecdotal reports. Subjects were exposed to pleasant or unpleasant smells for 30 minutes. A pleasant smell (citral—lemon) was judged less pleasant after adaptation than before, and an unpleasant smell (isobutyric acid—rancid butter) was judged less unpleasant.

Why is the hedonic aspect of smell so dominant? Olfaction is the only sense in which there are direct projections between the primary sensory cortex and the amygdala. In rodents 40% of neurons in the amygdala respond to olfactory stimulation (Cain and Bindra, 1972). The amygdala is well known to play a crucial role in generating emotional responses, as revealed by lesion studies and single-cell recording data (Aggleton, 1992). Zald and Pardo (1997) reported a PET brain-imaging study of the human brain regions activated by pleasant and unpleasant smells. The most significant increases in regional cerebral blood flow (rCBF) during exposure to a very unpleasant smell were bilaterally in the amygdala. Weaker activation was also found in the primary olfactory cortex. On the other hand, statistically non-significant increases in rCBF were found during presentation of pleasant odours. The greater power of aversive stimuli in this PET study is consistent with earlier reports that displeasure dominates odour perception, and with reports that the amygdala is particularly involved in the appraisal of danger and the emotion of fear (Scott, Young, Calder, Hellawell, Aggleton, & Johnson, 1997). It seems that one of the primary functions of olfaction is to alert the organism to the presence of danger indicated by decomposing vegetable or animal matter.

## THE VARIETY OF CHEMICAL RECEPTORS

The chemical senses are the most primitive of all senses, from an evolutionary perspective. Chemosensitivity undoubtedly emerged very early in the history of life on earth, in primitive bacteria immersed in a watery medium awash with chemicals. Present-day bacteria are known to possess chemoreceptors that they use to guide their movement, swimming towards nutrients and away from toxins (Koshland, 1980). Gustatory receptors clearly function primarily to detect and identify food-related chemicals, whereas olfactory receptors are also used to identify other animals (mates, predators, and prey) and for localisation (migration, navigation). The division of chemical senses into smell and taste has been questioned in the case of water-dwelling animals, though Atema (1977) argued that the two senses do remain distinct even in an aquatic environment. Many fish have very highly developed olfactory senses. They can detect blood and bodily fluids over considerable distances, and migrating salmon are believed to navigate to spawning grounds using olfactory signals (Smith, 2000).

Among land-dwelling animals, olfactory receptors are remarkably similar across phyla. Glomeruli similar to those found in the human olfactory bulb are found in a wide diversity of animals, from molluscs to arthropods (Delcomyn, 1998). Gustatory receptors, on the other hand, do show marked species differences. Many animals possess two gustatory systems. As well as gustatory receptors in the mouth, they have receptors on their external body surface, such as on antennae (snails), or tentacles (octopus), or legs (arthropods). The structure housing these external receptors is known as a "sensillum"—a small peg, pit, plate, socket, or hair usually open at the tip and covered in a small drop of viscous fluid in which substances diffuse before reception (Shepherd, 1988). Some female insects even have sensilli on their ovipositor (used for laying eggs in a suitable environment).

In addition to chemoreceptors that contribute to the sense of smell and taste, most animals (including humans) have a number of other chemoreceptors that monitor internal bodily chemicals, such as receptors for glucose levels, receptors for circulating toxins, and receptors for sensing the level of blood oxygenation in the carotid arteries. These receptors cannot be considered as part of a sensory system, since their responses are not processed in the same way as those of conventional sensory receptors and do not contribute to conscious experience. Many animals, especially insects, use a complex system of chemical signals to control social behaviour and mating. Moths that communicate by means of sex pheromones can have as many as 75,000 chemoreceptors on each of their antennae. Only one or two molecules of pheromone are required per receptor cell over a 2-second period in order to evoke a behavioural response from the insect (Delcomyn, 1998).

The chemoreceptors found in the human gustatory and olfactory senses thus represent just a small part of a broad spectrum of chemoreceptors that serve a number of different functions in different organisms.

# CHAPTER 3

## CONTENTS

# The body senses

## INTRODUCTION

The body senses provide information about surfaces in direct contact with the skin (touch), about the position and movement of body parts (**proprioception** and **kinesthesis**), and about the position and movement of the body itself relative to the external world (balance). All of this information is supplied by two anatomically separate sensory systems. The *somatosensory* system deals with touch, proprioception, and kinesthesis, while the *vestibular* system deals with balance.

## THE SOMATOSENSORY SYSTEM

Touch mediates our most intimate contact with the external world. We use it to sense the physical properties of a surface, such as its texture, warmth, and softness. The sensitivity of this system is exquisite, particularly at the most sensitive parts of the body such as the fingers and lips. Direct contact with other people is responsible for some of our most intense sensory experiences. Individuals who lack the sense of touch due to a physical disorder are severely disabled, since they lack the sensory information that is essential to avoid tissue damage caused by direct contact with harmful surfaces.

Compared to the sense of touch, proprioception and kinesthesis seem largely invisible. We are not conscious of making use of information about the position and movement of body parts, so it is naturally impossible to imagine being deprived of proprioception. Yet proprioception is vital for normal bodily functioning, and its absence is severely disabling. Some appreciation of its importance can be gained from individuals who have lost their sense of proprioception following illness. Cole and Paillard (1995) describe two such cases, identified by their initials, IW and GL. IW was a 19-year-old butcher when he suffered a flu-like viral illness. He became increasingly weak and at one stage fell down in the street. On admission to hospital, he had slurred speech, an absence of sensation in the mouth, no sense of touch on his body, and no awareness of body position. Although he retained an ability to move his body, he had no control over the movement. After recovery from the initial infection, IW spent 18 months in a rehabilitation hospital learning to control his movements, including learning to walk again, following which he was discharged and did not see a doctor for about 12 years. Later investigations established that IW's illness had

**KEY TERMS**
**Proprioception**: The sensory modality providing information about the position of body parts, served by mechanoreceptors in the musculoskeletal system.
**Kinesthesis**: The sensory modality providing information about the movement of body parts, served by mechanoreceptors in the musculoskeletal system.

destroyed the sensory nerves that supply the brain with information about touch and proprioception, though he can still sense pain and temperature. In the absence of proprioception, IW can only make controlled bodily movements with intense concentration, visual vigilance, and imagery. Once he had learned to walk, if he sneezed and thus broke his concentration, he would fall over. He must monitor the position of his moving feet and legs visually while walking. Even the act of sitting in a chair requires concentration to avoid falling out of it. IW avoids crowded spaces, for fear of being nudged by someone out of view. When navigating an unfamiliar environment he studies it beforehand, much like a mountaineer surveying a difficult climb, to judge the degree of slope in the ground surface, to measure the size of any gaps through which he must fit, and to estimate the strength of any wind. IW has made use of his acquired skill in assessing environments, and is now used as an adviser by holiday care services, reporting on the suitability of possible holiday locations for disabled visitors.

The case of IW is a vivid example of the importance of somatosensation.

## PHYSIOLOGY OF SOMATOSENSATION

The somatosensory system includes eight different kinds of receptor, and two separate pathways linking receptors to the primary receiving area in the cerebral cortex.

**FIG. 3.1**   Direct physical contact mediates some of our most powerful sensory experiences. Copyright © Patrik Giardino/Corbis.

### Somatosensory receptors

Table 3.1 below lists the eight types of receptor, their location, and their primary sensory function.

| TABLE 3.1 CLASSIFICATION OF SOMATOSENSORY RECEPTORS | | |
|---|---|---|
| **Receptor type** | **Location** | **Sensory function** |
| *Touch:* | | |
| Free nerve endings | All skin, superficial | Pain, temperature, tickle |
| Meissner's corpuscles | Glabrous skin, superficial | Light, dynamic touch |
| Merkel's disks | All skin, superficial | Static pressure |
| Pacinian corpuscles | All skin, deep | Pressure, vibration |
| Ruffini's corpuscles | All skin, deep | Stretching of skin |
| *Proprioception:* | | |
| Muscle spindles | Muscles | Muscle length |
| Golgi tendon organs | Tendons | Muscle tension |
| Joint receptors | Joints | Joint position |

## Touch receptors

Figure 3.2 illustrates the location of the five different **touch receptors** below the surface of the skin. As indicated in Table 3.1, some lie near the surface of the skin whereas others lie deeper below the surface. Free nerve endings do not have any structural specialisations for transducing stimuli, and it is not possible to determine their preferred stimulus on the basis of morphology. The mechanism of transduction is not well understood (Delcomyn, 1998), but they are known to mediate perception of pain from tissue damage, and perception of hot and cold. In the remaining four types of touch receptor the nerve ending is encapsulated within a specialised structure that governs the receptor's response to mechanical stimulation:

1. Pacinian corpuscles have an onion-like capsule in which layers of membrane lamellae are separated by fluid. Mechanical stimulation deforms the structure and leads to a response from the receptor. Pacinian corpuscles are able to vary their activity at a very high rate (250–350 Hz) in response to dynamic stimulation, allowing them to respond to high-frequency vibration of the skin, such as that produced by the movement of a fine-textured surface across the skin.
2. Merkel's disks and Ruffini's corpuscles, on the other hand, have a very sluggish temporal response, making them best-suited to signal relatively stable, unchanging mechanical stimulation.
3. Meissner's corpuscles have an intermediate temporal response (30–50 Hz), able to detect moderate dynamic stimulation.

It would be misleading to assume too neat a division in sensory function between different receptor types. Skin contact with an external surface produces a complex pattern of activation across all receptor types. One's perception of the properties of the surface depends jointly on the information provided by all of them.

> **KEY TERM**
> **Touch receptors**:
> Mechanoreceptors and free nerve endings below the surface of the skin, mediating perception of pain, temperature, pressure, vibration, stretch.

**FIG. 3.2** Cross-section through a region of hairless skin revealing five different types of touch receptor. Re-drawn from Purves et al. (2001). Copyright © 2001 Sinauer Associates. Reproduced with permission.

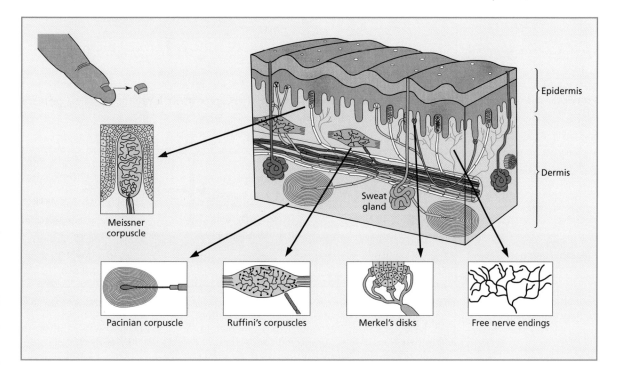

## Proprioception

Receptors for proprioception (**proprioceptors**) are found in and around the limbs, either in the muscles themselves, in the tendons that attach the muscles to bone, or in the joints. Muscle spindles are relatively well understood, whereas little is known about joint receptors. Muscle spindles consist of between four and eight specialised muscle fibres surrounded by a capsule of connective tissue. The axons of sensory nerves encircle the fibres within the capsule to provide information on muscle length. Large muscles that generate fairly coarse movements possess relatively few muscle spindles, while muscles used for very fine and accurate movements, such as those in the hand and surrounding the eyes, are well supplied with muscle spindles.

## Somatosensory pathways

The mechanoreceptors mediating somatosensation are modified sensory neurons. Their cell bodies are located in the **dorsal root ganglia**, which lie just outside the spinal column. Their peripheral axons end in various sensory specialisations below the surface of the skin, while their central axons project toward the brain. Mechanical stimulation of a particular sensory neuron provokes a graded change in receptor potential. When the receptor potential exceeds a certain minimum value, an action potential will be triggered, which travels along the cell's axon. The action potential will be transmitted along one of two routes, known as the **spinothalamic pathway** and the **lemniscal pathway**. The flowchart in Figure 3.3 summarises these two routes to the brain.

**KEY TERMS**
**Proprioceptors**:
Mechanoreceptors in muscles, tendons, and joints mediating perception of body position and movement.
**Dorsal root ganglia**:
Rounded swellings lying in the vertebrae just outside the spinal cord, each containing thousands of afferent cell bodies whose axons enter the spinal cord.
**Spinothalamic pathway**:
The ascending sensory pathway for pain and temperature signals from free nerve endings.
**Lemniscal pathway**: The ascending sensory pathway for somatosensory signals from mechanoreceptors.

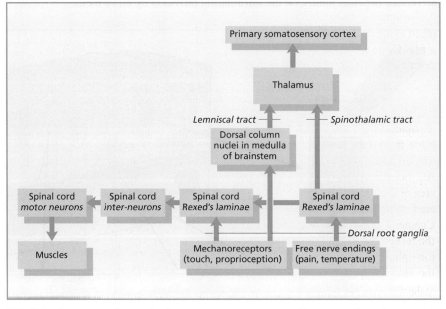

**FIG. 3.3** Sensory pathways in the somatosensory system. Responses from free nerve endings, mediating pain and temperature sensations, travel along the spinothalamic tract. Responses from mechanoreceptors mediating touch and proprioception travel along the lemniscal tract. Branching connections in Rexed's laminae of the spinal cord mediate reflexive withdrawal responses to harmful stimuli.

In the spinothalamic pathway (right-hand route in the flowchart), central axons carrying responses from free nerve endings (mediating pain and temperature sensation) terminate in the spinal cord in areas called Rexed's laminae I and II (Purves et al., 2001). Responses are then relayed to cells in laminae IV to VI, whose axons project all the way up the spinal cord to the thalamus. In the lemniscal pathway, central axons carrying responses from mechanoreceptors ascend the spinal cord as far as the brainstem. They terminate in the dorsal column nuclei of the medulla. Projections from the medulla terminate in the thalamus. In both the spinothalamic pathway and the lemniscal pathway, neurons in the thalamus send axons to the primary somatosensory cortex. Both pathways also contain branching projections in the spinal cord that are responsible for reflexes, such as withdrawal from painful stimuli, and the **knee-jerk reflex** (horizontal arrows in the flowchart).

Axons associated with mechanoreceptors in the lemniscal pathway are myelinated (covered in a laminated wrapping) and as a result have relatively fast conduction velocities of about 20 m/s. Axons in the spinothalamic pathway are only lightly myelinated or unmyelinated, and have relatively slow conduction velocities of about 2 m/s. This difference in conduction velocity can be sensed when a drop of hot water falls on the hand. The contact of the water drop on the hand can be sensed about half a second before its temperature (Delcomyn, 1998).

> In the case of IW described earlier, all myelinated fibres were destroyed by the disease, depriving him of all sensory information from mechanoreceptors.

## Cortical representation of somatosensation

The primary somatosensory cortex occupies a long, thin strip of cortical surface running from ear to ear across the head (the grey area in the side view of the cortex shown in the top left of Figure 3.4). The axons of thalamic neurons project to an area known as Brodmann's area 3 (sub-divided into a and b), but the adjacent areas 1 and 2 also represent somatosensation. The cross-section in Figure 3.4 (middle left) is taken along the line labelled A–A' in the top left, and shows the locations of the three areas. Close inspection of the properties of neurons in area 3 reveals a very high degree of selectivity and organisation.

### Receptive field properties

Mountcastle (1957) found that each cell in primary somatosensory cortex receives input from only one type of receptor. For example, one cell may be connected to Merkel disks, while another cell may receive inputs only from Meissner corpuscles. All the receptors projecting to an individual cortical neuron are located in a small area of the body. As a result, each cortical neuron responds to stimulation only in that area, which defines the cell's *receptive field*. Receptive fields were introduced in Chapter 1 to illustrate the principle of physiological selectivity. Figure 3.5 illustrates the receptive field of a typical somatosensory cortical neuron (the middle neuron on the right of the schematic cortical circuit). Projections from sensory receptors under the skin of the forearm converge on the cortical cell by means of intermediate synapses in the brain stem and thalamus. Consequently the neuron responds only to stimulation in that region of the body (shaded area).

Projections from receptors in area A of the receptive field are excitatory, and projections from receptors in area B provide **inhibition**, by means of inter-neurons coloured black in Figure 3.5. This kind of inhibition is a common feature in sensory pathways. The connections are organised in such a way that stimulation in the centre of

> **KEY TERMS**
> **Knee-jerk reflex (myotatic reflex)**: The reflexive extension of the lower leg following a hammer tap on the knee tendon, due to activation of a simple reflex circuit in the spinal cord.
> **Lateral inhibition**: Inhibition that travels across a neural network to impede the forward flow of activity.

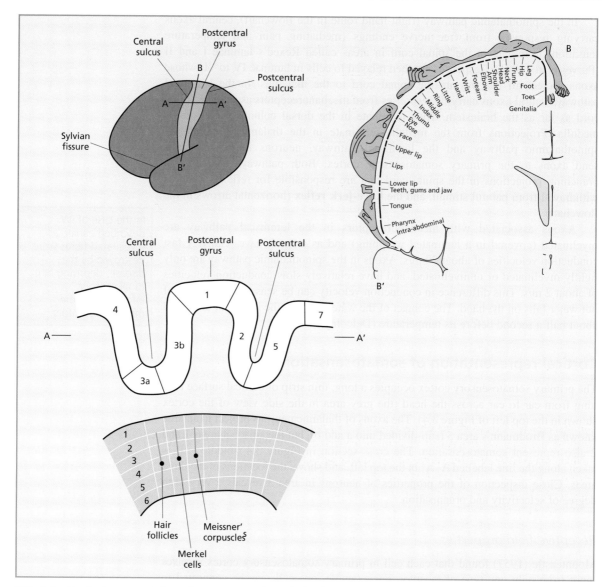

**FIG. 3.4**  Cortical representation of somatosensation. Thalamic neurons project to cells in a long, thin strip extending across the cortex from ear to ear (top left; a view of the cortex from the left side). Cross-sections along the line A–A' are shown in the lower left of the figure. In common with other areas of cortex, somatosensory cortex can be sub-divided into six different layers, labelled 1–6 moving down from the surface. Thalamic axons terminate in layer 4 of area 3. Within a thin column of cortex, cells in all layers receive inputs from just one receptor type. A larger scale cross-section along line B–B' is shown at the right of the figure. Each cell is selectively responsive to stimulation in a particular region of the body. Moving across the cortex from B to B', there is an orderly progression in the body part covered by the cells. Re-drawn from Smith (2000) and Penfield and Rasmussen (1950). Copyright © 2000 John Wiley & Sons Limited. Reproduced with permission.

the receptive field excites the cell, and stimulation in the periphery of the receptive field inhibits the cell. The top recording trace in the figure shows that neural activity increases in response to stimulation at point A in the receptive field. Stimulation in area B, on the other hand, causes a decrease in activity (middle trace) due to the inhibition transmitted laterally in the neural circuit. Stimulation at points A and B

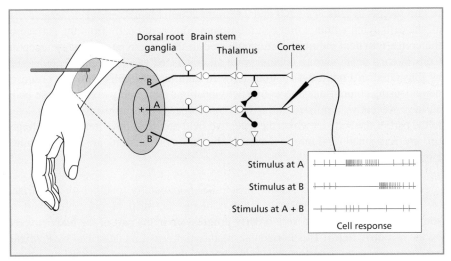

**FIG. 3.5** Cortical receptive fields. Stimulation of a small region on the forearm (left) generates a response that is recorded from the middle cortical cell on the right. This region of body surface represents the cell's receptive field. Excitation from receptors in region A of the receptive field is relayed via ascending projections in the spinal cord, brainstem, and thalamus. Inhibition from receptors in region B of the receptive field is generated by lateral connections (black in the figure). Stimulation in the central region (A) generates an increase in firing rate (top trace in the box). Stimulation in the outer region of the receptive field (B) causes a decrease in activity (middle trace). Stimulation in both A and B simultaneously does not change the activity level of the cell (bottom trace).

simultaneously leads to no net change in neural response (bottom trace). Receptive fields of this kind are often called antagonistic **centre–surround receptive fields**, for obvious reasons. Why is the receptive field organised in this way? Centre–surround antagonism means that the cell responds best to relatively small stimuli that fill the central excitatory area of its receptive field but do not encroach on the inhibitory surround. This makes the cell's response sensitive to very small changes in the position and/or size of the stimulus.

*Why is centre–surround organisation useful?*

## Cortical organisation

A basic principle of sensory physiology is the high degree of order shown by the arrangement of cells at each level of processing, as discussed in Chapter 1. Somatosensation offers a supreme example of this principle. Neurons connected to receptors on the left half of the body project to somatosensory cortex in the right-hand hemisphere, and neurons connected to receptors on the right half of the body project to the left-hand hemisphere. The properties of neighbouring cells in somatosensory cortex are closely related. Anatomical and electrophysiological studies over the last half-century have revealed that the somatosensory cortex is highly organised, both vertically and horizontally.

*Vertical organisation* Vertically, the mammalian cortex can be split into six distinct layers (see Figure 3.4, bottom left), on the basis of variations in cell number, density, and morphology. The axons of thalamic neurons terminate in layer 4 of Brodmann's areas 3a and 3b. Layer 4 cells connect with cells in other layers, which

> **KEY TERM**
> **Centre–surround receptive field**: A receptive field containing concentrically organised regions of excitation and inhibition, as a result of lateral inhibition.

The division of the whole neocortex into six layers and about 50 different areas, on the basis of histological features, was first described by the neuroanatomist Korbinian Brodmann in the early 1900s.

Penfield's findings are a dramatic demonstration of Muller's principle of specific nerve energy, introduced in Chapter 1.

Neurons in the spinal cord conveying pain signals from the internal organs also convey information about pain near the body surface. As a result, pain from internal organs is often "referred" to a more superficial part of the body sharing the same afferent neurons. Pain in the heart muscle, for instance, is referred to the chest wall and left arm (Purves et al., 2001).

in turn project to cells in areas 1 and 2 (Smith, 2000). Mountcastle (1957) found that all the cells lying within a thin column running down vertically from the surface of the cortex (**cortical column**) were connected to the same type of sensory receptor. Cells in each neighbouring column were all connected to a different receptor type, as illustrated in Figure 3.4 (bottom left). In addition, the cells within a group of neighbouring columns have receptive field locations that largely overlap on the body surface. Receptive field size varies between cortical cells, in a way that is related to the part of the body on which the receptive field lies. Receptive fields on the finger tips are very small (3–4 mm in diameter), but those on the trunk are over 100 times larger.

*Horizontal organisation* As one progresses horizontally (parallel to the surface of the cortex within a particular layer) along the strip of cortex devoted to somatosensation, there is a very orderly progression in the part of the body covered by the receptive fields. This horizontal organisation was first described by Penfield, a neurosurgeon who performed brain surgery during the early 1950s to relieve epilepsy. The patient was anaesthetised but awake during the operation, and Penfield applied small electric currents to the exposed surface of cortex by means of a small electrode. The patient reported any experiences that resulted from the stimulation. The purpose of the procedure was to identify critical areas of cortex to be avoided during surgery, but in the process Penfield made some startling discoveries. When stimulation was applied to the brain area now identified as somatosensory cortex, the patient reported tactile sensations on specific parts of the body. As Penfield systematically moved the electrode across the surface of the cortex, the bodily location of the sensation also moved systematically. Figure 3.4 (right) is re-drawn from Penfield and Rasmussen (1950), and represents a cross-sectional view of the cortex along the line B–B' in the figure. Notice that the body is mapped out across the surface of the cortex. The area of cortical surface devoted to different body parts is not in proportion to their size. For instance, relatively small areas of cortex contain cells with receptive fields on the back, or on the leg, whereas very large areas of cortex are devoted to the hands and to the lips. This effect is known as *cortical magnification*. Research on other species has discovered very different patterns of cortical magnification. In rodents, for example, the large facial whiskers are disproportionately represented in somatosensory cortex. The large spots or "barrels" apparent in the somatosensory representation of the star-nosed mole (Figure 1.2 in Chapter 1) each represent an individual whisker. The extent of cortical representation of a body part seems to reflect the importance of that body part for the survival of the animal.

## Cortical representation of pain

Although thalamic neurons conveying information about pain do project to somatosensory cortex, the cortical representation of pain is not well understood. Removal of the relevant region of cortex to alleviate chronic pain is not usually successful, though tactile sensation is impaired. There is a parallel projection of pain signals from the thalamus to the reticular formation, pons, and midbrain that is probably responsible for the arousing effects of pain. These projections would not be affected by cortical ablation. There are also descending projections from the cortex to the spinal cord, particularly to Rexed's lamina II. These projections are thought to play a role in the central control of pain, such as the surprisingly low intensities of pain reported by soldiers in battle.

# SOMATOSENSORY PERCEPTION

## Two-point acuity

Our ability to discriminate fine differences in touch stimulation can be measured using a pair of callipers, placing one or both points on the skin of the subject (Figure 3.6, top). The subject's task is to report whether they can feel a single point or a pair of points. As Figure 3.6 (bottom) shows, performance varies markedly in different regions of the body. Acuity is highest on the tongue and hands, where points separated by as little as 2 or 3 mm can be discriminated. Performance is worst on the back and legs, where points have to be over 50 mm apart to be discriminated. This pattern of performance closely reflects the variation in receptive field size and cortical representation mentioned earlier in the chapter. The area of cortex devoted to the fingers contains a great many neurons having small receptive fields, typically 1–2 mm in diameter. Consequently, if the callipers are placed on the fingers and gradually moved further apart, over a range of 3 or 4 mm, the activity of an individual neuron will change markedly (refer back to Figure 3.5). In addition, the points of the callipers will very soon stimulate different neurons, since the receptive fields are so small. These changes in cortical activity mediate fine touch discrimination at the fingers. The cortical representation of the back is relatively sparse, and receptive fields are large. Consequently, a change in position of 3 or 4 mm will have very little effect on the activity of individual cells, and therefore on discrimination.

*Think about how the activity of an individual cell varies with the position of the stimulus in its receptive field.*

**KEY TERM**
**Haptic perception**: The perception of shape, size, and identity on the basis of touch and kinesthesis.

## Object recognition

Although humans normally rely on vision for object identification, touch can also be used effectively. The perception of object properties on the basis of touch and kinesthesis is sometimes called **haptic perception**. When subjects are allowed to touch and manipulate objects without visual information, recognition rates are very high. Klatzky, Lederman, and Metzger (1985) investigated the ability of 20 blindfolded students to identify 100 common objects by touch. Objects included, for example, a ring, a golf ball, a sock, a tea bag, scissors, a fork, a key, and a screwdriver. Identification was 96% accurate, and 68% of responses occurred within 3 seconds of initial contact with the object. Subjects were clearly able to gather a great deal of useful information regarding object properties from a relatively brief manual inspection. Two objects in particular accounted for a high proportion of the errors, rice and a T-shirt.

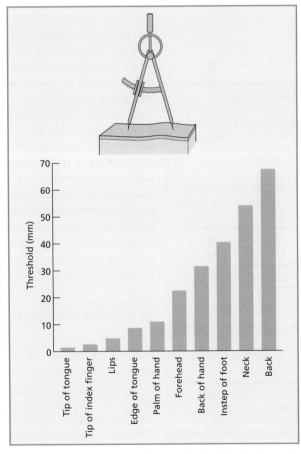

**FIG. 3.6** Two-point acuity for touch. A pair of callipers is placed on the skin surface, and the subject is required to report whether they feel a single point or a pair of points (top). The callipers are adjusted until the subject can just report the presence of a pair of points reliably (discrimination threshold). The bar graph shows the discrimination threshold on various parts of the body. Thresholds are smallest, in the region of 1–5 mm, on the mouth and fingers, and largest on the neck and back (50–70 mm).

# THE VESTIBULAR SYSTEM

Information about the orientation and movement of the body with respect to the external environment is vital for normal bodily function. It allows us, for example, to walk and run upright without falling over, and at the same time to maintain steady fixation on an object that may itself be moving. The speed and precision with which the mammalian brain can gather and use this information are evident in the supreme body control displayed by predators such as cats. When a cat falls from a tree or ledge, it can sense the orientation of its body relative to the ground and manoeuvre itself to land feet-first, even when falling from an inverted position.

## PHYSIOLOGY OF THE VESTIBULAR SYSTEM

The sensory system responsible for the beautifully executed movements of the cat, the vestibular system, is a prime example of exquisite biological engineering. It employs receptors that are sensitive to the forces of gravity and acceleration acting on the head. The two organs housing these receptors lie buried in deep cavities on either side of the skull known as vestibules. Consequently they are called the **vestibular organs**.

Figure 3.7 (top right) shows the position of the vestibular organs in the head. Each organ consists of a complex set of interconnected canals and otolith organs (utricle and saccule), known as the vestibular labyrinth. Another organ, the cochlea, is connected to each vestibular organ, and shares its afferent nerve, the VIIIth cranial nerve (see Figure 3.7, top left). The cochlea is a complex spiral-shaped canal that mediates hearing (discussed in the next two chapters). In both the vestibular organs and the cochlea, sensory reception is based on minute displacements of hair cells. In the vestibular canals, the hair cells are displaced by fluid movement caused by accelerations of the head. In the otolith organs, the hair cells are displaced by inertia or by gravity. In the cochlea, the hair cells are displaced by movements of a membrane, produced by fluid pressure waves.

## Vestibular receptors

Figure 3.8 depicts a group of vestibular hair cells on a patch of sensory epithelium. Notice that each hair cell gives rise to a single tall, thick hair known as a **kinocilium**, and a number of smaller, narrower hairs (**stereocilia**) grouped together on one side of the kinocilium. The stereocilia decrease in size with distance away from the kinocilium, and thin filaments connect the tip of each cilium to the side of its taller neighbour. This arrangement is crucial to the sensory properties of hair cells.

Unlike mechanoreceptors, hair cells do not have axons, and do not generate action potentials. Instead, pre-synaptic active zones around the base of each hair cell make synaptic connections with afferent nerve cells forming part of the VIIIth cranial nerve. Stimulation of a hair cell increases its receptor potential and causes the release of a chemical neurotransmitter from its pre-synaptic zones. This transmitter influences the pattern of action potentials generated by the sensory neuron. Movement of the stereocilia towards the kinocilium depolarises the hair cell and results in increases in sensory nerve activity. Movement of the stereocilia away from the kinocilium hyperpolarises the cell, reducing sensory nerve activity. In the patch of sensory epithelium shown in Figure 3.8 the stereocilia and kinocilia are all arranged in the

The contiguity of the vestibular organ and the cochlea led to early ideas that both organs were devoted to hearing, with the vestibular organ mediating auditory localisation. See Wade (2000).

**KEY TERMS**
**Vestibular organ**: A fluid-filled organ lying in a deep cavity on the side of the skull (one on each side); it provides information about the orientation and movement of the body relative to the external environment.
**Vestibular receptor**: A mechanoreceptor that produces an electrical response when hair-like protrusions are deflected as a result of external forces.
**Kinocilium**: The single, tall, hair-like structure projecting from each vestibular receptor.
**Stereocilia**: The small, hair-like structures projecting from each vestibular receptor to one side of its kinocilium; they are connected to the kinocilium by fine filaments.

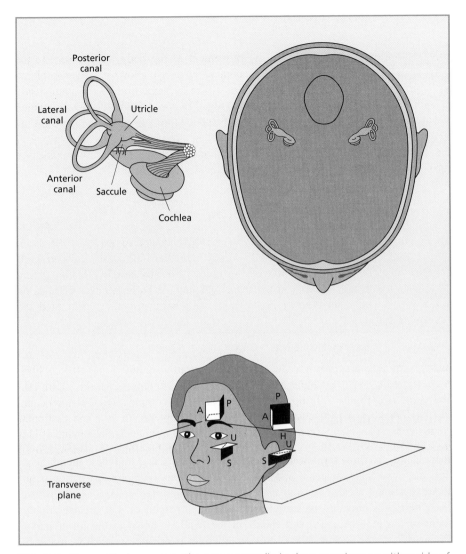

**FIG. 3.7**  The vestibular organs. The two organs lie in deep openings on either side of the skull. Each organ consists of three canals (posterior, anterior, lateral or horizontal) and two sacs (saccule and utricle), all of which are filled with fluid. Each structure also contains a small patch of sensory hair cells. Head movements result in fluid flow around the five structures, which displaces the hair cells and leads to sensory responses. The lower part of the figure shows the plane within which the head must move in order to excite each structure. P = posterior canal; A = anterior canal; H = horizontal or lateral canal; U = utricle; S = saccule.

same order, so that deflection to the left causes excitation, and deflection to the right causes inhibition. Resting potentials in hair cells generate a high level of spontaneous neural activity in sensory nerves (about 110 spikes per second), so the firing rate of vestibular nerve fibres can faithfully reflect the change in receptor potential, increasing or decreasing in accordance with the movement of the cilia. The significance of this biphasic response is that it allows nerve fibres to signal the direction of displacement of the hairs, which depends directly on the direction of tilt or acceleration of the head, as we shall see.

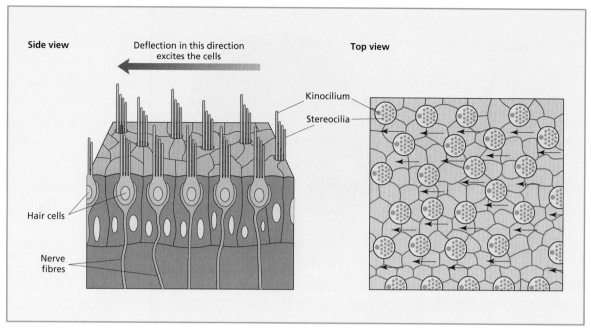

**FIG. 3.8**  Vestibular hair cells on a patch of sensory epithelium. Each cell consists of a single tall hair (kinocilium), and a number of smaller hairs (stereocilia) grouped on one side. Displacement of the hairs in the direction of the kinocilium, as shown, increases activity in the sensory nerve fibre. Displacement in the opposite direction decreases activity in the sensory nerve. Re-drawn from Purves et al. (2001). Copyright © 2001 Sinauer Associates. Reproduced with permission.

## The vestibular labyrinth

The labyrinth consists of two chambers (**otolith organs**), known as the utricle and the saccule, and three **semicircular canals** (see Figure 3.7). All of these membranous structures are interconnected and filled with fluid (endolymph). In each structure there is a small area of sensory *epithelium* containing hair cells. Displacement of these hair cells provides the stimulus for vestibular responses. The precise arrangement of the otolith organs and canals in the head is shown in the lower part of Figure 3.7. In the saccule, the sensory epithelium is oriented vertically, and in the utricle it is oriented horizontally. The three semicircular canals are oriented at right-angles to each other, as shown in the figure. The two vestibular organs on either side of the body are mirror images of each other. The significance of this arrangement becomes apparent when one considers the physics of head movement and the vertical direction of gravitational force.

### Planes and axes of head movement

Head movements can be defined in terms of three principal planes and three axes passing through the head, as illustrated in Figure 3.9.

*Planes*  The median plane passes vertically through the head from front to back. The frontal plane passes vertically through the head from side to side. Finally, the transverse plane passes through the head horizontally.

*Axes*  The *x*-axis runs from front to back, the *y*-axis runs from side to side, and the *z*-axis runs vertically (see Howard, 1982).

**KEY TERMS**
**Otolith organs**: Two fluid-filled sacs, the utricle and saccule, in each vestibular organ.
**Semicircular canals**: Three ring-shaped canals in each vestibular organ, arranged at right-angles to each other.

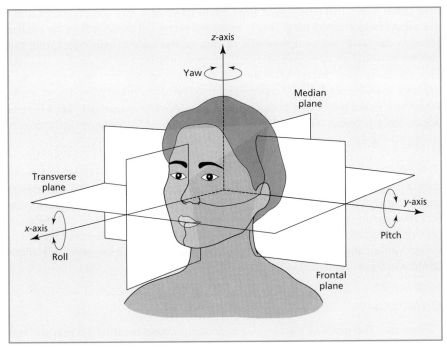

**FIG. 3.9**   Principal planes and axes of the human body. The body can move linearly along three possible axes; *x, y,* and *z*. The body can rotate within three possible planes; frontal, medial, and transverse. These movements define six degrees of freedom—the body can move in six possible ways, each independent of the others. Natural movements usually contain a combination of two or more of these movement components.

*Three components of translation*   Linear (translatory) head movements can be decomposed into three components, corresponding to translation along each of the three axes:

- Backward and forward along the *x*-axis
- Sideways along the *y*-axis
- Up and down along the *z*-axis

*Three components of rotation*   There are three possible rotational movements corresponding to rotation within each of the three planes:

- Rotation in the median plane about the *y*-axis, as in a "yes" nod, is called "pitch".
- Rotation in the transverse plane about the *z*-axis, as in a "no" shake, is known as "yaw".
- Rotation in the frontal plane about the *x*-axis, as in a sideways tilt of the head, is known as "roll".

*Natural head movements*   Head movements therefore have six different components; in other words, they have six degrees of freedom. Each of the six components can occur independently of the others. Natural head movements frequently contain a combination of two or more of these movement components. For example, as you

Decompose another
natural head movement
into its movement
components.

bend down to tie a shoelace, your head might move in a way that combines linear downward motion along the $x$- and $z$- axes, and rotational movement in the median plane as the head rotates downwards. A turn of the head to one side during this movement would add a second rotational component in the transverse plane. In order to maintain proper control of body and eye position, the nervous system must decompose such complex head movements into their component parts. For example, the presence of a translatory component of body movement may indicate a need to adjust one's balance, while the presence of a rotational component may require compensating eye movement to maintain a stable image in the eye.

*Vestibular responses to natural head movements* The otolith organs and semicircular canals are shaped and positioned very precisely so that their responses during natural three-dimensional head and body movements effectively decompose complex movements into their translatory and rotational components. The otolith organs provide information about linear movement components, and the semicircular canals provide information about rotational components. Precisely how they achieve this decomposition is explained in the following paragraphs.

### Otolith organs

*The macula* The patch of hair cells in each otolith organ is called the **macula**. It is covered by a gelatinous layer, which in turn is covered by a heavy fibrous carpet (otolithic membrane) containing calcium carbonate crystals (otoconia; see Figure 3.10). Linear acceleration of the head causes a shifting or shearing motion between the layer of hair cells and the otolithic membrane above them (similar to the movement of a loosely fitting hat placed on the head when the head is moved or tilted). The shearing motion displaces the hair cells and results in a sensory response, as shown in Figure 3.10 (right). Recall from the previous section that individual hair cells are directional in the sense that deflections toward the kinocilium are excitatory and deflections away from the kinocilium are inhibitory. Close examination of the arrangement of hair cells in the saccule and utricle reveals that the macula in each is split down the middle. All hair cells on one side of the division are excited by deflection in one direction but inhibited by deflection in the opposite direction, whereas hair cells on the other side of the division show the opposite pattern of response. This arrangement allows the organs to distinguish between opposite directions of shear on the basis of the pattern of excitation.

*Responses to linear acceleration* Since the macula of the utricle is approximately horizontal, and the macula of the saccule is roughly vertical, the two organs together can signal linear acceleration along any axis, since one or the other or both will always be activated. The otolith organs respond to acceleration rather than to movement at a constant velocity, because displacement of their hair cells is due to the initial inertia of the otolithic membrane. Once a steady speed of bodily motion is reached, the otolithic membrane catches up with the macula, so the hair cells return to their resting position.

It is important to note that the otolith organs provide static information about gravitational vertical acceleration as well as dynamic information about linear acceleration. This property arises from Einstein's equivalence principle, according to which a gravitational force field is equivalent to an artificial force field resulting from linear acceleration (the effect of gravity can, of course, be described in terms of

**KEY TERM**
**Macula**: The patch of vestibular receptors in each otolith organ.

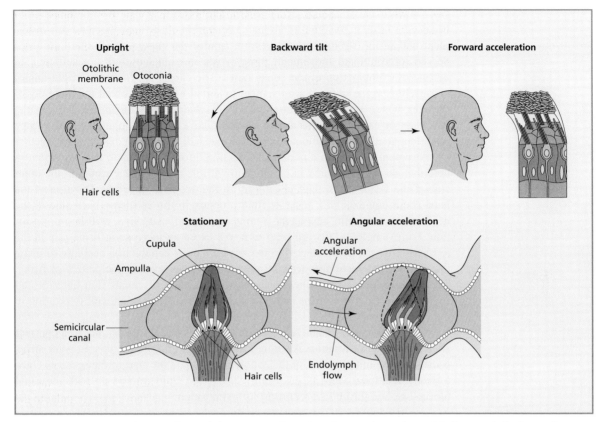

**FIG. 3.10** Sensory epithelia in the otolith organs and semicircular canals. In the utricle (top row) the hair cells are covered by a gelatinous carpet (otolithic membrane), itself covered with heavy calcium carbonate crystals (otoconia). Head tilts or accelerations lead to shearing motion between the otoconia and the hair cells, due to the inertia of the otoconia. The resulting displacement of hair cells leads to sensory responses. In the semicircular canals (bottom row), the hair cells form a bundle (crista) projecting across the canal inside a gelatinous mass (cupula). Head rotation causes a flow of fluid around the canal in the opposite direction, due to the inertia of the fluid. This current flow displaces the cupula and results in a sensory response. Re-drawn from Purves et al. (2001). Copyright © 2001 Sinauer Associates. Reproduced with permission.

acceleration toward the ground at a specific rate). Consequently, as illustrated in Figure 3.10, the shearing motion of the otolithic membrane produced by horizontal acceleration is identical to that produced by a static tilt of the head at an angle of 15°. This equivalence has important consequences for perception, described later in the chapter.

> Invertebrates possess a structure called the statocyst, which performs the same function as the vertebrate otolith organ. In shrimps, the statocyst has an opening through which the creature takes in grains of sand that perform the same function as otoconia. In a classic study in 1893, the sand in the creature's aquarium was replaced with iron filings. The shrimp's bodily orientation could then be influenced by the presence of a strong magnet placed outside the tank (Shepherd, 1988).

## Semicircular canals

*The crista* In each semicircular canal the bundle of hairs cells (known as the **crista**) stretches across the canal inside a gelatinous mass (the cupula). Rotational acceleration of the head causes a small deflection of the cupula and the hair cells, due to the inertia of the fluid. The hair cells are deflected by about 10 millimicrons for a relatively slow head movement, as shown in Figure 3.10 (bottom).

> **KEY TERM**
> **Crista**: The patch of vestibular receptors in each semicircular canal.

*Responses to rotational acceleration* The curved shape of the semicircular canals allows them to signal rotational acceleration of the head, because this movement will set up strong current pressure against the cupula. Since there are three degrees of rotational movement, three canals in each labyrinth are sufficient to detect any combination of the components. The canals are roughly at right-angles because this is the optimal arrangement to signal movement about the three possible axes, which are also at right-angles. Unlike hair cells in the utricle and saccule, hair cells in each canal are arranged with their kinocilium pointing in the same direction, so all cells within a particular canal will be excited or inhibited together by movement of fluid in a particular direction through the canal. It is important to note that each canal works in partnership with its mirror-image canal on the other side of the head, whose hair cells point in the opposite direction. Rotation of the head about any axis will generate fluid pressure in the canals on each side of the head, but the resulting responses from canals on opposite sides will be in opposition. For example, a leftward head turn will cause an increase in firing rate in the left vestibular nerve, connected to the left horizontal canal, but a decrease in firing rate in the right vestibular nerve. Rightward rotation reverses the pattern of firing. This arrangement also applies to the other two pairs of canals (left anterior and right posterior, left posterior and right anterior), which respond well to rotation in the $x$- and $z$- axes.

The semicircular canals respond only to angular acceleration, not to a constant angular velocity of rotation. As in the case of the otolith organs, this property arises because of the initial inertia of the endolymph fluid at the start of the rotation. Once a steady rotational velocity has been reached, the fluid catches up with the canal movement, and the cupula returns to its rest position.

## Central vestibular pathways

Hair cell responses are transmitted along the vestibular branch of the VIIIth cranial nerve. There are about 20,000 fibres on each side of the head (Shepherd, 1988), most of which terminate in several large groups of neurons in the brainstem called the **vestibular nuclei**. The remainder project directly to the cerebellum (see below). Projections from the vestibular nuclei can be grouped into four systems (see Figure 3.11), two ascending (thalamic and cerebellar), and two descending (spinal and ocular).

### The vestibulo-cerebellar system

Cells in the vestibular nuclei project to, and receive projections from the flocculonodular lobe of the cerebellum (see Carlson, 2004). The cerebellum is a large, complex neural structure that receives projections from and projects to many neurons in the cortex, brainstem, and spinal cord. One of its functions is to control movement by detecting and reducing differences between intended and actual movements. The vestibulo-cerebellar system regulates the movements that control posture and bodily equilibrium.

### The vestibulo-thalamic system

Thalamic cells receiving inputs from the vestibular nuclei project to two areas of the cerebral cortex (Purves et al., 2001). One area is just posterior to the primary

**KEY TERM**
**Vestibular nuclei**: Groups of nerve cells in the brain stem that receive axons from the vestibular receptors; they also receive inputs from the cerebellum, visual system, and somatosensory system.

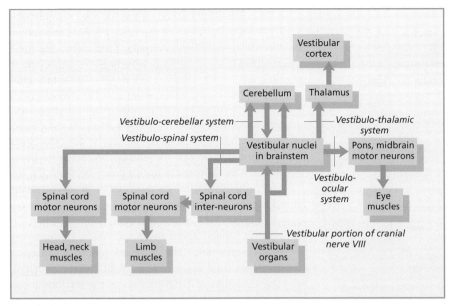

**FIG. 3.11** Sensory pathways in the vestibular system. Sensory nerve fibres from the hair cells project centrally along the vestibular portion of the VIIIth cranial nerve. Most of the fibres terminate in the vestibular nuclei of the brainstem. The vestibular nuclei act as major distribution centres, dividing responses among four major systems; vestibulo-cerebellar, vestibulo-thalamic, vestibulo-spinal, and vestibulo-ocular. These systems control reflex movements of the eyes and body, and provide a small cortical representation for vestibular signals.

somatosensory cortex near the representation of the face, and the other area is on the border between the somatosensory cortex and the motor cortex. These cortical projections may mediate perception of balance.

### The vestibulo-spinal system

This system carries projections to motoneurons in the spinal cord along two tracts, medial and lateral. The medial tract carries projections mainly from the semicircular canals to motoneurons controlling muscles in the neck and trunk. These projections are thought to be involved in reflexive control of body posture and head position in space. The lateral tract carries projections mainly from the otolith organs to motoneurons controlling limb muscles. These projections are thought to be important for the limb movements necessary to maintain balance. The small number of synapses between the vestibular organs and the motoneurons allows these reflexive movements to occur very rapidly. The high rate of resting discharge in vestibular afferent fibres supplies a continuous flow of excitation to the motor centres that control posture, helping to maintain the muscles in a steady state of contraction.

### The vestibulo-ocular system

This system carries projections to other nuclei in the brainstem, containing motoneurons that control eye movements. This neural circuit mediates reflexive eye movements (**vestibulo-ocular reflex**) that compensate for head movement and stabilise the visual image. The importance of the vestibulo-ocular reflex can be demonstrated

**KEY TERM**
**Vestibulo-ocular reflex:**
The reflexive eye movements that compensate for head and body movement to stabilise the visual image on the retinas.

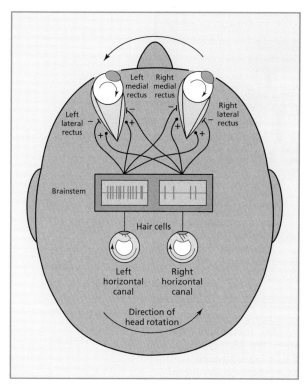

**FIG. 3.12**   Schematic representation of neural circuits in the vestibulo-ocular system. During head rotation to the left, fluid movement increases activity in afferent fibres of the left horizontal canal, and decreases activity in fibres of the right horizontal canal. These responses arrive in separate groups of neurons in the vestibular nuclei of the brainstem. There are both excitatory (+) and inhibitory (−) projections from the brainstem to the external muscles of the eyes. These connections are arranged in such a way that the imbalance in activity between left and right canals is translated into an imbalance in signals arriving at lateral and medial eye muscles. This imbalance produces a rightward rotation of each eye that is sufficient to compensate for the leftward head rotation.

easily. Hold your head stationary, and oscillate this book rapidly from side to side. Notice that the print becomes an unreadable blur. Now keep the book stationary but oscillate your head from side to side at the same rate, while fixating the page. The print should remain perfectly stable and readable, because your eyes move to stabilise the image. Signals from the vestibular organs are used to drive eye movements that compensate perfectly for the head movement. The eye movements are actually driven directly by differences in firing rate between the left and right vestibular organs, without the involvement of higher brain areas.

Figure 3.12 illustrates what happens when the head is rotated about the $z$-axis, as in turning your head to the left. The leftward rotary acceleration displaces fluid in the left and right horizontal canals. The direction of fluid motion in the left horizontal canal causes an increase in firing rate in its afferent fibres. Fluid motion in the right horizontal canal has the opposite effect, decreasing firing rate. Note the direction of fluid motion in each canal in relation to the kinocilia. These responses are collected by the left-hand and right-hand vestibular nuclei in the brainstem. Projections from the vestibular nuclei innervate the muscles surrounding each eye. There are both excitatory (+) projections and inhibitory (−) projections from each nucleus. Consequently, when the activity level in the two nuclei is equal, the eyes remain stationary. However, an imbalance between the nuclei leads to a bias in favour of signals to the muscle on one side of each eye, and a resulting eye movement. The greater level of activity in the left-hand vestibular nucleus during a leftward head turn, shown in Figure 3.12, results in compensatory eye movement to the right. Damage to the vestibulo-ocular system can result in unwanted jittering eye movements, even when the head is stationary, due to pathological differences in firing rates between the vestibular nuclei. Damage can also result in visual disturbances such as blurred vision during head movements, due to loss of image stabilisation.

## VESTIBULAR PERCEPTION

As we have seen above, the sensory information supplied by the vestibular system is used largely to control reflexive movements of the eyes and limbs. Its cortical representation is small relative to the representation of the other senses. In addition, information about the body's position and movement in the environment is available from vision as well as from the vestibular system. For example, contour orientation and texture gradients offer cues about the orientation of the ground plane relative to the body, and large-scale patterns of movement in the image ("optic flow", see

Chapters 10 and 11) offer reliable information on bodily movement. Vestibular responses tend to intrude on conscious experience only when there is a discrepancy between visual information and vestibular information. The resulting sensations of "motion sickness" can, however, be very powerful, often inducing confusion, disorientation, and nausea. The situations giving rise to such discrepancies typically involve subjecting the body to movements outside the range normally experienced.

## Perceptual effects attributable to vestibular responses

### The oculogyral illusion and Coriolis effects

Everyone has experienced the dizziness that results from rotating the body about the z- (vertical) axis very rapidly. Just as the spin stops there is a strong illusory sense of bodily movement, and loss of body equilibrium, accompanied by apparent visual movement in stationary objects and reflexive movements of the eyes. Graybiel and Hupp (1946) called the illusory visual movement the "**oculogyral illusion**". These effects can be attributed to responses in the semicircular canals. During initial acceleration into the spin, "backward" deflection of the cupula due to its inertia leads to appropriate vestibular signals concerning angular acceleration. During sustained rotation the cupula returns to its resting position. During and after deceleration as the spin stops, momentum in the fluid deflects the cupula "forwards" in the direction normally associated with a spin in the opposite direction. The resulting erroneous signals lead to disorientation and dizziness. The illusory impression of turning can persist for up to 30 or 40 seconds after stopping, during which time the vestibular system recovers to its resting state (Parsons, 1970).

*Think about how and why a ballet dancer moves her head during a pirouette.*

    **Coriolis effects** are experienced when the head is moved *during* a spin. Head movements modify the effect that the spin has on the semicircular canals. If the head rotates about the same axis as the spin, there is a momentary increase or decrease in the total angular acceleration of the head. If the head rotates about a different axis, then the angular accelerations produced by the spin and by the head rotation interact in a complex way, under forces known as Coriolis forces (similar to the forces that act on a spinning wheel if you try to turn its axis at right angles to itself). For example, if you are spinning in a leftward direction, and incline your head forward during the spin, the resultant stimulation of the canals produces a sensation that the head is being tilted sideways toward the left shoulder (see Howard, 1982, for more details). The mismatch with information supplied by the otolith organs and by vision induces dizziness and nausea.

### The oculogravic illusion

Illusory tilt that is perceived during linear acceleration is known as the **oculogravic illusion**. For example, a seated individual undergoing horizontal linear acceleration will experience a strong sensation of backwards tilt, and a corresponding apparent elevation of visible points positioned at eye level (e.g. Cohen, 1973). The illusion can be attributed to responses in the otolith organs. As discussed earlier, and illustrated in Figure 3.10, the macula cannot distinguish between displacements due to horizontal acceleration and displacements due to static head tilt. As a result, a displacement of the macula during acceleration may be attributed, at least partially, to head tilt. This illusion can have potentially disastrous consequences in modern transportation, as discussed in the tutorial section at the end of the chapter.

### Vection

Wood (1895) described a visit to a fairground attraction called the "Haunted Swing" at the San Francisco Midwinter Fair. Visitors entered a large cubical room containing various items of furniture, and sat on a large gondola that hung in the centre of the room. They experienced a swinging motion of the gondola, which eventually seemed to turn a complete revolution. In reality the swing was stationary, and the room moved (the furniture was fastened to the floor). Wood reports that "many persons were actually made sick by the illusion . . . [and could] . . . scarcely walk out of the building from dizziness and nausea". This kind of illusory motion is known as **vection** (Howard, 1982). Lishman and Lee (1973) constructed a moveable room similar to that used in the Haunted Swing to study one form of vection, apparent translation or "linearvection". The subject stood on a stationary platform inside the room, the walls and ceiling of which swung back and forth slowly. Adults experienced a sensation of body sway, and tended to sway in synchrony with the room to compensate for the apparent movement of the body. Infants who had recently learned to walk fell over as soon as the room began to move. Illusions of rotary movement of the body ("circularvection") can be induced by standing inside a large textured cylinder, and setting the cylinder to rotate very slowly. One might argue that vection is not truly a consequence of vestibular responses, because the subject is stationary, and the illusion is induced by movement of the surrounding scene. However, at a neural level, the distinction between visually generated and vestibular responses disappears. Neurons in the vestibular nuclei respond to both vestibular stimulation and visual stimulation, perhaps via signals from the cerebellum (Henn, Young, & Finley, 1974). This fusion of vision and movement probably explains why *visually* induced sensations of body motion (involving no direct stimulation of the vestibular organs) are indistinguishable from sensations induced by actual body motion. For example, if a person tilts their head while experiencing visually induced rotation of the body, they experience the same Coriolis effect that would be induced by real rotation (Dichgans & Brandt, 1973).

*Why is it difficult to balance on a narrow ledge high off the ground?*

## CHAPTER SUMMARY

The body senses provide information about surfaces in direct contact with the skin, about the position and movement of body parts, and about the position and movement of the body relative to the outside world.

### THE SOMATOSENSORY SYSTEM

● The somatosensory system contains eight different types of receptor distributed throughout the body, whose responses are conveyed to the brain along two parallel neural pathways.
● Each cortical neuron receives signals from just one of the eight receptor types, in a confined area of the body surface that defines the neuron's receptive field. Receptive fields on the hands and face are much smaller than those on the trunk and limbs.

**KEY TERM**
**Vection:** The illusion of body motion caused by visual stimulation.

- Cells with receptive fields at nearby body locations are themselves located near to each other in the cortex. Receptive field location changes systematically from cell to cell, so that the body is mapped out in an orderly manner across the cortex. The map is distorted so that a much larger area of cortex is devoted to some parts of the body than to others.
- Human ability to discriminate small differences in tactile stimulation varies in different regions of the body in a way that closely reflects the distortion of the cortical map.

## THE VESTIBULAR SYSTEM

- The sense of balance is mediated by sensory responses from hair cells in the vestibular organs.
- Separate neural structures within each organ signal angular acceleration and linear acceleration of the head through space.
- The vestibular nuclei in the brainstem are major distribution centres for vestibular signals. Descending projections to the spinal cord control reflexive movements of the head, neck, and limbs. Projections to the extra-ocular muscles control eye movements that compensate for head movement. The vestibular nuclei also project to the cerebellum and to the cortex (via the thalamus).
- Mismatches between vestibular information and visual information often induce "motion sickness"—feelings of disorientation, dizziness, and nausea.

# TUTORIALS

## PHANTOM LIMBS

A physician treating wounded soldiers during the American Civil War noticed that his patients reported the illusion that their amputated limb was still present. He used the term "**phantom limb**" to describe the effect (Ramachandran & Blakesee, 1998). Nine out of ten amputees have such experiences. The phantom limb feels much the same as a real limb in terms of its size, movement, and tactile sensations such as itching, sweating, and pain. Indeed pain is felt in about 70% of cases over the first few weeks following amputation, and persists for years in 50% of cases (Melzack, 1990). Over time, sensations from the phantom limb may change. It may, for example, appear to telescope into the stump so that the foot is perceptually located on the thigh, or the extremity may appear to be present in the absence of an intervening limb. Prostheses such as an artificial arm or leg may appear to be real, or filled with the phantom limb. Sensations from phantom body parts are not restricted to limbs, but can include many other innervated regions of the body such as the penis, breast, and bladder.

The traditional explanation for phantom limbs is based on neural responses arising in the stump of the amputated limb. Nerve endings that once innervated the missing limb may become irritated, and generate signals that duplicate those normally arising from the limb. Once these signals arrive in somatosensory cortex, they are perceptually localised on the missing limb. We know from the work of Penfield described earlier that direct stimulation of somatosensory cortex does evoke sensations of tactile stimulation that are localised on body parts, so this explanation seems plausible. However, phantom sensations occur even in patients whose spinal cord has been cut, so that there is no route for peripheral signals to reach the brain (Melzack, 1990). We must turn to signals within the brain, rather than signals arriving from the region of the stump, for an explanation of phantom limbs.

Merzenich, Nelson, Stryker, Cynader, Schoppmann, and Zook (1984) studied somatosensory cortical maps in adult monkeys before and after surgical amputation of one or two fingers. Before amputation, each finger was represented individually in the cortex (see Figure 3.13, top). Two months following amputation of digit 3, its cortical representation had disappeared entirely. The areas devoted to the adjacent fingers had expanded to occupy the area previously devoted to the amputated finger (see Figure 3.13, bottom). Pons, Garraghty, Ommaya, Kaas, Taub, and Mishkin (1991) reported more radical reorganisation in the somatosensory cortex of monkeys whose sensory nerves from one arm had been severed 11 years previously. Stimulation of a monkey's deafferented hand did not excite the hand area of cortex. However, stimulation of the monkey's face did evoke a response from the "hand" area. Recall from Penfield's map (Figure 3.4) and from Figure 3.13 that the face area of cortex is adjacent to the hand area. The "face" area of cortex had expanded to incorporate an area previously devoted to the hand.

These remarkable results demonstrate that even during adulthood the cortex is able to reorganise itself in response to altered sensory input. Recall that human tactile acuity in a particular body region is closely related to the area of cortex devoted to that region (see Figures 3.4 and 3.6). If cortical reorganisation also occurs in humans following amputation, one might expect improved acuity in the region surrounding the amputated limb. Haber (1955) reported just such an improvement in acuity.

It is tempting to relate the experimental findings of Merzenich et al. (1984) and Pons et al. (1991) to the phantom limb syndrome. On the basis of these studies we can assume that following amputation of a hand, for example, cortical cells formerly responsive to hand stimulation become responsive to stimulation in another part of the body (e.g. the face). We must also assume that, despite this re-wiring,

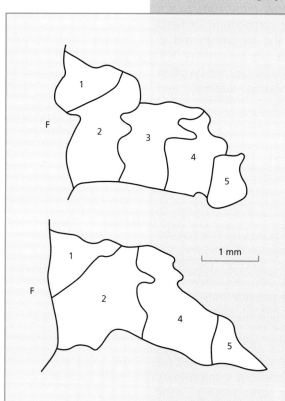

**FIG. 3.13** Maps of the somatosensory area of monkey cortex, showing the region devoted to the fingers of one hand before (top) and after (bottom) amputation of finger 3. Before amputation, each finger was represented individually in the cortex. After amputation, the representation of finger 3 disappeared, and the region devoted to adjacent fingers expanded to occupy its space. Re-drawn from Merzenich et al. (1984).

activity in these "hand" cells can still evoke a sensation that is localised on the missing hand. As a result, the amputee may experience sensations from a phantom hand when the face is stimulated. Ramachandran and Blakesee (1998) report observations that are consistent with this explanation. However, cortical re-mapping is unlikely to be a full explanation of the phantom limb syndrome. Haber (1955) did not find perceptual localisation errors with stimulation of the area surrounding an amputation. In addition, pain is a prominent feature of the syndrome and, as we saw earlier in the chapter, the central representation of pain is complex.

## MODERN TRANSPORTATION AND THE VESTIBULAR SYSTEM

The vestibular system evolved to deal with the restricted range of conditions that apply to natural bodily movements. The fastest human being can run no faster than about 50 km/h (31 mph), and gravitational acceleration is 9.8 m/s$^{-2}$ (32.2 ft/s$^{-2}$, or 1 G). Modern transportation can subject the body to velocities and accelerations far beyond these values. Surface transportation can reach speeds in excess of 500 km/h (310 mph), whereas the escape velocity for spacecraft is 40,000 km/h (25,000 mph). To reach this speed during take-off, spacecraft accelerate with a force of up to about 9 G. This means that the astronaut is pressed back into the seat by a force equal to nine times his or her body weight. Modern fairground attractions generate accelerations of several G. Velocities and accelerations outside the natural range can create abnormal vestibular responses that result in dizziness, disorientation, nausea, unstable vision, and disturbed motor control. These disturbances can obviously have disastrous consequences when experienced by a person in control of a vehicle.

> Sustained acceleration in excess of about 5 G actually causes loss of vision and consciousness, if applied in a standing position; astronauts lie in a reclined position during take-off to avoid blacking out.

### Effects of constant velocity

As we saw earlier in the chapter, bodily movement at a fixed velocity does not generate a vestibular response. Consequently humans can subject themselves to extreme velocities with no perceptual disturbances. Passengers in cars, airliners, and spacecraft feel no vestibular sensation of speed even at extreme velocities, provided that the velocity is constant. One can argue that it would make no sense to possess a vestibular system that was sensitive to constant velocity. As Einstein's theory of relativity made clear, in an abstract sense any measure of movement at a constant velocity is arbitrary since it depends on the frame of reference. If humans possessed a vestibular system that did signal constant velocity, would it report our speed relative to the surface of the earth, or the speed of the earth travelling in space? Humans can, of course, gain some sense of movement at constant velocity from the visual system. However, this information specifies *relative* velocity; speed in relation to the visible surroundings. Our perception of constant velocity movement is therefore vulnerable to variation in visual input. Underestimation of road vehicle speed in foggy conditions is due to the lack of both visual and vestibular information regarding velocity. A heightened sense of road speed is experienced in open or low-slung vehicles such as motorcycles and racing cars, where visual movement cues are particularly powerful.

## Effects of variation in velocity

Perceptual disturbances due to abnormal vestibular responses all arise from *changes* in vehicle velocity. Aircraft pilots are at particular risk of perceptual disorientation, leading to inaccurate perception of the attitude or motion of the aircraft relative to the earth's surface. According to one estimate, disorientation accounted for nearly 40% of fatal accidents in civil aviation in the period 1964–1972 (*United States Naval Flight Surgeon's Manual*, 1991). The oculogyral and oculogravic illusions described earlier in the chapter are common experiences for aircraft pilots.

The oculogyral illusion can occur following aircraft manoeuvres that involve complete revolutions in any of the three principal axes (turns, rolls, and spins). The pilot may experience an illusion of turning in the opposite direction just after the turn is completed. During and after such manoeuvres,

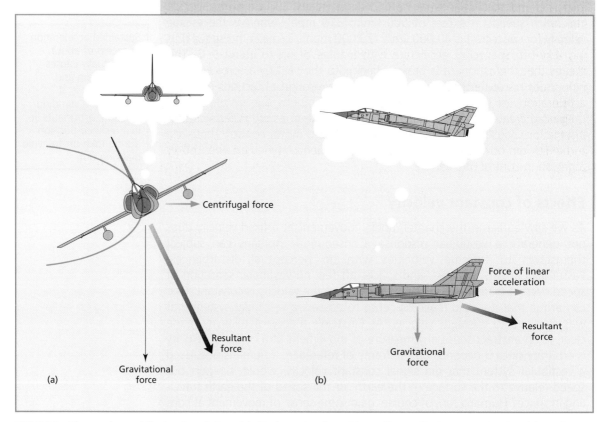

**FIG 3.14**   The oculogyral illusion in aviation. (a): During a bank and turn, the vestibular apparatus is subjected to both vertical gravitational force and horizontal centrifugal force. These forces combine to produce a resultant force that is slightly tilted from vertical. The pilot may interpret this resultant force as corresponding to gravitational vertical, and consequently perceive the plane to be flying straight and level. (b): During a catapult launch from an aircraft carrier, the vestibular apparatus is subjected to vertical gravitational force and to horizontal linear acceleration. The direction of the resultant force is tilted, and can lead the pilot to perceive the aircraft to be tilted backwards.

the vestibulo-ocular reflex is likely to trigger eye movements, in an attempt to stabilise vision during the spin. Since the aircraft's cockpit instrumentation obviously remains in a fixed position relative to the pilot's head, such eye movements succeed only in producing visual instability that obscures the instruments. Any head rotations executed during the spin heighten disorientation, due to Coriolis effects discussed earlier.

The oculogravic illusion can lead to the pilot mistakenly perceiving the aircraft to be level when it is in fact banking, or tilted when it is actually level. In the situation illustrated in Figure 3.14(a), the aircraft is executing a bank and turn. The pilot is subject to both gravitational and centrifugal forces, which combine to create a resultant force that is slightly tilted from gravitational vertical. The pilot may interpret this resultant force as gravitational vertical, and therefore perceive the plane to be flying straight and level. A second example is illustrated in Figure 3.14(b). During a catapult launch from an aircraft carrier, the aircraft is subjected to a peak forward linear acceleration that presses the pilot back in his or her seat with a force equal to 4.5 G. When combined with the downward gravitational force of 1 G, the resultant force acting on the otolith organs indicates a backwards tilt of the aircraft (though perceived tilt is much less than would be predicted by the direction of the resultant force). Inexperienced pilots may attempt to compensate for this apparent tilt by pitching the plane down towards the sea. The extreme disorientation experienced by pilots can impair and confuse their motor control to such an extent that they report an invisible "giant hand" interfering with their command of the control column.

Flying instruction draws attention to the dangers of misinterpreting vestibular signals. Pilots are taught to avoid flying "by the seat of the pants", and to rely on instrumentation for information about the altitude and motion of the aircraft.

# CHAPTER 4

## CONTENTS

# 4

# The physics and biology of audition

## INTRODUCTION

Humans are generally considered to be highly visual animals. However, visual information is restricted to the immediate field of view (an angle of approximately 200° centred on the line of sight in humans; see Chapter 7), and obviously relies on the presence of an adequate light source. Sound can be sensed in all directions around the body, and can even be sensed (within limits) through opaque occluding objects. Social and cultural communication in humans also relies heavily on sound stimuli, in the forms of language and music (see Figure 4.1).

Individuals lacking the sense of hearing are restricted in their ability to communicate with others, and are also at greater risk of injury from hazards outside the field of view. This chapter provides an introduction to the physical properties of sound, and to the biology of the sensory apparatus that humans use to sense sound. The following chapter concentrates on perceptual aspects of audition, building on the knowledge acquired here.

## SOUND AS A PHYSICAL STIMULUS

Sound consists of pressure waves carried by vibrating air molecules. It is usually produced by a vibrating surface. For example, when a gong vibrates after being struck, it pushes to and fro on the surrounding air molecules. The resulting pressure changes are passed on by collisions between air molecules, and the sound wave travels away from the gong at a speed of approximately 335 metres per second. Parts of the wave where air pressure is increased are called compressions, and parts where pressure is decreased are called rarefactions, as shown in Figure 4.2.

**FIG. 4.1** Auditory communication is an essential element of social interaction. Copyright © Leland Bobbe/Corbis.

## SIMPLE SOUNDS

*What is the mathematical relationship between frequency and wavelength (period)?*

The air pressure wave produced by the gong is called a longitudinal wave, because the particles that cause it vibrate back and forth in the same direction as the wave. The simplest sound wave, such as the pure tone produced by a tuning fork, can be described mathematically as a **sine wave**. This means that the repetitive alternation between compression and rarefaction as a function of distance from the sound source has the same shape as the variation in $sin(\theta)$ as a function of angle $\theta$, shown in Figure 4.3. Since sound pressure waves travel through air at a constant speed of 335 m/s, the horizontal axis of the waveform plot in Figure 4.3 can be scaled in terms of time, so representing the rate at which the alternations between compression and rarefaction are generated by the vibrating surface. The sinusoidal variation in sound pressure level has three important features: frequency, amplitude and phase.

> **KEY TERMS**
> **Sine wave**: A wave whose height varies smoothly so that it conforms to a mathematical sine function of time or distance (adjective: sinusoidal).
> **Frequency**: The number of cycles (periods) of a wave per unit of time or distance.
> **Amplitude**: The maximum height of a wave, measured from its mean value to its maximum value.
> **Decibel (dB)**: A measure of the difference between two quantities, based on the logarithm of their ratio (so equal ratios between the quantities correspond to equal dB differences).
> **Sound pressure level (SPL)**: A decibel measure of sound pressure relative to a fixed reference pressure.

### Frequency

A single alternation between compression and rarefaction is called one cycle of the wave. The wave's **frequency** corresponds to the number of alternations between compression and rarefaction that are generated in a 1-second period; in other words, the number of cycles per second. The unit of frequency is *hertz*, named after the 19th-century German physicist Heinrich Hertz. A sound pressure wave having a frequency of 1 Hz contains one compression/rarefaction cycle per second, a wave at a frequency of 2 Hz contains two cycles per second (as in Figure 4.3), and so on. The rate of vibration of the sound source determines the frequency of the resulting sound pressure wave. Variation in frequency relates perceptually to variation in perceived pitch. Low frequencies tend to be perceived as deep bass pitches, and high frequencies tend to be perceived as high treble pitches. However, the relation between frequency and pitch is complex, as we shall discover in the next chapter.

### Amplitude

The **amplitude** of a wave corresponds to the amount of change in pressure created by it (see Figure 4.3). Amplitude is usually expressed on the **decibel (dB)** scale, named after Alexander Graham Bell, the Scottish-American inventor of the telephone. The dB scale has two important properties.

#### The dB scale is relative

The dB **sound pressure level (SPL)** scale measures sound pressure relative to a fixed reference pressure, chosen because it is close to the minimum sound pressure detectable by humans (at 1000 Hz). So the dB SPL scale specifies that the amplitude of a particular sound is a certain number of times higher or lower than the standard pressure.

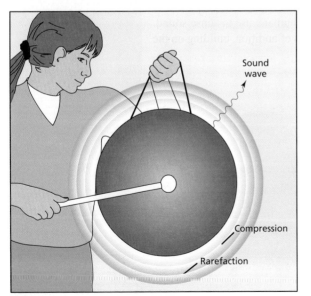

**FIG. 4.2**   The vibrating surface of a gong creates waves of fluctuating air pressure that emanate from the gong. The pressure wave consists of alternating phases of increased pressure (compression) and decreased pressure (rarefaction).

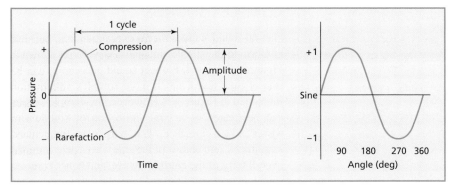

**FIG. 4.3**    A simple sound wave (left) can be described mathematically as a sine wave (right). Two critical parameters of the sound wave are its period (1/frequency) and its amplitude.

## The dB scale is logarithmic

Equal ratios of pressure level correspond to equal increments in dB level. For example, each ten-fold change in pressure equates to a decibel change of 20 dB. Similarly, each doubling (or halving) of pressure adds (or subtracts) 6 dB to the sound's decibel level. A logarithmic scale is used because it allows a very wide range of pressure levels (from 1 to 10 million) to be expressed in a compact range of dB values (from 0 to approximately 140).

Perceptually, SPL corresponds roughly with the apparent loudness of a sound although, as in the case of frequency and pitch, the relation between SPL and loudness is a complex one, to be discussed in the next chapter. The SPL produced by normal conversation is approximately 60 dB. The SPL of loud thunder or heavily amplified rock music is approximately 120 dB. Note that, because of the logarithmic nature of the dB scale, the pressure amplitude of the rock music is 1000 times greater than the amplitude of normal conversation. SPLs in the region of 140 dB can cause pain and hearing loss.

> The precise formula for dB SPL is:
> $$N_{dB} = 20 * \log_{10}(P_e/P_r)$$
> Where $N_{dB}$ is decibel level, $P_e$ is the SPL to be expressed in dB, and $P_r$ is the reference pressure. $P_e$ and $P_r$ are commonly expressed in the standard physical unit of pressure, dynes per square centimetre. $P_r$ is fixed at 0.0002 dynes/cm$^2$ (minimum sound pressure detectable by humans at 1000 Hz). The dB sensation level (SL) scale expresses dB above an individual's threshold at a given frequency.

## Phase

One complete cycle of a sine wave spans 360°, as shown in Figure 4.3. When the angular scale is applied to a sound wave, at 0° pressure is at resting level. Maximum pressure occurs at one quarter of a cycle (90°), and minimum pressure occurs at three-quarters of a cycle (270°). **Phase**, measured in degrees, refers to the part of the cycle that a sound wave has reached at a given point in time. Phase is often used to compare the timing of two sound waves.

Rows (b) to (d) in Figure 4.4 show three sound waves that differ in their timing from the wave in row (a). The angle at the end of each row specifies the phase of that sound wave relative to the wave in row (a). Each wave is phase-shifted relative to wave (a) by a specific angle. For example, wave (d) is phase-shifted relative to wave (a) by an angle of +270°. Note that, since sine waves are repetitive or periodic, we can also say that wave (d) is phase-shifted relative to wave (a) by −90°.

> **KEY TERM**
> **Phase**: A measure of the timing or position of a wave relative to a fixed point of reference, or to another wave.

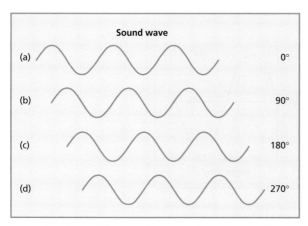

**FIG. 4.4**   Phase differences between sine waves. Each wave (a) to (d) differs from wave (a) by the phase angle shown on the right. Angles are based on the sine wave plot shown in Figure 4.3, so each point on wave (b) is shifted relative to the corresponding point on wave (a) by an angle of 90°, or one quarter of a complete cycle of the wave.

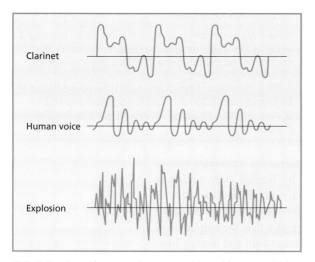

**FIG. 4.5**   Complex sound waves produced by a musical instrument, the human voice, and an explosion.

**KEY TERMS**
**Complex wave**: A wave that can be decomposed into a collection of simple, sinusoidal waves.
**Fundamental frequency**: The lowest sinusoidal frequency in a complex wave.
**Harmonic frequency**: A sinusoidal component of a complex wave, having a frequency that is an integer multiple of the fundamental frequency.

# COMPLEX SOUNDS

Natural sound sources hardly ever produce sounds that conform to the simple sinusoidal waveforms shown in Figures 4.3 and 4.4. Plots of sound pressure as a function of time reveal much more complex variation, as illustrated in Figure 4.5. However, any complex sound can be treated as a large collection of simple sine waves added together. The particular frequencies, amplitudes, and phases of the sine waves determine the overall form of the **complex wave**, and hence complex sound, they create. Figure 4.6 breaks the clarinet sound from Figure 4.5 into its component sine waves. The waveform in the top graph contains the series of sine waves shown in the middle graph. Notice how the components vary in frequency, amplitude, and phase.

The graph at the bottom left summarises the different sine wave frequencies contained in the clarinet note. The position of each dot on the horizontal axis identifies the frequency of that component, and the height of each dot specifies the component's amplitude. The graph at the bottom right plots the phase of each component, so the height of each dot specifies phase angle. The lowest frequency in the series is called the sound's **fundamental frequency**. The higher frequency components are equally spaced along the frequency axis, at integral multiples of the fundamental frequency. These components are known as **harmonics**, and are conventionally numbered in order of distance from the fundamental, which is assigned harmonic number 1. The fifth harmonic, for example, has a frequency that is five times higher than the fundamental frequency. Musicians sometimes call harmonics above the fundamental "overtones". The fundamental frequency of the note relates to its perceived pitch. A note with a higher fundamental frequency would appear to have a higher pitch. The amplitude of the harmonics relates to the timbre of the note played by the instrument. Different instruments playing a note at the same pitch (i.e. at the same fundamental frequency) sound different because they differ in terms of the relative levels of their harmonics.

Many natural sounds are not periodic, and do not contain a harmonic series of frequency components. Instead they contain a continuous "spectrum" of components in which all frequencies are represented. The particular amplitudes and phases of these components determine the overall form of the complex wave representing the sound.

## Fourier theory

A well-established mathematical procedure allows any complex sound, whether periodic or non-periodic, to be broken down into its sine wave components. The

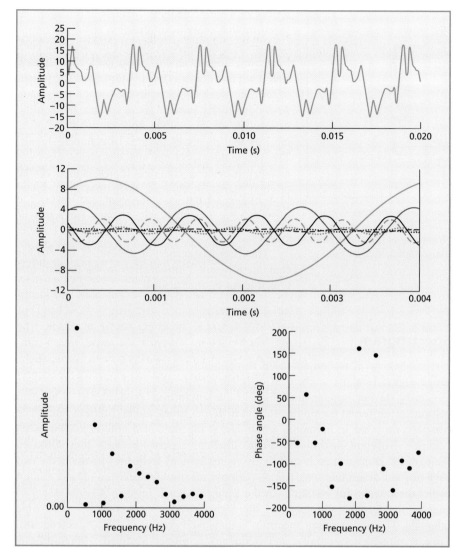

**FIG. 4.6** Top: A clarinet note. Middle: The series of sine wave components that add together to make the note. Bottom: Plots of the amplitude and phase of each component in the clarinet note. The component with the lowest frequency is called the fundamental, and gives the note its characteristic pitch. Higher frequency harmonics convey the timbre of the note.

mathematic theory underlying this procedure is called Fourier theory, after the 18th-century French mathematician who first developed it, Joseph Fourier. Some acquaintance with Fourier theory is crucial for a full understanding of the physical properties of sound, and of the biological system that processes sound. Indeed, Fourier theory has very wide scientific applications in many fields, including human vision.

## Fourier spectrum

As illustrated in Figure 4.7, any complex signal can be broken down into sine wave components by a procedure called **Fourier analysis**. Figure 4.6 illustrates part of the

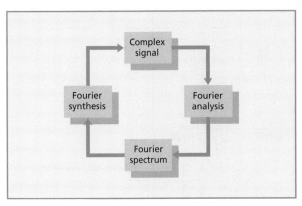

**FIG. 4.7** Fourier analysis decomposes a complex signal into its frequency components, which can be displayed visually in a Fourier spectrum. The original signal can be recovered by the reverse operation, called Fourier synthesis.

results of Fourier analysis, namely the magnitude spectrum that contains information about the amplitude, energy, or power in the original signal at each frequency. Fourier analysis also generates a **phase spectrum** that contains information about the phases of the sine wave components making up the signal. Textbooks rarely present phase spectra, but confine themselves to magnitude spectra, which capture most of the important features of complex signals. The magnitude spectrum and the phase spectrum together provide a complete representation of the original signal. It follows, then, that the original signal can be reconstituted perfectly by recombining the components, using a procedure called Fourier synthesis.

The Tutorials section at the end of the chapter contains a detailed introduction to the fundamental principles of Fourier theory.

## Spectrogram

The mathematical techniques used to compute Fourier spectra assume that the sound signal remains unchanged over an infinite period of time. Real signals obviously do not remain unchanged. In a single note produced by a musical instrument, different harmonics start at different times and at different rates. The complex variation in harmonic amplitude at the start of a note is known as its "attack". Different instruments sound distinctive partly because they differ in their attack. Human speech sounds also contain many frequency components that vary in their amplitude over time. A simple magnitude spectrum clearly cannot depict these temporal variations in the acoustic signal. Instead, it is necessary to analyse the frequency content of the signal over a succession of small time intervals. The time-varying spectrum is displayed graphically in a **spectrogram**. Time is plotted horizontally, and frequency is plotted vertically. Magnitude is represented by the darkness (or colour) of the plot. Figure 4.8 shows spectrograms of a musical note (top), and a speech sound (bottom). It is easy to see how the frequency content of each signal changes over time by inspecting the dark contours in each plot.

The spectrogram essentially represents a series of Fourier spectra from brief samples of the acoustic signals, taken over successive time windows. The restriction of each spectrum to such a short period of time limits its ability to distinguish between certain frequency components. In general, the frequency resolution of the spectrogram is equal to the reciprocal of the sampling window. For example, a sampling window of 10 ms would allow a frequency resolution of 100 Hz (two frequency components would have to differ by at least this amount to be resolvable as separate peaks in the spectrogram, see Moore, 1997). Spectrograms therefore must trade-off their ability to resolve variations over time with their ability to resolve variations over frequency. "Wideband" spectrograms opt for very good time resolution (typically around 3.3 ms) at the expense of relatively coarse frequency resolution (typically around a band of 300 Hz).

# Filters

As indicated in Figure 4.7, after Fourier analysis has been applied to a signal to yield its spectrum, the signal can be reconstituted exactly by the reverse procedure of Fourier synthesis. However, Fourier theory can be used to investigate how a particular transmitting device or medium modifies acoustic signals. The modification is assumed to involve changes in the amplitude of certain components in the signal's spectrum. When Fourier synthesis is applied to the modified spectrum, the resulting complex signal differs from the original because of the attenuation that has been applied to certain components. To give an example, suppose we wish to know what happens to a sound when it passes over a medium such as the human head (sounds arriving at the right ear from sources to the left of the head must pass around the head first). We can generate a complex sound and record its variation in pressure level at the source and at the ear (top row of Figure 4.9). What precisely has happened to the sound? Fourier analysis of the signal before and after passing around the head (bottom row of Figure 4.9) reveals that the obstruction caused by the head removes the higher frequency components from the signal. In Fourier terms, the head is said to act as a *filter* that allows low frequencies to pass by but attenuates or removes high frequencies; a low-pass filter.

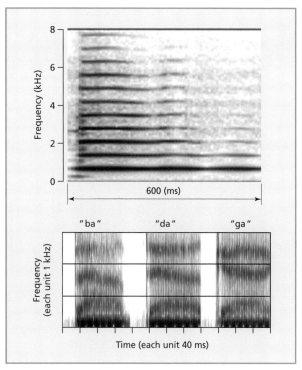

**FIG. 4.8** Spectrograms of two complex sounds: a note on a musical instrument (clarinet, top), and brief segments of human speech (bottom). Time is plotted horizontally and frequency is plotted vertically. Dark regions in the plot represent high amplitude components. Each spectrogram shows how the frequency components of the signal change progressively over time.

# Transfer functions

The middle plot in the bottom row of Figure 4.9 shows the **transfer function** of the head, in terms of the relative amplitude of the signal transmitted around the head as a function of frequency. Values close to 1 indicate very little attenuation. Values close to zero indicate that very little of the sound is transmitted around the head. If the transfer function of the head is known, then its effect on any complex signal can be calculated by (a) taking the spectrum of the signal; (b) multiplying the spectrum by the transfer function; and (c) applying Fourier synthesis to the output spectrum. The filtered signal transmitted around the head is revealed.

*Think of another example of an obstruction that acts as an acoustic filter.*

It is obviously crucial that the transfer function of the filter is known. How can it be derived? As mentioned earlier, the transfer function plots the amount of attenuation that is applied by the filter at each sine wave frequency present in a signal. The simplest way to derive the transfer function is to present the filter with a simple sinusoidal signal at a known frequency and amplitude, and measure the amplitude of the sine wave that is transmitted through the filter. The ratio of input amplitude to output amplitude defines the filter characteristic at that frequency. This procedure is repeated at a wide range of sine wave frequencies, to construct a complete representation of the filter's properties.

Filtering techniques provide powerful methods for describing the properties of acoustic filters and predicting their effects on an unlimited range of sound signals.

**KEY TERMS**
**Frequency filter**: Any process that modifies the frequency content of signals passing through it.
**Transfer function**: A function that describes a linear filter's frequency response, in terms of the degree of attenuation at each frequency.

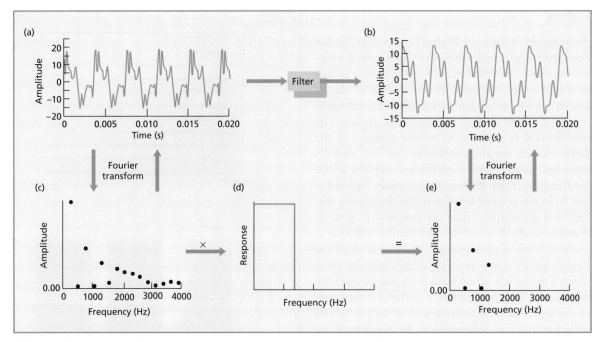

**FIG. 4.9**  Filtering using Fourier methods. When a complex sound signal (a) is transmitted through a linear acoustic filter such as the head, the output that results (b) is a modified version of the input. The effect of the filter on the frequency components of the signal can be computed by taking the Fourier spectrum of the input (c), and multiplying this spectrum by the transfer function of the filter (d). The resulting output spectrum (e) corresponds to the Fourier spectrum of the output signal (b).

They can be applied both to simple transmitting media and to more complex physical devices such as microphones and amplifiers. They can also be applied to the human auditory system. Each stage of auditory processing can be investigated to determine the way in which it filters the incoming acoustic signal.

## Linearity

The use of Fourier theory to analyse the properties of an acoustic filter depends critically on the assumption that the filter is **linear**. Such a filter must obey three rules:

1. The output of the filter never contains any frequency component that was not present in the input signal. In the simplest case, if a sine wave input is applied, then the output must consist of a sine wave at the same frequency (though its amplitude and phase may differ from the input).
2. If the amplitude of the input to the filter is changed by a certain factor, then the output should also change by the same factor. For example, if the amplitude of a sine wave input is doubled, then the amplitude of the sine wave output should also double.
3. If a number of sine wave inputs is applied to the filter simultaneously, then the resulting output should match the output that would be produced if the inputs had been applied separately, and their individual outputs summed.

The application of Fourier theory to linear systems that obey these rules is often called *linear systems theory*. A filter that violates at least one of these rules is called a **non-linear filter**. A non-linear system often adds distortions, in the form of additional frequency components that were not present in the input. Consequently, the filter's response to complex signals cannot be predicted straightforwardly from its response to simple sine wave inputs.

Figure 4.10 shows examples of linear and non-linear filter outputs in response to a pure sine wave. The leftmost graphs show the temporal waveform (upper), and the frequency spectrum (lower) of the signal. A pure sine wave contains only one frequency component. The output of a linear filter (middle graphs) is also a sine wave, though it may be delayed in time (phase-shifted), as the graph shows. One form of non-linearity is a failure to respond to low-intensity parts of the signal. The rightmost graphs show the output of a filter having such a non-linearity. The upper graph shows that parts of the input waveform below a certain intensity are truncated because the filter does not respond to them. The frequency spectrum of the truncated waveform is shown in the lower graph. It contains many other frequencies in addition to the original sine wave frequency, violating one of the rules of linearity.

*Why does truncating a waveform add new frequencies?*

Later in this chapter, and in the next chapter, it will become clear that some parts of the human auditory system can be considered approximately linear, while others are highly non-linear. Linear systems theory provides us with powerful mathematical tools to identify the non-linear parts of the auditory system, and to define the precise nature of the non-linearities.

> **KEY TERM**
> **Non-linear filter**: A frequency filter that distorts signals by adding new frequencies or by failing to respond at very low or high amplitudes.

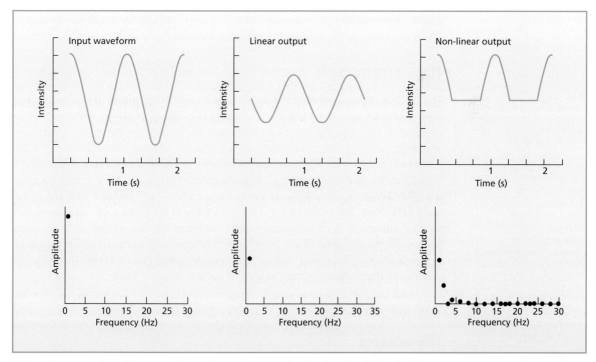

**FIG. 4.10**  Examples of linear and non-linear responses to simple stimuli. The left-hand pair of graphs show a single sine wave in terms of its waveform (upper) and its frequency spectrum containing a single component (lower). The middle pair of graphs show the output of a linear filter in response to the sine wave. The output is itself a sine wave. A non-linear filter may produce a non-sinusoidal output that contains a range of frequency components. The right-hand pair of graphs show the output of a non-linear filter, which does not respond to intensities below the mean intensity of the sine wave. The output waveform (upper) shows no modulation at lower intensities; the output spectrum (lower) shows the addition of many high-frequency components that were not in the signal.

# THE PHYSIOLOGY OF THE AUDITORY SYSTEM

Everyone knows that we hear sounds using our ears, two flexible flaps on either side of the head surrounding openings into the skull. The outer ear is the only visible part of the peripheral auditory system, a complex and sophisticated biological system that detects and encodes sound pressure waves. The peripheral auditory system includes the outer ear, the middle ear, and the inner ear. Neural responses generated by the inner ear are transmitted to the central auditory system, which includes populations of neurons in the brainstem and cerebral cortex.

It is fair to say that we know a great deal about how the peripheral auditory system detects and encodes sound, but relatively little about how the central auditory system mediates perception of sound. The neural circuits of the central auditory system, and the response properties of central auditory neurons, are very complex and only partly understood. This brief introduction will cover the whole auditory system, but will necessarily devote more space to those parts of it that are best understood.

The components of the peripheral auditory system are shown in Figure 4.11. The **outer ear** gathers sound energy and focuses it down the **ear canal** (**meatus**). A thin flexible membrane (the **tympanic membrane**) is stretched across the canal 2.5 cm inside the skull. Air pressure waves cause the membrane to vibrate. Three tiny interconnected bones (ossicles) in the middle ear transmit these vibrations to the cochlea, a spiral-shaped bony structure filled with fluid. Mechanical energy applied by the ossicles sets up ripples of movement in the cochlear fluid. Sensory hair cells in the cochlea generate neural responses when they are displaced by the fluid movement. These responses are transmitted to the brain stem and then to the cerebral cortex.

## THE OUTER EAR

The flexible flap surrounding the outer ear is known as the **pinna**. Its funnel-shaped inner part is known as the concha. The pinna is made up mostly of cartilage, and is attached to the skull by ligaments and muscles. In humans the pinna is virtually immobile, whereas other mammals such as horses and cats are able to move the pinna to orient it in the direction of a sound source. The shape and size of the human pinna, concha, and ear canal have two consequences for hearing. First, they act as an amplifier, boosting sound pressure for frequencies between 1500 and 7000 Hz, or 1.5 and 7 kHz (Yost, 2000). Second, the complex folds of the pinna act as an acoustic filter that attenuates high-frequency sound components. The extent of attenuation depends on the elevation of the sound source relative to the head, providing a cue as to the elevation of the sound source. The tympanic membrane is a cone-shaped semitransparent membrane covering an area of approximately 55 mm$^2$.

## THE MIDDLE EAR

### The ossicles

The three bones of the **middle ear** are housed in an air-filled chamber. Pressure in the middle ear is maintained at atmospheric pressure by means of the 3.5 cm long eustachian tube, which connects the middle ear chamber to the nasal cavity. The three interconnected bones are called the malleus (Latin for hammer), incus (anvil), and stapes (stirrup). The handle of the malleus is attached to the inner surface of the tympanic membrane. Its head is connected to the next ossicle, the incus. The smallest

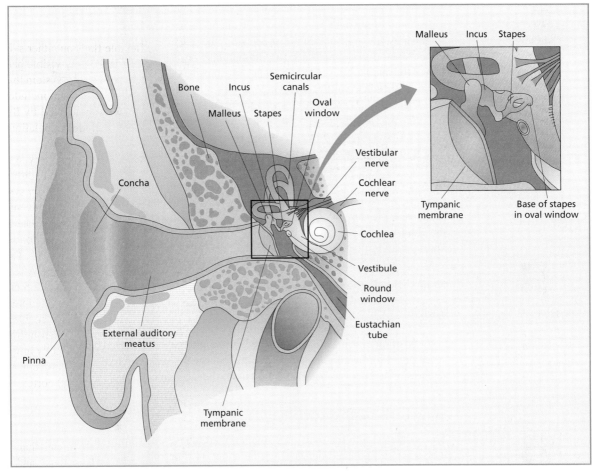

**FIG. 4.11**   Component parts of the human ear. The outer ear consists of the pinna, concha, and meatus. The middle ear includes the tympanic membrane and three ossicles. The inner ear includes the cochlea, a coiled structure filled with fluid. The vestibulo-cochlear nerve carries sensory responses towards the brain. Re-drawn from Purves et al. (2001). Copyright © 2001 Sinauer Associates. Reproduced with permission.

bone, the stapes (actually the smallest bone in the body), is connected to the incus at one end and to the cochlea at the other end. The point of attachment between the footplate of the stapes and the cochlea is a membrane-covered opening in the cochlea known as the **oval window**. The three ossicles are held in position by ligaments and muscles.

## Impedance matching

The tympanic membrane is thus connected mechanically to the oval window of the cochlea by the three ossicles. At first sight, this arrangement seems overly complicated. Why not have the tympanic membrane bear directly on the oval window? The reason is that the outer and middle ear cavities are filled with air, while the inner ear is filled with fluid. Air offers much less resistance to movement than

The muscles attached to the ossicles contract reflexively when the ear is exposed to intense sounds. The middle ear reflex is controlled by neurons in the brainstem, and may help to protect the ear from damage. However, the reflex acts too slowly to offer protection against sudden impulsive sounds such as gunshots. Another function of the reflex may be to dampen down the audibility of self-generated sounds to ensure that we are not deafened by the sound of our own voice.

**KEY TERM**
**Oval window**: The point of entry for sound energy into the inner ear; it is a small membrane-covered opening in the cochlea.

> **KEY TERMS**
> **Impedance**: The degree of resistance offered by a medium to an oscillating signal.
> **Impedance matching**: The boost in pressure at the oval window provided by the mechanical properties of the middle ear; it matches up the differing acoustic impedances of air and inner-ear fluid.
> **Inner ear**: The fluid-filled organ lying in the temporal bone, containing mechanoreceptors for hearing and balance.
> **Cochlea**: The spiral-shaped structure in the inner ear containing mechanoreceptors for hearing.
> **Scala vestibuli**: The tube running along the cochlea that contains the oval window at its base.
> **Scala tympani**: The tube running along the cochlea that contains the round window at its base.
> **Cochlear partition**: The flexible structure separating the scala vestibuli and scala tympani.
> **Basilar membrane**: The flexible structure on the cochlear partition that houses mechanoreceptors; it forms part of the organ of Corti.
> **Travelling wave**: The ripple of displacement that travels along the basilar membrane when sound vibrations are applied to the oval window.

does fluid. Consequently, if sound energy were to impinge directly on the oval window virtually all of it would be reflected back out of the ear. The bones of the middle ear act to maximise the transmission of sound from the outer ear to the inner ear. Technically, air and fluid differ in their acoustic **impedance**, or resistance to movement. The function of the middle ear is to match up the low impedance of the tympanic membrane with the high impedance of the oval window, known as **impedance matching**.

The middle ear achieves impedance matching in two ways. First, the diameter of the tympanic membrane (55 mm$^2$) is much larger than the area of the stapes in contact with the oval window (3.2 mm$^2$; Yost, 2000). Consequently, the force per unit area at the footplate of the stapes is much higher than that at the tympanic membrane. Second, the ossicles act as levers that increase the force at the tympanic membrane by a factor of 1.3. Buckling movement in the tympanic membrane also acts to increase pressure. Yost (2000) calculated that the combined effect of these actions is to increase pressure by a factor of 44, or 33 dB, counteracting the high impedance of the fluid behind the oval window. The middle ear is usually considered to be an approximately linear transmitter of sound energy, at least at normal listening levels.

## THE INNER EAR

Each **inner ear** consists of a series of bony, fluid-filled cavities in the temporal bone. The semicircular canals and otolith organs form the vestibular organ used to sense body position and movement (covered in the previous chapter). The **cochlea** is the sense organ for hearing, converting sound energy into neural impulses. Many critical features of hearing can be related directly to the mechanical properties of the cochlea.

### Structure of the cochlea

The cochlea (Latin for snail) is a small, coiled tube about 10 mm in diameter. If the tube were straightened out it would be about 34 mm long in humans. The cochlear tube or "duct" is divided along its length into two chambers, the **scala vestibuli** and the **scala tympani**, separated by the **cochlear partition** (see Figure 4.12).

The basal (outermost) end of the scala vestibuli contains the flexible oval window. The basal end of the scala tympani contains another flexible window called the round window. A small opening between the scala vestibuli and scala tympani known as the helicotrema allows the two chambers to share the same fluid, perilymph, which has the same composition as cerebrospinal fluid. The cochlear partition houses the **basilar membrane**, the structure that contains the cochlea's sensory hair cells. Before discussing the properties of these hair cells in detail, it is important to consider the mechanical response of the cochlea to vibrations applied to the oval window.

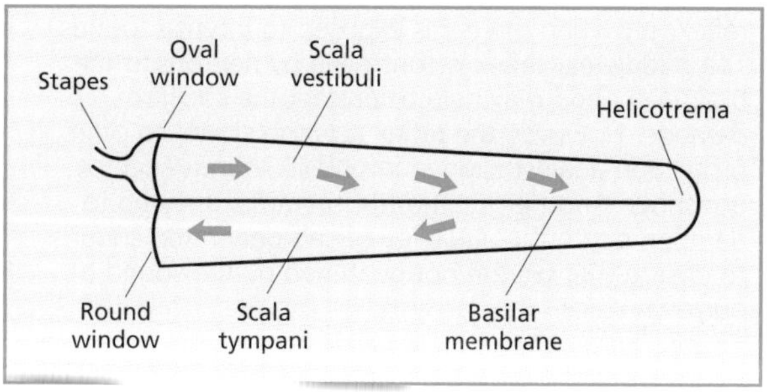


FIG. 4.12 Simplified cross-section through an uncoiled cochlea. Arrows indicate the direction of fluid displacement when the stapes pushes on the oval window. The basilar membrane lies between the two scala. It is narrow and stiff near the base, and wide and flexible near the apex.

### Mechanical properties of the cochlea

#### *Travelling waves on the basilar membrane*

Sound vibrations picked up by the tympanic membrane cause the stapes to push back and forth on the oval window at the same frequency as the sound wave. When the stapes pushes on the oval window, it displaces the fluid in the scala vestibuli. Since this fluid is incompressible, the pressure is transmitted across the cochlear partition into the scala tympani, deforming the basilar membrane. The increase in pressure in the scala tympani causes the round window to bulge outwards (see the arrows in Figure 4.12). When the stapes pulls back from the oval window, pressure is transferred through the cochlear chambers in the opposite direction, again causing a displacement of the basilar membrane.

The displacement of the basilar membrane takes the form of a wave that travels along the membrane from the basal end (where the wave originates) to the apical end. Figure 4.13 shows an example of a wave at four successive instants in time. The envelope of the wave is drawn through all the points of maximum displacement along the membrane as the wave travels along it.

### Frequency-to-place conversion

Displacement peaks at a particular place along the membrane. The mechanical properties of the basilar membrane vary considerably from base to apex. At the basal end, the membrane is relatively narrow and stiff, while at the apical end it is much wider and more flexible. As a result, the position of maximum displacement of the membrane depends on the frequency of vibration. Georg von Bekesy was the first to discover that the point of maximum displacement is near the apex for low frequencies, and near the base for high frequencies, as illustrated in Figure 4.13. This frequency-dependent displacement pattern is the key to the cochlea's ability to encode sound frequency.

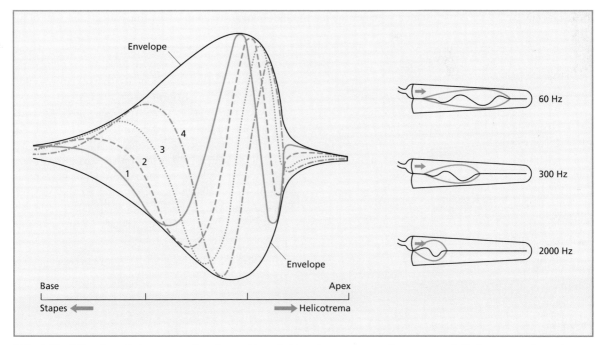

**FIG. 4.13**  Vibration of the stapes disturbs cochlear fluid and creates travelling waves of displacement along the basilar membrane. Left: A travelling wave on the basilar membrane at four instants in time. Right: Instantaneous waves and envelopes of travelling waves at three different frequencies. Re-drawn from Yost (2000). Copyright © 2000 Elsevier. Reproduced with permission.

When a pure sinusoidal input is applied to the cochlea, each point on the basilar membrane vibrates in an approximately sinusoidal manner, at the same frequency as the input sine wave. As we have seen in Figure 4.13, the magnitude of displacement is greater at some places on the membrane than at others. In a normal healthy ear each point on the basilar membrane is relatively sharply tuned to frequency, in that large displacements occur only for a relatively narrow band of sound frequencies. The left-hand plot in Figure 4.14 shows the sensitivity to sound at a specific place on the basilar membrane, as a function of sound frequency. Over a very narrow range of frequencies near 18 kHz, this particular place on the membrane requires very little sound in order to produce a displacement. At other frequencies, much greater sound levels are required to produce the same displacement. Such sharp frequency tuning is unlikely to reflect just the passive mechanical properties of the basilar membrane. As we shall see, an active physiological process involving outer hair cells contributes to the sharpness of tuning (bandwidth of auditory filters). The right half of Figure 4.14 is a drawing of the cochlea showing the place of maximum displacement over the full spectrum of audible frequencies. The basilar membrane achieves a "**frequency-to-place**" conversion (Moore, 1997). The frequency of vibration is encoded in terms of the place of maximum displacement.

### Linearity of basilar membrane displacement

KEY TERM<br>
Frequency-to-place conversion: The fact that the place of maximum displacement on the basilar membrane depends on the frequency of sound vibration.

One criterion for linearity is that the amplitude of basilar membrane displacement should double when the amplitude of the input wave doubles. The membrane obeys the rule only at very low and very high input amplitudes (Robles, Ruggiero, & Rich, 1986). At intermediate amplitudes the active physiological process mentioned above amplifies the response of the basilar membrane.

A second criterion for linearity is that when two pure sinusoidal tones are presented together the membrane should vibrate in a way that reflects the sum of the

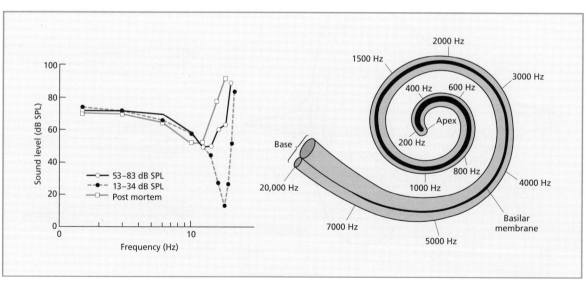

FIG 4.14   Left: Frequency tuning curves at a specific point on the basilar membrane in a live animal (filled symbols), and post mortem (open symbols). Data re-plotted from Moore (1997), Figure 1.10. Right: Map of the frequencies that produce maximum displacement at points along the basilar membrane. High frequencies displace the base of the membrane, and low frequencies displace the apex. Note the approximately logarithmic variation in frequency with distance along the membrane. For example, the distance between the 1000 Hz and 2000 Hz points is equal to the distance between the 2000 Hz and 4000 Hz points.

two individual responses. In other words it should show two peaks in displacement, at the locations appropriate for the two component frequencies. The basilar membrane obeys this rule only when the two tones are widely separated in frequency. When the tones are relatively close in frequency, their vibration patterns interact to produce non-sinusoidal displacements at certain locations. When the frequency difference is sufficiently small, the basilar membrane fails to resolve the components. It produces a single broad peak in displacement rather than two individual peaks.

## The organ of Corti

The basilar membrane forms part of a complex structure known as the **organ of Corti**, which separates the scala vestibuli from the scala tympani (see Figure 4.15). Sensory hair cells lie on top of the basilar membrane. Some of their stereocilia are embedded in the underside of a flexible overhanging structure called the

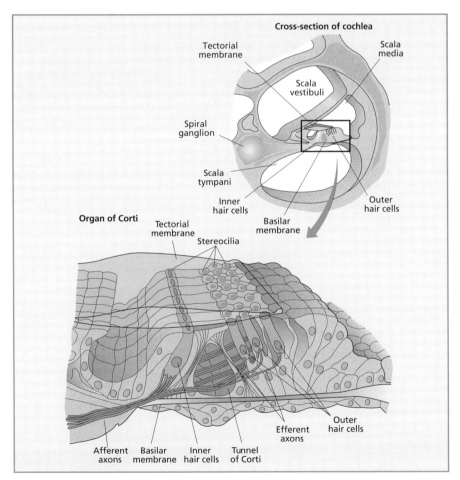

**FIG. 4.15** The organ of Corti, showing the detailed structure of the basilar membrane. Rows of inner and outer hair cells run along the length of the basilar membrane. Their stereocilia project into the space between the basilar membrane and the tectorial membrane. Outer hair cell stereocilia are actually embedded into the tectorial membrane. Re-drawn from Purves (2001). Copyright © 2001 Sinauer Associates. Reproduced with permission.

**KEY TERM**
**Organ of Corti**: The complex structure that forms part of the cochlear partition; it contains mechanoreceptors sandwiched between two flexible membranes.

**tectorial membrane**. The hair cells form four neat rows running along the length of the basilar membrane. One row lies on the inner side of the cochlear spiral (**inner hair cells**), and contains approximately 3500 hair cells. The other three rows lie closer to the outside of the spiral (**outer hair cells**) and contain about 12,000 hair cells (Moore, 1997). When fluid vibrations cause a displacement of the basilar membrane, it pivots about a point that is offset from the pivot point of the tectorial membrane. The up-and-down displacement of the two membranes is consequently transformed into a shearing motion between them, as shown in Figure 4.16. The inner hair cells are displaced by the fluid. The tips of the outer hair cells are embedded in the tectorial membrane, so are displaced by the relative motion of the basilar membrane and tectorial membrane.

## Inner hair cells

Cochlear hair cells are similar to the hair cells found in the vestibular organs, described in detail in the previous chapter, except that adult cochlear cells do not possess a single tall kinocilium (it disappears early in development). As in the vestibular system, cochlear hair cells produce graded receptor potentials in response to displacement of their stereocilia. Displacement towards the tallest stereocilia depolarises the cell (increasing voltage), and displacement in the opposite direction hyperpolarises the cell (decreasing voltage). It is remarkable that stereocilia displacements as small as 0.3 nanometres are sufficient to alter receptor potential. This distance corresponds to the diameter of atoms. Moreover, transduction can occur over a time period as small as 10 microseconds. Fluctuations in receptor potential can therefore reflect basilar membrane displacement quite faithfully. Palmer and Russell (1986) recorded receptor potentials in the guinea pig in response to pure tones. They found that receptor potential could follow the waveform of the tone only for frequencies up to 3000 Hz (note that one period of a 3 kHz tone lasts 300 microseconds).

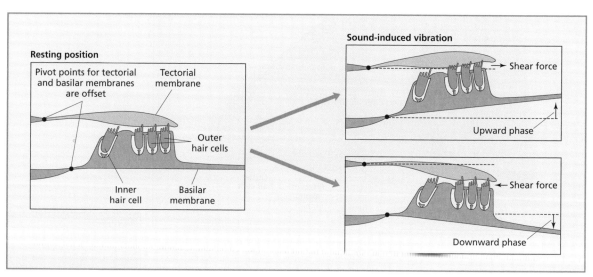

**FIG. 4.16**  Basilar membrane displacement produces shearing motion between the tectorial and basilar membranes, due to their different pivot points. Hair cells protruding into the gap between the two membranes are displaced by the shearing motion. Re-drawn from Purves et al. (2001). Copyright © 2001 Sinauer Associates. Reproduced with permission.

The base of each inner hair cell makes synaptic contact with afferent fibres of the auditory nerve. Approximately 90–95% of the estimated 50,000 afferent auditory nerve fibres make contact with inner hair cells. Each fibre attaches to a single inner hair cell. Since there are only 3500 inner hair cells, each hair cell has approximately 10 fibres attached to it. Most of the sensory information about sound is conveyed by inner hair cells.

## Outer hair cells

Since so few afferent fibres (5–10%) are connected to outer hair cells, the responses of these cells must convey very little useful sensory information about sound. On the other hand, there are far more outer hair cells than inner hair cells. What is the function of outer hair cells? Outer hair cells are able to change their size, expanding and contracting along their length. Inner hair cells do not have this ability. Outer hair cell motility seems to arise from two sources (Yost, 2000). First, they contain some crucial proteins supporting muscle-like contractions in response to stereocilia displacement. Second, they receive efferent stimulation from the cochlea nerve. It is known that there are about 1800 efferent fibres in the auditory nerve, which convey signals from the central auditory system out to the cochlea. Many of these fibres make contact with outer hair cells.

Since outer hair cells bridge the gap between the basilar membrane and the tectorial membrane, outer hair cell motility alters the mechanical coupling between two membranes. It is thought that the alteration in mechanical coupling effectively amplifies the response of the basilar membrane, so increasing the response of inner hair cells. The filled symbols in Figure 4.14 show the SPL required to produce a fixed basilar membrane displacement in the presence of outer hair cell motility (live animal). The open symbols show SPL required in the absence of outer hair cell motility (post mortem). Outer hair cell motility clearly increases the mechanical sensitivity of the basilar membrane, and narrows its frequency response.

> It is a remarkable fact that the ear itself can generate sounds, which can be detected by very sensitive microphones placed in the auditory meatus. These sounds are known as **oto-acoustic emissions** or *cochlear echoes*, since they are usually detected some 5–60 ms after the ear is stimulated with a click. Although the exact source of oto-acoustic emissions has not been identified, they are thought to originate in the non-linear amplification supplied by outer hair cells.

## Sound frequency coding in the auditory nerve

The intracellular resting potential of hair cells is $-70$ mV. Movement of the basilar membrane towards the tectorial membrane depolarises the inner hair cells, increasing their receptor potential. Movement of the basilar membrane away from the tectorial membrane hyperpolarises the hair cells. Neurotransmitter is released only when the hair cells are depolarised. As a result, auditory nerve fibres fire only when the basilar membrane moves towards the tectorial membrane. Since the basilar membrane vibrates in synchrony with an input sound wave, auditory nerve fibres fire during each positive phase of the wave, at least for low-frequency waves, as shown in the top half of Figure 4.17. This property of nerve fibre activity is known as **phase locking**. Neurons cannot produce action potentials at rates greater than 1000 spikes/s, since they have an absolute refractory period of 1 ms. Consequently, auditory nerve fibres cannot fire at every cycle of the wave for sound frequencies higher than 1 kHz. Although a particular nerve fibre does not fire at every cycle for

> **KEY TERMS**
> **Oto-acoustic emission**: A sound emitted from the ear, either spontaneously or following auditory stimulation.
> **Phase locking**: The firing of hair cells in synchrony with the variation of pressure in a sound wave.

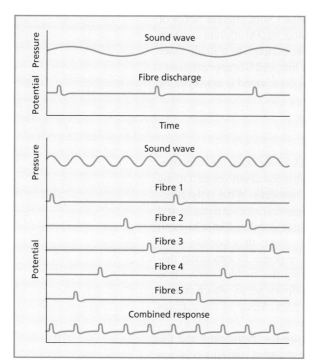

**FIG. 4.17** Phase locking of auditory nerve fibre activity in response to sounds at low frequency (top) and at high frequency (bottom). Since hair cells release neurotransmitter only when displaced in one direction, auditory nerve fibres fire only to one phase of the sound wave (the phase creating the necessary displacement). At low frequencies, a response can occur at every cycle of the sound wave (top). At high frequencies each fibre's response cannot occur at every cycle, but responses are still phase-locked. The combined response of a number of fibres can recover the frequency of the stimulating waveform (bottom).

*Think of a linking proposition (described in Chapter 1) to relate auditory nerve fibre responses to perceived pitch.*

sounds above 1 kHz, when it does fire the impulses occur at roughly the same phase of the wave each time. As a result, the interval between successive impulses is an integral multiple of the period of the waveform, as illustrated in the lower half of Figure 4.17. The response of the fibre is still phase-locked to the auditory signal. Even this form of phase locking collapses above frequencies of 4–5 kHz, because the inner hair cells cannot change their voltage fast enough (Palmer & Russell, 1986).

The mechanical and neural properties of the cochlea provide it with two methods of encoding the frequency of sound wave stimuli, place coding and frequency coding.

## Place code

Earlier in the chapter we saw that the basilar membrane performs a frequency-to-place conversion. As shown in Figure 4.14, each sound wave frequency is associated with a particular place of maximum displacement on the membrane. Since hair cells are distributed along the length of the membrane, the distribution of hair cell activity along the membrane provides an orderly *place code* for sound frequency. The place of maximum hair cell activity represents the frequency of the input sound wave. Each auditory nerve fibre connects to only a small number of hair cells in a particular region of the membrane. So the place code is preserved in the response pattern of auditory nerve fibres. The sound frequency that produces the greatest response from a particular nerve fibre is known as its *characteristic frequency*. The orderly spatial arrangement of characteristic frequency along a neural structure such as the basilar membrane is known as *tonotopic organisation*. We have already seen (Figure 4.13) that quite a large portion of the basilar membrane is displaced in response to a single input frequency, particularly at low frequencies. Consequently, any one auditory nerve fibre will respond to a broad range of sound frequencies, though it responds best to its characteristic frequency. Figure 4.18 plots frequency tuning curves derived from recordings in single auditory nerves of the cat (Palmer, 1995).

## Frequency code

Phase locking provides a second possible mechanism for encoding sound frequency. Since auditory nerve fibre impulses are phase locked to the sound wave, the response rate of a particular fibre should reflect the frequency of the stimulus. It should be noted that it is not necessary for an individual fibre to fire at every single cycle of the wave, only that when it does fire the impulse is locked to a particular part of the cycle. If the activity pattern from a whole ensemble of nerve fibres is combined, then the combined response should reconstruct the frequency of the stimulating waveform. Wever (1949) called this method of frequency coding the volley principle, illustrated in Figure 4.17.

There is still a degree of uncertainty about the roles of phase locking and place coding in sound frequency encoding. Place coding is likely to play a central role, since tonotopic organisation is found at every level of the auditory system. Phase locking is known to be important for sound localisation, and is also important for pitch perception at frequencies below 4 kHz (discussed in the next chapter).

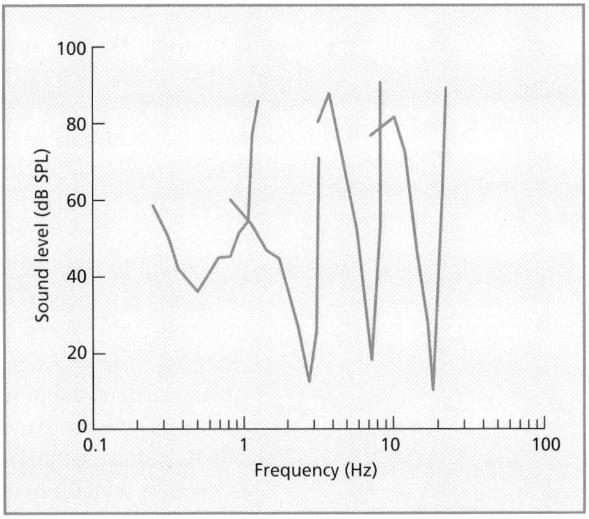

## Intensity coding in the auditory nerve

In the absence of stimulation, each auditory nerve fibre discharges at a steady spontaneous rate. Different fibres vary widely in their spontaneous firing rate. Most fibres have high resting firing rates (18–250 spikes/s), but a small number have very low spontaneous firing rates (below 0.5 spikes/s). In each fibre, SPL must exceed a certain threshold value in order to register a change in firing rate. At the other end of the intensity scale, above a certain SPL the fibre's activity level saturates, so that further increases in SPL result in no change in activity. The range of sound levels between threshold and saturation defines the fibre's **dynamic range**. Auditory nerve fibres have a dynamic range of between 20 and 50 dB. Human hearing has a dynamic range of at least 100 dB. How is this possible? Auditory nerve fibres with a high spontaneous firing rate have low thresholds, so they are sensitive to very quiet sounds, but their dynamic range extends only up to approximately 60 dB SPL (upper curve in Figure 4.19). Fibres with a low spontaneous firing rate have relatively high thresholds (up to 50 dB SPL), but their dynamic range extends up to about 100 dB SPL (lower curve in Figure 4.19). So information about sound intensities at different levels may be carried by different groups of fibres (Plack & Carlyon, 1995). Recall from earlier in the chapter that each inner hair cell has connections with multiple afferent fibres.

## Is the ear a Fourier analyser?

At the beginning of the chapter we discovered that, according to Fourier theory, each and every sound can be decomposed into a unique collection of sine-wave frequency

**FIG. 4.18** Frequency tuning curves of auditory nerve fibres in the cat. Each curve represents a single auditory nerve fibre, and plots the sound pressure level required to produce an above-threshold response from the fibre at different stimulating frequencies (re-plotted from Palmer, 1995, Figure 1).

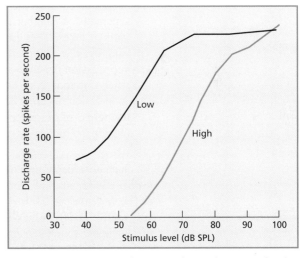

**FIG. 4.19** Activity as a function of sound pressure level, for a low-threshold and a high-threshold auditory nerve fibre (re-plotted from Palmer, 1995, Figure 9).

> **KEY TERM**
> **Dynamic range**: In auditory nerve fibres, it is the difference between the minimum SPL to which a fibre responds, and the SPL at the fibre's maximum firing rate.

components. Neural activity in the auditory nerve seems to encode input sounds in terms of their Fourier spectra. Frequency is encoded by the frequency-to-place conversion that occurs on the basilar membrane. Phase and intensity appear to be encoded directly in the patterns of activity in auditory nerve fibres. Although on this basis it is tempting to describe the ear as a Fourier analyser, such a view would be an oversimplification. The ear violates all three rules that must be satisfied by linear filters.

● According to the first rule described earlier, the ear should not introduce any frequency component that was not present in the input signal. One example of how the ear violates this rule is the phenomenon of oto-acoustic emissions described earlier. When the ear is stimulated with two tones at different frequencies, an echo may be detected at a third frequency, often corresponding to the difference between the input frequencies (Kim, Molnar, & Matthews, 1980). Human subjects often report hearing a pitch corresponding to the echoed frequency, which obviously represents a non-linear response generated within the ear.

● The second rule of linearity requires that the amplitude of the ear's output should vary in direct proportion to variations in input amplitude. But the basilar membrane's displacement is non-linear due to the cochlear amplifier described earlier in the chapter (the limited dynamic range of auditory nerve fibres, illustrated in Figure 4.19, also violates this rule).

● The third rule states that the ear's response to a combination of components should be equal to the sum of its responses to those components when applied separately. A number of researchers have studied auditory nerve responses to pairs of tones. They find that the response of a single fibre to one tone can be suppressed by the presence of a second tone (Sachs & Kiang, 1968). **Two-tone suppression** depends on the relative frequencies of the two tones. For example, when one tone is at or near the characteristic frequency of a particular fibre, suppression occurs when the second tone has a frequency that lies just outside the range of frequencies to which the fibre responds (in other words, just outside the tuning curve depicted in Figure 4.18).

Such gross departures from linearity clearly rule out the view that the ear performs a strict Fourier analysis on the incoming sound signal. However, the output of the ear can be viewed as an *approximation* to Fourier analysis, so the Fourier approach is still very useful. The frequency-to-place conversion of the basilar membrane does attempt to decompose sound signals into frequency components, and some representation of phase and intensity is carried in the patterns of firing in auditory nerve fibres. The non-linearities that rule out a faithful Fourier analysis can be viewed as adaptations that maximise the dynamic range of the system, or improve its ability to detect very faint sound signals. Given that the ear did not evolve with mathematical purity in mind, the extent of the similarity between Fourier analysis and auditory function is remarkable.

## THE ASCENDING AUDITORY PATHWAY

Cell bodies associated with the auditory nerve are located in the spiral ganglion of the cochlea. Each spiral ganglion cell sends a peripheral process to contact one or more hair cells, and a central process to form an auditory nerve fibre. Figure 4.20

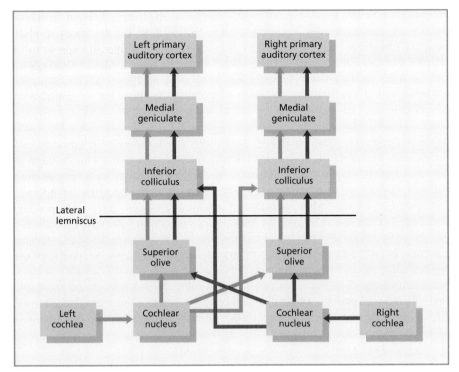

**FIG. 4.20** Schematic diagram of the ascending auditory pathway. Binaural responses appear first in the superior olive, which contains special neural circuits that compute "where" a sound originates in auditory space. The monaural projection from each cochlear nucleus to the inferior colliculi may carry information about "what" the sound is. Re-drawn from Moore (1997) and Yost (2000).

provides a simplified schematic view of the complete ascending pathway. Auditory nerve fibres terminate in the brainstem, where they form synapses with large groups of neurons in the **cochlear nuclei**. Fibres from the right ear arrive at the right cochlear nucleus, and fibres from the left ear arrive at the left cochlear nucleus. Most of the fibres leaving each nucleus cross over to the opposite (contralateral) side of the brain. The remaining fibres stay on the same side (ipsilateral). One group of fibres from each cochlear nucleus ascends directly to the contralateral inferior colliculus in the mid-brain. Another group of fibres projects only as far as the **superior olive** in the pons. Most fibres in this group project to the contralateral olive, while the rest project ipsilaterally. Neurons in the superior olives therefore receive inputs from both ears. Projections from each superior olive carry auditory responses centrally to the lateral lemniscus, then onwards to the inferior colliculus, and **medial geniculate nucleus**. Auditory signals finally arrive bilaterally in the primary auditory cortex.

The ascending auditory pathway involves a complex combination of serial and parallel processing stages. In the interests of simplicity, we will concentrate on how two important aspects of the sound stimulus are processed in the auditory pathway: *what* the sound is, and *where* it originates.

## "What" processing

The "what" attributes of a sound include its frequency composition and its temporal features such as phase properties, onset, and duration. On entering the cochlear

**KEY TERMS**
**Cochlear nucleus**: The mass of nerve cells in the brainstem where auditory nerve fibres terminate.
**Superior olive**: The complex of cells in the brainstem receiving projections from the cochlear nucleus; it contains binaural neurons that provide information about the location of sound sources.
**Medial geniculate nucleus**: The obligatory relay station for all ascending projections in the auditory system, en route to the cortex.

nucleus, each auditory nerve fibre branches into three separate regions, known as the anteroventral cochlear nucleus, posteroventral cochlear nucleus, and dorsal cochlear nucleus. The tonotopic organisation of the cochlea is preserved in each of these regions. Each cell in the dorsal and posteroventral cochlear nuclei receives inputs from several auditory nerve fibres. These cells have a more complex frequency response and a much wider dynamic range than auditory nerve fibres. Such complexity suggests that cells in the dorsal and posteroventral cochlear nuclei are concerned with processing the "what" attributes of sounds. The nucleus of the lateral lemniscus receives direct monaural projections from the contralateral cochlear nucleus (see Figure 4.20). Cells in the lateral lemniscus appear to signal the onset of sounds, as well as other attributes such as duration. Higher up in the auditory pathway, both the inferior colliculus and the medial geniculate nucleus contain cells that appear to convey "what" information, responding only to sounds that vary in frequency, or sounds of a specific duration. The ventral region of each medial geniculate nucleus shows tonotopic organisation, though the cells in this region have complex frequency responses. Other regions of the medial geniculate nuclei are not tonotopically organised, and contain cells that respond only to complex sounds. Some cells respond to more than one sense modality, by virtue of incoming signals from the somatosensory, vestibular, and visual systems. The ventral regions of the medial geniculate nuclei project to the primary auditory cortex. Other regions project to cortical areas surrounding primary auditory cortex.

## "Where" processing

An important attribute of a sound is the direction from which it originates. Sound local-isation allows us to orient ourselves to the potential danger of an unseen sound source such as a predator. It also helps us to segment complex sound stimuli into components from different sound sources. Unlike the retina of the eye, the cochlea offers no direct representation of sound location. However, as we have already seen, the filtering effect of the pinna provides a cue for the loca-tion of sound sources in the vertical plane. In addition, the physical arrangement of the ears on the head offers two cues for localisation in the transverse or horizon-tal plane (hearing researchers often call this plane the **azimuth**). The two ears are approximately 14 cm apart horizontally on the head, and separated by a mass of bone and tissue. There are two consequences for reception of sound signals from sources located to one side of the head, as illustrated in Figure 4.21. First, the sound signal has to travel slightly further to reach the contralateral ear than to reach the ipsilateral ear. As a result, the signal arriving at the contralateral ear is delayed or phase-shifted relative to the signal arriving at the ipsilateral ear. Second, the signal arriving at the contralateral ear must pass around the head, and may suffer some degree of attenuation as a result.

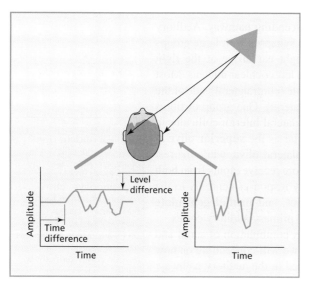

FIG. 4.21    Cues for auditory localisation in the transverse plane (azimuth). The signal arriving at the ear on the far side of the head has a lower amplitude and is slightly delayed relative to the signal arriving at the nearer ear. Re-drawn from Yost (2000). Copyright © 2000 Elsevier. Reproduced with permission.

Specialised neural circuits in the auditory pathway detect the very small differences in phase and intensity that can be used for sound localisation.

Cells in the superior olive receive bilateral projections from the anteroventral region of each cochlear nucleus. Circuits in the medial superior olive compute the minute time differences between the auditory signals arriving at the two ears (**inter-aural time differences**, or ITD). Circuits in the lateral superior olive compute the difference in intensity between the signals arriving at the two ears (**inter-aural level differences**, or ILD).

## Inter-aural time differences

Sounds originating directly opposite one ear arrive at that ear approximately 700 microseconds before they arrive at the opposite ear. This ITD becomes progressively smaller as the location of the sound source moves closer to the median plane (directly in front of or behind the head). Humans can detect ITDs as small as 10 microseconds. Such remarkable performance is mediated by neural circuits of the kind illustrated in Figure 4.22, first proposed by L.A. Jeffress in 1948. Figure 4.22 shows a row of cells (labelled A to E) in the right medial superior olive. Each cell receives one input from the ipsilateral cochlear nucleus (lower lines) and another from the contralateral cochlear nucleus (upper lines). Both inputs are excitatory

**KEY TERMS**
**Inter-aural time difference (ITD)**: A difference in the time of arrival of an auditory stimulus at one ear relative to the other.
**Inter-aural level difference (ILD)**: A difference in the intensity of an auditory stimulus arriving at the one ear relative to the other.

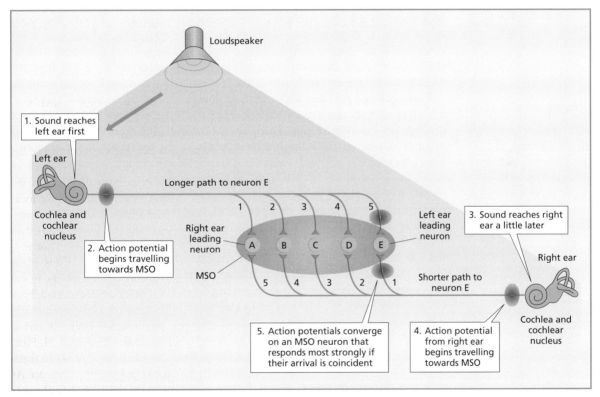

**FIG. 4.22**   Schematic diagram of a neural circuit in the medial superior olive that computes inter-aural time differences. Each neuron (A–E) receives one excitatory input from the left cochlea and a second from the right cochlea. Axon length varies systematically, so that the axon to neuron A from the right cochlea is longer than the axon from the left cochlea. The reverse applies to neuron E. As a result, neuron A responds best to sound located near to the right ear—although the sound reaches the right ear before the left, its signal is delayed due to the greater axon length. Right and left ear signals arrive at neuron A together. Neuron E responds best to sound located near to the left ear. Responses in the array of neurons A–E create a map of sound location. Re-drawn from Purves et al. (2001). Copyright © 2001 Sinauer Associates. Reproduced with permission.

(excitation–excitation, or EE), and each EE cell only fires when it receives coincident signals from the two cochlear nuclei. The axons projecting to the superior olive vary systematically in length, compensating for differences in the arrival time of signals at each ear. For example, a long axon projects to neuron E from the left cochlear nucleus, and a short axon projects to it from the right cochlear nucleus. As a result, a sound located nearer to the left ear than to the right ear will arrive at the left ear first, but its signal will take longer to travel up to the superior olive. Neuron E will fire strongly when the two signals arrive together. Activity in neuron E therefore encodes an ITD consistent with a sound source located near the left ear. Cells A to D are sensitive to other ITDs. Cell A, for example will respond strongly to sound sources located nearer to the right ear because the axon carrying signals from that ear is longer than the axon carrying signals from the left ear.

Responses based on ITDs require that the signal arriving from the ear is phase-locked to the auditory stimulus. As we saw earlier in the chapter, phase locking is only possible for sound frequencies below approximately 3 kHz.

### Inter-aural level differences

Sound frequencies above approximately 2 kHz are attenuated by the human head, which acts as a low-pass filter. Consequently, high-frequency signals originating on one side of the head have a higher intensity at the ipsilateral ear than at the contralateral ear. Neurons in the lateral superior olive respond according to these ILDs. Each lateral superior olive neuron receives an excitatory input from the ipsilateral anteroventral cochlear nucleus, and an inhibitory input from the contralateral anteroventral cochlear nucleus (via inhibitory neurons in the medial nucleus of the trapezoid body; excitation–inhibition, or EI). The net response of each EI neuron depends on the relative amount of excitation and inhibition it receives, which

*Think of linking propositions (described in Chapter 1) to relate responses in the superior olive to perceived direction.*

depends in turn on the relative activity levels in the ipsilateral and contralateral inputs. Response is strongest when the sound signal is more intense in the ear on the same side of the head. So cells in the right lateral superior olive respond to sounds located to the right of the head, and vice versa. Sounds originating in the median plane produce the weakest response in EI neurons, because the excitatory and inhibitory influences cancel out.

As in the case of the "what" pathway, responses in the "where" pathway pass through the inferior colliculi and medial geniculate nuclei on the way to the auditory cortex. Some cells in the inferior colliculi respond to ITD or ILD (Yost, 2000), elaborating the "where" information arriving from the superior olives. The inferior colliculus of the barn owl contains a topographic representation of auditory space, with different cells responding optimally to sounds originating in a particular region of space (Knudsen & Konishi, 1978). Many believe that the brains of other mammals are likely to possess topographic maps of auditory space (Purves et al., 2001). The superior colliculi lie adjacent to the inferior colliculi, and contain cells that respond to visual stimuli. Neural connections between the superior and inferior colliculi are important for co-ordinating responses to visual and auditory stimuli.

## AUDITORY CORTEX

The **primary auditory cortex** is located on Heschl's gyrus in primates, which lies on the superior temporal lobe, hidden from view in the lateral sulcus. Two areas of auditory association cortex surround the primary auditory cortex. The area immediately surrounding the primary auditory cortex is known as the "belt" region. This region is itself partially encircled by the "parabelt" region (see Kaas & Hackett, 2000). The top of Figure 4.23 shows a side view of the macaque cerebral cortex. Only the parabelt region is visible on the superior temporal gyrus. The bottom of Figure 4.23 also shows the areas hidden from view in the lateral sulcus.

The primary auditory cortex is mapped **tonotopically**. Cells with similar frequency preferences lie close to each other on the cortical surface. There is an orderly progression of preferred frequency across the cortex. The cortical surface can be divided into a series of bands containing cells with the same characteristic frequency (isofrequency bands), as shown in Figure 4.23. Cells within a column extending down from the surface of the cortex have similar characteristic frequencies. Figure 4.23 shows that there are actually three abutting "maps" of frequency space in primary auditory cortex, allowing the area to be sub-divided into three "core" areas (Kaas & Hackett, 2000). Cells in these core areas respond well to pure tones (Whitfield & Evans, 1965), and have narrow frequency tuning.

The belt regions surrounding primary auditory cortex (the **auditory association cortex**) are densely interconnected to it. Cells in these regions typically respond better to narrowband noise and frequency-modulated sweeps than to pure tones. Detailed examination of cells in the belt regions, and their connections with other areas of cortex, suggests that the distinction between "what" and "where" pathways is preserved in the cortex. Rauschecker and Tian (2000) propose that the "what" pathway involves projections from the anterior part of the parabelt region to orbitofrontal cortex. The "where" pathway involves projections from the posterior part of the parabelt region to posterior parietal cortex and dorsolateral prefrontal cortex (see Figure 4.23). As we shall see in later chapters, the visual system also appears to contain separate streams of neural information processing for "what" and "where" attributes.

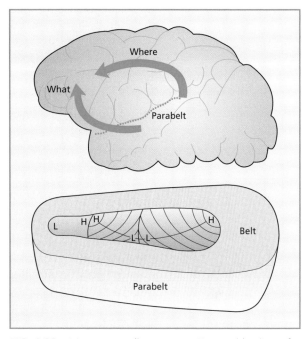

**FIG. 4.23** Macaque auditory cortex. Top: a side view of the cerebral cortex reveals only one visible area of auditory cortex, the parabelt region. Other areas of auditory cortex lie hidden in the lateral sulcus. Arrows indicate separate processing streams for the "what" and "where" attributes of sound stimuli. Bottom: Arrangement of three areas of auditory cortex in the lateral sulcus.

## THE DESCENDING AUDITORY PATHWAY

Descending fibre tracts run all the way from the auditory cortex to the cochlea, following a very similar route to the ascending fibres. En route, descending fibres form synapses in reverse order to those found in the ascending fibre tracts (cortex–medial geniculate nuclei–inferior colliculi–superior olives–cochlear nuclei–cochleas). The descending pathway contains both excitatory and inhibitiory connectons, and probably acts as a control system to select and shape the sensory input (Yost, 2000). Since the pathway extends all the way down to the ears, it probably contributes to the amplifying action of the inner hair cells and the acoustic reflex of the middle ear. It may also be involved in our ability to attend selectively to certain auditory stimuli.

# CHAPTER SUMMARY

## PHYSICS OF SOUND

- Sound waves consist of fluctuations in air pressure created by vibrating surfaces.
- A simple sound wave can be described as a sine wave having a specific frequency, amplitude, and phase.
- According to Fourier theory, a complex sound wave can be regarded as a collection of many simple sine waves added together. Fourier spectra and spectrograms offer graphical representations of the sine-wave frequency components of complex sounds.
- Any transmitting device or medium can be viewed as a filter that preserves some Fourier components in a sound, and attenuates or removes other components.
- The transfer function of the filter defines its ability to transmit sound components at different frequencies.
- Fourier theory can be used to characterise a filter's properties only if the filter can be assumed to be linear. The output of non-linear filters contains frequency components that were not present in the input.
- The auditory system can be viewed as a complex processing system that contains both linear and non-linear components.

## PHYSIOLOGY

The auditory system can be divided into a peripheral part and a central part.

### Peripheral auditory system

- The peripheral auditory system includes the outer ear, middle ear, and inner ear.
- The outer ear gathers sound energy and focuses it down the ear canal onto the tympanic membrane.
- Vibrations of the tympanic membrane are transmitted by the middle-ear ossicles to the inner ear. A major function of the middle ear is impedance matching.
- The organ of the inner ear, the cochlea, is spiral-shaped and filled with fluid.
- The basilar membrane divides the cochlea along its length into two chambers. Its mechanical response achieves a frequency-to-place conversion of sound signals.
- Inner hair cells distributed along the basilar membrane are tuned to different characteristic frequencies, by virtue of their location on the membrane, and their responses are phase-locked to the incoming sound waveform, for frequencies up to 1 kHz.
- Outer hair cells in the cochlea act to amplify and fine-tune the responses of the inner hair cells.
- Sound frequency is coded in the auditory nerve by the tonotopic organisation of the basilar membrane, and by phase locking of auditory nerve fibre impulses to the incoming sound wave.

- Sound intensity is coded in the auditory nerve by two populations of fibres, one responding at SPLs up to 60 dB, and the other responding to SPLs up to 100 dB.

## Central auditory system

- The central auditory system consists of several populations of cells in the brainstem and cerebral cortex.
- Auditory nerve responses from the hair cells arrive at the cochlear nuclei in the brainstem.
- A complex series of serial and parallel processing stages in the brainstem then conveys these signals to their destination in the auditory cortex.
- The "what" attributes of sound (frequency composition and temporal structure) are encoded by tonotopically organised neurons in the cochlear nuclei, and at higher levels of processing.
- The "where" attributes of sound (location of the sound source in auditory space) are encoded by binaural cells in the superior olive and higher levels of processing. Some binaural cells are sensitive to time differences, and others are sensitive to level differences.
- The auditory cortex preserves the distinction between "what" and "where" stimulus attributes in two streams of neural analysis.

# TUTORIALS

## FOURIER ANALYSIS

The mathematical foundations of Fourier analysis were established nearly 200 years ago by the French mathematician Jean Baptiste Joseph Fourier (1768–1830) from his work on the conduction of heat through solid bodies (see Bracewell, 1989). Fourier analysis is now widely used as a mathematical tool to solve a range of problems in science and engineering. It aids in understanding such physical phenomena as heat transfer, vibration, electrical current flow, sound conductance, and optical imaging. Fourier analysis is also a crucial tool in the fields of hearing and vision research. It provides a rigorous method of specifying the physical properties of stimuli and, with certain assumptions, how the stimulus is processed by the sensory system. This tutorial will introduce the basic concepts underlying Fourier analysis. A more rigorous mathematical introduction, including derivation of equations, can be found in Bracewell's (1978) standard text.

Fourier analysis, in essence, decomposes or divides up a waveform or function into sinusoidal waves of different frequency, known as frequency components or Fourier components. It identifies the different frequencies, amplitudes, and phases of the components. These components can, in turn, be summed to recreate the original waveform or function. In the context of hearing, the waveform represents sounds, such as a note produced by a musical instrument, or the call of a bird. Individual frequency components correspond to pure tones. Sound waveforms vary as a function of time, so the frequency components used in the examples below will be defined in terms of cycles per second or Hertz (Hz).

## Even and odd functions

A function is **even** if it is symmetrical about the vertical axis. In other words, when it is folded about zero on the horizontal axis, the positive and negative portions of the function match exactly. Figure 4.24 (top left) shows the even function $y = \cos(2\pi ft)$. The frequency term $f$ defines how rapidly the function modulates over time ($t$). Notice that the negative part of the waveform is a mirror image of the positive part. A function is **odd** if it is not symmetrical about the vertical axis; its positive and negative portions are not mirror images. Figure 4.24 (top right) shows the odd function $y = \sin(2\pi ft)$. The two functions in Figure 4.24 (top) are both sinusoidal. Notice that the cosine wave is identical to the sine wave except that it is shifted in phase by one quarter of a cycle of the wave.

## Inner products

The sine and cosine functions shown in Figure 4.24 (top) lie at the core of Fourier analysis. When a sound signal is subjected to Fourier analysis, the strength of a signal component at a given frequency is measured by calculating its **inner products** with sine waves and cosine waves at that frequency. The inner product of two functions is calculated by multiplying the two functions together point by point, and then summing the result of each multiplication. The inner product tells us how much one function has in common with the other. If the inner product is large, then the two functions are very similar, whereas if the inner product is zero then the two functions are unrelated. Decomposition of the signal waveform into frequency components therefore involves calculating inner products of the waveform with sine waves and cosine waves at all possible frequencies. The reason why inner products are calculated using both sine waves and cosine waves becomes clear when one considers how the result varies according to whether the original waveform itself is odd, or even, or intermediate between odd and even.

### Odd waveforms

If the waveform is odd, then the inner product of a sine wave (also odd) and the waveform is likely to be large, especially if the period of the waveform matches the period of the sine wave. Peaks in the waveform align with peaks in the sine wave. On the other hand, the inner product of an odd waveform and a cosine wave (even) of the same frequency will be zero. Peaks in the waveform align with zero in the cosine wave.

For example, the middle row of Figure 4.24 shows one cycle of a square-wave stimulus. Over the first half-cycle stimulus intensity is high, and over the second half-cycle it is low. Notice that the square wave is arranged in odd phase (zero on the horizontal axis corresponds to the start of the

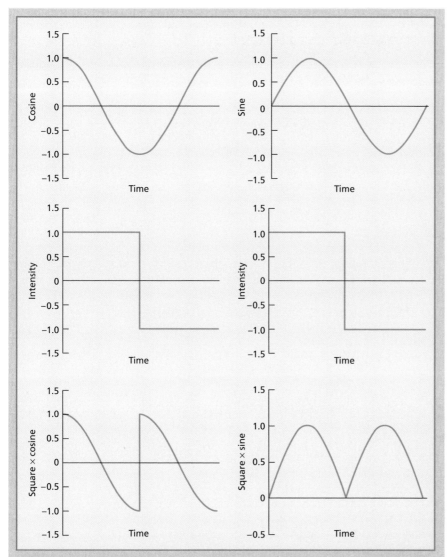

**FIG. 4.24** Top: Cosine function (left) and sine function (right). The cosine function has even phase, because it is symmetrical about zero on the *x*-axis. The sine function has odd phase, because it is asymmetrical about zero on the *x*-axis. Middle: A square wave arranged to have odd phase (at zero on the *x*-axis the wave is at the start of its high-intensity phase). Bottom: Point-by-point multiplication of the square wave with the cosine function (left) shows both positive and negative values that sum to zero. Point-by-point multiplication of the square wave with the sine function (right) has only positive values and a positive sum.

high-intensity part of the wave). The bottom row shows the result of multiplying the square wave point by point with the cosine and sine waves in the top row. The lower left graph is the product of the odd square wave and the even cosine wave. The sum of these products (inner product) equals zero, because for each positive value there is a matching negative value elsewhere in the product. The lower right graph shows the product of the odd square wave and the odd sine wave. Now all the products are positive, and the inner product sums to 1.273 (corresponding to $4/\pi$ in this simple waveform).

### Even waveforms

Similarly, if the waveform is even its inner product with a sine wave will be zero, whereas its inner product with a cosine wave will be large. Many waveforms are intermediate between odd and even, so their inner products with sine waves and cosine waves will both be non-zero.

If the square wave in Figure 4.24 was shifted to have even phase (so that zero on the time axis aligned with the middle of a peak or a trough rather than with the beginning of a peak), then the inner product with the cosine wave would become 1.273, and the inner product with the cosine wave would become zero.

Sines and cosines are thus used to ensure that frequency components are identified whether they be in odd phase, or in even phase, or in any intermediate phase. The relative magnitudes of the even and odd inner products specify the phase of the frequency component.

## Complex numbers

It follows from the preceding discussion that two values are required to represent the strength of a sinusoidal component at a given frequency, one representing its even part and the other representing its odd part. Mathematicians represent these even and odd pairs of values as a **complex number**, which contains a so-called *real* part and an *imaginary* part. The real ($R$) part of the number corresponds to the even, cosine part of the component. The imaginary ($I$) part of the number corresponds to the odd, sine part.

## Magnitude, energy, and phase

The real and imaginary parts can be combined to calculate the overall **magnitude** (sometimes called *amplitude*) of the component regardless of its particular phase. Magnitude is calculated by taking the square root of the sum of the two parts squared,

$$\sqrt{(R^2 + I^2)}.$$

The *energy* of the component at a given frequency is conventionally defined as the sum of the two parts squared, $(R^2 + I^2)$. Fourier analysis also provides a means to calculate the precise phase of a component at a given frequency from its even and odd parts. **Phase** is given by arctan $(I/R)$.

## Periodic waveforms

A periodic waveform, as we saw earlier, repeats itself at regular time intervals. The time interval separating successive repetitions defines the

**KEY TERMS**

**Complex number**: A number having two parts, called real and imaginary, from which other numbers can be computed; in Fourier analysis the parts represent the cosine and sine contributions to each component.

**Magnitude**: The strength of the contribution of a given frequency component in a waveform; it is calculated from the complex number for each component.

period of the waveform. The sound of a clarinet and of the human voice, depicted in Figure 4.5, are both periodic. Fourier theory states that all periodic waveforms can be decomposed into a set of discrete frequency components known as a **Fourier series**. The lowest frequency in the waveform is called the fundamental, and all other components in the waveform are at integer multiples of the fundamental frequency. The exact frequency, amplitude, and phase of the components depends on the particular form of the periodic waveform.

Table 4.1 shows how the frequency content of a complex wave can be calculated using inner products. It shows the inner product of the square wave in Figure 4.24 with sines and cosines at nine frequencies above the fundamental frequency ($f$). The first row at $f$ contains the inner products described previously. The square wave contains odd-numbered harmonic frequencies at $3f$, $5f$, $7f$, $9f$, and so on. All the components have odd phase, so all the cosine inner products are zero. Magnitude relative to the fundamental declines with frequency in the sequence 1/3, 1/5, 1/7, 1/9, and so on. The magnitude and phase values in Table 4.1 can be plotted in graphs, as shown in Figure 4.25. The plot of magnitudes is known as a magnitude spectrum, and the plot of phase is known as a phase spectrum. Compare Figure 4.25 to Figure 4.6, which shows the magnitude and phase spectra of a more complex periodic waveform. The complex waveform has components at many different frequencies and phases.

The standard formula for the Fourier series of a function $x(t)$ is:

$$x(t) = a_0/2 + \sum_{n=1}^{\infty} (a_n \cos 2\pi n f_0 t + b_n \sin 2\pi n f_0 t) \qquad (4.1)$$

where $a_0$ is the mean value of the function, $a_n$ and $b_n$ are the cosine and sine amplitudes of the $n$th frequency component, $f_0$ is the lowest (fundamental) frequency. The periodic waveform is composed of a series of sine and cosine components at integer multiples of the fundamental (the $n f_0 t$ term), at appropriate amplitudes (the $a_n$ and $b_n$ terms). The exact frequency, amplitude, and phase of the components depends on the particular form of the periodic waveform.

## TABLE 4.1 FREQUENCY COMPONENTS IN A SQUARE WAVE

| Component | Sine (I) | Cosine (R) | Magnitude | Phase (°) |
|---|---|---|---|---|
| $f$ | 1.273 | 0 | 1.273 | 90 |
| $2f$ | 0 | 0 | 0 | 0 |
| $3f$ | 0.424 | 0 | 0.424 | 90 |
| $4f$ | 0 | 0 | 0 | 0 |
| $5f$ | 0.255 | 0 | 0.255 | 90 |
| $6f$ | 0 | 0 | 0 | 0 |
| $7f$ | 0.182 | 0 | 0.182 | 90 |
| $8f$ | 0 | 0 | 0 | 0 |
| $9f$ | 0.14 | 0 | 0.14 | 90 |

**KEY TERMS**
**Phase**: The relative position of a given frequency component in a waveform; it is calculated from the complex number for each component.
**Fourier series**: A discrete series of frequency components making up a periodic (repetitive) waveform.

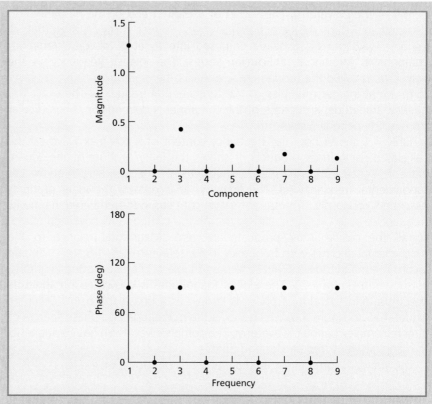

**FIG. 4.25** Magnitude and phase spectra showing the first five components of a square wave. Values correspond to those given in Table 4.1. In common with all periodic waves, the square wave contains a discrete sequence of frequency components.

## Non-periodic waveforms

Fourier analysis can also be applied to signals that do not have a repetitive periodic structure, called non-periodic signals. A simple example of a non-periodic waveform is a single pulse, as illustrated in Figure 4.26. As an auditory stimulus, this waveform would correspond to the sound of a click. Recall that the magnitude spectrum of any periodic waveform contains discrete components at intervals that are an integer multiple of the fundamental frequency. The magnitude spectrum of any non-periodic waveform contains a continuous array of frequency components, rather than a discrete series of components. Figure 4.26 shows the magnitude spectrum of the pulse. Although it contains energy at all frequencies, energy tends to decline progressively as frequency increases.

Whereas periodic signals are analysed using a Fourier series, non-periodic signals are analysed using a **Fourier integral**. The Fourier transform of a function of time, x(t), is a function of frequency F(f). The formula for the Fourier transform F(f) of x(t) is:

$$F(f) = \int_{-\infty}^{\infty} x(t)\exp(-j\,2\pi ft)\,dt \qquad (4.2)$$

**Key Term**
**Fourier integral**: A continuous spectrum of frequency components making up a non-periodic (non-repeating) waveform.

This formula appears markedly different from the formula for the Fourier series (4.1), in two ways. First, the summation term in formula (4.1) is replaced with an integral term in formula (4.2), because the Fourier integral contains an infinite array of frequency components. Second, the cosine and sine terms in formula (4.1) are replaced by a complex exponential in formula (4.2). According to **Euler's relation**, the sine and cosine parts of a complex number can be replaced by a complex exponential:

$$\cos\theta + j\sin\theta = \exp(j\theta) \tag{4.3}$$

The standard form of the Fourier integral (4.2) makes use of Euler's relation. A fundamental property of the Fourier transform is that the original function $x(t)$ can be recovered by an inverse Fourier transform, written mathematically as:

$$x(t) = \int_{-\infty}^{\infty} F(f)\exp(j2\pi ft)\,df \tag{4.4}$$

The presence of integrals extending to infinity in formulas for non-periodic waveforms (4.2 and 4.4) has two important consequences:

1. Both $F(f)$ and $x(t)$ are defined over times and frequencies from minus infinity to plus infinity. Negative time in $x(t)$ is a familiar concept, since it

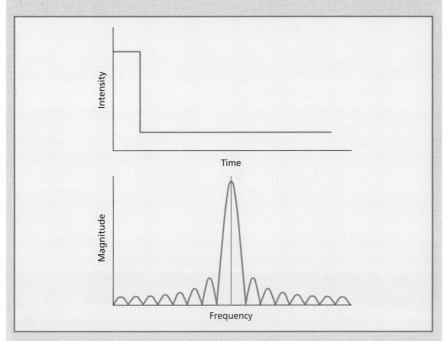

**FIG. 4.26** Top: A brief pulse, that would be heard as a click. Bottom: The amplitude spectrum of the pulse. Since the pulse is non-periodic, its amplitude spectrum contains energy at all frequencies, in contrast to periodic waves such as the square wave in Figure 4.25.

**KEY TERM**
**Euler's relation**: A mathematical rule that allows a sine and cosine pair to be represented as an exponential.

represents time in the past rather than time in the future. The concept of negative frequency in $F(f)$, on the other hand, may seem rather odd but is a mathematical consequence of the Fourier integral. Negative frequencies are displayed in the magnitude spectrum of the pulse (Figure 4.26). Fortunately negative frequencies make little difference to the interpretation of spectrum plots. Notice from Figure 4.26 that the magnitude of each negative frequency component exactly matches the magnitude of its positive counterpart. This property is generally true for real physical auditory or visual signals.

2.  The second consequence of the integrals is that the signal waveform is assumed to be infinitely long. No real sensory stimulus can be assumed to extend to infinity. Instead, we must assume that the signal extends for long enough to be considered effectively infinite.

## Fourier analysis in sensory systems

Both periodic and non-periodic signals are frequently encountered by all sensory systems. Isolated clicks, flashes of light, taps on the skin, and jerks of the head are all non-periodic. Voices, visual textures, rough surfaces drawn across the skin, and head bobs during running are all periodic. All sensory stimuli, whether periodic or non-periodic, can be subjected to Fourier analysis to identify the frequencies they contain. The neural response of each sensory system can also be subjected to Fourier analysis to discover which stimulus frequencies are attenuated, or whether the response contains frequencies not actually present in the stimulus:

*Think of other examples of sensory signals that can be subjected to Fourier analysis.*

● In the case of touch, neural responses depend on the vibration frequency of a mechanical stimulus. Some somatosensory neurons can respond to rapidly changing stimulation (high vibration frequencies), others can respond only to slowly changing stimulation (low vibration frequencies).

● In audition, cells in the cochlea respond according to the frequency and phase of incoming sound signals, described earlier in the chapter.

● In vision, neural receptive fields respond selectively to certain frequencies of light modulation over time and over space (discussed in more detail in Chapter 10).

Sensory neurons can therefore be viewed as frequency-tuned filters that respond to some stimulus frequencies but not others.

Fourier techniques help us to understand how a complex sensory stimulus is represented in the response of a population of sensory neurons (see Figure 4.9). However successful this approach is, it does not mean that the sensory system is actually performing Fourier analysis on the stimulus. As we saw earlier, Fourier analysis assumes strict linearity, but sensory systems exhibit many forms of non-linearity. Nevertheless, Fourier analysis helps us to identify the linear and non-linear parts of a sensory system, and to define the precise nature of the non-linearities.

## Calculating Fourier transforms

Although formulas have been included here in order to introduce the basic principles behind the technique, researchers do not need to know them in order to apply Fourier analysis to a data set. Standard numerical techniques have been developed that allow Fourier transforms to be computed quickly and easily from any array of numbers. A procedure known as the "**fast Fourier transform**", or FFT, is implemented in many scientific software packages, including spreadsheets. The Fourier transform in Figure 4.26 was produced using Excel's "fourier" function. For those wishing to add Fourier analysis to their own computer programs, code listings and libraries are widely available. As in the case of statistical analysis, modern software takes care of the computations, so researchers can concentrate on understanding what the results of the computations mean.

> **KEY TERM**
> **Fast Fourier transform (FFT)**: A numerical computational technique for performing Fourier analysis on an array of signal values.

# CHAPTER 5

## CONTENTS

# Perception of sound

## INTRODUCTION

The stimulus for hearing is a pair of sound pressure waves entering the two ears. In a natural sound field, these pressure waves are made up from a mixture of sounds generated by a variety of sources. Imagine that you are sitting in a bar talking with some friends. In addition to the sounds produced by your friends, perhaps talking simultaneously, each acoustic waveform may well include sounds from other conversations, from music playing on a jukebox, and from passing traffic.

The computational task facing the auditory system is to extract from these complex waveforms the discrete auditory objects that created them, such as individual voices, musical melodies, and car horns. Only by this means can you understand what each of your friends is saying, as well as enjoy the music playing in the background. The previous chapter described how the acoustic waveform is picked up by the peripheral auditory system and encoded as a stream of neural impulses travelling up the approximately 50,000 fibres that make up the auditory nerve. From this stream of impulses the brain builds a representation of basic perceptual attributes for each sound source, such as loudness and pitch, and of more complex objects such as speech sounds and musical melody. This chapter will present some of the theories that have been developed to bridge the gap between auditory nerve activity and perception. These theories make extensive use of concepts introduced in Chapter 1, including representation, computation, and linking propositions.

The chapter begins with a discussion of basic perceptual attributes (loudness, pitch, and location), before considering more complex representations (speech, auditory objects). The chapter ends with a discussion of hearing dysfunction.

**FIG. 5.1** In a noisy environment, the acoustic waveform may contain sounds emanating from many sources. Copyright © Ted Streshinsky/Corbis.

117

# LOUDNESS PERCEPTION

**Loudness** is the perceptual attribute of a sound that corresponds most closely to its physical intensity. Experimental studies of loudness perception have generally used two techniques to compare the loudness of different sounds: loudness matching and loudness scaling.

## LOUDNESS MATCHING

> The loudness level of a tone is sometimes expressed in *phons*, defined as the level (in dB SPL) of a 1 kHz tone to which the tone sounds equally loud. Each equal-loudness contour in Figure 5.2 defines a specific phon level. For example, a 50 Hz tone must be set to an SPL of approximately 60 dB in order to attain a phon level of 40.

In this technique, the subject is required to adjust the intensity of a sound (called the comparison stimulus) until it sounds as loud as a standard stimulus with a fixed intensity. The frequency dependence of loudness can be investigated by manipulating the frequency difference between the comparison stimulus and the standard stimulus. For example, a standard tone may be fixed at 1 kHz and 40 dB SPL, and the subject asked to adjust the intensity of a 2 kHz comparison tone until it appears equally loud. If this procedure is repeated for a range of comparison frequencies, then the resulting plot of comparison SPL as a function of frequency is known as an **equal-loudness contour**. The curve labelled "40" in Figure 5.2 shows the equal-loudness contour for a 1 kHz standard tone at 40 dB SPL. The whole procedure can be repeated at different standard intensity levels, to generate a family of equal-loudness contours, representing matched loudness at different sound levels. The other curves in Figure 5.2 show examples of these contours. Note that the lowest curve in the plot actually represents the absolute threshold for detecting the presence of a tone at different frequencies. The highest

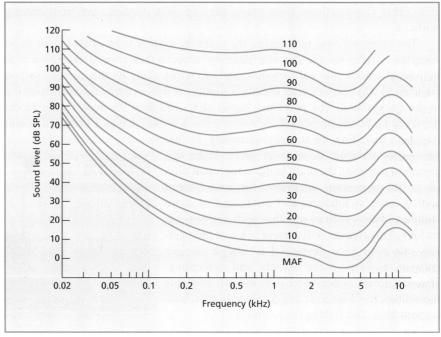

**FIG. 5.2** Equal-loudness contours for a range of comparison frequencies (shown on the abscissa), in relation to a standard frequency of 1 kHz. Different curves represent data at different standard SPLs. For this reason, reading up from 1 kHz on the abscissa (same frequency as the standard) each curve is at a height that matches its SPL (re-plotted from Moore, 1997).

curve shows that loudness matches are still possible at standard intensities in excess of 100 dB, indicating that the human auditory system has a very wide dynamic range.

It can be seen that equal-loudness contours tend to follow the absolute threshold curve at lower standard intensities, but flatten out at high intensities. At lower standard intensities low-frequency sounds must be set to a high intensity to appear equal in loudness to higher-frequency sounds. The "bass boost" control in audio reproduction equipment is an attempt to compensate for the lack of loudness in the low frequency region at low intensities. At high intensities the bass signal tends to appear relatively loud, due to the flattening of the equal-loudness curve.

## LOUDNESS SCALING

Equal-loudness contours provide a means of comparing the loudness of different sounds, but they cannot tell us how rapidly the loudness of a sound increases with its intensity; in other words, how loudness *scales* with intensity. The simplest method of estimating a loudness scale is to ask the subject to assign numbers to sounds at different intensities. For example, if the loudness of a standard tone is assigned the arbitrary number 100, and a second tone appears twice as loud, the subject should rate the loudness of the second tone with the number 200. This technique is known as magnitude estimation, and was discussed in Chapter 1. In common with other sensory magnitudes (see Figure 1.15), loudness does not increase linearly with intensity. Instead, loudness obeys a power law in which sensory magnitude grows in proportion to stimulus intensity raised to a power. According to Stevens (1961), the exponent for loudness is 0.3. This means that each time sound intensity increases by 10 dB, loudness increases by a factor of two, at least for sound levels above 40 dB SPL (Plack & Carlyon, 1995).

> Stevens devised the *sone* unit to define the loudness of a sound. 1 sone was arbitrarily defined as the loudness of a 1 kHz tone at 40 dB SPL. A sound judged to be twice as loud as this has a sone value of 2.

## MODELS OF LOUDNESS PERCEPTION

Auditory nerve fibre responses are known to be frequency selective, due to the frequency-to-place conversion performed by the cochlea. The simplest account of intensity coding in the peripheral auditory system is that intensity in a particular frequency region is coded by the firing rate of fibres tuned to that frequency region. As the firing rate of auditory nerve fibres increases, so does encoded intensity. How is encoded intensity linked to perceived loudness? The most successful model of loudness perception, the **excitation pattern model**, proposes that the overall loudness of a given sound is proportional to the total neural activity evoked by it in the auditory nerve. This model can account for experimental data on the loudness of both simple and complex sounds (Moore, 1997). Loudness meters incorporate a computation similar to that proposed by the excitation pattern model.

A potential problem for the excitation pattern model of loudness is that auditory nerve fibres have a relatively narrow dynamic range (about 60 dB; see Figure 4.19) compared to the dynamic range of loudness perception (about 120 dB; see Figure 5.2). However, as discussed in Chapter 4 and illustrated in Figure 4.19, different auditory nerve fibres cover different ranges of intensity. Fibres with low spontaneous firing rates saturate at intensities higher than approximately 60 dB SPL, and fibres with high spontaneous firing rates do not saturate until SPL exceeds 100 dB. Although individual auditory nerve fibres have a restricted dynamic range, the range covered by the whole population of fibres together is sufficient to account for the range of loudness perception.

A number of computational studies have investigated whether responses in auditory nerve fibres can account for human ability to discriminate different intensity levels.

> **KEY TERM**
> **Excitation pattern model:**
> A theory of loudness perception in which the loudness of a sound is proportional to the summed neural activity it evokes in the auditory nerve.

They have found that responses in as few as 10 auditory nerve fibres predict performance that is superior to human listeners over a wide dynamic range (e.g. Viemeister, 1983). This raises the question of why human performance is not better than one would expect on the basis of auditory nerve responses. Plack and Carlyon (1995) suggest that central limitations in the brain prevent it from making optimal use of the incoming neural information. One possible limitation is memory. Loudness comparisons require the listener to retain a memory trace of one sound in order to compare its loudness with that of a second sound. Decay of the trace may inject "memory noise" into the system, degrading the psychophysical judgement (see Chapter 1 for a discussion of noise in psychophysics).

# PITCH PERCEPTION

**Pitch** is the perceptual attribute of a sound that corresponds most closely to its frequency. In the case of pure tones, pitch is related to the frequency of the tone. In the case of complex tones, pitch is related to the frequency of the fundamental. Pitch perception allows us to order sounds on a musical scale extending from low bass notes to high treble notes. Since pitch is closely related to frequency, we shall begin by discussing frequency selectivity and discrimination by the auditory system as revealed by perceptual studies.

## FREQUENCY SELECTIVITY

Following on from earlier work by Ohm in the 19th century, Helmholtz (1877) believed that:

> *the human ear is capable, under certain conditions, of separating the musical tone produced by a single musical instrument, into a series of simple tones, namely, the prime partial tone, and the various upper partial tones, each of which produces its own separate sensation.*
> *(Helmholtz, 1877, translation by Ellis, 1954, p. 25)*

The assertion, now often called Ohm's law, that the auditory system constructs a separate representation for each frequency component of a complex sound has driven much psychophysical research since the time of Helmholtz.

## Psychophysical studies of frequency selectivity

There must, of course, be some limit to the auditory system's ability to select out the frequency components of a complex sound wave. The main psychophysical technique used to investigate the limits of frequency selectivity is **masking**. Everyday experience provides many examples of how one sound can be obscured by another. For example, ambient noise from the immediate environment can make it very difficult to hear the voice of a friend talking on your mobile phone. Systematic studies of masking typically measure a listener's ability to detect a simple sinusoidal signal in the presence of a noise mask. Noise in this context has a very particular meaning. It refers to a stimulus containing a wide range of frequency components having random phases but equal amplitudes. Subjectively, noise produces an unstructured hissing sound, similar to a de-tuned radio.

In the 1940s Fletcher used **band-pass noise** as a mask, centred on the frequency of the sinusoidal signal that the subject was required to detect. Band-pass noise contains only frequencies that fall within a certain band above and below its centre frequency. For example, band-pass noise with a centre frequency of 2000 Hz and a bandwidth of 400 Hz contains energy at all frequencies between 1800 and 2200 Hz, but no energy below 1800 Hz and above 2200 Hz.

Fletcher found, as illustrated by data from Schooneveldt and Moore (1989) in Figure 5.3, that the listener's ability to detect the signal became progressively worse as the noise bandwidth increased, but above a certain bandwidth detectability remained constant. Wider bandwidths had no effect on threshold. Fletcher inferred that the listener detects the signal using a band-pass filter somewhere in the auditory system that admits certain frequencies but removes others. He assumed that the most effective filter for detecting the signal is one centred on the same frequency as the signal. Only noise frequencies within the pass band of the filter affect the listener's ability to hear the signal. The noise bandwidth at which detectability flattens off can then be taken as an estimate of the bandwidth of the auditory filter. Fletcher called this bandwidth the *critical bandwidth*.

More recent masking experiments have used fixed bandwidth noise, and systematically varied the difference between mask centre frequency and signal frequency. The signal is fixed at a relatively low sound level (e.g. 10 dB SPL). Mask SPL is varied to find the level at which the signal can just be detected. Data from these experiments can be plotted as psychophysical tuning curves. Examples are shown in Figure 5.4, for several different signal frequencies. Notice that masking is most effective when the mask centre frequency is very close to the signal frequency. As mask centre frequency moves away from signal frequency, progressively higher mask SPLs are required to maintain the signal at threshold. Data of this kind have led to the view that hearing is served by a bank of overlapping band-pass filters stretching from low frequencies to high frequencies. The psychophysical tuning curves can be viewed as estimates of the filter shapes.

## Physiological basis of frequency selectivity and masking

Ever since the time of Helmholtz, the mechanical properties of the cochlea have been invoked to explain frequency selectivity. The point of maximum displacement on the basilar membrane varies with

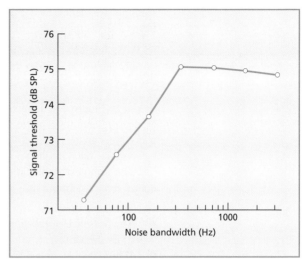

**FIG. 5.3**   Critical-band masking. The signal was a 2 kHz pure tone. The mask contained noise centred at 2 kHz. The abscissa plots the bandwidth of the noise, and the ordinate plots the threshold for detecting the signal in the presence of the noise. For very narrowband noise (50–400 Hz), detectability worsens as noise bandwidth increases. Once the noise bandwidth reaches 400 Hz further increases have no effect on signal detectability (re-plotted from Schooneveldt & Moore, 1989).

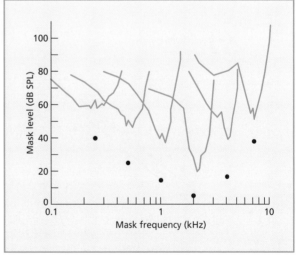

**FIG. 5.4**   Psychophysical tuning curves. The signal was a pure tone at one of six frequencies, fixed at a relatively low intensity (shown by the filled circles in the plot). The mask was also a pure tone, at one of the frequencies shown on the abscissa. Each curve represents the intensity of the mask required to just mask each signal, as a function of mask frequency. Low mask intensities are needed when the mask has a similar frequency to the signal, but progressively more intense masks are needed as mask frequency departs further from signal frequency (re-plotted from Vogten, 1974).

stimulus frequency (see Figure 4.14). So the frequency tuning of auditory nerve fibres reflects their place of innervation on the basilar membrane. It is therefore reasonable to propose a link between frequency-tuned responses in the peripheral auditory system, as revealed by physiological studies, and the auditory filters revealed by psychophysical studies. The frequency tuning curves of cat auditory nerve fibres shown in Figure 4.18 are remarkably similar to the psychophysical tuning curves shown in Figure 5.4. Evans, Pratt, and Cooper (1989) compared the bandwidths of guinea-pig auditory nerve fibres with filter bandwidths measured behaviourally using noise masking. There is very good agreement between the neural data and the behavioural data, as shown in Figure 5.5.

The simplest explanation of **critical-band masking** in psychophysical tasks makes three assumptions:

- The presence of the signal increases the level of activity in auditory filters tuned to its frequency.
- When this response increment exceeds some minimum value, the signal is detected by the listener.
- The mask also produces excitation in auditory filters, but this activity is obviously unrelated to the presence or absence of a signal.

If the mask and the signal activate *different* filters, then the presence of the mask should have no effect on the excitation produced by the signal, and therefore on its detectability. If the mask excites the *same* filter as the signal, the resultant activity will swamp the activity produced by the signal, impairing detectability. A more intense signal is required to reach the minimum increment in filter response required for detection.

**KEY TERM**
**Critical-band masking**: An experimental effect in which masking of a sinusoidal signal occurs only when the centre frequency of the noise falls within a certain band of frequencies surrounding the signal.

## FREQUENCY DISCRIMINATION

Studies of frequency discrimination measure a listener's ability to detect small changes in frequency. A common technique involves the successive presentation of two tones with slightly different frequencies. The listener is required to report whether the first tone or the second tone had a higher pitch. The differential threshold is taken as the change in frequency required for the listener to achieve a fixed percentage of correct responses (e.g. 75%; see Chapter 1 for more details on differential thresholds). Figure 5.6 shows differential threshold as a function of frequency, obtained in several studies.

It is clear that frequency discrimination is remarkably good at low frequencies. A change in frequency of less than 1 Hz can be detected reliably at frequencies below 1000 Hz. Discrimination deteriorates as frequency increases, but does not exceed 100 Hz even at frequencies over 10 kHz. This corresponds to a 1% change in frequency at threshold.

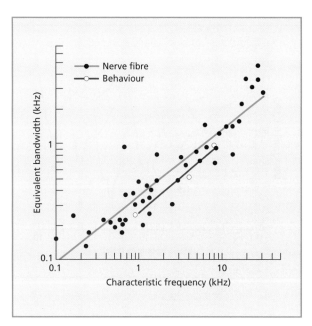

**FIG. 5.5**   Estimated auditory filter bandwidth as a function of characteristic frequency, in the guinea pig (re-plotted from Evans, Pratt, & Cooper, 1989). Filled circles represent estimates based on recordings directly from auditory nerve fibres. Open symbols represent estimates based on behavioural responses in a masking experiment.

What information do listeners use when making frequency discriminations? Experiments on frequency discrimination explicitly instruct the subject to attend to the pitch of the two tones. An adequate theory of pitch perception must therefore be able to explain why the differential threshold for frequency is so small.

## THEORIES OF PITCH PERCEPTION

A given sound stimulus produces a characteristic pattern of activity across neurons in the peripheral auditory system tuned to different frequencies. In simple terms, this activity pattern can be viewed as a smoothed sample of the sound's magnitude spectrum. The activity pattern is smoothed because each neuron responds to a range of frequencies centred on its characteristic frequency. It can be assumed, as the preceding section indicated, that frequency-tuned neurons bear a direct relation to the bank of auditory filters identified by psychophysical experiments. How is this activity pattern linked to our perception of the sound's pitch? The peripheral auditory system provides two ways to encode frequency:

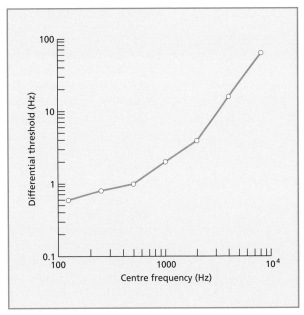

**FIG. 5.6**  Human differential threshold for frequency as a function of reference frequency, summarized from a number of early studies (re-drawn from Moore, 1997, Figure 5.1).

- The frequency-to-place conversion of the basilar membrane (see Figure 4.14).
- The timing of responses in auditory nerve fibres (see Figure 4.17).

The place and timing theories of pitch perception are linked directly to these two frequency-coding strategies.

### Place theory

Helmholtz (1877) believed that the basilar membrane vibrated in sympathy with the frequency of an incoming sound wave. He understood the implications of the membrane's variation in width, and noted that:

> *the parts of the membrane [vibrating] in unison with higher tones must be looked for near the round window, and those with the deeper, near the vertex of the cochlea.*
>
> *(Helmholtz, 1877, translation by Ellis, 1954, p. 146)*

From this fact he proposed the first theory of pitch perception, now called the **place theory**:

> *Hence every simple tone of determinate pitch will be felt only by certain nerve fibres, and simple tones of different pitch will excite different fibres… The sensation of pitch would consequently be a sensation in different nerve fibres.*
>
> *(Helmholtz, 1877, translation by Ellis, 1954, pp. 147–148)*

**KEY TERM**
**Place theory**: A theory of pitch perception, according to which pitch is determined by the place of maximum excitation on the basilar membrane.

### Is frequency discrimination in pure tones proportional to bandwidth?

*Think about why frequency discrimination should be related to critical-band masking.*

It follows directly from Helmholtz's theory that the frequency selectivity of auditory nerve fibres should be closely related to the ability of listeners to judge differences in the pitch of pure tones. If frequency selectivity is very fine, then only a small change in frequency should be required to produce a change in the activity pattern across the fibres that is detectable as a change in pitch. Broadly-tuned fibres would permit only relatively coarse frequency discrimination, because a small change in frequency would have very little effect on the activity pattern in the fibres. The breadth of frequency tuning in an auditory filter is measured by its bandwidth. So according to the place theory, frequency discrimination should be proportional to bandwidth.

A number of studies have used a psychophysical matching technique known as "**notched noise**" to estimate the bandwidth of human auditory filters. Figure 5.7 (left) summarises the results of several studies. For consistency with place theory, the frequency discrimination threshold at each frequency should be a fixed proportion of the filter bandwidth at the same frequency. In Figure 5.7 (right) the frequency discrimination thresholds shown in Figure 5.6 are expressed as a proportion of the auditory filter bandwidths shown in Figure 5.7 (left). Proportional threshold remains constant only up to approximately 2 kHz, and then increases markedly. Thus, there is only partial support for place theory.

### Frequency discrimination in brief tones

Another test of the place theory was performed by Moore (1973). He measured frequency discrimination for very briefly presented tones. Such stimuli produce very

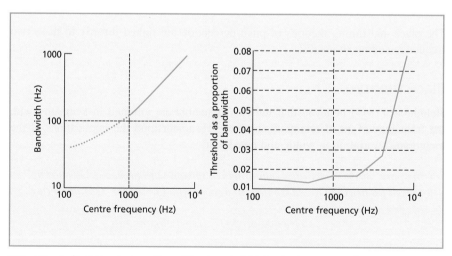

**FIG. 5.7** Left: Estimated auditory filter bandwidth in the human auditory system as a function of characteristic frequency, summarised from a number of masking studies (re-drawn from Moore, 1997, Figure 3.10). Right: Differential threshold for frequency (taken from Figure 5.6) expressed as a proportion of filter bandwidth (taken from Figure 5.7, left), as a function of characteristic frequency. For frequencies below 2 kHz, threshold is a constant proportion of filter bandwidth. Above 2 kHz, discriminability is worse than expected on the basis of filter bandwidth. Inspection of Figures 5.6 and 5.7 (left) indicates that this is due to a change in the rate at which threshold deteriorates at high frequencies.

broad patterns of displacement on the basilar membrane (brief pulses contain very many frequency components; see the tutorial section of Chapter 4). If frequency discrimination relies on the place of maximum displacement, performance should be relatively poor. Moore (1973) found that below 5 kHz discrimination was much better than that predicted on the basis of place coding.

*Why do brief pulses of sound contain so many frequency components?*

### Complex tones: The missing fundamental

Place theory has had only partial success in accounting for the perception of pure tones. Turning to complex tones, a phenomenon known as the "**missing fundamental**" presents a further problem for the place theory. Complex tones usually contain a fundamental frequency and a series of evenly spaced harmonics, as explained in Chapter 4. However, if the fundamental frequency of a complex tone is removed, its pitch is still heard at a frequency that corresponds to the fundamental. For example, a complex tone containing frequencies at 1000, 1200, and 1400 Hz appears to have a pitch corresponding to the fundamental at 200 Hz.

Helmholtz was aware of the phenomenon, and the difficulty it presented to the place theory. He attempted to explain it in terms of non-linear responses in the ear. Recall from Chapter 4 that one form of non-linearity is the presence of frequency components in a system's output that were not present in the input. Helmholtz argued that the ear reintroduces energy at a frequency corresponding to the fundamental. This explanation cannot be correct, because the missing fundamental is still heard even when masking noise is introduced in the region of a sound's spectrum corresponding to the fundamental frequency. If the fundamental is reintroduced by a non-linearity, then it should be masked by the noise.

> The missing fundamental can be heard every time you use the telephone. The small audio speakers in the handset only generate frequencies in the range of 300 Hz to 3 kHz. The male voice has a fundamental of approximately 150 Hz. Even in the absence of this fundamental, male voices heard over the telephone still sound male.

## Timing theory

### Phase locking to pure tones

As explained in Chapter 4, auditory nerve responses are phase-locked to the frequency of an incoming sound wave, at least for frequencies below 4–5 kHz. The timing of neural impulses therefore carries frequency information. The **timing theory** of pitch perception assumes that the listener discriminates the pitch of pure tones by means of differences in the time intervals between neural firings. Since phase locking breaks down at frequencies above 4 kHz, pitch perception based on timing information is possible only for low-frequency sounds. One line of evidence that supports the timing theory is the absence of apparent musical pitch for frequencies above 4 kHz.

### Complex tones: The missing fundamental

Timing theory was once thought to provide a convincing account of the missing fundamental phenomenon. Complex sound waves show periodic variations in SPL, known as **beats**. Beats occur because when sine waves at different frequencies are added together, they tend to cancel out at some parts of the wave, and augment each other at other parts of the wave (see the tutorial section of Chapter 4). The beat frequency for a set of harmonically related sine waves corresponds to their fundamental frequency. The temporal pattern of firing in the auditory nerve is known to

> **KEY TERMS**
> **Missing fundamental wave**: A complex wave from which the fundamental frequency has been removed.
> **Timing theory**: A theory of pitch perception, according to which pitch is determined by the timing of neural impulses in the auditory nerve.
> **Beat**: Regular changes in the amplitude of a wave when two or more sine waves at different frequencies are added together.

follow the beat frequency. So, it was argued, the pitch of a complex sound could be encoded in the pattern of firing at its beat frequency. The beat frequency is present in a complex sound even in when the fundamental component is absent, because the beat is produced by higher harmonics. Schouten called the pitch sensation produced by beats in higher harmonics "**residue pitch**".

Notice that, according to the timing theory's account of pitch perception in complex sounds, the higher harmonics must remain unresolved. The auditory system just encodes the frequency of the beats they produce. However, experiments by Plomp (1967) contradicted timing theory. He created complex harmonic stimuli in which the lower harmonics (which the auditory system can resolve individually) specified one pitch, and the higher unresolved harmonics specified a different pitch. Listeners heard the pitch defined by the resolved harmonics, not the pitch defined by beats in unresolved harmonics. The missing fundamental is no longer considered to provide crucial support for the timing theory of pitch perception.

## Pattern theory

The failure of Schouten's timing theory to provide an adequate account Plomp's (1967) result led to a new theory of pitch perception that can also explain the missing fundamental phenomenon. Goldstein's (1973) **pattern theory** proposed that the auditory system first resolves the individual sine wave components of a complex sound. It then tries to find a series of harmonically related frequencies that fits the components as closely as possible. Pitch is determined by the fundamental of the best-fitting harmonic series. Goldstein's theory clearly explains the missing fundamental effect, since the pitch of the fundamental is defined by the harmonics present in the stimulus, even when the fundamental is not present. The theory also explains Plomp's finding that resolved harmonics determine perceived pitch. On the other hand, pattern theory cannot explain why some impression of pitch can be formed even from stimuli that do not contain resolved harmonics (Moore & Glasberg, 1986).

**KEY TERMS**
**Residue pitch**: The pitch heard in a complex wave due to beats rather than to resolvable harmonic components.
**Pattern theory**: A theory of pitch perception in complex sounds, according to which pitch is determined by the harmonic series that best fits the pattern of frequencies in a sound.

A flexible cue-based approach of this kind has been very successful in the field of visual depth perception, as we shall see in Chapter 10.

## Evaluation

It is clear that none of the three theories outlined above can provide a complete account of pitch perception. Yet the empirical evidence indicates that each of them can play a part, at least for particular kinds of stimulus. The response of the peripheral auditory system provides several cues regarding the pitch of an incoming sound wave:

● Place cues are available in the place of maximum displacement on the basilar membrane, at least for relatively simple sounds of long duration.
● Periodicity cues are available in the temporal pattern of auditory response, at least for frequencies below 4 kHz.
● Pattern cues are available in the pattern of responses across the whole population of nerve fibres, at least for complex harmonic sounds.

The availability of each cue varies according to the nature of the sound stimulus, so pitch perception may be based on a flexible combination of different cues.

# AUDITORY LOCALISATION

Auditory localisation refers to a listener's ability to judge the direction and distance of a sound source. This information can be used to orient attention towards the source of the sound, such as a predator or prey animal. It can also be used as an aid in the segregation of individual sound sources from the complex wave arriving at the ears.

The direction of a sound source can be specified relative to two principal planes passing through the head. The direction of a sound source in the horizontal (left–right) plane is specified by an *azimuth* angle relative to straight ahead. Direction in the vertical (up–down) plane is specified by an angle of *elevation* relative to horizontal. For example, a sound source having an azimuth angle of 0° and an elevation of 90° would be located directly above the head. A sound source at 90° azimuth and 0° elevation would be directly opposite the left ear.

Perceptual research typically investigates sound localisation in one plane at a time, manipulating horizontal location while keeping vertical location constant, or vice versa. As was shall see, results indicate that horizontal localisation relies on binaural cues (comparisons between the signals arriving at the two ears). Vertical localisation relies on monaural cues (information available in the signal arriving at just one ear).

## LOCALISATION IN THE HORIZONTAL PLANE

### Minimum audible angle

Many psychophysical studies have measured the smallest change in azimuth angle that can be detected reliably by listeners, relative to a particular reference angle. The threshold angular change is known as the **minimum audible angle** (MAA). Figure 5.8 shows the MAA for sine wave stimuli as a function of stimulus frequency, for four different reference angles. The 0° data (filled circles) represent the smallest change in direction from straight ahead that listeners could reliably detect. Below approximately 1000 Hz a shift as small as 1° can be detected. There is a pronounced elevation of thresholds for frequencies in between 1500 and 1800 Hz. This region of poor performance is also present for all the other reference angles plotted in the figure.

**KEY TERM**
**Minimum audible angle (MAA)**: The smallest change in the azimuth angle of a sound source that can be detected reliably.

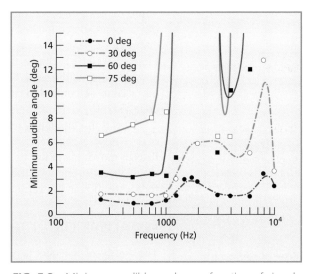

**FIG. 5.8** Minimum audible angle as a function of signal frequency. A pure tone was presented at one of four azimuth angles, and the ordinate plots the minimum change in angle that listeners could detect reliably (re-plotted from Yost, 2000).

### The duplex theory

Over 120 years ago, John William Strutt (Lord Rayleigh) identified two potential cues for the localisation of sound sources in the horizontal plane: inter-aural level differences (ILD) and inter-aural time differences (ITD):

- ILDs arise because the ear farther from the sound source lies in the acoustic shadow cast by the listener's head. As a result the intensity of the signal arriving at the farther ear is lower than the intensity of the signal arriving at the nearer ear.

● ITDs occur because the two ears are approximately 14 cm apart, so sounds from a source nearer to one ear will arrive at that ear slightly before they arrive at the other ear.

Rayleigh's **duplex theory** proposed that the two cues are complementary: ITDs are effective at low sine-wave frequencies, and ILDs are effective at high frequencies. The neural coding of ILD and ITD was considered in detail in Chapter 4 (see Figure 4.21). Specialised neural circuits in the superior olive encode the ILDs and ITDs created by lateralised sound sources. Responses in these neural circuits are the presumed neural substrate of Rayleigh's duplex theory. Central processes in the auditory cortex must compute a single estimate of azimuth angle on the basis of information concerning ILD and ITD.

We can infer that the deterioration in performance shown in Figure 5.8 occurs at the transition between localisation based on ITDs (below 2 kHz), and localisation based on ILDs (above 2 kHz). In this frequency region neither cue operates effectively. The MAA of 1° obtained at low frequencies corresponds to an ITD of only 10 μs.

For complex natural sounds such as speech, ITDs in lower frequencies appear to dominate the computation of azimuth angle. Wightman and Kistler (1992) generated stimuli in which ITDs indicated one azimuth angle, but ILDs indicated another azimuth angle. When the stimuli contained low frequencies, ITDs determined apparent direction. When low frequencies were removed, ILDs were more important for apparent direction.

## Cones of confusion

Despite the obvious utility of binaural cues for sound localisation, they are not sufficient to define direction uniquely. A given set of cue values is usually consistent with a range of possible sound directions, in addition to the true direction. For example, a sound source located directly in front of a listener provides the same binaural cue values as a sound source located directly behind the listener. The curved line in Figure 5.9 (left) is drawn through all locations in the horizontal plane (seen from above) that yield the same ITD between the ears. This curve can be rotated to sweep out a **cone of confusion**, shown in Figure 5.9 (right). All sounds located on the cone's surface yield the same ITD, so their locations are confusable.

How is this ambiguity resolved? The key lies in the observation that each position of the listener's head relative to the sound source has its own cone of confusion. If the listener moves his or her head, then only a very small number of possible directions would be consistent with the different cones of confusion. Listeners can also use cues for localisation in the vertical plane.

## LOCALISATION IN THE VERTICAL PLANE

The ability of listeners to judge elevation is much better than would be expected on the basis of binaural cues and head movements (Moore, 1997). The auditory system must therefore exploit other cues to establish elevation. The main cue for vertical localisation is thought to be the interaction of the sound with the external ear. This cue is necessarily monaural, and is based on the way that sound waves are reflected off the external ear into the ear canal. The complex folded structure of the

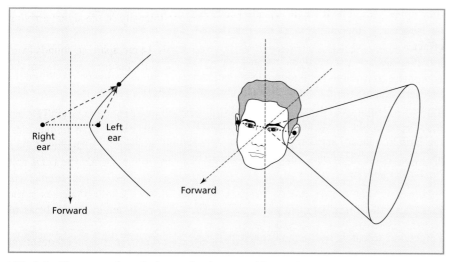

**FIG. 5.9** The cone of confusion. Left: The curved line is drawn through all horizontal locations (seen from above the head) that yield the same ITD between the two ears. Right: The curve on the left has been rotated to sweep out a conical surface. Sound sources located anywhere on the surface yield the same ITD. These locations are therefore confusable.

pinna acts as an acoustic filter, selectively modifying both the amplitude and phase properties of frequency components in the incoming sound wave. The small, asymmetrical shape of the human pinna has two crucial effects on its filtering properties. First, the effect of the pinna is restricted to frequencies above 6 kHz, because only these frequencies have sufficiently short wavelength (below 6 cm) to be affected by the pinna. Second, the filtering effect of the pinna depends on the direction of the sound source. Given a complex broadband stimulus, the pinna tends to introduce peaks and valleys in the high frequency region of the sound's spectrum. As the elevation of the sound source increases, these peaks and valleys tend to move towards higher frequencies.

Gardner and Gardner (1973) compared localisation performance with and without pinna effects. They removed any contribution of the pinna by filling the cavities in the outer ear with moulded rubber plugs. Localisation was worse when the effect of the pinna was removed, especially for bands of noise with high centre frequencies.

*Think about why some animals have larger ears than others.*

## THE PRECEDENCE EFFECT

In a cluttered natural environment, the sound emanating from a given source may reach our ears via several paths. As well as the direct path from the source to the ear, there may be many other paths that involve reflections off nearby surfaces such as rocks or walls (echoes). With several echoes from different directions, there is a great deal of scope for confusion about the true direction of the sound source. However, listeners do not normally experience such confusion. Sounds can be localised accurately even in highly reverberant conditions. This accuracy is achieved because the earliest arriving sound wave is given precedence over later echoes. If two brief sounds are presented to an observer, 5–50 ms apart in time,

Sounds heard via headphones tend to appear localised inside the listener's head, because they bypass the pinna. The pinna appears to alter sounds in a way that leads them to be perceived as external to the listener. Sounds recorded using microphones placed in the ear canal of a dummy head with realistic outer ears still appear externalised even when played through headphones.

they appear fused as a single sound. The apparent direction of the fused sound is determined by the direction of the first sound. This is known as the **precedence effect**.

*Demonstrate the precedence effect using your own stereo system.*

Precedence can be demonstrated easily at home using stereo reproduction equipment to listen to a monophonic signal, such as a mono radio station. When the listener is facing the two speakers and positioned midway between them, the sound appears to come from directly ahead. When the listener moves closer to one speaker than the other, the sound appears to come entirely from the nearer speaker. However, the farther, unheard speaker still makes a contribution to the loudness and apparent spatial extent of the sound. This can be verified by listening to the effect of unplugging the farther speaker.

## DISTANCE JUDGEMENTS

Perceptual research has demonstrated that several cues are used by the auditory system to estimate the distance of a sound source. Other things being equal, more distant sounds are quieter than nearer sounds. In fact, sound intensity decreases by a factor of four each time distance doubles (the inverse square law). So sound intensity provides a simple cue to distance, and it is well known that louder sounds appear closer than quieter sounds. Distance also alters the spectrum of sounds. Air molecules absorb energy at higher sound frequencies more than at lower sound frequencies. As a result sounds from more distant sources appear muffled. Thunder, for example, is heard as an extremely loud crack from nearby, but as a quiet rumble from a far distance.

Intensity and spectral profile are most effective as cues to distance when the sound is familiar to the listener. Otherwise it is not possible to disentangle the effect of distance from the inherent intensive and spectral characteristics of the sound. Distance judgements of unfamiliar sounds are consequently rather inaccurate: errors of 20% or more are not uncommon (Moore, 1997).

**KEY TERMS**

**Precedence effect**: A phenomenon in which apparent sound source direction is determined by the earliest sound to arrive at the ear.

**Formant frequency**: The distinctive frequency at which the vocal tract (the tube of air between the larynx and lips) vibrates to create a certain vowel sound.

The smallest unit of sound that allows different words to be distinguished is defined as the *phoneme*. The word "dog", for example, contains three phonemes. Changes to the first, second, and third phoneme respectively produce the words "log", "dig", and "dot". English is said to contain 40 different phonemes, specified as in /d/, /o/, /g/ for the word "dog".

## SPEECH PERCEPTION

### THE PRODUCTION OF SPEECH SOUNDS

Speech and musical sounds are produced by a vibrating sound source that is filtered by a resonant chamber. In the case of speech, the vibration is produced by air forced through the vocal cords by the diaphragm. This vibration creates a harmonic sound whose fundamental frequency depends on the rate of vibration. When this harmonic sound reaches the vocal tract, its spectrum undergoes radical modification because the vocal tract acts as a resonator. Certain frequencies are amplified, because the vocal tract tends to vibrate or resonate more at those frequencies than at other frequencies. These resonant frequencies are called **formant frequencies**, and show up as distinct peaks of energy in the sound's frequency spectrum. Formants are numbered in ascending order starting with the formant at the lowest frequency. Formants often display a smooth change in their frequency during the first 50 ms or so of the speech sound. These frequency glides are known as *formant transitions*. Figure 5.10 shows a simplified spectrogram for three different speech sounds, heard as /ba/, /da/, and /ga/. The sounds differ in terms of their formant transitions.

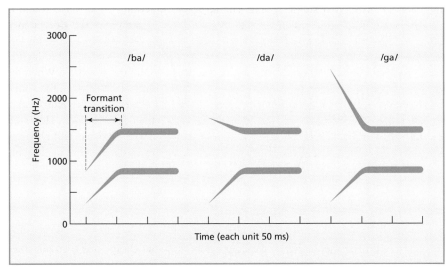

**FIG. 5.10**   Simplified spectrograms of three speech sounds, /ba/, /da/, and /ga/. Each sound contains concentrations of energy at particular frequencies (formants), due to resonance in the vocal tract. The frequency of each formant changes progressively over the first 50 ms or so of the sound (formant transition). Different speech sounds are distinguishable in terms of their formant frequencies and transitions.

## SPEECH MODE

It has long been argued that speech perception involves a special mode of auditory processing, known as the **speech mode**. Advocates of the existence of a speech mode make two claims about speech processing. First, they argue that the perceptual processing of speech sounds is qualitatively different from the processing of non-speech sounds. Second, they argue that specialised neural structures are dedicated to speech processing.

## Qualitative differences between speech and non-speech processing

Processes that differ *qualitatively* use completely different kinds of computation. It should not be possible to convert one process into the other by changing some details of the computation, such as increasing the bandwidth of a filter, or adding an extra step in the computation (see the distinction between analogue computation and symbolic computation in Chapter 1). Some have argued that the speech processing is qualitatively different from the processing of non-speech sounds because it supports **categorical perception**.

### Categorical perception

When the frequency content of non-speech sounds is altered in some way, listeners report relatively gradual and continuous changes in their perceptual attributes. For example, the pitch of a sound varies smoothly with changes in its fundamental frequency. A small change in frequency produces a slight change in pitch, while a large change in frequency produces a very marked change in pitch. Different speech sounds vary in terms of their formant frequencies or formant transitions, as we have seen

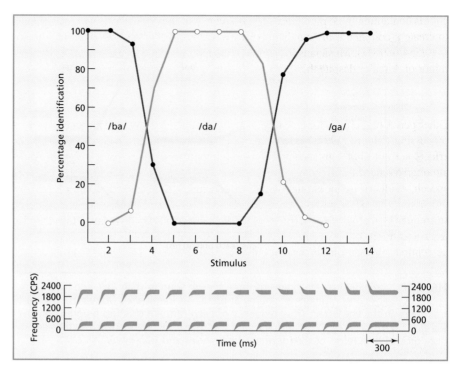

**FIG. 5.11**   Phoneme boundaries. Liberman, Harris, Hoffman, and Griffith (1957) created a set of 14 synthetic speech sounds in which the formant transition of the second formant varied continuously between the values specifying the three sounds shown in Figure 5.10. Spectrograms of the 14 sounds are shown along the bottom of the figure. Listeners were asked to identify each synthetic sound as a /ba/, /da/, or /ga/. Identification data show very sharp transitions between perceived phonemes (re-drawn from Liberman et al., 1957).

in Figure 5.10. It is possible to create synthetic speech stimuli that contain formants lying in between those defining different speech sounds. Liberman, Harris, Hoffman, and Griffith (1957), for example, created a set of 14 stimuli in which the formant transition of the second formant varied continuously between the three values illustrated in Figure 5.10. The spectrograms at the bottom of Figure 5.11 show the stimulus set.

What do listeners perceive when presented with these intermediate stimuli? Do they report a gradual change in their perception of the phoneme, similar to the change in pitch of non-speech sounds? The answer is negative—there is no gradual shift from perception of one phoneme to perception of another. Instead, there is a sudden switch when the formant frequency reaches a particular value. The three curves in Figure 5.11 show the percentage of time each stimulus was identified as /ba/, /da/, and /ga/ in Liberman et al.'s (1957) experiment. The transition from one phoneme to the next was very sudden, as seen in the steepness of the curves. The sharpness of the perceptual boundary between phonemes has been taken as evidence that listeners group speech sounds into discrete perceptual categories (e.g. Liberman et al., 1957). The switch from one category to another occurs when the formant frequency reaches a **phoneme boundary**. On this basis it has been argued that there is a special speech mode of auditory processing. The argument is weakened by evidence for categorical processing of non-speech sounds. For example, Locke and Kellar (1973) studied the identification and discrimination of chords by musicians and non-musicians. Stimuli were musical

**KEY TERM**
**Phoneme boundary**: A formant frequency defining the boundary at which perception switches from one phoneme to another.

chords containing three pure tones. The frequency of the middle tone was manipulated to create a continuum of sounds in between A minor (440/523/659 Hz) and A major (440/554/659 Hz). Musicians in particular tended to categorise the sounds as either A minor or A major despite the relatively small changes in frequency involved.

### Evaluation

Other perceptual effects have also been taken as support for a special speech mode of processing (Moore, 1997). However, as in the case of categorical perception, these effects are not unique to speech, but are also found using non-speech signals. Thus, although a range of different studies does indicate that there is something special about speech, evidence is not strong enough to conclude that there is a mode of auditory processing that is unique to speech. Speech may be special because it is encountered so frequently that listeners become expert at processing speech signals. This expertise leads to differences between speech and non-speech perception. In a similar way, pitch perception in expert musicians may differ from pitch perception in non-musicians.

## Physiological specialisation in the processing of speech sounds

Evidence that specialised neural structures are dedicated to processing speech sounds has come from two sources: neuropsychological studies of brain damage, and brain imaging.

### Neuropsychology

Neuropsychological research has identified an area in the left hemisphere of the human brain, where damage is associated with disturbed speech perception. In the late 1800s the German neurologist Carl Wernicke found that damage in a small area of the left cortical hemisphere resulted in an inability to comprehend speech. The area he discovered became known as **Wernicke's area**, and the disorder is commonly called Wernicke's aphasia.

Figure 5.12 shows that Wernicke's area lies on the posterior portion of the temporal lobe, posterior to primary and secondary auditory cortex. Patients suffering from Wernicke's aphasia are unable to understand speech, but do not show evidence of marked sensory impairments of hearing. Wernicke's aphasia does not offer clear-cut evidence for a special speech mode of auditory processing. The disorder may reflect a disturbance in the neural system that links the auditory representation of speech sounds with their meanings.

### Brain imaging

Research in this area has attempted to isolate regions of the cortex where activity is uniquely associated

> **KEY TERM**
> **Wernicke's area**: An area in the left hemisphere of the human cortex where damage results in disordered speech perception (Wernicke's aphasia).

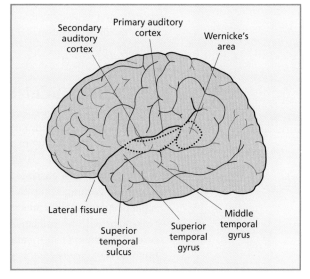

**FIG. 5.12** Human cortical areas involved in speech processing. Primary auditory cortex lies on Heschl's gyrus, hidden on the upper surface of the temporal lobe inside the lateral fissure. Secondary auditory cortex encircles this primary area, covering part of the superior temporal gyrus. Wernicke's aphasia (inability to understand speech) is associated with damage to the posterior portion of the left temporal lobe, posterior to auditory cortex. Brain-imaging studies of cortical activation in response to speech stimuli (e.g. Scott et al., 2000) find activity in auditory cortex and in an area anterior to secondary auditory cortex on the superior temporal gyrus.

with auditory processing of speech sounds. Scott, Blank, Rosen, and Wise (2000), for example, used PET to study the brain areas activated solely by intelligible speech, regardless of acoustic complexity. They used a variety of speech and speech-like sounds that were carefully designed to be equivalent in terms of acoustic complexity, but variable in terms of their intelligibility as speech. In addition, Scott et al. used a passive listening task in which subjects were not required to make semantic decisions regarding the content of the speech stimuli. In keeping with earlier neuropsychological research, Scott et al. (2000) found preferential activation of the left hemisphere by speech stimuli. Sounds that were comparable in complexity to speech, but totally unintelligible, activated areas previously identified as secondary auditory cortex on the superior temporal gyrus (see Figure 5.12). Intelligible speech activated an adjacent area in the anterior superior temporal sulcus. Scott et al.'s results are consistent with single-cell recording studies in primates that reveal a "what" auditory processing stream that advances anteriorly from primary auditory cortex, extracting more complex features from auditory stimuli (see Chapter 4).

### Evaluation

Neuropsychological and brain-imaging studies do not provide clear evidence for a special speech mode of auditory perception. Brain imaging indicates that neural processing of speech forms part of a general "what" stream of auditory processing. Wernicke's area is separate from, and posterior to, the presumed "what" stream. This may indicate that Wernicke's area stores memories for the constituent sounds of speech, and is responsible for linking the auditory representations of speech with their meanings (Martin, 1998; Scott et al., 2000), but it may not tell us much about auditory processing per se.

## AUDITORY SCENE ANALYSIS

This chapter began with an example of a natural acoustic environment, likely to be encountered while sitting in a bar talking with some friends. The sound waves reaching each ear may include contributions from friends' voices, from music playing on a jukebox, and from passing traffic (see Figure 5.1). The auditory system must partition the incoming complex signal into each of these components in order to build separate perceptual representations of the objects or events generating the sounds. Only then will the listener be able to follow the conversation, enjoy the music, and so on. Bregman (1990) called the perceptual process that achieves this decomposition *auditory scene analysis*. Parts of the complex acoustic signal that are grouped together form an **auditory stream**, in Bregman's (1990) terminology, which is identified with a discrete object or event in the world that created the sound (your friend, the jukebox, a car outside the bar). The auditory system groups sound components into streams on the basis of their physical characteristics. Bregman (1990) distinguished between two forms of auditory grouping—sequential and simultaneous.

## SEQUENTIAL GROUPING

In sequential grouping the auditory system assigns successively occurring sounds to specific auditory streams. Some simple examples of sequential grouping are shown in Figure 5.13.

KEY TERM
**Auditory streaming**: Grouping of parts of a complex acoustic signal into discrete auditory objects.

The stimulus consists of six tones presented in a repeating sequence, with three tones at higher pitch interleaved with three tones at lower pitch. In the case of the left-hand sequence, listeners perceive a single auditory stream in which the "melody" contains alternating high- and low-pitched notes. When the same sequence of tones is presented more rapidly (middle stimulus) the tones tend to separate into two streams, one containing the higher-pitch notes and the other containing the lower-pitch notes. A similar effect occurs when the presentation rate stays constant, but the frequency difference between the two sets of notes increases (right-hand stimulus).

The stimuli in Figure 5.13 illustrate two sequential grouping cues, based on temporal proximity (middle), and frequency similarity (right). Other cues for sequential grouping include harmonic similarity and spatial location (Darwin, 1997). In the case of complex harmonic sounds, rather than the tones in Figure 5.13, streaming is influenced by the overall spectral properties or timbre of harmonic sequences. Grouping can depend on the ear at which successive sounds arrive, so spatial location is important. For example, tones played to the same ear tend to be grouped together in the same stream.

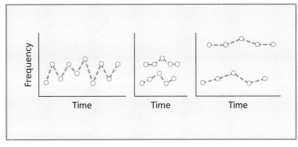

**FIG. 5.13**  Sequential auditory grouping. The stimulus contains a repeating sequence of six notes, with three low-pitch notes alternating with three high-pitch notes. In the left-hand stimulus, the notes form a single perceptual stream or melody whose pitch rises and falls alternately (dashed line). If the time interval between notes is shortened (middle), or if the frequency difference between the high notes and the low notes is increased (right), the stimulus tends to segregate into two streams, one containing the high notes and the other containing the low notes.

*Think about the auditory streams you perceive in emergency sirens. Are they stable?*

## SIMULTANEOUS GROUPING

In this form of grouping, the auditory system assigns simultaneously occurring sounds to specific auditory streams. It attempts to determine, at any given instant in time, how many different sound sources are present in a complex waveform. The most important cue for simultaneous grouping is pitch (Darwin, 1997). The conversation in the bar provides a very good example of simultaneous grouping on the basis of pitch. Men tend to speak at a lower pitch (fundamental frequency) than women, and individuals differ in the precise pitch of their voice. So if two friends are talking simultaneously, the difference in the pitch of their voices is a major cue enabling the listener to correctly separate the utterances into two streams.

The fundamental frequency of each complex sound is so important for simultaneous grouping because it determines the frequencies of all the sound's harmonics. As we saw in Chapter 4, the harmonics of a complex sound are equally spaced in frequency at exact multiples of the fundamental frequency. So if two complex sounds have different fundamentals, their harmonics form different harmonic series, which can be segregated into different auditory streams.

Inter-aural timing differences (ITDs) are a powerful cue for localising complex sounds, as we discovered earlier. However, ITDs are surprisingly ineffective at producing simultaneous grouping. Darwin (1997) suggested that ITDs rely on prior grouping, rather than act as a cue to grouping. ITDs are encoded by frequency-selective neurons in the brainstem (see Chapter 4). Natural sounds usually contain many frequency components. If several sounds are present simultaneously, the auditory signal will contain many frequency components having a range of ITDs. The auditory system can only deduce location from the ITDs of a set of components after

*Why is it a good idea to wear earplugs at heavily amplified music concerts?*

those components have been grouped together as belonging to the same source. ITD cannot therefore act as a simultaneous grouping cue itself.

# HEARING DYSFUNCTION

Human hearing is mediated by a complex system of mechanical and neural structures. Consequently there are many sources of dysfunction that result in hearing loss. Dysfunctions are broadly classified into two categories, *conductive* and *sensori-neural*. **Conductive hearing loss** is associated with problems in the mechanical structures of the outer and middle ear. **Sensori-neural** dysfunction arises from damage to neural structures in the cochlea, auditory nerve, or central auditory system. Tinnitus, or ringing in the ears, cannot be readily classified as a conductive disorder or a sensori-neural disorder, since its origin has not yet been identified. Figure 5.14 summarises the main forms of dysfunction.

## CONDUCTIVE HEARING LOSS

Apart from blockages in the outer ear due to wax or a foreign body, conductive hearing loss is usually associated with damage to the tympanic membrane or impeded transmission via the ossicles.

### Damage to the tympanic membrane

Holes or perforations in the eardrum can be caused by violent stimulation or by infection. This damage reduces the efficiency with which the eardrum transmits sound pressure waves to the middle ear. Scar tissue formation during healing may increase the stiffness of the membrane, again reducing its efficiency.

### The ossicles

Infection or otosclerosis can impede the ability of the ossicles to transmit energy, by restricting their ability to move. Infection is common in childhood, and may result in the development of scar tissue around the bones. Otosclerosis may fuse the ossicles against the bony structure of the middle ear.

**FIG. 5.14**   Classification of hearing dysfunction.

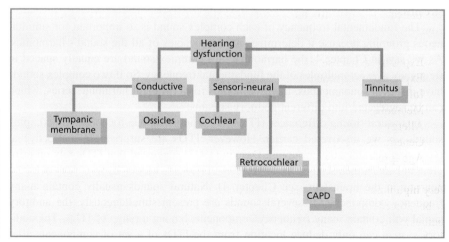

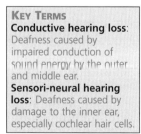

**KEY TERMS**
**Conductive hearing loss**: Deafness caused by impaired conduction of sound energy by the outer and middle ear.
**Sensori-neural hearing loss**: Deafness caused by damage to the inner ear, especially cochlear hair cells.

The middle ear cavity is normally filled with air, which allows free movement of the ossicles. Fluid build-up in the middle ear can impede the movement of the ossicles, and is the most common cause of hearing loss. It arises from blockages that prevent fluid produced by the lining of the middle ear from draining into the nasal cavity through the Eustachian tube.

## Consequences and treatment of conductive hearing loss

All conductive dysfunctions impede the conduction of sound energy to the cochlea. As a result, auditory thresholds are raised by as much as 40–50 dB in the most severe cases. Subjectively, very quiet sounds will be inaudible, while louder sounds will seem muffled. A crucial feature of conductive hearing loss that aids diagnosis is the relatively uniform elevation of threshold at all sound frequencies.

Fortunately, most forms of conductive hearing loss can be treated either by drugs to attack the infection, or by some form of mechanical intervention. Damaged tympanic membranes heal or can be repaired using grafting techniques. Damaged ossicles can be replaced with prosthetic ossicles. Fluid in the middle ear can be drained by inserting a grommet (tiny plastic tube) through the eardrum (though resulting damage to the eardrum is a risk).

All these interventions can return hearing sensitivity to normal or near-normal levels. In cases that cannot be treated by drugs or surgery, a simple hearing aid can be effective because it amplifies the signal to compensate for the loss in conduction efficiency.

> Grommet surgery has become so common that health care providers now consider the financial implications of the procedure carefully before approving surgery.

## SENSORI-NEURAL HEARING LOSS

Neural damage can be located in the cochlea, in the auditory nerve, or in central structures. Damage located in the auditory nerve is usually called *retrocochlear dysfunction*. Damage to central structures is sometimes termed *central auditory processing disorder* (CAPD).

## Cochlear damage

The delicate sensory structures of the cochlea are vulnerable to damage resulting from:

1. Exposure to intense sounds
2. Exposure to ototoxic drugs (e.g. antibiotics, solvents)
3. Infection
4. Metabolic disturbance
5. Allergy
6. Genetic disorders
7. Age (presbyacusis).

Very high noise levels, for example, can cause the elastic limit of the organ of Corti to be exceeded. This may result in structural damage to the stereocilia, tectorial membrane, and basilar membrane. Damage consequently has a major impact on the sensory function of the hair cells, particularly outer hair cells.

> Mammalian hair cells do not regenerate once they have been damaged, so cochlear hearing loss is permanent. On the other hand, some species such as birds and fish do have the ability to regenerate hair cells following damage. The origin of these species differences is not clear.

Cochlear damage usually has three perceptual consequences:

- Raised thresholds
- Broader frequency tuning
- Loudness recruitment.

*Think about how outer hair cell loss affects the functioning of the basilar membrane.*

As in the case of conductive disorders, cochlear damage leads to elevated thresholds for detecting sounds. Unlike conductive losses, however, the problem cannot be solved satisfactorily by simply amplifying the incoming signal. Sufferers report that sounds appear unclear and distorted, and find understanding speech particularly difficult. These problems can be attributed to the effect of cochlear damage on frequency tuning in the auditory nerve. Loss of outer hair cell function leads to a broadening in the frequency tuning of individual nerve fibres (see Figure 4.14). Broader tuning means that the listener cannot separate simultaneous frequency components in complex signals. The ability to segregate a speech signal from background noise and from other speech signals is severely impaired.

**Loudness recruitment** refers to an abnormally rapid growth of loudness as the intensity of a sound is increased. Sufferers find very quiet sounds difficult to hear, but may be able to hear louder sounds as well as normal listeners. Hence raising your voice so that it can be heard by an elderly relative often leads to the complaint "no need to shout!" Loudness recruitment is closely associated with cochlear damage and, as in the case of broadened frequency tuning, is probably related to outer hair cell damage. The cochlear amplifier described earlier enhances sensitivity to faint sounds, but has little effect on sensitivity to louder sounds. Outer hair cell motility is thought to be responsible for this effect. Without the amplification of faint sounds, loudness grows very rapidly as sound intensity increases.

As mentioned earlier, one cause of cochlear hearing loss is ageing. **Presbyacusis**, as it is known, probably starts when a person is in their 20s, but may not become noticeable until they have reached 50. Hearing loss begins at extremely high frequencies, and progresses down the frequency scale with advancing age. The effect is thought to reflect a progressive loss in hair cell efficiency. In other words, the hair cells wear out. Hair cells at the base of the cochlea bend in response to all sound frequencies, whereas cells at the apex only bend at low frequencies. Cells at the base are therefore likely to wear out sooner than those at the apex. Since, according to the place theory of frequency coding, cells at the base code high frequencies, presbyacusis progresses from high to low frequencies.

## Retrocochlear dysfunction

Retrocochlear dysfunction arises from disorders that affect the auditory nerve. The vestibular nerve runs alongside the auditory nerve. Tumours growing on the vestibular nerve can damage the auditory nerve, resulting in unilateral hearing loss and tinnitus (ringing in the ears). Treatment involves surgical intervention to remove the tumour, which results in complete and permanent hearing loss in the affected ear.

**KEY TERMS**
**Loudness recruitment**: Abnormally rapid growth in loudness with SPL, resulting from damage to outer hair cells in the cochlea.
**Presbyacusis**: Age-related hearing loss associated with deterioration of the cochlea.

## Central auditory processing disorder

A group of clinical patients present themselves with hearing problems in noisy environments, yet standard tests reveal no sensory deficits. This condition is gradually becoming known as *central auditory processing disorder*, or CAPD (e.g. Paul-Brown, 1996). The precise cause or causes of the disorder have not yet been identified. Treatment is confined to measures that improve the perceptibility of the signal against noisy backgrounds.

## Tinnitus

Tinnitus is the perception of a ringing sound that appears to originate inside the head, and to occur in the absence of any obvious external source. Transitory episodes of tinnutus are quite common, but in a small number of individuals the experience is so persistent that it becomes debilitating. Although the phenomenon probably originates in the peripheral auditory system, its exact causes have proved very difficult to identify (apart from tinnitus associated with retrocochlear dysfunction). One form of tinnitus is due to otosclerosis causing changes in impedance across frequency. Current therapeutic approaches emphasise a three-way interaction between the auditory system, the limbic system (involved in emotional responses), and the sympathetic nervous system (involved in arousal). Therapy may involve measures to intervene in each system. Auditory interventions may include the use of in-ear sound generators to promote habituation to the sound. Relaxation techniques and counselling attempt to minimise the arousal and anxiety produced by the phenomenon.

## CHAPTER SUMMARY

### LOUDNESS

- Perception of loudness is studied experimentally using matching and scaling tasks.
- Sound intensity appears to be coded by the rate of firing in frequency-tuned auditory nerve fibres. The excitation pattern model of loudness perception proposes that the overall loudness of a given sound is proportional to the total neural activity evoked by it in the auditory nerve.
- Human loudness discrimination is worse than one would expect on the basis of auditory nerve responses, indicating that central factors limit the ability of the brain to make use of intensity information.

### PITCH

- Pitch is related to a sound's frequency.
- Psychophysical tuning curves are remarkably similar to the frequency tuning curves of individual auditory nerve fibres.
- There are three major theories of pitch perception:

  - Place theory;
  - Timing theory;
  - Pattern theory.

- None of the theories provides a complete account of pitch perception. Their relative utility varies according to the nature of the sound stimulus:

  - Place coding is most useful for pitch perception in higher-frequency simple tones.

- Timing information can be used for lower-frequency simple tones, and in complex tones with unresolved harmonics.
- Pattern information is particularly useful in complex tones with resolved harmonics.

## LOCALISATION

- Rayleigh's influential duplex theory proposes that localisation in the horizontal plane makes use of two different binaural cues over different frequency ranges:
    - Inter-aural time differences are used at low frequencies;
    - Inter-aural level differences are used at high frequencies.
- Localisation in the vertical plane depends on the filtering effect of the pinna.
- Localisation is accurate even in highly reverberant environments, because the earlier arriving direct sound wave takes precedence over later echoes.

## SPEECH PERCEPTION

- Speech sounds are complex harmonic sounds that vary continuously over time.
- Evidence for a special speech mode of auditory processing is inconclusive:
    - Effects previously considered to be unique to speech (e.g. categorical perception) are also obtained using non-speech sounds;
    - Recent brain-imaging studies do not provide clear evidence for a special-purpose speech mode of auditory processing in the cortex.

## AUDITORY SCENE ANALYSIS

- Auditory scene analysis involves dividing up the components of a complex sound wave into auditory objects, on the basis of grouping cues.
- Sequential grouping of sounds is based on similarity in frequency, harmonicity and spatial location, and on temporal proximity.
- Simultaneous grouping is based on pitch.

## HEARING DYSFUNCTION

- Disorders of hearing can be grouped into two categories: conductive and sensori-neural.
- Conductive hearing loss is associated with disorders in the mechanical structures of the outer and middle ear.
- Conductive disorders impede the transmission of sound energy to the cochlea, and can be treated with an amplifying hearing aid.
- Sensori-neural dysfunction arises from damage to neural structures in the cochlea, auditory nerve, or central auditory system.
- Sensori-neural disorders can cause abnormal growth in loudness with stimulus intensity and broadened frequency tuning, usually due to damage in the outer hair cells of the cochlea. Simple amplifying hearing aids are therefore of limited utility.

# TUTORIALS

## MUSIC PERCEPTION

Music is a universal feature of all human cultures, both past and present. Crude musical instruments have been found in the remnants of the earliest civilisations. Music is so important in present-day culture that it supports a huge worldwide industry. In the UK alone, annual turnover in the music industry amounts to several hundred million pounds.

Curiously, there is no universally agreed definition of what constitutes music. Carterette and Kendall (1999, p. 726) provide a general definition of music as "temporally organised sound and silence that is areferentially communicative in a context". A crucial distinction between music and speech is that speech is referential because speech sounds act as references to words. Setting aside issues of definition, certain acoustic stimuli are recognised as musical by most members of a given culture, even when those stimuli have never been heard before. Recognition is based on a set of universal perceptual features of musical sounds.

## Features of musical sounds

### Musical tone

Tone is the primary quality of musical sound in western music. It has three important characteristics: pitch, loudness, and timbre (Rasch & Plomp, 1999).

- *Musical pitch* is related to the fundamental frequency of a complex harmonic sound, and is heard for fundamental frequencies between 20 Hz and 5000 Hz.
- *Loudness* is less important than pitch. Western musical notation allows for only five levels of loudness (from soft or pianissimo to loud or forte).
- *Timbre* gives a tone its distinctive character, and allows two tones to be distinguished even if they have the same pitch and loudness. Timbre is related to the harmonic composition of the tone, as well as to its temporal properties such as rise time and vibrato.

Theories of how pitch, loudness, and timbre are analysed by the auditory system were discussed in detail earlier in the chapter.

### Consonance

When two tones are played simultaneously, they may sound pleasant and harmonious, or *consonant*. Alternatively the combination may sound unpleasant and rough, or *dissonant*. Pure tones separated by more than one critical bandwidth (described earlier in the chapter) sound consonant. Tones having smaller differences in frequency sound dissonant (Rasch & Plomp, 1999). Complex tones blend harmoniously to produce chords when their fundamental frequencies are in simple ratios, such as 2:1, so that several of their harmonics coincide in frequency. Otherwise the harmonics tend to beat.

*What role does auditory streaming play in melody perception?*

### Melody

When the pitch of a musical sound varies progressively over time, it creates a pitch "contour" that is heard as a melodic, flowing form. This contour retains its character even when the sequence of tones defining it is transposed to a different pitch range. Rosner and Meyer (1982) found that untrained subjects classify musical melodies into a small number of standard schemes, such as a "gap-fill" scheme involving a melodic leap (usually upward) followed by a gradual progression back to the starting note. Melodic contours are probably constructed by listeners using the processes of auditory scene analysis described earlier in the chapter.

### Rhythm

Melody involves musical structure over time periods extending over many seconds. Rhythm relates to relatively short-term temporal structures. Lerdahl and Jackendoff (1983) argued that rhythm has two components:

● *Segmentation* or the grouping of repeating elements over different time scales.
● *Metre* or the regular alternation of strong and weak elements.

The strong beat heard in popular music is a good example of metre. Metrical music has a prominent motor component—listeners respond to the beat by tapping their feet or by moving their body in synchrony. The association between music and dance is ancient.

## Functional significance of music

Our ability to hear the distinctive features of music can be explained using the same perceptual processes discussed earlier in the chapter in the context of non-musical sound processing, such as pitch and loudness analysing mechanisms, and auditory grouping processes. However, these explanations do not address the fundamental question as to why music has become such a powerful feature of human culture. It is plausible to suppose that music is a biological adaptation, since its features are universal across cultures and recorded history, and it can be appreciated with no formal training. There are two alternative accounts of the origin of this biological adaptation.

### Music and language

One account draws on the close parallels between language and music. Both are forms of communication found in all human cultures, and involve discrete acoustic elements structured hierarchically into sequences according to a set of rules. The assumption is that our ability to perceive music is a by-product of the evolution of language, and has no evolutionary function of its own. This view is exemplified in Pinker's (1997) provocative remark that music is no more than "auditory cheesecake". The characteristics of music perception are primarily useful features of language processing. Pitch and timbre, for example, may represent identifying properties of individual voices. Melody and rhythm in music relate to intonation and prosody in speech.

## Music and evolution

The alternative view is that music evolved because it is adaptive. There are several variants of this argument (see Miller, 2000; Cross, 2001). One advocates the Darwinian view that music is important for sexual selection, because it functions as a courtship display to attract sexual partners. Another variant emphasises the role of music in promoting social cohesion and cooperation. Rhythmic songs help a group of people to work together in a co-ordinated way, perhaps improving teamwork in hunting or reducing intergroup conflict. A third variant of the evolutionary argument proposes that music plays a central role in socialisation. Musical communication is prominent in early mother–infant interactions and, according to this view, promotes emotional bonding and social awareness.

The issue of whether music is a by-product of language or an adaptation in its own right is still unresolved. Support for the linguistic view of music comes from studies of the syntatic structure of music and language, and from brain-imaging research, which shows that music and language activate overlapping areas of the cortex (Patel, 2003). On the other hand, neuropsychological case studies show that some individuals can have impaired music perception but no impairment in language processing, or vice versa (Peretz & Coltheart, 2003), indicating that at least part of music processing is distinct from language processing.

# CHAPTER 6

# The physics of vision—light and the eye

## INTRODUCTION

Before we can begin to understand visual perception, we must consider the basic properties of the physical stimulus, light. Answers to fundamental questions about vision, such as why we have a light sense and how our sense organs gather information from light, depend on understanding the nature of the physical stimulus.

The physical nature of light has puzzled philosophers and scientists throughout history, and is still not completely understood. The Ancient Greeks believed that vision was due to a "fire" that is emitted by the eyes to strike objects and so reveal their shape. Plato distinguished three kinds or "fire"—daylight from the sun, fire of the same kind emitted by the eye, and fire streaming off objects to interact with the fire emitted from the eyes (see Gregory, 1981). We now know, of course, that the eye does not emit light (except as a reflection) but only receives it. Issues concerning the nature of light itself have taxed some of the greatest minds in the history of science, including Isaac Newton, Christian Huygens, Max Planck, and Albert Einstein.

## WHAT IS LIGHT?

Light is a form of radiant energy that is capable of stimulating receptors in the eye and evoking a visual sensation. The behaviour of light can be described in three apparently incompatible ways: as rays, as particles, and as waves. One of the major successes of modern theoretical physics has been to resolve the apparent inconsistencies between these descriptions.

### LIGHT AS RAYS

Everyday experience tells us that light normally travels in straight lines or rays from a light source at such a high speed that it can be considered instantaneous. Light rays are emitted from a point on a source in all directions (see Figure 6.1). Opaque occluding objects in the path of the rays create well-defined shadows. Light rays are

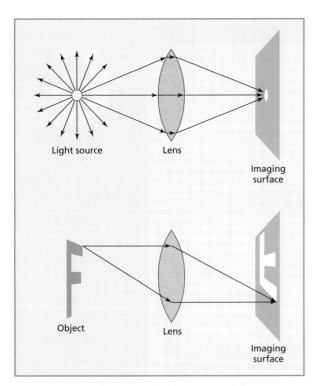

**FIG. 6.1** Image formation by lenses. Top: Light emanates from a point source in all directions. When some portion of the rays passes through a lens, refraction causes the rays to converge back to a point. An image of the point is created on an appropriately positioned imaging surface. Bottom: An extended object can be considered as a spatially distributed collection of points. The lens produces a spatially distributed image of the object on the imaging surface.

deflected (**refracted**), as they pass from one transmitting medium, such as air, into another, such as glass or water. This behaviour is crucial to our understanding of how images can be formed by lenses and mirrors.

## Lenses

A suitably shaped lens will refract incident rays emanating from a point so that they converge back to a point after they emerge from the lens. An image of the point on the source is created if an imaging surface is placed at the correct distance from the lens. If the source is a spatially distributed object comprising many points, then the lens will form a spatially distributed image of the object on the imaging surface.

The image will be inverted relative to the object, but it will preserve the topology of the object (the geometrical relations between individual points), as shown in Figure 6.1. The field of geometrical optics provides very precise descriptions of the ray behaviour of light. The tutorial section of this chapter provides a more detailed introduction to optics.

## LIGHT AS PARTICLES: ISAAC NEWTON

The question of what light rays contain was addressed by Isaac Newton (1642–1727). He believed that light rays were composed of a stream of particles or "corpuscles" that travelled in straight lines. He argued that reflections occurred when these particles bounced off an opaque surface. Refractions occurred as the particles entered a transparent medium at an oblique angle and were deflected in their path. Newton explained the spectrum of colours observed when sunlight is refracted through a prism by supposing that rays of different colours are "differently refrangible".

## LIGHT AS WAVES

### Christian Huygens

Christian Huygens (1629–1695), who was a contemporary of Newton in the 1600s, proposed that light propagates from a source in waves similar to water waves. This wave theory was seen as a direct competitor to Newton's particle theory.

### Thomas Young

The authority of Newton was such that Huygens' wave theory received little attention until a critical experiment was published by Thomas Young in 1801. He passed light through two adjacent slits in an opaque screen, and observed the pattern created on a second screen (see Figure 6.2, left).

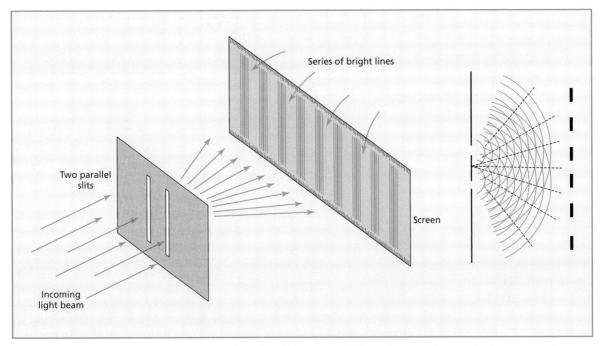

**FIG. 6.2** Young's double-slit experiment. Left: When light is passed through two adjacent slits in a screen, the image formed behind the screen consists of alternating light and dark lines. Right: The lines are created by interference between the two wavefronts emanating from the slits. Where the peaks in the two wavefronts coincide (dotted lines on the right), bright bars are created on the screen. Young's experiment provided strong evidence for the wave properties of light. Copyright © 1982 John Wiley & Sons Limited. Reproduced with permission.

Young observed a pattern of alternating dark and light bands. It was clear that light added to light could result in darkness. He had observed the phenomenon now known as **interference**, which can be explained by supposing that light travels in waves. When two wavefronts cross, they can either augment each other or cancel each other out (see Figure 6.2, right), in the same way that water waves can interact to create a bigger wave or to cancel each other out. Notice from Figure 6.2 that as the original wavefront passes through each slit, it spreads laterally to create two new wavefronts. This effect is known as **diffraction**. The concentric circles emanating from each slit in Figure 6.2 (right) represent adjacent peaks in the advancing wavefronts. The radiating lines are drawn along directions in which peaks in the two wavefronts add together (constructive interference). Bright lines appear at locations where these lines strike the screen. In between the lines the waves tend to cancel each other out (destructive interference) because peaks in one wave meet troughs in the other wave.

## James Clerk Maxwell

What kind of waves make up light? This question was answered by James Clerk Maxwell's (1831–1879) famous electromagnetic field equations, according to which light waves can be described as transversely oscillating electrical and magnetic fields that propagate at finite speed. Maxwell described light as "an electromagnetic disturbance in the form of waves".

The full **electromagnetic spectrum** of wavelengths extends from wavelengths as small as $10^{-13}$ m ($\gamma$-rays) to wavelengths spanning several kilometres (radio

**KEY TERMS**
**Interference pattern:** The pattern formed when two sets of waves overlap, producing mutual reinforcement at some locations and cancellation at others.
**Diffraction:** The scattering or bending of a wave as it passes around an obstacle or through a narrow opening.
**Electromagnetic spectrum:** The full range of frequencies that characterises electromagnetic radiation; only a tiny portion of it is visible as light.

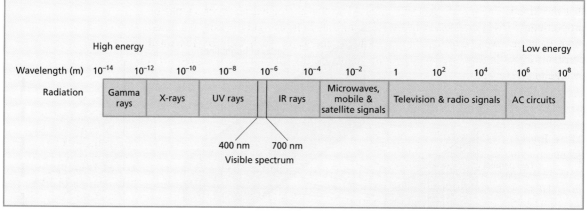

**FIG. 6.3**   The electromagnetic spectrum. The wavelength of electromagnetic radiation spans a huge range. The energy associated with the radiation co-varies with wavelength, so very short wavelength gamma rays have extremely high energy. The portion of the spectrum capable of producing a visual sensation occupies a narrow band of wavelengths, from 400 to 700 nm.

waves), as shown in Figure 6.3. Wavelengths that can stimulate the receptors in the eye to produce a visual sensation occupy only a very narrow band of wavelengths in this spectrum (between 400 and 700 nm). As we shall see later, the wavelength of light is closely associated with visual sensations of colour.

## THE DUALITY OF LIGHT

By the end of the 19th century, Newton's corpuscular theory had been eclipsed by the electromagnetic wave theory developed by Maxwell. However, a series of major empirical and theoretical developments in the first decade of the 20th century re-defined views on the nature of light, and led to the development of quantum mechanics.

### Max Planck

> Planck's equation is one of the most famous in physics:
>
> $E = hf$
>
> Where $E$ is the energy transferred by a quantum, $f$ is the frequency of the quantum, and $h$ is Planck's constant ($6.63 \times 10^{-34}$ Joules).

At the turn of the century the German physicist Max Planck (1858–1947) was attempting to derive equations to describe the radiation emitted by a black body at different temperatures. He found that his equations worked only if he assumed that the radiation was emitted as a stream of discrete packets or **quanta** of energy. Planck proposed that each quantum vibrated at a specific frequency, giving quanta the wave-like properties observed by previous physicists. The energy of a quantum is proportional to its frequency, according to Planck's equation.

### Phillip Lenard

> **KEY TERM**
> **Quantum:** The smallest discrete unit of energy in which radiation may be emitted or absorbed.

At about the same time another German physicist, Phillip Lenard (1862–1947), was making empirical observations that were entirely consistent with Planck's quantum theory and inconsistent with wave theory. He reported a phenomenon known as the *photoelectric effect*. He found that electrons can be released from a metal surface when it is struck by light. Observations of the kinetic energy measured in the released electrons did not agree with predictions of the wave theory of light. According to the theory, the energy of a light is proportional to its intensity. This would predict that the kinetic energy of electrons released in the photoelectric effect should be proportional to light intensity. Observations indicated that as light intensity increased more electrons were emitted, but the kinetic energy of each electron remained constant. Changing the frequency of the light, on the other hand, did produce a change in kinetic energy.

## Albert Einstein

Albert Einstein (1879–1955) used Planck's notion of quanta to explain the photoelectric effect in a major theoretical paper published in 1905. This paper laid the foundations of the theory of quantum mechanics, according to which light (and indeed all matter) can be considered to be both particles and waves.

> Einstein published two other theoretical papers in 1905, while working as a clerk in the Swiss Patent Office in Bern. One paper concerned the random motion of small particles, and the other concerned the special theory of relativity. Einstein received a Nobel Prize for this work in 1921. Lenard and Planck also received Nobel Prizes for their work, in 1905 and 1918 respectively.

## Light is a wave *and* a particle

How can light be both a particle and a wave? The behaviour of light is certainly consistent with both descriptions, since it propagates through space as a wave, yet behaves like particles during emission and absorption. It must be recognised that quanta of light are fundamentally different from the particles that we can see and touch in everyday experience, such as pebbles or grains of sand. Light quanta are sub-microscopic units of energy that have no mass and do not even seem to have a discrete location. Light is both a ray, a wave, and a stream of particles. All three aspects of behaviour are important for understanding visual perception:

1. Ray properties are especially useful when attempting to understand how images are formed by optical devices such as eyes.
2. Wave properties are important when considering the behaviour of light at a much finer scale, such as when dealing with passage through small apertures (e.g. the pupil) or along very narrow waveguides (e.g. photoreceptors).
3. The quantal nature of light intrudes on visual perception when light intensity is so low that quantum absorptions can be counted individually.

Both wave and particle models of light can be related to the colour sensations produced by light. According to wave theory, colour depends on frequency (the frequency of violet light is about twice that of red light). According to particle theory, colour depends on energy (violet quanta transfer twice as much energy as red quanta). The two models are related via Planck's equation (see the box to the left). Discussions of colour vision generally prefer to use the wave model.

> Light quanta are also known as *photons*. This term was introduced by Lewis (1926).

# SOME IMPORTANT PROPERTIES OF LIGHT

## ABSORPTION, REFLECTION, TRANSMISSION

When light strikes the interface between two substances (e.g. between air and glass), it may be transmitted, absorbed, or reflected, as shown in Figure 6.4. All three properties are crucial for vision.

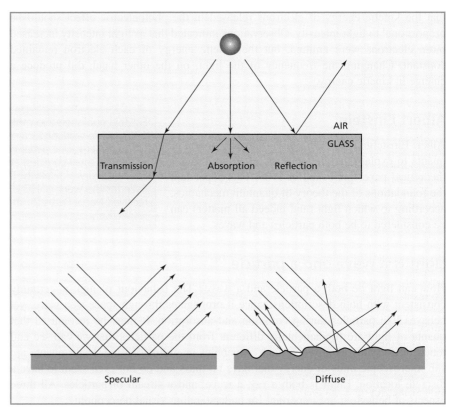

**FIG. 6.4**   How light interacts with surfaces. Top: When light strikes an interface between two media, such as air and glass, it may be transmitted, absorbed, or reflected. All three possible events are important for vision. Bottom: Reflections can be either specular (such as those seen in mirrors) or diffuse (such as those seen on rough surfaces like wood and fabric).

## Absorption

Heat is, of course, radiant energy that is re-emitted from the hot surface in the infrared region of the spectrum. In a greenhouse, or a car, longer wavelength sunlight heats up the interior, but the glass of the greenhouse or vehicle is opaque to the infrared heat waves, trapping the energy inside. A similar effect occurs when sunlight enters the earth's atmosphere and heats the surface of the earth—hence the "greenhouse effect".

During absorption, light quanta are taken up by the substance and converted into thermal energy. Substances that absorb a high proportion of incident radiation, such as dark clothing and black-painted metal, heat up rapidly when exposed to sunlight.

Light must be absorbed to be seen. Photoreceptors in the eye must absorb light energy and convert it into electrical signals, otherwise the process of vision cannot begin.

## Reflection

During reflection, light rays are scattered backward at the interface. According to the first law of reflection, rays are reflected so that the angle of incidence equals the angle of reflection. Rays can be reflected in two ways (lower part of Figure 6.4):

● *Specular reflection* occurs when the surface is smooth (irregularities are small relative to the wavelength of light). Light rays are reflected regularly in a predictable direction.
● *Diffuse reflection* occurs when the surface contains larger irregularities. Each ray obeys the law of reflection, but rays are reflected in random directions.

Reflected light is crucial for vision, since it conveys information about the properties of surfaces present in the environment.

## Transmission

During transmission through a medium, quanta of certain wavelengths may be scattered by the molecules they hit. In low-density media such as air, light is scattered laterally. Air molecules scatter light in the blue region of the spectrum, resulting in the bluish appearance of the sky. In dense, uniform media such as glass there is very little lateral scattering, due to destructive interference. Scattering occurs mostly in the forward direction. The interference between the original wave and waves produced by forward scattering results in a retardation of the wavefront as it passes through the medium.

### Refraction

An important consequence of the retardation of light during transmission through a medium is *refraction*, a change in the direction of the path of light rays as they enter a transmitting medium obliquely. The degree of change in direction depends on the extent to which the wavefront is retarded, and this in turn depends on the **refractive index** of the transmitting medium. Materials with higher indices retard light more, and consequently produce greater angles of refraction. Air has a refractive index close to 1.0, meaning that light is retarded very little during its transmission. Glass has a refractive index of approximately 1.5, so when light strikes an interface between air and glass it will change direction.

Refraction is a crucial property of light for vision, because it is the principle underlying the formation of images by lenses. Figure 6.5 shows two glass prisms receiving parallel light rays. Due to refraction, as the light rays enter and leave the glass, the rays begin converging when they exit the prisms. This effect illustrates the basic principle underlying the ability of lenses to form images, as seen in Figure 6.1 earlier. The surface of the lens is curved so that parallel light rays entering the lens from a distant point will converge on a point behind the lens. The distance of this point of focus from the lens defines the lens's **focal length**. Further details can be found in the tutorial section later in the chapter.

## INTENSITY

The intensity of a light source ultimately depends on the number of quanta it emits per unit of time. A range of physical units, known as **radiometric** units, has been developed to measure intensity. However, the effectiveness of light quanta as a stimulus for vision depends on their wavelength properties, since the human visual system is more sensitive to some

**KEY TERMS**
**Refractive index:** The ratio of the velocity of propagation of an electromagnetic wave in a vacuum to its velocity in a given transmitting medium.
**Focal length:** The distance from the centre of a lens to its focal plane (the plane in which parallel light rays are brought into sharp focus).
**Radiometry:** The measurement of electromagnetic radiation.

*Think about why your vision is blurred under water.*

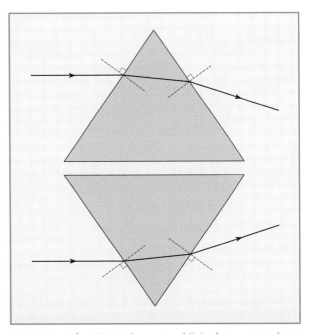

**FIG. 6.5** Refraction. When rays of light from a wavefront strike a transmitting medium such as glass obliquely, their direction of travel is deflected (refracted) due to the retardation in the wavefront. When parallel rays strike two glass prisms, they begin converging when they emerge from the prisms. This illustrates the basic principle behind image formation by lenses.

wavelengths than to others. So in the context of vision, light intensity is usually specified in **photometric** units that take account of human sensitivity. The most commonly used unit is "candelas per square metre" (abbreviated to $cd/m^2$, or equivalently $cd \cdot m^{-2}$), which measures the intensity of the light emanating from a surface relative to that of a standard light. Further details on different measures of light intensity can be found in the tutorial section.

Table 6.1 gives typical **luminance** values (in $cd/m^2$) for six light sources (based on data in Makous, 1998, and Land & Nilsson, 2002). Corresponding numbers of photons emitted per second are shown in the middle column, calculated according to formulae given in the tutorial section. Light intensities experienced by organisms living on the surface of the earth seem very high indeed when measured in terms of quanta emitted. Even viewed in moonlight, white paper emits $10^{15}$ quanta per second ($10^6$ is a million). In sunlight the paper emits nearly a million times more quanta.

On this basis we might be tempted to disregard the quantal nature of light when considering it as a stimulus for vision. However, it is important to consider natural light intensities in terms of the number of quanta available for vision. As we shall see below, the human eye responds to light by means of many photoreceptor cells distributed around its inner surface. Light is brought to focus on these receptors by the optical apparatus of the eye (cornea, pupil, and lens). The right-hand column of Table 6.1 estimates the number of quanta hitting each receptor per second at the six different light levels (based on Land & Nilsson's, 2002, estimate that photon numbers are reduced by a factor of $10^{15}$ when one takes into account the optics and dimensions of photoreceptors). In the brightest conditions, each photoreceptor receives 100,000 quanta per second. In the dimmest borderline conditions supporting human vision, each receptor receives only 0.01 quanta per second. In other words, minutes may elapse between successive strikes on any one receptor. The quantal nature of light thus becomes an important issue at low light levels (individual photoreceptors are capable of responding to individual quantal strikes).

We can see from Table 6.1 that the visual diet experienced by an organism on earth spans a very wide range (increasing by a factor of 10,000,000, or $10^7$, from starlight to sunlight). Individual photoreceptors can respond over a range of intensities spanning less than one hundredth of this range (roughly two rows of the table). Yet humans can see adequately both by starlight and in the midday sun. How, then, does the visual system cope successfully with such a huge range of light levels? At any one moment the intensity in a scene, from the darkest shadow to the brightest surface, varies only by a factor of less than 1 in 100 (see below), a tiny fraction of the full range available on earth. As one moves from well-shaded, interior, or night-time

*Why do so few photons reach each photoreceptor, relative to the number entering the eye?*

**TABLE 6.1 LUMINANCE VALUES AND PHOTON COUNTS FOR SIX LIGHT SOURCES**

| Light source | Luminance ($cd \cdot m^{-2}$) | Photons $m^{-2} \cdot sr^{-1} \cdot s^{-1}$ | Photons per receptor |
|---|---|---|---|
| Paper in starlight | 0.0003 | $10^{13}$ | 0.01 |
| Paper in moonlight | 0.2 | $10^{15}$ | 1 |
| Computer monitor | 63 | $10^{17}$ | 100 |
| Room light | 316 | $10^{18}$ | 1 000 |
| Blue sky | 2 500 | $10^{19}$ | 10 000 |
| Paper in sunlight | 40 000 | $10^{20}$ | 100 000 |

conditions into bright outdoor conditions, the relatively narrow range of light levels experienced slides up the intensity scale. The visual system possesses mechanisms that adjust the operating range of photoreceptors so that it too slides up and down the intensity range, and thus receptor responses remain well matched to prevailing illumination conditions. This process of adjustment is known as light and dark adaptation, and is discussed in detail in Chapter 8.

## CONTRAST AND REFLECTANCE

Unless the observer looks directly at a light source (not recommended in the case of the sun, as it is likely to result in permanent eye damage), the pattern of light and dark entering the eye is due to reflections from surfaces in the scene. Some surfaces reflect a very high proportion of the light that strikes them. White paper reflects approximately 75% of the incident light. Other surfaces absorb a high proportion of the incident light. Black paper and paint, for instance, reflect only 5% of the incident light. Black velvet reflects about 2%.

> The proportion of incident light reflected by a surface is known as its **reflectance**. Highly reflecting surfaces appear whitish, and have values approaching unity. Snow, for example, has a reflectance of 0.93, whereas newspaper has a reflectance of 0.38 (Makous, 1998). Surfaces with reflectance values approaching zero appear very dark.

Consequently, even in a scene containing the extreme combination of both black velvet and white paper, intensity will vary only by a factor of 1 in 38 (the paper will reflect 38 times more light than the velvet). A useful measure of relative luminance is **contrast** (C) defined as:

$$C = (L_{max} - L_{min})/(L_{max} + L_{min})$$

Where $L_{max}$ is the higher luminance value and $L_{min}$ is the lower luminance value. Contrast can vary between 0 and 1.

It is very important to realise that contrast is independent of the absolute level of illumination and (in the absence of variations in illumination such as shadows) is determined by surface reflectance. For example, assume that the velvet and paper are viewed in moonlight: $L_{max}$ corresponds to the luminance of the paper, 0.2 cd·m$^{-2}$; $L_{min}$ corresponds to the luminance of the velvet, 0.0053 cd·m$^{-2}$. The contrast between the paper and the velvet is 0.948, according to the equation above. When viewed in sunlight, the luminances of the paper and velvet are 40,000 cd·m$^{-2}$ and 1066.7 cd·m$^{-2}$ respectively. Contrast is again 0.948.

Absolute luminance is relatively uninformative about the properties of surfaces, whereas contrast provides information about surface reflectance. So early neural processes in the visual system are specialised to encode contrast but discard information about absolute luminance.

*Think about why luminance is less informative about objects than contrast.*

## WAVELENGTH

Humans are able to detect wavelengths in the region between 400 nm and 700 nm. Wavelength is correlated with sensory impressions of colour. Moving down the wavelength scale from 700 to 400 nm, colour varies through the following sequence: red–orange–yellow–green–blue–indigo–violet. The acronym ROYGBIV is some-times used as a mnemonic. The wavelength composition of light actually reflected from a surface depends jointly on the spectral power distribution of the illuminating light and the spectral reflectance of the surface.

> **KEY TERMS**
> **Reflectance:** The proportion of incident light reflected from a surface.
> **Contrast:** A measure of the difference between the highest luminance and the lowest luminance emitted or reflected from a surface.

## Spectral power distribution of light sources

Commonly experienced light sources emit radiation across a broad spectrum of wavelengths. Figure 6.6 plots relative energy as a function of wavelength (spectral power distribution) for sunlight and for an incandescent lamp. The vertical lines mark the limits of the visible spectrum. Notice from Figure 6.6 that incandescent lamps such those used in domestic rooms have much more energy in the yellow–red end of the spectrum than daylight.

## Spectral reflectance functions

Surface reflectance (the proportion of incident light reflected) generally varies as a function of wavelength to define the surface's spectral reflectance function. Figure 6.7 plots **spectral reflectance functions** for a range of surfaces. Snow reflects a high proportion of light at all wavelengths, whereas grass absorbs light quite efficiently at most wavelengths. Notice the distinct peak in the reflectance of grass at wavelengths in the green region of the spectrum. Natural surfaces tend to have smooth, slowly changing reflectance functions, and generally reflect more light at longer wavelengths than at shorter wavelengths.

## Spectral power distribution of reflective surfaces

As stated earlier, the spectral power distribution of light reflected from a surface depends jointly on the power distribution of the illuminant (e.g. Figure 6.6), and the

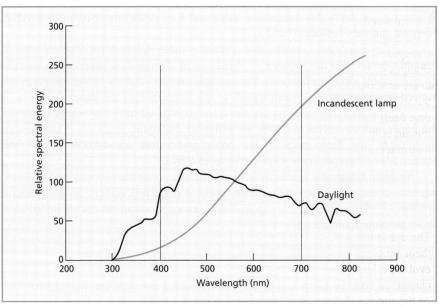

**KEY TERM**
**Spectral reflectance function:** The proportion of light reflected from a surface as a function of the wavelength of the incident light.

FIG. 6.6  Emission spectra of two common light sources, the sun and an incandescent lamp (domestic lightbulb). Vertical lines represent the borders of the visible spectrum. Daylight has a peak in energy at wavelengths in the short wavelength region (450 nm) that appears bluish to humans, whereas lamps emit more and more energy at higher wavelengths that appear yellowy-red (graphs based on CIE standard illuminants A and D$_{65}$).

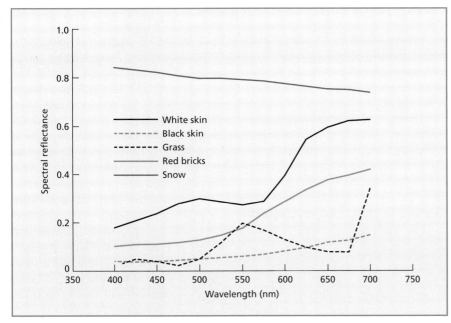

**FIG. 6.7**  Spectral reflectance functions of several familiar surfaces. Notice that some surfaces such as snow reflect a much higher proportion of incident radiation than other surfaces. In addition, the preponderance of different wavelengths in the reflected energy varies between surfaces. Grass, for example, has a peak in the green part of the spectrum (550 nm) (data re-plotted from Wyszecki & Stiles, 1982).

surface's reflectance function (e.g. Figure 6.7). The two functions are multiplied, wavelength by wavelength, to arrive at the power distribution of the reflected light. Changes in the power distribution of the illuminant can therefore result in marked changes in the power distribution of light reflected from a surface. Surfaces viewed under artificial light, for instance, reflect much more energy in the yellow region of the spectrum than when viewed under daylight, due to the marked differences in incident energy shown in Figure 6.6. However, our perception of surface colour tends to remain constant in the face of such changes. This phenomenon is known as *colour constancy*, and is discussed in detail in Chapter 12.

## THE EYE

The eye is the peripheral organ of vision. Its function is to catch photons and direct them onto photoreceptors in order to begin the process of vision. Animals have evolved a huge variety of organs that respond to light, only some of which can be classed as eyes. Some invertebrates such as worms have single receptors distributed on the surface of their skin. The minimum qualification for such an organ to be called an eye is that it must form some kind of image on a sheet of photoreceptors. Images are vital for effective vision because they preserve the spatial arrangement of the points in space from which the light rays emanated. With suitable neural processing, a great deal of information about the world can be extracted from images, as we shall discover in the rest of the book.

## STRUCTURE OF THE HUMAN EYE

Humans, in common with other mammals, birds, and reptiles, have single-chambered eyes. Figure 6.8 shows the main structures of the human eye. It is a roughly spherical, light-tight chamber, the inside surface of which is lined with a sheet of photoreceptors. An opening in the chamber, covered by a transparent membrane, admits light.

The transparent membrane is known as the **cornea**. Having passed through the cornea, incoming light then enters an aperture known as the **pupil**. The pupil is formed by a muscular diaphragm known as the iris (idiosyncratic pigmentation in the iris determines eye colour, and is increasingly used as a form of identification). After passing through the lens, situated behind the pupil, light strikes the photoreceptor sheet, known as the retina. The structure of the retina is very complex, and will be described in detail in the next chapter.

The interior of the eye is filled with two substances, vitreous humour and aqueous humour. Vitreous humour is a viscous gel that fills the large posterior chamber of the eye, maintaining its shape and holding the retina against the inner wall. The watery aqueous humour is pumped into the eye continuously, entering the eye near the attachment of the lens (ciliary processes) and leaving near the margins of the iris (canal of Schlemm). It flows in both the small anterior chamber (behind the cornea) and the main posterior chamber. Rate of flow is such that the entire volume of the fluid is replenished approximately every 45 minutes. The functions of the aqueous humour are to nourish the lens and to keep the eye inflated.

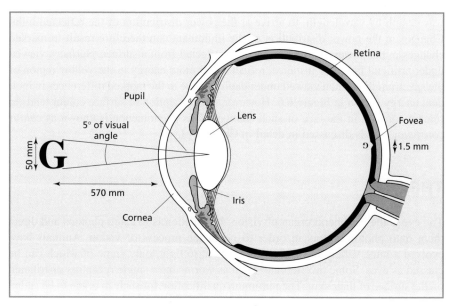

**FIG. 6.8**  Major components of the human eye. Dimensions are also shown for the image produced by a 50 mm tall letter viewed at a distance of 570 mm (similar to a large newspaper headline viewed at arm's length). The angle subtended by the letter at the nodal point of the eye is 5°. The retinal image of the letter is 1.5 mm tall, and spans approximately 500 photoreceptors.

## VISUAL ANGLE

How should we specify the size of an object? Linear size in millimetres is obviously the most appropriate measure for most everyday situations, such as when deciding whether a given item of furniture will fit into an available space. However, when studying the images of objects as stimuli for vision, the most appropriate measures of size relate to the size of the image projected onto the retina. The most frequently used measure is **visual angle**: the angle subtended by the object at the centre (nodal point) of the lens. Visual angle depends jointly on the size of the object and its viewing distance. If visual angle is relatively small (10° or less) it can be calculated easily from trigonometry using the formula:

$$\text{Tan } \theta = s/d$$

Where $\theta$ is visual angle, $s$ is object size, and $d$ is viewing distance. One degree is divided into 60 minutes (abbreviated to 60′), and one minute is divided into 60 seconds (abbreviated to 60″). So 0.25° can also be expressed as 15′, and 0.01° can be expressed as 36″.

The importance of the nodal point of the lens is that light rays pass through it without being refracted (because they strike the surface of the lens at right-angles). So the angle subtended by the image on the retina is equal to the angle subtended by the object at the nodal point. It is sometimes useful to convert this angular subtense into linear units, so specifying the size of the retinal image in millimetres. Image size in linear units depends on eye size. For a given angular subtense, the farther away the retina is from the lens, the larger will be the retinal image. In the case of human eyes, one degree of visual angle is equal to 0.288 mm on the retina. The issue of eye size is discussed in more detail later in the chapter. Retinal image size will be specified in either angular or linear units or both in the remainder of this chapter, as appropriate.

To give an example, Figure 6.8 includes a letter G and the image it projects onto the retina. Values given correspond to a 50 mm tall headline in a newspaper viewed at approximately arm's length (570 mm). The letter subtends a visual angle of 5°, and projects an image 1.5 mm tall on the retina. The width of a thumb held at arm's length corresponds to approximately 2° of visual angle on the retina.

*Which would be preferable, a television 50 cm wide viewed from 3 m away, or a cinema screen 6 m wide viewed from 40 m?*

## OPTICAL PROPERTIES OF THE EYE

### Cornea and lens

*Optical power*

Refraction occurs at an interface between media having different refractive indices. In the case of the eye, refraction occurs at four surfaces, namely:

- Anterior (front) corneal surface
- Posterior (back) corneal surface
- Front surface of the lens
- Rear surface of the lens.

The combined effect of these surfaces is to create an optical system with a focal length of 16.8 mm. This means that in a normal, relaxed eye the image of a distant object will fall into focus 16.8 mm behind the centre of the lens system, a distance

> **KEY TERM**
> **Visual angle:** The angle an object subtends at the centre of a lens; it is used to measure the size of an object as a stimulus for vision.

that corresponds precisely to the location of the retina. As discussed in detail in the tutorial section, optical power is conventionally expressed in **dioptres** (D), which correspond to (1/focal length in metres). The power of the eye's optical system is therefore ($1/16.8 \times 10^{-3}$), or 59.52 D.

The degree of refraction at an interface between two media depends on the difference in refractive index of the media, as described in the tutorial. The refractive indices of air, cornea, ocular fluid, and the lens are 1.009, 1.376, 1.336, and 1.413 respectively. We can therefore see that the greatest degree of refraction in the eye's optical system occurs at the interface between air and the cornea, because of the large difference in refractive index. In fact, approximately 48 D of the eye's optical power is contributed by refraction at the anterior surface of the cornea.

## Accommodation

Although the optical power of the eye is sufficient to focus parallel rays from far objects on the retina, diverging rays from near objects come into focus behind the retina. There are two ways to bring the image back into focus on the retina. The first is to move the lens further away from the retina. Certain fish (and cameras) adopt this strategy. The alternative is to increase the optical power of the lens. This latter strategy is adopted by reptiles, birds, and mammals, including humans. The lens is deformable, and ciliary muscles located around the margins of the lens where it attaches to the eye can adjust its shape to accommodate objects at different distances. The process of focusing is actually known as **accommodation**. Zonular fibres attach the lens to the ciliary muscles. When the muscles are relaxed, intra-ocular pressure stretches the zonular fibres, which in turn pull the lens into a thin shape. In this shape the lens has a focal length of 59.52 D, appropriate for far objects. When the muscles are tense, they relieve the pressure on the zonular fibres, which allows the lens to relax into a thicker shape with a shorter focal length. In young healthy eyes accommodation can increase the optical power of the eye by up to approximately 8 D, allowing objects as close as 250 mm to be brought into focus. This distance is known as the *near point*. Lens flexibility declines with age, so that the near point moves progressively farther away. Beyond the age of 50 there is typically little scope for accommodation left, a condition known as **presbyopia**.

*How can presbyopia be treated?*

*Accommodative errors* Two kinds of error are commonly found. The optical power of the eye can be either too great or too weak, given the size of the eye, resulting in image blur at the retina.

● **Myopia**, or short-sight occurs when the optical power is too great. Rays from distant objects come into focus in front of the retina, and accommodation is no help because it brings the point of focus even further forward. Near objects do fall into focus, and accommodation is required only for very near distances.
● **Hyperopia** or long-sight occurs when the optical power is too weak. Rays from distant objects come into focus behind the retina. In this case accommodation does help, but it comes into play at distances that should not normally require it.

*What kinds of lenses must spectacles contain?*

Both kinds of accommodative error can be corrected in two ways. The traditional solution is to wear corrective lenses, either as spectacles or as contact lenses, which adjust the optical power of the eye to remove the error. A more recent solution, known as *photorefractive keratectomy*, is to shave a very small amount of material from the surface of the cornea using a laser. This has the effect of altering the radius of curvature of the cornea in such a way as to alter the optical power of the cornea and correct the accommodative error.

## Pupil

The diameter of the pupil can vary between approximately 2 mm and 8 mm. The resultant change in area equates to a sixteen-fold variation in retinal illumination. Since this is a tiny fraction of the range of illumination levels experienced on earth, as explained earlier, we can safely assume that the function of the pupil is not solely to control retinal illumination. Its function may be more subtle, in regulating the balance that must be struck between maximising the eye's sensitivity and retaining its resolution (ability to resolve detail), as explained later in the chapter.

Pupil size is influenced by emotional responses. Large pupils are associated with positive or pleasurable emotions, whereas small pupils are associated with negative emotions. For example, in a study by Hess and Polt (1960), the pupils of male and female subjects were photographed while they viewed a range of photographs. Figure 6.9 plots the mean change in pupil size as a function of subject matter. Male subjects showed a large increase in pupil size while viewing pictures of nude females, and very small increases while viewing landscapes. Female subjects showed large increases while viewing pictures of mother and baby, and nude males, but decreases while viewing landscapes.

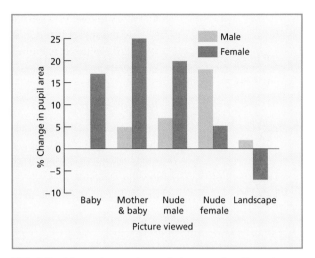

**FIG. 6.9** Mean change in pupil size as a function of image viewed, for male and female subjects. Male subjects show a large increase in pupil diameter only when viewing pictures of nude females. Female subjects show increases in pupil diameter when viewing pictures of babies and nude males. An increase in pupil size is usually interpreted as an indicator of positive emotional responses (data re-plotted from Hess & Polt, 1960).

> Other old studies (e.g. Hess, 1975) also claim that large pupils make female faces appear more attractive, perhaps because they indicate an interest in the viewer.

## Photoreceptors

The retina of each eye contains over 100 million photoreceptor cells, responsible for converting light energy into neural activity (transduction). Each photoreceptor is a long, thin tube consisting of an outer segment that contains light-sensitive pigment and an inner segment that in effect forms the cell body. A detailed discussion of how photoreceptors achieve transduction will be postponed until the next chapter. The discussion here will concentrate on the optical properties of photoreceptors.

### Rods and cones

Human photoreceptors fall into two classes, called **rods** and **cones** on the basis of the shape of their outer segments. Rods and cones differ in several important respects:

- They contain different light-sensitive pigments (discussed in the next chapter). Rod pigment is very sensitive at low light levels. Cones are 30–100 times less sensitive, so function only at high light levels.
- There are far more rods in each eye (approximately 120,000,000) than cones (approximately 6,000,000).

> **KEY TERMS**
> **Rod:** A type of photoreceptor that is specialised for responses at low light levels.
> **Cone:** A type of photoreceptor that is specialised for responses at high light levels.

● They differ in width, length, and retinal distribution. An important landmark on the retina is the *fovea*, a small pit at the optical centre of the retina, 0.5 mm (1.7°) wide. It is entirely devoid of rods and contains only cones (more details below).

### Photoreceptor width

The light-sensitive portion of each cone has a diameter of approximately 1–4 μm in the fovea, and 4–10 μm outside the fovea. Rods have a diameter of 1 μm near the fovea (Wandell, 1995). The width of each photoreceptor obviously imposes a limit on the spacing between adjacent photoreceptors. Spacing, in turn, determines the ability of the retina to resolve detail. As we shall see in a moment, reducing the spacing between receptors increases their ability to resolve fine spatial detail. So why are the photoreceptors not narrower still? The answer to this question lies in the wave properties of light. As each photoreceptor's width approaches the wavelength of visible light (0.4–0.7 μm) it becomes unable to retain light by total internal reflection. Instead, some of the light leaks out through the sides of the photoreceptor, and excites adjacent receptors. This "cross-talk" between receptors reduces the effective resolution of the retinal mosaic, because each photoreceptor's response depends not just on the light striking it, but also on the light striking its neighbours. There is consequently nothing to be gained in terms of resolution from having photoreceptors narrower than 1 μm, and indeed none have been found in the eyes of any animal.

### Photoreceptor length

The light-sensitive portion of each human cone is up to 80 μm long in the fovea and 40 μm long outside the fovea; rods are 60 μm long (Wandell, 1995). The proportion of incident light absorbed by a photoreceptor depends on its length. Inside the fovea, cones absorb up to 50% of incident light. Outside the fovea, cones absorb 33% of incident light. Rods absorb 42% of incident light (see Warrant & Nilsson, 1998).

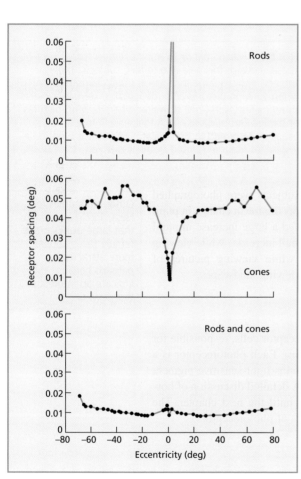

**FIG. 6.10** Distance between adjacent photoreceptors in the human retina as a function of retinal position for rods, cones, and all receptors combined. Cones are concentrated in the fovea, where no rods are found. Taking both receptor types together, spacing remains fairly stable across the retina (data taken from Osterberg, 1935, which were expressed as photoreceptors per square mm; the data plotted were calculated as the square root of his values, to give an approximate value for spacing).

### Photoreceptor spacing

Figure 6.10 plots photoreceptor spacing for cones, for rods, and for both combined, as a function of retinal location. Cone spacing is smallest in the fovea—0.003 mm (0.01°, or 0.6′ arc). Moving outside the fovea, cone spacing increases fourfold to approximately 0.013 mm (0.045°, or 2.7′ arc), while rod spacing is 0.003 mm (0.01°, or 0.6′ arc). Taking both classes of photoreceptor together, Figure 6.10 indicates that spacing is surprisingly stable across the retina, at a value (3 μm) approaching the minimum available given the wavelengths of visible light.

## Resolution and sensitivity

The *resolution* of the eye is its ability to resolve fine spatial detail in the retinal image. *Sensitivity* refers to the eye's ability to respond at very low illumination levels. Both aspects of performance are important for vision, but they place different demands on the optical components of the eye.

### Resolution

Figure 6.11 illustrates how photoreceptor spacing affects resolution. It shows a black-and-white test image (upper left) along with corresponding patterns superimposed on three imaginary retinal mosaics with different receptor spacing. Each circle represents an individual photoreceptor.

The test image includes a **grating** consisting of alternating black and white bars. Gratings are used very frequently to assess spatial resolution, for reasons that will become clear in Chapter 8. Notice that the finest mosaic (top right) can represent both the grating pattern and the broken circle faithfully. The coarsest mosaic (bottom right) cannot resolve individual grating bars, and provides only a crude rendition of the broken circle. Mathematical procedures allow us to calculate the finest grating bars that can be resolved by a given photoreceptor spacing. In simple terms, the grating can be resolved faithfully if each adjacent light and dark bar falls on a separate receptor. Each pair of light and dark bars constitutes one cycle of the grating pattern. So there must be two receptors per grating cycle in order accurately to represent the grating. With fewer receptors it is not possible to distinguish all the bars of the grating.

Photoreceptor spacing is limited by photoreceptor width which, in turn, is limited by the wavelengths of visible light. Once the minimum photoreceptor width is achieved, the only other way to increase the resolving power of the retina is to increase the size of the image. Larger images allow greater detail to be resolved because they are sampled by more photoreceptors. Larger images require larger eyes, since image size or **magnification** is a function of focal length (see the tutorial

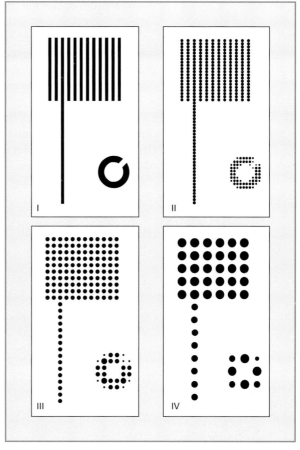

**FIG. 6.11** Effect of receptor spacing on acuity. The stimulus pattern (top left) consists of a vertical grating and a broken circle. This pattern was superimposed on retinal mosaics at three different spacings: small (top right), medium (bottom left), and large (bottom right). Each circle represents a receptor positioned over an element of the pattern. Small receptor spacings permit a faithful rendition of the pattern—all grating bars and the break in the circle are visible. At the largest receptor spacing individual grating bars cannot be resolved, and the break in the circle is lost (re-drawn from Pirenne, 1948).

> **KEY TERMS**
> **Grating:** A pattern of alternating light and dark bars, widely used in vision research.
> **Magnification:** The size of the image produced by a lens; it depends on the focal length of the lens.

*How well would a miniature person, say 20 cm tall, be able to see?*

section at the end of the chapter). In the case of the human eye (focal length 16.8 mm), an object 50 mm tall viewed from a distance of 570 mm (such as the headline in a newspaper held at arm's length; see Figure 6.8) would cast an image 1.5 mm tall on the retina. This image would span 500 photoreceptors. An eye half the size of the human eye would produce an image half as tall, spanning half as many photoreceptors (assuming constant photoreceptor spacing).

*Inter-receptor spacing* Receptor spacing ($s$) and eye size or focal length ($f$) jointly determine the **inter-receptor angle** ($\Delta\Phi = s/f$). This angle is the defining feature of the eye's resolving power. For example, eyes with an inter-receptor angle $\Delta\Phi$ of 0.01° can resolve successive dark bars in a grating no closer than 0.02°, corresponding to a grating spatial frequency of 50 cycles per degree of visual angle (cpd). Assuming that photoreceptor spacing is close to its optical limit, resolution is governed by eye size. Other things being equal, animals with small eyes have less acute vision than animals with large eyes. Cats, for example, have poorer spatial resolution than humans.

## Sensitivity

Sensitivity is limited by **photon noise**, as Figure 6.12 illustrates. It shows an array of 400 photoreceptors (small circles), receiving an image of a central dark disk (large circle) on a light background. Each white small circle represents a photon strike on a receptor. At high illumination levels (IV, bottom right), photon strikes define the image accurately. As light level falls towards the absolute threshold for vision (I, upper left), the image becomes less distinct due to the uncertainty associated with individual photon strikes (photon noise).

Retinal illumination at low light levels naturally depends on pupil diameter. Eyes capable of very large pupil diameters have an advantage in terms of sensitivity, since they admit more light. Image degradation due to lens imperfections at wide apertures is not an issue, since resolution is limited by photon noise as Figure 6.12 illustrates. At higher illumination levels there are so many photons available that photon noise is no longer relevant. In these conditions smaller pupil diameters are called for in order to minimise the deleterious effects of lens imperfections. A pupil diameter of 2–3 mm is considered optimal for retinal image quality. Pupil diameters smaller than 2 mm suffer increased blur due to the effects of diffraction. At diameters greater than 3 mm the effects of **chromatic** and **spherical aberration** become more pronounced (a detailed discussion of diffraction and aberration can be found in the tutorial section).

## Optimal eye size

The foregoing discussion would indicate that both resolution and sensitivity are best served by larger eyes, which have the smallest possible inter-receptor angles and large maximum pupil diameters. This observation begs the question—why are human eyes not larger than 24 mm in diameter? Eyes are expensive organs, because they occupy a significant amount of space in the head, and they consume a large amount of energy. It has been estimated, for example, that 10% of the oxygen consumption of a walking fly is devoted to phototransduction (Laughlin, de Ruyter van Steveninck, & Anderson, 1998). It therefore makes sense for eyes to be no larger than strictly

**KEY TERMS**
**Inter-receptor angle:** The visual angle between two neighbouring photoreceptors; it determines the resolving power of the eye.
**Photon noise:** The inherent natural variation in the rate at which photons strike a receiving surface such as the retina.
**Chromatic aberration:** The property of an optical system that causes light rays at different wavelengths to be focused in different planes, so degrading the image.
**Spherical aberration:** The failure of light rays striking all parts of a lens to converge in the same focal plane, so degrading the image.

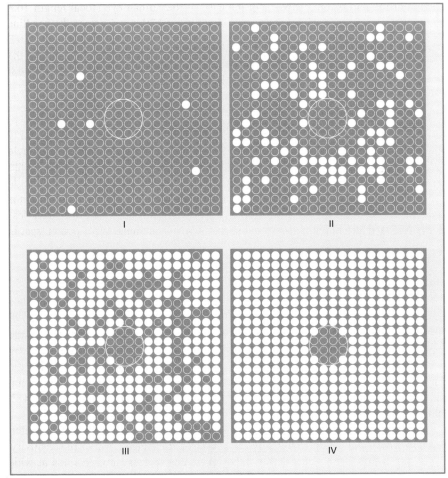

**FIG. 6.12**  Effect of photon noise on acuity. The small circles represent locations of individual photoreceptors, with white circles representing active receptors. The large circle in the centre of each panel shows the position of a large dark disk presented as an image against a white background for a short time. The four panels represent photoreceptor responses at four different light levels. Under extremely dim illumination (top left), when few photons are emitted, the probability that any one receptor will be struck by a photon is very low. Just six active receptors are shown. As illumination level and photon numbers rise, the probability of activity in each receptor also rises. At the highest level (bottom right), so many photons are emitted that all receptors are activated by the light region of the image. The ability of the photoreceptor mosaic to resolve the pattern at low light levels therefore depends on the number of photons emitted, not on the fineness of the mosaic or blur in the image (re-drawn from Pirenne, 1948).

necessary given the visual requirements of their host. Once the eyes have achieved the level of resolution required by their host in order to catch prey, avoid predators, and so on, pressures on energy consumption and cranial real estate limit further increases in eye size. Nocturnal and deep-sea dwelling animals have the largest eyes, in the interests of maximising sensitivity at low levels of ambient illumination. Deep-sea squid possess the largest eyes of all, with a diameter of 40 cm (Land & Nilsson, 2002).

*Rods versus cones*

The relatively constant spacing of rods and cones combined (Figure 6.10) might lead one to expect that our ability to resolve detail is also constant across the retina. However, as mentioned earlier, rods and cones operate at different light levels, with rods operating at low light levels and cones operating at high light levels. The differing distributions of rods and cones aim to strike a balance between maximising resolution while retaining sensitivity. In high illumination, resolution is very high (near the 50 cpd optical limit of the eye) but only in central vision, since this is where cone spacing is smallest. Outside the fovea, resolution drops to a value dictated by rod spacing—only 11 cpd. On the other hand, the fact that we have any sensitivity at all at low illumination levels is due to rods outside the fovea.

# EYE MOVEMENTS

## The eye muscles

Humans have six extra-ocular muscles that allow the eyes to rotate quickly and accurately about any combination of the three possible axes. Figure 6.13 illustrates the attachment points of the muscles. They work as three antagonistic pairs. The medial and lateral recti control side-to-side rotation about the vertical axis (known as adduction and abduction); the superior and inferior recti control up-and-down rotation around the horizontal axis running from side to side across the head (known as elevation and depression); and the superior and inferior obliques control rotation about the visual axis itself around the horizontal axis running from front to back through the head (known as intorsion and extorsion).

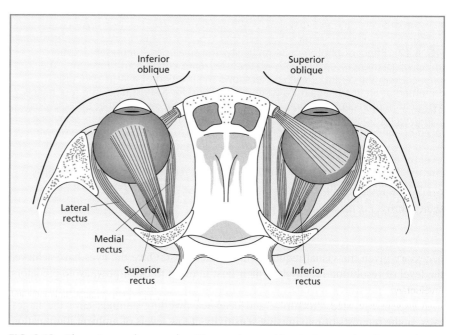

**FIG. 6.13**  The extra-ocular muscles. Six muscles working in three pairs allow each eye to rotate in its socket about the three possible axes (based on Walls, 1963).

## Types of eye movement

There are six types of eye movement, which can be categorised in terms of whether they are voluntary (under conscious control) or involuntary (under reflex control), and whether they are *conjugate* or *disjunctive*. The latter classification relates to how the two eyes move together.

In conjugate movements, the two eyes move by the same amount and in the same direction (e.g. both eyes turn to the left). In disjunctive movements, the two eyes move by the same amount but in opposite directions (e.g. the eyes both turn inwards towards the nose, so that one becomes cross-eyed).

Table 6.2 categorises the six different types of movement according to the two classifications:

- **Saccades** are rapid, voluntary shifts in eye position between steady fixations, which typically last only 45 ms or less. Saccade means "jerk" in French.
- Voluntary *pursuit* movements are engaged when the eyes lock on to a moving target and track it as it moves across the visual field. It is impossible to initiate smooth pursuit movements without having a target to track.
- Vergence eye movements can be divided into *convergent* movements in which the visual axes of the two eye move further away from parallel (becoming more cross-eyed), and *divergent* movements in which the visual axes of the eyes move towards parallel (becoming less cross-eyed).
- *Vestibulo-ocular* movements are triggered by signals generated in the vestibular system in response to head acceleration or deceleration. These movements were considered in detail in Chapter 3.
- *Optokinetic nystagmus* is triggered by image motion. It consists of an alternating series of saccadic and smooth pursuit movements. Optokinetic nystagmus is easily experienced when looking sideways out of a moving train or car. Your eyes involuntarily latch onto a stationary point in the scene outside, track it back smoothly for a short distance, and then flick or saccade forward to latch onto another stationary point.

## Why do the eyes move?

There are two general reasons why it is useful to have mobile eyes—preservation of spatial resolution, and binocular registration.

### Spatial resolution

An immobile eye would be prone to poor spatial resolution partly due to variation in acuity across the retina and partly due to image motion.

**TABLE 6.2 CLASSIFICATION OF EYE MOVEMENTS**

|  | Conjugate movement | Disjunctive movement |
|---|---|---|
| Voluntary | Saccade | Convergence |
|  | Pursuit | Divergence |
| Involuntary | Vestibulo-ocular |  |
|  | Optokinetic |  |

**KEY TERM**
**Saccade:** The rapid, jerky eye movement used to shift gaze direction.

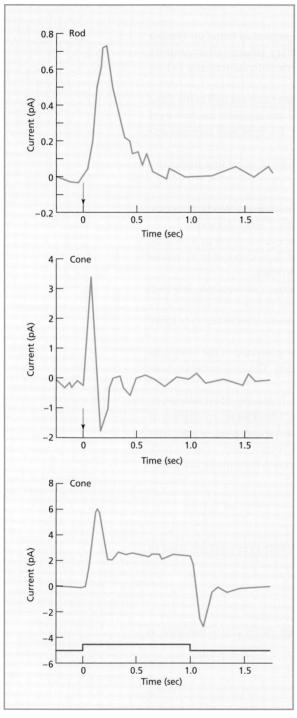

**FIG. 6.14** Time course of photoreceptor responses to a brief, dim flash of light (top two traces), and a 1 second pulse of light (bottom trace) (re-plotted from recordings in macaque monkey photoreceptors reported by Schnapf & Baylor, 1987).

*Acuity variation* As we saw in the previous section, the ability of the retina to resolve fine spatial detail varies with retinal location and with illumination level. Cones operate only in bright conditions, so resolution is much higher near the visual axis in the fovea than elsewhere on the retina. Eye movements allow the most acute portion of the retina to be brought to bear on a particular region of interest in the visual field. For this reason humans tend to adopt a fixate–saccade strategy. Short periods of fixation, typically lasting 300 ms, alternate with saccades to ensure that the eyes are always directed at the centre of current interest. It seems that relatively little specific detail about the content of the visual scene is stored in the visual system from one saccade to the next, though more general information may be retained. This explains why saccades occur so frequently—if detailed information is required, the eye simply executes a saccade to acquire it.

*Image motion* Any movement of the image across the retina degrades the quality of the information provided by photoreceptors, because photoreceptor responses are relatively slow. Figure 6.14 shows the time course of responses in photoreceptors to a brief flash of light. It can take a tenth of a second or more for receptor response to reach its peak, and each response lasts at least 100 ms even for very brief flashes. Imagine that you are fixating steadily on a stationary point as a person walks across your field of view at a distance of 10 metres. The image of the person will move across your retina at a speed of $8° \, s^{-1}$, passing over photoreceptors at a rate of one every 1.25 ms (assuming a walking speed of 5 kph or 140 cm $s^{-1}$). At this speed the image of the person will not dwell on each photoreceptor long enough for that receptor to reach its maximum response before the image moves on—there will be a reduction in effective contrast. Since each photoreceptor's response lasts tens of milliseconds, at any one instant in time a whole array of receptors will be responding. Receptors that were passed over many milliseconds ago will still be responding when new responses are just building in other receptors. Consequently, the image of the moving figure will be spread over many receptors, an effect known as **motion blur**. The deleterious effects of image motion can be overcome by moving the eyes to compensate for the movement and stabilise the position of the image on the retina. Voluntary pursuit movements and optokinetic nystagmus keep the centre of interest—a moving object—stationary on the retina (at the cost of blurring and contrast reduction in the background). Vestibulo-ocular movements stabilise the retinal image of the stationary world during head movements.

Saccadic eye movements themselves generate motion of the image across the retina. Chapter 11 on motion perception contains a discussion of why we are not aware of this motion.

### Binocular registration

We have already seen that in order to maximise acuity each eye must be positioned so that the centre of interest in the image is projected onto the fovea. The eyes are necessarily located a short distance apart in the head. This means that if both eyes are to engage in foveal fixation on the same point in the world, their optical axes must be made to converge using vergence eye movements. The degree of convergence depends on viewing distance. Points very close to the observer require large convergence angles, while very distant points require extremely small convergence angles.

Even when converged to fixate on the same object, the two eyes receive slightly different views of the world, due to their different positions in the head. These slight differences provide a very powerful visual depth cue, discussed in detail in Chapter 10, which also contains more information about convergence.

# CHAPTER SUMMARY

## LIGHT

Light is a form of energy that can be described as both a ray, a wave, and a stream of particles:

- The particle or quantal nature of light is important for understanding how light is emitted and absorbed, especially at low intensities.
- Ray properties are useful for understanding large-scale properties of light, including how it is refracted during transmission through optical devices.
- Wave properties are useful for understanding much finer scale effects such as diffraction.

Three important aspects of light as a stimulus for vision are:

- Intensity (number of quanta emitted per second)
- Contrast (ratio of the lightest to the darkest parts of an image)
- Wavelength (emission spectra of light sources, and reflectance functions of object surfaces).

## THE EYE

- Humans have single-chambered eyes. The cornea and lens refract incoming rays to form an image on the light-sensitive inner surface of the eye (the retina). Two-thirds of the optical power of the eye is provided by the cornea.

KEY TERM
**Motion blur:** Smearing in an image caused by movement of an object relative to the imaging surface.

- Variation in lens shape allows the eye to adjust its optical power to maintain a focused image of objects at different distances.
- Photoreceptor cells called rods and cones catch incoming photons and generate electrical currents that are transmitted through the network of neurons in the retina to the optic nerve.
- The optical properties of the photoreceptors (width, length, and distribution) place fundamental limits on the information transmitted up the optic nerve.
- The structure of the eye represents a compromise between properties that maximise spatial resolution and sensitivity to light.
- Eye movements are mediated by six extra-ocular muscles. Their functions are to maintain spatial resolution in the face of image movement across the retina, and to allow binocular registration of objects seen through both eyes.

# TUTORIALS

## OPTICS

## Lenses

The surface of an illuminated or self-luminous object can be regarded as a large collection of point sources. Rays emanate from each point radially in all directions. Figure 6.1 (page 146) shows one such point, placed in the vicinity of a lens. Hecht (2002) defines a lens as "a refracting device that reconfigures a transmitted energy distribution" (p. 150). Some portion of the rays emanating from the point passes through the lens. In the case of a convex or converging lens, the bundle of rays from a far object converges on a point some distance behind the lens, known as the focal point ($F_1$ at the top of Figure 6.15). A *real image* of the point would be formed if an imaging surface were placed at the focal point, to form a focal plane. In the case of a concave or diverging lens, the bundle of rays diverges on leaving the lens, as if emanating from a point in front of the lens ($F_2$ in Figure 6.15). No image would appear on a screen placed at focal point $F_2$, since it is just a projection from the path of the diverging rays, so the image at $F_2$ is known as a *virtual image*. The distance of the focal point from the centre of the lens is known as the *focal length, f,* of the lens. The power of a lens if often expressed in terms of the reciprocal of focal length ($1/f$). If $f$ is expressed in metres, then power is measured in *dioptres* (D).

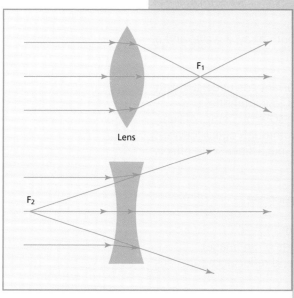

**FIG. 6.15** Converging and diverging lenses. Top: a converging lens forms a real image of an object at its focal point ($F_1$). An imaging surface placed at this point would show an image of the object. Bottom: In a diverging lens rays emanate as if from an object positioned at focal point $F_2$. The image at $F_2$ is known as a virtual image, since no image would appear on a surface placed at $F_2$ (the rays do not actually reach $F_2$).

## Refraction

Refraction is the principle underlying the formation of images by lenses. As mentioned earlier in the chapter, the effective speed with which a light wavefront passes through a medium may be retarded (even though individual quanta always travel at the speed of light), due to interference between the original wave and waves produced by forward scattering. An important consequence of the retardation of light during transmission through a medium is *refraction*, a change in the direction of the path of light rays as they enter a transmitting medium obliquely (see Figure 6.16). Refraction occurs because the retardation of the wavefront skews its direction of travel as it enters the medium, similar to the way a moving vehicle's direction would be skewed if one front wheel left the road and entered gravel at the roadside. Imagine that rays *a* and *f* in Figure 6.16 were the wheel tracks of a vehicle as it left the road (air), and entered gravel (glass). Wheels in track *a* would reach the gravel and begin slowing down before the wheels in track *f*. As a result, the direction of the vehicle's travel would be skewed towards the slow side of the vehicle.

Media that transmit light have an *index of refraction*, which defines the extent to which a light wavefront is retarded during transmission. The index of refraction, *n*, is defined as follows:

$$n = c/v$$

where $c$ is the speed of light in a vacuum, $v$ is its speed in the medium. Air has a refractive index $n$ of 1.00029. For water $n$ equals 1.333, for glass $n$

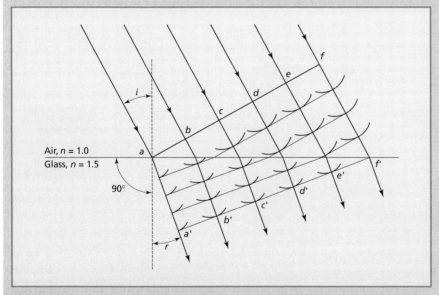

**FIG. 6.16**   Refraction. A wavefront containing the bundle of rays *a–f* is shown striking a glass surface. The wavefront is retarded as it enters the glass. Since waves in one part of the wavefront (*a*) are retarded before waves at other parts (e.g. *f*) have reached the glass, the direction of the wavefront is skewed once it enters the glass. The angle of each refracted ray (*r*) differs from the angle of each incident ray (*i*) by an amount that depends on the refractive indices of air and glass.

equals approximately 1.5, and for the cornea (outermost surface of the eye) $n$ equals 1.376. The degree to which light rays are deflected or refracted as they pass from one medium into another depends on the refractive index of each medium. The angle of refraction is defined in Snell's Law:

$$\sin i/\sin r = n_2/n_1$$

where $\sin i$ is the angle of the incident light ray as it strikes the interface between medium 1 and medium 2, $\sin r$ is the angle of the refracted light ray travelling through medium 2, and $n_2$, $n_1$ are the indices of refraction of the two media (see Figure 6.16). The angle through which light rays are refracted on entering a given medium is higher for media with larger refractive indices.

## Airy disk

According to ray or geometric optics, the real image of the point source in Figure 6.1 should itself be a point. However, images formed by actual lenses never conform to this ideal. Even in the best lenses, the image of a point is always slightly blurred. To understand why this is so, we must consider image formation in terms of wave or physical optics rather than geometrical optics. Light from a point strikes the lens as a wavefront, shown as $W_1$ in Figure 6.17 (rays are lines at right-angles to the wavefront).

The part of the wavefront passing through the centre of the lens is delayed more than the part passing through the edge of the lens, because the lens is thinner at its edges. Consequently, the wavefront that emerges from the lens

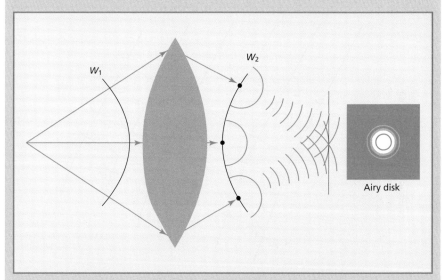

**FIG. 6.17**  Formation of the Airy disk. The wavefront ($W_1$) emanating from a point is curved in an arc centred on the point. After this wavefront has passed through a lens, it is curved in an arc centred on the focal point of the lens ($W_2$). Each point on a wavefront can be considered as the source of new wavefronts. Three points are shown on $W_2$. As these wavefronts interact when they reach the focal point, constructive and destructive interference produces a central bright disk (the Airy disk) surrounded by dimmer rings.

is curved in an arc centred on the focal point ($W_2$ in Figure 6.17). As the various parts of the wavefront meet at the focal point, they interfere to create an interference pattern of the same kind as that observed by Thomas Young. The pattern has a central bright spot, known as the **Airy disk**, surrounded by an alternating series of faint dark and bright rings. Figure 6.17 illustrates how interference produces the Airy disk. Each point on the wavefront emanating from the lens ($W_2$ in the figure) can be considered as the source of a new wavefront. Three such wavefronts are shown in the figure. Just as in the case of Young's double slit experiment (see Figure 6.2), when these different wavefronts cross they interact to either cancel out or augment each other. All of the wavefronts combine constructively at the focal point to create a bright spot, but alternating destructive and constructive interference creates a series of rings surrounding this spot.

Optical systems, including eyes, usually have a circular aperture placed between the light source and the lens in order to control light intensity and depth of field. The radius of the Airy disk depends on the diameter of the aperture, according to the following equation:

$$r \approx 1.22 \cdot f\lambda/D$$

Where $r$ is the radius of the disk (radius to the first dark ring), $f$ is focal length, $D$ is aperture diameter, and $\lambda$ is the wavelength of the light (all measures in mm). The width of the Airy disk is inversely proportional to aperture diameter—wider apertures create smaller disks. You may be able to understand

**KEY TERM**
**Airy disk:** The image of a point light source created by an optical system; it contains a bright central spot surrounded by several faint rings.

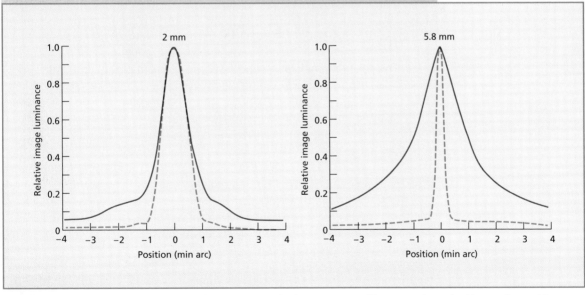

**FIG. 6.18**  Linespread functions. These functions plot the luminance profile across the retinal image formed by a thin bright line. The functions on the left relate to a pupil diameter of 2.0 mm, and the functions on the right relate to a pupil diameter of 5.8 mm. The solid functions show the actual luminance profile of the line. The broken functions show the profiles predicted on the basis of diffraction effects illustrated in Figure 6.17. The difference between the solid and broken functions can be attributed to aberrations of the kind shown in Figure 6.19, which become more severe as pupil diameter increases (re-plotted from Campbell & Gubisch, 1966).

why this is so from inspection of Figure 6.17. An aperture placed in front of the lens limits the size of the wavefront emanating from the lens. A narrow aperture, for example, would remove the more peripheral (top and bottom) wavefronts and so broaden the interference pattern at the focal point.

Figure 6.18 plots the intensity of the retinal image created by a very thin line, at two different pupil diameters. The dotted line is the **linespread** expected on the basis of diffraction effects alone. The solid line is the actual image measured by Campbell and Gubisch (1966). At the narrower pupil diameter, the actual linespread is very close to that predicted by diffraction—the image is said to be *diffraction-limited*. At the wider pupil diameter, diffraction effects predict a narrower spread, according to the equation above. Actual linespread at wider pupil diameters is much worse than that predicted by diffraction—optical imperfections play a much greater role in determining image quality. Small pupil diameters are therefore optimal for preserving image quality.

## Aberrations

The two most significant optical imperfections that affect image quality are spherical aberration and chromatic aberration.

### Spherical aberration

A lens with a spherical surface will not bring all rays to focus at the same point. Peripheral rays are refracted more than central rays (see top of Figure 6.19), so the image of a point will be a blurred circle. One solution to this problem is to use an appropriately non-spherical surface. The surface of the human cornea has a hyperbolic shape for this reason. A second solution, also adopted in human and other eyes, is to vary the refractive index of the lens material, adjusting the angle of refraction across the lens to compensate for the focusing error. This solution requires that the lens has a gradient of refractive index from high in the centre to low at the periphery. Even after such measures are taken to avoid spherical aberration, slight deviations from a perfect hyperbolic shape, or refractive index, will introduce some degree of blurring in the image.

### Chromatic aberration

Chromatic aberration arises from the manner in which the wavefront emanating from a light source is retarded during its passage through a refracting medium. The degree to which the wavefront is retarded varies with frequency, because the retardation is due to interference between the original wave and forward scattered waves. Shorter wavelengths are retarded more than longer wavelengths. Since refraction (a change in the direction of the path of light rays as they enter a transmitting medium obliquely; refer back to page 169) depends on retardation, the angle through which a light ray is refracted depends on its frequency. Shorter (violet) wavelengths are deflected more than longer (red) wavelengths. If the refracting device is a prism, then white light (composed of many wavelengths) will be dispersed into a rainbow spectrum of colours. If the refracting device is a lens, then each different wavelength will have a different

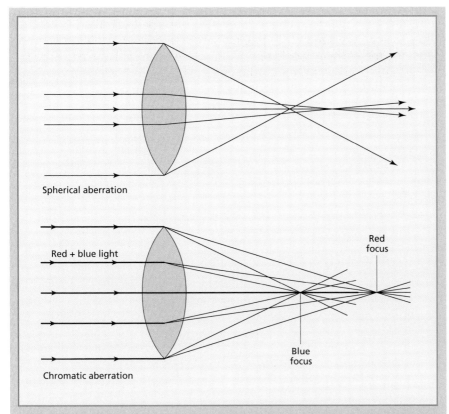

**FIG. 6.19** Lens aberrations. Top: Spherical aberration. Light rays passing through the lens near its centre come into focus at a farther distance than rays that pass through the lens near its edges. Consequently, an imaging surface placed at either distance will reveal a blurred image. Bottom: Chromatic aberration. Light rays at longer (red) wavelengths come into focus at a farther distance from the lens than rays at short (blue) wavelengths. Hence an imaging surface placed at a particular distance will show colour fringes from out-of-focus wavelengths.

focal point (see bottom of Figure 6.19). The image of light from a white point will be a blurred circle of coloured fringes. Cameras attempt to compensate for this effect by combining two lenses of different material and different shape, so that their aberrations cancel out. Eyes attempt to deal with the problem by reducing sensitivity to wavelengths at the short end of the visible spectrum.

## Lens equations

Lens equations allow us to calculate the size and location of the image produced by a lens. For a thin lens, the distance ($d_i$) of the image from the focal plane depends on the distance of the object ($d_o$), as defined in the Newtonian lens equation (which first appeared in Isaac Newton's *Opticks* in 1704):

$$d_i = f^2/d_o$$

For an object very far away from the lens ($d_o$ essentially infinite), $d_i$ is effectively zero, so the image falls in the focal plane of the lens. As the object approaches the lens, $d_i$ grows progressively because the point of focus falls beyond the focal plane of the lens. An imaging surface fixed in position at the focal plane would render a blurred image of the object. In order to maintain a focused image, one of two things must happen. The imaging surface could be moved back away from the lens until it coincides with the point of focus. This is the solution used in many cameras. Alternatively, the power (focal length) of the lens could be adjusted to maintain focus on a fixed imaged plane. As objects move closer to the lens, its power must be increased to maintain focus. This is the solution adopted in human eyes.

The size of the image, $H_i$, is an important consideration for eyes. The following equations specify image height:

$$H_i/H_o = f/d_o, \quad \text{or}$$

$$H_i = H_o \cdot (f/d_o)$$

Thus, for a given size of object (i.e. $H_o$ fixed), at a given distance away (i.e. $d_o$ fixed), the size of the image scales directly with focal length $f$. Lenses with small focal lengths project smaller images than those with long focal lengths. The human eye has a focal length of approximately 16.77 mm (59.6 D, see Land & Nilsson, 2002). So a person 1.8 m (6 ft) tall standing 15 m away would project an image in your eye that was 2 mm tall. The ability of an eye to resolve fine detail is partly governed by the size of the image projected by the lens, so animals with smaller eyes are inherently limited in their ability to resolve detail.

## MEASURING LIGHT INTENSITY

Light intensity can be measured according to two different systems, the *radiometric* system and the *photometric* system.

### The radiometric system

The radiometric system for measuring light intensity uses physical energy units that can be traced back to photons. Measures fall into four categories, as shown in the left-hand column of Table 6.3.

#### Total radiant energy

The total energy emitted by a source, also called *radiant energy* or *radiant flux*, is measured in watts. One watt corresponds approximately to $10^{18}$ photons at a wavelength of 555 nm.

#### Radiant energy from a point source

Energy emitted by a point source emanates in all directions, so it is usually more convenient to specify the range of directions over which the measured amount of energy is emitted. The convention is to consider a point source as positioned at the centre of a sphere, and to divide the sphere into conical

**TABLE 6.3 PHOTOMETRIC AND RADIOMETRIC MEASURES OF LIGHT INTENSITY**

| Measure | Radiometric term | Radiometric unit | Photometric term | Photometric unit |
|---|---|---|---|---|
| Total energy emitted | Radiant energy or flux | Watts (W) | Luminous flux | Lumen (lm) |
| Energy from a point source | Radiant intensity | Watts per steradian ($W \cdot sr^{-1}$) | Luminous intensity | Lumens per steradian ($lm \cdot sr^{-1}$), known as candelas (cd) |
| Energy from an extended source | Radiance | Watts per square metre per steradian ($W \cdot m^{-2} \cdot sr^{-1}$) | Luminance | Lumens per square metre per steradian ($lm \cdot m^{-2} \cdot sr^{-1}$), or candelas per square metre ($cd \cdot m^{-2}$) |
| Energy received at a surface | Irradiance | Watts per square metre ($W \cdot m^{-2}$) | Illuminance | Lumens per square metre ($lm \cdot m^{-2}$), known as lux |

sectors. These sectors are measured in units of solid angle known as *steradians*. A complete sphere contains $4\pi$ steradians. Energy emitted by a point source, also called *radiant intensity*, is therefore specified in watts per steradian.

### Radiant energy from an extended source

Most light-emitting sources, such as TV and computer screens, are extended over space. The appropriate measure of intensity for such sources must therefore specify the unit of surface area over which it applies. Energy emitted by an extended source, also called *radiance*, is therefore specified in watts per square metre per steradian.

### Radiant energy received at a surface

Energy falling on a receiving surface can simply be specified in terms of watts received per square metre of surface area, also called *irradiance*. The amount of energy received depends on both the energy emitted by the source and the distance between the receiving surface and the source. Irradiance $E_e$ can be calculated from radiant intensity $I_e$ using the following relation:

$$E_e = I_e/r^2$$

Where *r* is the distance between the source and the receiving surface. Energy falling on the surface declines according to the square of the distance, known as the *inverse square law*. Each doubling in distance results in a four-fold decline in irradiance. This occurs because as distance increases, energy emanating over a particular range of directions falls on a progressively greater area of the receiving surface (the same effect occurs with sound intensity, for the same reasons). Strictly speaking, the inverse square law holds only for point sources. Practically speaking, it operates with an error of less than 1% if the diameter of the source is less than 1/10th of the distance to the receiving surface (Pokorny & Smith, 1986).

## The photometric system

Light was defined at the beginning of the chapter as energy that is capable of evoking a visual sensation. Since this definition includes a reference to perception, purely physical radiometric measures of light are not sufficient. The majority of frequencies in the spectrum of radiant energy are invisible to humans, and even the visible frequencies vary in their effectiveness. Radiometric measures do not therefore accurately represent light intensity as a stimulus for vision. The photometric system of light measurement was developed by the Commission Internationale de l'Eclairage (CIE) to take account of human sensitivity to different wavelengths.

### Spectral luminous efficiency functions: $V(\lambda)$ and $V'(\lambda)$

The *spectral luminous efficiency function* specifies the relative sensitivity of the eye to different wavelengths. There are a number of ways to estimate the spectral luminous efficiency function, but in 1924 CIE adopted a standard function $V(\lambda)$ based on the average of estimates obtained in a number of different laboratories. Most of the estimates were obtained using a technique known as heterochromatic flicker photometry, in which a fixed reference light alternates rapidly with a comparison light to create flicker. The observer adjusts the intensity of the comparison light to minimise or eliminate the sensation of flicker. In this way lights of many different wavelengths can be defined in terms of their sensory "efficiency" relative to a light of standard intensity. Figure 6.20 shows the luminous efficiency function for the standard observer defined by CIE in 1924. This function was obtained at high light levels, known as **photopic vision**. But relative sensitivity has been found to change slightly at low light levels. So in 1951 CIE introduced a second standard function $V'(\lambda)$ appropriate for lower light levels, known as **scotopic vision**, also shown in Figure 6.20.

Units in the photometric system of measurement are based on corresponding units in the radiometric system, adjusted for the relative efficiencies defined in $V(\lambda)$ and $V'(\lambda)$, as shown in Table 6.3.

**KEY TERMS**

**Photopic vision**: Vision at high illumination levels (above approximately 4 cd·m$^{-2}$), mediated by cone photoreceptors.

**Scotopic vision**: Vision at low illumination levels (below approximately 1 cd·m$^{-2}$), mediated by rod photoreceptors.

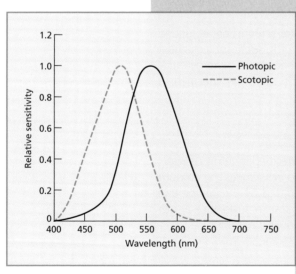

**FIG. 6.20** Photopic and scotopic luminous efficiency functions, as defined by CIE. These show the relative sensitivity to light of different wavelengths at high (photopic) illumination levels (solid line), and low (scotopic) illumination levels (broken line). The peak sensitivity of human vision shifts to shorter wavelengths under scotopic viewing conditions.

## Total luminous energy

Total energy emitted, or *luminous flux*, is specified in *lumens*. One lumen is defined as the luminous flux of 1/683 W of monochromatic radiation at a wavelength of 555 nm (Makous, 1998), or approximately $4 \times 10^{15}$ photons. The total luminous flux emitted by a source is calculated by multiplying the radiant flux at each wavelength by its luminous efficacy defined on the luminous efficiency function, and summing the products.

## Luminous energy from a point source

Energy emitted by a point source, or *luminous intensity*, is specified in lumens per steradian, also known as *candelas* (cd).

## Luminous energy from an extended source

Energy emitted by an extended source, or luminance, is specified in candelas per square metre (lumens per square metre per steradian), abbreviated to $cd \cdot m^{-2}$.

## Luminous energy received at a surface

Energy received at a surface, or illuminance, is specified in lux (lumens per square metre).

Photometric units are used very frequently in the research literature, the most commonly used unit being candelas per square metre ($cd \cdot m^{-2}$), since this measures surface luminance of visual stimuli. Luminance is usually measured by pointing a telescopic spot photometer at the surface to be measured. The photometer is similar in size and shape to a small camcorder. The centre of its viewfinder contains a small grey spot. A digital display on the photometer reports the luminance of the area covered by the spot, in $cd \cdot m^{-2}$.

## Retinal illumination

Even photometric luminance units may not provide a sufficiently precise measure of stimulus intensity in certain situations. Light enters the eye via the pupil, and variation in the diameter of the pupil can result in significant variation in the amount of light that falls on the retina of the eye (see earlier in the chapter for a discussion of the pupil). **Troland** units (td) specify retinal illuminance, taking pupil size into account. One troland is defined as the retinal illumination that would result from viewing a surface at 1 $cd \cdot m^{-2}$ through a pupil with an area of 1 mm² (Makous, 1998). There are two limitations on the accuracy of troland measures. First, troland value does not make any correction for absorption by ocular media. Second, troland value does not take into account the part of the pupil through which light enters the eye. Light entering near the edge of the pupil is less effective than light entering near the centre of the pupil, due to the optical properties of the retinal photoreceptors (light rays that strike the photoreceptors obliquely are less effective than rays that strike them straight on). This effect is known as the **Stiles-Crawford** effect.

**KEY TERMS**
**Troland:** A photometric unit specifying retinal illuminance, which takes into account pupil diameter.
**Stiles-Crawford effect:** The variation in the sensitivity of the retina with the place of entry of light rays at the pupil.

# CHAPTER 7

## CONTENTS

# Visual physiology

## INTRODUCTION

When light strikes the network of cells that line the inside surface of the eye, it initiates a chain of neural events in the visual system that leads, 100 milliseconds or so later, to a conscious visual experience. The visual system comprises all the neurons responsible for seeing. It can be broken down into three major components: the retina, the visual pathway, and the visual cortex, as illustrated in Figure 7.1.

- The retina contains the neural circuitry connecting photoreceptors to the ganglion cells, whose fibres form the optic nerve.
- The visual pathway includes the optic nerve, the cell nuclei to which its fibres project, and the onward projection to the cortex.
- The visual cortex includes all cortical areas that contain cells responsive to visual stimuli.

This chapter will review the major features of each component, following the route of neural signals as they travel through the system from the photoreceptors to cortical cells.

## THE RETINA

Figure 7.2 contains a cross-section sketch of the human eye, with an enlarged cross-section of the human retina shown in a photomicrograph. The retina is a layered network containing five different types of cell, whose nuclei are grouped into three layers:

- Photoreceptor cells in the outer nuclear layer are responsible for transducing light energy into neural signals.
- Ganglion cell fibres in the ganglion cell layer carry neural signals out of the eye and along the visual pathway towards the brain.
- The complex retinal circuitry of the inner nuclear layer connects photoreceptors to ganglion cells. It contains bipolar cells, amacrine cells, and horizontal cells.

Separating these layers are plexiform layers that contain the fibres and synapses connecting the cell layers together. There are far more photoreceptors (over 100 million)

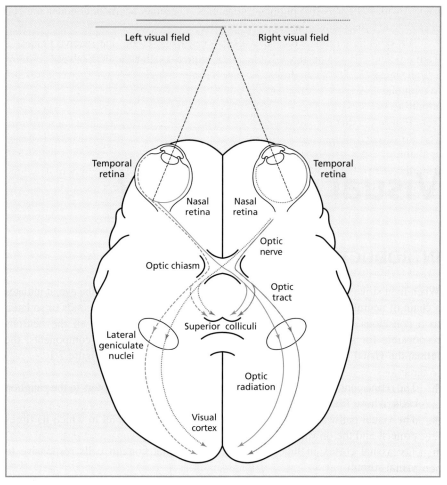

**FIG. 7.1**   The visual system includes the retinas, the visual pathway connecting the retinas to the brain, and the visual cortex. The two eyes' fields of view overlap (top). The human visual system is arranged so that binocular information from the right half of the visual field arrives in the left hemisphere, and binocular information from the left half of the visual field arrives in the right hemisphere.

than there are ganglion cells (approximately 1 million). The massive convergence of signals from the outer nuclear layer to the ganglion cell layer is achieved by the cells in the inner nuclear layer. This convergence is executed with such precision and selectivity that by the time signals travel up the fibres of ganglion cells, they contain a highly encoded representation of the retinal image, the first stage of image analysis in the visual system. Our journey through the visual system begins with photoreceptors in the outer nuclear layer.

## OUTER NUCLEAR LAYER

### Photoreceptor components

As we learnt in the previous chapter, receptors in the outer nuclear layer fall into two classes, rods and cones. The outer segment of each receptor contains a stack of disks

> Disk turn-over is such that all the disks in each photoreceptor are replaced approximately every 12 days (Purves et al., 2001).

packed with light sensitive pigment molecules. The inner segment contains the cell nucleus and synaptic terminals (see Figure 7.3).

The synaptic terminals contain pockets or synaptic clefts that receive processes from bipolar cells and horizontal cells in the adjacent retinal layer. Each rod contains a single synaptic cleft that admits two horizontal cell processes and between two and five bipolar processes. Cones, on the other hand, have several synaptic clefts, each admitting two horizontal cell processes and two or more bipolar processes. Notice from Figure 7.2 that the photoreceptors actually face away from the incoming light. The tip of each outer segment abuts a layer of the retina known as the pigment epithelium. When receptor disks are expended after exposure to light, they are shed from the end of the outer segment and absorbed into the pigment epithelium, which regenerates the photopigment and transports it back to the receptors.

## Photon absorption

The probability that a photon will be absorbed by a photoreceptor depends on its direction of travel and on its frequency.

### Photon direction

Photons arrive at the photoreceptors from a range of directions, depending on where they pass through the pupil. Photons travelling through the centre of the pupil arrive in a direction that is nearly parallel to the long axis of each receptor, while photons travelling near the edge of the pupil arrive at a slight angle to the receptor's long axis. Photons arriving from non-parallel directions are less likely to be absorbed, an effect known as the Stiles-Crawford effect (discussed in Chapter 6). This effect occurs because photons are guided onto the receptor's outer segment as they pass through the inner segment. This guidance is most effective when photons travel the full length of the photoreceptor. The Stiles-Crawford effect is more marked for cones than for rods, so rods absorb 60% more photons from a dilate pupil than do cones.

### Photon frequency

The probability that a photon at a given frequency will be absorbed by a photopigment molecule depends on the spectral sensitivity of the molecule. As shown in Figure 12.8 (see colour plates), there are three distinct classes of cone photopigment, which have different spectral sensitivities from each other and from rod photopigment. If a photon happens to have a frequency near the peak sensitivity of the receptor it strikes, it is more likely to be absorbed.

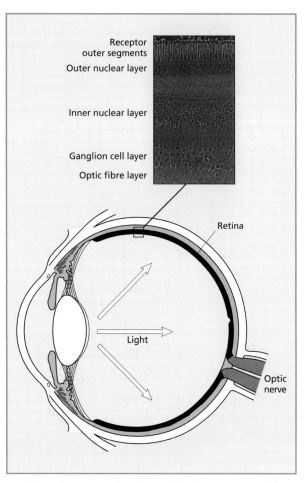

**FIG. 7.2**  A cross-section through the human eye, with a photomicrograph showing the layered structure of the retina. Light must pass through all the lower layers before it reaches the outer segments of the photoreceptors at the top.

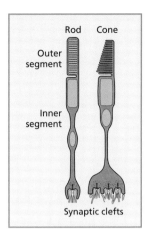

# Photoreceptor responses

Even once a photon has been absorbed, there is no guarantee that it will lead to
a visual response. Only two-thirds of the photons absorbed by a photoreceptor
actually result in a response. Energy from the remaining photons is dissipated as
heat (Rodieck, 1998). Any responses that do occur are mediated by a process
known as *photoisomerisation* in the visual pigment molecules that all photoreceptors
contain.

## Photoisomerisation

Each molecule consists of a protein portion (known as *opsin*), and a light-catching
portion (known as a *chromophore*). All mammalian pigment molecules use 11-*cis*
retinal as their chromophore, and are known as *rhodopsins*. Rods and cones contain
different variants of rhodopsin, giving them different wavelength sensitivities. Visual
responses are initiated when an absorbed photon causes a change in the shape of the
chromophore molecule (*photoisomerisation*). A cascade of biochemical events then
occurs within the outer segment of the photoreceptor, which results in a change in
receptor membrane potential.

## Graded potentials

The distance over which signals are transmitted through the layers of retina from
photoreceptors to ganglion cells is so small (less than 0.2 mm) that it does not require
the generation of action potentials. Instead, photoreceptors generate graded changes
in membrane potential and correspondingly graded changes in the rate of neurotransmitter release within their synaptic cleft. In total darkness photoreceptors have
a membrane potential of $-40$ mV. Increases in retinal illumination cause the
potential to become more negative (hyperpolarisation), until it reaches saturation at
$-65$ mV. So the rate of neurotransmitter release is actually higher in the dark than it
is in the light.

At very low light levels, rods can produce a reliable change in potential after a
single photon strike, but they reach saturation with the absorption of only approximately 100 photons per second. Cones require approximately 30–100 photons to
produce a reliable change in potential, but can respond without saturating at very
high rates of absorption (50,000 photons per second).

Rods and cones also differ in their temporal response. The two traces of
Figure 7.4 show the change in membrane current in a rod and a cone in response to
a very brief flash of light (marked on the trace below each response; the black bar
represents 500 ms; re-drawn from Schnapf & Baylor, 1987). The rod does not reach
its peak response until roughly 200 ms after the flash. The cone responds about four
times faster. A number of other differences between rods and cones were discussed
in Chapter 6, including their retinal distribution and spectral sensitivity.

## Univariance

Each photon that photoisomerises a pigment molecule has the same effect on
the molecule as any other photon that photoisomerises it, regardless of photon
frequency. The photoreceptor has no way of distinguishing between photoreceptors
at different frequencies. All it can do is report the rate at which it is catching photons.

This principle of photoreceptor behaviour is known as the *principle of univariance*. Of course the probability that a photon will be absorbed by a given receptor depends jointly on its frequency and the spectral sensitivity of the photoreceptor. Photons of a particular frequency will tend to be captured more by some receptor types than by others. So later stages of visual processing must integrate information across the different photoreceptor types in order to infer the frequency characteristics of the incident photons.

## INNER NUCLEAR LAYER

Cones connect to a complex network of postsynaptic cells in the retina, whereas rods' connectivity involves relatively simple retinal circuitry. As a result, although there are far fewer cones than rods in the retina, there are 8–10 cone-driven neurons for every rod-driven neuron. Figure 7.5 is a highly schematic representation of the pattern of connectivity in the inner nuclear layer. It shows how bipolar, horizontal, and amacrine cells collect the signals from receptors and funnel them towards the ganglion cells.

## Bipolar cells

Bipolar cells transmit responses "vertically" through the retinal network from photoreceptors down towards ganglion cells. Like the photoreceptors to which they are connected, bipolar cells transmit graded potentials.

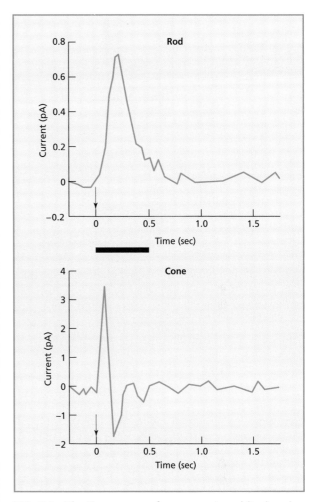

**FIG. 7.4**  The time course of responses in rod (top) and cone (bottom) photoreceptors. A brief flash of light was presented at the point marked by the arrow on the horizontal axis. The bar between the two plots represents 500 ms. Re-drawn from Schnapf and Baylor (1987).

*ON versus OFF bipolars*

Bipolar cells can be sub-divided into two types, *ON* and *OFF*.

● ON bipolars are activated by an increase in the photon catch of receptors. In other words, they depolarise (increase the rate of transmitter release).
● OFF bipolars are activated by a decrease in the photon catch of receptors. In other words, they hyperpolarise (decrease the rate of neurotransmitter release).

Table 7.1 summarises the change in the graded potential of photoreceptors and bipolars in response to increases or decreases in photon catch.

Notice that the response of OFF bipolars has the same sign as the response of photoreceptors, whereas the response of ON bipolars is inverted relative to the photoreceptors. This distinction between ON and OFF responses is of major importance for visual processing, and is preserved at later levels of analysis.

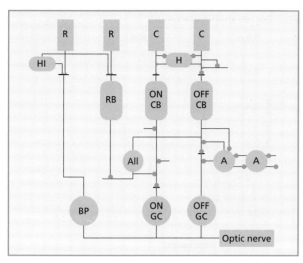

**FIG. 7.5** Retinal circuitry connecting photoreceptors (top: rods, R; and cones, C) to ganglion cells (bottom: GC). Circuitry differs between the different receptor types. Cone bipolars (CB) connect cones to ganglion cells; ON variants (ON CB) increase transmitter release when cone photon catch increases, while OFF variants (OFF CB) decrease transmitter release when photon catch increases. Rod bipolars (RB) are all ON, and connect rods to ganglion cells via AII amacrine cells and cone bipolars. The laterally spreading dendrites of horizontal cells (H, HI) terminate in the synaptic clefts of photoreceptors alongside bipolar cell processes. Amacrine cells (A, AII) connect to each other, to bipolar cells, and to ganglion cells. Large dots indicate excitatory connections, small dots indicate inhibitory connections.

*Why is retinal circuitry dominated by cones?*

### Rod versus cone bipolars

Some bipolar cells connect only to cones. Others connect only to rods. Each cone bipolar makes contact with between 1 and 10 cone photoreceptors, whereas rod bipolars contact 30–50 rods.

* **Cone bipolars** can be divided into ON and OFF variants, and connect with ganglion cells, as shown in Figure 7.5 (labelled ON CB and OFF CB).
* **Rod bipolars** (RB in Figure 7.5), on the other hand, have only ON responses, and mainly connect to a class of amacrine cells known as *AII*, rather than to ganglion cells. These amacrine cells in turn make connections with cone bipolar cells. Some connect to ON cone bipolars; others connect to OFF cone bipolars.

So ON signals from rods "piggyback" onto both the ON and OFF bipolar circuitry that connects cones to ganglion cells (Rodieck, 1998). It seems that the relatively simple circuitry for rod signals is superimposed on pre-existing cone circuitry (there is also evidence for some direct connections between rod and cone receptors at their inner segments; Sharpe & Stockman, 1999).

### Horizontal cells

**Horizontal cells** each have an axon that extends laterally across the retinal network up to a distance of 1 mm or more. Dendrites reach out from both the cell body and the axon, terminating in the synaptic clefts of photoreceptors. These clefts also receive processes from bipolar cells, and horizontal cells serve to modulate the signals that are passed from photoreceptors to bipolar cells. Stimulation of horizontal cells by photoreceptors is fed back to reduce the influence of the photoreceptors on bipolar cells. This effect is known as *lateral inhibition*; it spreads across the retina

**TABLE 7.1 CHANGES IN THE GRADED POTENTIAL OF PHOTORECEPTORS AND BIPOLARS IN RESPONSE TO INCREASES OR DECREASES IN PHOTON CATCH**

|  | Increase in photon catch | Decrease in photon catch |
|---|---|---|
| Photoreceptors | Hyperpolarise (more negative) Decrease in neurotransmitter | Depolarise (more positive) Increase in neurotransmitter |
| ON bipolars | Depolarise (more positive) Increase in neurotransmitter | Hyperpolarise (more negative) Decrease in neurotransmitter |
| OFF bipolars | Hyperpolarise (more negative) Decrease in neurotransmitter | Depolarise (more positive) Increase in neurotransmitter |

along horizontal cell axons. Consequently, activation of any one photoreceptor tends to reduce the activation of the surrounding photoreceptors.

## Amacrine cells

**Amacrine cells** make synaptic contacts with bipolar cells, with other amacrine cells, and with ganglion cells. Amacrine cells outnumber both horizontal cells and **ganglion cells**, and account for the majority of synapses onto ganglion cells. They can be classified into many different types that appear to serve different roles, mostly still ill-defined (Masland, 2001). The AII amacrines convey rod signals to cone bipolars, as we have seen. Other types of amacrine cell may serve to modulate the signal carried by bipolar cells and ganglion cells, over both short and long periods of time.

## GANGLION CELL LAYER

As its name suggests, this layer contains the cell bodies of ganglion cells, though it also contains some amacrine cell bodies.

## Cell types

Ganglion cells can be classified into four major types on the basis of their anatomical properties (namely shape and connectivity). There are:

- **Biplexiform**
- **Bistratified**
- **Midget**, and
- **Parasol ganglion cells**.

### Biplexiform cells

Biplexiform ganglion cells are the only type that connect directly to photoreceptors, depolarising in response to increases in photon catch. They have processes in both the upper plexiform layer (between the outer and inner nuclear layers), and the lower plexiform layer (between the inner nuclear layer and the ganglion cell layer). The upper processes connect directly to rod photoreceptors, bypassing the influence of bipolar and amacrine cells. Nevertheless, biplexiform ganglion cell responses can be influenced by both rods and cones, presumably due to inter-receptor contacts, or via their processes in the lower plexiform layer. The precise role of these cells in visual processing is not clear. They may provide information on ambient light level, useful for controlling pupil diameter and diurnal body rhythm (Rodieck, 1998).

### Bistratified, midget, and parasol cells

Much more is known about the other three types of ganglion cell. Their distinctive response properties are crucial for higher-level processing of spatial, temporal, and chromatic information. All three cell types generate action potentials at a rate that is influenced by activity levels in the amacrine and bipolar cells that connect with them. The precise response properties of each ganglion cell type arise from the specific connections they make with amacrine and bipolar cells, which in turn make selective contacts with photoreceptors.

---

**KEY TERMS**

**Amacrine cell**: A class of retinal cell that has extensive contacts with bipolar cells, ganglion cells, and other amacrine cells; it serves a number of functions.

**Ganglion cell**: The class of retinal cell that provides the output signal from the retina; ganglion cell axons form the optic nerve.

**Biplexiform ganglion cell**: A class of ganglion cell that connects directly to photoreceptors.

**Bistratified ganglion cell**: The least numerous ganglion cell class; it responds only at high light levels, has no spatial opponency, but shows blue–yellow spectral opponency.

**Midget ganglion cell**: The most numerous class of ganglion cell; it responds only at high light levels, shows spatial opponency, and may also show red–green spectral opponency.

**Parasol ganglion cell**: The only class of ganglion cell that remains active at low light levels; it shows spatial opponency but does not show spectral opponency.

# Response properties of bistratified, midget, and parasol cells

Table 7.2 summarises the major response properties of, midget, parasol, and bistratified ganglion cells.

We have already seen that there are far fewer cones than rods in the primate retina (7 versus 120 million), both connecting to approximately 1 million optic nerve fibres. Given the relative incidence of different ganglion cell classes, and their luminance response, we can infer the following. During daylight, an average of seven cone photoreceptors must converge onto each active ganglion cell. At night, an average of 600 rod photoreceptors must converge onto each active parasol ganglion cell. It is therefore inevitable that the eye's resolving power is much lower at night than during daylight. However, such simple ratios do not allow for the fact that different ganglion cells may receive information from different numbers of receptors.

## Luminance response

All three ganglion cell types are active during daylight (photopic light levels). At dusk the midget ganglion cells fall silent, but parasol and bistratified cells remain active. After nightfall (scotopic light levels), only the parasol cells remain active, driven by rod responses. Since midget ganglion cells account for 70–80% of all ganglion cells, it seems that the primate retina is designed primarily for daytime vision. Vision at night is mediated by only a small fraction of the optic nerve fibres projecting to the brain, since parasol cells account for just 8–10% of all ganglion cells.

## Spatial response

Every ganglion cell has a *receptive field*, which defines the area of retina within which light must fall in order to influence the response of the cell. This area corresponds to the array of photoreceptors whose responses can find a route to the ganglion cell through the intervening retinal cell network. Many ganglion cell receptive fields exhibit a crucial property known as **spatial opponency**, in which the cell is excited when light falls in one part of its receptive field, and inhibited when light falls in another part. The excitatory and inhibitory regions of the receptive field are arranged in a centre–surround configuration, as shown in Figure 7.6 (left).

Centre–surround organisation in ganglion cells is a consequence of bipolar and horizontal cell influences. The centre response reflects the influence of bipolar cells, and the opposing surround response is due to lateral inhibitory signals from horizontal cells. We saw earlier that there is a distinction between ON bipolars and OFF bipolars. This distinction is inherited by ganglion cells.

*Which other sensory system is known to possess centre–surround receptive fields?*

**KEY TERM**
**Spatial opponency:**
Excitatory responses generated in one part of the retinal receptive field are opposed by inhibitory responses in another part.

| TABLE 7.2 MAJOR RESPONSE PROPERTIES OF MIDGET, PARASOL, AND BISTRATIFIED GANGLION CELLS | | | |
|---|---|---|---|
| | **Midget ganglion** | **Parasol ganglion** | **Bistratified ganglion** |
| Incidence | 70–80% | 8–10% | Below 10% |
| Luminance response | Photopic only | Photopic and scotopic | Photopic only |
| Spatial response | Opponent | Opponent | Non-opponent |
| Spectral response | L versus M (central) L + M (peripheral) | L + M | S versus (L + M) |
| Temporal response | Sustained | Transient | |
| Projection | Parvo LGN | Magno LGN | Konio LGN |

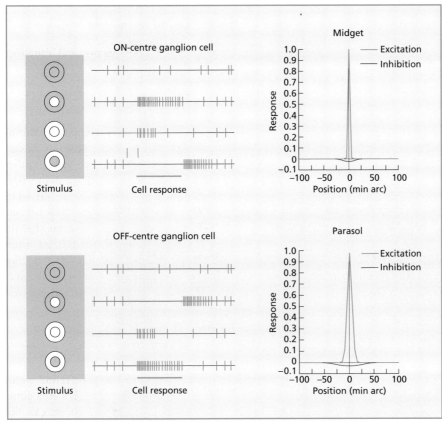

**FIG. 7.6**  Spatial responses in ganglion cells. Left: Stimuli are shown superimposed on concentrically organised receptive fields. The trace adjacent to each stimulus shows neural activity as a function of time. The thick horizontal bars mark the duration of each stimulus. Cells with an excitatory centre and inhibitory surround (top four traces) respond best to the onset of small light spots and offset of small dark spots. Cells with an inhibitory centre and excitatory surround (bottom four traces) show the opposite pattern of response; they respond best to the onset of small dark spots and the offset of small light spots. Right: Cross-sections of midget and parasol ganglion cell receptive fields. Midget ganglion cells have smaller receptive fields than parasol ganglion cells. In both cell types the centre and surround influences conform to a spatial Gaussian (bell-shaped or normal) distribution. The centre is more dominant than the surround.

- ON-centre ganglion receptive fields have an excitatory centre and inhibitory surround (as in Figure 7.6, top left). Small light spots that fill the centre of the receptive field produce the best response.
- OFF-centre receptive fields have the opposite arrangement; an inhibitory centre and excitatory surround (bottom left). Small dark spots produce the best response.

Midget cells have smaller receptive fields than parasol cells. The two right-hand profiles in Figure 7.6 show cross-sections of typical ON-centre midget and parasol receptive fields (taken across the middle of the receptive field map on the top left). The blue lines show the excitatory input to each receptive field, and the grey lines show the inhibitory input. Notice that the strength of each input follows a bell-shaped or normal distribution across the receptive field. Individual ganglion cells vary in the

Centre–surround ganglion cell responses were first observed in a mammal (the cat) by Stephen Kuffler in 1953, at Johns Hopkins Hospital, USA.

height and width of the two components, but the surround is always much wider than the centre (usually by a factor of four or more), and the centre input is always more dominant than the surround input. In central vision, the receptive field centre of a midget cell may be so small as to be driven by a single cone, to maximise acuity (see below under "Information processing"). Receptive field size increases towards the retinal periphery.

### Spectral response

Cone photoreceptors can be divided into three classes on the basis of their spectral sensitivity (see Chapter 6):

- "Blue" or short wavelength (S)
- "Green" or medium wavelength (M)
- "Red" or long wavelength (L).

The manner in which a given ganglion cell responds to the wavelength properties of incident light depends on how different cone classes contribute to its receptive field. If the excitatory and inhibitory inputs to the cell are each drawn from all cone classes, then the cell will not show any selectivity in its spectral response. If there is an imbalance between the cone classes in their contributions to excitation or inhibition, then the ganglion cell will exhibit some degree of **spectral opponency**: the cell will be excited by light from one portion of the spectrum, and inhibited by light from another portion of the spectrum. Spectral opponency can be broadly classified into two types:

- Blue–yellow opponent
- Red–green opponent.

### Relation between spectral opponency and spatial opponency

Figure 7.7 summarises the various receptive field types found in bistratified, midget, and parasol ganglion cells.

Blue–yellow opponency is a property of bistratified ganglion cells (Figure 7.7, bottom). Most of the cells discovered so far are excited by blue and inhibited by yellow (so-called blue–ON cells; see Dacey, 2000), and do not show spatial opponency.

Red–green opponency is mediated by midget ganglion cells in the centre of the retina. Parasol cells, and midget cells in the peripheral retina, do not show spectral opponency, but do show spatial opponency.

Notice that short-wavelength (S) cones have their own class of ganglion cell. The segregation of S cone responses in bistratified ganglion cells probably has

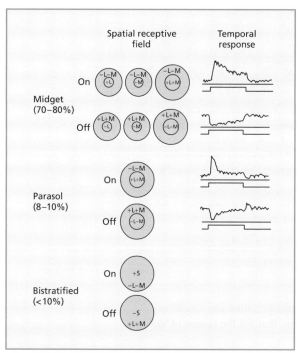

**FIG. 7.7** Summary of the spatial, spectral, and temporal response properties of the three major ganglion cell types. Percentages represent the relative preponderance of different cell types. L, M, and S refer to the cone classes providing inputs to each region of the receptive fields (L = long; M = medium; S = short); either excitatory (+) or inhibitory (−). Temporal responses show the effect of presenting a small spot of light at the centre of the receptive field for 450 ms (horizontal traces; re-plotted from de Monasterio, Gouras, & Tolhurst, 1976).

an evolutionary origin. The S cone pathway is present in all non-primate mammals, and may represent a very early mammalian colour coding circuit. The L and M pathway is mostly restricted to Old World monkeys and is associated with the more recent evolution of separate L and M cone types (Dacey, 2000).

Why is the red–green opponent system restricted to central vision? The answer may lie in the distribution of cone types on the retina, and how they connect to ganglion cells. Roorda, Metha, Lennie, and Williams (2001) created photographic images of the living human retina that revealed the spatial arrangement of S, M, and L cones. Photoreceptors are arranged in an approximately hexagonal lattice pattern.

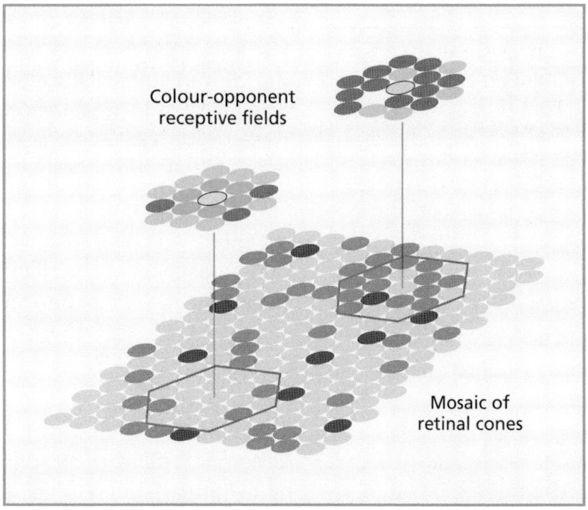

S cones appear to be distributed non-randomly, but are relatively rare. On the other hand, the distribution of M and L cones is essentially random, allowing clumps of cones of the same pigment type. There appears to be no special circuitry segregating L and M cone signals on their way to the ganglion cells in order to create clean spectrally opponent responses. Rather, spectral opponency may be a by-product of small receptive field sizes in central retina. Here, midget cell receptive fields are created from a dominant input from a single M or L cone at the centre of the receptive field, and weak non-selective inputs from M and L cones in the surround (horizontal and amacrine connections are not selective for cone type). This is sufficient to create strong red–green opponency (Lennie, Haake, & Williams, 1991). Figure 7.8 shows two midget receptive fields superimposed on the retinal mosaic from which they are drawn. The centre of both receptive fields is dominated by input from a single L cone. In the receptive field on the right, the surround is largely drawn from M cones, so the cell will show strong spectral opponency. The receptive field on the left shows surround inputs from L cones, and will therefore show weak spectral opponency. Further into the retinal periphery, ganglion cells connect with many tens of cones, again drawn randomly from M and L cones on the basis of their retinal distribution. Both centre and surround will include contributions from both L and M cones, so the receptive fields will lack wavelength selectivity. Although the scheme in Figure 7.8 is attractive in its simplicity, recent research shows that the origin of spectral opponency in the retina is still not fully understood (Reid & Shapley, 2002, Dacey & Packer, 2003).

**FIG. 7.8** Origin of spectral opponency in small midget ganglion cell receptive fields. Dominant centre input from a single photoreceptor and weak surround inputs from a random mixture of photoreceptor types are sufficient to confer spectral opponency (after Lennie, 2000). Key: dark grey = S cones; light grey = M cones; blue = L cones. Copyright © 2000 Elsevier. Reproduced with permission.

L cones outnumber M cones by a ratio of 1.6:1, but this ratio varies by at least a factor of four between individuals. Nevertheless, colour perception seems relatively stable across individuals (Lennie, 2000).

## Temporal response

The temporal response of a cell describes the time course of its activity following the appearance or disappearance of a stimulus. Midget and parasol cells have distinctively different temporal responses. Midget ganglion cells have a so-called *tonic* or **sustained temporal response**, which means that their level of activity remains at a relatively high level during the presence of a visual stimulus. Parasol ganglion cells have a *phasic* or **transient temporal response**, which means that they show a brief change in activity at stimulus onset and offset, but relatively little activity during constant stimulation. Figure 7.7 includes examples of midget and parasol temporal responses

**KEY TERMS**
**Sustained temporal response**: A change in response is sustained at a relatively high level for the whole duration of stimulation.
**Transient temporal response**: A change in response occurs only at the onset and offset of stimulation.

*What is the functional significance of a cell's temporal response?*

to a small spot of light presented in the centre of the receptive field for 450 ms (from de Monasterio et al., 1976). ON-centre cells respond with an increase in firing level, and OFF-centre cells respond with a decrease in firing level. Amacrine cell influences may play a role in generating the distinctive temporal responses of ganglion cells.

## Information processing by ganglion cells

Ganglion cell responses carry a very selective representation of the retinal image. Certain aspects of the image are preserved, while others are removed. In this sense ganglion cells act as information-processing filters.

### Spatial filtering

A ganglion cell's activity level reflects the combined responses of all the photo-receptors within its receptive field. Since small receptive fields sum over a smaller retinal area than large receptive fields, they can resolve higher levels of detail. This is illustrated in Figure 7.9.

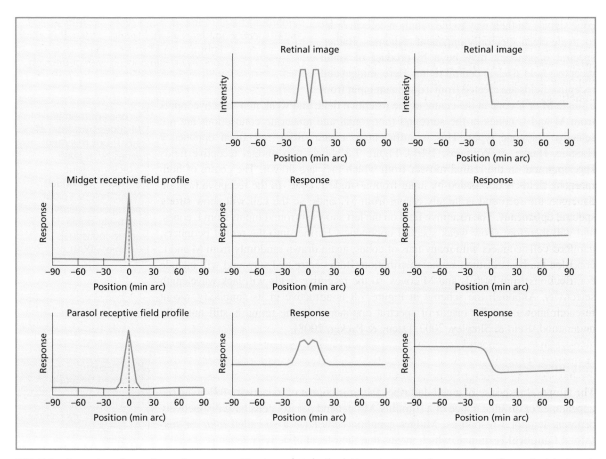

**FIG. 7.9** Examples of ganglion cell responses. The two plots in the leftmost column show cross-sections of midget and parasol spatial receptive fields (the same cells as plotted in Figure 7.6). The two plots in the top row show two stimulus profiles, a double-bar stimulus (left) and a step edge (right). Reading down from each stimulus, and across from each receptive field, the plot at each intersection shows the response of the receptive field to the respective stimulus.

The left-hand column shows the ON-centre midget and parasol receptive fields also plotted in Figure 7.6, this time as net response (the difference between excitation and inhibition at each point in the receptive field). The top row shows two retinal light distributions: a pair of thin bars (left), and a step change of intensity (right). The profiles below each retinal stimulus show the response of each receptive field type to the stimulus.

Consider first the response of the midget receptive field to the double-bar stimulus. The graph plots the response generated by receptive fields centred on each retinal position shown on the horizontal axis. Receptive fields positioned at the middle of each bar generate a high response, because the bright bar just fills the ON centre. Receptive fields positioned in the dark surround generate a lower level of response, since there is less light falling on them. The larger parasol receptive field's response to the double-bar stimulus is markedly different. The receptive field is so large that its response combines the two bars into one. In other words, the large receptive field filters out fine-scale detail in the image (the gap between the bars), and retains coarse-scale detail (the general shape of the pair of bars). The right-hand column in Figure 7.9 shows responses to a step edge. The parasol response is spread over a greater retinal area than the midget response. Because of this, large receptive fields are sometimes said to create **neural blur**.

> Centre–surround receptive fields are sometimes called edge finders, because they are described as responsive to edges but not to regions of even illumination. This description is only correct when there is perfect balance between the excitatory and inhibitory influences on the receptive field. Ganglion cell receptive fields are invariably weighted in favour of the centre, producing edge responses of the kind shown in Figure 7.9. The tutorial section of this chapter explains how receptive field profiles are defined mathematically, and how they are used to compute the activity levels shown in Figure 7.9.

## Chromatic filtering

The opponent nature of chromatically selective ganglion cell responses creates antagonistic pairs of colours that cannot co-exist. The antagonistic pairs isolate three dimensions in separate information processing channels, two **chromatic channels** and one **achromatic channel**:

*Relate channel structure to the theoretical principles introduced in Chapter 1.*

- Red versus green (midget ganglion cells)
- Blue versus yellow (bistratified ganglion cells)
- Dark versus light (parasol cells and midget cells).

The implication is that perception of colour along the red–green dimension is mediated by activity in the red–green channel. Similarly perception along the blue–yellow axis depends on activity in the blue–yellow channel, and perception of intensity is mediated by the achromatic channel. Chromatic opponency forms the basis of one theory of colour perception, known as *opponent-process* theory, which was actually developed long before ganglion cells were discovered. Chapter 12 provides a detailed discussion of this and other theories of colour perception.

**KEY TERMS**
**Neural blur**: The removal of spatial detail in neural responses, as a result of neural processes rather than optical effects.
**Chromatic channel**: A channel of processing in the visual system that conveys information about the chromatic or colour properties of the image.
**Achromatic channel**: A channel of processing in the visual system that conveys information about the luminance or light–dark properties of the image.

## Temporal filtering

The characteristically different temporal responses of parasol and midget cells (see Figure 7.7) have led to the view that there are two separate channels conveying temporal information to the brain. The two channels have become known as the parvo (P) and magno (M) systems, on the basis of the lateral geniculate neurons to which midget and parasol ganglion cells connect. The P system has sluggish, sustained temporal responses inherited from midget cells, and is supposed to convey information primarily about static form. The M system has fast, transient temporal responses inherited from parasol cells, and is supposed to convey information primarily about motion. The M versus P distinction is discussed in more detail later in the chapter.

### ON and OFF systems

It is important for the visual system to respond both to light increments and to light decrements. As we saw earlier, ON and OFF cells both respond to increments and decrements, but in opposite directions. For example, ON cells increase their firing rate and OFF cells decrease their firing rate in response to light increments in their receptive field. Since both cell classes respond to both directions of luminance change, why are separate ON and OFF systems required? In the absence of stimulation, spontaneous activity levels in ganglion cells are relatively low. Consequently, a given cell is much more able to convey information by raising its activity level than by lowering it. It therefore makes sense for both light increments and light decrements to be signalled by increases in activity. Light increments are signalled by ON cells, and decrements are signalled by OFF cells (Schiller, Sandell, & Maunsell, 1986).

## THE VISUAL PATHWAY

The fibres of retinal ganglion cells form the optic nerve. In all vertebrates these fibres terminate at six locations within the brain. Each termination site consists of a large agglomeration of neuronal cell bodies, often called a nucleus. The relative numbers of fibres arriving at each site vary across species. In primates the major projection is to the lateral geniculate nuclei, which receives approximately 90% of ganglion cell fibres. The remaining 10% is shared among the other sub-cortical nuclei, though most goes to the superior colliculi (Perry, Oehler, & Cowey, 1984). The importance of these minor projections should not be underestimated. Even 10% of optic nerve fibres exceeds the combined central projections from hearing, taste, and smell.

## DESTINATIONS OF OPTIC NERVE FIBRES

### Lateral geniculate nuclei

Two nuclei in the thalamus, known as **lateral geniculate nuclei** (LGN; also called the dorsal LGN or LGN$_d$) receive the major projection from the retina in primates (see Figure 7.1). LGN cell fibres project in turn to the cortical receiving area for vision, known as striate cortex or V1. Signals travelling along the path through the LGN to the cortex (the *geniculo-striate* pathway) are thought to be responsible for conscious visual awareness. This pathway is discussed in much more detail in a later section.

## Superior colliculi

Two nuclei in the midbrain known as the superior colliculi also receive major projections from the retina. It is the most important projection site in many non-primate species such as birds, reptiles, and fish. The superior colliculi are thought to be involved in integrating visual and auditory signals, and in directing visual attention.

## Suprachiasmatic nuclei

The suprachiasmatic nuclei form part of the hypothalamus, and project to the pineal gland. They are thought be the brain's "biological clock", regulating the daily rhythms of sleep and wakefulness. Visual input to the suprachiasmatic nuclei should allow the clock to remain synchronised to the cyclical variation in light levels at the earth's surface.

## Pretectum

The pretectum lies in the path of optic nerve fibres travelling towards the superior colliculi (in non-mammalian vertebrates the superior colliculus is know as the tectum). Neurons in the pretectum project to neurons in the Edinger-Westphal nucleus that play a role in controlling the constrictor muscle in the iris. Hence the pretectum is thought to be important for regulating pupil diameter.

## Pregeniculate

The pregeniculate in primates lies adjacent to the $LGN_d$, and probably corresponds to the ventral lateral geniculate nucleus ($LGN_v$) of other vertebrates. The function of the pregeniculate/$LGN_v$ remains mysterious. It does not project to the cortex, but to the suprachiasmatic nuclei, so may be involved in regulating the biological clock.

## Accessory optic system

Some optic nerve fibres branch away from the main tract to terminate in midbrain nuclei that form the accessory optic system. The precise function of the accessory optic system is not known, though it seems to play a role in stabilising the retinal image during head movements (Rodieck, 1998).

## THE GENICULO-STRIATE PATHWAY

## Representation of the visual field

### Binocular convergence

Figure 7.1 shows that in primates, as in many other predators, the two eyes face forward so their fields of view overlap substantially. Consequently, a given object will project images onto the retina of both the right eye and the left eye. For example, the words to the right of the word you are presently reading will project an image onto the outer (temporal) half of your left eye's retina, and onto the inner (nasal) half of your right eye's retina. Important information about depth and distance can be inferred from comparisons between the images projected onto the two eyes (see Chapter 10). The left eye's view of a given image feature must be compared to the right eye's view of the same feature in order to extract this information. The comparison is achieved by neurons in the visual system that receive signals from both eyes, so-called **binocular neurons**. These neurons are located in the visual cortex, as we shall see below. The representation of the visual field in the visual pathway is designed to achieve binocular convergence of signals from the two eyes onto cortical neurons.

Notice from Figure 7.1 that the left visual field (solid lines) is represented binocularly in the right cortical hemisphere. The right visual field (dashed lines) is represented binocularly in the left cortical hemisphere. The key to achieving binocular convergence is partial decussation.

### Partial decussation

When the optic nerve fibres from each eye meet at the optic chiasm (from the Greek letter *chi*, or X) half the fibres from each eye cross over to the other (contralateral) hemisphere of the brain, and half remain in the same hemisphere (ipsilateral), so achieving **partial decussation** or partial crossing-over. The eye of origin and retinal location of each ganglion cell's receptive field determine whether its fibre crosses over or not, as shown in Figure 7.1.

*Left visual field*  Fibres originating in the left visual field of each eye (solid lines in Figure 7.1) converge on the right hemisphere:

- Fibres in the left visual field of the left eye (nasal retina) cross over.
- Fibres in the left visual field of the right eye (temporal retina) do not cross over.

*Right visual field*  Fibres originating in the right visual field of each eye converge on the left hemisphere:

- Fibres in the right visual field of the left eye (temporal retina) do not cross over.
- Fibres in the right visual field of the right eye (nasal retina) cross over.

Consequently, the left LGN, and the cortex to which it projects, receive information from both eyes, but only from the right half of the visual field. The right LGN, and the cortex to which it projects, receive information from the left half of the visual field in both eyes.

## Structure of the LGN

### LGN layers

Figure 7.10 (top) is a cross-section through the LGN revealing its six major layers, numbered from 1 to 6. Layers 1 and 2 contain large cell bodies, so these layers are called *magnocellular* or **magno layers**. Layers 3 to 6 contain small cell bodies, so these layers are called *parvocellular* or **parvo layers**. Each major layer contains two sub-layers. The upper, *principal* sub-layer contains most of the cell bodies, and the lower *koniocellular* or **konio sub-layer** contains fewer, smaller cell bodies. Each sub-layer can be identified by a letter—P for principal parvo, M for principal magno, and K for konio—and a number between 1 and 6. So there is a total of 12 LGN layers—$M_1$ to $M_2$, $P_3$ to $P_6$, and $K_1$ to $K_6$ (bottom of Figure 7.10).

There are four important features of the LGN's layered structure: eye of origin, ganglion cell type, topography, non-retinal input.

---

**KEY TERMS**
**Binocular neuron**: A neuron that has a receptive field in each eye.
**Partial decussation**: Partial cross-over of each eye's optic nerve fibres in the visual pathway, so that half stay on the same side of the brain, and half cross over.
**Magno layers**: Layers in the LGN with large cell bodies; they receive projections from parasol ganglion cells.
**Parvo layers**: Layers in the LGN with small cell bodies; they receive projections from midget ganglion cells.
**Konio layers**: Sub-layers of LGN magno and parvo layers that contain the smallest cell bodies; they receive projections from bistratified ganglion cells.

---

The names attached to different layers are based on Latin or Greek words. Magnus means large and parvus means small in Latin; konis means dust in Greek. Fitzpatrick, Itoh, and Diamond (1983) found that average cell body size in LGN magno layers was 154 $\mu m^2$. Parvo cell bodies measured 119 $\mu m^2$, and cells in the intercalated or konio layers were 76 $\mu m^2$.

## Eye of origin

Each LGN cell within each major layer receives information originating from only one eye. With one exception, the eye of origin alternates in successive layers, as shown in the Figure 7.10. Cells in layers 1, 4, and 6 receive optic nerve fibres from the contralateral eye. Cells in layers 2, 3, and 5 receive optic nerve fibres from the ipsilateral eye.

## Ganglion cell type

There is a highly organised projection from different ganglion cell types to LGN layers. Although there is still some uncertainty about connections to the LGN, the following points appear to be well established:

- Midget ganglion cell fibres terminate in the four principal parvo layers, $P_3$–$P_6$.
- Parasol ganglion cell fibres terminate in the two principal magno layers, $M_1$–$M_2$.
- Small bistratified ganglion cell fibres terminate in two koniocellular layers, $K_3$ and $K_4$.

## Topography

The receptive fields of cells within each layer of the LGN are arranged topographically, creating a map of the visual field in each layer. Furthermore, the maps in different layers are in register. So the central visual field is represented near the centre of each layer. Consequently, if a small visual stimulus is presented at a particular location in the visual field, it will activate cells lying along a line passing through the layers of the LGN perpendicular to its surface (approximately parallel with the column of numbers in Figure 7.10, top).

## Non-retinal input

The retinal input to the LGN accounts for only 10% of the synapses on its neurons. Descending fibres from the visual cortex provide 30% of the input (Sillito & Jones, 2002). Cortical input is topographically organised, and different groups of cortical neurons provide input to the magno, parvo, and koniocellular layers of LGN. Other inputs to the LGN also arrive from midbrain sites such as the superior colliculus and reticular formation.

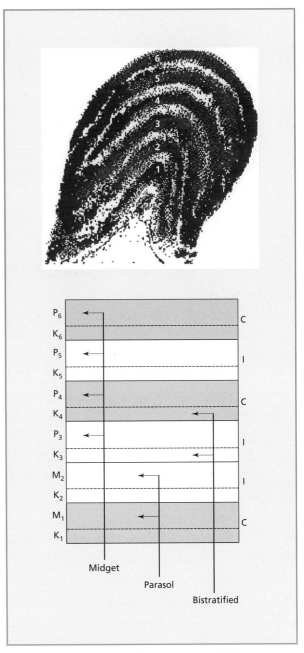

**FIG. 7.10**   The lateral geniculate nucleus (LGN). A cross-section through the LGN (top) reveals six major layers. The bottom two layers are magnocellular layers, because they contain large cell bodies; the top four layers are parvocellular layers because they contain small cell bodies. Each layer contains a principal sub-layer (labelled $M_1$ to $M_2$ and $P_3$ to $P_6$), and a koniocellular sub-layer (labelled $K_1$ to $K_6$). Eye of origin varies from layer to layer: layers receiving input from the contralateral eye (C) are shaded; the rest receive input from the ipsilateral eye (I).

## Signal processing in the LGN

No new response properties emerge at the level of the LGN. Cells have centre–surround receptive fields similar to those of the incoming optic nerve fibres. The preponderance of non-retinal inputs indicates that the function of the LGN is to modulate the flow of information from retina to cortex. Three particular functions have been proposed (Sillito & Jones, 2002):

● To sharpen spatial responses by modifying the centre–surround organisation of the receptive fields, perhaps increasing surround inhibition.
● To begin the process of integrating information across larger retinal areas by promoting synchronous activation of ascending LGN signals.
● To enhance the salience of sudden changes in stimulation by modulating the firing patterns of LGN neurons.

# THE VISUAL CORTEX

Much of the posterior half of the cerebral cortex is devoted to vision. Anatomical, electrophysiological, and brain-imaging studies have revealed at least 10 distinct areas, each with its own retinotopic map of the visual field. Area V1, also known as **striate cortex**, is the receiving area for LGN fibres. All the other areas (often called **"extrastriate" cortex**) largely depend on V1, either directly or indirectly, for their visual input. The next section discusses striate cortex in detail. Extrastriate cortex is discussed later in the chapter.

## STRIATE CORTEX

### Anatomical connections

*Layers*

Striate cortex is so called because of its characteristically striped appearance in anatomical sections, such as the example at the top right of Figure 7.11.

Striate cortex is approximately 1.5 mm thick, and is divided into six layers numbered from 1 (nearest the surface) to 6 (deepest). Layer 4 is actually sub-divided into separate sub-layers labelled 4A, 4B, 4Cα, and 4Cβ (see Figure 7.11).

*LGN inputs*

Fibres from the LGN terminate in different layers (Fitzpatrick et al., 1983):

● Magno fibres terminate primarily in layer 4Cα.
● Parvo fibres terminate primarily in layer 4Cβ.
● Konio fibres terminate in superficial layers 2 and 3.

*Internal connections*

There are rich interconnections between cells in different cortical layers, particularly from layer 4 cells to cells in layers 2 and 3, and from these superficial layers down to layers 5 and 6.

## Connections to extrastriate cortex

Fibres project from the striate cortex to several destinations:

- Cells in layers 2, 3, and 4B project to extrastriate cortex.
- Cells in layer 5 project to midbrain structures such as the superior colliculus and pons.
- Cells in layer 6 project to the LGN. Projections are highly selective, with cells in different parts of layer 6 projecting to different layers in the LGN.

Striate cortex also receives reciprocal connections from extrastriate cortex. The rich interconnections between cortical cells allow them to generate new forms of stimulus selectivity, particularly selectivity for spatial orientation, motion direction, binocularity, and wavelength.

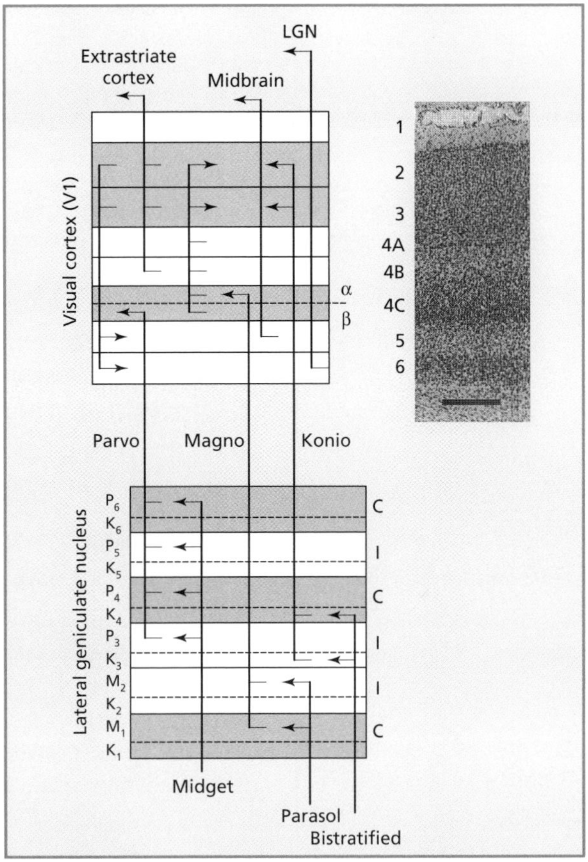

## Cell properties

Striate cortical cells have much larger receptive fields than LGN cells (Sceniak, Hawken, & Shapley, 2001; see Table 7.6 in the Tutorial section). Indeed the difference in receptive field size is so great that it cannot be explained solely by the spread of connections within striate cortex. Sceniak et al. (2001) suggest that feedback connections from extrastriate cortex play a role in shaping striate receptive fields. The relatively large receptive fields of cortical cells have a high degree of stimulus specificity.

**FIG. 7.11** Primary visual cortex, or V1, contains six anatomically distinct layers. Layer 4 is divided into four sub-layers (4A, 4B, 4Cα, 4Cβ). Parvo, magno, and konio divisions in the LGN project selectively to different layers. The predominant input is to layer 4C (magno to 4Cα and parvo to 4Cβ). Konio cells project to superficial layers. There are forward projections from V1 to extrastriate cortex, as well as descending projections to the LGN and the midbrain.

## Orientation tuning

The majority of cortical cells show selectivity for stimulus orientation. For a given cell, lines or bars at a specific orientation produce the greatest response. A change in orientation away from the cell's preferred orientation, even by a few degrees, produces a marked drop in response, as shown in Figure 7.12.

Orientation-tuned cells can be classified as either **simple** or **complex**, using Hubel and Wiesel's (1962) original criteria. Simple cells have receptive fields that can be mapped into excitatory and inhibitory zones just like retinal ganglion and LGN cells. Orientation tuning arises because the zones are elongated rather than circularly symmetrical (see Figure 7.12, top), so that the optimal stimulus is also elongated. The stimulus must be aligned appropriately with the cell's excitatory and inhibitory zones in order to produce a strong response. Complex cells respond to the same kinds of stimuli as simple cells, but their receptive fields are much larger, and they do not contain identifiable excitatory and inhibitory zones. Each cell's response does not depend critically on the precise position of

*What is the functional significance of cortical cell selectivity?*

**KEY TERMS**

**Simple cell**: An orientation selective cell in visual cortex with an elongated retinal receptive field containing excitatory and inhibitory zones.

**Complex cell**: A cell in visual cortex with a relatively large receptive field that does not contain identifiable excitatory or inhibitory zones, but nonetheless is orientation selective.

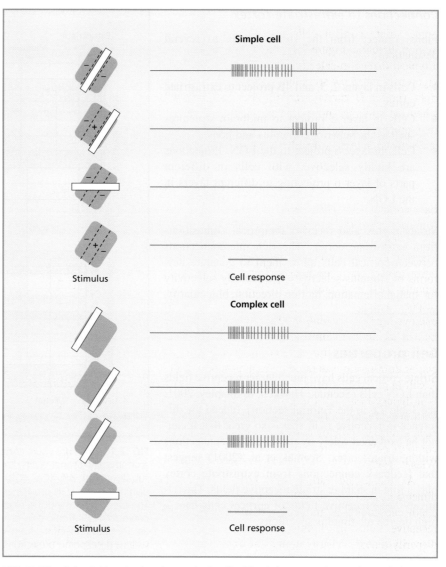

**FIG. 7.12**   Orientation tuning in cortical cells. The leftmost column shows bar stimuli at different orientations and positions, superimposed on a simple cell receptive field (top) and a complex cell receptive field (bottom). The trace adjacent to each stimulus shows neural activity as a function of time. The thick horizontal bars mark the duration of each stimulus. Simple cell receptive fields have elongated excitatory and inhibitory zones, and produce the strongest response to a line or edge at the optimal orientation and position. Different cells prefer different orientations. Complex cells also respond best at certain orientations, but their receptive fields cannot be mapped into excitatory and inhibitory regions. Their response does not depend critically on stimulus position.

Hubel and Wiesel (1962) also described a third, rare, class of cells called *hypercomplex*, whose response seemed to depend critically on stimulus length as well as orientation. More recent research indicates that some degree of length tuning is present in many cortical cells, and that some of these cells may actually be tuned to stimulus curvature rather than length. The "hypercomplex" label is no longer widely used.

the stimulus in the receptive field (see Figure 7.12, bottom). Complex cells are the most common type of cortical cell, accounting for over two-thirds of striate cells. Simple cells are relatively uncommon, at about one in ten striate cells (Hubel & Wiesel, 1968).

## Direction selectivity

Some striate cortical cells respond selectively to motion direction. Figure 7.13 shows the response of a typical **direction-selective cell**. The cell responds vigorously when the stimulus moves up towards the right (preferred direction), but does not respond when the stimulus moves in the opposite direction (non-preferred or null direction). Direction selectivity is discussed in greater detail in Chapter 11.

## Binocularity

Each cortical hemisphere receives signals originating from both eyes, by virtue of partial decussation in the visual pathway. A given cortical cell can be assessed in terms of its ability to respond to stimulation presented to each eye. Some cells respond equally well to stimulation of either eye. Others respond much more vigorously to stimulation of one eye than to stimulation of the other, a property known as **ocular dominance**. Hubel and Wiesel devised a classification scheme in which a cell's ocular dominance was rated on a seven-point scale. A cell in group 1 is influenced only by the contralateral eye, and a cell in group 7 is influenced only by the ipsilateral eye. Cells in group 4 are driven equally by both eyes. Figure 7.14 plots the relative proportions of striate cells belonging to each group, in monkey cortex. Simple cells tend to belong in groups 1 or 7, while complex cells are spread more evenly across ocular dominance groups (Hubel & Wiesel, 1968).

As mentioned earlier, binocularity is important for depth coding. Three-dimensional scenes project slightly different images to the two eyes, creating a depth cue known as **binocular disparity**. Some binocular cortical cells do have receptive fields in slightly different locations in the two eyes, making them disparity-tuned. Disparity tuning and depth coding are discussed in much more detail in Chapter 10.

## Wavelength

Our understanding of wavelength responses in striate cortex is still incomplete. It is clear, however, that a significant proportion of cortical cells show selective responses to wavelength. Johnson, Hawken, and Shapley (2001) found that 41% of striate cells gave chromatically opponent responses. Most of these cells responded equally well to luminance variation and to wavelength variation, and exhibited **double opponency**. This means that the cell has a spatially opponent receptive field containing excitatory and inhibitory zones, but spectrally opponent responses can be found in both zones. For example, a given cell's receptive field may have one zone in which it is excited by red and inhibited by green light, and an adjacent zone in which it is inhibited by red but excited by green light. The role of chromatically opponent cells in colour vision is discussed in Chapter 12.

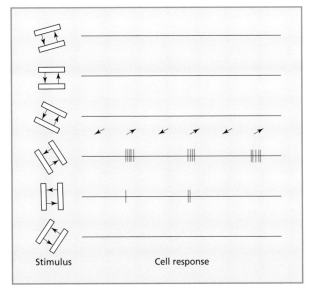

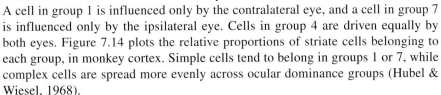

**FIG. 7.13**   Direction selectivity in cortical cells. The stimulus (leftmost column) was a bar that oscillated back and forth repetitively, shown by the arrows. The trace adjacent to each stimulus denotes neural response. The cell responded only during phases when the bar moved up and to the right.

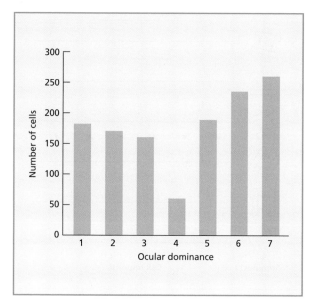

**FIG. 7.14** The distribution of ocular dominance in striate cortical cells. Cells in group 1 are driven only by the contralateral eye; cells in group 7 are driven only by the ipsilateral eye; cells in group 4 are driven equally by the two eyes. The great majority of cells show a clear preference for one eye or the other (data from Hubel & Wiesel, 1968).

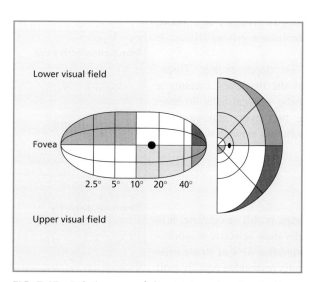

**FIG. 7.15** Relative area of the striate cortex devoted to different regions of the visual field. The right half of the visual field is shown on the right, sub-divided into zones centred on the fovea. The surface of the contralateral striate cortex is shown on the left, marked and shaded to match the visual field diagram. A very small central portion of the visual field occupies a large proportion of cortical surface.

### Origin of cortical cell receptive field properties

Hubel and Wiesel favoured a hierarchical scheme to explain the construction of cortical receptive fields. A simple cell with an orientation-tuned receptive field could receive inputs from several LGN cells whose concentric receptive fields are aligned on the retina to form a row at a specific orientation. Cells with large, complex receptive fields could be constructed using inputs from a group of simple cells with overlapping, small retinal receptive fields that have the same orientation tuning. Although attractive, there is no direct evidence in favour of the hierarchical scheme, and some contradictory evidence. As mentioned at the start of this section, Sceniak et al. (2001) found that cortical receptive fields are too large to be explained by simple convergence of LGN receptive fields. In addition, several lines of evidence indicate that complex receptive fields are created in parallel with simple receptive fields, rather than in series (see Wilson, Levi, Maffei, Rovamo, & De Valois, 1990). It is likely that striate receptive fields emerge from a combination of complex circuitry within striate cortex, and reciprocal connections with extrastriate cortex.

## Functional architecture

The previous section detailed some of the stimulus specificities that emerge in individual striate cortical cells. In this section we consider how these neurons are distributed within the cortical tissue, an aspect of the cortex known as its functional architecture. Are cells that share certain stimulus specificities grouped together, and if so, how? It is important to bear in mind that a given cell is selectively responsive to a combination of stimulus attributes, such that the optimal stimulus must have an appropriate retinal location, orientation, binocularity, and (frequently) motion direction. If grouping principles do apply to the layout of cells in the cortex, we must also consider how the ordered arrangements of different specificities intersect.

### Topography

It should come as no surprise now to learn that cells are distributed across the cortex so that their receptive field locations form an ordered topographic map of the visual field. Figure 7.15 (right) shows the right half of the visual field. Central, foveal locations are at the centre of the bull's-eye pattern at 0°. The black circle shows the location of the optic disc, where optic nerve fibres leave the eye. Figure 7.15 (left) shows the surface of the contralateral (left) striate cortex in humans, marked with the visual field location of receptive fields at each point on the cortical surface. Although the visual field is mapped in a very orderly way, the map is hugely distorted. About half of the cortical surface is devoted to the central 10° of the visual field, which occupies only 1% of the visual field.

## Layers

As mentioned earlier, the cortex can be divided horizontally (parallel to its surface) into six layers. Hubel and Wiesel (1962, 1968) found that different cell types tended to be more numerous in some layers than in others. Cells in layer 4 tended to have either circularly symmetrical receptive fields, or elongated "simple" receptive fields. Cells in the more superficial (1–3) and deeper (5–6) layers tended to have "complex" receptive fields. Wavelength selective cells are found in all layers, but are concentrated especially in layers 2 and 3 (Johnson et al., 2001). This organisation makes sense in the context of the anatomical connections between layers described earlier.

## Columns

Hubel and Wiesel (1962, 1968) discovered that the cortex can also be divided vertically (perpendicular to its surface) into columns on the basis of receptive field properties. They found columnar organisation of two response properties, **ocular dominance** and **orientation**. Cells lying along a line drawn vertically through the cortex have similar ocular dominance and orientation preferences. Moving horizontally across the cortex, ocular dominance shifts gradually and repetitively between left-eye and right-eye dominant. At the same time, preferred orientation changes progressively. Ocular dominance columns are much wider than orientation columns. A distance of 1 mm on the cortical surface is sufficient to cover a complete ipsilateral–contralateral cycle of ocular dominance, and a total shift in preferred orientation of 180°.

Figure 7.16 (top) is a schematic depiction of striate cortical architecture, showing the columnar arrangement of orientation and ocular dominance

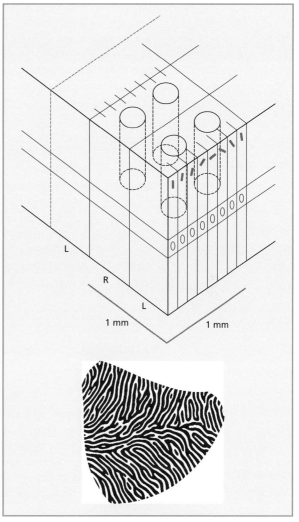

**FIG. 7.16**   Top: Schematic depiction of a striate cortical hypercolumn, covering a 1 mm × 1 mm region of the cortical surface. Cells are grouped according to their ocular dominance, with the dominant eye alternating roughly every millimetre. Preferred orientation changes progressively but more rapidly than ocular dominance, so that a complete set of orientation preferences occupies approximately 1 mm of cortical distance. Cytochrome oxidase blobs are found in superficial layers, centred on the ocular dominance columns. Bottom: View of the cortical surface from above, showing how the tops of ocular dominance columns form a swirling, striped pattern not unlike a fingerprint.

*Compare the architecture of striate cortex with the architecture of somatosensory cortex outlined in Chapter 2.*

columns. Orientation columns generally cross the borders between ocular dominance columns perpendicularly, and converge in pinwheel-like patterns at the centres of ocular dominance columns (not shown in Figure 7.16). Viewed from above the surface of the cortex, the tops of ocular dominance columns form a striped pattern across the cortex, as shown in Figure 7.16 (bottom).

## Blobs

Layers 2 and 3 of striate cortex contain clusters of cells, called **blobs**, that were identified over 20 years ago (Wong-Riley & Carroll, 1984) using a histological stain that detects high levels of metabolic activity. These blobs have been the subject of intense scrutiny, and some controversy, since their discovery. They are cylindrical pillars roughly 0.5 mm apart, and arranged in parallel rows centred on ocular dominance columns (Livingstone & Hubel, 1982; see Figure 7.16). Cells in the blobs receive afferents from koniocellular LGN fibres, as well as from other cells within striate cortex. The receptive fields of cells within the blob regions are often poorly tuned for orientation, and many are colour selective (Landisman & Ts'o, 2002).

## Hypercolumns

Although receptive fields are laid out on the cortex topographically, the local scatter in receptive field position is such that one must traverse a distance of approximately 2 mm on the cortical surface to move from one region of the visual field to the next. This distance is sufficient to include one complete cycle of ocular dominance, and a full range of preferred orientations. Hubel and Wiesel (1974) therefore argued that a 1 mm$^2$ region of cortex can be viewed as a functional unit called a **hypercolumn** that contains all the neural machinery required to analyse a particular region of the visual field. In central vision, each hypercolumn would cover an area of the visual field spanning about 0.25° or less. In peripheral vision (20° eccentricity), each hypercolumn would cover an area over 30 times this size.

## EXTRASTRIATE CORTEX

Beyond striate cortex, a large number of visually responsive cortical areas have been identified on the basis of several criteria, including topographic organisation, anatomical connections, and cell response properties. Figure 7.17 illustrates the 30 cortical areas identified in the macaque monkey.

Some of these areas have also been identified in human cortex using brain-imaging techniques (Tootell, Hadjikhani, Mendola, Marrett, & Dale, 1998). The functional significance of these diverse areas is still largely unclear. Some have attempted to organise the visual areas hierarchically on the basis of anatomical connections, to reveal the order in which visual processing advances from one area to the next (Felleman & van Essen, 1991). However, with approximately 300 projections between different areas, the number of possible hierarchical schemes is extremely large, making it difficult to draw firm conclusions about hierarchical processing, at least beyond the first five or six areas (Hilgetag, O' Neill, & Young, 1996). Some hints about the role of areas closest to V1 can be gleaned from their detailed properties,

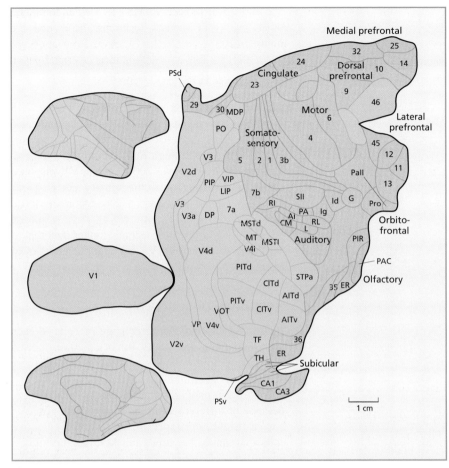

There is still some debate about the best way to characterise areas V3, V3A, and VP. Some authors view V3 and VP as a single area, since they both share borders with V2, and cover the lower and upper visual field respectively. Others prefer to include V3A in the grouping. For simplicity, all three areas will be treated as a single complex labelled V3/V3A in this discussion.

**FIG. 7.17**   Cortical areas of the macaque monkey that contain cells responsive to visual stimuli (shaded areas re-drawn from Felleman & van Essen, 1991). The small insets show an intact brain, viewed from each side. The large map represents a flattened view of one hemisphere. Copyright © 1991 Oxford University Press. Reproduced with permission.

some of which are summarised in Figure 7.18 (based on Lennie, 1998 and Schmolesky et al., 1998).

## Size

Each cortical area in Figure 7.18 is drawn in proportion to its relative area. On this basis alone it can be seen that areas V1, V2, and V4 are responsible for the bulk of early visual processing.

## Connectivity

The values adjacent to the arrows connecting areas in Figure 7.18 show estimates of the percentage of fibres in each projection pathway (calculated in the manner described by Lennie, 1998). V1 projects primarily to V2. V2 in turn has roughly equal projections to V3/V3A and to V4. V3/V3A projects predominantly to V4. The largest projection from V4 is to IT. Area MT receives very small projections from V1,

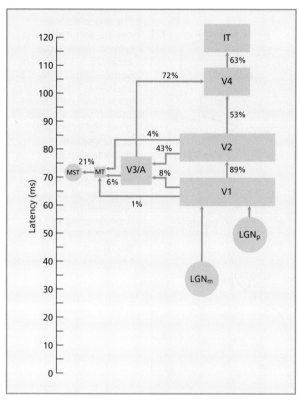

**FIG. 7.18**   Some distinctive features of the largest visual cortical areas. The relative size of the boxes reflects the relative area of different regions. The arrows labelled with percentages show the proportion of fibres in each projection pathway. The vertical position of each box represents the response latency of cells in each area, as measured in single-unit recording studies. V3/A includes areas labelled as V3, V3A, and VP in Figure 7.17; IT includes areas labelled as PITd, PITv, CITd, CITv in Figure 7.17.

V2, and V3. It projects to MST as well as to several other areas (not shown), including the frontal eye fields (FEF).

## Response latency

The vertical position of each area in Figure 7.18 represents the response latency of its cells (indicated by the scale on the left), as reported by Schmolesky et al. (1998) from single unit recordings (see also Lamme & Roelfsema, 2000). Area V1 responds earliest, as befits its role as the primary receiving area for LGN fibres. However, a succession of dorsal areas (V3/V3A, MT, and MST) have response latencies only a few milliseconds longer than that of V1. More ventral areas (V2, V4, and IT) have slower latencies.

## Response properties

Figure 7.19 shows the percentage of cells in each area displaying selectivity for orientation, motion direction, colour, and binocular disparity. All these selectivities are found in all areas. Areas V1, V2, and V3 are broadly similar in terms of the preponderance of different stimulus selectivities. Area V4 has a higher proportion of colour selective cells than any other area, and MT has the highest proportions of motion and disparity selective cells.

Notice that the values in Figure 7.19 exceed 100%. This means that cortical cells have multiple stimulus specificities. A given cell may show selective responses to both orientation and movement direction, or binocular disparity. So although cells show a high degree of specificity, they cannot be viewed as feature detectors that respond only in the presence of a single stimulus attribute.

Although cells in different areas have broadly similar stimulus specificities, closer inspection reveals some marked differences. For instance, receptive field sizes are substantially larger in extrastriate cortex, as shown in Table 7.3 (figures from Lennie, 1998).

Extrastriate cells also show more sophisticated response properties than striate cells. Motion selective cells in MT, for instance, respond to more complex motion properties than striate cells (discussed in more detail in Chapter 11). Cells in MST appear to prefer large-field motion such as expansion or rotation (Tanaka & Saito, 1989). Cells in IT prefer highly specific spatial patterns, such as geometrical shapes or even faces (Tanaka, 1993; Perrett, Rolls, & Caan, 1982).

## Architecture

Detailed study of extrastriate cortex has revealed highly ordered architectural features. Cytochrome oxidase staining of V2 reveals **stripes**, in contrast to the blobs of

V1 (Tootell, Silverman, De Valois, & Jacobs, 1983). The projection from V1 cells to V2 cells is still not clear (Xiao & Felleman, 2004). MT cells appear to be grouped according to speed preference (Liu & Newsome, 2003) and disparity tuning (De Angelis & Newsome, 1999), whereas V2 cells show some grouping according to colour preference (Xiao, Wang, & Felleman, 2003).

## Lesion studies

Several studies have used reversible lesions, in which area V1 is temporarily deactivated by cooling before neural responses in adjacent areas are recorded. Results of these experiments are consistent with the pattern of connections shown in Figure 7.19. Deactivation of V1 causes a complete loss of responsiveness in V2 and V4 neurons, and partial loss in V3 (Girard, Salin, & Bullier, 1991). There is relatively little change in MT responses during V1 deactivation (Girard, Salin, & Bullier, 1992).

Behavioural studies shed light on the perceptual consequences of cortical lesions (e.g. Newsome, Wurtz, Dursteler, & Mikami, 1985; Merigan, Nealey, & Maunsell, 1993; Merigan, 1996):

- V1 lesions result in a complete loss of visual function in the affected area.
- V2 lesions produce impaired form and texture discrimination.
- V4 lesions also produce impaired form and texture discrimination.
- MT lesions cause pronounced deficits in motion perception.

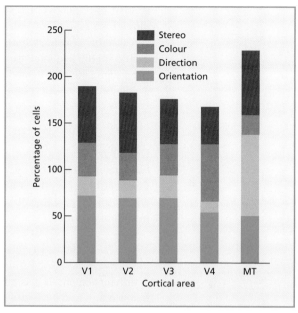

**FIG. 7.19**  Percentage of cells in each of the first five cortical areas selective for orientation, motion direction, colour, and binocular disparity. Total percentage in each area exceeds 100% because cells respond selectively to more than one stimulus attribute. The full range of stimulus specificities is found in all areas, though relative proportions vary from area to area.

**TABLE 7.3 RELATIVE RECEPTIVE FIELD SIZE IN DIFFERENT CORTICAL AREAS**

| Relative RF size | Cortical area |
| --- | --- |
| 1 | V1 |
| 2–3 | V2 |
| 4–5 | V3/VP |
| 5–6 | V4 |
| 7–10 | MT |

## The "two streams" theories of cortical function

The dominant view of visual cortical function is that beyond V2 it forms two parallel **streams of processing**, each containing several successive stages of analysis. One stream analyses movement and depth, and courses through more **dorsal** visual areas including V3, MT, and MST. The other stream analyses spatial form, and courses through several **ventral** areas including V4 and IT. Several more specific versions of the two streams theory have been proposed.

### Magno versus parvo

Some authors argue that the motion and form streams are a direct continuation of the magno and parvo division that can be traced right down to the parasol and midget cells of the retina. There is some evidence for segregation of signals as they pass through V1 and V2 towards the two streams: Layer 4B in V1 has projections to thick cytochrome oxidase stripes in V2, which then project to area MT; layers 2/3 in V1 project to thin and interstripe regions in V2, which then project to area V4. However, strict segregation of magno and parvo signals does not seem to occur in V1 (Nealey & Maunsell, 1994).

### "What" versus "where"

One of the earliest theories preferred to characterise the difference between the two streams as a "what" versus "where" distinction (Ungerleider & Mishkin, 1982). The ventral stream deals with what objects are, while the dorsal stream deals with where objects are. Recall from Chapter 5 that a similar division has been proposed in auditory cortex.

### "Perception" versus "action"

A different emphasis was offered by Goodale and Milner (1992). Rather than viewing both streams as contributing to conscious visual awareness, they argued that only the ventral stream subserves conscious vision. Information in the dorsal pathway is used for the unconscious control of actions, such as movements of the body guided by visual input.

### Evaluation

A division into two cortical streams of processing is consistent with the features summarised in Figure 7.18, but there is no general consensus as to which form of the two-streams theory offers the best view of visual cortex. Much of the continuing debate revolves around the interpretation of neuropsychological case studies, and controversial evidence from visual illusions (reviewed in Carey, 2001). A more detailed discussion can be found in Bruce, Green, and Georgeson (2003). The following observations offer some hints:

1.  There is a large disparity in size between areas in the two streams. The total cortical area devoted to the ventral stream areas in Figure 7.18 (V4, IT) is 2.5 times larger than the area devoted to the dorsal stream areas (V3/A, MT, MST). This indicates that the dorsal stream has a more specialised and/or simpler function than the ventral stream.
2.  There is a marked difference in latency between the two streams. The three dorsal areas have almost identical, fast latencies. Responses in ventral areas are up to twice as slow. This indicates that the two streams do not act in parallel, at least in the sense of response timing, and hints that the dorsal stream carries more time-critical information.
3.  There are extensive reciprocal connections between areas forming the two streams, indicating a high degree of cross-talk between them.
4.  There is no clear dichotomy between the streams in terms of cell response properties. The full range of stimulus specificities is found in both streams, though in different proportions. Along with the previous observation, this hints that the two streams are not strictly segregated modules dedicated to processing separate stimulus attributes.

# CHAPTER SUMMARY

The visual system can be divided into three major components: the retina, the visual pathway, and the visual cortex.

## THE RETINA

The retina is a layered network of cells lining the inner surface of each eye:

- The outer nuclear layer contains over 120 million photoreceptor cells that generate graded changes in neurotransmitter release in response to changes in illumination.
- The inner nuclear layer contains a complex network of bipolar, horizontal, and amacrine cells through which the photoreceptor responses converge onto ganglion cells.
- The ganglion cell layer contains 1 million cell bodies of ganglion cells, whose axons form the optic nerve.
- Two major types of ganglion cell, midget and parasol, both have opponent centre–surround receptive fields, with either an ON centre or an OFF centre. Centre response is mediated by bipolar cells, and surround response is mediated by horizontal cells.
- Midget, parasol, and bistratified receptive fields vary in their spatial, temporal, and spectral response.

## THE VISUAL PATHWAY

The visual pathway carries responses from the retina to the visual cortex:

- In mammals the major termination site for optic nerve fibres is the lateral geniculate nucleus (LGN) in the thalamus.
- Due to partial decussation, fibres carrying responses from the left visual field of each eye terminate in the right LGN, and responses from the right visual field arrive in the left LGN.
- Each LGN contains four magnocellular layers and two parvocellular layers, each separated by a koniocellular layer.
- Parvo, magno, and konio layers receive selective projections from midget, parasol, and bistratified ganglion cells respectively.
- LGN cells project to the primary receiving area in visual cortex, V1.
- The preponderance of non-retinal input to the LGN indicates that its main function is to modulate incoming responses on the way to the cortex.

## THE VISUAL CORTEX

- The visual cortex comprises the major receiving area V1, also known as striate cortex, and numerous extrastriate areas.
- Cortical cells respond selectively to stimulus orientation, movement direction, colour, and binocular disparity.
- Extrastriate cortical cells have larger receptive fields and more complex responses than striate cells.

- In all cortical areas, cells are distributed in a highly ordered pattern.
- The precise function of many extrastriate areas is not clear, but a broad division between two parallel streams is a central element in current theories. One stream includes a series of ventral areas, and the other passes through more dorsal areas.
- One major theory characterises the different roles of the two streams in terms of information regarding "what" versus "where" objects are in the image; another argues for a distinction in terms of information for perception versus action.

# TUTORIALS

## WHY DO WE NEED TO KNOW ABOUT VISUAL PHYSIOLOGY?

This chapter has presented a very detailed introduction to the physiology of the visual system. Since this book is really concerned with visual perception rather than visual physiology, it is reasonable to ask why a knowledge of physiology is important in order to explain vision.

One way to answer this question is to look back at theories of vision that pre-dated single-cell studies. The anatomy of the connections between eye and brain has been known since the turn of the 20th century. However, knowledge of neural circuit layout alone is not enough to infer function. Before recordings of activity in individual cells became available in the 1950s, theories of perception were inspired by anatomy. The brain was known to contain huge numbers of cells, massively interconnected (but only over short distances) in circuits that are similar over the whole cortex. Studies of localised brain damage (e.g. following gunshot wounds) also showed that the visual cortex was mapped topographically. These facts inspired the *Electrical Field Theory* of perception. Visual patterns were thought to set up corresponding fields of electrical activity across the surface of the cortex. Perceptual organisation in complex displays was said to be governed by interactions between these current fields. Experimental tests of the theory included attempts to short-circuit the electrical fields by pinning metallic strips across the surface of the cortex in rhesus monkeys, and then performing tests of visual functioning (e.g. Lashley et al., 1951).

Of course we now know that, despite anatomical uniformity, functional properties vary markedly from cell to cell and from area to area in the cortex. The key word is specialisation rather than uniformity of function. The known functional properties of cells, and the architecture of the cortex, place fundamental constraints on the nature of perceptual theories. Later chapters will discuss in some detail theoretical approaches to understanding, for example, spatial vision, colour vision, and motion perception. All these theories are intimately linked to our knowledge of the underlying physiology and would not exist in their present form with this knowledge.

A second way to answer the question would be to attempt an explanation for a well-known phenomenon in visual perception that avoids all reference to physiological entities such as photoreceptors, receptive fields, stimulus-specific neurons, or cortical processing.

# MODELLING CELL RESPONSES

Mathematical techniques are available that allow us to compute precisely how an array of cells in the visual system responds to a specific visual stimulus. Computational modelling is a crucial tool in vision research, because it reveals exactly which aspects of stimulation are preserved in cell responses, and which are discarded. It provides a rigorous method for comparing the predictions of theoretical models against actual data (obtained either from cells, or from behaving organisms). This tutorial offers a general introduction to the field of computational modelling, at least in the context of relatively low-level cells in the visual system, which makes minimal assumptions about prior mathematical knowledge.

Cells in the visual system can be viewed as simple **information processing devices**, consisting of an input, an output, and a process that transforms one into the other. In order to compute the output (response) of a given cell to a given visual stimulus, we need to specify:

- *Input*—A description of the stimulus.
- *Process*—A description of the cell's receptive field, and a mathematical process for applying the receptive field to the stimulus.

## Visual stimuli

Stimuli are represented by arrays of numbers, corresponding to the intensity of the image at regular intervals across the retina. A one-dimensional cross-section through a visual image can be represented using a one-dimensional array of numbers. For example, Table 7.4 shows the intensity of the image in the region of the double bar plotted in Figure 7.9.

Intensity is constant at 100 (arbitrary) units, except at the locations of the bars (5 to 10, and −5 to −10′ arc) where intensity rises to 200 units.

## Receptive fields

A one-dimensional cross-section through a receptive field can also be represented by an array of numbers. Table 7.5 shows the responsiveness profile of the midget receptive field plotted in Figure 7.9.

How was this responsiveness profile generated? As shown in Figure 7.6, receptive fields can be decomposed into opposing centre and surround components. Single-cell studies beginning with Rodieck (1965) have shown that each response component can be approximated quite well using a bell-shaped,

> **KEY TERM**
> **Information processing device**: A "black box" description of a physical system in terms of an input signal, an output signal, and an intervening process that converts one into the other.

**TABLE 7.4 INTENSITY PROFILES IN A DOUBLE-BAR LUMINANCE PROFILE**

| Position (min) | −40 | −35 | −30 | −25 | −20 | −15 | −10 | −5 | 0 | 5 | 10 | 15 | 20 | 25 | 30 | 35 | 40 |
|---|---|---|---|---|---|---|---|---|---|---|---|---|---|---|---|---|---|
| Intensity | 100 | 100 | 100 | 100 | 100 | 100 | 200 | 200 | 100 | 200 | 200 | 100 | 100 | 100 | 100 | 100 | 100 |

**TABLE 7.5 RESPONSIVENESS PROFILE OF A MIDGET RECEPTIVE FIELD**

| Position (min) | −20 | −15 | −10 | −5 | 0 | 5 | 10 | 15 | 20 |
|---|---|---|---|---|---|---|---|---|---|
| Response $R(x)$ | −0.003 | −0.007 | −0.013 | −0.008 | 0.98 | −0.008 | −0.013 | −0.007 | 0 |

or Gaussian, distribution (probably because of the way dendrites spread out across the retina from their cell bodies). The responsiveness of a centre–surround ganglion cell can therefore be calculated as the difference between two Gaussian functions (often called a **difference-of-Gaussians**, or *DoG* function). A convenient mathematical formula for a DoG function is:

$$R(x) = \exp^{-(x/\sigma_c)2} - [A \cdot (\sigma_c/\sigma_s)^2 \cdot \exp^{-(x/\sigma_s)2}]$$

where $x$ represents retinal position. Only three parameters, $\sigma_c$, $\sigma_s$, and $A$, are needed to specify the receptive field profile. $\sigma_c$ and $\sigma_s$ are **space constants** that determine the width of the centre and surround components respectively. The scaling factor $A$ sets the balance between the centre and surround components. If $A$ equals 1.0, then the centre and surround are perfectly balanced. This means that there is no net response from the cell when the whole receptive field is evenly illuminated. If $A$ is less than 1.0, then the response is biased in favour of the centre, so the cell does respond to even illumination.

Estimates of the three parameters are available in the single-cell recording literature. Table 7.6 shows some typical values, based on the means or medians of samples of cells studied in each of the research papers. Estimates vary due to differences between species, cell classes, visual stimuli, retinal location, and even the anaesthetic employed.

The profiles plotted in Figures 7.6 and 7.9 were calculated using averages of the estimates provided by Croner and Kaplan (1995) and Lee, Kremers, and Yen (1998). For the midget cell, $\sigma_c = 2.33$ min arc, $\sigma_s = 14.59$ min arc, and $A = 0.80$. For the parasol cell, $\sigma_c = 6.73$ min arc, $\sigma_s = 30.25$ min arc, and $A = 0.59$.

**KEY TERMS**
**Difference-of-Gaussians (DoG)**: A mathematical description of a receptive field profile as the difference between two Gaussian or normal distributions; one is excitatory and the other is inhibitory.
**Space constant**: The parameter specifying the width of a Gaussian or normal distribution; mathematically it corresponds to the standard deviation of the distribution.

**TABLE 7.6 REPRESENTATIVE ESTIMATES OF CONCENTRIC RECEPTIVE FIELD PARAMETERS**

| Paper | Cell type | $\sigma_c$ (min arc) | $\sigma_s$ (min arc) | $(\sigma_c/\sigma_s)$ | $A$ |
|---|---|---|---|---|---|
| Rodieck (1965) | Cat ganglion | 35.4 | 106.2 | 0.33 | 0.80 |
| Enroth-Cugell and Robson (1966) | Cat X ganglion | 23.2 | 156.4 | 0.15 | 0.90 |
| Linsenmeier et al. (1982) | Cat X ganglion | 21.6 | 86.4 | 0.25 | 0.94 |
|  | Cat Y ganglion | 52.8 | 79.2 | 0.66 | 0.75 |
| Derrington and Lennie (1984) | Macaque parvo LGN | 1.68 | 10.14 | 0.17 | 0.65 |
| Croner and Kaplan (1995) | Macaque midget ganglion | 3.0 | 25.2 | 0.12 | 0.73 |
|  | Macaque parasol ganglion | 10.2 | 48 | 0.21 | 0.31 |
| Lee et al. (1998) | Macaque midget ganglion | 1.55 | 3.97 | 0.31 | 0.80–0.92 |
|  | Macaque parasol ganglion | 3.35 | 12.5 | 0.26 | 0.80–0.92 |
| Sceniak et al. (2001) | Macaque V1 | 60 | 126 | 0.48 | 0.63 |

As mentioned earlier in the chapter, computational models frequently use receptive fields that are perfectly balanced ($A = 1.0$), because they respond only in the region of luminance edges. However, balanced cells are encountered only rarely in single-cell studies, as is clear from the values for $A$ in Table 7.6. The example responses used here are more representative of realistic cells.

## Receptive field responses

Table 7.5 quantifies the responsiveness of the cell at each position in its receptive field. The centre of the receptive field falls at position 0 min arc. The response of the cell to a stimulus that covers its receptive field can be calculated by summing the responses at each point in the receptive field. The response at each point is found by multiplying the responsiveness at that point by the intensity of the stimulus at the same point.

The second row of Table 7.7 shows the intensity profile of a step-edge stimulus, with higher intensity to the left of position zero. The third row is the responsiveness of a receptive field centred at zero. Values represent responsiveness at each location in the receptive field (taken from Table 7.5). The fourth row is the product of stimulus intensity and responsiveness at each position. The fifth row contains the net response of the receptive field centred at position zero (obtained by summing all the responses in the fourth row). It is possible to compute the summed response of cells with receptive fields centred at each other location using the same procedure. The bottom row shows net response of receptive fields at different locations on either side of the edge. The leftmost and rightmost responses show the response of receptive fields positioned wholly on the light side and wholly on the dark side of the edge, respectively. Two points are worthy of note:

- First, the receptive field does respond to even illumination, since the leftmost response is higher than the rightmost response (due to the receptive field's imbalance in favour of the receptive field centre).
- Second, the influence of the edge extends some distance on either side. Only at $+/-20$ min arc does response settle down to a stable value. The receptive field introduces neural blur, as described earlier in the chapter.

**TABLE 7.7  COMPUTED RESPONSE OF CONCENTRIC RECEPTIVE FIELDS TO A STEP EDGE (CONVOLUTION)**

| Position (min) | −40 | −35 | −30 | −25 | −20 | −15 | −10 | −5 | 0 | 5 | 10 | 15 | 20 | 25 | 30 | 35 | 40 |
|---|---|---|---|---|---|---|---|---|---|---|---|---|---|---|---|---|---|
| Intensity | 200 | 200 | 200 | 200 | 200 | 200 | 200 | 200 | 100 | 100 | 100 | 100 | 100 | 100 | 100 | 100 | 100 |
| Responsiveness at 0 | | | | | −0.003 | −0.007 | −0.013 | −0.008 | 0.98 | −0.008 | −0.013 | −0.007 | 0 | | | | |
| Response | | | | | −0.6 | −1.4 | −2.6 | −1.6 | 98 | −0.8 | −1.3 | −0.7 | −0.3 | | | | |
| Sum | | | | | | | | | 88.7 | | | | | | | | |
| Response sum at each position | 183.6 | 183.6 | 183.6 | 183.6 | 183.9 | 184.6 | 185.9 | 186.7 | 88.7 | 89.5 | 90.8 | 91.5 | 91.8 | 91.8 | 91.8 | 91.8 | 91.8 |

The mathematical procedure illustrated in Table 7.7 is known as **convolution**. It is the standard technique for modelling receptive field responses, and is easy to apply using standard spreadsheet formulas such as SUMPRODUCT(). Some of the plots in Figure 7.9 are graphical representations of the arrays in Table 7.7.

## Modelling with more dimensions

The stimulus and receptive field profiles used so far have been cross-sections showing intensity or responsiveness along one dimension of space. Natural images and receptive fields actually vary in three dimensions; two spatial dimensions (*x* and *y*), and one temporal dimension (*t*). The computational method described in the previous section extends readily to two or three dimensions. Consider a two-dimensional image, which contains variation of intensity in both *x* and *y*. Table 7.8 shows a simple 2-D image containing a tilted light bar.

The responsiveness of a receptive field can also be described in two dimensions. Indeed centre–surround receptive fields are 2-D by definition. The upper 9 × 9 cells of Table 7.9 show a simple version of a small cortical receptive field in which the excitatory and inhibitory zones confer a preference for the same orientation as the line in Table 7.8. Excitation exactly balances inhibition (the summed responsiveness of the cell is zero).

We can compute the response of this receptive field to the stimulus in Table 7.8 using convolution, as before:

- The centre of the receptive field is superimposed on a specific cell of the stimulus array.
- Response at each point is computed by multiplying stimulus intensity in each cell by responsiveness in the corresponding cell of the receptive field.

**TABLE 7.8 A SIMPLE 2-D IMAGE CONTAINING A TILTED LIGHT BAR**

| | *x*-position | | | | | | | | | |
|---|---|---|---|---|---|---|---|---|---|---|
| | 200 | 100 | 100 | 100 | 100 | 100 | 100 | 100 | 100 | 100 |
| | 100 | 200 | 100 | 100 | 100 | 100 | 100 | 100 | 100 | 100 |
| | 100 | 100 | 200 | 100 | 100 | 100 | 100 | 100 | 100 | 100 |
| | 100 | 100 | 100 | 200 | 100 | 100 | 100 | 100 | 100 | 100 |
| *y*-position | 100 | 100 | 100 | 100 | 200 | 100 | 100 | 100 | 100 | 100 |
| | 100 | 100 | 100 | 100 | 100 | 200 | 100 | 100 | 100 | 100 |
| | 100 | 100 | 100 | 100 | 100 | 100 | 200 | 100 | 100 | 100 |
| | 100 | 100 | 100 | 100 | 100 | 100 | 100 | 200 | 100 | 100 |
| | 100 | 100 | 100 | 100 | 100 | 100 | 100 | 100 | 200 | 100 |
| | 100 | 100 | 100 | 100 | 100 | 100 | 100 | 100 | 100 | 200 |

**TABLE 7.9 RESPONSE PROFILES OF SIMPLE ORIENTATION-SELECTIVE RECEPTIVE FIELDS**

| | | |
|---|---|---|
| 2 | −1 | −1 |
| −1 | 2 | −1 |
| −1 | −1 | 2 |
| | | |
| −1 | −1 | 2 |
| −1 | 2 | −1 |
| 2 | −1 | −1 |

**KEY TERM**
**Convolution**:
A mathematical procedure used to combine a receptive field profile with a stimulus profile, in order to model the response of the receptive field.

**TABLE 7.10 RESULT OF CONVOLVING THE UPPER RECEPTIVE FIELD IN TABLE 7.9 WITH THE IMAGE IN TABLE 7.8**

| | | | | | | | |
|---|---|---|---|---|---|---|---|
| 600 | −200 | −100 | 0 | 0 | 0 | 0 | 0 |
| −200 | 600 | −200 | −100 | 0 | 0 | 0 | 0 |
| −100 | −200 | 600 | −200 | −100 | 0 | 0 | 0 |
| 0 | −100 | −200 | 600 | −200 | −100 | 0 | 0 |
| 0 | 0 | −100 | −200 | 600 | −200 | −100 | 0 |
| 0 | 0 | 0 | −100 | −200 | 600 | −200 | −100 |
| 0 | 0 | 0 | 0 | −100 | −200 | 600 | −200 |
| 0 | 0 | 0 | 0 | 0 | −100 | −200 | 600 |

**TABLE 7.11 RESULT OF CONVOLVING THE LOWER RECEPTIVE FIELD IN TABLE 7.9 WITH THE IMAGE IN TABLE 7.8**

| | | | | | | | |
|---|---|---|---|---|---|---|---|
| 0 | −200 | 200 | 0 | 0 | 0 | 0 | 0 |
| −200 | 0 | −200 | 200 | 0 | 0 | 0 | 0 |
| 200 | −200 | 0 | −200 | 200 | 0 | 0 | 0 |
| 0 | 200 | −200 | 0 | −200 | 200 | 0 | 0 |
| 0 | 0 | 200 | −200 | 0 | −200 | 200 | 0 |
| 0 | 0 | 0 | 200 | −200 | 0 | −200 | 200 |
| 0 | 0 | 0 | 0 | 200 | −200 | 0 | −200 |
| 0 | 0 | 0 | 0 | 0 | 200 | −200 | 0 |

- Overall response is computed by summing responses at each point.
- This procedure is repeated at each location in the stimulus array.

Table 7.10 shows the convolution output (the location of the line is shown by white cells). The balanced receptive field produces zero response in locations where it is covered uniformly, but a very high response at the location of the line. For comparison, Table 7.11 shows the response of the lower receptive field in Table 7.9, whose optimal orientation is perpendicular to the line. In this case there is no response at the location of the line, and weak, inconsistent responses nearby.

These examples illustrate how to perform computational modelling in two spatial dimensions. But natural images vary over time as well, when objects in the scene move. The temporal response of a receptive field can be specified by an array representing responsiveness as a function of time after stimulus onset. The response plots in Figure 7.7 are taken from arrays of numbers representing responses at different time intervals. It is therefore possible to model cell responses to stimuli that vary over time, as well as over space. A comprehensive model would perform convolutions in all three dimensions ($x$–$y$–$t$). Researchers in motion perception often find it sufficient to compute responses to motion over just two-dimensions, the time dimension plus one spatial dimension ($x$–$t$ space). Chapter 11 describes $x$–$t$ space in much more detail.

# CHAPTER 8

## CONTENTS

# Spatial vision

## INTRODUCTION

Chapter 7 surveyed the neural structures that subserve vision. All perceptual experience depends on the functioning of these structures. Certain basic phenomena in spatial vision can be linked directly to the underlying neural structures. We know, for example, that vision at high light levels is mediated by cones, while vision at low light levels is mediated by rods. Several aspects of vision at different light levels can be related to the properties of the cone and rod photoreceptor systems. This chapter begins by discussing some of these fundamental perceptual phenomena. They will provide a platform in the perceptual domain on which we can build later discussions of more complex phenomena in spatial vision, as well as phenomena associated with motion and colour perception.

## FUNDAMENTAL FUNCTIONS

### PHOTOPIC AND SCOTOPIC VISION

As Table 8.1 shows, rod-mediated vision at low light levels is called **scotopic vision**. Cone-mediated vision at high light levels is called **photopic vision**. The differing properties of the two photoreceptor systems have several consequences for vision at different levels of illumination, summarised in the bottom four rows of the table.

**TABLE 8.1 DIFFERENCES BETWEEN SCOTOPIC AND PHOTOPIC VISION**

| | Scotopic vision | Photopic vision |
|---|---|---|
| Photoreceptors | Rods (120,000,000) | Cones (6,000,000) |
| Light levels | Below 0.01 cd/m$^2$ | Above 10 cd/m$^2$ |
| Dark adaptation | Slow (35 min) | Fast (10 min) |
| Colour vision | Monochromatic | Trichromatic |
| Peak spectral sensitivity | 507 nm | 555 nm |
| Peak spatial and temporal sensitivity | 1 cpd low-pass below 3Hz | 3 cpd 8 Hz |

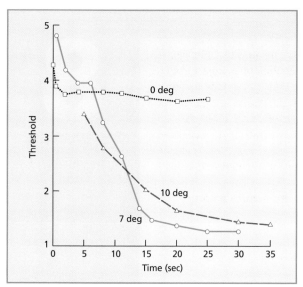

**FIG. 8.1** Dark adaptation curves re-plotted from Pirenne (1962) Figures 1, 7, and 8. The solid line shows results using a 3° diameter spot viewed at an eccentricity of 7° (both rods and cones); the dotted line shows results using a 2° spot at an eccentricity of 0° (cones only); and the dashed line shows results using a 2° spot at an eccentricity of 10° (rods only). Threshold is expressed in picolamberts (1 lambert = 3183 cd/m²). The vertical position of the 7° data has been shifted to facilitate comparison with the other data.

## Dark adaptation

The shift from photopic vision during during daylight to scotopic vision after sunset takes over half an hour to complete. So when moving abruptly from daylight into a dark room such as a movie theatre, we initially experience blindness. Very little of the visual scene in the theatre is perceptible at first, but more detail gradually becomes visible. The process of adjusting to dark conditions is known as dark adaptation.

The two photoreceptor systems adapt at different rates. Cones adapt more rapidly than rods, so if one measures the time course of dark adaptation using a method that allows contributions from both rods and cones, the dark adaptation curve has a characteristic scalloped shape. The solid line in Figure 8.1 shows such a dark adaptation curve, obtained by measuring the detectability of a small spot of light placed 7° into the periphery (which contains both rods and cones). When rod and cone contributions are isolated, the two limbs of the dark adaptation curve are revealed.

The dotted line shows results when the experiment is repeated in the rod-free fovea, and the dashed line shows results in the periphery at 10° eccentricity, where cones are scarce. When the process of dark adaptation is incomplete (after 5 to 10 minutes of adaptation, or around dusk), neither system of photoreceptors is operating at its peak efficiency. Subjectively, the world takes on a murky, indistinct character at these so-called **mesopic** light levels.

## The Purkinje shift

Figure 6.20 in Chapter 6 showed the differing spectral sensitivities of the rod and cone photoreceptors. Rods are most sensitive to light wavelengths in the region of 507 nm, whereas cones are maximally sensitive in the region of 555 nm. This difference in maximum sensitivity has consequences for the appearance of coloured surfaces at different illumination levels. In photopic conditions, a surface emitting wavelengths near 555 nm will appear brighter than one emitting wavelengths near 507 nm, because cones are more sensitive to wavelengths of 555 nm. In scotopic conditions, wavelengths near 507 nm will appear brighter, since their perception is mediated by rods. This shift in brightness is called the Purkinje shift, after the Bohemian physiologist J. E. Purkinje who first observed it in 1825.

Figure 6.20 also reveals why vehicle instrument panels are often illuminated by red light at night. Long wavelengths are visible to the high-acuity cone system, provided that intensity is high enough. They fall beyond the rod system's sensitivity range, so do not affect the driver's state of dark adaptation, and his or her ability to see in the darkness outside.

**KEY TERM**
**Mesopic vision**: Vision at ambient light levels intermediate between photopic and scotopic levels, typical of dusk, mediated by both rods and cones.

*Think of other differences between rod and cone systems that might affect driving performance.*

# SPATIAL CONTRAST SENSITIVITY

Spatial vision relies fundamentally on the detection of spatial features in the image. We would not be able to perform everyday tasks, such as recognition of an object from its outline shape, or interpretation of road traffic signs, without some representation in the visual system of spatial image features. Spatial features are defined by spatial variations of image intensity. A simple measure of the salience of a spatial feature is the contrast between its brightest and darkest parts (contrast was defined more precisely in Chapter 6). Our present understanding of how the visual system builds representations of spatial features began with studies of the minimum amount of contrast in a simple spatial pattern required for an observer to detect its presence. The standard laboratory stimulus for measuring contrast detection thresholds is the **luminance grating**.

## Luminance gratings

Luminance gratings contain alternating bright and dark bars. Four defining properties of a grating are its *contrast*, *spatial frequency*, *orientation*, and *phase* (illustrated in Figure 8.2).

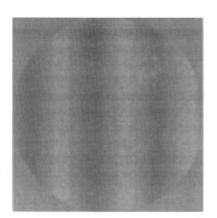

**FIG. 8.2**  Stimulus dimensions of luminance gratings. The two left-hand gratings differ in luminance contrast, with the lower contrast at the bottom. They also differ in spatial phase, as revealed by the misalignment of their bars. The two left-hand gratings have a low spatial frequency, while the two right-hand gratings have medium (top) and high (bottom) spatial frequencies. The two right-hand gratings differ in orientation.

### Contrast

Contrast relates to the magnitude of the intensity difference between the lightest part of the luminance distribution (peak) and the darkest part (trough). The lower left grating in Figure 8.2 has low contrast, and the upper left grating has high contrast. Contrast can vary between 0 and 1.0. A contrast of zero corresponds to a uniform field (no difference between peak and trough in the luminance distribution), and very high contrast patterns approach a contrast of 1.0 (contrast can only reach 1.0 if the darkest part of the luminance distribution has a luminance of zero). The formula for calculating contrast can be found in Chapter 6.

### Spatial frequency

The **spatial frequency** of a grating relates to the fineness of its bars, since it specifies how many bars the grating contains per unit of distance. The two left-hand gratings in Figure 8.2 have a low spatial frequency, and the right-hand gratings have a high spatial frequency. We saw in Chapter 6 that distances in retinal images are expressed in degrees of visual angle. Spatial frequency is therefore defined as the number of grating cycles per degree of visual angle, where one cycle of the grating is the distance from a given point on the waveform to the nearest corresponding point (e.g. between adjacent peaks). The fingers of an outstretched hand held at arm's length create a grating pattern with a spatial frequency of 0.25 cycles per degree (cpd); each finger subtends approximately 2°, so adjacent fingers (one cycle of your hand grating) are roughly 4° apart.

### Orientation

Orientation relates to the slant of the grating's bars. Two gratings in Figure 8.2 are vertical, one is horizontal, and the fourth has an orientation of −45° with respect to vertical.

> Psychophysical experiments often use *sinusoidal* gratings in which luminance varies smoothly from bright to dark and back again, with a profile that conforms to a mathematical sine function. You may recall that sine waves were also discussed in Chapter 4 in the context of sound waves (see Figure 4.6). To learn more about sinusoidal gratings, and why they are used so frequently in experiments, refer to the tutorial section at the end of the chapter.

*What is the auditory equivalent of a sine wave grating?*

### Phase

Phase relates to the position of the bars in the grating with respect to some fixed point on a display surface, or relative to the bars of another grating. The two vertical gratings on the left of Figure 8.2 differ in phase, since their bars are in different relative positions. Phase is usually specified in phase angle. One complete cycle of a grating corresponds to 360°. So a phase difference of, say, 180° corresponds to a difference in relative position of one half a cycle. The gratings on the left of Figure 8.2 differ by 180° of phase; bright bars in the top grating line up with dark bars in the bottom grating.

## Contrast thresholds for gratings

Grating sensitivity at a given spatial frequency is established by measuring the minimum amount of contrast required for an experimental observer reliably to discriminate the grating from a uniform field. In a classic psychophysical experiment, Campbell and Robson (1968) generated a grating pattern on a display screen much

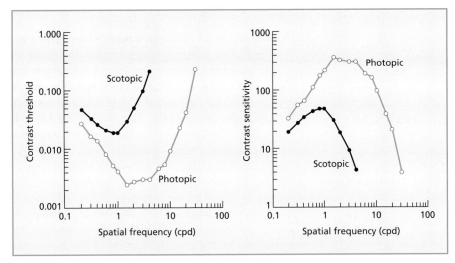

**FIG. 8.3**   Grating sensitivity, as measured in psychophysical threshold experiments. The left-hand graph shows the luminance contrast required to detect the presence of a grating, as a function of its spatial frequency and mean luminance. The subject requires least contrast to detect gratings at medium spatial frequencies. The right-hand graph re-plots the data in terms of contrast sensitivity (1/contrast) as a function of spatial frequency. Data are taken from Campbell and Robson (1968).

like a television. At each of a range of spatial frequencies, the observer adjusted the contrast of the grating until the pattern was barely detectable. The mean of either five or ten such settings defined the observer's contrast threshold for that spatial frequency (page 153).

Figure 8.3 (left) plots contrast threshold as a function of spatial frequency at two levels of illumination. In photopic conditions (500 cd/m$^2$; open symbols) the observer required least contrast to detect gratings of 3 cpd, but could not detect gratings higher than about 40 cpd whatever their contrast. In borderline scotopic conditions (0.05 cd/m$^2$; closed symbols) more contrast was needed to detect gratings at any frequency. Thresholds were lowest at 1 cpd, and the high frequency cut-off (beyond which gratings were no longer visible at any contrast) fell to about 8 cpd. These curves have been replicated in numerous studies.

## Contrast sensitivity

Contrast threshold values are often converted into contrast sensitivity values by calculating the reciprocal of **contrast threshold** (1/contrast). For example, a threshold contrast of 0.05 becomes a **contrast sensitivity** of 20, and a threshold of 0.2 becomes 5. The right-hand graph of Figure 8.3 plots the data in the left-hand graph in terms of contrast sensitivity. These plots are called **contrast sensitivity functions**, or CSFs. The main advantage of plotting data in terms of CSFs is that higher sensitivities produce higher values in the graph.

## Origins of the spatial contrast sensitivity function

What determines the shape of the CSF? Sensitivity is governed by two factors: optical limitations and neural responses.

Since the advent of computer-controlled psychophysical techniques, the preferred method of measuring thresholds is the Method of Constant Stimuli. See the tutorial section of Chapter 1.

**KEY TERMS**
**Spatial contrast threshold:** The minimum contrast between the lightest and darkest parts of a pattern required for it to be reliably detected by an observer; lower values indicate better performance.
**Spatial contrast sensitivity:** The reciprocal of spatial contrast threshold (1/threshold); higher values indicate better performance.
**Contrast sensitivity function (CSF):** A graph of spatial contrast sensitivity to luminance gratings, plotting sensitivity as a function of grating spatial frequency.

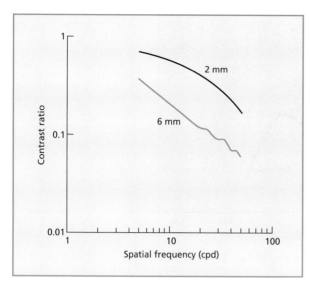

**FIG. 8.4** Optical transfer functions of the human eye, at two pupil diameters. Each line shows the ratio between contrast in a grating stimulus and contrast in its image, as a function of stimulus spatial frequency. Ratios close to 1.0 indicate that the stimulus is transmitted with relatively little attenuation. Ratios close to zero indicate that the stimulus is severely attenuated during its passage through the system. The optics of the eye act as a low-pass filter. Low spatial frequencies are transmitted well, but attenuation increases progressively as spatial frequency increases. Image quality is generally higher at the smaller pupil diameter, as indicated by the higher contrast ratios. Data based on Ijspeert, Van Den Berg, and Spekreijse (1993).

*Why does pupil diameter affect the OTF?*

## Optical limitations

In Chapter 6 we discovered that all optical systems suffer from diffraction and aberrations, which introduce image blur. The image of a very thin bright line is spread over some distance in the image to form a line spread function, as shown in Figure 6.18. If a second line is placed sufficiently close to the first, then their blurred images merge into each other; the two lines are not resolved. Similarly, gratings of sufficiently high spatial frequency disappear entirely from the image because their bars are too close together. The ability of an optical system to resolve a high contrast grating of a given spatial frequency is assessed by comparing the original contrast of the grating with the contrast present in its image. The ratio between the contrast of the grating's image and its original contrast specifies how well the optical system transmits the grating. **Contrast ratios** close to 1.0 indicate near-perfect transmission; ratios near zero indicate that the grating is very poorly resolved by the optical system. Figure 8.4 plots contrast ratio as a function of spatial frequency for the human eye at two pupil diameters, one typical of photopic intensities (2 mm) and the other typical of scotopic intensities (6 mm). These plots are called **optical transfer functions**. Notice that progressively more contrast is lost from the image as spatial frequency increases. The optical transfer function clearly sets an upper limit on the highest spatial frequencies that human observers can detect. Although the upper limit of the CSFs in Figure 8.3 is reasonably close to the limit imposed by optics, the decline in sensitivity at high frequencies is much steeper than that attributable to optics.

## Neural responses

The shapes of the CSFs in Figure 8.3 are very different from the optical transfer functions in Figure 8.4. Not only is the high frequency decline in sensitivity steeper than that predicted by the optics, but there is a marked decline in low frequency sensitivity even though low frequencies are preserved well in the optical image. These differences are due to the neural machinery used by the observer to detect the presence of the gratings.

As we saw in the previous chapter, the response of a neuron in the visual system depends on how well its retinal receptive field matches the spatial pattern in the image (see Figures 7.6 and 7.12). Many neurons in the early stages of visual analysis (at least up to striate simple cells) have receptive fields made up of excitatory and inhibitory sub-regions. A grating of a given spatial frequency will selectively activate cells whose receptive field sub-regions match the width of its bars. As Figure 8.5 illustrates, a low spatial frequency grating (left) will activate large receptive fields well (a bright bar fills the excitatory centre), but produces little response in small

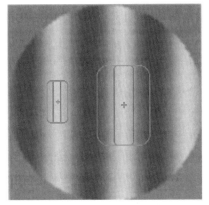

**FIG. 8.5** Spatial frequency selectivity in cortical cell receptive fields. The left-hand panel shows a low spatial frequency grating, and the right-hand panel shows a high spatial frequency grating. Two receptive fields are shown in each panel, one small and one large. Each receptive field will only generate an excitatory response if more light falls on its centre than on its surround. The small receptive field is well matched to the width of the bars in the high frequency grating, but is swamped by the bars of the low frequency grating. The large receptive field, on the other hand, is best suited to the low frequency grating.

receptive fields (a bright bar fills the whole receptive field). On the other hand, a high spatial frequency grating (right) will be ineffective for large receptive fields (no difference in average illumination between the centre and flanks), but will drive small receptive fields very well. The shape of the CSF is presumed to reflect the responsiveness of the underlying receptive fields. From the CSFs in Figure 8.3 we can infer that:

1.  There are fewer, less responsive receptive fields present at the extreme sizes (very small and very large), resulting in the inverted-U shape of the CSF.
2.  Receptive field sizes are larger in scotopic conditions, since peak sensitivity occurs at a lower spatial frequency in scotopic conditions than in photopic conditions. This may reflect the greater role played by parasol ganglion cells at low light levels (see Table 7.2 and Figure 7.6).

## TEMPORAL CONTRAST SENSITIVITY

Natural visual images are never entirely stationary on the retina. Our eyes move incessantly, and real-world objects have a tendency to move either under their own steam or due to the effect of gravity. It is therefore important to establish how well the visual system responds to images that vary over time—its **temporal contrast sensitivity**. The simplest way to measure temporal sensitivity is to present an observer with a small flickering light, and find the smallest amount of flicker that the observer can detect. In other words, we find the smallest luminance contrast between the bright phase and the dark phase of the flicker that is required for the observer to just detect that the light is flickering rather than steady. Sensitivity has been found to depend on the rate of flicker, usually called the **temporal frequency** of the light.

Figure 8.6 illustrates different flicker rates in a small bright spot. The intensity of the spot is shown at several different times during the course of one second. In

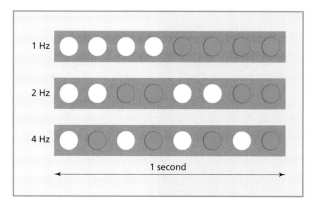

**FIG. 8.6**    An illustration of flicker rate in a small bright spot. The spot alternates in intensity between light and dark. The rate of alternation defines its flicker temporal frequency. When each light and dark phase lasts 500 ms (top), one cycle of alternation lasts 1 s, so temporal frequency is 1 Hz. When each light and dark phase lasts 125 ms (bottom), one cycle lasts 250 ms, so temporal frequency is 4 Hz (four cycles per second).

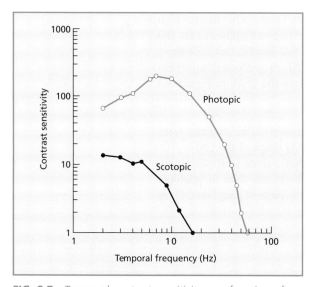

**FIG. 8.7**    Temporal contrast sensitivity as a function of flicker rate, at two illumination levels. Sensitivity is highest (in other words, thresholds are lowest) at a flicker rate of approximately 8 Hz in photopic conditions. Data are re-plotted from de Lange (1958).

**KEY TERM**
**Temporal contrast sensitivity function.**
A graph of temporal contrast sensitivity, plotting sensitivity as a function of flicker temporal frequency.

the top row the spot is bright for 500 ms, and dark for 500 ms. In the middle row the spot is bright (or dark) for periods of 250 ms, and in the bottom row the spot is bright (or dark) for periods of 125 ms. Flicker rate is expressed as cycles per second, or hertz, where one cycle is a single alternation from bright to dark. The lights in the three rows have flicker rates of 1, 2, and 4 Hz reading from top to bottom.

## Temporal contrast sensitivity function

When temporal sensitivity is measured at a range of flicker rates, the results can be plotted in a **temporal contrast sensitivity function**, as shown in Figure 8.7 (from de Lange, 1958). The figure shows sensitivity at two different illumination levels: photopic (159 cd/m²; open symbols), and borderline scotopic (0.06 cd/m²; closed symbols). Sensitivity declines rapidly at high temporal frequencies, and frequencies above 50 Hz are not visible at any contrast. Peak sensitivity at high intensities occurs at approximately 8 Hz, and sensitivity drops away gently at lower frequencies.

## Origins of the temporal contrast sensitivity function

The shape of the temporal contrast sensitivity function is determined entirely by neural responses in the visual system. Rods and cones have different temporal responses, as shown in Figure 7.4 in the previous chapter. Both receptor types contribute to retinal ganglion cells, and the complex neural circuitry associated with these cells has a major bearing on their temporal response (Masland, 2001). For example, differences in the timing of excitatory and inhibitory inputs to a cell will influence how its response fluctuates over time. So even at the ganglion cell level, temporal responses represent a complex interaction between multiple inputs. Temporal responses at the next level in the neural hierarchy, the LGN, will show additional influences as a result of descending inputs from the cortex. Further modifications to temporal responses occur in the cortex, due to intra-cortical circuitry.

Psychophysically measured temporal sensitivity therefore represents the combined effect of multiple neural processing stages. A clearer understanding of the origin of the contrast sensitivity function emerges when one considers temporal sensitivity and spatial sensitivity together—*spatiotemporal sensitivity*.

## SPATIOTEMPORAL SENSITIVITY

The previous two sections have shown how we can investigate spatial sensitivity and temporal sensitivity using very similar techniques. Both involve the measurement of contrast thresholds for a periodic stimulus. In the case of spatial sensitivity, the stimulus is periodic over space (a grating). In the case of temporal sensitivity, the stimulus is periodic over time (a flickering light). Contrast sensitivity in the two domains looks very similar. Figures 8.3 and 8.7 show that in both cases sensitivity is optimal at intermediate frequencies, declines rapidly at higher frequencies, and declines more gradually at lower frequencies. The link between the spatial and temporal domains is closer still. In both, the subject's task is simply to detect the presence of a stimulus. One can therefore measure sensitivity to stimuli that contain both spatial *and* temporal periodicity (**spatiotemporal contrast sensitivity**; see overleaf for key term definition).

### Stimuli

Spatiotemporal sensitivity is measured with a flickering grating. The alternating black and white bars of the grating define its spatial periodicity. Over time, each light bar gradually becomes dark at the same time as each dark bar becomes light, so the grating reverses in contrast. The bars then reverse in contrast again to return to their original intensity, as shown at the top of Figure 8.8. The rate at which each bar completes one cycle of contrast reversal defines the temporal frequency of the grating. Notice that a horizontal slice through the **space–time plot** (see overleaf for key term definition) in Figure 8.8 represents a spatial pattern at an instant in time, and shows the spatial periodicity of the grating. A vertical slice through the *space–time* plot represents a temporal pattern at a given location, and shows the temporal periodicity of the grating.

### Sensitivity

Experiments to measure spatiotemporal sensitivity have found that the spatial and temporal properties of the grating interact: spatial contrast sensitivity depends on the grating's temporal frequency, and vice versa. Figure 8.8 plots contrast sensitivity as a function of spatial frequency for gratings at four different temporal frequencies, taken from Robson (1966). The

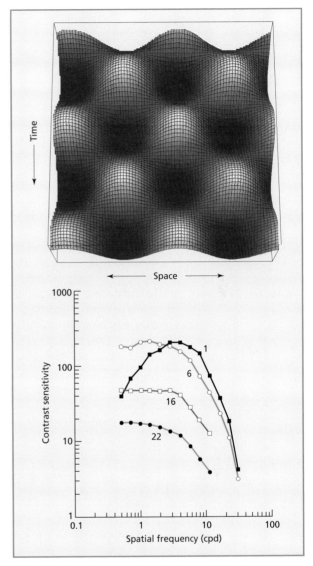

**FIG. 8.8** Spatiotemporal contrast sensitivity. Top: Space–time plot of a spatial grating that repetitively reverses in contrast over time. The grating's spatial frequency is defined by the rate of contrast alternation across space (horizontal slices through the panel). The grating's flicker temporal frequency is defined by the rate of contrast alternation across time (vertical slices through the panel). Bottom: Contrast sensitivity for flickering gratings as a function of their spatial frequency (horizontal axis) and temporal frequency (different curves), re-drawn from Robson (1966). Spatial sensitivity is band-pass at low temporal frequencies (filled squares), but low-pass at high temporal frequencies (filled circles).

low temporal frequency curve (filled squares) is similar to that shown in Figure 8.3, with a pronounced peak at medium spatial frequencies (known as band-pass).

However at the highest temporal frequency (filled circles), spatial sensitivity becomes low-pass.

## Origins of variation in spatiotemporal sensitivity

We saw earlier that neural factors account for the shape of the spatial and temporal CSFs. The interaction between spatial and temporal frequency evident in Figure 8.8 can also be attributed to the properties of visual neurons. There are two alternative accounts of how the properties of centre–surround receptive fields can explain the **spatiotemporal CSF**. One account is based on changes in the receptive field organisation of a single cell population, and the other is based on differing responses of two distinct populations of centre–surround cells.

### Receptive field organisation

We saw in the previous chapter that centre–surround receptive fields can be broken down into the separate contributions from their centre and surround. Figure 7.6 showed that each component conforms to a normal or Gaussian spatial distribution. Excitation and inhibition tail off gradually from their maximum values at the centre of the receptive field. The net response of the receptive field is given by the difference between the two distributions. Figure 8.9 (left) shows another example of centre, surround, and net responses. The centre and surround components have different widths, so they respond to different ranges of spatial frequency. Both have a low-pass frequency response, but the centre responds to higher frequencies than the surround. The black and dotted lines in Figure 8.9 (right) show the spatial frequency

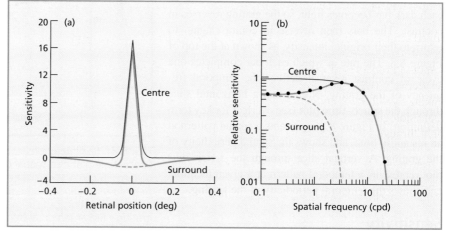

**FIG. 8.9** Decomposition of centre–surround receptive fields into centre and surround components (left) that have different spatial frequency responses (right). The centre is narrower, and therefore responds to higher spatial frequencies. The overall shape of the receptive field, and its spatial frequency response (thick lines), is given by the difference between the centre and surround responses (left). The spatiotemporal contrast sensitivity function shown in Figure 8.8 can be explained by an alteration in the relative weights of centre and surround components at different temporal frequencies, either in a single population of cells or in separate populations of cells. Equal weighting between the centre and surround produces narrow frequency selectivity, whereas unequal weights produce broad, lower-pass selectivity. (Based on Bruce et al., 2003, Figure 2.1, p. 41.) Copyright © 2003 Psychology Press.

response of each component. The difference between them (thick blue line) has a band-pass response.

This explanation of the spatiotemporal CSF assumes that the balance between excitatory and inhibitory components varies with temporal frequency (Kelly, 1985). At low temporal frequencies, the two components have similar weight, so the receptive field has a band-pass characteristic (filled squares in Figure 8.8). Inhibition is less effective at high temporal frequencies. The influence of the surround becomes weaker, so the low-pass spatial response of the centre becomes dominant.

Evidence in support of this theory comes from single-unit recording data. Derrington and Lennie (1984) measured the contrast sensitivity of individual primate parvo and magno LGN cells. They found the minimum contrast of a flickering grating required to produce a criterion level of response in each cell, as a function of spatial and temporal frequency. Both parvo and magno cells showed a band-pass spatial frequency response at low temporal frequencies, and a low-pass temporal response at high temporal frequencies. The optimum spatial frequency was approximately 8 cpd for parvo cells, much like the human psychophysical data shown in Figure 8.8, and 1 cpd for magno cells.

## Parallel pathways

According to this explanation, the spatiotemporal CSF actually reflects the contributions of two different populations of cells. Psychophysical experiments conducted after Robson's (1966) study led to the conclusion that information is processed in two separate and parallel pathways or *channels* in the human visual system (Tolhurst, 1973). One channel conveys information about pattern and shape, and is the most sensitive channel at high spatial frequencies and low temporal frequencies (filled squares in Figure 8.8; also known as the **sustained channel** due to the nature of its temporal response). The other channel conveys information about movement, and is the most sensitive channel at low spatial frequencies and high temporal frequencies (filled circles in Figure 8.8; also known as the **transient channel**). The characteristics of putative sustained and transient channels map neatly on to the differing response properties of cells in the parvo and magno divisions of the visual pathway respectively (refer back to Figure 7.7). This idea is attractive because it provides a linking hypothesis between a large body of human psychophysical data and the neurophysiological parvo versus magno division that, according to some views, runs right through to extrastriate visual cortex.

*Compare the response properties of the psychophysical transient and sustained channels with the magno and parvo systems (Chapter 7).*

Merigan and Eskin (1986) attempted to establish the neural substrate of contrast sensitivity in an experiment that combined psychophysical observations with physiological intervention. They trained macaque monkeys to perform a task measuring their contrast sensitivity. The monkeys were presented with a grating on one of two screens and pressed a button to select the screen containing the grating. One group of monkeys was given a neurotoxin that causes selective degeneration of ganglion cells projecting to the parvo layers of the LGN. When the treated monkeys were compared with untreated monkeys, they showed reduced contrast sensitivity only for gratings that were both high in spatial frequency and low in temporal frequency. Sensitivity at combinations of low spatial and high temporal frequency was barely affected by the neurotoxin. Contrast sensitivity losses in patients suffering certain clinical conditions mirrors the selective losses observed by Merigan and Eskin (Plant, 1991).

These results favour the parallel pathways interpretation of the contrast sensitivity function. They indicate that basic perceptual functions can be dissected into contributions from cells in the parvo and magno divisions of the visual pathway. However,

**KEY TERMS**
**Sustained channel**: A channel of processing in the visual system that is most sensitive at high spatial frequencies and low temporal frequencies.
**Transient channel**: A channel of processing in the visual system that is most sensitive at low spatial frequencies and high temporal frequencies.

there are two important limitations:

- It would be an oversimplification to assume that the visual system just switches between the two cell divisions as stimulus parameters change. Contrast sensitivity is likely to reflect contributions from both divisions, though their relative importance may vary with stimulus conditions. Bright, centrally viewed but spatially extended visual stimuli, for example, are likely to activate both cell divisions in different regions (parvo cells at the fovea, and magno cells in the periphery).
- Contrast sensitivity experiments, by definition, tell us only about the detectability of visual stimuli. Experiments that require *discrimination* of stimulus attributes such as orientation, size, motion direction, and velocity, are likely to reflect more complex cortical processes in which parvo and magno responses are combined in some way.

## REPRESENTATION AT MULTIPLE SPATIAL SCALES

### SPATIAL SCALE

Visual images contain detail at many different spatial scales. Coarse-scale detail carries information about the general shape and structure of objects in the image, while fine-scale detail carries information about sharp edges and surface textural properties.

For example, the left-hand image of Figure 8.10 shows a photograph of a human face. The middle image represents only the coarse-scale information in the photograph. The only information preserved at this scale conveys the general shape of the head and hair, and the locations of relatively large features such as the eyes and mouth. The right-hand image represents only the fine-scale information, conveying the precise shape of the eyes and mouth, but discarding large-scale luminance variation such as the colour of the hair. Coarse-scale information may be useful for identifying the shape as a human face, and locating the approximate positions of the eyes, nose, and mouth. Fine-scale information, on the other hand, may be useful for estimating the age of a person from the skin texture of their face. Natural images generally contain different kinds of information at different spatial scales. In images of landscapes, coarse-scale detail might allow identification of trees and rock formations, while fine-scale detail conveys textural properties such as leaf shape and rock surface markings. In a traffic scene, coarse-scale detail may indicate the location of vehicles and road signs, while fine-scale detail reveals the make of the vehicle, and the lettering on road signs.

*Think of other examples of natural scenes in which information at different spatial scales can be used in different ways.*

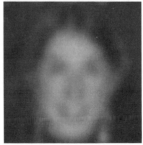

**FIG. 8.10**   Left: A photograph of a face. Middle: A low-pass filtered version of the face, retaining only coarse-scale or low spatial frequency information. Right: A high-pass filtered version of the face, retaining only fine-scale or high spatial frequency information.

# SPATIAL SCALE AND SPATIAL FREQUENCY

## Fourier theory

There is a close relation between spatial scale in natural images and spatial frequency in gratings. Low frequency gratings contain only coarse-scale information, and high frequency gratings contain only fine-scale information. According to a mathematical theory called Fourier theory, any natural image can be decomposed into a large collection of sine wave gratings at various spatial frequencies, contrasts, orientations, and phases. Each image has a unique collection of sine wave components that make it up. Fourier theory was introduced in Chapter 4 in the context of complex sounds. Any complex sound waveform can be decomposed into a collection of harmonic components, as illustrated in Figure 4.6. Exactly the same principle applies to visual images. Since visual images are two-dimensional, spatial Fourier analysis must take account of component orientation, but in other respects the mathematical principles are the same as those introduced in Chapter 4. More details on the application of Fourier analysis to vision can be found in the tutorial section at the end of this chapter.

## Spatial filtering

As the flowchart in Figure 4.7 shows, when Fourier analysis is applied to a complex signal the resultant Fourier spectrum contains the frequency components present in the signal. In spatial vision the complex signal is a two-dimensional image, and the frequency components in the Fourier spectrum are sine wave gratings. Fourier synthesis reconstitutes the image. As Figure 4.9 goes on to demonstrate, it is possible to remove certain components from the Fourier spectrum before synthesising the image. This operation amounts to filtering some spatial frequencies from the image.

*What is the visual equivalent of an auditory click? Think about their frequency content.*

Returning to the example of the face on the left of Figure 8.10, the left-hand plot in Figure 8.11 shows its Fourier spectrum. Each point in the plot

> The preponderance of low frequencies in the spectrum of the face in Figure 8.10 is typical of natural images. In general, amplitude falls in proportion with the reciprocal of spatial frequency (1/f). There has been much debate in the literature on the significance of this fact (Field, 1987).

**FIG. 8.11**   Fourier spectra of the images shown in Figure 8.10. Each point represents a spatial frequency component. Spatial frequency increases with radial distance from the centre of the plot. Orientation is given by the angle of the line joining each component to the centre of the plot. The amplitude of each component is represented by its intensity. The spectrum of the original image (left) contains a full range of frequency components, while in the filtered spectra (middle and right) components within a certain range have been removed.

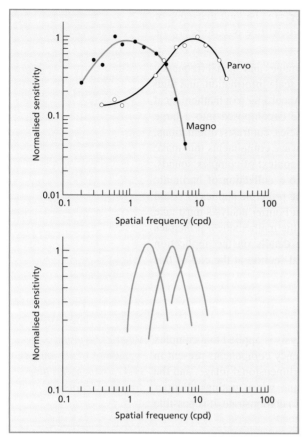

**FIG. 8.12**   Contrast sensitivity functions of cells in the visual system. Top: Parvo (open symbols) and magno (filled symbols) LGN cells, re-plotted from Derrington and Lennie (1984, Figures 3A and 10A; curves are based on best-fitting difference-of-Gaussian functions). Bottom: Striate cortical cells (re-plotted from De Valois, Albrecht, & Thorell, 1982). Cortical cells have much narrower spatial frequency tuning than LGN cells.

The contrast in tuning width between LGN and cortical cells bears out the observation in Chapter 7 that cortical cell receptive fields are not simply created by aggregating LGN receptive fields. Intra-cortical processing is required, and this is likely to involve operations that combine magno and parvo signals in various ways.

represents a particular spatial frequency component. Distance from the centre of the plot corresponds to spatial frequency, with lower frequencies nearer the centre. The angle of the line joining each component to the centre of the plot corresponds to the orientation of the component. The intensity of each point represents the amplitude of the corresponding component. The original photograph contains a wide range of component frequencies and orientations, though lower frequency components have the greatest amplitude.

When the photograph is blurred to preserve only the coarse-scale information (Figure 8.10 middle) the effect is to filter out all the higher frequencies, as can be seen in the middle of Figure 8.11. The filter which produces this effect is a low-pass filter. The version of the photograph that contains only fine-scale detail has been high-pass filtered to remove all the low frequencies and preserve all the high frequencies.

## Multiple spatial filters in the visual system

The visual system preserves the diverse information present at different spatial scales in the responses of different populations of neurons. In frequency terms, different populations of neurons encode information over different ranges of spatial frequency in the Fourier spectrum; in other words, the neurons act as narrowly tuned spatial frequency filters. The CSF of a given neuron in the visual system can be viewed as an estimate of its spatial frequency response, since it represents how well the neuron responds to gratings at various frequencies.

Figure 8.12 (top) shows the CSFs of parvo and magno LGN cells recorded by Derrington and Lennie (1984). These functions are so broad that they basically divide up the frequency spectrum into just two components—too coarse a representation for useful spatial frequency analysis. Figure 8.12 (bottom) shows the CSFs of cells in the striate cortex, recorded by De Valois, Albrecht, and Thorell (1982). Cortical CSFs are much narrower than those in the LGN, and do a much better job of dividing up the frequency spectrum into bands of spatial frequencies.

In the next section we consider psychophysical evidence that the human visual system also contains such narrowly tuned spatial frequency filters. Later sections consider how the visual system makes use of these filters in the early stages of visual processing. There are two major caveats to bear in mind. First, in the interests of simplicity, the foregoing discussion has disregarded temporal sensitivity. However, it was emphasised earlier that spatial sensitivity cannot be regarded as independent of temporal sensitivity. A more comprehensive treatment of spatial vision would consider *spatiotemporal* frequency analysis. This would require consideration of three-dimensional Fourier spectra (two spatial dimensions, plus a third dimension to represent temporal frequency). A discussion of such spectra is beyond the scope of this chapter, though simple spatiotemporal receptive fields will be introduced in the context of motion perception (Chapter 11). Second, the idea that the visual system performs a frequency analysis on the image using frequency-tuned filters should not be taken to mean that the visual system actually uses Fourier analysis to represent and recognise objects. Fourier transforms involve some strict assumptions:

- They are global, integrating across the *whole* image, whereas visual receptive fields are local.
- They represent each frequency component in the image independently of all other components, while visual receptive fields admit a range of components (Figure 8.12), and interact with each other.
- They assume that the response of the system is linear. Linearity was discussed in Chapter 4, and the same restrictions apply in the case of vision as in the case of hearing. Some aspects of visual responses can be considered linear, but many others are grossly non-linear.

Fourier analysis just provides a powerful mathematical tool for analysing the information available in visual images, and characterising certain response properties of visual neurons.

## PSYCHOPHYSICAL EVIDENCE FOR MULTIPLE SPATIAL FILTERS

Psychophysical evidence for the existence of multiple spatial filters in the human visual system is provided by two techniques: adaptation and masking.

## Adaptation

Adaptation is one of the most widely used techniques in visual psychophysics. The basic paradigm involves three stages:

- Pre-adaptation psychophysical measurement
- Adaptation to an inducing stimulus
- Post-adaptation psychophysical measurement.

A comparison between pre-adaptation and post-adaptation measurements will reveal the effect of the adapting stimulus on performance. Measurements involve either threshold or suprathreshold stimuli.

### Threshold measurements

If an observer views a high-contrast grating for several minutes, their ability to see a low-contrast test grating is reduced for a while afterwards. A comparison of contrast thresholds before and after the period of adaptation reveals **threshold elevation**: more contrast is required for detection after adaptation than before adaptation. Blakemore and Campbell (1969) measured threshold elevation as a function of the difference in spatial frequency between the adapting and test gratings. They found that threshold elevation was generally maximal when adapting and test spatial frequencies matched, and declined progressively as the difference between the two

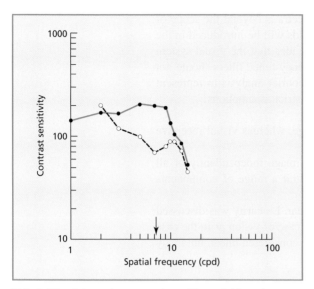

**FIG. 8.13** Adaptation to gratings. The solid line shows contrast sensitivity as a function of spatial frequency, prior to adaptation. Note the similarity with the graph in Figure 8.3. The broken line shows contrast sensitivity after a period of adaptation to a high-contrast grating at the spatial frequency shown by the arrow on the horizontal axis. Adaptation reduces sensitivity to gratings whose frequency is similar to the adapting spatial frequency. Data are re-plotted from Blakemore and Campbell (1969).

frequencies increased. Figure 8.13 shows some of their data. The solid curve shows contrast sensitivity before adaptation. The dashed curve shows sensitivity after adapting to a spatial frequency of 7.1 cpd (arrowed on the abscissa). Sensitivity is depressed only for similar spatial frequencies.

We can assume that adaptation depresses the sensitivity of neural filters responsive to the adapting spatial frequency. So the specificity of the adaptation effect reflects the specificity of the underlying filters. When adapting and test frequencies are very similar, the *same* filters respond to both, so threshold elevation occurs. On the other hand, when adapting and test frequencies are very dissimilar, they stimulate *different* filters and no threshold elevation occurs. The spatial frequency specificity of contrast adaptation is therefore evidence for the existence of multiple spatial filters.

Contrast adaptation is orientation tuned. When adapting and test gratings are sufficiently different in orientation then no threshold elevation is found, even if the gratings have the same spatial frequency (Movshon & Blakemore, 1973). Contrast adaptation is also binocular, in the sense that it can be obtained when the adapting grating is presented to only one eye, and the test grating is presented to the other eye (Blakemore & Campbell, 1969). These findings indicate that the spatial filters involved in contrast adaptation correspond to binocular, orientation-tuned cells in striate cortex.

### Suprathreshold measurements

Adaptation can also affect the appearance of high-contrast stimuli, also known as *suprathreshold* stimuli. Figure 8.2 showed several examples of suprathreshold sine wave grating stimuli. The reader should have no difficulty in detecting these gratings, and judging their frequency and orientation accurately. However, the apparent frequency or orientation of a grating can be influenced by prior exposure to an adapting grating:

● **Size after-effect** Blakemore and Sutton (1969) reported that a given test spatial frequency grating appears to have a lower frequency following adaptation to a high frequency grating, and appears to have a higher frequency following adaptation to a low frequency grating.

● **Tilt after-effect** An analogous effect is found in judgements of orientation (Gibson & Radner, 1937). Adaptation to lines tilted slightly clockwise from vertical makes vertical lines appear tilted slightly anti-clockwise; adaptation to anti-clockwise lines makes vertical lines appear tilted clockwise from vertical.

These after-effects can be explained using spatial filters selectively tuned to spatial frequency and orientation. We must assume that the apparent frequency or tilt of a stimulus is determined by the relative activity it evokes in filters tuned to different values along the relevant stimulus dimension (spatial frequency or orientation). The computation underlying our perception of frequency or tilt can be likened to a tug-of-war between differently tuned filters. Normally, filters optimally tuned to a given test stimulus respond the most, and win the tug-of-war to determine its appearance. After adaptation to a higher frequency, filters tuned to frequencies slightly lower than the actual test frequency respond the most and win the tug-of-war. Similarly, adaptation to a spatial frequency slightly lower than the test frequency skews the pattern of response towards filters tuned to slightly higher frequencies. The same explanation can be used for the tilt after-effect. Indeed, adaptation effects in motion perception can also be explained by a tug-of-war between filters tuned to different directions (see Figure 11.5 in Chapter 11 for an illustration of the tug-of-war explanation).

*Relate this explanation for after-effects to the population coding ideas discussed in the first three chapters.*

## Masking

Contrast threshold at a given spatial frequency is elevated when a high-contrast masking grating is superimposed on the test pattern. The magnitude of elevation depends on the difference in frequency between the test grating and the masking grating. Masks at the same frequency as the test stimulus produce the greatest threshold elevation. The masking effect declines steadily as the difference in frequency increases, in much the same way that adaptation declines as the difference between adapting and test gratings increases.

> **KEY TERM**
> **Masking:** A rise in the contrast threshold for a test stimulus in the presence of a second, masking stimulus.

We can assume that masking is effective because it corrupts the response of filters tuned to the test spatial frequency (it injects activity that is not correlated with the presence of a signal). When the mask and test frequencies are sufficiently close in frequency to stimulate the same filter, threshold elevation occurs. When the two frequencies are so different that the mask stimulates a different filter from the test, no threshold elevation occurs. So the specificity of masking provides an estimate of the spatial frequency selectivity of the underlying filters. Figure 8.14 shows estimates of the frequency selectivity of spatial filters, based on masking data (Wilson, McFarlane, & Phillips, 1983). The similarity with the frequency tuning of cortical cells (Figure 8.12) is striking.

> Masking techniques were also discussed extensively in Chapter 5, because they can be used to infer the selectivity of filters in the auditory system tuned to narrow ranges of sound frequency. As in the case of vision, the similarity between physiological and perceptual estimates of filter bandwidth is remarkable (see Figure 5.5).

## USES OF SPATIAL FILTERS

So far we have seen that natural images contain information at many different spatial scales or frequency ranges. The visual system possesses filters that respond selectively to different ranges of spatial frequency. In neural terms, these mechanisms correspond to populations of spatial frequency-selective neurons in the visual cortex. In this section we consider in more detail how the visual system might make use of the information provided in spatial frequency-tuned neural filters.

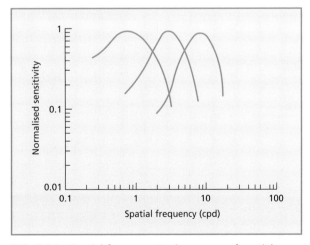

**FIG. 8.14** Spatial frequency tuning curves of spatial filters in the visual system, estimated psychophysically using contrast masking. The similarity with cortical cell tuning (Figure 8.12) is remarkable. Data are re-plotted from Wilson, McFarlane, and Phillips (1983).

## EDGE LOCALISATION

The visual system uses the output of spatial frequency-tuned filters to assign locations to (or *localise*) intensity edges in the image.

### The importance of edges

Intensity edges in an image correspond to the points at which luminance changes most steeply across space. Figure 8.15 shows a greyscale image. The graph below the image plots luminance as it varies along the horizontal line drawn across the middle of the image. The edges (steepest luminance changes in the profile) mark the boundaries of surfaces and objects in the scene. Information on edge location is therefore necessary to distinguish objects from their background, and establish their shape and position. So edge localisation is a crucial early step in the process of scene analysis and object recognition.

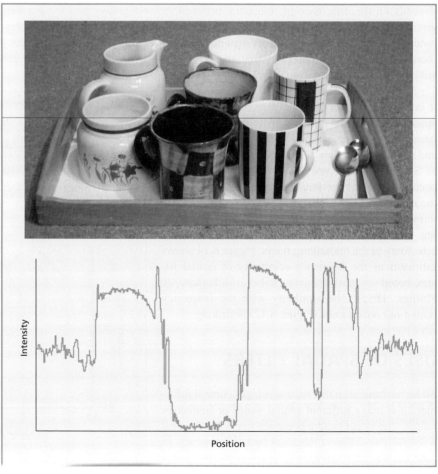

**FIG. 8.15** Intensity edges in images are defined by steep changes in luminance across space. The graph below the image plots luminance along the horizontal line drawn across the image. Edges occur at the boundaries of surfaces and objects, as well as at surface markings.

Observers are highly efficient at locating edges. A standard laboratory test of edge localisation is **Vernier acuity**, illustrated in Figure 8.16. The observer's task is to report whether the top line is displaced to the left or to the right of the bottom line. In optimal conditions, observers can reliably report displacements as small as 5″ arc (Westheimer & McKee, 1977). In linear units, this distance corresponds to an offset of less than 1/70th of a millimetre at arm's length, or of 5 mm viewed from a distance of 200 meters. A 5″ arc is also less than one-sixth of the distance between adjacent photoreceptors on the retina. Performance at such high levels of precision has been called **hyperacuity** (Westheimer, 1975).

## Explaining hyperacuity

How can observers perform acuity tasks with a precision that seems to defy the resolution of the retinal mosaic? Figure 8.17 (top) shows the retinal luminance profile of a thin line at two positions, 0′ and 0.2′ arc (12″ arc). Due to the optical effects discussed in Chapter 6 (see Figure 6.18), the line's profile is spread over a distance spanning more than 4′ arc. Foveal cones are spaced at intervals of approximately 0.6′ arc (36″ arc), and the vertical dashed lines in the top graph represent the centres of adjacent cones in the retinal mosaic. The middle bar graph shows the response of each photoreceptor in the presence of the line at its two positions (given by summing the light that falls in each 0.6′ arc interval). Notice that the shift in line position causes a slight change in the response of each photoreceptor. Some receptors increase their response, while others decrease their response. The bottom bar graph shows the ratio of photoreceptor responses at the two line positions. Some receptors increase their response by over 25% and others decrease their response by a similar amount, even though the change in line position is much smaller than the distance between adjacent photoreceptors. This shift in the pattern of photoreceptor response can be detected by a mechanism that compares the responses of nearby photoreceptors. Centre–surround receptive fields are well suited to the job of comparing photoreceptor responses. The visual system requires a mechanism that can infer the location of intensity edges from the pattern of responses in centre–surround receptive fields (see Barlow, 1979; Morgan & Watt, 1982 for more detailed discussions).

*Why are centre–surround receptive fields important in explaining hyperacuity?*

## Theories of edge localisation

In general terms, then, hyperacuity can be achieved by receptive fields integrating across a number of photoreceptors. Several theories have been developed to explain exactly how the outputs of spatial receptive fields are used to localise edges and lines, including:

- Zero-crossing model (Marr & Hildreth, 1980)
- MIRAGE model (Watt & Morgan, 1985)
- Local-energy model (Morrone & Burr, 1988)
- MIDAAS model (Kingdom & Moulden, 1992)
- Derivative-peaks model (Georgeson, 1992).

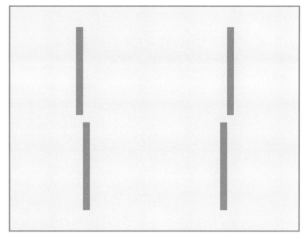

**FIG. 8.16** A standard psychophysical test of edge localisation performance involves Vernier alignment. In each trial a pair of lines is presented, one above the other. The observer must report whether the upper line is displaced to the left of the lower line (as on the left) or to the right (as on the right). Vernier acuity is defined by the displacement that reaches a criterion level of response, usually 75% correct reports of displacement direction.

**KEY TERMS**
**Vernier acuity:**
An observer's acuity for detecting the direction of small spatial offsets between collinear lines or edges.
**Hyperacuity:** Acuity performance in which the observer can detect changes in spatial location that are smaller than the distance between adjacent retinal photoreceptors.

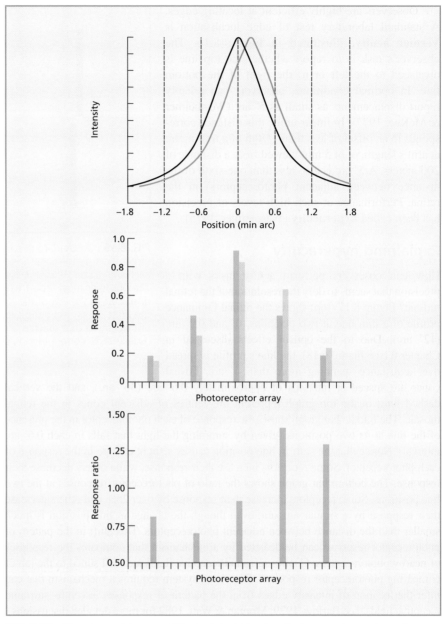

**FIG. 8.17**  How to explain our ability to detect Vernier displacements much smaller than the distance between adjacent photoreceptors. Top: Retinal light distributions across two lines displaced by a distance of 12″ arc (typical of Vernier acuity thresholds). The vertical dashed lines mark the centres of adjacent photoreceptors. Light from each line is spread over more than 4′ arc and six photoreceptors, but the shift in the peak of the distribution is a fraction of the spacing between photoreceptors. Middle: Response at each photoreceptor, assuming that response is given by summing the light over each 0.6′ arc interval in the top graph. Dark-blue bars correspond to the left-hand line, and light-blue bars correspond to the right-hand line. Bottom: The change in response at each photoreceptor caused by the shift in line position. Some receptors increase their response by about 25%, while others decrease their response by the same amount. Thus, even though the line displacement is relatively small, there is a significant change in response across a number of photoreceptors.

Most theories involve the series of processing stages illustrated in Figure 8.18.

## Spatial filtering

All models begin by applying a bank of spatial frequency-tuned filters to the image, in order to extract information at different spatial scales. Early theories such as Marr and Hildreth's (1980) **zero-crossing** model assumed that these filters corresponded to neurons in the visual pathway with concentric receptive fields. More recent discussions acknowledge that these cells are too broadly tuned, and that the most likely candidates are cortical cells (Morgan & Watt, 1997). All the models use balanced centre–surround receptive fields, which produce no net response to uniform illumination and narrow frequency tuning (see Figures 8.9 and 8.24).

## Feature extraction

All models also contain a stage of feature extraction, in which the filter outputs are interpreted to extract a limited set of features that describe the spatial structure of the image, such as edges, lines, and bars. The rules governing this interpretation are based on the distinctive "signature" of different features. Each edge, for example, creates a zero-crossing in filter output (where filter response changes from positive to negative) at the location of the edge, and a **peak** in response nearby. Marr and Hildreth's (1980) rules are based on zero-crossings, whereas MIRAGE's rules are based on peaks.

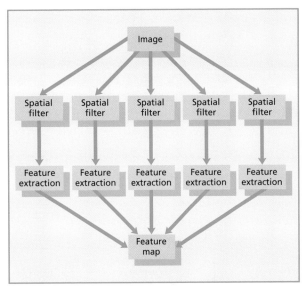

**FIG. 8.18**   Processing stages involved in current theories of edge localisation in the visual system. A bank of spatial frequency-tuned filters extracts image detail at different spatial scales. Filter outputs are used to detect the presence of features in the image, such as edges, lines, and bars. Finally, the features extracted at each spatial scale are reconciled to create a single, integrated feature map. Specific theories differ in the detailed operations performed at each stage, and one model argues that filter outputs are combined before feature extraction, rather than after.

## Feature map

The output of all models is a map containing the locations of all extracted features. Grouping processes (discussed in Chapter 9) are assumed to use the map to extract large-scale spatial structures and shapes. Marr and Hildreth (1980) called the output of their model the **primal sketch**, and this term is now often used to refer to any low-level map of local spatial structure (Bruce et al., 2003).

*At what stage does the representation in each model become symbolic?*

## Filter combination

A distinctive aspect of different models concerns when and how filter outputs are combined:

- *When:* Most theories assume that feature extraction occurs *before* filter combination, as depicted in Figure 8.18. Watt and Morgan's (1985) MIRAGE favours the reverse order; feature extraction *after* filter combination.
- *How:* Some theories sum across different spatial frequency bands, but separately for ON- and OFF-centre filters (Watt & Morgan, 1985). Others sum within frequency bands and then across frequency bands (Morrone & Burr, 1988; Georgeson, 1992).

**KEY TERMS**

**Zero-crossing**: A point where the value of a function such as a receptive field response changes from positive to negative.

**Peak**: A point where the value of a function such as a receptive field response reaches its maximum.

**Primal sketch**: A relatively primitive representation of local spatial structure in an image, produced by the initial stages of visual processing.

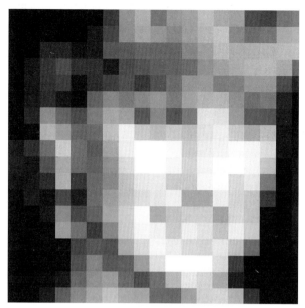

**FIG. 8.19** A photograph that has been block-quantised by dividing the image into blocks, and setting the intensity of each block to the average intensity of the region covered by the block. It is very difficult to identify the subject of the photograph, unless the image is blurred (Harmon & Jules, 1973).

### Which model is best?

All models are capable of explaining some basic perceptual facts about edge appearance and localisation, as one would expect given their design brief. There are no psychophysical data available that critically test all models against each other. This is partly because each model involves a complex sequence of computations, and a comprehensive empirical test would have to implement all of them in order to derive predictions from each; a major undertaking. A deeper problem is that many of the differences between models are rather subtle, making it extremely difficult to devise a critical test (or at least a test that can withstand attempts to iron out difficulties by tweaking details of specific models; a favoured pastime of modellers). A detailed discussion can be found in Bruce et al. (2003).

### Block quantisation effects

*The effect* As an example of the difficulty in distinguishing between the models, consider the well-known "Abraham Lincoln" demonstration, which offered the prospect of telling us about how the outputs of spatial frequency-selective filters are combined in early spatial vision. In the original demonstration, a photograph of Abraham Lincoln was subjected to block quantisation as follows. The image is divided up into tiles or blocks. The intensity of each block is set to the average intensity of the region of the photograph covered by the block.

Block quantisation preserves the low spatial frequency content of the image, corresponding in size to the width of the blocks. But it introduces arbitrary high spatial frequencies, carried by the edges of the blocks, that are not related to the content of the image. As you will see from Figure 8.19, block quantisation makes it very difficult to identify the person in the photograph. However, low-pass filtering the image (by removing your spectacles, if you wear spectacle corrections, or de-focusing your eyes) allows the person's identity to become obvious.

*Explanations* Both early and late feature extraction models offer explanations for block quantisation effects:

● MIRAGE assumes that the outputs of filters in different frequency bands are combined *early* in the process of edge localisation. Before edges are extracted, the high-frequency information introduced by the edges of the blocks is summed with the low-frequency information correlated with the photograph, resulting in interference with recognition. Blurring improves recognition because it physically removes the spurious high frequencies that influence edge extraction.

● Advocates of *late* filter combination such as Morrone, Burr, and Ross (1994) argue that features are first extracted at each scale, and a final feature map is derived by combining the scale-specific maps. The high-frequency features "drag" the features at coarser scales with them, so distorting the representation in the final feature map and causing interference.

The Abraham Lincoln demonstration is not a very good testbed for theories of edge localisation. It does tell us that information in different frequency bands is combined, as all models assume, but it cannot tell us much more.

## TEXTURE ANALYSIS

In everyday terms, texture refers to the physical properties of an object's surface, such as whether it is rough or smooth, glossy or matt, patterned or uniform. If two surfaces differ in physical texture, the images of those surfaces will differ in spatial structure or **visual texture** (provided that the texture can be resolved by the imaging system). The visual system can use visual texture to unify its representation of a surface, and to segment a shape or object from its background. Spatial frequency-selective filters can play a role in texture analysis because their output depends on spatial structure in the image. If two regions of the image differ in terms of spatial structure, and we apply an array of spatial frequency- and orientation-tuned filters to them, we can assume that at least some of those filters will respond more to one region than to the other. This variation in filter response forms the basis for current models of texture segregation (reviewed in Landy & Graham, 2004). The general scheme, known as **filter–rectify–filter (FRF)**, is illustrated in Figure 8.20 alongside an example of its operation. The example at the top of Figure 8.20 shows an image in which a central region contains lines tilted at + 45° from vertical, and a surrounding region containing lines tilted at −45° from vertical.

### Spatial filtering

The first stage of analysis (second row) involves filtering by an array of filters tuned to different spatial frequencies and orientations. The example shows the output of filters with receptive fields tuned to respond selectively to an orientation of +45°. These receptive fields have an excitatory central region and inhibitory flanks (e.g. ON-centre cortical simple cells). Excitation is represented in the output image by light points, and inhibition is represented by dark points. Regions of no response are represented by grey values in the output image. Notice that filter output shows large positive and negative responses to the central region, and no response to the surrounding region. Lack of response in the surround is to be expected since the preferred orientation of the filter is perpendicular to the orientation of the bars. Response in the centre varies between excitation

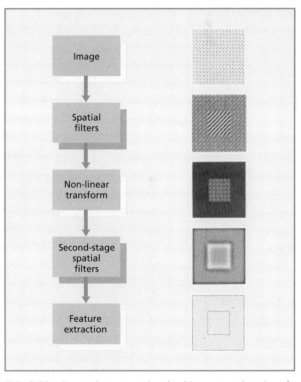

**FIG. 8.20**   Processing stages involved in current theories of texture analysis in the visual system (left), with an example of their operation (right). A bank of filters is applied to the image. Selective tuning for orientation causes a greater modulation of response in the centre region of the example texture (grey level represents activity level). A non-linear transform converts variations in response modulation into variations in mean response level, to produce a higher level of activity in one region of texture. A second stage of spatial filtering is used to allow detection of spatial features in the transformed responses. (From Bruce et al., 2003, Figures 6.27 and 6.28.) Copyright © 2003 Psychology Press.

and inhibition because of the varied alignment between individual bars and the excitatory and inhibitory sub-regions of receptive fields at different positions (refer back to Figure 6.12, top). Cells with inhibitory centres and excitatory flanks (e.g. OFF-centre cortical simple cells) will show a pattern of responses that is the opposite of that shown in Figure 8.20 (i.e. excitation where Figure 8.20 shows inhibition, and vice versa).

Linearity was discussed earlier in this chapter, and in Chapter 4, as an assumption of Fourier methods. Since non-linearities are central to processing schemes of the kind depicted in Figure 8.20, these schemes are sometimes called *non-Fourier* or *second-order*. They are particularly useful for texture analysis and have also been proposed to explain the perception of texture-defined movement (see Chapter 11).

## Non-linear transform

The aim of this stage in the process is to transform the responses of the filters so that they are all excitatory or positive, rather than both positive and negative (for reasons that will become clearer in the next paragraph). In full-wave rectification (shown in the example), negative responses are transformed into positive responses. Such transforms are non-linear because after they have been applied it is not possible to reverse them. Once all responses have been converted into positive ones, there is no way to determine which were originally positive and which were negative.

Rectification or similar operations can be achieved in a variety of ways in the visual system, for example by cortical complex cells that receive excitatory input from both ON- and OFF-centre simple cells.

## Second-stage spatial filtering and feature extraction

In the example of Figure 8.20, rectification of filter outputs produces a neural image in which the central region is "brighter" (i.e. has a higher average level of neural response) than the background region. In order to find the border separating the two regions of texture, standard edge-localisation methods are used of the kind discussed earlier in the chapter: spatial filtering followed by feature extraction. The second stage of spatial filtering must necessarily involve frequency-selective filters tuned to lower spatial frequencies than those used in the first stage, which responded to individual elements.

## Psychophysical evidence on texture edge localisation

The FRF scheme depicted in Figure 8.20 can be used to localise texture edges, as opposed to the luminance edges localised in the scheme in Figure 8.18. The low-frequency second-stage filters wipe out any representation of the individual texture elements themselves, but retain a representation of texture boundaries. Nothdurft (1993) provided psychophysical evidence that texture segmentation depends specifically on the differences between texture elements at the borders between texture regions, as would be expected on the basis of an edge localisation scheme. Evidence for low-frequency second-stage filtering was provided by Gray and Regan (1997) and Mather and Smith (2002):

● Gray and Regan (1997) compared Vernier acuity for luminance- and texture-defined edges. Acuity for texture edges was an order of magnitude worse than acuity for luminance edges (6' arc or more for the former, compared to 30" arc or less for the latter), as expected on the basis of low-frequency second-stage filtering. Morgan (1986) had previously reported Vernier thresholds in the region of 40" arc for stereoscopically defined texture edges.

- Mather and Smith (2002) measured observers' ability to discriminate different degrees of blur in luminance edges and in texture edges. Blur discrimination thresholds were much larger for texture edges than for luminance edges, consistent with the idea that lower-frequency filters are used for texture edges than for luminance edges.

*Why should acuity be worse using lower-frequency filters?*

## STEREO AND MOTION

Spatial frequency selective receptive fields lie at the heart of neural processes dealing with the extraction of stereoscopic depth and motion:

- Accurate stereoscopic vision relies on the visual system correctly matching features extracted from the image in one eye with the corresponding features extracted in the other eye. This matching problem is very difficult to solve. Some computational theories make use of spatial frequency selectivity to simplify the problem by restricting the search for matches to certain bands of spatial frequency.
- Motion analysing processes must deal with images that move across the retinal mosaic at high speed. For example, the image of a human walking across your field of view at a distance of 10 metres will traverse 800 photoreceptors per second (assuming the eyes are stationary). Precise localisation is not a priority for motion processes, so relatively large, low spatial frequency receptive fields can be used. They have the advantage that they are able to integrate over a greater portion of the motion trajectory and therefore produce a more reliable estimate of velocity and direction.

These processes will be discussed at length in later chapters.

## CHAPTER SUMMARY

### FUNDAMENTAL FUNCTIONS

- The shift from cone vision to rod vision (dark adaptation) takes approximately 30 minutes. Dark adaptation is accompanied by a shift in the relative brightnesses of surfaces that reflect different wavelengths, due to the differing spectral sensitivities of rods and cones (the Purkinje shift).
- The spatial contrast sensitivity function shows that human observers are most sensitive to gratings of medium spatial frequency (3 cpd). Sensitivity to spatial frequency declines rapidly at higher frequencies, and gradually at lower frequencies.
- The temporal contrast sensitivity function shows maximum sensitivity to medium flicker rates (8 Hz). Sensitivity to temporal frequency declines rapidly at higher frequencies and more gradually at lower frequencies.

- Spatiotemporal contrast sensitivity depends jointly on spatial frequency and temporal frequency: Sensitivity to spatial frequency is band-pass at low temporal frequencies, and low-pass at high temporal frequencies. The shape of the spatiotemporal contrast sensitivity function can be explained by the properties of parvo and magno cells in the visual pathway.

## REPRESENTATION AT MULTIPLE SPATIAL SCALES

- Natural images contain information at many different spatial scales, or spatial frequencies.
- Fourier theory provides a method of decomposing complex images into their spatial frequency components.
- Cells in the visual system can be viewed as spatial frequency filters tuned to respond to only a sub-set of spatial frequencies.
- Psychophysical evidence for multiple spatial filters in the human visual system comes from contrast adaptation and from masking experiments.

## USES OF SPATIAL FILTERS

- Spatial frequency-tuned filters in the human visual system are used for localising luminance edges, for texture analysis, and in the early stages of stereo and motion processing.
- Theories of luminance edge localisation combine the outputs of multiple spatial filters to infer the presence of features such as edges and lines. Some theories extract features before combining information at different spatial scales. Other theories extract features after combining the outputs of filters at different spatial scales.
- Theories of texture analysis include additional intermediate processing stages in which a non-linear transform is applied to the filter outputs before second-stage low spatial frequency filtering and feature extraction.

# TUTORIALS

## FOURIER ANALYSIS APPLIED TO VISION

Fourier analysis was introduced in Chapter 4 as a tool for studying complex auditory waveforms and their representation in the auditory system. Fourier analysis is widely used in the study of vision as well. This tutorial introduces the basic principles of Fourier analysis in the visual domain. It assumes that the reader has already studied the tutorial on Fourier analysis in Chapter 4.

### One dimensional (1-D) spatial images

Auditory stimuli can be described in terms of variation along a single dimension, namely time. So Fourier analysis of an auditory waveform produces a frequency spectrum that contains variation in amplitude along a single dimension representing temporal frequency. The direct spatial equivalent in vision is a one-dimensional image that contains variation in light intensity along a single spatial dimension, which has the appearance of a stripy texture. Fourier analysis decomposes any complex one-dimensional spatial pattern into sinusoidal component waves of different spatial frequency, amplitude, and phase. Visually, each spatial frequency component is a sine-wave grating. Figure 8.21 shows a simple example.

The image at top left shows a one-dimensional pattern containing a single vertical sine wave. Luminance is constant along the vertical axis, but varies sinusoidally along the horizontal axis (the luminance distribution is shown below the grating). The image in the next row (left) shows another grating at three times the spatial frequency of the top grating, alongside the result of summing the two gratings (right). The sequence continues in lower rows, showing the addition of gratings at five and seven times the frequency of the top grating. The four gratings are actually the first four components of a square wave. As each is added in turn, the resultant image approximates the luminance profile of a square wave more closely. The auditory equivalent of this Fourier series was shown in Table 4.1 and Figure 4.25. So any periodic one-dimensional spatial pattern can be decomposed into a Fourier series of sine-wave gratings (as in the case of audition, a strict application of Fourier theory requires that the waveform is infinitely long, though this restriction is often disregarded).

## Two-dimensional (2-D) spatial images

Natural images vary in two spatial dimensions, vertically (y-axis) and horizontally (x-axis). Fourier analysis can also be applied to these images, and results in two-dimensional spectra. Each component in the frequency spectrum of a complex 2-D

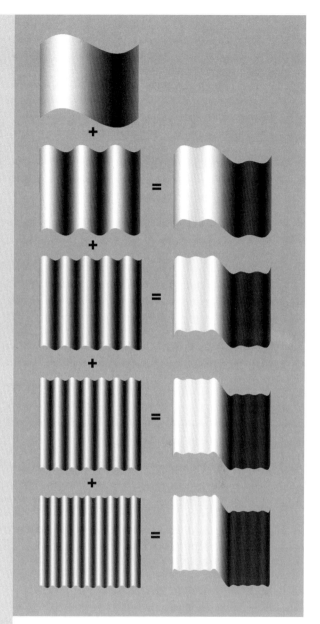

**FIG. 8.21** Summation of 1-D spatial frequency components to create complex spatial waveforms. As a series of components are added progressively to the waveform, the resultant image approximates a square wave more closely. The components correspond to those shown in Table 4.1 and in Figure 4.25.

pattern has both a vertical spatial frequency and a horizontal spatial frequency. Consider the case of the spatial frequency grating shown in Figure 8.22 (top). Vertical and horizontal cross-sections across this grating (Figure 8.22, middle) reveal the horizontally and vertically oriented spatial frequencies of the grating respectively. The representation of this component in a 2-D

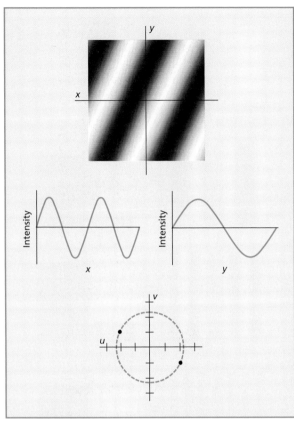

**FIG. 8.22** Top: A tilted sine-wave grating. Middle: The vertical and horizontal spatial frequencies of the grating, given by its modulation along the vertical and horizontal lines through the middle of the grating. Bottom: Representation of the grating in a 2-D frequency spectrum. The y-axis represents modulation along the vertical axis, and the x-axis represents modulation along the horizontal axis. Each point identifies the vertical and horizontal frequency of the grating. As discussed in Chapter 4, frequency spectra contain both positive and negative frequencies at symmetrically opposite locations.

frequency spectrum is shown in Figure 8.22 (bottom). The y-axis represents modulation along the vertical axis (horizontally oriented frequency, conventionally labelled v), and the x-axis represents modulation along the horizontal axis (vertically oriented frequency, conventionally labelled u). As with the spectra shown in Chapter 4, the frequency spectrum contains both positive and negative frequencies. The component in Figure 8.22 is represented by a pair of points at the appropriate uv locations in frequency space. Notice that if the grating was rotated to a different orientation, its vertical and horizontal spatial frequencies would change, even though the width of its bars remained constant. If the grating was rotated to a vertical orientation, its spatial frequency along the vertical axis would become zero (no variation along the y-axis), and its spatial frequency along the horizontal axis would correspond to the frequency given by the width of its bars. Whatever orientation the grating is given, its location in uv space will always lie at some point around the circle in the frequency spectrum. Different points around the circle involve different combinations of horizontal and vertical spatial frequency, and correspond to different grating orientations. The orientation (θ) and spatial frequency (f) of the grating can be calculated trigonometrically from its horizontal (u) and vertical (v) spatial frequencies as follows:

$$\theta = \arctan(u/v)$$
$$f = \sqrt{(u^2 + v^2)}$$

According to Fourier theory, any complex 2-D spatial pattern can be decomposed into a set of frequency components. Each component is identified by its vertical frequency, its horizontal frequency, its phase, and its amplitude. Frequency spectra provide a very useful visual summary of the information content of images. Most natural images contain a preponderance of low spatial frequencies, but can vary markedly in terms of the preponderance of energy at different orientations.

Figure 8.23 shows several 2-D images and their frequency spectra, organised in two columns. One column has been randomly re-ordered. As a test of your understanding of Fourier spectra, try to pair up each image in one column with its spectrum in the other column. An interesting point, which may help you to solve the problem, is that an image and its spectrum form a Fourier transform pair—one is the Fourier transform of the other. So you can either treat the left-hand column as images and the right-hand column as frequency spectra, or vice versa. The solution can be found at the end of the tutorial.

## Spatial frequency filtering

As Figures 8.10 and 8.11 demonstrated earlier in the chapter, spatial frequency filtering amounts to the removal of certain spatial frequencies from an image by setting the amplitude of components at those frequencies to zero. An inverse Fourier transform applied to the modified spectrum reveals the effect on the spatial image. When high frequencies are removed (Figures 8.10 and 8.11, middle), the image appears blurred and lacking detail. When low frequencies are removed (Figures 8.10 and 8.11, right), the image contains only fine-scale lines.

Individual visual cortical neurons can be viewed as spatial frequency filters tuned to respond only to certain grating frequencies and orientations. The response selectivity of these neurons can be visualised in the spatial frequency domain, as shown in Figure 8.24 (bottom). Each ellipse in the plot represents the responsiveness of an individual neuron. The distance of each ellipse from the centre of the plot represents each neuron's preferred spatial frequency, and the angular position of each ellipse represents its preferred orientation. The area of each ellipse encloses the range of frequencies and orientations to which the neuron responds. Each cortical neuron in Figure 8.24 samples a relatively small region of frequency space, though some cells are more selective than others. LGN cells, on the other hand, are very broadly tuned for spatial frequency and orientation. Figure 8.24 (top) shows the selectivity of two such cells.

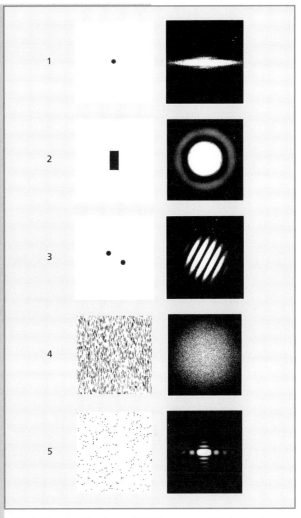

FIG. 8.23   A collection of 2-D images and their Fourier transforms. One column represents the images, and the other represents their transform (the two labels are interchangeable, since one column is the Fourier transform of the other). The order in one column has been randomly re-ordered relative to the other column. The correct order is given at the end of the tutorial. Images are based on those in Harburn, Taylor, and Welberry (1975).

## Spatiotemporal images

Visual images vary over time as well as over space. We can therefore add a third, temporal, dimension to our representation of visual images, to create an *xyt* representation. The Fourier transform of an *xyt* image is also three-dimensional. Two dimensions correspond to horizontal and vertical spatial frequency, as described in the previous section. The third dimension corresponds to temporal frequency. The tutorial on spatiotemporal approaches to motion processing in Chapter 11 contains examples of *xyt* images. Three-dimensional *xyt* images and their Fourier transforms are time-consuming to compute, and difficult to interpret, so many researchers restrict themselves to two of the three dimensions of the *xyt* space, according to the task in hand. The 2-D *xy* representation discussed in the previous section is

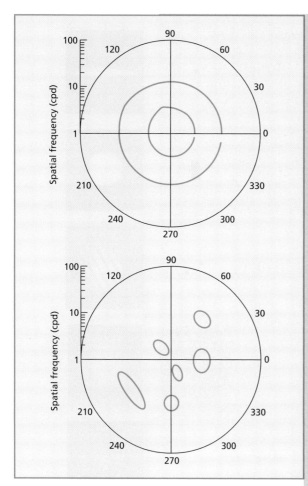

**FIG. 8.24** Polar plots of LGN (top) and cortical (bottom) cell receptive fields estimated from single-cell recordings, arranged to resemble a 2-D spatial Fourier spectrum. Each ellipse encloses the spatial frequencies and orientations to which a single cell responds. Cortical cells are much more selectively tuned than LGN cells (re-plotted from De Valois et al., 1982).

useful for studying spatial vision, and can be viewed as a cross-section through $xyt$ space in the $xy$ (spatial) plane. We can also slice $xyt$ space in the $xt$ (or $yt$) plane, illustrated in Figure 11.17. An $xt$ image contains the temporal dimension ($t$) and one spatial dimension ($x$), and is particularly useful for studying motion processing.

If we return to Figure 8.22 (top), the vertical axis can be re-labelled to represent the temporal dimension. The grating now shifts progressively along the $x$ (spatial) axis as one advances along the $y$ (temporal) axis. In other words, the grating is *moving* along the horizontal axis. Consider the vertical slice through the grating, shown in the middle of Figure 8.22. This now represents how the intensity at a specific $x$ location in the image varies over time ($y$). Notice that the intensity of the point modulates repetitively at a particular temporal frequency as successive grating bars drift past (recall Figure 8.8). So in the frequency spectrum of the $xt$ image the $v$ axis becomes temporal frequency. The pair of points representing the grating component in the frequency spectrum (Figure 8.22, bottom) now identify its spatial frequency ($u$) and its temporal frequency ($v$).

Visual movement therefore creates oriented contours in $xt$ space (spatiotemporal orientation). If the grating in Figure 8.22 was re-drawn to move at a higher velocity, its orientation in $xt$ space would be farther away from vertical (stationary), and its temporal frequency would be higher. Changes in the velocity of a grating at a fixed spatial frequency shift the position of its Fourier component vertically along the temporal frequency axis. Note that this is an important difference between $xy$ and $xt$ representations. In $xy$ space, changes in the orientation of the grating correspond to rotations in the $xy$ spatial domain, and rotations of its frequency component in the Fourier domain. In $xt$ space, on the other hand, grating motion corresponds to shearing of the grating along the $x$-axis, and shearing of its frequency component in the Fourier domain along the $u$-axis (both of which preserve its spatial frequency).

## Fourier analysis in theories of vision

Two-dimensional Fourier representations of visual images, whether as $xy$ or as $xt$ space, are widely used in vision research. As in the case of audition, Fourier techniques have allowed researchers to develop theories in which responses at certain processing stages faithfully represent the Fourier energy in the stimulus, while responses at other stages contain significant non-linear components. This approach has proved valuable in the development of theories of texture segmentation (see the discussion of texture analysis earlier in this chapter, and in Chapter 9) and of motion processing. Theories of motion processing, for instance, distinguish between Fourier and non-Fourier motion detectors. Fourier-based motion detectors are also known as first-order detectors. Their response is thought to be governed by energy in the spatiotemporal Fourier spectrum. The response of non-Fourier detectors, also known as second-order detectors, contains significant non-linear components so the relation between Fourier energy in the stimulus and detector response is much more complex (see Chapter 11).

## Solutions for Figure 8.23

Images are paired (L–R) as follows:

1–2
2–5
3–3
4–1
5–4

# CHAPTER 9

# 9

# Shape and object perception

## INTRODUCTION: THE THREE-STAGE MODEL

The processes described in Chapter 8 provide a piecemeal representation of visual structure, containing information about the edges and lines present at each location in the image. This representation is sometimes called the *primal sketch*, because it provides a simple, sparse description of local image features. However most visual tasks, such as recognition and visually guided action, require sophisticated representations of discrete, meaningful objects rather than an unstructured patchwork of locally encoded detail. Theories of visual processing therefore presume that at least two further levels of analysis are required after the primal sketch, as shown in Figure 9.1, to create a three-stage model of shape and object processing. In the second stage, the visual system builds a representation of the larger-scale shapes and surfaces present in the visual scene. In the third stage, the visual system constructs representations of objects present in the scene.

## NEUROPSYCHOLOGICAL EVIDENCE

Neuropsychological case studies provide general support for the three-stage model of visual analysis shown in Figure 9.1:

1. Patients with damage to the earliest visual cortical areas, particularly striate cortex, are blind in the area of the visual field lying in the damaged area. These areas of cortical blindness are called *scotomas*.
2. Patients with brain damage to extrastriate visual cortical areas seem to have intact lower level visual functions, including complete visual fields, and near-normal colour, depth, and movement detection and acuity (stage 1 in Figure 9.1), but suffer from disordered object perception or **agnosia** (stages 2 or 3 in Figure 9.1).

Lissauer (translated in Yantis, 2001) drew a distinction between two forms of agnosia, *apperceptive* and *associative*, which seem to map on to the two higher stages of the three-stage model:

- Apperceptive agnosia involves deficient shape representation (stage 2). A patient studied by Benson and Greenberg (1969), for example, could not name, copy, or

There is some evidence that patients with scotomas can, when pressed, reveal access to some primitive perceptual representation, probably in sub-cortical structures (*blindsight*; see Weiskrantz, 1986).

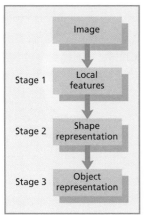

**FIG. 9.1** Three stages of visual processing. The first stage, discussed in Chapter 8, builds a piecemeal representation of local image properties. The second stage builds a representation of larger-scale shapes and surfaces. The third stage matches shapes and surfaces with stored object representations to achieve recognition.

match even simple shapes. In a shape matching task he incorrectly matched a triangle with a circle.

● Patients suffering from associative agnosia *are* able to copy and match shapes normally but cannot identify objects from their images (stage 3). Recognition based on touch or sound is unimpaired.

There is a continuing debate among neuropsychologists about how many other forms of agnosia can be distinguished, and precisely what functional impairments they involve (reviewed in Farah, 1999). Some argue in favour of a finer grained distinction between agnosias, which would indicate that the three-stage model of Figure 9.1 is too coarse. Furthermore, there is no universal agreement among researchers as to what visual processes are involved in shape analysis and object representation, as we shall see in this chapter. Nevertheless, it is convenient for the present purposes to partition visual processing into the three broad stages illustrated in Figure 9.1. Stage 1 was considered in the previous chapter. The various proposals for stages 2 and 3 are surveyed in the following sections. A crucial distinction between stages 2 and 3 is that operations performed in stage 2 do not involve any knowledge about the objects present in the scene, whereas stage 3 involves stored representations of objects.

## SHAPE REPRESENTATION

### GESTALT LAWS

The process that creates a representation of shape must necessarily integrate local information provided in the primal sketch over relatively large distances in the image. In the first part of the 20th century the Gestalt psychologists formulated a set of rules or "laws" of perceptual organisation, which demonstrate how the visual system seems to have in-built preferences for grouping parts of the image together on the basis of certain visual properties. These properties include:

● Proximity
● Similarity of colour
● Similarity of size
● Common fate
● Good continuation.

Figure 9.2 illustrates some of these principles in operation (common fate, not illustrated, involves grouping on the basis of common movement properties). The Gestalt psychologists attempted to relate their grouping laws to events in the brain that are isomorphic to the corresponding perceptual experience. Isomorphism assumes that the brain event has the same shape as the perceptual event, so that a perceived circle, for instance, creates a circular trace in the brain. Gestalt theories were obviously handicapped by lack of knowledge concerning the

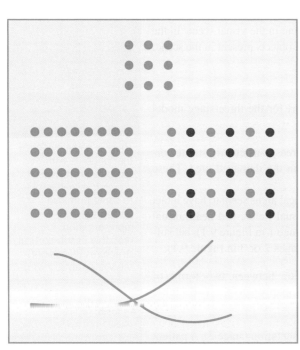

**FIG. 9.2**   Examples of Gestalt grouping laws in action.

physiology of the visual system (see the tutorial section of Chapter 7). Later discoveries concerning the physiological substrate of perception offered no support for the Gestaltists' ideas about isomorphism, leaving behind a set of descriptive principles with no theory of perceptual processing.

> "Gestalt" is a German word whose closest English equivalents are "pattern", "shape", or "configuration". The Gestalt movement began with the work of Wertheimer in Germany in the early 20th century (see Wertheimer, translated in Yantis, 2001; and Rock & Palmer, 1990).

Nevertheless, Gestalt laws do capture some consistent aspects of perceptual organisation. It is therefore worth asking why and how the laws work. In answer to "why", it is plausible to argue that Gestalt laws are built in to the visual system because they reflect the properties of real-world objects.

## Proximity

Most objects are made of cohesive, opaque material. So in general two nearby points in the image are more likely to originate from the same object than two points that are far apart. The law is not cast-iron, of course. Translucent or transparent objects, such as a net or a dirty window, violate this law and are known to stretch theories of shape analysis to their limit.

## Similarity

Object surfaces tend to be made of relatively few materials, so their visual texture is relatively uniform. It therefore makes sense to group local image regions together if they contain similar visual texture (e.g. size and colour). Animals and military vehicle designers try to avoid detection by breaking up their surface into discordant textures (camouflage).

## Common fate

As in the case of proximity, this law is motivated by the fact that objects are made of cohesive, opaque material. If an object moves, its parts tend to move together. Consequently, if different image regions contain movement that has a common direction and velocity, they are likely to have originated from the same object. The dirty window mentioned in the case of proximity also raises issues for models of motion analysis (discussed in Chapter 11).

## Good continuation

Object shape tends to vary smoothly, with relatively few very sharp corners or edges, especially if the object has been moulded by natural forces of erosion. A very good natural example would be a beach pebble. When attempting to delineate the contours of objects, it therefore makes sense to bias grouping in favour of contours that vary smoothly rather than sharply (Geisler, Perry, Super, & Gallogly, 2001).

Marr's (1982) theory of vision recognised the value of Gestalt laws as assumptions about the world. Marr built Gestalt-like grouping constraints into his computational theory. Having answered the "why" of Gestalt grouping, we are left with the question of how perceptual grouping is achieved. There are probably several answers to this question.

## SHAPE SEGMENTATION PROCESSES

### Texture-based segmentation

*Review the operation of the FRF process described in Chapter 8.*

The outputs of spatial frequency-tuned filters can be used to unify image regions on the basis of visual texture, as discussed in Chapter 8, using a filter–rectify–filter (FRF) processing sequence (Figure 8.20). Grouping on the basis of proximity and similarity can be explained by FRF processing.

#### *Proximity*

When texture elements are closer together in one region than in another, the spatial frequency content (and average luminances) of the two regions are likely to differ. Spatial frequency-tuned filters are sensitive to these differences, so FRF processing would achieve segmentation.

#### *Similarity*

Grouping on the basis of similarity in size, shape, or colour can also be driven by variations in the output of spatial frequency-tuned filters, since filter response will vary as a function of these attributes. The orientation-defined shape illustrated in Figure 8.20 is detected using the FRF process.

### Motion- and depth-based segmentation

The Gestalt psychologists did not actually describe a grouping law based on common disparity, perhaps because the nature of this cue was not fully understood at the time.

The Gestalt law of *common fate* can be explained by specialised motion and depth processes. In both cases, cooperative interactions between motion- or depth-sensitive neurons lead to segmentation on the basis of common motion or stereoscopic disparity. Detailed discussions of motion and stereo processing can be found in later chapters, but it should be borne in mind that they provide important routes to shape segmentation.

### Symbolic segmentation

Texture, motion, and depth processes operate in the domain of neural images. The outputs of spatial frequency-, motion-, or disparity-selective filters form a neural image of the corresponding image attribute. Specialised processes such as FRF sequences can be applied to the neural image to achieve segmentation. An alternative, influential approach to segmentation is based on symbolic computations (the distinction between image-based and symbolic computations was introduced in Chapter 1 during the discussion of representation).

Marr's (1982) original conception of the primal sketch was as a symbolic representation. It consisted of a list of the local features or **primitives** in the image (edges, bars, and so on), each annotated with its properties (position, orientation, contrast, length, width).

Collections of primitives can be grouped on the basis of similarities in their symbolic properties. Marr (1982) proposed that grouping is based on:

**KEY TERM**
**Primitive:** A symbolic description of a local image feature such as an edge or bar segment.

- Average local intensity
- Average size
- Local density

- Local orientation
- Local distances between neighbouring pairs of similar items
- Local orientation of the line joining neighbouring pairs of similar items.

Marr (1982) described the grouping process as follows (p. 91):

> One initially selects roughly similar items from it [the primal sketch] and groups or clusters them together, forming lines, curves, larger blobs, groups, and small patches to the extent allowed by the inherent structure of the image.

The result of grouping, in Marr's view, is a new set of symbolic primitives representing the larger spatial structure of more localised primitives.

## CONTOUR INTEGRATION

The segmentation processes discussed so far divide up the image into regions on the basis of shared texture, motion, or depth properties. The contours between regions are important because they describe the boundaries of objects or their parts. Silhouettes, for example, present only the bounding contours of an object, yet they are often sufficient to support identification. Figure 9.3 shows some objects represented as silhouettes.

Contour representation at the earliest levels of visual analysis (stage 1 in Figure 9.1) is limited to local information about the position, contrast, and orientation of edges and lines. In order to represent extended contours, the visual system must integrate this local information over relatively long distances in the image. The Gestalt law of good continuation is an example of contour integration. As in the case of shape segmentation, theories of contour integration can be divided into two classes. Some theories involve image-based processes, and others involve symbolic computations.

### Image-based contour integration

Psychophysical research has produced two hypothetical mechanisms for image-based contour integration—collector units, and cooperative interactions.

#### Collector units

In this mechanism, a sequence of local edge responses that lies along a relatively smooth contour in the image is collected together by neurons in the visual cortex that basically sum all the local responses. The output of these **collector units** signals the presence of extended contours. Morgan and Hotopf (1989) proposed such units (illustrated in Figure 9.4) to explain the illusory diagonal lines seen in certain tartan patterns.

**FIG. 9.3** The silhouettes of objects are often sufficient for recognition, demonstrating the importance of bounding contours in object representation.

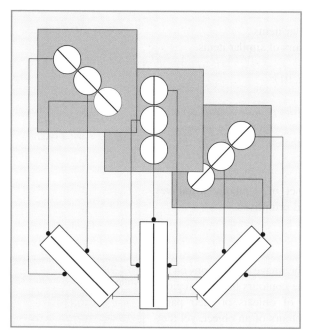

**FIG. 9.4** Hypothetical collector units with long receptive fields (large rectangles) integrate contour signals from smaller receptive fields (circles) to construct responses to extended contours (after Morgan & Hotopf, 1989).

Moulden (1994) offered a similar explanation (*collator units*) to account for his psychophysical data on the detection of co-linear line segments embedded in a dense array of randomly oriented line segments (see also Moulden & Kingdom,1987). Field, Hayes, and Hess (1993) found that observers are able to detect the presence of disconnected line or bar segments that follow a smooth path across the image against dense backgrounds of randomly oriented segments.

## Cooperative interactions

In this mechanism neurons providing local edge responses do not feed forward to a higher level integrating unit, but laterally to other neurons at the same level. Reciprocal connections between the neurons responding to different edge segments produce mutual facilitation when all neurons are active simultaneously, enhancing responses in the presence of a long, smooth contour. In support of this proposal, Polat and Sagi (1994) found that contrast thresholds to detect a patch of grating were lower when another grating was present at an adjacent location, provided that the bars of the two gratings were co-linear (see also Pettet, McKee, & Grzywacz, 1998).

## Symbolic contour integration

Marr (1976) described a symbolic process he called *curvilinear aggregation*, defined as "the assembly of place-tokens that contain an orientation into a group that preserves it" (p. 502). He believed that this form of grouping was "by far the most important kind", because it generates the bounding contours of shapes. Marr conceived of the process as operating in successive stages:

● First, local primitive features are grouped into a contour only if they have matching orientation, contrast, type (edge, line, etc.), and "fuzziness", and are very close to one another. This typically produces quite long segments of 20 or more local edge or line segments. The ends of each segment are given an entry as a "node" in the symbolic description of the image. Each entry includes a list of other nodes that could possibly match it.

● In the second stage, possible node matches are evaluated and resolved. Marr (1976) suggested that physiological evidence consistent with his aggregation theory would be the discovery of cells responsive to the overall direction of aggregation independently of the orientation of the local elements.

## Physiological correlates

Some physiological data are consistent with the presence of cortical cells with long-range connections (Gilbert & Wiesel, 1985; Gilbert, 1995; Bosking, Zhang, Schofield, & Fitzpatrick, 1997). However, physiological evidence does not yet allow us to discriminate between the contour integration processes that have been proposed.

# SURFACE PARSING

Nakayama, He, and Shimojo (1995) argue that shape segmentation alone is insufficient to serve as a precursor for object representation. The problem is that natural scenes are cluttered with numerous surfaces, many of which occlude each other. Consequently, segmented regions and shapes are likely to have arbitrary configurations that reflect the spatial arrangement of surfaces as well as their intrinsic shapes. Nakayama et al. (1995) therefore argue that surface parsing is an essential part of shape representation processes (stage 2 in Figure 9.1). Shapes that are disconnected in the image, yet belong to the same surface on an object, are grouped together by the visual system. Nakayama et al. (1995) call this grouping operation **parsing**. It can be achieved with no knowledge of the objects to which the surfaces belong.

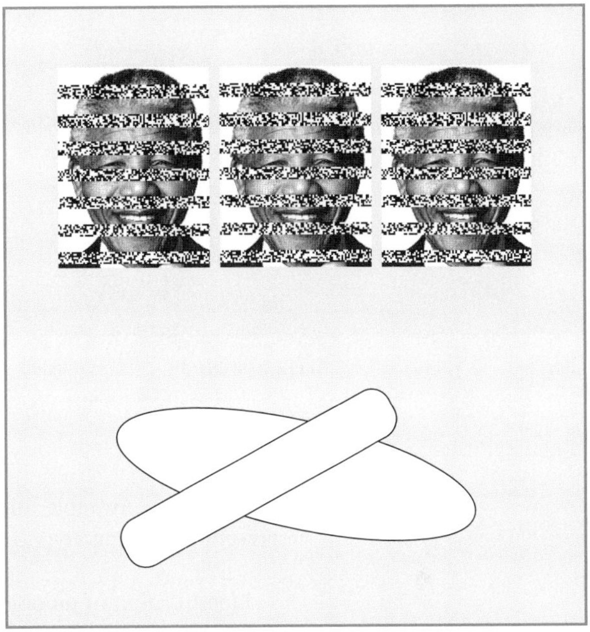

Depth cues are crucial for parsing image regions into surfaces, since they provide information about the depth ordering of different regions. Stereoscopic disparity is a particularly powerful parsing cue, as illustrated in Figure 9.5 (based on Nakayama, Shimojo, & Silverman, 1989). The figure shows an image of a face interleaved among horizontal strips of texture. When stereoscopic disparity is added to place the strips belonging to the face behind the texture strips, the face strips are parsed into a common surface, and the face is readily perceived. When disparity places the face strips in front, they are no longer parsed into a single surface, disrupting our perception of the face.

Though a powerful cue, stereoscopic disparity is not essential for surface parsing. The line drawing in Figure 9.5 shows a collection of arbitrary closed forms. We do not perceive three arbitrary shapes, but two surfaces arranged in depth, with one partially occluding the other. In this case surface parsing is based on the intersections between contours. "T"-junctions are strong occlusion cues. The surface to which the top of the "T" belongs is parsed as in front of the surface to which the upright of the "T" belongs.

In some situations, several alternative surface interpretations of an image may be available. In these circumstances, Nakayama et al. (1995) propose that the visual system selects the most likely interpretation, which assumes that the surfaces are being viewed from a "generic" vantage point as opposed to an "accidental" vantage point. A **generic viewpoint** is one of a large set of possible vantage points that all give roughly the same view. An **accidental viewpoint** is one that is uniquely associated with a very specific view of the scene. In Figure 9.5, for example, the generic constraint would parse the image into two shapes. It is also possible, though extremely unlikely, that the scene does actually consist of three separate shapes whose contours happen to line up with each other precisely at a specific vantage point. The generic view constraint is an example of a Bayesian approach to visual theories, discussed in the tutorial section.

**FIG. 9.5** Demonstrations of surface parsing. Top: the image of a face is interleaved with strips of texture. When the strips belonging to the face have far disparity, allowing them to be parsed into a single surface, the face is readily perceived (stereo viewing of this demonstration requires crossed free fusion, described in the next chapter). Bottom: monocular cues from T-junctions of contours are sufficient for surface parsing.

**KEY TERMS**
**Parsing:** A process that divides input signals into discrete, meaningful units.
**Generic viewpoint:** A viewpoint providing a perspective on an object that is typical of many other viewpoints.
**Accidental viewpoint:** A viewpoint providing a highly unusual, perhaps unique, perspective on an object.

*Think of some examples of generic and accidental views of everyday objects, such as a bucket or pen.*

**FIG. 9.6** A collection of objects, illustrating the various tasks that require object representations: recognition (a mug versus a jug); discrimination (my mug versus your mug); interaction (pour the milk from a jug into a mug).

# OBJECT REPRESENTATION

Imagine that you have made some teas and coffees for a group of friends, and have carried the mugs, milk, sugar, and so on, to the table (Figure 9.6). In order for each of your friends to pick up the correct drink, they need to:

1. Identify the mugs in the presence of other items such as milk jugs, sugar bowls, spoons, and biscuits.
2. Distinguish between their personal mug and other mugs.
3. Reach out and pick up their mug.

This everyday example illustrates some of the visual tasks that require object representations, namely:

- Identification of an object as belonging to a particular class (e.g. a mug versus milk jug).
- Discrimination of different objects within a class (e.g. my mug versus your mug).
- Interaction with objects (pour the milk without spillage).

Although most people complete these tasks without difficulty or effort, their underlying complexity is revealed when computer scientists attempt to build machines that can perform the same tasks. The main computational difficulty arises from the fact that images of objects reflect both intrinsic factors and extrinsic factors (Riesenhuber & Poggio, 2000):

- Intrinsic factors define the character of an individual object, in terms of its shape and surface properties.
- Extrinsic factors cause significant changes in the image of the object that are not related to its intrinsic properties. They include the viewpoint of the observer relative to the object; the nature of the light source such as its direction; the presence of occluding surfaces; and the nature of the background. Figure 9.7 illustrates the effect of extrinsic factors on the image of a mug.

**FIG. 9.7** Demonstration of how extrinsic factors affect the image of a mug. The images are very different, yet they all depict the same object.

Low-level features and surfaces extracted during earlier stages of visual processing reflect both instrinsic and extrinsic factors. Theories of object processing vary in the way they accommodate extrinsic factors. **View-independent** theories attempt to remove all extrinsic influences and build representations of objects that reflect only their intrinsic properties. **View-dependent** theories incorporate viewpoint effects into their object representations. Both kinds of theory include propositions for how a novel internal representation is created, and how novel representations are compared against stored representations of previously viewed objects.

## VIEW-INDEPENDENT THEORIES

View-independent theories propose that the visual system represents objects in terms of a **structural description** of their component parts, and the relations between those parts, independent of extrinsic factors. They are symbolic, containing a list of parts descriptors with associated properties. Marr and Nishihara (1978) offered an influential analysis of models based on structural descriptions, and some specific proposals for human vision.

### Marr and Nishihara's (1978) generalised cones

In Marr and Nishihara's (1978) theory, the basic descriptor for all object parts was a three-dimensional *generalised cone*, as illustrated in Figure 9.8.

A generalised cone corresponds to the volume created by moving a cross-section of constant shape but variable width along an axis. The shape in Figure 9.8 was created using a circular cross section. Generalised cones can form a variety of shapes including pyramids, spheres, and cylinders. Marr and Nishihara's description of a human figure, for example, was similar to a stick figure, as shown in Figure 9.9. Generalised cones forming cylinders capture the relative lengths and positions of the limbs.

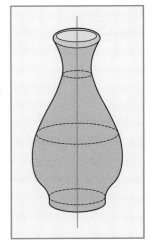

**FIG. 9.8** Marr and Nishihara's generalised cones, used to represent the shape of a vase. (From Bruce et al., 2003, Figure 9.15, p. 277.) Copyright © 2003 Psychology Press.

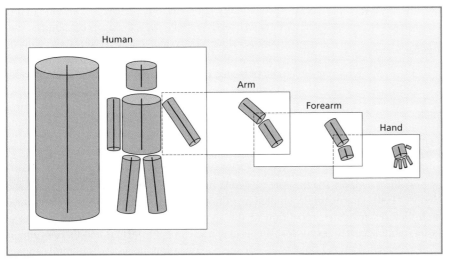

**FIG. 9.9** Marr and Nishihara's structural description of the human figure as a hierarchical arrangement of cylindrical shapes. From Marr and Nishihara (1978). Reprinted with permission of the Royal Society.

**KEY TERMS**
**View-independent representation:** An object representation that reflects only the intrinsic structure of the object; also known as an object-centred representation.
**View-dependent representation:** An object representation that reflects the structure of the object as seen from a specific viewpoint; also known as a viewer-centred representation.
**Structural description:** A view-independent representation containing a description of an object's parts, and the relationship between the parts.

Marr and Nishihara's 3-D object models were hierarchical in that component parts could themselves be decomposed into parts. Figure 9.9 shows models of the body, the arm, and the hand. Recognition was achieved by matching a model description derived from the image with stored 3-D model descriptions.

A crucial aspect of Marr and Nishihara's theory was the axis along which to sweep the cross-section of the generalised cone describing the object. Marr and Nishihara restricted their analysis to objects whose primary axis can be derived from its axis of symmetry or elongation. Marr (1977) had previously shown that the outline or silhouette of an object is sufficient to derive its primary axis (hence Marr's statement quoted earlier on the importance of contour integration). However, perceptual evidence that the visual system uses axis-based descriptions is not convincing (Quinlan & Humphreys, 1993).

## Biederman's (1987) geons

Marr and Nishihara's approach has been highly influential, even though their specific proposals have been disputed. Biederman's (1987) model of recognition is also based on structural descriptions, and owes a large debt to Marr and Nishihara's analysis. In contrast to Marr and Nishihara's generalised cones, Biederman's parts descriptors are a limited set of basic geometric shapes, or *geons*. Examples of proposed geons include wedges, cylinders, and bricks, as shown on the left of Figure 9.10. Example objects containing these geons are shown on the right of Figure 9.10. Geons are derived from a 2-D image representation, rather than the 3-D representation proposed by Marr and Nishihara.

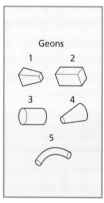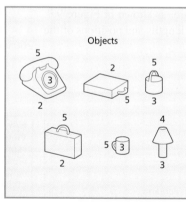

FIG. 9.10    A selection of Biederman's geons, and their combination to form objects. Reproduced from Biederman (1987) with permission © 1987 IEEE.

Biederman proposed that geons are detected on the basis of certain "non-accidental" properties of contours in the image, such as linearity, parallelism, curvilinearity, and symmetry. His assumption was that these image properties are more likely to reflect certain regularities in the world than to arise accidentally. For example, curved contours in the image usually reflect curved edges on objects, and parallel contours reflect parallel edges on objects. Specific non-accidental properties are used to detect the presence of specific geons. Parallel contours, for example, are used to detect the presence of "brick" geons. The structural description of a given object defines the spatial arrangement of the geons making it up.

Biederman and his co-workers reported a series of psychophysical experiments, which they interpreted as providing support for the role of geons in object representation. Biederman and Cooper (1991), for example, studied repetition priming. When subjects are presented with pictures to name, repetition of the same picture in different trials results in faster, more accurate responses. Biederman and Cooper (1991) found that priming is reduced when depicted objects do not share geon components. A limitation of these experiments is that they were not designed to critically test predictions from competing models. It is therefore not clear how well other models can account for the results.

Biederman's use of non-accidental properties is another example of Bayesian approaches to vision, discussed in the tutorial section of this chapter.

Models based on structural descriptions have several weaknesses:

- Since all objects are described using the same limited set of components, it is difficult to make fine discriminations between objects in the same class.
- It is possible to decompose any object in a number of ways, depending on what component parts are extracted. An "A", for example, can be decomposed into either three lines or five lines (Edelman, 1997). Indeed some objects, such as a shoe or a loaf, may have no structural decomposition at all.
- It has proven to be extremely difficult to find the lines and junctions from which to infer the presence of components in a natural (photographic) image. Implementations of Biederman's geon model have therefore restricted themselves to labelled line drawings.

## VIEW-DEPENDENT THEORIES

This class of theory does not attempt to construct a view-invariant, abstract model of objects. Instead, known objects are stored in terms of a small number of discrete prototypical forms. Recognition is achieved by comparing a novel view of an object against stored prototypes.

## Alignment

Ullman's (1998) model uses features such as surface markings and junctions between surfaces, which are particularly informative about the disposition of the object's surfaces. Each prototype stores the image positions of these features. Intermediate views can be created by interpolating between the positions of corresponding features in different prototypes. During recognition of an object from a novel viewpoint, the system attempts to create an intermediate view that matches the novel view. Figure 9.11 (top), for example, shows two prototypical views of the same car. Figure 9.11 (middle) shows a view that is intermediate between the two stored views, created by combining the positions of certain features in the two views. Figure 9.11 (bottom) shows a novel view of the car superimposed on the intermediate view (blue). The interpolated view is a good match with the novel view.

## Feature space

Edelman and Duvdevani-Bar's (1997) model is also based on comparisons between novel views and interpolated prototypical views, but uses a more complex form of prototype representation, and

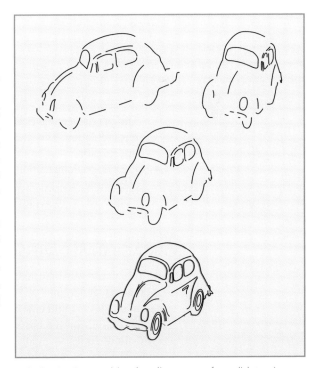

**FIG. 9.11** Recognition by alignment of candidate views with a novel view of an object. Top: Two prototypical views of a car. Middle: An intermediate view created by combining the two prototypical views. Bottom: A match between the intermediate view (blue) and a novel view (black). Modified from Ullman (1998).

**FIG. 9.12**  Recognition by interpolation between a novel object view and stored prototypical views. Each prototypical animal shape occupies a specific location in a multidimensional representation space (collapsed onto just two dimensions in the figure). The distance between prototypical shapes reflects their similarity. The similarity of a viewed shape (kangaroo) to stored prototypes is measured by their distances in the shape space. Re-drawn from Edelman (1995). Reproduced with kind permission of Springer Science and Business Media.

different mathematical procedures to achieve matching. Each prototype occupies a specific location in a multidimensional feature space (Ullman's model uses 2-D image space), which represents the many dimensions of variation along which shapes can vary. The distance between prototypical shapes in this representation reflects their similarity. A viewed shape is given a location in feature space, and can be categorised according to the prototypical shapes closest to it. In the example of Figure 9.12, the shapes of different animals are positioned according to their similarity.

Although the specific proposals of view-based models have not been subjected to perceptual tests, there is strong support for the general idea that human object recognition involves view-dependent representations. Palmer, Rosch, and Chase (1981) found that many objects have "canonical" views, from which subjects prefer to imagine, view, or photograph them. Object naming is faster using canonical views. Bulthoff and Edelman (1992) required subjects to learn complex unfamiliar shapes. Later recognition was poorer when the shapes were presented from novel viewpoints, even though the learning phase was sufficient to form a 3-D view-independent representation.

The main weaknesses of view-dependent theories are that:

● The precise geometrical structure of objects is usually not made explicit in the representation. This makes the representation unsuitable for tasks requiring such information.

● Present implementations include only a limited set of object prototypes. It is not clear how well view-dependent theories can be scaled up to accommodate a large set of object prototypes.

## IMAGE-BASED VERSUS SYMBOLIC PROCESSING

By this point you may have noticed that at every stage of processing theoretical approaches divide into two camps. Image-based theories perform computations on neural images to build new representations. The FRF process, for example, segments texture regions on the basis of variation in filter responses. In the opposing camp, symbolic theories manipulate symbols in order to build new symbolic representations. The two camps represent fundamentally different processing modes, yet there is no universal agreement as to which mode is used at each level of processing. Two points of agreement are that:

● At the lowest levels, such as retinal processing, visual analysis involves image-based computations.

- At the highest levels of processing the brain operates in symbolic mode, since the meanings attached to known objects are abstract. Your knowledge of an umbrella, for example, extends beyond its visual properties to include symbolic information about how to use it, and what function it serves.

There is a presumption that at some point during visual analysis, processing switches over from imaged-based to symbolic computations. However, there is no consensus regarding when the switch occurs. Only one theorist has attempted to build a complete theory of human vision that extends from retinal responses to object representations. David Marr's (1980) theory switched from image-based computations to symbolic computations as early as possible, after the outputs of low-level receptive fields. Marr's primal sketch is a symbolic representation. His early switch to symbolic computations has been problematic, because symbolic computational systems have been found to be very difficult to implement. On the other hand, more sophisticated (and tractable) image-based computations have been developed that can achieve representations previously thought not possible in this processing mode.

The presumption of a simple switch from image-based to symbolic computations once processing reaches a specific stage may be incorrect. The idea that different object representation systems operate in parallel, discussed in the next section, opens up the possibility that different processing modes may be used in parallel as well. Structural descriptions are inherently symbolic, whereas view-dependent representations lend themselves to image-based processing.

## MULTIPLE REPRESENTATIONAL SYSTEMS?

The debate between view-independent and view-dependent theories has been a lively one (see, e.g. Biederman & Gerhardstein, 1993; Tarr & Bulthoff, 1995). For example, advocates of structural descriptions have criticised experiments such as Bulthoff and Edelman's (1992) on the grounds that they used objects with no distinguishing geons. On the other hand, advocates of structural description theories tend to restrict themselves to objects that have a clear decomposition into component parts.

Testing for viewpoint dependence in recognition is not a decisive way to discriminate between theories, since all current models predict some perceptual effect of viewpoint. According to Marr and Nishihara's theory, views that obscure an object's major axis can be expected to impair performance. Biederman's geon theory predicts worse performance from viewpoints that introduce accidental properties leading to inappropriate geon decomposition.

Much of vision research operates on the basis that different theories are mutually exclusive, and one of the aims of researchers is to devise experiments that can critically distinguish between them. The field of object representation may not be amenable to this approach. Object representations are used in a variety of ways, as indicated earlier in the tea-serving example. In addition, humans can identify and discriminate an infinite variety of objects (if one considers each individual living form as a unique example). It may be too ambitious to expect a single representational system to cope with this variety of tasks and visual forms. Instead, the visual system may use multiple object representation systems for different tasks and/or different classes of object (Logothetis & Sheinburg, 1996; Foster & Gilson, 2002). In this scenario, both view-dependent and view-independent representations are used for different purposes. View-independent representations may be used for object classification, and view-dependent representations may be used for discriminations within an object class (Tarr & Bulthoff, 1995). Some have argued that face recognition requires a separate, specialised representational process (reviewed in Bruce & Humphreys, 1994).

The idea of multiple representational systems, using different modes of processing, finds an echo in the ideas discussed in previous chapters concerning parallel neural streams of processing ("what" versus "where", dorsal versus ventral, perception versus action).

# CHAPTER SUMMARY

Higher levels of visual processing can be divided into two broad stages:

- Shape representation
- Object representation.

## SHAPE REPRESENTATION

- Gestalt laws describe the tendency for image elements to be grouped together on the basis of such properties as proximity, similarity, common fate, and good continuation. Gestalt laws reflect the properties of real-world objects, such as cohesiveness and opacity.
- Shape segmentation can be achieved using texture analysis, common motion and depth properties, and symbolic grouping.
- Shape representation may also involve a parsing operation to link together disparate shapes that belong to the same, partially occluded object surface. Motion, depth, and T-junctions of contours are powerful parsing cues.

## OBJECT REPRESENTATION

- Object representations serve several purposes: recognition of an object as belonging to a general class; discrimination of particular objects within a class; interaction with objects.
- Object processing is computationally difficult because images of objects reflect both intrinsic factors and extrinsic factors. Theories of object processing differ in how they deal with extrinsic factors.
- View-independent theories propose that the visual system removes all extrinsic influences to create a structural description of objects in terms of their component parts and the relations between parts. Marr and Nishihara's (1978) model is based on generalised cones. Diederman's (1987) model is based on geons.
- View-dependent theories store objects in terms of a few discrete prototypical views. Recognition involves comparing a novel 2-D view with intermediate views between prototypes (Ullman, 1998), or comparing

the positions of novel views and prototypical views in higher dimensional feature space (Edelman & Duvdevani-Bar, 1997).

- Available evidence cannot distinguish decisively between different theories. There is no universal agreement as to which type of theory offers the best account of human object representation.
- Given the multiplicity of functions served by object representations, and the infinite variety of objects, it is possible that two or more different representational systems are used in parallel for different tasks and/or classes of object.

# TUTORIALS

## PASSIVE VERSUS ACTIVE PROCESSING

### Passive processing

The dominant view of visual processing, expressed in all the theories discussed in this chapter, is that the visual system is a *passive* information-processing device. When a visual stimulus impinges on the system, it triggers a cascade of computations as the information courses down through progressively deeper levels of analysis. The computations are pre-defined to work autonomously and automatically, in the same way on every occasion. They are also assumed to be exhaustive, in the sense that they attempt to build a representation of the whole scene. For example, in Marr's (1982) theory, "a key goal of early processing is the construction of something like an orientation-and-depth map of the visible surfaces around a viewer" (p. 129). Likewise Watt's (1988) theory of visual processing requires a "full scene description".

Passive, exhaustive computational theories are inspired by traditional image-processing programs implemented on computers using preset procedures or recipes (a list of instructions to be executed in sequence to complete a specific task). This traditional approach to computational modelling is not the only one available.

### Active processing

An alternative approach views visual processing as *active*, in the sense that it is flexible and selective. Flexible processing is tailored to the requirements of the task in hand at a given time. While driving a car, for example, the bulk of visual processing effort may be devoted to a fine-grained analysis of motion flow fields. While looking for a friend in a crowded room, on the other hand, processing effort may be directed towards subtle discriminations of facial features. Selective processing does not build a complete representation of the scene, but a partial representation only of those aspects of the scene relevant to the task in hand, perhaps structured in terms of the objects present (Pylyshyn & Storm, 1988; Kahneman, Treisman, & Gibbs, 1992).

## Physiological evidence

Several lines of physiological evidence are consistent with active control of processing.

### Single cell recordings

Electrophysiological studies have recorded activity in single neurons in the primate visual system while at the same time manipulating the animal's attention using a visual discrimination task. They have found that neural responses to stimuli at an attended location are enhanced, while responses to stimuli at an unattended location are reduced. Attentional modulation of this kind has been reported in several of the earliest cortical processing areas (e.g. Treue & Trujillo, 1999).

### Reciprocal connections

We saw in Chapter 7 that reciprocal connections are found between all cortical areas, and travel back as far as the lateral geniculate nuclei. A plausible role for these connections is the active control of processing.

### Inhomogeneity

The marked inhomogeneity of the retina and visual cortex presents a problem for theories which claim that the visual system builds a complete representation of the whole scene. Half the striate cortex is devoted to the central 1% of the visual field. Peripheral areas of the visual field are represented only in very coarse form (see cortical magnification in Figure 7.15). It could be argued that eye movements allow the visual system to scan the scene and build up a complete high-resolution representation that is stored in visual memory. However, psychophysical evidence described below shows that relatively little detailed information is retained from one glance to the next.

## Psychophysical evidence

### Acuity variation

The marked decline in spatial acuity away from central vision is a direct perceptual consequence of structural inhomogeneity. Figure 9.13 illustrates this decline graphically, and is based on charts devised by Anstis (1974). The equal-sized letters in the left-hand chart are legible only near the centre of the chart, assuming fixation on the central dot. Acuity declines roughly equally in all directions away from central vision. The letters in the right-hand chart progressively increase in size in inverse proportion to the decline in acuity, so that they remain equally discriminable at all positions. Changes in viewing distance (or actual size) make no difference: bringing the chart closer to the eyes (or enlarging it) increases the size of all letters, but also pushes them further out into the periphery. The visual system uses sudden, rapid eye movements (saccades) to direct an area of interest onto the central portion of the visual field where acuity is highest.

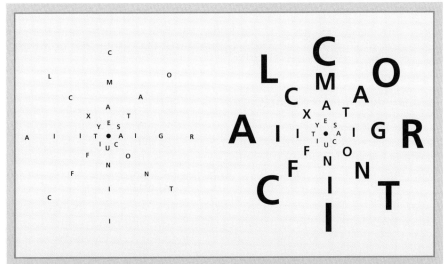

**FIG. 9.13**   Left: With strict fixation on the central spot, only the letters near the centre are clearly legible, due to variation in acuity with retinal position. Right: Each letter is equally legible because it is about 10 times its threshold size.

## Inattentional blindness

A number of recent experiments indicate that the visual system retains relatively little information from one glance to the next. Observers are unable to detect even gross changes in image content when they occur during saccades or simulated saccades, especially if the change occurs away from the focus of interest. This effect is called *inattentional blindness*, and has been demonstrated using a variety of experimental paradigms (see Simons & Levin, 1997). It indicates that observers never form a complete and detailed representation of their surroundings. Only partial representations are constructed, under the guidance of attention (Rensink, O'Regan, & Clark, 1997). In the context of natural eye movements the implication is that scene details are not retained from one glance to the next. A vivid demonstration of the transitory nature of sensory representations was described by Ballard, Hayhoe, Pook, and Rao (1997), who gave subjects a simple construction task illustrated in Figure 9.14. They were shown a pattern of coloured blocks on a computer screen (top left), and were required to reproduce it (bottom) by moving blocks from a stockpile using a mouse (top right). Eye movement records showed that subjects checked the model very frequently. Furthermore, surreptitious changes to the pattern of blocks in the model during the task (when the eyes were directed elsewhere) were not usually detected by the subject.

It seems that much less scene information is encoded and retained with each glance than

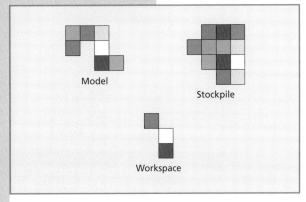

**FIG. 9.14**   In this computer-based task, the subject is shown a pattern of coloured blocks on a computer screen (model at top left). He must reproduce the pattern by dragging blocks from the stockpile (top right) to the workspace (bottom) using a computer mouse.

one would expect on the basis of passive, exhaustive processes. Instead, processing resources are allocated under the control of attention. Recent psychophysical research demonstrates the importance of attentional effects in visual processing.

### Spatial resolution of attention

Acuity variation is often invoked to explain why text is legible only over a short distance on either side of fixation. Each word in this line is legible at the point where you fixate, but words a short distance to the left or right of fixation are not legible. As well as acuity limitations, an effect known as "crowding" contributes to illegibility. When a single letter is placed by itself away from the centre of gaze, it may be legible, as in the top panel of Figure 9.15 (fixate on the upper dot at the left). When the same letter forms part of a word, it is no longer possible to distinguish it clearly (fixate on the lower dot at the left of the top panel). The letters appear to crowd each other out. This kind of crowding can be explained by assuming that there is a limit to how finely we can focus our spatial attention (He, Cavanagh, & Intriligator, 1997). An example is shown in the bottom panel of Figure 9.15. When the central spot is fixated, it is possible to resolve the individual bars in the gratings both to the left and to the right. However, the bars on the left are too closely spaced to be resolved attentionally. We cannot direct our attention to individual bars, or count through them without moving fixation from the central spot. The bars on the right are more widely spaced, so attention to each bar is possible. An equivalent effect exists in the temporal domain. When a spot flickers on and off repeatedly at a slow rate, its bright and dark phases can be perceived and counted individually. At faster rates (above 4–6 Hz), individual phases cannot be separated and counted.

### Object-based attention

It is possible to divide attention between several different objects simultaneously, provided that the objects do not suffer from the crowding effects described above. The clearest demonstration of this effect comes from studies of multiple object tracking, illustrated in Figure 9.16. The observer views a computer display containing, say, nine disks (left panel). When the disks first appear, four of them flash briefly. Then the disks all begin moving around the display randomly (middle panel). The observer's task is to keep track of the four disks that had flashed briefly at the start. After 10 seconds or so the observer is asked to pick out the four disks that had flashed (right panel). Observers can perform this task successfully, selecting the correct disks almost

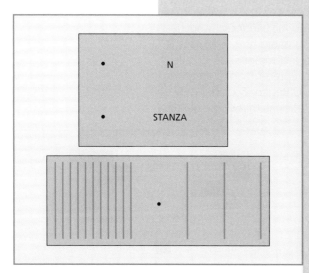

**FIG. 9.15** Upper panel: While fixating the dot at the top, the letter N to the right can be seen clearly. While fixating the dot below, the letter N cannot be seen clearly, due to crowding by the other letters in the word. Lower panel: While fixating on the central spot, it is possible to attend to each of the bars on the right individually, and count them. Although the bars on the left can be resolved, it is not possible to attend to each individually, or to count them.

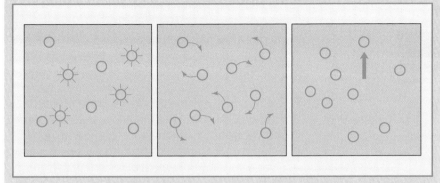

**FIG. 9.16** Nine disks appear on-screen (left), and four of them flash briefly. All nine disks then move randomly around the screen (middle). After a short while all the disks stop, and the observer must select which four disks had flashed at the beginning (right).

nine times out of ten (Pylyshyn & Storm, 1988). However, errors increase dramatically when observers are asked to track more than four objects simultaneously, indicating that processing effort is applied selectively rather than exhaustively.

### Attentional modulation

Even relatively low level visual processes are amenable to modulation by attention. For example, a number of effects in motion perception, such as adaptation, are influenced by manipulations of attention (Raymond, 2000).

## Mixed modes of processing

To a certain degree the passive versus active dichotomy maps onto the distinction between image-based and symbolic processing modes discussed earlier. Image-based operations are readily implemented as passive information-processing procedures, while symbolic computations are by their very nature selective representations of certain properties. However, it is possible to conceive of an active processing system that contains both image-based and symbolic computational sub-systems. Ullman (1984a) introduced the notion of *visual routines*, which are special self-contained processes that perform certain tasks, such as counting, indexing, and tracking, and are actively invoked by attention. Some of these routines may be autonomous image-processing procedures, invoked as and when required. Others may involve symbolic computations. According to this view, the visual system contains a collection of specialised processing modules performing a variety of computations, that are invoked as and when required by the attentional system.

## BAYESIAN MODELS OF VISUAL PERCEPTION

Visual images are generally ambiguous in the sense that the same sensory data can be interpreted in a number of different ways. The simple example

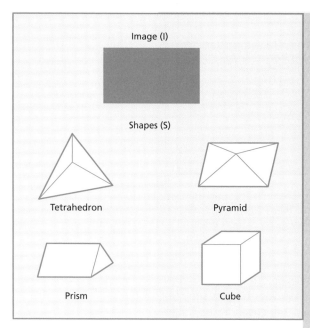

**FIG. 9.17**   An image containing an arbitrary geometrical shape, and four 3-D objects that could all have given rise to it.

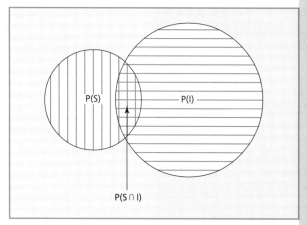

**FIG. 9.18**   Venn diagram to illustrate Bayesian probability. The area of P(I) represents the probability of an individual experiencing indigestion. The area of P(S) represents the probability of suffering from a stomach ulcer. The overlap between the two areas represents the probability of suffering from indigestion and a stomach ulcer at the same time.

shown in Figure 9.17 depicts a dark rectangular shape projected onto the retina. What real-world object created this image?

Four possible 3-D objects are shown. How does the visual system select one of these alternatives as its interpretation of the image? One solution is to use prior experience of real-world objects as a basis for rejecting interpretations that are unlikely to be true. Bayes' theorem provides a rigorous mathematical framework for modelling how prior knowledge should be combined with sensory data to make inferences about the world.

## Bayesian probability

Bayesian probability is best explained with a concrete example. Assume that I is a medical symptom, indigestion, and that S is a medical condition, a stomach ulcer. P(I) is the probability of an individual experiencing indigestion, and P(S) is the probability of suffering from a stomach ulcer. Both of these probabilities can be estimated empirically by physicians. The Venn diagram in Figure 9.18 represents P(I) and P(S) as two sets. The relative areas of the sets represent their relative probabilities. Indigestion is more likely to occur than a stomach ulcer, because it can arise from a variety of causes. The overlap in the circles (cross-hatched area) represents the probability of suffering indigestion *and* a stomach ulcer at the same time, shown as P(S ∩ I).

Physicians have learnt that indigestion is a symptom associated with stomach ulcers, and can estimate the probability of suffering indigestion given the confirmed presence of a stomach ulcer. This probability is known as a conditional probability, and is denoted by P(I/S). It corresponds to the probability of both S and I occurring together as a proportion of the overall probability that S occurs. In the Venn diagram, it is the cross-hatched area P(S ∩ I) as a proportion of the P(S) area. Conditional probability P(I/S) is formally defined as follows:

$$P(I/S) = P(S \cap I)/P(S) \qquad (9.1)$$

We can rearrange the terms in equation (9.1) so that

$$P(S \cap I) = P(S) \cdot P(I/S) \qquad (9.2)$$

Similarly, the conditional probability of a stomach ulcer given that indigestion is present corresponds to the cross-hatched area P(S ∩ I) as a proportion of the P(I) area. It is formally defined as follows:

$$P(S/I) = P(S \cap I)/P(I) \qquad (9.3)$$

Rearranging again,

$$P(S \cap I) = P(I) \cdot P(S/I) \qquad (9.4)$$

Since the left-hand side of equations (9.2) and (9.4) is the same, we can see that:

$$P(I) \cdot P(S/I) = P(S) \cdot P(I/S) \qquad (9.5)$$

Equation (9.5) can be rearranged to form Bayes' theorem:

$$P(S/I) = P(S) \cdot P(I/S)/P(I) \qquad (9.6)$$

Equation (9.6) is the basis of Bayesian inference. The left-hand side, P(S/I), is an inference or diagnosis, usually called a posterior probability. In our medical example, it expresses the probability of suffering a stomach ulcer given that the symptom of indigestion is present. The terms on the right-hand side are measurable probabilities. P(S) expresses our knowledge about the probability of a stomach ulcer being present (prior probability). P(I/S) is the likelihood that the indigestion could have arisen from the presence of a stomach ulcer. P(I), the probability of the symptom occurring, can be considered as a normalising constant when we are making inferences about diseases in the presence of I, so

$$P(S/I) \approx P(S) \cdot P(I/S) \qquad (9.7)$$

This form of Bayes' theorem is commonly used in Bayesian approaches to vision. It has been applied in a wide range of areas, including shape analysis, motion illusions, contour integration, and colour constancy (reviewed in Kersten & Yuille, 2003). The attractiveness of Bayesian approaches to vision comes from the way they combine Helmholtz's notion of perceptual inference with explicit probabilistic descriptions of prior knowledge and image data.

## Bayesian inference in shape analysis

Returning to the example in Figure 9.17, image I is equivalent to the symptom of indigestion in the medical example. It indicates the presence of a shape, but is actually consistent with several shapes. Each shape S is equivalent to a different disease, any of which could have created image I. For each shape we must calculate the posterior probability that it is present given image I, namely P(S/I). From Bayes' theorem (equation (9.7)), we can see that this probability depends on:

- Prior knowledge about the probability that the shape could exist in the real world, P(S). Given the constraints of the real-world objects, some shapes are much more likely to exist than others. In the arbitrary example in Figure 9.17, we shall assume that a prism is the most commonly encountered object. Table 9.1 provides illustrative values for P(S).
- The likelihood that the image could have arisen from the shape P(I/S). In our example, we shall assume that the shape, whatever it is, is viewed side-on to one of its sides. So the likelihood associated with each shape is based on the proportion of its sides having a silhouette that matches the image I. The cube has the highest likelihood because all its sides match the silhouette. Table 9.1 gives P(I/S) values for all four possible shapes.

Table 9.1 also shows the posterior probability of each shape, calculated by multiplying its prior probability by its likelihood. Now the visual system must apply a decision rule to determine which shape interpretation to select. The best guess is usually taken as the most likely shape, namely the prism. A more detailed introduction to Bayesian methods, based on an example similar to that illustrated in Figure 9.17, can be found in Knill, Kersten, and Yuille (1996). We can see from this example how the interpretation depends jointly on prior knowledge about the world P(S) and on how well each shape accounts for the sensory data P(I/S). A change in either can alter the interpretation.

## Bayesian inference in signal combination

Bayes' theorem can also be used in situations where a number of different signals must be combined to produce a single value. In motion analysis, different local motion detectors may provide separate estimates of the velocity of an image element. Bayes' theorem provides a method of combining these signals to yield a single estimate of element velocity. Weiss, Kemmler, Deisenhammer, Fleischhacker, and Delazer (2002) proposed a model in which the prior P(S) assumes that slower velocities are more likely than faster velocities. Their likelihood function P(I/S) assumes that local motion responses tend to be noisy, resulting in greater noise at lower stimulus contrasts.

**TABLE 9.1 ILLUSTRATIVE BAYESIAN PRIORS FOR THE SHAPES IN FIGURE 9.17**

| Object | P(S) | P(I/S) | P(S/I) |
|---|---|---|---|
| Tetrahedron | 0.1 | 0 | 0 |
| Pyramid | 0.3 | 0.2 | 0.06 |
| Prism | 0.4 | 0.6 | 0.24 |
| Cube | 0.2 | 1 | 0.2 |

Estimated velocity is based on the most likely velocity in the resulting posterior distribution (which was also the mean of the posterior distribution). Weiss et al. (2002) applied the model to a range of motion stimuli, and found that the estimated velocity agreed with that reported psychophysically.

In depth analysis, different depth cues may provide separate estimates of the depth of an image element. For example, an observer may be required to judge the depth depicted in a stimulus containing both motion and texture cues. Bayesian approaches propose that the two cues are combined by a weighted average:

$$d = (w_m \cdot d_m) + (w_t \cdot d_t)$$

where $d$ is the combined depth estimate, and $d_m$ and $d_t$ are estimates of depth provided by the motion and texture cues respectively. These values are Bayesian estimates that maximise their posterior probabilities $P(d/m)$ and $P(d/t)$. The weights attached to each cue in the average, $w_m$ and $w_t$, sum to one and are based on a comparison of the variances of the $P(d/m)$ and $P(d/t)$ distributions. For example, if the variance of $P(d/m)$ is high, and the variance of $P(d/t)$ is low, then the weights are biased in favour of texture over motion since that cue is more reliable (see Jacobs, 2002).

These examples illustrate how Bayesian approaches can be applied in a wide variety of perceptual tasks. They provide a method of computing perceptual inferences that make optimal use of the information available. As such, Bayesian inferences provide a benchmark or *ideal observer* against which to compare the performance of real observers.

# CHAPTER 10

## CONTENTS

# Depth perception

**10**

## INTRODUCTION

It is essential to construct a representation of depth in order to interact in various ways with a three-dimensional (3-D) world, such as reaching out to pick up objects, walking over uneven terrain, or assessing how far away a dangerous predator may be (Figure 10.1).

The images cast onto our retinas vary in only two spatial dimensions. Image elements can be specified in terms of their vertical ($y$) location, and their lateral ($x$) location. The third dimension of depth, or $z$ location, is missing. Yet this dimension is crucial for dealing with the 3-D world. The visual system must recover this missing dimension from the clues available in the two-dimensional image, and in the state of the muscles both inside and outside the eye.

**FIG. 10.1** Many everyday activities require perceptual judgements of three-dimensional depth and distance. Copyright © David Butow/Corbis Saba.

## THE MULTIPLICITY OF DEPTH CUES

Retinal images contain multiple visual cues regarding the depth of objects within view. Additionally, the visual system can make use of non-visual cues from the oculomotor muscles controlling eye position and accommodative state. Several cues provide **metric** information that can be used to make precise quantitative estimates of how far away an object is, or at least how much farther one object is than another. Other cues provide **ordinal depth** information, which can only be used to establish the depth ordering of different parts of the scene (no quantitative information). We shall begin by discussing cues available in the image projected on a single retina, or in the position of a single eye, the so-called **monocular cues**.

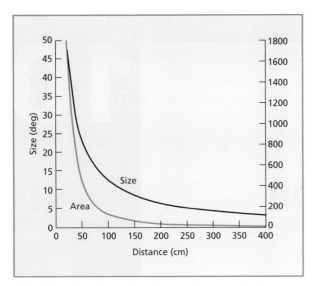

**FIG. 10.2** Graph showing the variation in projected image size and area of a football as a function of distance from the viewer. Variation in size and area is highly non-linear. Most of the range of variation is confined to distances of less than 3 metres.

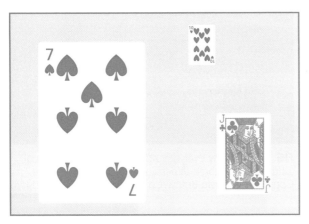

**FIG. 10.3** Demonstration of relative size as a distance cue. The three playing cards appear to be at different distances because their images differ in size. This effect relies on the assumption that the three cards have the same actual size.

# MONOCULAR CUES

## Retinal image size

The most basic cue to depth arises from the geometric fact that an object of fixed actual size will project a progressively smaller image onto the retina as it is viewed from more distant viewpoints (see Chapter 6 to review geometrical optics). The retinal area covered by the object decreases at a faster rate than its size, as illustrated in Figure 10.2.

The graph shows the imaged diameter and visual area of a football as a function of its distance from the eye (starting from a distance of 20 cm, a typical value for the near point of accommodation). Notice that the variation in size and area is highly non-linear. Retinal size is halved each time distance doubles. Once the ball reaches a distance of approximately 2 metres, 90% of its range of variation in size has occurred. The range of variation in area asymptotes more quickly; 90% of its range of variation is reached at a distance of less than 3 metres.

Retinal image size varies in a lawful and systematic way with distance. So if we are viewing two objects of equal actual size, and the image of one is half the size of the other, we can infer that it is twice as far away. The usefulness of image size as a depth cue is limited by the fact that it requires some knowledge of actual size, or at least similarity in size. Nevertheless, in many viewing conditions this limitation does not preclude the use of retinal size as a cue, since many commonly viewed classes of object, such as trees, humans, and cars, are similar in size. Figure 10.3 is based on the experiment of Ittelson (1951).

## Height in the visual field

Imagine that you are standing on a level surface outdoors (usually called the *ground plane* in the perceptual literature) and looking toward the distant horizon. The position in the visual field of surface markings or of objects resting on the ground depends on their distance. We can express visual field position in degrees, where 0° corresponds to the horizon, and 90° corresponds to a position at your feet (perpendicular to your line of sight). As elements on the surface move farther away, their position rises progressively from near 90° to near zero. Figure 10.4 shows **height in the visual field (HVF)** as a function of distance. HVF varies with the tangent of visual field position (shown in the inset). HVF therefore offers an indication of distance.

The upper plot represents HVF from the point of view of a human of average height (160 cm). The lower plot represents HVF from the point of view of a crawling infant, or a domestic cat (20 cm). Cue variation is much more rapid when the eyes are closer to the ground. Equivalent distances also project to more central locations in the image. A point 400 cm away on the ground plane is only 3° below the line of sight from the point of view of a cat, but over 20° away from the line of sight from the viewpoint of an adult human.

The cue plotted in Figure 10.4 can be used as either a visual cue or a non-visual cue. A comparison of the vertical position of two elements in the visual field provides the visual cue of height. The change in angle of elevation of the eyes as one shifts fixation between the two elements provides a non-visual cue, assuming that information is available from the extra-ocular muscles that control eye position.

There has been relatively little psychophysical research on the use of HVF as a depth cue (Epstein, 1966; Wallach & O'Leary, 1982; Ooi, Wu, & He, 2001). In a recent paper, Ooi et al. (2001) measured apparent distance using two tasks. One task required a blindfolded subject to walk to a previously seen spot on the ground. The other task required the subject to throw a beanbag to a visible target on the ground. Ooi et al. (2001) manipulated the HVF cue by having subjects wear prisms that displaced the image vertically. They found evidence that HVF does indeed influence perceived distance.

The utility of height in the visual field as a cue to distance has a major limitation. The relation between height and distance shown in Figure 10.4 applies only to objects or markings on horizontal ground plane surfaces. When objects move off the ground plane and into the air, height in the image is an unreliable indicator of distance. When surfaces depart from horizontal, height is determined by surface slant as well as distance. While reading a page in a book held up in front of you, for example, text on different lines varies markedly in vertical position but relatively little in viewing distance. On the other hand, the *rate* at which text varies in size at different vertical positions in the image (an example of a texture gradient) can be used to infer surface slant.

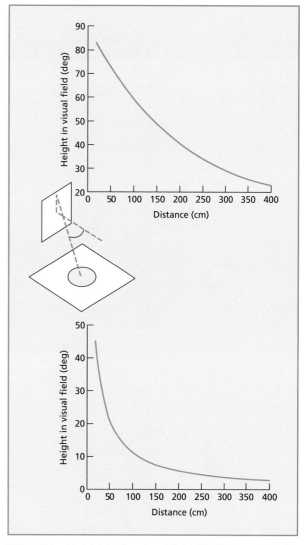

**FIG. 10.4**  Height in the visual field (HVF) of an object on the ground surface as a function of its distance from the viewer, assuming a horizontal ground plane and fixation on the horizon. The upper plot shows HVF from the point of view of a human of average height (160 cm), while the lower plot shows HVF from the point of view of a crawling infant or domestic cat (20 cm). The inset shows the angle plotted in the graphs.

## Texture gradients

The image of a textured surface that is slanted away from an observer, such as the ground plane or the book discussed above, contains highly structured variations in the shape and density of elements located on the surface. Gibson (1950) noted that

> **KEY TERM**
> **Texture gradient:**
> A monocular cue to the orientation and depth of a textured surface; it is based on graded variation in the size, shape, and density of texture elements.

texture gradients provide visual cues about surface orientation and depth. Figure 10.5 (top) shows an example of a textured surface slanted away from the viewpoint. Three separable components of texture gradient are evident as one moves across the image in the direction of surface slant (vertically in Figure 10.5).

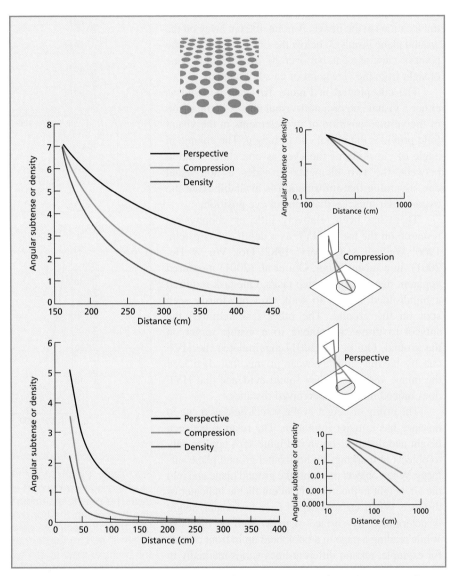

**FIG. 10.5**   Top: The image of a textured surface slanted away from the viewer. There is a graded variation in texture properties as one moves across the image in the direction of increasing distance: element width or separation decreases (perspective gradient); element height decreases (compression gradient); and texture density (elements per unit area in the image) increases. (From Bruce et al., 2003, Figure 7.14A, p. 189.) Middle and bottom: Graphs plotting the three components of texture gradient for a ground plane surface from the point of view of a human of average height (middle), and a crawling infant or domestic cat (bottom). Inset: The inset drawings show the angles plotted for compression and perspective; 1/density is plotted in the graphs to allow comparison with the other quantities. The inset graphs re-plot the data from the large plots on logarithmic axes, revealing the power-law relationship.

## Perspective gradient

Element *width* or separation at right-angles to the slant varies systematically. Convergence or linear perspective is a special case of this gradient, the most familiar example of which is the convergence of rail tracks as they disappear into the distance.

## Compression gradient

Element *height* in the direction of slant varies progressively, due to the foreshortening effect of surface slant.

## Density gradient

The number of elements per unit of area in the image varies progressively. At the bottom of the image in Figure 10.5 (nearest part of the surface), there are relatively few texture elements per unit of image area, while at the top of the image (farthest part of the surface) there are many texture elements in an equal-sized image area.

The graphs in the lower part of Figure 10.5 plot these three components of texture gradient for a ground plane surface as a function of distance from the viewer's eyes. The upper graph plots texture variation from the point of view of an adult human, and the lower graph plots texture variation from the point of view of a domestic cat or crawling infant. Both graphs plot the projected height, width, and density of equally sized and spaced elements on the ground plane. All three texture cues vary with distance according to a **power law** (inset). Cue variation is more gradual for taller observers, because the degree of slant in the surface along a given line of sight is lower.

The projection in the visual image of texture elements distributed on any planar surface, such as the wall of a building, will obey the power-law function shown in Figure 10.5. The steepness of the function depends on surface slant. Knill (1998) measured the ability of observers to discriminate small changes in the slant depicted in a planar textured surface, for slants ranging from zero (a vertical surface parallel to the plane of the image) to 70° (nearly horizontal). He found that performance was very poor for slants near vertical, but improved markedly as depicted slant increased. Knill (1998) concluded that texture gradients were useful only for slants in excess of 50°. When viewing a horizontal ground plane from the height of an adult, this would correspond to the slant visible when fixating on a point on the ground at least 2 metres away. From the point of view of a cat, this slant would occur while fixating at a distance of only 25 cm. Of the three gradients described above, Knill (1998) found that compression seemed most important for slant judgements.

The utility of texture gradients clearly relies on the presence of textured surfaces. Strictly speaking, elements should have uniform size, shape, and spacing on the surface for the cue to operate reliably. However, Knill (1998) and others have shown that the visual system is able to make use of texture gradient cues even when texture elements vary somewhat in size, shape, or spacing.

## Image blur

In a real retinal image of a slanted surface, such as that depicted in Figure 10.5, some parts of the scene will inevitably be more spatially blurred than others. Eyes, like cameras, have a limited **depth of field**. Assume that the eye (or camera) is focused on a point at a given distance. Within a certain range of distances, points lying

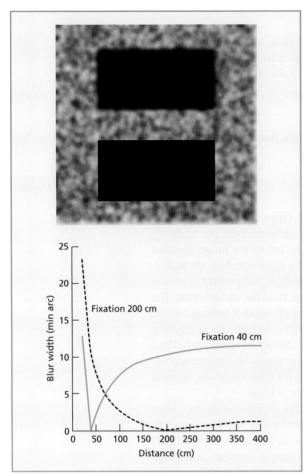

**FIG. 10.6** Image blur as a depth cue. Top: Two black rectangles against a blurred texture background. The rectangle with sharply-defined borders appears closer than the rectangle with blurred borders. Bottom: Degree of blur in the image of a point in a 3-D scene as a function of the distance of the point from the viewer. The solid line shows image blur when the observer fixates on a point at a distance of 40 cm; the broken line depicts blur assuming fixation at 200 cm. Blur is absent for scene points at fixation distance, but increases for nearer or more distant points. Values were calculated using equations in Mather and Smith (2000).

Leonardo da Vinci was a pioneer in the use of atmospheric perspective in paintings. He developed a technique known as *sfumato* ("smoky" or "hazy" in Italian), which involved the application of thin translucent glazes to reduce contrast and so create a sense of distance.

nearer or farther away than the point of focus will appear sharply defined in the image. This range of distances defines the optical system's depth of field. Points lying beyond these limits will appear blurred in the image, by an amount that depends lawfully on distance. The graph in Figure 10.6 (bottom) shows how the magnitude of blur varies with distance from the point of fixation. Two fixation distances are plotted, 40 cm and 200 cm. Blur is absent at fixation distance, and increases more sharply for nearer distances than for farther distances. Depth of field is defined by the smallest increase in blur on either side of fixation that is perceptible to the observer (Campbell, 1957).

Blur in a region of the image therefore offers a cue to the distance of surfaces in that region (Pentland, 1987), and several computational algorithms have been proposed for estimating depth from image blur. Perceptual evidence indicates that image blur does influence perception of depth (Marshall, Burbeck, Ariely, Rolland, & Martin, 1996; Mather, 1996). Figure 10.6 (top) shows a synthetic image in which blur provided a cue to the differing depths of the black rectangles.

The utility of blur as a depth cue is limited by two factors. First, depth of field depends on the diameter of the entrance pupil. So a point at a given distance from fixation will appear more blurred when viewed through a relatively wide pupil than when viewed through a narrow pupil. Second, human observers are relatively insensitive to small changes in blur extent (Mather & Smith, 2002). Consequently, regional blur differences probably provide relatively coarse ordinal depth information, indicating that two surfaces lie at different depths.

## Atmospheric perspective

Light from distant objects has to travel through more atmosphere than light from nearby objects. Atmospheric particles, including dust, air, and water molecules, scatter light. Consequently, distant objects appear reduced in contrast, as shown in Figure 10.7 (there is also a slight shift toward bluish hues). The degree of attenuation in contrast depends on the atmosphere's attenuation coefficient. Figure 10.7 (bottom) plots contrast as a function of distance for different attenuation coefficients. Contrast does seem to be a cue to ordinal depth.

O'Shea, Blackburn, and Ono (1994) reported that higher contrast shapes are judged as nearer than

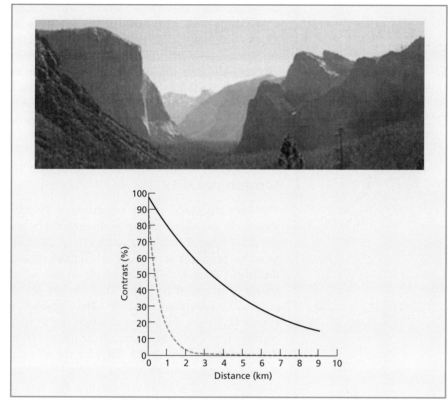

**FIG. 10.7**   Contrast attenuation due to light scattering by atmospheric particles (dust, air, and water molecules). The photograph at the top demonstrates the reduction in contrast in the image of more distant hills compared with nearer hills. The graph at the bottom plots contrast as a function of distance for two different atmospheric conditions, clear (solid line), and light fog (dashed line; re-drawn from Fry, Bridgman, & Ellerbrock, 1949). Notice that the distance scale covers several kilometres.

lower contrast shapes. Given the relatively slow change in contrast with distance, it is best viewed as a coarse, ordinal depth cue used in images that contain a very wide range of distances.

## Accommodation

If an observer shifts fixation between points in the scene lying at different distances, the lens of the eye must change shape (accommodate) in order to maintain a sharply focused image of the fixated point. Accommodation is controlled by the ciliary muscles of the eye. The lens is at its thinnest when the muscles are relaxed, optimal for distance vision (shown at the top left of Figure 10.8). Fixation on a relatively near point requires that the muscles contract to release the tension on the lens's suspensory ligaments, allowing the lens to assume a thicker shape (top right of Figure 10.8). Information on the state of the ciliary muscles therefore offers a non-visual cue to absolute fixation distance.

Figure 10.8 also shows a plot of accommodation as a function of fixation distance. In an eye free of refractive error, no accommodation is required for objects

The range of accommodation shrinks with age. By the time most people reach their 50s, there is virtually no accommodative range left, due to loss of flexibility in the lens (hence the need for reading glasses).

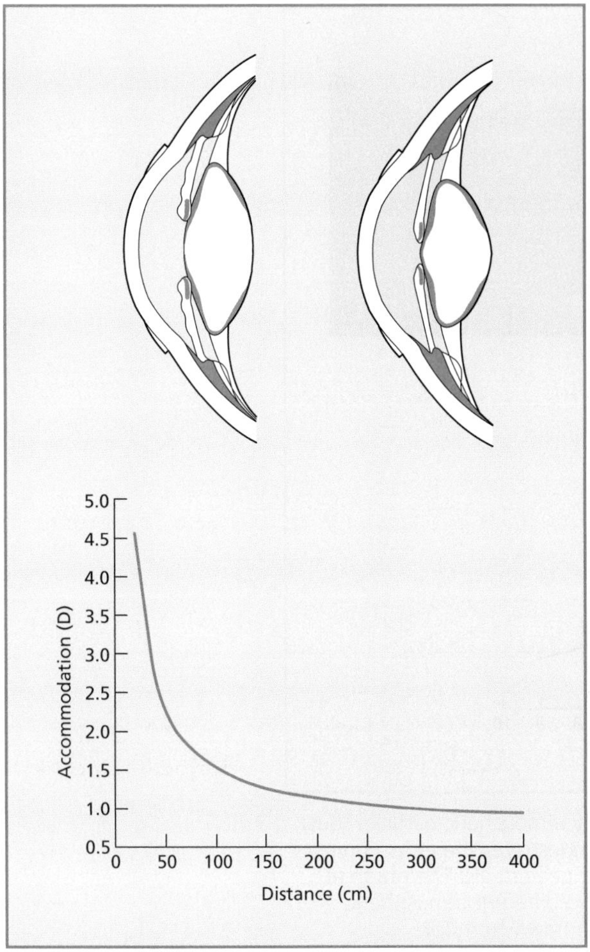


**FIG. 10.8** Top: The eye's lens changes shape to maintain a sharply focused retinal image of scene points at different distances. When fixating distant points (left), the ciliary muscles are relaxed and the lens is quite thin, producing relatively little convergence of incoming light rays; for near points (right), the ciliary muscles are tensed to allow the lens to take on a thicker shape, producing greater convergence of incoming rays. Bottom: Graph showing accommodation in dioptres (D) as a function of object distance from the eye (re-plotted from Charman, 1991, Figure 5.30a; recall from the tutorial section of Chapter 6 that the converging power of a lens is measured in dioptres).

at very far distances. The nearest distance to which young adults can accommodate is approximately 15 cm. The range of distances over which accommodation changes significantly with distance extends only from about 15 to 300 cm. Fisher and Ciuffreda (1988) and Mon-Williams and Tresilian (2000) report that within this range accommodation probably provides only relatively coarse, ordinal depth information.

## Motion parallax

The cues discussed so far are available in static scenes. If the observer moves through the scene, the movement of image elements across the retina provides powerful depth cues. Movement through the world creates motion gradients in the retinal image, which bear a close relation to the texture gradients described earlier. The graphs in Figure 10.5 show the projected height and width of equally sized elements located on the ground plane. Projected height and width decrease for elements located at progressively farther distances. We can also view the graphs as representing the velocity of elements that move through equal distances on the ground plane, rather than elements that are equal-sized.

### *Optic flow*

In the case of *height* variation (compression), the graphs show the projected velocity of points on the ground at different distances, moving *towards* the observer at a constant speed. The lengths of the arrows in Figure 10.9 (top) show velocity in different parts of the image. This pattern of movement is often called *optic flow*.

### *Motion parallax*

In the case of *width* variation (perspective) plotted in Figure 10.5, the graphs show the projected velocity of points at different distances moving *across* the observer's field of view at a constant speed. The lengths of the arrows in Figure 10.9 (middle) show velocity at different distances. This pattern of movement is often called *motion parallax*.

**KEY TERM**
**Motion parallax:** Movement in one part of an image relative to another, as can be produced by objects moving at different distances from the observer.

The examples in Figures 10.5 and 10.9 assume that the observer's gaze remains fixed on the horizon. If the observer fixates on one of the moving points, then that point becomes a stationary reference in the image, and the projected movement of all other points in the field will be expressed relative to that point. For example, in the case of motion parallax, if the observer tracks a point in the middle distance, the movement pattern shown in Figure 10.9 (bottom) will result. Points nearer than the fixated point are moving more rapidly, so will continue to move in the same direction as previously. Points farther away than the fixated point are moving more slowly, so will move in the opposite direction. Psychophysical experiments have shown that optic flow and motion parallax are sufficient to support high-precision depth perception even when no other depth cues are available (Rogers & Graham, 1979; M. G. Harris, 1994). The success of Imax theatres is testament to the power of dynamic depth cues. Motion processing is discussed in more detail in Chapter 11. That chapter also discusses a phenomenon known as the kinetic depth effect, in which the three-dimensional structure of an object can be inferred solely on the basis of its movement properties.

## Shadows

Directional illumination creates two kinds of shadow. *Cast shadows* are shadows from one object that fall on the surface of another object. *Attached shadows* are those cast by the object onto its own surface. Both kinds of shadow provide depth information. Kersten, Knill, Mamassian, and Bulthoff (1996) demonstrated how the position and movement of cast shadows determine perceptual interpretations of depth. Figure 10.10 (top) reproduces the effect studied by Kersten et al. (1996). The texture gradient on the surface provides a 3-D context for the spheres, but the perceived position of the spheres depends on their cast shadows.

Figure 10.10 (bottom) shows how attached shadows provide powerful cues to 3-D object structure. Koenderink, van Doorn, and Kappers (1996) found that shading cues are important for judging 3-D shape (though their stimuli also contained texture cues). Many sculptures are carved from materials that provide no cues to

**FIG. 10.9** Motion parallax provides powerful depth cues, illustrated by these images depicting an outdoor scene from the viewpoint of a moving observer (based on illustrations in Gibson, 1950). Top: When the observer translates across the ground plane towards the horizon, while fixating on the horizon, scene points translate across the image in a highly structured expanding pattern, often called optic flow. Retinal velocity increases as scene points approach the observer. Middle: When the observer translates to the left, while maintaining fixation on the horizon, the pattern of retinal flow again provides information about distance. The retinal velocity of a given point depends on its distance from the viewer. Bottom: When the observer fixates on a point in the middle distance (F) while translating leftwards, point F becomes stationary on the retina, while other points move leftward or rightward. Image points that were moving rightward more rapidly than the point in the middle distance continue to move rightwards; points that were moving more slowly now move leftwards.

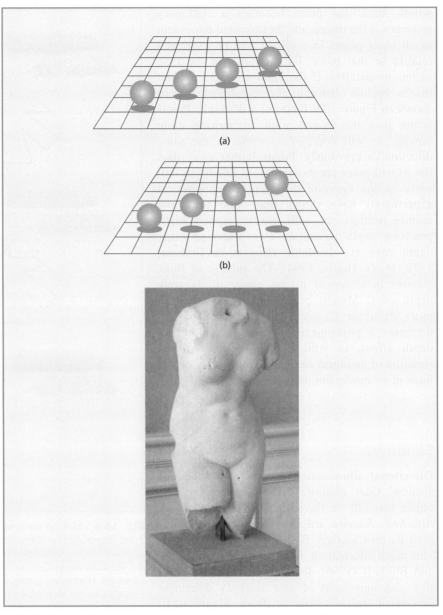

**FIG. 10.10**  Top: Texture and shape cues provide a 3-D context for the spheres, but each sphere's apparent position in the scene is influenced by its cast shadow. If the shadow is close to the spheres, then the spheres are perceived as near the ground plane. Bottom: Attached shadows provide information about three-dimensional form.

*Analyse a painting of an outdoor scene in terms of the cues used by the artist to convey an impression of depth.*

depth other than attached shadows, yet convey a strong impression of three-dimensional form.

When interpreting shadow effects, the visual system tends to assume that light is directed from above, and that objects are convex rather than concave. Correct interpretation of shading also requires assumptions that the illumination is uniform, and that object surfaces are uniform, diffuse reflectors. In situations where these assumptions do not hold, interpretations based on shadows alone are liable to be inaccurate.

## Interposition

**Interposition** is a monocular depth cue that is also discussed in Chapter 9 in the context of surface representation. As Figure 9.5 shows, the partial occlusion of a far object by a near object creates characteristic "T"-shaped intersections of contours. These intersections provide an ordinal depth cue.

## BINOCULAR CUES

Two depth cues are available only when information from both eyes is combined. One cue is non-visual (vergence), and the other cue is purely visual (binocular disparity).

## Vergence

When both eyes fixate on the same point in space, their visual axes must converge in order to project an image of the point onto the fovea in each eye. The **vergence angle** formed by the intersection of the two visual axes depends on distance, as shown at the top of Figure 10.11.

The graph at the bottom of Figure 10.11 plots vergence angle as a function of distance. Vergence angle is controlled by the extra-ocular muscles (see Chapter 6). Information on the state of the extra-ocular muscles therefore offers a cue as to the absolute distance of the fixated point. As with other depth cues, vergence angle varies non-linearly with distance. By a distance of 200 cm, 90% of the full range of vergence angles has been used up.

There has been a longstanding debate in the literature regarding the importance of vergence angle as a depth cue. It appears weak beyond 2 metres (not surprising, given the the physical cue variation plotted in Figure 10.11), and seems to lead to depth underestimation at these distances. Viguier, Clement, and Trotter (2001) investigated vergence cues at relatively near distances (below 80 cm). They found that distance perception mediated by vergence was accurate below 40 cm, but showed consistent underestimation at greater distances. One difficulty facing those studying vergence cues is that vergence and accommodation are yoked together in the visual system. When accommodation changes, so does vergence, even when one eye is occluded (an effect called *accommodative vergence*). It can therefore be difficult to separate out the contribution of the two cues to distance perception.

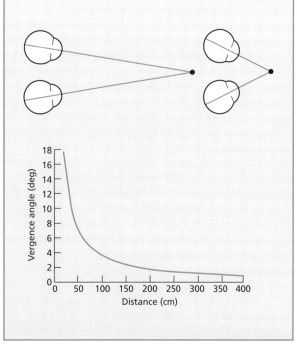

## Binocular disparity

In humans, the two eyes are typically 6.3 cm apart. Consequently, they receive slightly different views of the world. These slight differences provide one of the most powerful cues to depth, binocular disparity, which is responsible for stereo vision (*stereopsis*).

**FIG. 10.11**   Top: The eyes must converge to fixate on a near object. (From Bruce et al., 2003, Figure 7.2, p. 171.) Bottom: Graph showing converge angle as a function of object distance. Notice that most of the range of variation in vergence angle is confined to distances that are within 2 metres from the observer. Copyright © 2003 Psychology Press.

Figures 10.12 and 10.13 illustrate the detailed basis of the cue. They show two eyes viewing a pair of rectangles, one slightly closer than the other. The view from each eye is shown below. The two views are superimposed at the bottom, with the left eye's view in blue, and the right eye's view in black. The slight difference in viewing position produces small differences between the two eyes' images.

While fixating on the centre of the small *near* rectangle (Figure 10.12), its vertical edges fall on corresponding positions in the two eyes (the blue and black edges are superimposed). Notice that the vertical edges of the far rectangle fall on non-corresponding locations in the two eyes. The right eye's view of these edges is displaced to the right relative to the left eye's view. The difference in horizontal image position between the two eyes is called **horizontal binocular disparity**.

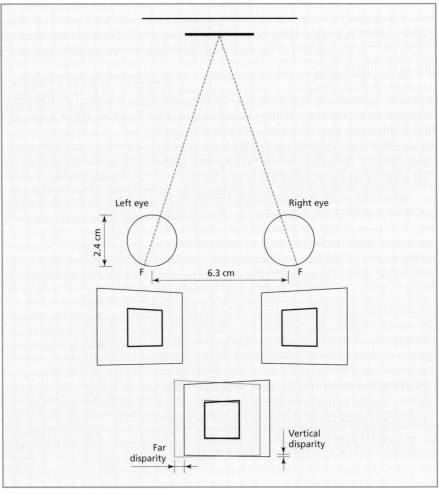

**FIG. 10.12**    Top: Plan view of a simple scene in which a binocular observer views a small vertical rectangle positioned in front of a larger rectangle. The observer is fixating on the centre of the nearer rectangle. Middle: The scene as viewed from the left eye and the right eye. Bottom: The left- and right-eye views are superimposed to show the small differences resulting from the slightly different viewpoints of the two eyes. While the observer fixates on the nearer rectangle, there are differences in both the horizontal and the vertical positions of the edges of the far rectangle.

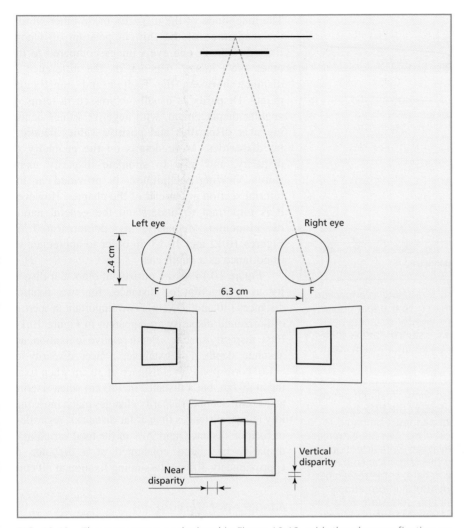

**FIG. 10.13**  The same scene as depicted in Figure 10.12, with the observer fixating on the far rectangle. Notice that the pattern of disparities between the two eyes' views is different: the edges of the near rectangle now show horizontal disparities.

## Horizontal binocular disparity

When fixation shifts to the large *far* rectangle (Figure 10.13), its vertical edges now fall on corresponding positions in the two eyes, but the vertical edges of the nearer non-fixated rectangle fall on non-corresponding positions. Now the right eye's view is displaced to the left relative to the left eye's view, in the opposite direction to the displacement shown in Figure 10.12. In general, the sign of horizontal binocular disparity depends on the sign of the difference in depth between fixated and non-fixated points in the image:

- **Far (uncrossed) disparity**: The non-fixated point is farther away, and the right eye's view of the point is shifted to the right relative to the left eye's view.
- **Near (crossed) disparity**: The non-fixated point is nearer, and the right eye's view of the point is shifted to the left relative to the left eye's view.

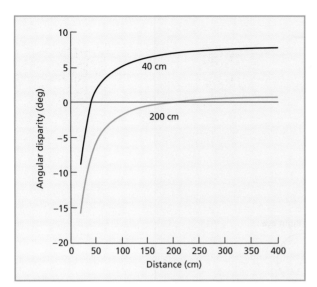

**FIG. 10.14** Horizontal binocular disparity as a function of distance, for two fixation distances. Notice that disparity is zero at fixation distance, is negative for distances nearer than fixation, and is positive for distances farther than fixation. Binocular disparity provides information about distance relative to fixation.

Figures 10.12 and 10.13 also show small differences in the vertical position of edges in the two eyes' images, known as vertical disparities. Compared to horizontal disparities, vertical disparities are extremely small. They have received relatively little attention in psychophysical studies, and their significance has been the subject of intense debate; some researchers believe that they can provide useful information about absolute depth (Cumming, Johnston, & Parker, 1991; Rogers & Bradshaw, 1993; Matthews, Meng, Xu, & Qian, 2003).

The magnitude of the disparity or, in other words, the magnitude of the shift in position of a non-fixated point in one eye's image compared to the other eye's image, depends on the difference in distance between the fixated and non-fixated points. Disparity is usually expressed in terms of angular displacement, with negative values denoting near disparities and positive values denoting far disparities. More details on the geometry of disparity, and how to simulate disparity using stereo viewing techniques, is provided in the tutorial section at the end of the chapter. However, it is important to understand the general nature of binocular disparity, as demonstrated in Figures 10.12 and 10.13, in order to appreciate its importance as a depth cue.

Figure 10.14 shows horizontal binocular disparity as a function of distance, for two fixation distances (40 and 200 cm). Two important properties of horizontal disparity are apparent in Figure 10.14. First, disparity specifies depth relative to fixation, not absolute depth. For example, a near disparity of $-1.0°$ corresponds to a distance of 36 cm when fixating at 40 cm, but a distance of 130 cm when fixating at 200 cm. Second, disparity changes much more rapidly at near distances than at far distances, regardless of fixation distance, and 90% of the total variation in disparity has been consumed at a distance of approximately 300 cm (assuming fixation at 40 cm).

### Random-dot stereograms

Far more research on depth perception has been devoted to horizontal disparity than to any other depth cue. Much of this attention was prompted by the development of **random-dot stereograms (RDS)** by Bela Julesz in the late 1960s. An RDS (shown in Figure 10.15) contains two dense arrays of random dots. A stereo viewing technique is employed to deliver one array of dots to the left eye, and the other to the right eye.

If the two arrays are identical, the observer perceives a single fused image of a vertical planar surface. It is possible to create a horizontal disparity cue by selecting particular dots, and shifting their horizontal position in one eye's view relative to the other eye's view. The direction of the shift (left versus right) determines whether the displacement creates a far disparity or a near disparity. In the example of Figure 10.15, a central rectangular region of dots is shifted to the right in the left eye's view (the region vacated by some of the dots is filled with new dots). When subjects view the RDS, they perceive the rectangle of dots to be nearer than the remaining dots. It is important to realise that any arbitrary shape can be depicted in this way, though textbook examples generally involve simple rectangular shapes.

The crucial aspect of an RDS is that it presents disparity in isolation from all other depth cues, and therefore demonstrates that disparity alone is sufficient to mediate depth perception.

## Psychophysics of stereopsis in RDS stimuli

A great deal of psychophysical research has been conducted on the ability of observers to discriminate depth in RDS stimuli. The smallest disparity that can be discriminated reliably (the lower disparity limit) is typically less than 6″ of arc (Howard & Rogers, 1995; Badcock & Shor, 1985). When fixating at arm's length (57 cm), this corresponds to a change in distance of less than 1/60th of a centimetre. At the other extreme, the largest disparity that can be discriminated reliably in RDS stimuli, known as the upper disparity limit, is in the region of 20′ arc (Glennerster, 1998). With fixation at arm's length, this upper limit corresponds to a change in distance of 3 cm. Disparity limits are influenced by a range of stimulus parameters (e.g. Wilcox & Hess, 1995; Burt & Julesz, 1980). The typical values obtained psychophysically for the lower and upper disparity limits imply that stereopsis is particularly useful for making very fine discriminations of depth at distances quite close to fixation distance.

## Diplopia

At very large (or small) disparities vision tends to become *diplopic*; we see double images. To demonstrate this effect, fixate on the end of a finger held about 30 cm in front of the eyes. If you direct your attention to objects farther away, while maintaining fixation on the finger, you will see two images of each object. Similarly, if you place another finger much closer to your eyes it will also appear diplopic while fixating on the more distant finger.

## Physiology

As mentioned in Chapter 7, many cells in the visual cortex are selectively sensitive to disparity, by virtue of binocular receptive fields lying in different relative positions in the two eyes. Poggio and Talbot (1981) found that these cells can even respond appropriately to RDS stimuli. They found that cells fell into three classes, according to whether their preferred stimulus contained near, far, or near-zero disparity. Such findings have contributed to the view the binocular disparity is pre-eminent among depth cues because it is extracted at such an early stage in processing.

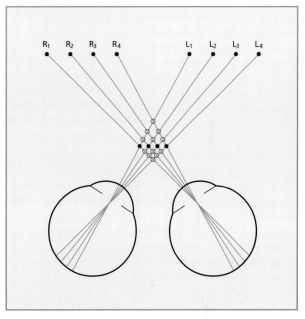

**FIG. 10.15** Top: Construction of a random dot stereogram. One image is delivered to each eye (see Figure 10.20 for delivery methods). The two images contain identical arrays of dots, except that a sub-set of dots in one image is shifted in position relative to their position in the other image (black dots; colour for illustration only). The shift introduces a disparity cue when the images are viewed binocularly. Bottom: The correspondence problem. When a row of four identical dots is viewed binocularly, the visual system must match each image in the left eye ($L_1$–$L_4$) with its corresponding partner in the right eye ($R_1$–$R_4$). Perceived depth is correct only if the correct matches are made (filled circles). Each false match (open circles) lies at an incorrect depth. (From Bruce et al., 2003, Figure 7.7, p. 178.) Copyright © 2003 Psychology Press.

*Stereo-blindness*

In order to make use of binocular disparity in depth estimation, the observer obviously must possess two eyes that can execute vergence eye movements, and disparity selective neurons in their visual cortex. Surprisingly, 5–10% of the general population does not satisfy these requirements, and is consequently stereo-blind. The most common aetiology of stereo-blindness is as follows. In the first few years of life, an imbalance in the extra-ocular muscles results in poorly co-ordinated eye movements. The infant has a squint (technically known as a *strabismus*), and is unable to maintain binocular fixation.

Consequently, the images projected onto the retinas of the two eyes contain very little of the correlation that is required to drive binocular cortical neurons. These neurons shift their sensitivity to become monocularly driven. If the strabismus is not corrected in the first 5 years of life, during which cortical responses are malleable, then no binocular cortical neurons will be left in the cortex, and stereopsis will be not be possible. In adulthood, individuals with this history are often unaware of their lack of stereo vision until they encounter RDS stimuli, but have relied on the many alternative cues to depth and distance.

*The correspondence problem in RDS*

When researchers began to consider in detail how a visual processing system (whether natural or artificial) can extract depth from RDS stimuli, they encountered a severe problem, known as the **correspondence problem**. Figure 10.15 illustrates a very mild form of the problem. It shows a row of four dots presented to two eyes. The left-eye images of the dots are labelled $L_1$ to $L_4$, and the right-eye images are labelled $R_1$ to $R_4$. The left image of the leftmost dot ($L_1$) could, in principle, be matched with any one of the four dots visible in the right eye. Only the correct match (shown by the leftmost filled circle) will be encoded at the correct depth. Each of the other possible matches will be encoded at incorrect depths defined by the retinal positions of the two images. These incorrect or false matches are shown by open circles. Across all four left- and right-eye dots, there are four correct pairings, and 12 incorrect pairings. How does the visual system select the correct matches and reject the incorrect matches? This is the correspondence problem. It has been the subject of much psychophysical and computational research.

The problem is much more severe in the case of full RDS arrays, since they contain many thousands of dots in each eye's image. From a purely computational viewpoint, the information available in the image is not sufficient to arrive at a unique solution that rejects all false matches and retains only correct matches. However, it is possible to arrive at a correct solution if certain assumptions are made that rule out many potential matches on the grounds that they are impossible (or at least extremely unlikely to occur) in images of real three-dimensional scenes. A number of constraining assumptions have been identified in both psychophysical and computational research, including similarity, continuity, and epipolar geometry.

*Similarity* Binocular matches are only admissible if they involve elements in each eye that have similar spatial properties such as contrast and orientation (Marr & Poggio, 1976; Mayhew & Frisby, 1981).

*Continuity*  If there are several candidate matches, the visual system selects the match offering the smoothest and/or least change in disparity across the image (Marr & Poggio, 1976; Pollard, Mayhew, & Frisby, 1985).

*Epipolar geometry*  A plane passing through a point at a given depth and the optical centres of the eyes (**epipolar plane**) projects to a straight line in each eye's image. These lines are called **epipolar lines**. Thus, for a given image point in one eye, all the possible matching points in the other eye must lie along an epipolar line (more details on epipolar geometry can be found in the tutorial section). On this basis the search for correspondence can be restricted to epipolar lines, greatly simplifying the problem. The epipolar constraint has received a great deal of attention in computational research (e.g. Zhang, Deriche, Faugeras, & Luong, 1995), but its relevance for stereopsis is still unclear (Stevenson & Schor, 1997; Schreiber, Crawford, Fetter, & Tweed, 2001).

Some constraints, such as similarity and continuity, can be implemented readily in terms of the properties of or interactions between disparity-tuned cortical cells. No firm conclusions have been reached regarding which assumptions are the most important for human vision. Human stereopsis is not captured adequately by current computational models (e.g. Gillam & Borsting, 1988; Weinshall, 1989). A detailed discussion of theories of stereopsis can be found in Bruce et al. (2003).

# CUE COMBINATION

The preceding sections have demonstrated that multiple cues are available to the visual system, each offering its own estimate of depth. A single depth estimate of a particular surface or object is required in many natural situations, such as when deciding whether to jump safely from a ledge, or whether to apply the brakes in a car to avoid a road collision, or whether a coffee cup is within reach. How does the system make use of different cues to arrive at a single estimate of depth? Before considering research on cue combination, it is worthwhile considering how well different cues agree in physical terms.

## CORRELATIONS BETWEEN CUES

Looking back over the depth cues surveyed in the previous section, it is clear that most offer metric information about depth. Cue magnitude varies in a lawful quantitative manner with distance. Cues derived from elements lying on the ground plane (perspective and compression, with corresponding motion cues of flow and parallax) vary according to a power law at a rate that depends on eye height (see Figure 10.5). When the metric information available in the other cues is compared, it becomes clear that different cues are very highly correlated. Figure 10.16 re-plots cue values for disparity, blur, vergence, accommodation, and size from previous figures as a function of distance, in a manner that allows direct comparisons between cues. It plots cue magnitude relative to its value at fixation (40 cm in Figure 10.16), as a proportion of its maximum value (estimated at a distance of 1000 cm). In this plot all cues are zero at fixation distance, and rise towards their maximum at far distances. Remarkably, the cues collapse onto a single function. Cue magnitude initially rises sharply, and then levels off. As the inset graph shows, cue magnitude varies linearly with the reciprocal of distance (1/distance).

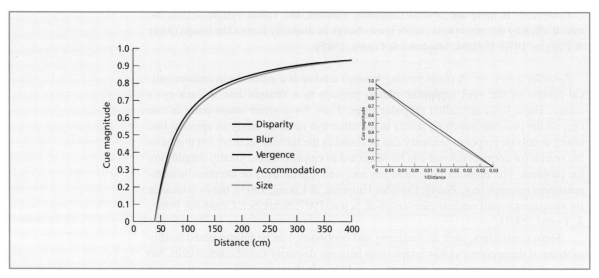

**FIG. 10.16**   Cue variation for disparity, blur, vergence, accommodation, and size as a function of distance, re-plotted from previous Figures (assuming fixation at 40 cm). Cue magnitude relative to its value at fixation is expressed as a proportion of its maximum value (1.0). Different cues are very highly correlated. In all cases, cue magnitude varies linearly with the reciprocal of distance (shown in the inset).

## WEIGHTED AVERAGES OF CUES

The depth cues shown in Figure 10.16 must be encoded by neurons in the visual system if they are to influence depth perception. Given the contrasting nature of the cues, we can assume that they are encoded by different populations of neurons. Since the cues are highly correlated, a simple strategy for combining estimates from different neural sub-systems would be to take the average of the estimates. However, as the preceding sections explained, cues are likely to vary in their availability and reliability. For example:

● Texture gradients are available only in scenes containing evenly textured surfaces;
● Motion parallax cues rely on the presence of object or observer motion;
● Image blur varies with ambient illumination (pupil diameter);
● Accommodation varies with the age (and refractive state) of the observer;
● Size cues rely on knowledge about real size.

It would not, therefore, make sense to take a simple average across the cues in all situations. It would be more appropriate to rely more on some cues in certain situations, and on other cues in other situations. So a number of researchers have proposed that the visual system does indeed take the average of different cues, but it weights the contribution of each cue according to context (see Bulthoff & Mallot, 1988). Heavily weighted cues have a greater influence on the average depth estimate than lightly weighted cues. Much of the recent research on depth perception has been

*Think of other factors that might influence the weight attached to particular cues.*

devoted to cue combination. Psychophysical studies indicate that the amount of weight assigned to a given cue varies with stimulus conditions, and across observers (Buckley & Frisby, 1993; Johnston, Cummings, & Landy, 1994). For example, Johnston et al. (1994) studied stereo and motion cues, and found that stereo cues were more heavily weighted at near distances, but motion cues were more heavily weighted at far distances.

A coherent theoretical basis for variation in cue weight is provided by Bayesian approaches to vision (discussed in detail in the tutorial section of Chapter 9). The basic idea is that cues that are highly reliable in a given context (in other words, show low variability) are assigned more weight than cues that are relatively unreliable.

# CHAPTER SUMMARY

## THE MULTIPLICITY OF DEPTH CUES

- A wide range of cues can provide information about depth.
- Monocular cues include:

  - Retinal image size
  - Height in the visual field
  - Texture gradient (height, width, and density)
  - Image blur
  - Atmospheric perspective
  - Accommodation (a non-visual cue)
  - Motion parallax
  - Shadows
  - Interposition.

- Binocular cues include:

  - Vergence (a non-visual cue)
  - Binocular disparity.

- All cues have limitations that constrain their utility.
- Binocular disparity is generally considered to be the most important depth cue, because it is extracted at a very early stage of neural processing, and observers are very sensitive to small changes in depth signalled solely by disparity.
- Theories of disparity coding employ constraints that allow the visual system to solve the stereo correspondence problem successfully.

## CUE COMBINATION

- Most cues provide quantitative information about depth:

  - Texture gradient and motion parallax obey a power law.
  - Image size, blur, accommodation, vergence, and disparity are highly correlated, and vary linearly with the reciprocal of distance (1/distance).

- In order to arrive at a single estimate of depth, the visual system must combine the estimates available from different cues.
- Research indicates that the visual system takes the weighted average of the estimates provided by different cues. Cue weight varies according to stimulus conditions and across observers.

# TUTORIALS

## THE GEOMETRICAL BASIS OF STEREOPSIS

### Horizontal disparity

The 6.3 cm separation between the two eyes creates small differences in the images projected onto their retinas. Figure 10.17 (top) shows a plan view of two eyes fixating on point F. Images of F fall on the left and right foveas. If another point is present in the visual field at the same distance from the observer as the fixated point, then a second image will appear in each eye. The retinal distance of this second image from the image of the fixated point will be the same in the two eyes. As such, this image is said to fall on corresponding positions in the two eyes. The *horopter* is a line drawn through all points that project to corresponding retinal positions in the two eyes, and appear to be located at the same distance as the fixated point. Figure 10.17 (top) shows the horopter with two points projecting to corresponding retinal locations.

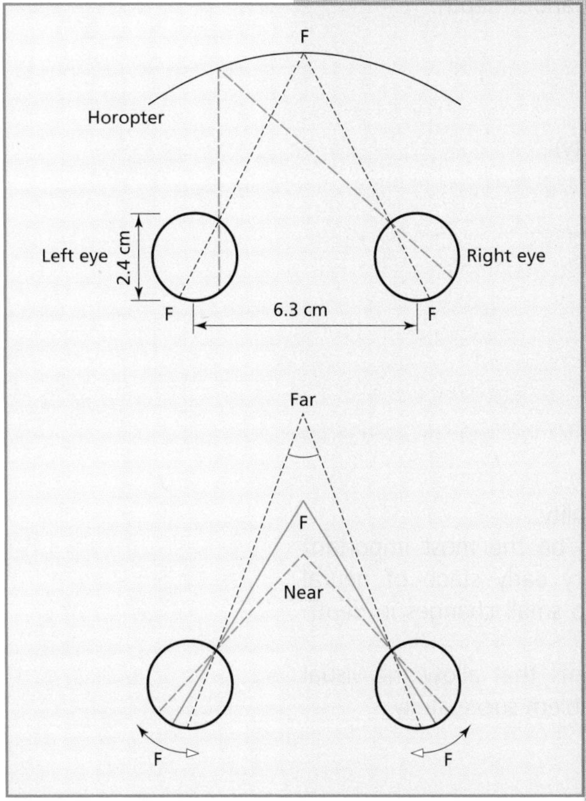

The images of points located nearer to or farther away from the observer than the fixated point fall on non-corresponding retinal positions. Figure 10.17 (bottom) shows one nearer point and one farther point. Notice the lack of correspondence in their image positions between the two eyes, which is called *binocular disparity* or just *disparity*. Two properties of binocular disparity are crucial for depth perception:

● The *sign* or direction of disparity depends on the sign of the depth difference between the fixated and non-fixated points. Notice in Figure 10.17 (bottom) that the images of the far point are displaced inward towards the nose (nasally) in each eye relative to the images of the fixated point (open arrows). The images of the near point are displaced outwards towards the temples (temporally) in each eye (filled arrows). Near disparities are also called crossed disparities, and far disparities are called uncrossed disparities. One way to remember this is to think of how vergence would change if you moved your eyes to the disparate point. To fixate on a more distant point you would have to uncross your eyes, while to fixate on a nearer point you would have to cross your eyes.

**FIG. 10.17**  The geometrical basis of binocular disparity. Binocular fixation on point F produces images of F on the two foveas. Top: If a second point is present at the same distance as point F, a second image appears in each eye. The distance of this second image from the fovea is the same in the two eyes, so these images are said to fall on corresponding retinal positions. The line joining all points that lie at the same distance, and so project to corresponding retinal positions, is called the horopter. Bottom: Points lying nearer or farther away than the fixated point fall on non-corresponding retinal positions. The images of a far point shift inwards or nasally in the two eyes (open arrows); the images of a nearer point shift outwards or temporally (filled arrows).

- The *magnitude* of the disparity depends on the magnitude of the depth difference between the fixated and non-fixated points. Imagine that the more distant point in Figure 10.17 (bottom) was positioned much farther away than is shown here. Its image in each eye would swing around on the retina so that it was much farther away from the image of the fixated point. Figure 10.14 earlier in the chapter shows how the magnitude of disparity varies with distance. Mathematically the magnitude of binocular disparity actually corresponds to the difference in vergence angle between the fixated and non-fixated points.

## Epipolarity

Figure 10.18 shows two eyes and a point (F) in the visual field. Each eye's nodal point is shown by the black dots (light rays pass through this point without being bent by the lens). A plane can be drawn so that it passes through point F and through the nodal point of each eye. This plane is called the *epipolar plane* (outlined with dashed lines in Figure 10.18). The projection of this plane on each eye's retina is a line, known as an *epipolar line* (thick lines in Figure 10.18). The images of point F in the left and right eyes must lie along these epipolar lines, a geometrical fact that is potentially very useful for solving the stereo correspondence problem. Recall from earlier in the chapter that in order to code depth from disparity accurately, the visual system must match a given image point in one eye with the image point in the other eye that arose from the same point out in the visual field. Epipolar geometry greatly simplifies the matching problem, because it means that searches for correspondence can disregard most of the image and be confined to epipolar lines. For a given image point in one eye, its correct partner in the other eye is guaranteed to lie along an epipolar line belonging to the same epipolar plane. The use of epipolar geometry in theories of stereo processing was discussed earlier in the chapter.

## Stereograms and stereoscopes

Stereopsis is based on the slightly different images received by the two eyes when viewing a real three-dimensional scene. A number of techniques have been developed to create stereo images artificially. All involve a pair of images (*stereogram*) depicting the left- and right-eye views, that are usually delivered to the two eyes using an instrument called a *stereoscope*. Figure 10.19 shows a variety of stereograms.

### Mirror stereoscope

Sir Charles Wheatstone (1802–1875) designed the first instrument, based on mirrrors, which he

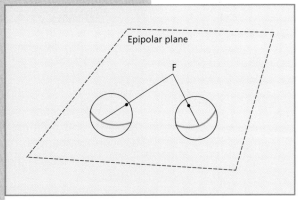

**FIG. 10.18** Epipolar geometry. During binocular fixation on point F, a plane can be drawn so that it passes through point F and through the nodal point of each eye (epipolar plane). Light rays pass through the nodal point without changing direction. So the images of point F must lie somewhere along the lines where the epipolar plane intersects each retina (thick lines). This fact simplifies the solution to the correspondence problem, because it means that the search for correct matches can be restricted to epipolar lines.

**FIG. 10.19** Examples of stereograms. When viewed through a stereoscope (shown in Figure 10.20) or with free fusion, a compelling impression of depth is perceived.

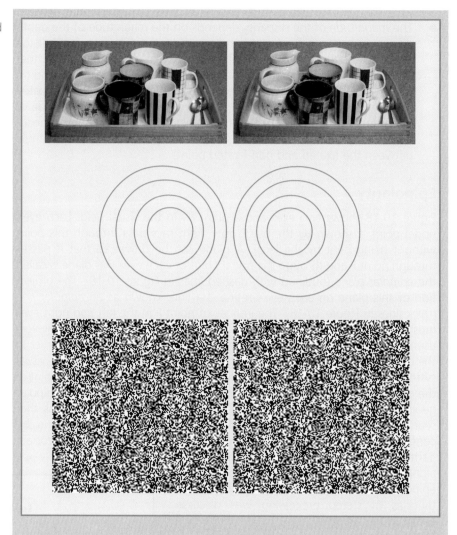

called a stereoscope (published in 1838). Figure 10.20A illustrates its design. The left- and right-eye images (sometimes called half-images) are viewed through two mirrors. The angle of convergence of the eyes required to fuse the images into a single percept can be adjusted for accuracy.

### Prism stereoscope

Sir David Brewster (1781–1868) studied Wheatstone's stereoscope and designed his own version of the instrument. In Brewster's stereoscope the half-images were placed side by side and viewed through prisms that created the required angular convergence of the eyes (Figure 10.20B). Wheatstone and Brewster entered into an acrimonious dispute about who first invented the stereoscope, but Wheatstone is now generally regarded as the creator of the first instrument (see Wade, 1983). Prism stereoscopes became a popular

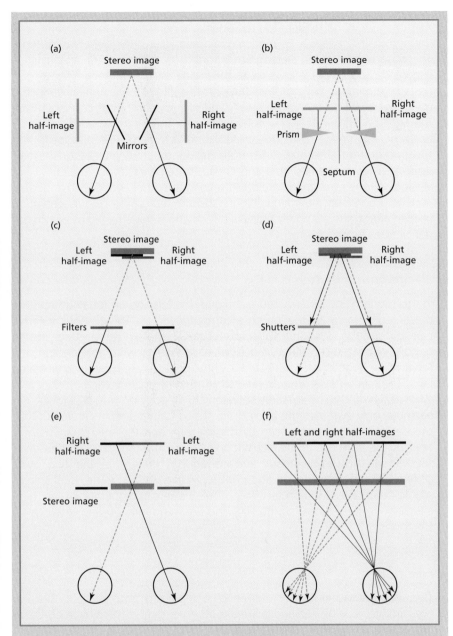

**FIG. 10.20** A wide variety of methods have been devised for delivering stereo-pairs of images to the eyes. A: Mirror stereoscope; B: Prism stereoscope; C: Anaglyphs; D: Electro-optical shutters; E: Free fusion; F: Autostereograms.

Victorian amusement, particularly after the enthusiasm shown by Queen Victoria at the Great Exhibition in 1851.

### Anaglyphs

In this technique the left and right half-images are superimposed in a single image, but are printed or projected in different colours. For example, the left half-image may be rendered in red against a neutral light background, and the right half-image may be rendered in green against the same background. The observer views the stereogram through coloured red and green filters (Figure 10.20C). If the left eye views the image through a green filter, the red parts of the image will not pass through the filter, so will appear dark. The green parts will be transmitted well, and will appear indistinguishable from the light background. In the right eye's view through the red filter, green parts of the image will appear dark and red parts will disappear into the background. The filters therefore deliver different images to the two eyes. This technique is simple and cheap, but suffers from cross-talk. Faint versions of one eye's image are often seen in the other eye, due to imperfect matching between the image colours and the filters. The colour separation used in anaglyphs is a purely physical effect, and is not affected by any colour deficiencies in the observer.

### Electro-optical shutters

In this modern computer-based technique, the left and right half-images are presented in rapid alternation on a computer screen. The observer wears a pair of goggles containing electro-optical shutters. The shutters in the goggles allow the computer to occlude each eye's view completely and very rapidly (the goggles are connected to the computer via a lead or an infrared link). The computer is programmed to alternately occlude each eye's view in synchrony with the alternation between the images on the display, so that each eye only ever sees the appropriate stereo half-image. In Figure 10.20D, the dashed image is only seen by the left eye, and the solid image is only seen by the right eye. If the alternation rate is sufficiently high, the observer sees apparently simultaneous and continuous images in the two eyes. Differences between the left and right half-images provide the usual stereoscopic depth cue. Modern electro-optical shutters can operate at very high alternation rates (exceeding 60 Hz), and are frequently used in research on stereopsis.

### Free fusion

The simplest technique for delivering stereograms is to present the two eyes' images side by side and invite the observer to fuse them by freely crossing or uncrossing their eyes. As shown in Figure 10.20E, if the eyes are crossed sufficiently, the two eyes' images superimpose to create a stereo image. The technique is difficult to master, partly because of the distraction of two unpaired half-images in the visual field (middle of Figure 10.20E), and partly because changes in vergence angle tend to produce concomitant changes in accommodation. A special kind of free fusion stereogram known as the *autostereogram* was developed by Tylor and Clarke (1990), and later inspired a large number of "magic eye" books and posters. The idea was to make free fusion easier by dividing the left and right half-images into thin vertical strips placed side by side (Figure 10.20F). Now the observer requires only a relatively small change in vergence to make each left-eye strip superimpose on the abutting right-eye strip, even when the stereo image is very wide. Left-eye views in Figure 10.20F are shown by dashed lines, and right-eye views are shown by continuous lines (depth is actually created by varying the repetition width of the strips). Notice from the intersections of left- and right-eye sight lines that a given strip serves as the right-eye partner for the strip on its left, but the left-eye partner for the strip on its right. This results in the repetitive structure visible in autostereograms.

An ablity to free-fuse is very useful for viewing stereograms presented in books and journal articles. Although Figures 10.20E and 10.20F illustrate crossed free fusion, it is also possible to achieve uncrossed free fusion by uncrossing one's eyes (looking beyond the image) rather than crossing one's eyes to look in front of the image. Some observers prefer crossed free fusion, while others prefer uncrossed free fusion. As an aid to crossed free fusion it sometimes helps to fixate on an object such as a pencil held in front of the stereogram. If the object is moved back and forth while fixating on it, it should be possible to find a position at which the two halves of the stereo-gram superimpose to create a fused stereo image. As an aid to uncrossed free fusion, place a sheet of clear glass or rigid plastic on the stereogram, and view the reflection of a distant object in the surface of the glass. If an appro-priate distance is selected, the two halves of the stereogram should fall into register to create a stereo image.

## Vertical disparity

This tutorial has concentrated on horizontal binocular disparity, but natural binocular images also contain vertical disparities. Figures 10.12 and 10.13 show the left- and right-eye views of two fronto-parallel rectangles. The rec-tangles appear trapezoidal because each eye is viewing them from a slightly oblique angle (the slightly nearer side of each rectangle appears longer than the opposite side). Consequently, when the two eyes' views are superimposed (bottom of Figures 10.12 and 10.13) there are slight differences in vertical location between the eyes. These differences are called vertical disparities. At far viewing distances the difference in viewpoint between the eyes becomes negligible, so the images of the rectangles actually appear rectangular. Mayhew and Longuet-Higgins (1982) showed that as one advances horizontally across the image, the rate at which vertical disparity changes depends on viewing distance. In the rectangles of Figure 10.12 and 10.13, for instance, as one advances along one of the horizontal sides the vertical separation between the two eyes' views increases progressively. What Mayhew and Longuet-Higgins showed was that the rate of increase is determined by the absolute distance from which the rectangle is viewed.

Vertical disparities are therefore potentially very useful because they provide a visual measure of absolute viewing distance. Horizontal disparities reflect only relative distance, not absolute distance (see Figure 10.14). However, vertical disparities are actually very small, except at large retinal eccentricities, and there has been a long-running debate about whether the visual system really does make use of them to estimate viewing distance.

# CHAPTER 11

# Visual motion perception

## INTRODUCTION

When an object or surface moves across the visual field, its image moves across the surface of the retina (provided that the eyes do not track the object). Even the simplest sighted animals have an ability to sense this image motion, which can be used in several ways:

- *Figure–ground segregation* Shapes and objects that are invisible while static (e.g. camouflaged animals) are revealed as soon as they move relative to the background. Prey animals that prefer to remain hidden as much as possible, such as small lizards and rodents, have evolved an ability to move in short, rapid bursts to minimise the time that they are visible in this way to predators.

- *Extraction of three-dimensional structure* When any solid object moves, the images of its various parts that are cast on the retina move relative to each other. For example, when you view a rotating globe, surface markings near the equator move across your field of view more rapidly than markings near the poles (see Figure 11.1). This highly structured variation in speed conveys information about the 3-D structure of the shape.

- *Visual guidance of action* As we move about the world, image detail "flows" across the retina (see Chapter 10). A great deal of information can be extracted from the pattern of optic flow, including the speed and direction of self-motion. For example, as you drive down a road, focusing on the horizon, image details arising from road markings, signposts, and pedestrians appear at the horizon and then flow through your field of view to create an expanding flow field. The rate of flow provides information on your speed.

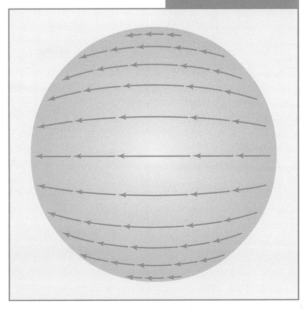

**FIG. 11.1** Arrows represent the speed and direction of surface markings on the sphere as it rotates. Markings near the poles move more slowly and follow a more curved path than those near the equator.

The importance of visual motion is dramatically illustrated by the unfortunate case of a woman who lost the ability to sense motion following brain damage (Zihl, Von Cramon, & Mai, 1983). She had difficulty, for example, in pouring tea or coffee into a cup because the fluid appeared to be frozen, like a glacier. She found face-to-face conversations difficult because she could not see the movements of the speaker's face and mouth. Crowded rooms or streets made her feel unwell, because "people were suddenly here or there but I have not seen them moving". This problem was particularly acute when attempting to cross a road with moving traffic, although she had no difficulty in actually identifying the cars.

## DETECTING MOVEMENT

Responses from individual photoreceptors on the retina contain no information about image motion. Consider the image of a static scene, such as an empty road, falling on an array of photoreceptors. Receptors responding to the image of the road surface will register low levels of illumination. If a light-coloured car moves into view, some of these receptors will register a sudden increase in illumination as the car passes over them.

In Figure 11.2, for example, receptor A's response increases from zero to ten units of activity as the image of the car reaches it, and then falls back to zero once the car has passed by. However, the change in this response alone can tell us nothing about the movement of the car. The same change in response would have occurred if

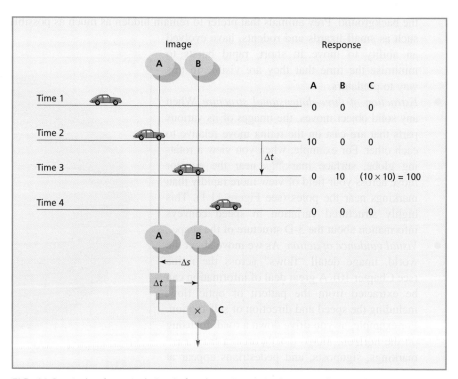

**FIG. 11.2**   A simple neural circuit for detecting retinal motion from left to right. Numbers on the right refer to activity levels in the three cells A, B, and C. A detailed explanation can be found in the text.

the car had moved in the opposite direction. In addition, response level can change for a variety of other reasons. For example, a cloud may pass by, or the sun may be setting, or the street lighting may have been switched on.

This simple example illustrates the basic point that motion detection is not straightforward. Theories of how the visual system detects motion divide into two camps. One camp views motion perception as a relatively high-level perceptual inference; if the image of the car used to be at location A, but is now at location B, then an intelligent system might infer that the car had shifted position (see Chapter 1). The other camp views motion perception from the point of view of neural circuits designed specifically to encode retinal movement. As will become apparent later in the chapter, there is support for both kinds of theory. The next section explains how simple neural circuits can detect motion. Later sections will discuss high-level influences on motion perception.

## PRINCIPLES OF NEURAL MOTION DETECTION

### Neural motion detectors

In order to signal movement, we need to compare the change in response of one receptor with the change in response of a neighbouring receptor. As a moving image advances across the retina a whole series of receptors in turn will register a transitory change in illumination. This sequential activation can be detected by simple neural circuits to encode retinal movement. A circuit for an elementary **motion detector** is shown in the lower part of Figure 11.2. Two retinal receptor cells, A and B, transmit signals to a third comparator neuron, C. The comparator neuron performs motion detection as follows. The two receptors are positioned a short distance apart on the retina ($\Delta s$), and the transmission line from receptor A to the comparator is subject to a brief temporal delay ($\Delta t$). The level of output at the comparator depends on the product of the signals arriving from A and B (in other words, their activities are multiplied together). So the comparator's output is very much higher when strong signals from the two receptors arrive together than when one or the other arrives alone. Motion detectors of the kind depicted in Figure 11.2 are commonly called **Reichardt detectors**, after the person who first proposed them from observations of beetles and flies (Reichardt, 1961; strictly speaking, Reichardt's scheme involved pairs of detectors responsive to opposite directions).

### Direction selectivity in motion detectors

We can examine the output of the comparator during the passage of the image of the car across the retina from left to right (see the right-hand side of Figure 11.2). At time 2 the car's image falls on receptor A, evoking a large response (10 units of activity) that begins travelling towards the comparator. The response will take one time period to reach the comparator. By the next time interval (time 3) the image has reached the second receptor, B. Response at receptor A drops back to zero, but the high response at receptor B (10 units of activity) reaches the comparator immediately. Thus, at time 3 the two responses from A and B arrive together at the comparator, creating a very large response (100)—motion is detected.

Figure 11.3 shows the pattern of responses when the car moves in the opposite direction. In this case the two receptors' signals arrive at the comparator at different times. At time 1 receptor B's response travels immediately to the comparator C,

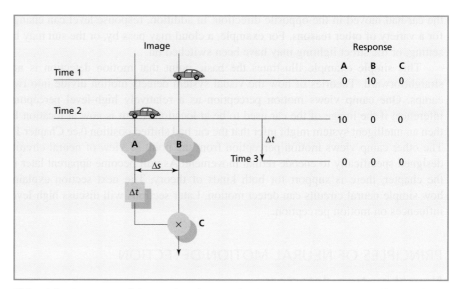

**FIG. 11.3** Response of the motion detector in Figure 11.2 to movement from right to left. The wiring of the circuit makes it selectively responsive to motion only in one direction.

*Why do spinning wheel spokes sometimes appear to rotate backwards in TV images?*

provoking a low response. At time 2 the image of the car has passed on to receptor A. The resulting response does not arrive at the comparator until time 3, resulting in no response from the comparator. The neural circuit is thus selectively responsive to motion from left to right. A motion detector selectively responsive to motion from right to left can be made simply by re-wiring the circuit so that the temporal delay is imposed on the line from receptor B to the comparator instead of on the line from receptor A.

## Aliasing

Motion detectors of this kind are very sensitive to the properties of the motion stimulus. In particular, the velocity of the stimulus has to be such that the time taken for it to traverse the distance from A to B matches the temporal delay in the circuit. Only then will the signals from A and B arrive at C together, even for the preferred direction. If there is a mismatch because the stimulus moves too slowly or too rapidly, the detector may fail to signal motion at all—it is velocity sensitive. In certain conditions (e.g. if a succession of vehicles pass by at high speed) it may even respond to motion in the opposite direction, an effect known as "aliasing". An example is shown in Figure 11.4.

The motion detector is tuned to respond to rightward motion, as in Figures 11.2 and 11.3. Two vehicles pass the two receptors, moving rapidly from right to left. At time 1 the image of the first vehicle arrives at receptor A, having already passed receptor B. At time 2 the image of the second vehicle arrives at receptor B, and its response arrives at the comparator at the same time as the response from receptor A. As a result, the comparator erroneously signals the presence of rightward motion even though the vehicles are moving leftward.

The error arises because each receptor receives a rapid sequence of images as each vehicle passes, and responds to all of them. The comparator cannot pair up

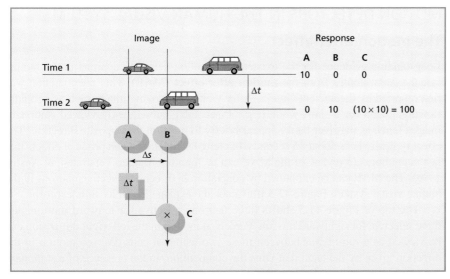

**FIG. 11.4**  Aliasing. The motion detector is tuned to rightward motion, but in certain circumstances it also responds to leftward motion.

stimuli arriving at each receptor correctly. A simple way to avoid the confusion between different images is to make each receptor selectively respond only to certain images. For example, if each receptor responded only to images having certain spatial structure (e.g. size, texture), or temporal structure (e.g. flicker rate) it is likely to respond only to the car, or only to the bus in the example.

As mentioned earlier, the detectors shown in Figure 11.2 are velocity sensitive. In order to deal with a range of image velocities, the visual system requires a population of detectors that vary in terms of the temporal delay and/or spatial offset built in to their circuits (for more details on velocity coding, see the tutorial at the end of the chapter).

## Direction selective cells in primates

All the features of motion detectors that we have discussed are easy to implement in neural hardware. Similar circuits were found by Barlow and Hill (1963) in the retina of the rabbit. The primate visual system seems to possess neural motion detectors based on the same principles (Mikami, Newsome, & Wurtz, 1986). In primate motion detectors, the inputs (A and B) are not individual photoreceptors, but intermediate neurons that collect information from a group of receptors, probably retinal ganglion cells (or cells in the LGN or cortex linked to ganglion cells; see Chapter 7 for more details on the physiology of the visual pathway). The receptive fields of these cells have spatial and temporal response selectivities that prevent aliasing, as described earlier. The direction-selective comparator neuron is a cortical cell. The temporal delay in the circuit arises because the cells in one branch of the circuit have more sluggish responses and lower conduction velocities than the cells in the other branch. Recall from Figure 7.18 that signals from parvo LGN cells arrive at the cortex slightly later than signals from magno cells. This latency difference could be used in cortical motion-detecting circuits.

Motion-detecting receptive fields can be characterised in terms of their spatial frequency and temporal frequency tuning functions. See Chapter 8.

# MOTION DETECTORS IN THE HUMAN VISUAL SYSTEM

## The motion after-effect

Longstanding evidence for the existence of motion-detecting neurons in the human visual system comes from the **motion after-effect (MAE)**. This phenomenon was first reported by the ancient Greeks. After viewing a moving image such as a rapidly flowing stream for a short while (e.g. 60 seconds), subsequently viewed stationary images (such as the river bank) appear briefly to move in the opposite direction. The effect typically lasts about 15 seconds, but lengthy adaptation can produce effects that last many hours (a review of the MAE can be found in Mather, Verstraten, & Anstis, 1998). The MAE can be explained by adaptation in direction-selective neurons in the human visual system. Figure 11.5 illustrates the explanation in its simplest form.

The top of Figure 11.5 shows three neurons selective for leftward motion, and three selective for rightward motion. Perceived motion in the left–right dimension can be viewed as a tug-of-war between these two teams of cells. We see motion in the direction given by the team that wins the competition. In the presence of a stationary pattern there is only moderate activity (effort) from either team, so no motion is seen. During exposure to rightwards motion (middle) the "right" team is highly active, but the "left" team is relatively weakly activated, so rightward motion is perceived. After a period of rightward adaptation and in the presence of a stationary pattern (bottom) the "right" team is fatigued, allowing the moderate activity of the "left" team to win the contest and signal leftward motion.

Figure 11.5 illustrates the classic opponent-process account of the MAE. A similar theory of opponent colour coding will be described in Chapter 12. It is important to realise that this account is too simple to offer a serious account of the MAE. One reason is that perceived direction of motion involves a comparison of activity in cells tuned to a wide range of directions, rather than just the opposites shown in Figure 11.5 (Mather's, 1980, "distribution-shift" account of the MAE; see also Snowden, Treue, Erickson, & Andersen, 1991). One way to imagine this more complex explanation is in terms of many tug-of-war teams pulling on ropes joined together to create a radial pattern (inset of Figure 11.5). Each team pulls in its own direction, and the direction perceived is that given by the direction in which the centre of the rope shifts relative to its neutral position. If one team is weakened by adaptation, then the centre of rope will tend to move toward the opposite direction, if all other teams are equally active.

*Compare the motion after-effect and its explanation with the tilt and size after-effects described in Chapter 8.*

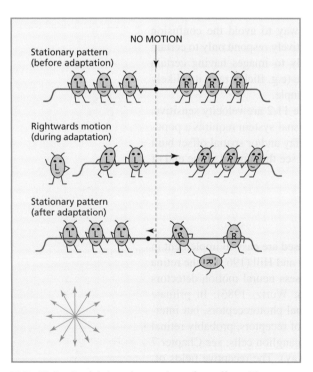

**FIG. 11.5** Explaining the motion after-effect. The classic opponent-process account assumes that the perceived direction of motion depends on a competition or tug-of-war between detectors selectively responsive to opposite motion directions. Adaptation reduces the responsiveness of one team, allowing the opposing team to signal motion even in the presence of a stationary pattern.

## Direction-specific threshold elevation

Strong evidence for motion detectors in the human visual system also comes from the existence of

**direction-specific threshold elevation**. Pantle and Sekuler (1968) measured the threshold for detecting upward or downward moving bars, before and after observers were adapted to upward moving bars. Upward adaptation had no effect on observers' ability to detect downward bars, but elevated their threshold for detecting upward bars. In other words, adapation made it harder to detect the presence of weak stimuli moving in the adapting direction. This effect is called *direction-specific threshold elevation*. It can be explained by changes in the responsiveness of direction-specific cells. Direct recordings from individual direction-selective neurons in cat and monkey cortex have confirmed that adaptation leads to a depression in responsiveness (Giaschi, Douglas, Marlin, & Cynader, 1993; Petersen, Baker, & Allman, 1985).

Motion adaptation effects show *inter-ocular transfer*: an effect is still obtained when the subject views the adapting stimulus with one eye only, and is later tested using the other eye only (e.g. Moulden, 1980). Inter-ocular transfer is clear evidence that the neurons involved in adaptation are located in the cortex, rather than earlier in the visual system, since only in the cortex are cells found that can be driven by stimulation from either eye. Brain-imaging studies of observers experiencing motion after-effects have found peaks of activity in an area of the human brain that is thought to be homologous to an area in monkey cortex that is known to be rich in motion-detecting cells (Tootell et al., 1995; see Chapter 1 for more details on brain imaging).

## OBJECT MOTION AND OBSERVER MOTION

Motion detectors respond to movement of the image across the retina. This movement can arise either from movement of an object in the world, or from movement of the observer's eyes or body (in the absence of object motion), or from a combination of both. For example, you may be standing at a roadside waiting to cross. If you stand perfectly still as a car moves past, its image will move across your retina (upper part of Figure 11.6). As you turn your eyes and head to glance up and down the road along rows of parked cars, their images also move across the retina, even though they are stationary (lower part of Figure 11.6). In order to cross the road safely you must correctly partition retinal motion signals into those arising from object motion and those arising from your own bodily movements. How does the brain solve this important problem? Three different strategies appear to be used.

### Saccadic suppression

During rapid shifts in eye position (saccades), vision is suppressed. Burr, Morgan, and Morrone (1999) argue that this saccadic suppression specifically targets the responses of neurons early in the visual pathway that feed into motion detectors. The motion system is in effect switched off during saccades, so avoiding the problem of attribution.

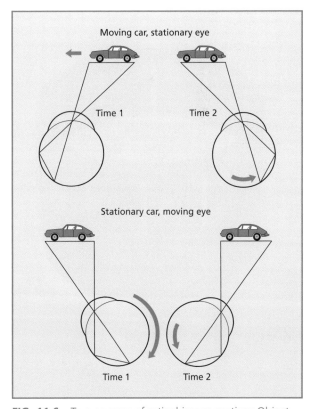

**FIG. 11.6** Two sources of retinal image motion: Object movement with a stationary eye (top), and observer movement with a stationary object (bottom).

## Eye movement commands

For slower movements of the eyes, the visual system seems to compare a record of the commands sent to the ocular muscles to initiate eye movements against signals arriving from motion detectors. If these two signals are equal and opposite, they cancel each other out and no motion is perceived. For example, when one's eyes move to the right, image detail translates to the left in the visual field. If the leftward motion signals exactly balance the rightward eye motion commands, then no motion is seen. If a residual motion signal remains, it is attributed to motion of an object in the scene. This theory can be tested very easily by creating eye movements in the absence of eye motion commands. Press your eye gently with a finger against the lid, rocking it from side to side; the world will appear to swing to and fro (Bridgeman & Delgado, 1984).

## Large-scale motion

Observer motion generally results in highly structured, large-scale movement patterns across the retina (optic flow). For example, as you move your eyes to the right, the whole retinal image slides to the left (see Figure 10.9 in Chapter 10). On the other hand, object motion generally results in smaller scale movement relative to the background, such as moving vehicles against a background of stationary roadside buildings. As a final method of disambiguating retinal motion signals, the visual system tends to assume that large-scale movements reflect observer motion rather than world motion, whereas localised relative motion is assumed to reflect object motion (L. R. Harris, 1994).

> **KEY TERM**
> **Stroboscopic apparent movement**: Apparent movement seen in patterns that are briefly flashed in different spatial positions.

**FIG. 11.7**   The daedalus or zoetrope, a Victorian device for creating the illusion of apparent movement.

## REAL MOVEMENT VERSUS APPARENT MOVEMENT

Imagine that you are at a theatre watching a performance on stage. As the actors move around, their movements project images onto your retinas that vary smoothly and continuously over time—so-called "real" movement. If you visit the cinema to watch a movie film, you are presented with a series of static images or frames, presented stroboscopically (i.e. briefly flashed), with 24 different frames being flashed every second. Each is presented three times to create a flash rate of 72 Hz (Why? See Chapter 8). Any movement that you perceive can be viewed as an illusion, since the image itself contains only static information—"apparent" movement.

The effectiveness of **stroboscopic apparent motion** has been known for well over a century. A variety of mechanical devices were built as parlour amusements during the 1800s. The daedalus or zoetrope, for example, consisted of a rotating drum with a series of thin regularly spaced vertical slots cut around its side (Horner, 1834; see Figure 11.7). A paper strip containing a series of static drawings was placed inside the drum, and the drum was spun fairly rapidly. When an observer peered through the slots of the spinning drum, each successive static image was visible in turn through the slots, creating an entertaining impression of movement. Cinema projectors and modern televisions operate on the same basic principle of presenting a series of static images successively to create apparent motion.

## EXPLAINING PERCEPTION OF APPARENT MOVEMENT

Why do stroboscopically presented static images create an impression of motion? A common fallacy is that the illusion results from the persistence of vision. According to this explanation, each static image persists in our vision for a short time, so that successively presented static images blend together into one apparently continuous scene. However, briefly presented stationary images remain visible only for about one-tenth of a second (e.g. Hogben & DiLollo, 1974), yet apparent motion can be seen between stationary images separated by temporal intervals of up to half a second (Kolers, 1972; Burt & Sperling, 1981). Farrell (1984) and Farrell, Pavel, and Sperling (1990) measured the visible persistence of stroboscopically moving images, and found that visible persistence actually decreased as presentation rate increased. This effect may be due to the poor ability of the motion processing system to resolve spatial detail (Burr & Morgan, 1997). It is clear that persistence cannot explain the effectiveness of apparent motion.

The success of apparent motion stimuli is almost certainly due to their ability to activate motion selective neurons in the visual cortex. Newsome, Mikami, and Wurtz (1986) recorded neural responses in visual areas V1 and MT to stroboscopically presented bars, as a function of the spatial and temporal intervals between successive presentations. Small spatial intervals (displacement distances) and temporal intervals (inter-stimulus intervals) produced reliable direction-specific responses, but at large intervals neural responses become inconsistent (see Figure 11.8).

*How does the perception of stroboscopic apparent motion relate to the spatiotemporal contrast sensitivity function discussed in Chapter 8?*

Combinations in the bottom-left corner of the graph produced reliable direction-specific responses; combinations in the top-right corner of the graph were ineffective. The filled symbols in Figure 11.8 show the borderline combinations separating effective and ineffective stimuli. Direction-selective responses were obtained for spatial intervals up to approximately 1°, and temporal intervals up to 100 ms. MT cells (filled squares) responded to larger spatial intervals than V1 cells (filled circles).

Newsome et al. also studied the apparent motion seen by human observers using exactly the same stimuli. They measured the maximum spatial interval at which observers reported seeing motion. Apparent motion was seen consistently at small spatial and temporal intervals, but not at longer intervals. Open circles in Figure 11.8 show the borderline combinations of spatial and temporal interval. There was good agreement between the psychophysical data and the cell responses, and particularly with MT cell responses. Newsome et al. concluded that motion-selective neurons in visual areas V1 and MT are the neural substrate of apparent motion perception.

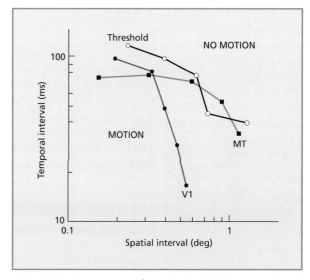

**FIG. 11.8** Comparison of psychophysical data on apparent motion perception (open symbols) and electrophysiological data from cortical cells (filled symbols; data re-plotted from Newsome et al., 1986, Figure 4).

# THE INTEGRATION OF MOTION DETECTOR RESPONSES

Each neural motion detector can only respond to motion in a very small portion of the image, namely the area covered by the detector's receptive field. Yet we are able to perceive meaningful motion in complex shapes and objects, moving either rigidly (e.g. moving cars, tumbling boulders) or non-rigidly (e.g. running animals, fluttering flags), even though local responses vary widely at different locations. For this reason, it is universally agreed that a second stage of motion processing occurs after initial detection. In this stage local detector responses are combined or integrated to encode the motion of the shape or object from which the responses arose.

*Motion integration theories exemplify the principle of population coding introduced in the first chapter.*

Theories of motion integration do not try to accommodate all possible instances of complex object motion in a single process, but restrict themselves to a sub-class of moving objects. Some theories restrict themselves to encoding the motion of rigid planar objects. Others restrict themselves to the motion of solid three-dimensional objects such as tumbling boulders, or the motion of articulated natural forms such as animal and human figures. These different approaches are not necessarily mutually exclusive.

## PLANAR SURFACES

Rigid planar surfaces are perfectly flat, like the surface of a wall or table. The most widely known models of motion integration restrict themselves to the analysis of rigid planar surfaces moving in the frontal plane. This means that all parts of the surface move in the same direction at the same speed, in a plane that is perpendicular to the line of sight. To experience this motion, hold the surface of the book directly in front of you, and move the book from side to side. An example of rigid planar motion is shown in Figure 11.9a.

A geometrical shape is shown in two successive positions as it drifts horizontally across the visual field (central arrow). Local motion direction and speed vary around the shape, as shown by the arrows along each edge. The circles in Figure 11.9b represent the receptive fields of neural motion detectors in cortical area V1, responding to the local motion of each edge. Although we correctly perceive the shape to move horizontally, none of the local signals is actually in the horizontal direction. The visual system must somehow unite the differing local signals to extract the movement of the shape. The problem caused by the limited receptive field size of motion detectors is usually called the **aperture problem**. The **velocity space** model of motion integration (also known as the *intersection-of-constraints* model; Adelson & Movshon, 1982; Simoncelli & Heeger, 1998) provides a mechanism for combining these local responses to encode the motion of the shape.

## The velocity space model

Integrative neurons in visual area MT are assumed to receive inputs from a range of neural detectors in area V1, as shown in Figure 11.9c. This part of the Figure illustrates a group of V1 detectors that all project to a cell in MT signalling horizontal movement. Arrows represent preferred direction and speed. With inputs from this set of V1 detectors, the MT cell will respond to rigid shapes moving horizontally rightwards. A sub-set of these V1 cells is activated by the geometrical shape in Figure 11.9a (shaded cells in Figure 11.9c), resulting in a response from the MT cell.

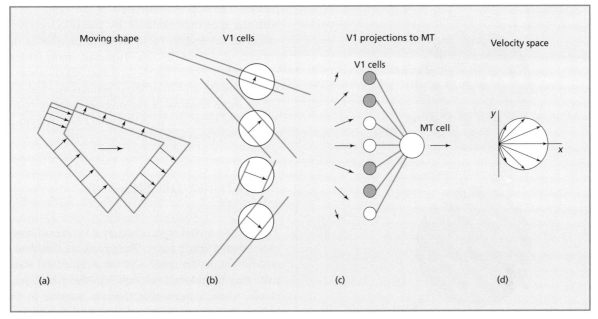

**FIG. 11.9** The "velocity space" model of motion integration. (a) A rigid shape moving rightwards; (b) Local responses from motion-sensitive neurons in V1; (c) Connections to a motion-sensitive cell in MT that responds to global motion. Shaded cells are those activated by the shape; (d) Velocity space representation of the local motion components in a horizontally moving shape.

To understand the logic behind this scheme, we need to represent the local signals in a *velocity space* diagram (see Figure 11.9d). This simply represents each motion signal by an arrow (also called a vector). The angle of each arrow represents the direction of that signal, and the length of the arrow represents its speed. In Figure 11.9a and 11.9b, notice that the speed associated with each signal depends on the angle between that signal and the motion of the shape. Signals in directions very close to the direction of shape motion are relatively fast (long vectors). Signals in directions nearly at right-angles to the shape motion are relatively slow (short vectors). If vectors in different directions are plotted in velocity space, as in Figure 11.9d, it becomes apparent that their end points lie around the circumference of a circle (assuming rigid motion). The circle passes through the origin (zero velocity perpendicular to the object motion) and through the point corresponding to the actual velocity of the object (maximum velocity in the direction of the object). If an integrative neuron is wired such that it receives inputs from a group of motion detectors having preferred directions and speeds that fall on this circle, as in Figure 11.9c, then the neuron will encode horizontal motion of any rigid shape. Other directions of shape motion can be encoded by combining responses from other sets of motion detectors.

## Plaid patterns

There is a good deal of psychophysical and physiological evidence that motion integration does involve some form of velocity space computation. Much of this evidence has come from studies of **plaid** stimuli, made by superimposing two gratings drifting in different directions (see Figure 11.10). Adelson and Movshon (1982) found that the two gratings often appear to lock together, moving as a single plaid

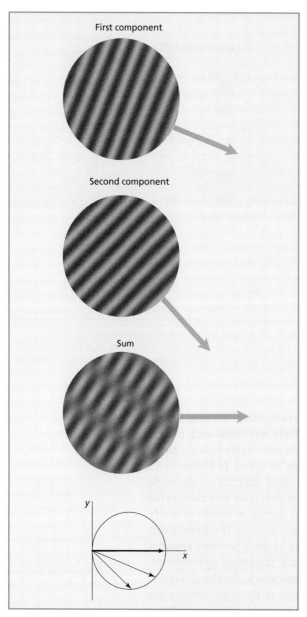

First component

Second component

Sum

$y$

$x$

**FIG. 11.10**   A "plaid" pattern made by superimposing two drifting sine-wave patterns. Although each sine wave alone drifts down to the right (arrows), the plaid pattern appears to drift horizontally. The velocity space representation (bottom) can explain this effect.

**KEY TERM**
**Kinetic depth**: The impression of depth seen in the two-dimensional image of a moving three-dimensional object; the depth is apparent only when the object moves.

pattern. The apparent direction of the plaid agreed with the direction predicted by the velocity space model of integration (bold arrow in the plot at the bottom of Figure 11.10). However, more recent research has found that the apparent plaid direction sometimes departs from these predictions, and has led to some revision of the original velocity space model (for example, Yo & Wilson, 1992; Wilson & Kim, 1994; Bowns, 2001).

## RIGID THREE-DIMENSIONAL OBJECTS

Three-dimensional objects occupy a volume of space rather than a single plane. Their parts are distributed at different depths relative to the viewer (and some parts may be hidden from view by other parts). As a result, when a rigid object moves relative to the viewer, the images of its parts move relative to each other on the retina. In the rotating sphere described at the start of the chapter (Figure 11.1), points near the equator move across the field of view faster than points near the poles. This pattern of motion is clearly more complex than the rigid translation described above, in which all points move at the same speed. Observers readily perceive coherent three-dimensional structure from this kind of motion stimulus. The percept is called "**kinetic depth**". A sphere that is completely transparent and invisible except for many dots of light randomly scattered on its surface appears to be a flat, unstructured cloud of dots when stationary. When it moves its 3-D structure becomes clear despite the absence of shape cues. This shows that movement alone is sufficient to convey the 3-D structure of the object. Theories to explain kinetic depth fall into two categories: position-based and motion-based.

## Position-based theories of kinetic depth

In position-based theories, the visual system keeps track of the positions of features in the image over a series of static snapshots of the moving object. The 3-D structure of the object is inferred from changes in the position of its features over time. Ullman's (1984b) incremental-rigidity algorithm is an example of such a theory. It is based on Ullman's (1979) earlier proof that 3-D structure can be inferred from the positions of at least four points on the object at three different times.

## Motion-based theories of kinetic depth

In motion-based theories, 3-D structure is inferred from the retinal velocities of points in the image, rather than from their positions. Retinal velocity signals are provided by simple motion detectors of the kind discussed earlier. Hildreth, Ando, Anderson, and Treue's (1995) theory computes 3-D velocities that maximise the rigidity of the moving shape, but are as consistent as possible with the retinal velocities.

## Psychophysical evidence

Psychophysical evidence on kinetic depth perception favours motion-based theories rather than position-based theories. Several studies have used displays containing elements with very short lifetimes (e.g. Todd, Akerstrom, Reichel, & Hayes, 1988; Dosher, Landy, & Sperling, 1989; Mather, 1989; Dick, Ullman, & Sagi, 1991). In some studies the whole display was presented for a very short time. In other studies the display lasted much longer, but each dot in the display appeared only for a brief time before being replaced by a new dot elsewhere in the display. Subjects could perceive complex 3-D surfaces even in displays where each dot lasted only two frames, but only over temporal intervals below 80–100 ms and displacement distances of below 15′ arc. These limits are comparable to those found for the perception of simple apparent motion stimuli, as described earlier (Newsome et al., 1986) and below. Andersen and Bradley (1998) argue that neurons in cortical area MT, and perhaps MST, are responsible for the computation of 3-D structure from the 2-D motion signals provided by V1 neurons.

## ARTICULATED BIOLOGICAL FORMS

### Biological motion

The bodies of humans and animals are made from rigid parts (e.g. limbs) joined together at points of articulation. The visual system is able to build rich perceptual representations from minimal displays of moving biological forms. Johansson (1973) filmed actors wearing patches of retro-reflective material on their joints (shoulders, elbows, wrists, hips, knees, and ankles), in lighting conditions which ensured that only the patches were visible against a dark background (see Figure 11.11). When the film was shown to naïve observers, they spontaneously reported the perception of moving human figures. This effect has been replicated many times, and is known as **biological motion**.

> **KEY TERM**
> **Biological motion:** The perception of a moving biological form, either human or non-human, when the body is visible only by means of light points attached at joints.

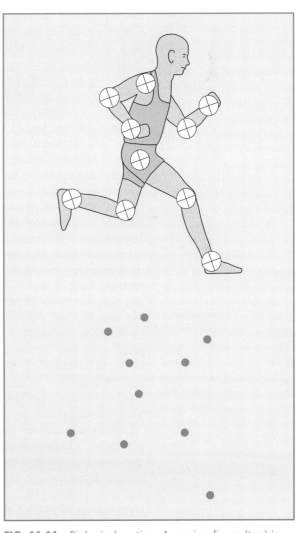

**FIG. 11.11** Biological motion. A moving figure (top) is represented by isolated points positioned at major joints (bottom). When the dots are animated, naïve observers perceive a moving human figure.

The display contains no explicit connections between the dots, and has no apparent structure when stationary. As soon as motion is added, the visual system is able to establish the pattern of connectivity between the dots. Observers can discriminate the gender and even the identity of the walker, from the pattern of dot movements in the display (e.g. Kozlowski & Cutting, 1977). Recent research (e.g. Mather, Radford, & West, 1992; Neri, Morrone, & Burr, 1998) has employed computer-generated synthetic walkers, based on an algorithm from Cutting (1978).

## Explanations of biological motion

Johansson (1973) attempted to explain the perception of biological motion using a theory of *visual vector analysis* that he had developed to explain the motion seen in more simple patterns. The starting point for his theory was the observation that the motion observed in each spot of light attached to the walker contains contributions from several sources. For example, the movement of a spot attached to the walker's knee represents the combined effect of several movements—translatory motion of the body relative to the environment, oscillatory motion of the hip relative to the body, and pendular movement of the knee relative to the hip. Johansson proposed that the visual system can separate out these contributions to each dot's movement, so inferring the articulated structure of the walker's body. Cutting and Proffitt (1981) argued that the visual system builds the representation sequentially, beginning with dots on the hip and shoulder because the torso provides the reference point for all other structures of the body. Analysis then proceeds to dots located on more peripheral parts of the body.

The movement of each dot in a biological motion display is almost certainly encoded by responses in neural motion detectors of the kind described earlier. Johansson (1976) found that perception of biological motion was possible even at exposure durations below 200 ms. He concluded that analysis "is accomplished at the initial stage of physiological signal recording and that it is a consequence of receptive field organisation" (p. 379). Mather et al. (1992) reported that the spatial and temporal limits of biological motion perception are similar to those found for the detection of translatory motion in dot patterns, universally attributed to the response properties of neural detectors (see earlier). Young infants and cats can perceive biological motion (Fox & McDaniel, 1982; Blake, 1993), leading Blake (1993) to conclude that biological motion analysis is likely to be accomplished by neurons responsive to complex motion patterns. Consistent with this view, Perrett, Harries, Mistlin, and Chitty (1990) found cells in monkey temporal cortex (superior temporal sulcus) that appear to be highly selective for biological motion.

Biological motion used to be treated as distinct from the rest of motion perception, an example of "event perception". Recent research has led to the view that biological motion can be explained by processes similar to those used to explain other motion phenomena, including low-level and high-level motion analysing neurons. Brain-imaging studies implicate a visual area in the superior temporal sulcus (STS, Grossman & Blake, 2002) that lies adjacent to other areas such as MST, known to be involved in processing other kinds of complex motion patterns. Evidence also indicates that form analysing processes can contribute to the perception of biological motion (Beintema & Lappe, 2002), so there is presently no universally agreed theory to explain biological motion.

# MULTIPLE PROCESSES IN MOTION PERCEPTION

We have seen that neural motion detectors play a central role in theories of motion perception. However, over the years many researchers have argued that we can also perceive motion independently of activity in neural detectors, mediated by higher level inferences or by attentional processes. According to the perceptual inference theory (e.g. Braddick, 1980), motion perception can arise from perceptual problem solving to explain the appearance and disappearance of shapes in apparent motion displays. In the "attention-based" theory of motion perception (e.g. Cavanagh, 1992), visible features in the image attract the attention of the viewer. As those features change position in the image, the resultant shift in attention gives rise to the perception of motion. Advocates of such high-level processes do not see them as inconsistent with the notion of lower level neural motion detection, but rather as a second system that co-exists with low-level detection.

## THE SHORT-RANGE VERSUS LONG-RANGE DISTINCTION

Much of the early justification for two motion processes came from the results of experiments using two very different motion displays: random-dot kinematograms and classical apparent motion displays.

## Random-dot kinematograms (RDKs)

RDKs contain many randomly positioned black and white dots. In a simple two-frame RDK, the two fields of dots are presented sequentially, separated by a brief inter-stimulus interval. All the dots in the second frame are shifted a certain distance relative to the first frame (see Figure 11.12). The observer's task is to report the direction of the shift. Using relatively small dots that appear and disappear suddenly, direction can be reported reliably only for short displacement distances (below approximately 0.25°) and short inter-stimulus intervals (below approximately 80 ms).

The squares in Figure 11.13 show RDK data re-plotted from Baker and Braddick (1985). The direction of RDK displacement could be reported reliably (less than 5% errors) only for combinations of spatial interval and temporal interval that fell in the area of the graph between the open squares and the filled squares. Notice that the upper limit for motion discrimination in RDKs (filled squares in the graph) agrees quite well with the data reported by Newsome et al. (1986) and re-plotted in Figure 11.8. This supports the long-held assumption that apparent motion seen in

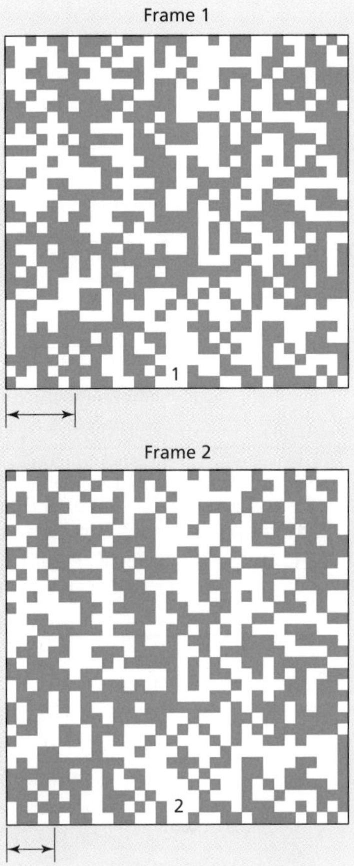

**FIG. 11.12** A two-frame random-dot kinematogram. The arrows identify the relative displacement of dots between frames.

*Compare random-dot kinematograms, and their theoretical significance, with random-dot stereograms described in Chapter 10.*

**KEY TERM**
**Random-dot kinematogram (RDK)**: A two-frame motion sequence containing pseudo-randomly arranged dots; some or all dots shift location in one frame relative to the other to offer a signal for motion detection.

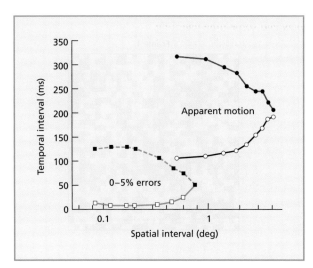

**FIG. 11.13** Comparison of direction discrimination data in RDKs (squares, re-plotted from Baker & Braddick, 1985, Figure 6 CLB), and apparent motion in classical displays (circles, re-plotted from Kolers, 1972, Figure 3.2).

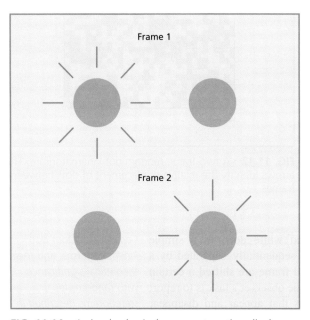

**FIG. 11.14** A simple classical apparent motion display. Two lights flash on and off in alternation. In ideal conditions, they create the illusion of a single light moving back and forth.

RDKs is due to the activity of low-level neural motion detectors (Braddick, 1974). As Figure 11.12 demonstrates, simple visual inspection of the two frames of an RDK does not reveal the direction of pattern displacement, yet motion is readily seen when the two frames are animated.

## "Classical" apparent motion

Classical displays contain a small number of elements that shift position from one frame to the next. Kolers (1972) reported data gathered by Neuhaus in 1930 using a pair of lights flashed on and off in alternation (see Figure 11.14). The spatial separation between the lights, and the time interval between each light flash, were varied systematically. Subjects reported whether they saw "good" apparent motion between the lights (a single light moving back and forth), or apparent simultaneity (two lights apparently illuminating almost simultaneously), or apparent succession (two independent lights appearing to illuminate successively). The circles in Figure 11.13 re-plot some of these data. Combinations of spatial interval and temporal interval that fell in the area of the graph between the open and filled circles supported good apparent motion. Combinations above the filled circles yielded apparent succession, and combinations below the open circles yielded apparent simultaneity. The limits of apparent motion in classical displays are clearly much higher than those reported for RDKs. A temporal interval of 100 ms represents the lower boundary for perceiving motion in classical displays, but the upper boundary for direction discrimination in RDKs.

## The two-process theory of apparent motion

This empirical dichotomy between RDK data and classical apparent motion data led to the proposal that two separate processes mediated the perception of apparent motion, a low-level neural motion system (responsible for motion seen in RDKs), and a higher level "cognitive" motion system (responsible for motion seen in classical displays)—the two-process theory. The two motion systems became known as the "short-range" system and the "long-range" system, respectively (Braddick, 1974), for obvious reasons. There is ample evidence from adaptation studies and from studies of cortical cells, discussed earlier, for the existence of the short-range system. Why would the visual system need the long-range system as well? In natural images, moving objects often disappear behind occluding surfaces, reappearing some distance away and some time later (e.g. animals moving behind trees in a wood). A perceptual system that could track such movement would allow us to maintain a stable representation of object identity.

## Reappraisal of the two-process theory

In the late 1980s there was a critical reappraisal of the two-process theory of apparent motion. It is still universally agreed that only a low-level neural process can account for the apparent motion seen in dense RDKs. However, the empirical justification for two qualitatively different motion processes operating over different ranges was called into question (Cavanagh & Mather, 1989). Morgan (1992) found that maximum displacement or Dmax in RDKs can be extended to nearly 2° by using very large or blurred dots. Mather and Tunley (1995) found that maximum inter-stimulus interval or Tmax in RDKs can be extended to nearly 500 ms by using frames that appear and disappear smoothly rather than suddenly. The scope of the short-range process now appears to extend into the stimulus space previously occupied solely by the long-range system, depending on the nature of the stimulus. This raises the possibility of explaining the full range of apparent motion phenomena using only motion detectors of the kind proposed for the short-range system. Notice that the classical apparent motion data and the RDK data in Figure 11.13 show a similar dependence on stimulus parameters, but occupy a different region of the graph. This lends credence to the idea that the two sets of data arise from the same kind of process. Different stimuli may excite different populations of cells. For example, data obtained using RDKs may reflect the properties of small motion-detecting receptive fields, with relatively small $\Delta t$ and $\Delta s$ values. Classical apparent motion displays, on the other hand, may reflect contributions from relatively large receptive fields having larger $\Delta t$ and $\Delta s$ values.

Despite the criticism of the two-process theory, there is still evidence that multiple processes play a role in motion perception. A new dichotomy has become widely accepted, between *first-order* and *second-order* motion processes.

## FIRST-ORDER VERSUS SECOND-ORDER MOTION

All the motion displays described so far contain shapes that are distinguishable by a difference in luminance, such as light bars or spots against a dark background. Cavanagh and Mather (1989) called such displays **first-order**, because the moving shape is defined by a difference between the intensity values of individual image points inside the shape (e.g. light) and image points outside the shape (e.g. dark). A number of experiments have employed displays in which the moving shape has no consistent point-by-point differences against the background, but differs instead in textural properties. Two examples are shown in Figure 11.15. In the upper two-frame stimulus, the dots in each frame have completely different spatial arrangements, but in both arrangements a central square region is distinguishable from the background. In the central square region of the first frame the dots tend to occur in horizontal runs. In the central region of the second frame, the dots tend to occur in vertical runs. Background dots are completely different (uncorrelated) across the two frames. The location of the square is shifted in one frame relative to the other to create a stimulus for apparent motion.

Notice that the central square of each frame in Figure 11.15 has the same point-by-point intensities as the background, but it differs in terms of the intensities of pairs

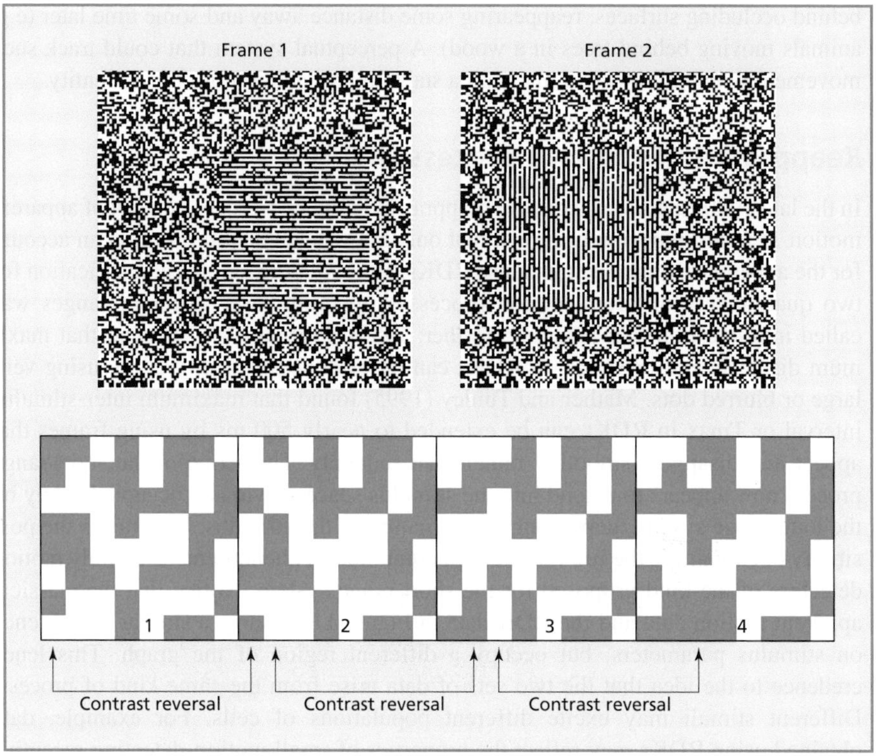


FIG. 11.15 Two kinds of second-order motion stimulus. Top: A square shape defined by a difference in second-order texture shifts position from frame 1 to frame 2. Bottom: Travelling contrast reversal. In frame 2, the leftmost column of dots from frame 1 reverses in contrast; in frame 3 the second-left column from frame 2 reverses in contrast; in frame 4 the third-left column from frame 3 reverses in contrast; and so on.

of points. In the centre of the first frame, for example, horizontally separated pairs of points are more likely to have the same intensity than pairs of points at other orientations. In the surrounding dots, the probability that any pair of points has the same intensity is the same at all orientations. Thus, the difference between the centre and surround is defined by the properties of pairs of points, rather than the properties of single points. Cavanagh and Mather (1989) called such displays **second-order displays**. The lower stimulus in Figure 11.15 consists of four frames from a motion stimulus containing a field of random light and dark dots. From frame to frame, a single vertical column of dots (arrowed) reverses contrast (dark dots become light, and vice versa). The column selected for reversal advances across the pattern with each frame to create a stimulus for apparent motion. In this case the moving shape is defined by the properties of pairs of points separated in time rather than in space. Outside the column, luminance contrast does not change from frame to frame. Inside the column, contrast reverses from frame to frame.

**KEY TERM**
**Second-order motion display**: A motion stimulus containing shapes defined by variations in texture, with no corresponding variation in luminance.

Observers readily perceive apparent motion in second-order displays similar to those in Figure 11.15 (e.g. Ramachandran, Rao, & Vidyasagar, 1973; Lelkens & Koenderink, 1984; Chubb & Sperling, 1988). Yet neural motion detectors of the kind described earlier would not be activated by second-order displays. These detectors respond to the movement of first-order intensity patterns, containing bright or dark bars, edges, and dots. For this reason they are now sometimes called first-order

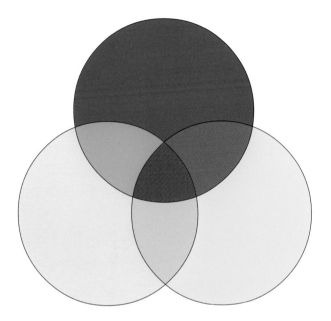

**FIG. 12.3** Typical colours used in reproduction systems based on subtractive mixing. Areas of overlap indicate the colour seen in mixtures of the primary colours.

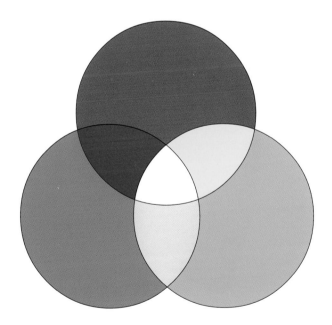

**FIG. 12.4** Additive mixtures of three primary lights. The areas of overlap show the colour seen in mixtures of the primary colours.

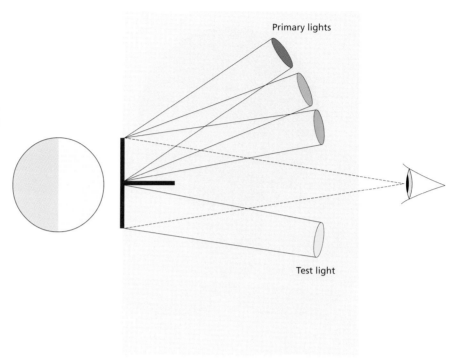

**FIG. 12.5** Apparatus used to study additive colour mixing. The observer views a bipartite field. One side of the field is illuminated by a monochromatic (single-wavelength) test light. The other side is illuminated by a mixture of three primary wavelengths. The subject can achieve a subjective match between the two halves of the field by adjusting the relative intensities of the primary lights.

Primary lights

Test light

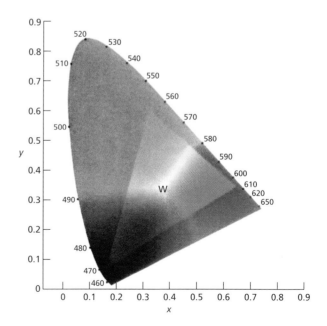

**FIG. 12.6** The CIE chromaticity diagram. Pure spectral colours are arranged around the perimeter of the shape. Additive mixtures of wavelengths lie inside the shape. The colour seen in a mixture of two wavelengths lies along a straight line joining the two wavelengths. Mixtures falling on the location labelled W appear white. The small triangle in the space represents the gamut of colours available in a typical display monitor.

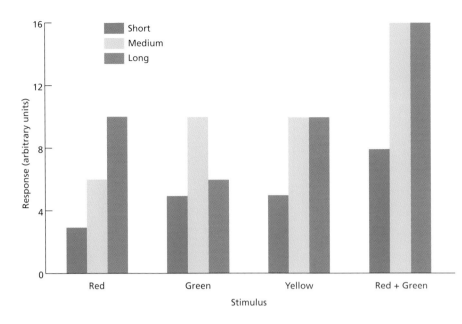

FIG. 12.7 A simple explanation of additive colour mixture. The leftmost group of three bars shows the triad of cone responses to a "red" wavelength light. The middle-left group shows the triad of cone responses to a "green" wavelength. The middle-right group shows the triad of cone responses to a "yellow" wavelength. The rightmost group shows the triad of responses to an additive combination of the "red" and "green" wavelengths. Notice that the relative response of the three cone classes to the mixture is identical to that produced by the pure "yellow" wavelength. Hence the mixture appears yellow.

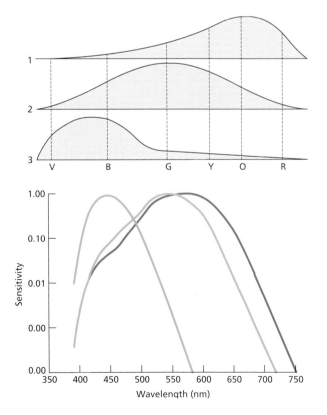

FIG. 12.8 Top: Helmholtz's estimate of three kinds of "fibre" responsible for colour sensations, produced in the later 1800s. Bottom: Estimates of cone photoreceptor spectral absorbances based on direct measurements taken in the late 1900s (re-plotted from Stockman & Sharpe, 2000).

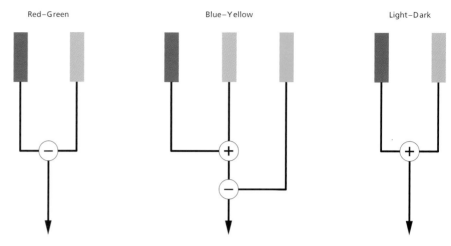

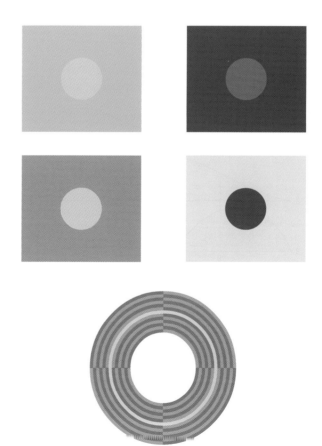

**FIG. 12.11** Colour after-images. After fixating on the centre of the upper display for approximately 60 seconds, transfer your gaze to the lower display. You should experience a colour after-image.

**FIG. 12.14** Luminance and chrominance signals in a natural scene. The original image is shown at the top. The lower-left image shows only its luminance signal. The lower-right image shows only its chrominance signal. The original image is basically the sum of the luminance and chrominance components.

motion detectors. The borders defining the moving shape in second-order displays are not defined by intensity differences, but by textural differences, and would be invisible to these detectors. For example, there is no difference in intensity across the border of the square in the upper display in Figure 11.15, because there is an equal number of light and dark dots on each side of the border. The distribution of the dots (i.e. texture) varies across the border, but the dots themselves are uncorrelated. First-order motion detectors would produce essentially random responses to movement of the texture-defined shape, driven by random pairings between the dots in each frame.

## Explaining the perception of second-order motion

If first-order detectors cannot respond to second-order displays, what visual process mediates the perception of movement in second-order displays? Two ideas have been proposed to explain the perception of second-order motion, feature tracking, and second-order motion detectors.

### Feature tracking

This explanation revives the old long-range process, and proposes that motion perception in second-order displays is mediated by a relatively high-level feature-tracking process. This process identifies individual features and shapes in the image, however they are defined, and tracks changes in their position over time.

### Second-order motion detectors

According to this explanation, motion detectors can be sub-divided into two classes. One class encodes the motion of first-order patterns, and the other class encodes the motion of second-order patterns. How can neural motion detectors respond to second-order motion? Second-order motion detectors are assumed to have extra stages of processing inserted in between the input receptive fields and the comparator neuron, which allow them to respond to texture variation. The filter–rectify–filter or FRF scheme discussed in Chapter 8 (see Figure 8.20) offers a mechanism for detecting texture-defined borders.

### Both?

These two explanations of second-order motion are not mutually exclusive. Indeed, available evidence indicates that both explanations are probably correct.

*Second-order motion detectors* Evidence consistent with second-order motion detectors includes the following:

- *Physiology* Several papers have reported that visual cells in cat and monkey cortex can respond to second-order motion (Albright, 1992; Zhou & Baker, 1993; O'Keefe & Movshon, 1998). O'Keefe and Movshon (1998) compared cell responses to first-order motion (drifting intensity gratings) and to second-order motion (similar to the lower display in Figure 11.15). All cells responded to first-order motion; 25% of cells studied in area MT, and 9% of cells studied in V1 also responded to second-order motion. Albright (1992) reported a much higher proportion of MT cells (87%) responding to second-order motion. Second-order responses were usually weaker than first-order responses.

● *Psychophysics* Ledgeway and Smith (1997) and Nishida and Sato (1995) report adaptation to the motion of second-order patterns. Apparent motion is seen in second-order RDKs, and is limited in the same way that first-order motion is (Mather & West, 1993). The general consensus from these studies is that the visual system possesses two populations of neural motion detector (e.g. Nishida, Ledgeway, & Edwards, 1997; Sperling & Lu, 1998). One population contains first-order detectors, and deals with first-order motion. It corresponds to the neural detectors described earlier in the chapter. The other population contains second-order detectors, and deals with second-order motion. Detectors in this population receive inputs from receptive fields that respond to texture borders.

*Feature tracking* A number of papers have reported motion phenomena that are very difficult to explain using neural detectors, either first- or second-order, but are consistent with feature-tracking. Seiffert and Cavanagh (1998), for example, studied the perception of motion in slowly moving grating patterns. They found that observers' ability to detect the motion of first-order gratings depended on velocity. Observers' ability to detect the motion of second-order gratings, however, depended on displacement distance rather than on velocity. Seiffert and Cavanagh reasoned that velocity dependence is a feature of motion detectors (as discussed earlier), whereas position dependence reflects the operation of a feature-tracking mechanism that depends on position change. They concluded that, at least under the conditions they used, motion perception was mediated by feature tracking. Data presented by Smith (1994), by Sperling and Lu (1998), and by Bex and Baker (1999) also support the existence of a motion process based on the attentive tracking of features.

## OTHER HIGH-LEVEL INFLUENCES ON MOTION INTERPRETATION

Other research provides evidence that high-level, interpretive processes influence motion perception. Michotte (1946, translated 1963) described a number of phenomenological observations in which collisions between elements in a dynamic display lead to the impression that the elements "cause" each other to move. The impression of causality depended on the spatial and temporal parameters of the display. Michotte (1950, translated by Thines, Costall, & Butterworth, 1991) also described the following phenomenon:

> One projects onto a screen any coloured shape, such as a circle, and suddenly changes its colour, size, or shape. . . . Under these conditions, one can have the impression that the object has undergone a change while remaining "itself". The same coloured circle has become greenish, for example, or has dilated, or become oval.
>
> (p. 125)

> In fact, the change is so rapid that it always appears to be a partial evolution of the object, and it then occurs as a "growing into", and by virtue of this has its own anterior temporal limits.
>
> (p. 137)

Michotte believed that the phenomena he observed arose from visual processes that serve to make explicit the functional relations between real-world objects; how one object acts on another, for instance, or how an object changes its shape.

Tse, Cavanagh, and Nakayama (1998) later studied the apparent motion that Michotte had originally observed when different shapes are presented in rapid succession, and called the effect *tranformational apparent motion*. When the two frames in Figure 11.16 are presented in succession, observers perceive a smooth transformation in shape, rather than an abrupt switch. Tse et al. found, as did Michotte, that the apparent motion seen during such transformations is influenced by contour continuity, colour, texture, and shape. They argued that the importance of form implicates a high-level matching or "parsing" process in the generation of apparent motion. A discussion of surface parsing can be found in Chapter 8.

Kersten, Mamassian, and Knill (1997) devised several compelling "shadow motion" displays, in which the apparent motion of an object is influenced by the movement of its shadow. For example, in a display containing a stationary object with a moving shadow, observers consistently report that the shape appears to move. Kersten et al. explain the misattribution of motion in terms of an inbuilt assumption by the visual system that light sources generally remain stationary over very short time periods. Hence, moving shadows are best "explained" by moving objects.

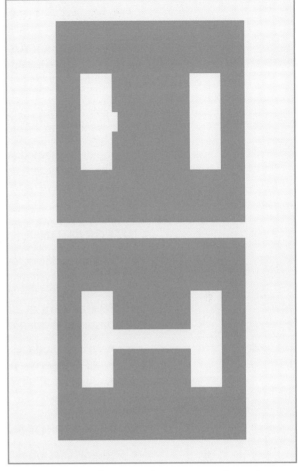

**FIG. 11.16** Transformational apparent motion. When these two images are presented repeatedly in alternation, observers see the horizontal bar smoothly growing and shrinking across the central gap.

## CONCLUSIONS

Our understanding of motion perception has made very significant advances over the last 15 or so years. At a neural level, there is a general consensus that the major processing stream for motion runs from cortical area V1 through area MT, and on to MST and STS; the dorsal route discussed in Chapter 7. Local motion is encoded in V1. MT cells respond to more complex rigid motion. MST and STS appear to play central roles in the processing of complex motion such as optic flow and biological motion (e.g. Tanaka, 1998; Grossman & Blake, 2002).

Psychophysical research has led to a proliferation in the number of putative processes involved in motion analysis, including different types of motion process, different integrative mechanisms, and different high-level tracking systems. It is not yet clear how these processes relate to each other, or to the neural substrate. The precise role of tracking mechanisms in motion perception is still an open question, though emerging evidence demonstrates that both neural motion detectors and higher level tracking mechanisms participate in motion perception (e.g. Smith & Ledgeway, 2001).

## CHAPTER SUMMARY

### DETECTING MOVEMENT

- There is ample evidence that many organisms detect retinal motion using specialised neural circuits.
- Psychophysical evidence for neural motion detectors in humans includes the motion after-effect and direction-specific threshold elevation.
- These detectors can also explain the perception of apparent motion in rapidly presented static displays.
- The visual system uses several strategies to discount the retinal movement caused by eye movements, including saccadic suppression, eye movement commands, and large-scale motion.

### INTEGRATION

- Motion detector responses are ambiguous (the aperture problem). So the visual system must integrate the responses of many detectors to disambiguate the local signals.
- Several forms of integration have been proposed, to deal with different classes of moving object:
  - Planar surfaces—velocity space
  - 3-D objects—position-based and velocity-based models
  - Biological motion—vector analysis and neural motion-detecting processes.

### MULTIPLE PROCESSES

- Several lines of evidence indicate that multiple processes contribute to motion perception.
- The different results obtained with RDKs and classical displays led to the two-process theory.
- More recent evidence favours a distinction between first-order and second-order neural detectors.
- Evidence also indicates that feature tracking and surface parsing play a role in motion perception.

## TUTORIALS

### SPATIO-TEMPORAL APPROACHES TO MOTION PROCESSING

#### Motion as spatio-temporal orientation

Retinal images of shapes or objects obviously contain variations of intensity in two dimensions, x and y. When these shapes move, a third dimension of variation is added to the image—change over time, t. We can therefore represent motion in a space–time volume with dimensions x, y, and t. The top image in Figure 11.17 shows a car moving rightwards. The mid-left image depicts this moving image in a 3-dimensional $x$–$y$–$t$ volume. As the car moves across the image, it sweeps out a volume in $x$–$y$–$t$ space. We can slice through this volume horizontally at a particular $y$ value to reveal a cross-section, shown on the mid-right. This cross-section reveals the image variation in two of the three dimensions, $x$ and $t$. The two dimensions are plotted as $x$–$t$ or space–time graphs in the bottom images of Figure 11.17. Note that rightward motion leads to an oriented structure in the space–time plot. Motion at a different velocity or in the opposite direction would alter the space–time orientation seen in the plot, because the slope of the pattern corresponds to velocity. For example, a car moving at 30 km/h (lower left) travels a distance of 8.3 metres in one second. A car moving at 20 km/h travels 5.6 metres in one second (lower right). Note the difference in slope between the two plots, corresponding to the difference in speed. Space–time plots provide a very convenient means of depicting the stimulus properties of moving images, and the response properties of motion detectors, as we shall see.

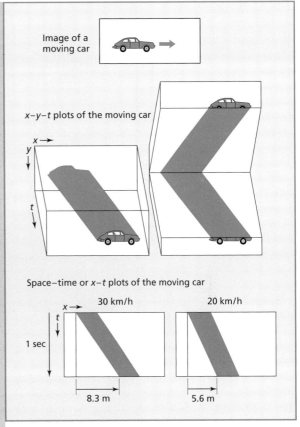

**FIG. 11.17** Representing a moving image in $x$–$y$–$t$ and $x$–$t$ plots.

## Motion detectors in space–time plots

How do neural motion detectors described earlier in the chapter fit into this form of representation? Motion detectors sample two different locations in the image at two different times, defined by their $\Delta s$ and $\Delta t$ constants, as shown at the top left of Figure 11.18.

The two inputs to each detector can therefore be drawn in a space–time plot as two sampling points separated by a distance in space equal to $\Delta s$, and a difference in time equal to $\Delta t$, as shown in the left-hand space–time plot of Figure 11.18. Notice that the detector's input receptive fields fall along a tilted line in the space–time plot. For this reason, motion detectors can be said to respond to spatio-temporal orientation. The orientation of the receptive field defines its optimal velocity.

Adelson and Bergen (1985) proposed that cortical direction-selective simple cells were tuned to spatio-temporal orientation. The receptive field of the cells in Adelson and Bergen's model contained both excitatory and inhibitory regions, so that the response of each cell depended on how well a moving stimulus aligned with its receptive field structure. There is strong evidence in support of this model. The upper space–time plot in Figure 11.19 illustrates the receptive field structure of a simple cell in V1 of the cat

**FIG. 11.18** Representing a motion-detecting receptive field in space–time plots.

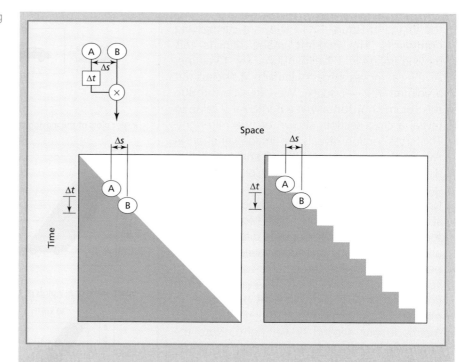

(McLean & Palmer, 1989). The white regions are responsive to bright stimuli, and the dark regions are responsive to dark stimuli. The cell clearly has a preference for rightwards moving stimuli, as indicated by the tilted line at its preferred spatio-temporal orientation. Adelson and Bergen (1985) also proposed that complex cortical cells receive inputs from pairs of simple cells having different receptive field arrangements, so that complex cell responses would not depend on how the moving pattern aligns with receptive field structure. Adelson and Bergen (1985) called these complex cells "motion energy detectors". Data from complex cells in cat cortex (Emerson, Bergen, & Adelson, 1992) are consistent with this second stage of the model. A more detailed description of the motion energy model can be found in Bruce et al. (2003).

There is good psychophysical evidence that the human visual system also contains motion detectors tuned to spatio-temporal orientation. Burr, Ross, and Morrone (1986a) estimated receptive field structure by measuring contrast sensitivity to movement in the presence of masking gratings at various spatial and temporal frequencies. The lower plot of Figure 11.19 illustrates their estimate of a human motion-sensitive receptive field. As in the case of the cat cell, it contains antagonistic sub-regions, and is optimally responsive at a particular velocity (shown by the tilted line).

## Velocity coding

Image velocity corresponds to spatio-temporal orientation. Each motion detector is tuned to a particular spatio-temporal orientation. However, any single detector's response does not uniquely specify velocity, since response depends on stimulus contrast as well as velocity. Even at the preferred velocity, the response to a particular stimulus will depend on how effectively it stimulates the antagonistic sub-regions of the receptive field. So in order to encode velocity unambiguously, the visual system must compare the outputs of detectors tuned to different velocities. How many different velocity-tuned detectors are there? Psychophysical evidence indicates that there may only be two types of detector, one sensitive to "fast" velocities, and the other sensitive to "slow" velocities (Bruce et al., 2003). The ratio of their responses provides a code for stimulus velocity, increasing as velocity increases. Smith and Edgar (1994) and Hammett, Champion, Morland, and Thompson (2005) found that changes in perceived speed following adaptation to motion could be explained by such a fast versus slow velocity ratio code.

## Apparent motion in space–time plots

Discontinuously moving images generate staircase patterns in space–time plots. The right-hand plot in Figure 11.20 shows an edge moving discontinuously. At regular intervals the edge shifts rapidly to a new position (horizontal edges in the plot), but in between shifts it remains stationary (vertical edges in the plot). The result is a staircase pattern in the space–time plot. These patterns do effectively stimulate detectors with receptive fields at the appropriate spatio-temporal orientation, as the superimposed receptive field in Figure 11.18 shows. It is easy to see from Figure 11.18 that responses in neural motion detectors can explain both perception of real motion (left-hand plot), and perception of apparent motion (right-hand plot).

However, discontinuous motion weakly stimulates detectors tuned to the direction opposite to the direction of displacement. This happens because discontinuous motion actually contains motion components in both directions. If one adds segments of reversed motion to a smoothly drifting pattern, the result is discontinuous motion (Morgan, 1980). The left-hand space–time plot in Figure 11.20 depicts a line drifting continuously and smoothly rightwards. The middle plot depicts a line that repeatedly drifts leftward and then flicks rapidly back to its original position. The resulting pattern is known as a sawtooth wave. The right-hand

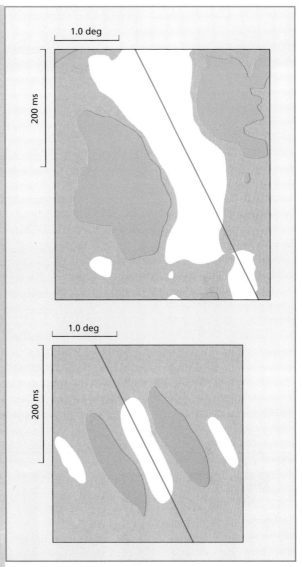

**FIG. 11.19** Space–time plots of motion-sensitive receptive fields. The upper plot is based on recordings from a simple cell in cat V1 (re-drawn from McLean & Palmer, 1989, Figure 1E). The lower plot is based on psychophysical masking data (re-drawn from Burr, Ross, & Morrone, 1986a, Figure 8).

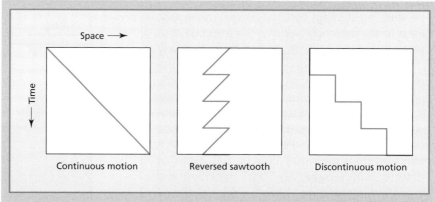

**FIG. 11.20**   Space–time decomposition of discontinuous motion (right) into two components; a continuous forward component (left), and a reversed sawtooth component (middle). The velocity of reversed motion (middle) exactly cancels out the velocity of continuous forward motion (left) to create the discontinuous motion in the right. Only when the relatively high-frequency sawtooth pattern is detectable can an observer tell the difference between continuous motion and discontinuous motion.

plot is the motion that results when the continuous motion and sawtooth motion are combined in a single line. The line moves discontinuously rightward, because the reversed drift of the sawtooth component cancels out the forward drift of the continuous component, leaving only the rapid rightward flicks.

The presence of this sawtooth motion "hidden" in discontinuous motion helps us to explain some properties of apparent motion. First, our ability to distinguish between real motion and apparent motion probably depends on visual responses to the sawtooth component. When the sawtooth component is detectable by the visual system, observers perceive the discontinuity in the apparent motion, but when it is too rapid to be detectable, all that is left is the continuous component, so the apparent motion is perceptually indistinguishable from real motion (Morgan, 1980; Burr, Ross, & Morrone, 1986b). Second, observers sometimes make errors in their reports of motion direction in apparent motion stimuli (Morgan & Cleary, 1992). This effect is probably due to motion responses to the reversed motion in the sawtooth component.

## Second-order motion in space–time plots

Figure 11.21 shows a space–time plot of the contrast-reversing second-order motion stimulus illustrated in Figure 11.15 (lower). An array of randomly bright and dark elements is shown on

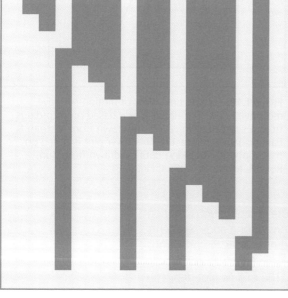

**FIG. 11.21**   Space–time plot of the contrast-reversing second-order motion display shown in Figure 11.15.

the *x*-axis of the plot (corresponding to one row in the 2-D pattern). Over a series of time intervals (*y*-axis), each element in turn reverses in contrast to create a spatio-temporally oriented texture border. Notice that the moving border contains no consistent intensity difference. At some positions it is defined by a decrease in intensity over time. For example, the blocks in the two leftmost columns are initially dark but become light. At other positions, the border is defined by an increase in intensity over time. For example, the block in the third column from the left is initially light, but becomes dark. A first-order motion-sensitive receptive field similar to those shown in Figure 11.19 would produce no consistent response to the border because there is no consistent pattern of intensity that can align with the receptive field sub-regions. The motion can be encoded by a detector that is selectively responsive only to decreases in luminance over time, or only to increases, as described earlier.

# CHAPTER 12

## CONTENTS

# 12

# Colour vision

## INTRODUCTION

The power of colour as a perceptual experience is vividly illustrated by the unfortunate case of a painter who lost his ability to see in colour following a closed head injury he suffered in a minor traffic accident. Sacks and Wasserman (1987, p. 26) describe his experiences as follows:

> He saw people's flesh, his wife's flesh, his own flesh, as an abhorrent grey; "flesh-coloured" now appeared "rat-coloured" to him... The "wrongness" of everything was disturbing, even disgusting... He turned increasingly to black and white foods—to black olives and white rice, black coffee and yoghurt. These at least appeared relatively normal, whereas most foods, normally coloured, now appeared horribly abnormal.

He confused many things, such as grey and yellow socks, red and green peppers, mustard and mayonnaise. He could no longer see clouds, since they were indistinguishable from the apparently pale-grey sky.

As the description of this case indicates, colour is especially important for judging the appearance of food, and many believe that the evolution of colour vision was influenced by the need of our ancestors to discriminate red-brown berries against a predominantly green background (see the tutorial section of this chapter).

The physical and physiological basis of colour vision was reviewed extensively in previous chapters. As discussed in Chapter 6, colour relates to the wavelength properties of light emitted or reflected from a surface. Chapter 7 showed that neural processing of wavelength begins with three classes of cone receptor having different spectral sensitivity curves. Visual neurons with wavelength selective receptive fields use chromatic opponency to encode wavelength. This chapter will review the major psychophysical properties of colour vision, and relate them to the physical and physiological properties discussed earlier. Before proceeding, it is important to recall Newton's observation that light waves or particles are not coloured. Colours are constructed by neural processes in the brain on the basis of the spectral composition of the incoming light. But there is no one-to-one mapping from wavelength to colour. The term "colour perception" is tautological, because colour *is* a perception.

*Review the physics and physiology of colour in Chapters 6 and 7.*

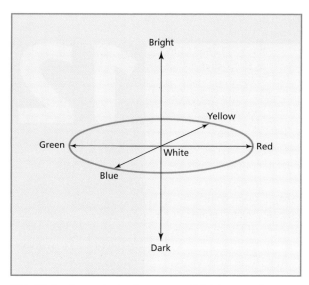

**FIG. 12.1** Perceptual colour space. Brightness varies vertically, hue varies around the circumference of the circle in the horizontal plane, and saturation varies radially in the horizontal plane (from neutral at the centre of the circle).

## COLOUR SPACE

It is generally agreed that descriptions of colour make use of only three attributes: hue, saturation, and brightness:

● *Hue* corresponds to the colour itself, such as "red", or "blue".
● *Saturation* corresponds to the purity of the colour, often described in terms of how much neutral colour (white) is present. Pink, for example, is a desaturated red.
● *Brightness* corresponds most closely to the perceived intensity of the light.

Traditionally these three attributes are depicted in a three-dimensional space, as shown in Figure 12.1.

The vertical axis represents brightness. The horizontal plane contains colours of equal brightness but varying chromaticity. Neutral white light lies at the centre of the circle. Colour becomes progressively more saturated moving out from the centre along any given radius. Hues are arranged around the circumference of the circle, in order of similarity. Most colours around the circle can be described as intermediate between other colours. Orange, for example, is intermediate between red and yellow—a reddish yellow; aquamarine is intermediate between green and blue—a greenish blue. But four particular colours are said to be "unique" in that they cannot be described as intermediates of other hues. These unique colours are red, green, blue, and yellow. They define the *cardinal directions* of chromaticity, the compass points against which all other points are referenced in colour descriptions.

## OPPONENT COLOURS

The existence of two cardinal axes in perceptual colour space led Ewald Hering, a German physiologist (1834–1918), to propose an opponent theory of colour, as follows:

> *Therefore, since redness and greenness, or yellowness and blueness are never simultaneously evident in any other colour, but rather appear to be mutually exclusive, I have called them* opponent colours. *To begin with, this term is used to characterise the way they occur without implying any sort of explanation.*
>
> (Hering, 1905–1911/1964, p. 50)

Hering also proposed an opponency between light and dark sensations. The notion of opponency along the red–green and blue–yellow axes of colour space has been very influential in the development of colour theories, as later sections in the chapter will show.

# COLOUR MIXTURE

The colour space in Figure 12.1 is a useful way of summarising the ways that humans describe individual colours. However, it is of limited use in understanding what happens when colours are mixed. What colour is seen in the mixture, and what does that imply for theories of colour? There are two fundamentally different ways of mixing colours. One is known as additive mixing, and the other is known as subtractive mixing. Additive mixing is much more useful as a tool for developing colour theories.

## SUBTRACTIVE MIXTURES

Subtractive colour mixing involves the removal of wavelength components from a stimulus patch by absorption or by scattering. Colours created using pigments or dyes are based on **subtractive colour mixture**. A simple hypothetical example is shown in Figure 12.2.

The two curves show the reflectance spectra of two ink pigments. One pigment appears blue when illuminated by broad-spectrum (white) light, because it absorbs all wavelengths except those in the blue region. The other pigment appears yellow because it absorbs all wavelengths except those in the yellow region. When the two pigments are mixed together the result appears green in broad-spectrum light, because the only wavelengths spared from the combination are in this part of the spectrum (shaded region). If more pigments were put into the mix, the resulting colour would become a murky grey as a wider range of wavelength components were absorbed. Ink-based colour reproduction systems, such as those in inkjet printers, use three differently coloured inks, called *subtractive primaries*, chosen because their mixture gives the broadest gamut of available colours. Figure 12.3 illustrates three typical subtractive primaries (cyan, magenta, and yellow), and the colours that result from their combination.

Subtractive colour mixing is of great practical value for painted or printed reproduction of colour, but is of limited use as a tool for developing colour theories. Unlike **additive mixture**, the colour seen in one mixture cannot be predicted straightforwardly from the colour seen in other mixtures.

## ADDITIVE MIXTURES

Additive mixing involves the addition of wavelength components to a stimulus by the superimposition of multiple light sources. To give an example, a stimulus patch emitting light at a wavelength of 700 nm appears red (in a neutral context; see "Colour constancy" below). A patch emitting light at 560 nm appears green. What colour is seen when the two patches are superimposed to create a stimulus that emit both 560 nm and 700 nm wavelengths? Yellow is seen, as a result of a perceptual effect known as additive colour mixing. If a third wavelength is available, in the blue region of the spectrum, then seven different colours are seen in the various combinations of the three wavelengths, as illustrated in Figure 12.4.

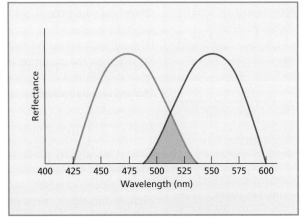

**FIG. 12.2** Hypothetical illustration of subtractive colour mixture. The two curves represent the reflectance spectra of two pigments, one "blue" and the other "yellow". A mixture of the two appears green because only these wavelengths are spared by both pigments (shaded area).

Why might the colour of a garment appear different in a photograph or on TV?

Colour mixture is investigated in the laboratory using the apparatus illustrated in Figure 12.5. The observer views a circular stimulus patch that is split vertically into two halves. One half receives monochromatic light of a given wavelength and intensity, known as the test light. The other half of the stimulus patch receives light containing a mixture of wavelengths, known as primaries. The observer adjusts the relative intensities of the primaries until the stimulus patch appears uniform.

Once a colour match is achieved, the two halves of the stimulus patch contain **metameric colours**, or *metamers*, defined as a pair of stimuli that have the same colour but physically different spectra. In the example of Figure 12.4, the yellow seen in the mixture of 560 and 700 nm may appear identical to a monochromatic light from the yellow region of the spectrum, provided that the relative intensities of the 560 and 700 nm components are appropriate. Additive colour mixtures generally obey two simple laws.

## Laws of additive mixture

### Linearity

In a linear system, the response to a stimulus containing several components corresponds to the sum of the responses produced when the components are presented separately. For example, assume that a test patch matches the colour of a combination of primaries when the primary intensities are set to appropriate values. A second test patch matches the same primaries at a different pair of intensities. If the two test patches are added together, what primary intensities are required to match this new mixture? Matching intensities can be found simply by adding together the primary intensities that were required to match the original tests when they were presented separately. A further consequence of linearity is that when a new wavelength component is added equally to both members of a metameric pair of colours, then their metameric identity is preserved (though their apparent colour may change).

### Trichromacy

**KEY TERM**
**Metameric colours**: Two colours that appear the same hue but emit or reflect physically different light wavelengths.

Observers with normal colour vision can match any given test colour with a combination of no more than three appropriately chosen primary colours. Colour matching is therefore said to be *trichromatic* (three-coloured). The choice of primaries is restricted by the condition that one primary cannot be metameric to a mixture of the other two. In practice, primaries are chosen on the basis of empirical convenience, and are usually as widely spectrally separated as possible.

The choice of red, green, and blue primaries in colour displays was largely pragmatic because it allowed the largest gamut of colours to be reproduced. No specific attempt was made to match the spectral properties of the primaries with the spectral sensitivities of photoreceptors.

### Uses of additive mixture

These two laws of additive colour mixing play an essential role in modern image reproduction systems such as colour televisions, liquid crystal displays (LCDs; used in computers, cameras, and phones), and projectors. Such systems are based on additive mixing of three primaries. In the case of television and LCDs, the inner surface of the screen is covered with many tiny triads of phosphor or liquid crystal dots that emit light in the red, green, and blue portions of the spectrum when excited. The triads of dots are too small to be resolved by the visual system, so the colour seen from the light emitted by each triad is equivalent to an additively mixed colour. The wide gamut of colours seen on these displays relies on varying the relative intensities of the red, green, and blue components.

# COLOUR MATCHING: THE CIE CHROMATICITY DIAGRAM

Since additive colour matching is so lawful, it is possible to create a new colour space based on colour matching data, rather than the descriptive dimensions used in Figure 12.1. A universally agreed, metric colour space was produced by the Commission Internationale de l'Eclairage (CIE) in 1931 using matching data from large groups of observers. Unlike the colour space shown in Figure 12.1, the CIE chromaticity diagram is two-dimensional. There is no need to include the brightness axis because mixture linearity means that colour matches are independent of intensity. The CIE chromaticity diagram plots proportions of light rather than absolute intensities. It is reproduced in Figure 12.6.

Pure spectral colours are plotted along the perimeter of the space, labelled with their wavelength. Mixtures of wavelengths lie inside the perimeter. Saturation decreases toward the centre until, at the location marked W, mixtures appear neutral or white. The colour created by an additive mixture of any two primary wavelengths lies along a straight line across the space joining the two wavelengths. The location of the mixture along the line is determined by the relative intensities of the two primaries. If a mixture line passes through the neutral point at the centre of the space, the wavelengths at each end are said to be **complementary**, since the colour of one can be balanced out completely by the other to produce white.

## The shape of the chromaticity diagram

The characteristic shape of the colour space is determined by the need to depict colour mixtures along straight lines. The straight section in the lower part of the perimeter arises because the most saturated purples can only be created by a mixture of the shortest and longest visible wavelengths (440 nm and 700 nm respectively). The line represents differing proportions of the two wavelengths.

## Chromaticity co-ordinates

Notice that the colour space in Figure 12.6 is located within two axes, *x* and *y*. Any colour can be identified by its location on the *x*- and *y*-axes, known as its **chromaticity co-ordinates**. This provides a universally agreed system for specifying colour, essential both in scientific research and in industrial applications. Modern instruments can be used to identify the chromaticity co-ordinates of a given colour patch, allowing researchers to reproduce each other's stimuli. Table 12.1 shows the chromaticity co-ordinates of some standard light sources.

> **KEY TERMS**
> **CIE chromaticity diagram**: A standard graphical representation of the hue and saturation attributes of colour, based on colour matching data obtained from large groups of observers.
> **Complementry colours**: Colours that cancel each other out when mixed together, producing neutral white or grey.
> **Chromaticity co-ordinates**: The *xy* co-ordinates of a colour in the CIE chromaticity diagram.

| TABLE 12.1 CHROMATICITY CO-ORDINATES OF SOME STANDARD LIGHT SOURCES | | |
|---|---|---|
| **Source** | **x** | **y** |
| Fluorescent lamp | 0.35 | 0.37 |
| Sun | 0.32 | 0.33 |
| Red display phosphor | 0.68 | 0.32 |
| Green display phosphor | 0.28 | 0.6 |
| Blue display phosphor | 0.15 | 0.07 |

Although mixture of pigments is subtractive, there is one way to create a form of additive colour mixture using pigments. The *pointillist* technique in art involves constructing a painting by placing very small dots of colour next to each other. When viewed from a distance at which the individual dots cannot be resolved, the dots merge together additively to create new colours.

The vertices of the pale triangle in Figure 12.6 are located at the chromaticity co-ordinates of the three display phosphors given in Table 12.1. The gamut of colours available with these three primaries lies inside the triangle. Colours outside the triangle cannot be seen in a computer display. They generally correspond to colours having the most extreme levels of saturation.

## ORIGIN OF ADDITIVE COLOUR MIXTURE

Additive colour mixture can be explained by retinal processes. As Chapter 7 explained, the human eye contains three classes of cone photoreceptor, with differing spectral sensitivities (S, M, and L cones; see Figure 12.8). The response of each cone class obeys the principle of univariance. The response of the photopigment is the same to all wavelengths, but the cone classes differ in terms of the probability that they will respond to a quantum of a given wavelength. The only way to infer the wavelength of the incident light is to compare the responses of different cone classes. A short-wavelength light, for example, will produce a greater response in S cones than in M or L cones. Additive colour mixture can be explained by the simple proposition that colour is determined by the relative activation levels of the three cone classes. Metamers appear identical because they create the same ratio of responses across the triad of cone classes.

Figure 12.7 illustrates this very important point. The first three groups of bars in Figure 12.7 show hypothetical activation levels of three cone classes to three wavelengths. The leftmost bars show relative responses to a light in the red portion of the spectrum. The light appears red because it produces the greatest activation in L cones. Similarly, the green and yellow wavelengths produce greatest activation in the M and (M and L) cones, respectively. The rightmost bars show the pattern of cone response to a combination of the red and green wavelengths. The pattern of activation corresponds to the sum of the two individual activations (see "Linearity" above). It is identical to the pattern of activation produced by spectral yellow. Consequently, this combination will appear identical to spectral yellow.

Maxwell and Young were renowned British physicists who made major contributions in several fields (see Chapter 6 on the physics of light). Helmholtz was a hugely influential German physiologist. Palmer, by contrast, was an obscure figure, better known in Continental Europe than in his native Great Britain. He was a glass merchant specialising in coloured glass, who spent much of his time in Europe, and also published in French (Mollon, 1993).

## Trichromacy theory

The fact that metameric matches can be achieved with no more than three primaries led to the proposal that human colour vision was trichromatic long before the three cone classes were discovered. The origins of **trichromacy theory** can be traced back to four individuals, whose work was published between 1777 and 1909: George Palmer, Thomas Young, James Clerk Maxwell, and Herman von Helmholtz.

The earliest account of trichromacy was published in 1777 by Palmer. He believed that light was actually composed of only three differently coloured rays (red, yellow, and blue), and proposed that:

**KEY TERM**
**Trichromacy theory**: The theory that human colour vision involves three primary colour sensations.

*the surface of the retina is compounded of particles of three kinds, analogous to the three different rays of light; and each of these particles is moved by its own ray.*

(quoted in Sherman, 1981, p. 17)

In 1802, Thomas Young (who may have encountered Palmer's work while a student in Gottingen, according to Mollon, 1993) proposed that the three primary colours were red, green, and violet. To test his theory, Young performed additive colour mixing experiments using spinning disks with sectors painted in different colours. Maxwell also conducted many quantitative experiments on additive colour mixture using spinning disks. Writing in 1856, Maxwell supported Young's trichromacy theory as follows:

> We are capable of feeling three kinds of colour-sensations. Light of different kinds excites these sensations in different proportions, and it is by the different combinations of these three primary sensations that all the varieties of visible colour are produced.
>
> (quoted in Helmholtz, 1911/1962, p. 143)

Helmholtz (1911/1962) proposed that the three primary sensations were conveyed to the brain by three kinds of nervous fibre, and estimated the spectral response of the fibres using the graph reproduced in Figure 12.8 (top).

He called the three fibres red-sensitive, green-sensitive, and violet-sensitive, on the basis of their peak response. The curves in Figure 12.8 (top) are remarkably accurate estimates of the spectral absorbance curves of the three cone classes (Figure 12.8, bottom), discovered over 150 years later. The durability of trichromatic theory is a tribute to the insights and empirical ingenuity of Palmer, Young, Maxwell, and Helmholtz. The theory is often called the *Young-Helmholtz Theory*, but this name does not give due recognition to the contributions of Palmer and Maxwell.

## DUAL-PROCESS THEORY

Notice the discrepancy between trichromacy and the perceptual colour space depicted in Figure 12.1. The latter has two principal chromatic axes, red–green and blue–yellow, which inspired Hering's opponency theory. Yet trichromacy implicates only three colours; red, green, and blue. The apparent discrepancy between trichromatic and opponent theories was resolved in the second half of the 20th century. Hurvich and Jameson (1957) developed a dual-process theory that contained trichromatic photoreceptors in the first stage, and an opponent-process second stage. Like its predecessors, Hurvich and Jameson's model was developed without the benefit of modern electrophysiological data. Instead, Hurvich and Jameson estimated the spectral response of putative opponent mechanisms using a perceptual cancellation technique. For the red–green pair, for example, Hurvich and Jameson measured the amount of light from the green region of the spectrum that was required to cancel the reported "redness" of a patch containing light from the red region of the spectrum. Hurvich and Jameson were able to use the cancellation technique to estimate the spectral sensitivities of the colour-opponent channels.

Later experiments confirmed the main features of Hurvich and Jameson's theory: the retina does indeed contain three classes of cone photoreceptor, and opponent responses are found in ganglion and LGN cells. As shown in Figure 12.9, the trichromatic stage involves three photoreceptors with peak sensitivities at long (red), medium (green), and short (blue) wavelengths. The opponent stage involves three opponent pairs; red–green, blue–yellow, and light–dark. The three pairs are sometimes called "channels", two **chromatic** and one **achromatic**:

- *The red–green chromatic channel* receives opposing input from long and medium wavelength cone classes.
- *The blue–yellow chromatic channel* receives opposing input from short cones, and a combination of long and medium cones.
- *The light–dark achromatic channel* receives non-opponent input from long and medium cones. The light–dark response of this channel is provided by spatial opponency.

*Colour processing involves ratios of cell responses. What other perceptual dimensions appear to involve ratio coding?*

Compare the schematic diagram of Figure 12.9 with the ganglion cell receptive fields shown in Figure 7.7. Midget ganglion cells carry the red–green opponent signal, bistratified ganglion cells carry the blue–yellow opponent signal, and both parasol and midget cells carry the light–dark opponent signal (Dacey, 2000). These three ganglion cell classes basically encode the three dimensions of perceptual colour space depicted in Figure 12.1. Red–green and blue–yellow ganglion cells encode the two cardinal directions of chromaticity; achromatic cells encode the brightness dimension.

# COLOUR INTERACTIONS

## COLOUR CONTRAST AND ADAPTATION

Colour matches that can be explained lawfully by triplets of cone responses are only obtained when stimulus surfaces are viewed against a chromatically neutral background. When a coloured surface is viewed in a spatial or temporal context that contains other colours, the colours interact. Several forms of **colour interaction** have been described.

### Simultaneous colour contrast

When a coloured surface is placed against a coloured background, the background may change the surface's hue, saturation, and brightness. A green disk placed against a more saturated green background appears less green than when it is placed against a red background (Figure 12.10, upper left). Similarly, a blue disk placed against a more saturated blue background appears less blue than when it is placed against a yellow background (Figure 12.10, upper right). Particularly vivid effects can be created using patterned surrounds, as shown in the lower half of Figure 12.10. In general, colour contrast shifts the hue of a surface away from the hue of its background and in the direction of the complementary hue.

### Colour adaptation

**KEY TERMS**
**Chromatic channel**: A channel of processing in the visual system that conveys information about the chromatic or colour properties of the image.
**Achromatic channel**: A channel of processing in the visual system that conveys information about the luminance or light–dark properties of the image.
**Colour interaction**: A change in the apparent hue, saturation, or brightness of a coloured surface in the presence of, or following exposure to, an inducing colour.

When one colour is viewed for a short time, and then replaced by a differently coloured test surface, the colour of the test surface is influenced by the adapting colour. Similar test colours appear less saturated. Neutral test colours take on the complementary hue to the adapting colour. An example of the latter effect is shown in Figure 12.11.

# ORIGIN OF COLOUR INTERACTIONS

Contrast and adaptation effects can be explained using triads of cone responses. The hue of a surface is determined not just by the triad of cone responses to it, but by a comparison of responses to the surface and responses to the contextual colour. A surface looks more red if the triad of responses to it shows a greater preponderance of red signals than the triad of responses to its context. Figure 12.12 shows in more detail how comparisons of response triads can explain contrast and adaptation. The vertical bars containing red, green, and blue sections depict the relative cone response to the stimulus arrowed below each bar. The upper half of Figure 12.12 illustrates the explanation for simultaneous colour contrast, and the lower half illustrates the explanation for colour adaptation.

## Explaining colour contrast

Consider the contrast effect in Figure 12.12 (reproduced from Figure 12.10, upper left). The central bar in Figure 12.12 (upper) depicts the relative responses of red, green, and blue cone classes to the green disk. The right-hand bar in Figure 12.12 (upper) depicts the relative cone responses to the red background. The disk appears a saturated green because of the relatively large green response to the disk compared with the background. The left-hand bar in Figure 12.12 (upper) depicts the relative cone responses to a saturated green background. Now the disk appears de-saturated, because of the lower preponderance of green signal in its response compared with the background.

## Explaining colour adaptation

To explain adaptation, we must assume that the adapting colour reduces the responsiveness of the cone classes sensitive to it. The triad of responses to subsequently viewed colours will be biased in favour of the other two cone classes. The lower-left bar in Figure 12.12 shows the unadapted response to a grey surface. Roughly equal responses from the three cone classes mean that the surface appears a neutral colour. The middle bar in Figure 12.12 (lower) shows the relative cone responses while adapting to a blue field. Blue cones are most active, and will show the greatest reduction in responsiveness. When the grey surface is viewed after adaptation, the blue response is weak compared with the response of the red and green cone classes. Hence the grey field takes on a yellowish hue.

## Physiology

Chromatically selective receptive fields in the visual pathway and cortex are likely to play an important role in encoding relative cone responses. Recent studies of primate cortical area V1 have found cells that appear to signal colour contrast (reviewed in Hurlbert, 2003). Wachtler, Sejnowski, and Albright (2003) found colour selective cells whose response is influenced by background colours well outside their conventional receptive field. These background colours do not evoke a response when presented alone, but modify the neuron's response to stimuli falling inside its receptive field. Wachtler et al. (2003) found that a cell which responded well to a bluish patch on a grey background responded less well when the patch was presented on a blue background. These neural effects shared certain features in common with perceptual contrast effects studied with the same stimuli. The similarity between neural and perceptual contrast effects supports the view that V1 "plays an important role in the neural processing that leads from the sensory signals to our percept" (Wachtler et al., 2003, p. 689).

## COLOUR CONSTANCY

What is the functional significance of colour contrast and adaptation, and the cells that create these effects? The spectrum of wavelengths reaching the eye from an object depends jointly on the spectral reflectance properties of the object and the spectrum of the illuminating light (see Chapter 6). Relatively gross changes in the illuminating spectrum are not uncommon in everyday life. For instance, the spectrum of daylight varies markedly during the day from daybreak, through midday, to sunset. Artificial light has a greater preponderance of longer wavelengths than daylight, as shown in Figure 6.6. Despite such large changes in illumination, an object's colour (namely, our perception of its spectral reflectance) remains relatively stable. This effect is known as **colour constancy**.

The spectral reflectance of an object is an inherent property of it that can be used for recognition and classification, so colour constancy is clearly beneficial for object perception. How is it achieved? Foster and Nascimento (1994) computed cone excitations from a variety of reflective surfaces viewed under different illuminants. They found that the ratio of cone responses remains invariant under different illuminants. For example, if surface *a* excites red cones twice as much as surface *b* under a given illuminant, it will also excite red cones twice as much under other illuminants. Cone excitation ratios therefore provide a stable measure of surface reflectance properties, and offer a means for the visual system to discount the contribution of the illuminant.

Local contrast and adaptation phenomena can be viewed as evidence that cone excitation ratios are actually used to assign colour. Indeed local contrast and adaptation have been identified as cues for colour constancy. Other proposed constancy cues include (Hurlbert, 1999):

- Global contrast, based on cone responses averaged over the whole scene.
- Luminance maxima or highlights, which usually represent specular reflections from glossy surfaces. As mirror reflections of the light source, highlight colour depends on its spectrum.
- Mutual reflections from one object to another in the scene, creating secondary light sources.
- The range of colours in the scene, which is indicative of the range of wavelengths in the illuminant.

**KEY TERM**
**Colour constancy**: The apparent hue of a reflective surface remains constant even when changes in the spectral power distribution of the illuminant alter the wavelengths reflected from it.

A recent study of colour constancy by Kraft and Brainard (1999) produced evidence that local contrast makes the largest contribution to colour constancy, though other cues are also used. Kraft and Brainard showed observers a realistic scene containing various small objects and papers. Their task was to adjust the chromaticity of a test surface in the scene until it appeared neutral grey. Kraft and Brainard varied the illuminant and the cues available. Baseline observations revealed that colour constancy was by no means perfect (i.e. 100% resistant to illuminant changes), but attained a level of 83%. Kraft and Brainard found that when local contrast cues were removed, constancy fell to 53%. So, although local contrast is important, it is not the only cue used. Kraft and Brainard (1999) also found evidence for the use of global contrast and luminance maxima. With all these cues removed, constancy was still above zero, at 11%.

Although perceptual research has provided information on what visual cues are used to establish colour constancy, there is as yet no universally agreed computational theory of colour constancy.

# COLOUR DEFICIENCY

A frequently asked question about colour vision is "How do I know that the colour I see is the same as the colour you see?" There is no way to answer this question definitively, of course, since colours are mental states. Most people use colour names in the same way, and make the same judgements of the similarities and dissimilarities between colours. A fabric that I might describe as "crimson", for example, would be given the same description by most other observers. However, about one in twelve people have very different colour experiences from the rest of us. They may confuse crimsons with blues, and scarlets with greens. Such individuals are commonly called "colour-blind", though this label is a misnomer since most of them do see colours, but in a different way from normal observers. The more accurate clinical term is *colour deficient*, because there is a reduced capacity to discriminate between colours. The existence of colour deficiency has been known for centuries, but only in the last century was its cause traced to the properties of cone photopigments.

As discussed earlier, normal colour vision is trichromatic in the sense that observers require three primaries to achieve a subjective match with any colour. Colour deficient observers behave differently in colour matching experiments. They can be divided into three groups on the basis of their performance:

- *Anomalous trichromats* require three primaries to achieve metameric matches, but in proportions different from those required by normal observers;
- *Dichromats* require only two primaries to achieve metameric matches;
- *Monochromats* require only one primary.

Normal trichromacy can be related to the presence of three distinct classes of cone in the retina. Not surprisingly, colour deficiency is linked to abnormal properties in the cones.

## ANOMALOUS TRICHROMACY

The eye of the anomalous trichromat possesses three cone classes, but the spectral sensitivity of the cones is shifted relative to normal trichromats. The two major forms of anomalous trichromacy are protanomaly and deuteranomaly:

- In *protanomaly* the peak response of the long (red) wavelength cone class is shifted to shorter wavelengths, so that it is closer than normal to the peak of the medium (green) wavelength cone class. As a result, protanomalous observers are more sensitive to green wavelengths than normal observers.
- In *deuteranomaly* the peak response of the medium (green) wavelength cone class is shifted to longer wavelengths, so that it is closer than normal to the peak of the long (red) wavelength cone class. As a result, deuteranomalous observers are more sensitive to red wavelengths than normal observers.

Both protanomalous and deuteranomalous observers have poorer than normal colour discrimination, due to the greater overlap in the spectral sensitivities of the medium and long wavelength cone classes.

**KEY TERMS**
**Colour deficiency**: A reduced capacity to discriminate between colours, caused by an abnormality in cone photopigments.
**Anomalous trichromacy**: A form of colour deficiency in which the individual possesses three different cone classes, but their spectral sensitivity is shifted relative to normal trichromats.

## DICHROMACY

The dichromatic eye contains a normal number of cones, but lacks cones of one class. Any one of the three cone classes may be missing:

- In *protanopia*, long (red) wavelength cones are missing.
- In *deuteranopia*, medium (green) wavelength cones are missing.
- In *tritanopia*, short (blue) wavelength cones are missing.

Protanopes and deuteranopes cannot distinguish between reds and greens, since one or the other arm of the red–green chromatic axis is missing. They have no ability to distinguish between wavelengths greater than 520 nm (Ruddock, 1991). Tritanopes cannot distinguish between blues and yellows, since one arm of the blue–yellow chromatic axis is missing. They have no ability to distinguish wavelengths between 450 nm and 480 nm.

All dichromats have a *neutral point* on the spectrum; a wavelength that appears neutral grey to them. Normal trichromats, of course, have no neutral point because each wavelength is associated with a colour experience. For protanopes, the neutral point is at 492 nm, while for deuteranopes it is at 498 nm. Tritanopes have a neutral point at 575 nm (Ruddock, 1991).

## MONOCHROMACY

Monochromats have no ability to distinguish different colours, and can match any given colour with a single primary wavelength of the appropriate intensity. Monochromats presumably experience the world as shades of grey, rather like the view on a black and white television. The poor visual acuity of most monochromats is consistent with the view that their vision is mediated entirely by rods. A few monochromats appear to have near-normal acuity, and at least some receptors that resemble cones, though in relatively small numbers (Ruddock, 1991).

## INCIDENCE OF COLOUR DEFICIENCIES

Colour deficiency is genetically transmitted. The relevant genes are located on the X chromosome, and behave recessively. The normal allele is dominant. Males have only one X chromosome, inherited from their mother, so are colour deficient if this chromosome carries the trait. Females have two X chromosomes (one from each parent), so are colour deficient only if both carry the trait. It is not, therefore, surprising that male colour deficients outnumber female colour deficients by a factor of 22:1.

The prevalence of colour deficiency varies markedly between racial groups, with Caucasians showing a higher incidence than other racial types. For example, Caucasian males have the highest prevalence of red–green deficiency, at nearly 8%, while Native Americans have the lowest prevalence, at 2.5% (Jaeger, 1972). Table 12.2 shows the incidence of the different forms of colour deficiency in the Caucasian population, taken from Piantanida (1991).

> **KEY TERMS**
> **Dichromacy**: A form of colour deficiency in which the individual possesses only two cone classes.
> **Monochromacy**: A form of colour deficiency in which the individual possesses very few or no cones, and is therefore unable to discriminate between colours.

**TABLE 12.2 INCIDENCE OF COLOUR DEFICIENCY IN THE CAUCASIAN POPULATION**

| Deficiency | Prevalence (%) |
| --- | --- |
| Protanomaly | 1.73 |
| Deuteranomaly | 4.78 |
| Protanopia | 0.81 |
| Deuteranopia | 0.48 |
| Tritanopia | 0.45 |
| Rod monochromacy | 0.30 |
| Monochromacy (cones) | 0.0001 |
| Total | 8.55 |

Anomalous trichromacy is much more common than dichromacy or monochromacy, accounting for three-quarters of all reported colour deficiencies.

A great deal is also known about the genes coding photopigments; see Nathans (1989).

## DIAGNOSIS OF COLOUR DEFICIENCY

A range of clinical tests has been developed to assess colour vision. One of the most common tests involves so-called **pseudo-isochromatic plates**, on which are printed dots of varying hue, brightness, and saturation. The dots are arranged so that dots of similar colour form a recognisable shape, such as a letter against a background of dissimilar dots. An example is shown in Figure 12.13. The observer's task is to identify the number. The number seen depends on the form of colour vision possessed by the observer. The most well-known test is named after its inventor, Ishihara.

## CHAPTER SUMMARY

### COLOUR SPACE

- Colour descriptions are based on three dimensions: hue, saturation, and brightness.
- Hering proposed that the hue dimension contains two opponent pairs of colours, red–green and blue–yellow.

### COLOUR MIXTURE

- Subtractive mixtures of pigments involve the removal of wavelength components from a stimulus.
- The colours seen in subtractive mixtures cannot be predicted straight-forwardly from their constituent pigments.
- Additive mixtures of light sources involve the addition of wavelength components to a stimulus.
- The colours seen in additive mixtures can be predicted on the basis of two rules: linearity, and trichromacy.
- The CIE chromaticity diagram represents additive colour mixtures in a standardised, metric colour space.
- A metameric match to any colour can be achieved with an additive mixture of no more than three primaries. This fact led to the trichromatic theory of colour vision.
- Metameric matching can be explained by the ratio of responses across the cone classes. Two colours with matching cone ratios appear identical.

### DUAL-PROCESS THEORY

- The apparent discrepancy between Hering's opponent colours theory and the trichromatic theory can be reconciled by a two-stage theory in which trichromacy forms the first stage and opponent-processing forms the second stage.

**KEY TERM**
**Pseudo-isochromatic plate**: A pattern of coloured dots, used in the diagnosis of colour deficiency; the shape seen in the dots varies according to the observer's colour vision.

## COLOUR INTERACTIONS

● When a surface is surrounded by another colour, its hue may be altered (contrast).

● When one colour is viewed for a short time and then replaced by a test colour, the latter may be influenced by the adapting colour (adaptation).

● Colour contrast indicates that the colour of a surface is not determined solely by the triad of cone signals it generates. Instead, a surface's colour is determined by comparing its triad of cone responses with the triad of responses generated by the surrounding colour.

● Colour selective cortical cells show contrast effects analogous to those found in perceptual experiments, indicating that they play a role in encoding colour contrast.

● In colour constancy, the colour of an object remains stable even in the face of changes in the spectral composition of the illuminating light.

● Colour contrast is one of the most basic mechanisms for achieving colour constancy, though several other cues are also involved.

## COLOUR DEFICIENCY

● Observers with deficient colour vision fall into three categories:

  ● Anomalous trichromats, who require three primaries for metameric matches, but in abnormal proportions.

  ● Dichromats, who require only two primaries to achieve metameric matches.

  ● Monochromats, who require only one primary and therefore cannot discriminate colour at all.

● Colour deficiency is inherited genetically via a recessive gene on the X chromosome, so its incidence is much higher in males than in females.

# TUTORIALS

## WHY THREE CONE CLASSES?

An ability to detect variations in the spectral composition of light reflected from objects (*chrominance*) is extremely useful for distinguishing between objects in natural scene. As an example, Figure 12.14 shows a photograph of natural foliage. The original image is shown at the top. The version in the lower left contains only the original image's luminance signal, while the version in the lower right shows only the chrominance signal. It is clear that different kinds of leaf can be discriminated much better on the basis of chrominance than on the basis of luminance. One complication with luminance variation is that it confuses variation in surface reflectance with variation in illumination (shading and shadows), while chrominance is unaffected by illumination level. In general terms, then, colour vision has obvious benefits. The minimum requirement for chrominance discrimination is the presence of two photoreceptor classes with different spectral sensitivities. A change in wavelength composition will then produce a change in relative photoreceptor response even when there is no change in illumination. In principle, chrominance discrimination should improve as the number of receptor classes increases. Two specific questions are frequently asked about human colour vision:

- Why do we possess only three different classes of cone?
- Why are their spectral sensitivities distributed in the manner shown in Figure 12.8, namely two largely overlapping and one set apart?

## Spatial resolving power

One way to answer these questions is to consider the consequences of possessing many photoreceptor classes having relatively narrow spectral sensitivities. The problem with this arrangement is that each cone class would have to share the retina with all the others. The average spacing between adjacent receptors of the same class would necessarily be relatively large. This would have a disastrous effect on the spatial resolving power of the retina, as discussed in Chapter 6 (see Figure 6.11). Each doubling of receptor spacing would halve the maximum spatial resolution of the receptor array. Moreover, the effective resolving power of the retina would vary with the spectral composition of the stimulus. Stimuli that excited only one photoreceptor class would be resolved very poorly, whereas stimuli that excited several classes would be resolved much better.

Fine spatial discriminations are best served by having very few photoreceptor classes (ideally just one), while fine chromatic discriminations are best served by having more photoreceptor classes. The visual system strikes a balance between these competing requirements by having three classes with relatively broad spectral sensitivities. In fact, the central retina possesses just two photoreceptor classes whose spectral sensitivities overlap extensively, since S cones are absent.

## Visual ecology

We can also gain clues about trichromacy by considering its evolutionary origins. The dominant view is that colour vision evolved for finding food. Indeed, the spectral sensitivity of the L and M cone classes seems to be finely tuned to detect small differences between the leaves and fruit eaten by our ancestors. Leaves and fruit tend to have high reflectance in the red–green part of the spectrum. It was even suggested by Grant Allen in the 1800s that trichromacy in primates and the reflectance functions of certain fruits are well matched because they co-evolved as a seed dispersal system. Both parties benefited from this relationship, since the animal acquired food while dispersing the plant's seeds. According to this idea, the colours we see in fruits such as apples and oranges actually arose because of the colour sensations themselves. Regan, Julliot, Simmen, Vienot, Charles-Dominique, and Mollon (2001) found evidence consistent with the co-evolution hypothesis from their investigation of primate trichromacy and fruit colouration. For example, many plants from different branches of the evolutionary tree produce similar fruits. However, trichromatic vision is also found in primate species that eat only leaves, so it likely that our cone classes evolved for discriminating young leaves as well as fruit.

### Evolutionary genetics

Another reason for the similarity in spectral sensitivities of the M and L cone classes is their evolutionary genetics. They are thought to have evolved from a common ancestor relatively recently (35 million years ago), long after the emergence of the S cone class. S cone photopigment is coded by an autosomal (not sex-linked) gene. The genes coding L and M cone photopigments are adjacent to each other on the X chromosome, and are 98% identical in terms of their DNA.

There is still a great deal of debate concerning the evolutionary origin of the L and M cones, and about the evolutionary benefits of trichromatic vision. For recent discussions, see Gegenfurtner and Kiper (2003), and Surridge, Osorio, and Mundy (2003).

### SYNAESTHESIA

Some people experience a colour sensation not from visual stimulation, but from auditory stimulation. "Coloured hearing" or *synaesthesia* (literally meaning a union of the sensations) is most commonly associated with speech sounds. Different sounds evoke different colours so, for example, each spoken letter or number might evoke a specific colour sensation. There are also reports of colour sensations evoked by non-speech sounds, by touch, and by smell.

As a test of whether synaesthesia is a genuinely sensory phenomenon rather than learned associative pairings of colours and sounds, Baron-Cohen, Harrison, Goldstein, and Wyke (1993) investigated the consistency of the pairings over time. Nine experimental subjects who reported synaesthetic experiences were asked to report the colours evoked by 122 words, letters, and phrases. A matched group of control subjects were asked spontaneously to generate a colour to associate with each stimulus, and encouraged to use a mnemonic to aid recall. Both groups were re-tested on 10% of the words, one year later in the case of the experimental group, and one week later in the case of the control. 93% of the experimental group's colour responses were identical on re-testing after a year, but only 37.6% of the control group's responses were identical after one week. Baron-Cohen et al. (1993) concluded that the phenomenon is a genuinely sensory one. They found that the initial letter of the word tended to determine the colour it evoked. Colours reported were generally idiosyncratic to different individuals, though the vowels "i", "o", and "u" were consistently associated with the same colours in different individuals: "i" was grey, "o" was white, and "u" was yellow.

Further evidence for the sensory nature of synaesthesia comes from a brain-imaging study. Paulesu et al. (1995) used PET to study brain activation while blindfolded synaesthetic subjects and controls were presented with spoken words or pure tones. Both groups showed activation of cortical language areas when words were presented as opposed to tones. In the case of synaesthetic subjects, several extrastriate visual cortical areas were also activated during word stimulation, though there was no activation in V1, V2, and V4.

A population study (Baron-Cohen, Burt, Smith-Laittan, Harrison, & Bolton, 1996) found a prevalence of 1 case of synaesthesia in every 2000 people. Many more women than men reported synaesthesia; the female:male ratio is 6:1. One third of the cases identified by Baron-Cohen et al. (1996) reported familial aggregation. It seems that synaesthesia is likely to have a genetic origin, but its physiological basis is still unknown. The most popular suggestion is that the brains of synaesthetic individuals possess neural links between areas serving different senses, such that activity in neurons serving one sensory modality is transferred to neurons serving another modality. Paulesu et al.'s (1995) PET study found direct evidence for such activity. Brain growth during childhood is known to involve rapid proliferation of neural connections beyond adult levels, followed by pruning back (Webb, Monk, & Nelson, 2001). Perhaps in synaesthetic individuals certain connections between cells serving different modalities survive the pruning process.

# CHAPTER 13

# 13

# Individual differences in perception

## INTRODUCTION

Chapter 12 ended with a discussion of a major source of individual differences in perceptual experience, namely colour deficiency. Earlier chapters contain occasional references to clinical conditions such as anosmia, deafness, scotoma, and agnosia, which also introduce differences in perceptual experience. However, the bulk of the text has concentrated on aspects of perception that are assumed to be universal among the majority of adult humans with a healthy, fully functioning sensory system. This does not mean, however, that the perceptual experiences of this population are identical. Several factors are known to produce consistent individual differences in perception. This chapter will review some of the evidence regarding the effects of age, sex, culture, and expertise on perception.

## AGE

### CHANGES IN PERCEPTUAL CAPACITY OVER THE LIFESPAN

Many studies have measured perceptual capacities at different stages of the lifespan. But studies of infant perception face particularly demanding methodological problems. Experimental procedures used to study adults are generally not suitable for research on infants. So a range of techniques has been developed specifically to cater for infants. The tutorial at the end of the chapter describes some of these techniques. When we compare data from infant studies against data collected from adults at various ages, a general pattern emerges of rapid early improvement followed by gradual decline. The peak in perceptual capacity tends to occur in the late teens and early 20s. Figure 13.1 shows representative data from four sensory modalities.

*Review the section on contrast sensitivity in Chapter 8.*

### Visual acuity

Figure 13.1(a) is based on data in Atkinson (2000) and Owsley, Sekuler, and Siemsen (1983). It shows that visual acuity (the ability to resolve fine spatial detail) improves dramatically over the first year of life but does not reach adult levels until

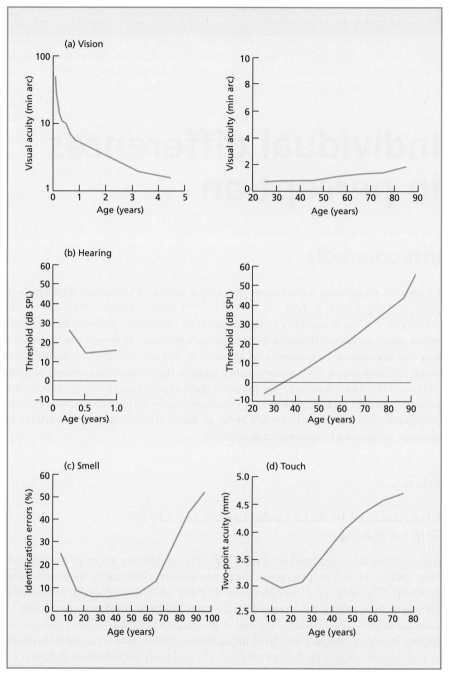

**FIG. 13.1**   Perceptual capacity over the lifespan, in four sensory modalities. Data are plotted so that smaller values on the y-axis correspond to better performance. (a) Visual acuity (re-plotted from Atkinson, 2000, and Owsley, Sekuler, & Siemsen, 1983; note the different x- and y-axes in the two graphs); (b) Hearing threshold (re-plotted from Olsho, Koch, Carter, Halpin, & Spetner, 1988, and Morrell, Gordon-Salant, Pearson, Brandt, & Fozard, 1996; note the different x-axis in the two graphs); (c) Odour identification errors (re-plotted from Doty, Shaman, Applebaum, Giberson, Sikorski, & Rosenberg, 1984); (d) Touch discrimination (re-plotted from Louis, Greene, Jacobson, Rasmussen, Kolowich, & Goldstein, 1984).

the age of 4 or 5. There is a much more gradual decline in performance in the later decades of life (assuming that appropriate optical corrections are worn). Notice that even a 90-year-old's acuity is five times better than that of a 6-month-old infant. Contrast sensitivity for spatial frequency gratings shows the same trend: infant sensitivity is up to 10 times worse than an adult's, and peaks at a much lower spatial frequency (approximately 0.5 cpd, as opposed to 3 cpd in adults). Why does infant acuity improve so dramatically, and what underlies the decline in later life? We shall begin the search for possible causes in the peripheral visual system, namely in the optical and neural properties of the eye.

> Even within the same individual, perceptual functions are likely to vary as a result of such factors as diurnal rhythm, life events, intake of psychoactive substances (nicotine, alcohol, caffeine), and so on.

## Developmental changes in the eye

The poor vision of newborn infants cannot be attributed to optical aberrations or accommodation defects. The newborn eye is relatively free of optical defects, though accommodation is relatively inaccurate (Atkinson, 2000). There are, however, marked structural changes in the retina over the first few months of life, which mirror the changes in acuity. The packing density of foveal cones does not reach adult levels until after the age of 4 years. Figure 13.2 (top) is an idealised representation of the cone mosaic of an infant (right) relative to an adult (left; based on Banks & Bennett, 1988).

*Why does cone packing density affect visual acuity?*

Notice the markedly coarser sampling of the image in the infant retina. In addition, cone outer segment length increases by a factor of 10 or more during infancy (Youdelis & Hendrickson, 1986). Figure 13.2 (bottom) shows human foveal cones at different ages. Short cones are much less sensitive to light than long cones, as explained in Chapter 6. A further limitation on the sensitivity of infant eyes is their small size. Overall, retinal factors certainly do limit the visual capabilities of infants. However, Banks and Bennett (1988) estimate that only about half of the difference between infant and adult acuity can be attributed to retinal factors. The remainder must reflect limitations in post-receptoral neural processing.

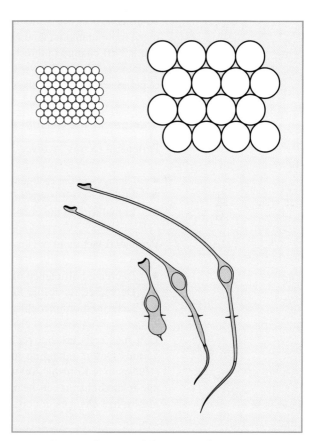

## Senescence in the eye

Some of the deterioration in vision during old age can be traced to decreasing efficiency in the eye:

- Reduced mobility of the pupil (*pupillary miosis*), which results in a tendency for pupils in elderly observers to remain quite small even in dim illumination, with consequent reduction in retinal illumination.
- Reduced flexibility in the lens, leading to reduced accommodative range and longsightedness (*presbyopia*).

**FIG. 13.2** Developmental changes in the retina. Top: Idealised representation of the retinal receptor mosaic of a neonatal infant (right) and an adult (left, based on Banks & Bennett, 1988). Centre-to-centre separation is approximately 0.5′ arc in the adult receptor mosaic, and 2.3′ arc in the neonate. Bottom: Drawings of human foveal cones at different ages. Left—newborn; middle—15 months old; right—45 months old.

- Increased light absorption by the lens (*senile cataract*), reducing retinal illumination and increasing light scatter.
- Degeneration of the central retina (*age-related macular degeneration*, or AMD).
- Photoreceptor loss due to the disappearance of the retinal pigment epithelium results in a progressive loss of central vision.

However, as in the case of early development, peripheral factors alone cannot account for all the effects of senescence (Weale, 1991). Central factors will be discussed following a review of other sensory modalities.

## Hearing level

Data in Figure 13.1(b) are taken from Olsho, Koch, Carter, Halpin, and Spetner (1988) and Morrell, Gordon-Salant, Pearson, Brant, and Fozard (1996), and represent the threshold for detecting a 4 kHz tone as a function of age. There are significant improvements in sensitivity over the first year, amounting to a change in threshold of 10 dB SPL between 3 months and 12 months of age. The deterioration later in life is much more dramatic, amounting to a 60 dB loss of sensitivity by the age of 90 (recall that a 3 dB change in threshold is equivalent to a halving of sensitivity). Age-related deafness is known as *presbycusis* (see Chapter 5). As in the case of vision, a number of peripheral factors are thought to be involved in age-related changes in hearing level.

### Changes in the peripheral auditory system over the lifespan

Peripheral factors involved in developmental improvements in sensitivity include:

- Changes in the resonance of the outer ear.
- Middle ear effusions in very young infants.
- Immaturity in the cochlea.

Peripheral factors in presbycusis include:

- Decreased efficiency of sound transmission through the middle-ear ossicles.
- Decreased flexibility in the basilar membrane.
- Deterioration in cochlear hair cells.

Lost hair cells are not replaced, so their number declines throughout life due to various factors including infections, ototoxic drugs, and exposure to loud sounds (Hudspeth & Konishi, 2000). Nozza (1995) and Frisina and Frisina (1997) argue that age-related changes in hearing are not entirely the result of peripheral effects, but also reflect changes in cortical auditory processing.

## Odour identification

Figure 13.1(c) plots errors in an odour identification task as a function of age, from Doty, Shaman, Applebaum, Giberson, Sikorski, and Rosenberg (1984), based on a range of 40 odours. After developmental improvements up to the age of 10, presumably attributable to experience, performance remains relatively stable up to the 60s, when decline sets in. Doty et al. (1984) argue that declining performance in the elderly is not due to deterioration in memory, since there is no significant correlation between scores in the odour identification task and scores in standard memory tests. On the other hand, there is evidence for deterioration in the peripheral olfactory system, perhaps caused by the cumulative effects of viruses and chronic inflammatory diseases. Rawson, Gomez, Cowart, and Restrepo (1998) compared the odour selectivity of olfactory receptors in young and old subjects, and found a marked decrease in selectivity in older subjects. Meisami, Mikhail, Baim, and Bhatnagar (1998) compared the number of glomeruli and mitral cells in young and old adults and found a significant decline with age. Young subjects had over three times the number of glomeruli and mitral cells found in elderly subjects.

*Why should the number of glomeruli affect odour identification?*

## Touch discrimination

Figure 13.1(d) plots two-point discrimination of touch stimuli applied to the hand as a function of age, taken from Louis, Green, Jacobson, Rasmussen, Kolowich, and Goldstein (1984; see also Shimokata and Kuzuya, 1995; two point-discrimination was described in Chapter 3, and illustrated in Figure 3.6). Performance peaks in the late teens and early 20s, and declines monotonically thereafter. This steady decline can be partly attributed to changes in the mechanical properties of the skin (decreasing elasticity), and reductions in the number of touch receptors with age (Bolton, Winkelmann, & Dyck, 1966).

## CHANGES IN THE BRAIN OVER THE LIFESPAN

It is clear from the preceding discussion that changes in peripheral sensory structures play a role in age-related changes in perceptual capacity. However, in many cases peripheral changes cannot entirely account for age-dependent effects. We must also consider the effects of age on the brain itself.

Figure 13.3 shows data on brain weight as a function of age, taken from Dekaban and Sadowsky (1978). Brain weight increases rapidly during the first few years of life, reaching a peak at the age of 20. Between the ages of 20 and 80 brain weight declines by 9%. The change in brain weight generally mirrors the change in perceptual

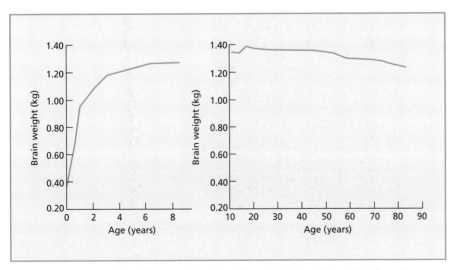

**FIG. 13.3**   Brain weight in kg as a function of age (re-plotted from Dekaban & Sadowksy, 1978). Note the different *x*-axes in the two graphs.

capacity over the lifespan. In the next section we consider what neuronal changes in the brain may underlie the change in weight.

## Developmental changes

Cortical development during the first years of life is characterised by growth in both dendrites and axons:

● Dendritic growth involves proliferation in the connections between neurons during infancy. In visual cortex, for example, synaptic density at birth is only 17% of the adult level (Huttenlocher & de Courten, 1987). This period of growth is followed by regression or pruning of connections back to adult levels during late childhood and adolescence (Webb, Monk, & Nelson, 2001).

● Cortical regions rich in axons are called **white matter**, whereas regions rich in neuronal cell bodies are called **grey matter**. **Myelin** is an insulating fatty sheath surrounding axons that promotes rapid and efficient neural transmission. Studies of white matter indicate that axon diameter and myelination continue to develop throughout childhood (Paus et al., 1999).

These structural changes in the brain must play an important role in the developmental improvements in sensory performance shown in Figure 13.1. They are likely to be regulated by sensory experience, so that the sensory systems attune themselves to the growing individual's environment. Classic experiments on selective rearing (e.g. Wiesel, 1982; Blakemore & Cooper, 1970) illustrate the degree to which sensory systems can mould themselves to their environment. Blakemore and Cooper (1970), for example, exposed kittens to patterns of only vertical stripes for the first 15 months of life. Afterwards, the cats seemed blind to horizontal stripes. Electrophysiological recordings revealed that cats reared in a normal environment possessed orientation-selective cortical cells at all orientations. Selectively reared cats, on the other hand, possessed orientation-selective cells preferring only vertical orientations. Analogous effects have been found following selective exposure to stroboscopic motion (Cynader, Berman, & Hein, 1973).

## Senescence

What does the brain lose as its weight declines in old age? For many years the dominant view was that brain ageing involves progressive cortical cell death. Anatomical studies conducted in the 1950s had indicated that up to 40% of cortical neurons were lost during senescence. However, recent research indicates that these early studies grossly overestimated cell loss (Morrison & Hof, 1997; Peters, 2002). Early estimates were based on cell counts in mounted brain sections, and were biased by shrinkage of brain preparations, and by the inadvertent inclusion of brains with neuro-degenerative diseases. It now appears that there is no drastic loss of cells, or of synapses, in the elderly brain. On the other hand there is evidence for myelin breakdown and degeneration. A reduction in white matter by as much as 15% has been reported. This change may explain much of the decline in brain size shown in Figure 13.3. Myelin breakdown is likely to have important consequences for sensory and cognitive functioning. It will cause reductions in the conduction velocity of neural signals, and disrupt the timing of signals in neural circuits. Precise synchronisation of neural firing is thought to be important during the construction of complex

**KEY TERMS**
**White matter**: Tissue in the brain and spinal cord containing cell axons.
**Grey matter**: Tissue in the brain and spinal cord containing neuronal cell bodies.
**Myelin**: A fatty sheath covering certain cell axons; it facilitates the transmission of neural impulses.

perceptual representations (Engel & Singer, 2001), so disrupted timing is likely to impede processing.

## SEX

A huge number of experiments have been conducted to investigate differences in perceptual functions that can be linked to sex. Baker's (1987) extensive review found a female advantage in many functions, including tone sensitivity, taste sensitivity, odour recognition (see Figure 2.3 in Chapter 2), and touch acuity. Male subjects performed better in tests of spatial vision. It is very important to note that scores vary from one individual to the next even within each sex. Although the mean scores of male and female subjects may be different, this sex difference is usually small relative to the variability of scores within each sex.

To illustrate this point, Figure 13.4 shows mean performance in male and female subjects aged between 20 and 30 for several sensory modalities. The error bars mark the first and third quartiles in each distribution of scores: the lower error bar cuts off

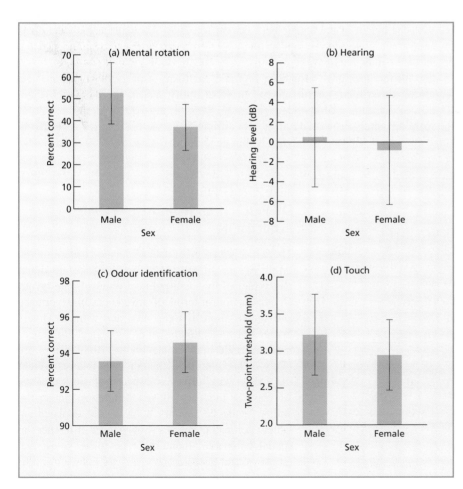

**FIG. 13.4**  Male and female performance in four sensory modalities. (a) Mental rotation (data from Collins & Kimura, 1997); (b) Hearing (data from Morrell et al., 1996; dB SPL for 30 years at 4 kHz); (c) Odour (data from Doty et al., 1984); (d) Touch (data from Louis et al., 1984). Error bars indicate the first and third quartiles (25% and 75% of scores were lower than the values indicated by the bars, respectively). NB in the two left-hand plots, better performance gives higher scores in the graph, and in the right-hand two plots better performance gives lower scores in the graph.

Scores tend to be normally distributed and the difference between mean male and female scores rarely exceeds 0.5 standard deviations. See Halpern (2000) for a detailed discussion of the statistics of gender differences.

the lowest 25% of scores, and the upper error bar cuts off the highest 25% of scores. Mean male performance exceeds female performance in three of the four modalities, but there is extensive overlap in the distribution of scores, as indicated by the overlap in the error bars.

The largest sex difference in performance is usually found in variants of the **mental rotation** task (Voyer, Voyer, & Bryden, 1995). Two variants used by Collins and Kimura (1997) are shown in Figure 13.5. The test shape is shown on the left, and four comparison shapes are shown on the right, labelled (a) to (d). The subject's task is to select the comparison shape that matches the test shape, but viewed from a different angle. The upper variant contains three-dimensional shapes similar to those used by Shepard and Metzler (1971). The correct shape (c) must be rotated in depth (about the $y$-axis) in order to create the same view as the test shape. The lower variant contains two-dimensional shapes. The correct shape (d) must be rotated in the picture plane (about the $z$-axis) to create the same view as the test shape (rotate the page by approximately 150°).

In common with many other studies, Collins and Kimura (1997) found that men performed better at this task than women. The data in Figure 13.4(a) show Collins and Kimura's results for the 3-D task in Figure 13.5 (calculated from Collins & Kimura, 1997, Figure 3). On average, male subjects recorded over 15% more correct responses than female subjects. We can see from the error bars that 75% of male scores exceeded the average female score (compare the lower error bar in the male bar with the height of the female bar), but the top 25% of female scores were close to the average male score (compare the upper error bar in the female bar with the height of the male bar).

Sex differences have also been reported for many aspects of cognition. The largest female advantage occurs in tests of verbal ability, such as speed of articulation, fluency, and accuracy of speech production (Weiss et al., 2002). As in the case of the male advantage in spatial ability, the difference between the sexes is relatively small compared with the variability within gender.

**KEY TERM**
**Mental rotation**: The manipulation of an internal mental image of a shape, so that is visualised from a different viewing angle.

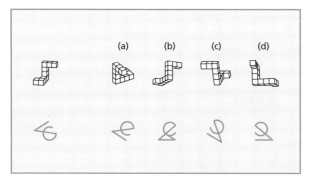

**FIG. 13.5** Typical stimuli in a mental rotation task. The test shape on the left is shown alongside four comparison shapes, labelled (a) to (d). The subject's task is to select the comparison shape that matches the test shape, viewed from a different angle. The version in the upper row contains line-drawn, three-dimensional shapes, as used by Shepard and Metzler (1971). The version in the lower row contains two-dimensional shapes, as used by Collins and Kimura (1997). Copyright © 1997 by the American Psychological Association. Adapted with permission.

## THE ORIGINS OF SEX DIFFERENCES IN PERCEPTUAL FUNCTION

There has been a great deal of debate concerning the origin of sex differences in performance, no doubt partly fuelled by socio-political issues. Some favour an explanation in terms of differences in experience and socialisation between men and women. Others favour an explanation based on biological differences between male and female brains. Both factors are likely to be important, though their relative weight may vary with different aspects of performance. At least in the case of sex differences in spatial ability, evidence favours a biological explanation. Other mammalian species show gender differences in spatial behaviour, including rats, mice, voles, and monkeys, and testosterone levels are known to influence performance in spatial tasks (Jones, Braithwaite,

& Healy, 2003). Evolutionary pressure may have led to a gender difference in spatial ability. According to this argument, ancestral males who were best at navigation would have been the most successful hunters, and would have encountered more potential mates. On the other hand, female reproductive success would have been best served by reduced mobility, leading to greater energy conservation and reduced predation (Jones et al., 2003).

# CULTURE

Studies of cultural influences on perception have concentrated on two questions: (1) Do subjects from different cultures vary in **pictorial competence**?; (2) Does the ecology of the visual environment influence perception?

## PICTORIAL COMPETENCE

This issue focuses on the idea that subjects from cultures lacking pictorial representations find it difficult to interpret pictures. There are many anecdotal accounts of this kind in, for example, the writings of missionaries (Deregowsky, 1989), but relatively little systematic research. Hudson (1960) developed an influential test of picture perception based on images of the kind shown in Figure 13.6.

Subjects were asked three questions about each picture:

1. What do you see?
2. What is the man doing?
3. Which is nearer the man, the elephant or the antelope?

> **KEY TERM**
> **Pictorial competence**: The ability of an observer to make meaningful and accurate interpretations of pictorial images.

Responses were classified as "3-D" if the subject responded that the hunter was aiming at the antelope, and that the antelope was nearer than the elephant. Hudson (1960) administered his test to several groups of subjects in South Africa, classified as "schooled" or "unschooled", and as "white" or "black". The mean percentage of subjects in each group giving 3-D responses is shown in Table 13.1 (calculated from Hudson, 1960, Table 2).

Schooled subjects gave many more 3-D responses than unschooled subjects, and Hudson concluded that:

> *formal schooling and informal training combined to supply an exposure threshold necessary for the development of the process [3-D perception]. Cultural isolation was effective in preventing or retarding the process.*
>
> (Hudson, 1960, p. 207)

However, there are serious reservations about the validity of Hudson's picture test. Jahoda and

**FIG. 13.6** Typical line drawing from Hudson's test of picture perception, used in studies of cultural influences on perception. From Deregowsky (1989). Copyright © 1989 Cambridge University Press. Reproduced with permission.

**TABLE 13.1 RESPONSES TO HUDSON'S PICTURE TEST IN DIFFERENT CULTURE GROUPS**

|  | Unschooled | Schooled |
|---|---|---|
| Black | 8.56% (n = 204) | 66.22% (n = 111) |
| White | 15.33% (n = 60) | 58.61% (n = 187) |

McGurk (1974) and Hagen and Jones (1978) argued that the results of pictorial competence studies are heavily biased by the methodology. Hagen and Jones (1978) reviewed several picture perception studies in which results were significantly altered by the nature of the experimental instructions. Culture is likely to have influenced subjects' attitudes to instructions and test-taking, regardless of sensory effects. Furthermore, Hudson's pictures were relatively impoverished and geometrically inaccurate line-drawings, lacking textural detail and grey-level gradation. Notice from Table 13.1 that one in three responses of even "schooled" subjects was incorrect. Hagen and Jones (1978) argue that any test of picture perception that:

> *fails to generate nearly 100% three-dimensional responding in educated Western adults has faults of either design or procedure or both which leaves its validity open to serious question. It seems to us very unlikely that some 30% of educated Scots are* incapable *of seeing depth in pictures stylistically indigenous to their culture.*
>
> (p. 191, their emphasis. Jahoda and McGurk, 1974, tested Scottish and Ghanaian subjects)

## ECOLOGY: THE "CARPENTERED WORLD" HYPOTHESIS

A number of studies have explored the idea that subjects living in highly industrialised environments perceive angles and straight edges differently from subjects living in environments lacking rectangular manufactured structures.

### Illusion studies

The standard technique in early studies was to measure the magnitude of geometric illusions in groups of subjects from different cultures.

#### Ames Window

Allport and Pettigrew (1957) employed the rotating trapezoid illusion, or Ames Window. A sheet of metal is cut to form a trapezoidal window, and rotated about a vertical axis (see Figure 13.7(a)). Subjects generally report seeing the window oscillate from side to side rather than rotate, so that the longer vertical edge always appears closer to the viewer. Allport and Pettigrew (1957) used rural Bantu boys and urban African or European boys as subjects. They reported that in "optimal" conditions of distant, monocular viewing, both rural and urban subjects reported seeing the illusion (87.5% and 92.5% of reports, respectively). In "marginal" conditions of near, binocular viewing, fewer rural subjects saw the illusion than urban subjects (35% and 60% of reports, respectively).

#### Geometrical illusions

Segall, Campbell, and Herskovits (1963) measured the magnitude of the Müller–Lyer, Sander Parallelogram, and Vertical–Horizontal illusions in urban and tribal subjects in the USA, Africa, and the Philippines. Examples of these illusions are shown in Figure 13.7 (parts (b)–(d)). They reported that urban subjects showed larger illusion magnitudes than tribal subjects, for the Müller–Lyer and the Sander Parallelogram. Results for the Vertical–Horizontal illusion were mixed, with some non-urban subject groups showing a larger effect, and others showing a smaller effect than urban subjects.

Leibowitz and Pick (1972) studied the magnitude of the Ponzo illusion (Figure 13.7(e)) in college students (both US and Ugandan) and in rural Ugandans. They reported that rural Ugandans saw no illusion at all, while college students saw a relatively strong illusion.

### The utility of illusion studies

It is unfortunate that geometrical illusions featured so prominently in early research on visual ecology. The classical psychophysical methods used in this research are notoriously vulnerable to bias effects introduced by instructions, or by observer attitudes, or even by experimenter attitudes (see the tutorial on psychophysical methods in Chapter 1). A further source of bias is the quality of the retinal image, which may have varied systematically between subject groups. The incidence of uncorrected refractive error was almost certainly higher in non-industrialised, rural subjects, but was not measured in the studies reviewed above. In addition, different racial groups vary in terms of pigmentation of the lens, iris, and fundus. Such optical factors are claimed to produce significant variations in illusion magnitude and picture perception (e.g. Coren, 1989; Pollack, 1989).

So any obtained differences in measured illusion magnitude confound sensory effects and bias effects. Even if one sets aside issues of bias, data on illusion magnitude are of limited use because there is no universally agreed explanation for the illusions themselves, despite claims to the contrary in some of the cross-cultural literature. Indeed many illusions are likely to reflect the combined effect of several causes (Morgan, 1996). The lack of clarity on illusion causation makes it difficult to judge the significance of any differences in illusion magnitude.

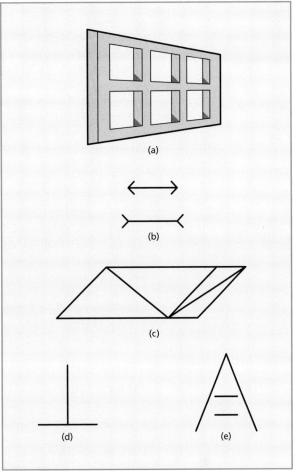

**FIG. 13.7** Examples of geometrical illusions used in studies of cultural influences on perception. (a) The Ames Window appears to oscillate back and forth when it is rotated about the vertical axis; (b) The Müller–Lyer illusion. The line with outward-facing arrowheads appears longer than the line with inward-facing arrowheads; (c) Sander Parallelogram. The two diagonals appear unequal in length, but are actually equal; (d) The Vertical–Horizontal illusion. The vertical line is the same length as the horizontal line, but appears longer; (e) The Ponzo illusion. The two horizontal lines are equal in length, but the top line appears longer.

## The oblique effect

Annis and Frost (1973) approached the "carpentered world" hypothesis from a different angle. They investigated a well-known perceptual effect, known as the **oblique effect**. Many studies of subjects from industrialised cultures have shown that visual acuity is greater for lines oriented vertically or horizontally than it is for lines oriented obliquely. One explanation for the effect is that a "carpentered world" provides selective visual experience that favours vertically and horizontally oriented contours (recall the

**KEY TERM**
**Oblique effect**: Reduced visual acuity for oblique lines and gratings, relative to vertical and horizontal orientations.

experiments on selective rearing by Blakemore and Cooper, 1970, mentioned earlier). Annis and Frost (1973) measured the oblique effect in urban Euro-Canadians and in non-urban Cree Indians. They found a larger oblique effect in the former than in the latter, which they interpret as supporting the "carpentered world" hypothesis. However, Timney and Muir (1976) took the same measurements from another two ethnic groups of subjects, one Caucasian and one Chinese, who were both raised in urban carpentered environments. Timney and Muir obtained effects similar in size to those found by Annis and Frost (1973). Chinese subjects showed a smaller oblique effect than Caucasian subjects. Timney and Muir (1976) argue that variations in the magnitude of the oblique effect may reflect genetic factors rather than environmental effects.

## CULTURE EFFECTS?

Data from cross-cultural studies are claimed by some to support the conclusion that perception is influenced by culture (e.g. Deregowski, 1989; Gregory, 1998). However, much of the evidence is either weak or subject to alternative interpretations. A rare piece of convincing evidence in favour of cultural effects comes from Werker and colleagues, who studied phoneme discrimination (phonemes are elementary units of speech, see Chapter 5 and Figure 5.10). They and others have found that infants younger than 12 months old are able to discriminate phonemes from all the world's languages, whereas older infants and adults cannot discriminate some phonemes not used in their native language (see Werker and Desjardins, 1995).

## EXPERTISE

### FORMAL TRAINING

There are several examples of perceptual differences linked to the level of expertise of the subject, as indicated by formal training.

### Musicians

Crummer, Walton, Wayman, Hantz, and Frisina (1994) studied the discrimination of timbre in notes produced by variants of several musical instruments (cellos, violas, flutes, and tubas). Recall from Chapter 5 that different instruments produce different complex sounds even when playing the same note, giving each instrument its characteristic timbre. Crummer et al. (1994) found that all subjects could discriminate timbre reliably, but trained musicians had a slight advantage over non-musicians. Musicians showed larger and faster event-related potentials (ERPs, brain waves) than non-musicians.

A few people possess *perfect pitch*, which means that they can identify the absolute pitch of a sound without aids, while most people require a reference pitch and/or rehearsal in order to identify absolute pitch. Crummer et al. (1994) found that individuals with perfect pitch had the shortest ERP latencies of all.

Beauvois and Meddis (1997) studied auditory grouping. As described in Chapter 5 and illustrated in Figure 5.13, when two tones are presented in a repeated sequence, a higher-frequency tone alternating with a lower-frequency tone, one of two percepts is heard. Rapid alternation leads to the perception of two streams, one high-pitched and the other low-pitched. Relatively slow alternation leads to perception of a single rhythmic form (a musical trill). Prolonged exposure (adaptation) to a streaming sequence biases subjects' perception of subsequent test sequences in favour of streaming, but this bias effect dissipates if a silent interval is interposed between adaptation and testing. Beauvois and Meddis (1997) found consistent differences in streaming responses between musicians and non-musicians, as shown in Figure 13.8.

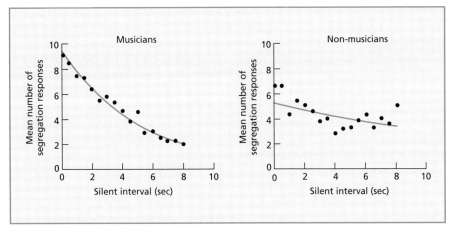

**FIG. 13.8** Strength of auditory streaming as a function of the duration of the interval between adaptation and testing (re-plotted from Beauvois & Meddis, 1997). Musicians (left-hand graph) showed more streaming than non-musical subjects (right-hand graph), and the effect dissipated more slowly.

Musicians showed more perceptual segregation than non-musicians, as is evident from the height of the curves in Figure 13.8 at short silent intervals. In addition, musicians required a longer silent interval to dissipate the bias than non-musicians. Musicians apparently have a more finely tuned ability to perceive musical trills.

## Visual artists

Thouless investigated shape and size constancy in a series of classic psychophysical experiments published in the 1930s. **Shape constancy** is the tendency for perceived shape to remain relatively constant even when variations in viewing conditions produce marked changes in the retinal image. For example, if a flat circular disk is placed on a table top, and an observer views it from an oblique angle, the image of the disk on the retina will be elliptical due to foreshortening, as illustrated in Figure 13.9 (foreshortening was explained in Chapter 10, Figure 10.5). However, the observer tends to perceive the retinal projection of the disk as more circular than it really is.

In Thouless's experiments, observers were asked to match the shape of the disk as seen from their viewpoint with a series of alternative elliptical shapes varying in their degree of eccentricity. An observer showing perfect shape constancy would select the circle as the matching shape, since this is the actual shape of the disk. An observer showing no shape constancy would select the shape that matches the elliptical retinal image of the disk exactly. Most observers show partial shape constancy, selecting a shape intermediate between these two extremes. Thouless called this effect "phenomenal regression to the real object", and measured it in a large number of subjects. He expressed constancy scores on a scale from 0 (no constancy) to 1.0 (perfect constancy). Thouless (1931) compared the degree of constancy shown by trained artists and by non-artists, and Figure 13.10 shows his data (taken from Thouless, 1931, Table 12).

Artists showed much less constancy than non-artists. Shape constancy is probably responsible for the difficulties most people experience when they attempt to create realistic life-drawings of three-dimensional scenes. It thwarts attempts to render

*Compare shape constancy with colour constancy, described in Chapter 12.*

**KEY TERM**
**Shape constancy**: The apparent shape of an object remains constant despite gross changes in its retinal image caused by variations in viewing position.

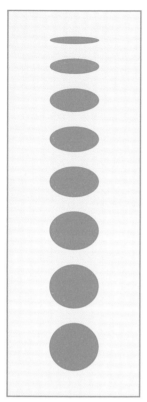

**FIG. 13.9** Illustration of shape constancy. In the images of mugs in Figure 9.6, the tops of the mugs project elliptical images on the retina. When an untrained observer is required to select the ellipse in this Figure that matches the image of the top of a mug, they tend to select an ellipse that is more circular than the image (phenomenal regression to the real object). The mug images in Figure 9.6 have aspect ratios corresponding to the two topmost ellipses in Figure 13.9.

viewed shapes accurately in a drawing, since it distorts perceptual impressions towards real object shapes. Trained artists counteract constancy more successfully than non-artists, but note that some constancy is present even in artists (their scores in Figure 13.10 are below 1.0). To overcome this residual tendency, artists have traditionally used aids such as Albrecht Dürer's device, a viewing window divided into squares using a wire grid. The three-dimensional scene is reproduced on paper divided up into a corresponding number of squares. Artists today generally use *sighting* to overcome constancy. Image dimensions, such as the projected width and height of the disk in Figure 13.9, are measured using a thumb positioned along a pencil or brush handle held at arm's length.

More recently, Kozbelt (2001) compared art students against novice artists in several visual tasks including mental rotation, identification of blurred photographs, embedded figures, and fragmented pictures. He found no difference between the groups in mental rotation scores. But art students performed markedly better than novices in the other three tasks involving degraded images, by as much as 52%.

## PRACTICE

At least some of the difference in performance between formally trained and untrained subjects must reflect a straightforward practice effect rather than innate ability as a musician or artist. Formally trained subjects spend a large proportion of their time, perhaps over many years, absorbed in relevant activities, such as artistic performance or observation and analysis of other artists' work. So there is plenty of scope for practice effects. Laboratory studies have shown that practice at even simple sensory tasks leads to consistent improvements in performance, as the following examples show.

### Odour

Rabin (1988) studied the ability of subjects to discriminate between unfamiliar odours. He found that a practice session in which subjects became familiar with the smells improved performance significantly relative to control subjects who were given no practice. Practised subjects achieved 94% correct odour discrimination in the test phase, while control subjects achieved 81% correct discrimination. In a second experiment, Rabin (1988) found that detection rates for contaminants in familiar odours were higher than for contaminants in unfamiliar odours, especially when the contaminant itself was familiar. Detection was 20.5% better using familiar contaminants in familiar odours than when both were unfamiliar. This research bears out anecdotal claims that expert perfumiers and wine tasters can make finer discriminations than unpractised subjects.

### Vision

A number of studies have found that practice at simple visual discriminations improves performance significantly. The practice effects show a surprising degree of specificity. Fahle and Morgan (1996) employed two tasks that involved judging the relative positions of three small dots. One task involved judging the alignment of the dots, and the other involved judging the spacing between the dots. An hour of practice at either task improved discrimination performance by between 6% and 12%. When subjects switched from one task to another, the benefits of practice were eliminated and performance returned to a level similar to that shown in entirely unpractised subjects. Beard, Levi, and Reich (1995) also used simple visual discrimination tasks. They found partial transfer of training between tasks, but no transfer to new retinal locations. When subjects were trained and tested using the same stimuli presented at the same location in the right eye, performance improved by 13.06%. When subjects were tested using the same stimuli but presented at a different location in the same eye, there was very little practice effect (2.34%). Such a high degree of specificity indicates that practice causes changes to occur in very early, retinally localised perceptual processes rather than in higher level cognitive processes.

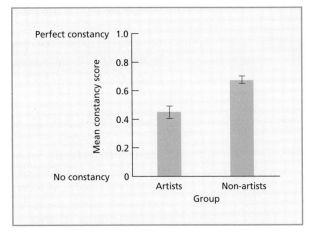

**FIG. 13.10** Shape constancy scores reported by Thouless (1931) in trained artists and non-artists. Scores ranged from 0 (no constancy; judgements governed by image dimensions) to 1.0 (perfect constancy; judgements governed by object shape). Error bars indicate the standard error of the mean.

## NEURAL CORRELATES OF EXPERTISE

We have already seen that differences in perception resulting from age and sex can, to a large extent, be traced to physical differences in the brain. Can differences resulting from expertise be linked to differences in brain structure? Several studies have reported physical differences between the brains of trained and untrained subjects.

Elbert, Pantev, Wienbruch, Rockstroh, and Taub (1995) used magnetic source imaging to compare the primary somatosensory cortex of experienced string musicians against a group of control subjects. They found evidence that the cortical representation of the fingers of the left hand is larger in string musicians than in control subjects. The magnitude of the difference between expert and control subjects was significantly correlated with the age at which the expert had begun to play their instrument, indicating a role for experience.

Maguire et al. (2000) took MRI scans of the brains of licensed London taxi drivers and of age-matched control subjects. They found that the posterior hippocampus was larger in taxi drivers than in control subjects. Hippocampal volume was correlated with the amount of time served as a taxi driver. Figure 13.11 shows hippocampal volume as a function of length of service.

The hippocampus is thought to play an important role in spatial tasks, and particularly in navigation. So Maguire et al. concluded that professional dependence on spatial navigation skills results in a redistribution of grey matter in the hippocampus. The correlation with experience supports their view that variations in hippocampal volume are acquired through experience.

Schwartz, Maquet, and Frith (2002) conducted an fMRI experiment to investigate the neural substrate of learning a visual texture discrimination task. They found, as had previous studies, that intensive practice

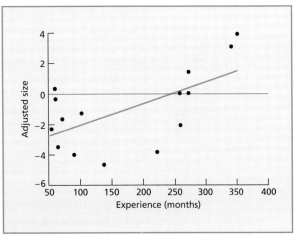

**FIG. 13.11** Volume of grey matter in the right hippocampus as a function of time spent as a London taxi driver (data from Maguire et al., 2000). The hippocampal volume was significantly correlated with experience ($r = 0.6$; $p < .05$).

at the task using one eye improved performance using that eye but not using the other eye. Moreover, they found greater fMRI activation using the trained eye than using the untrained eye. The difference in activation level was restricted to early visual cortex (V1). Schwartz et al. (2002) concluded that training induced neural changes in the earliest stage of cortical processing.

## IDIOSYNCRATIC INDIVIDUAL DIFFERENCES

If one controls for all the important factors discussed above, namely age, sex, culture, and expertise, do some idiosyncratic individual differences in perceptual function persist? No study has yet been conducted with the level of control required to answer this question definitively. Several studies have reported marked individual differences in performance on perceptual tasks, but controls for age, sex, and expertise were incomplete. For example:

● Ginsburg and colleagues found threefold variations in spatial contrast sensitivity in a large group of air force pilots, but controlled only for visual acuity (see Ginsburg, 1986).

● Halpern, Andrews, and Purves (1999) tested 20 subjects between 20 and 30 years of age (all members of Duke University, USA) using seven visual tasks ranging from orientation discrimination to form identification. They found large inter-subject differences in performance. Scores in most tasks tended to co-vary, so if an individual scored highly in one task, he or she tended to score highly in other tasks. It is possible that at least some of the variation reported by Halpern et al. (1999) reflected differences due to expertise and sex, since these factors were not partitioned in data analysis.

There is some evidence for differences between individual brains, but in the absence of adequate controls for age, gender, and expertise it is not possible to identify the origin of these differences. Andrews, Halpern, and Purves (1997) took postmortem measurements of the visual system in a sample of normal human brains. They measured the area and volume of several neural structures, including the optic tract, lateral geniculate nucleus, and primary visual cortex. Andrews et al. (1997) reported a two- to threefold variation in the size of these components between individuals. They also found a high correlation between the size of the components, so brains with a large visual cortex also tended to have a large optic tract and lateral geniculate nucleus. The same research group later reported significant individual differences in performance on a range of visual tasks (Halpern et al., 1999, described above). The authors were tempted to conclude that: "interindividual variation in the amount of neural circuitry devoted to vision gives rise to differences in human visual ability" (Halpern et al., 1999, p. 524).

At least some of the variability in brain structure reported by Andrews et al. (1997) may reflect differences resulting from sex, age, and expertise. Andrews et al.'s (1997) donors ranged in age from 28 to 86 and their background (formal qualifications, occupation, pastimes, etc.) was not reported. As yet no study has attempted a direct correlation between individual task performance and brain structure with adequate controls to separate out the effects of age, gender, and expertise. So the question of idiosyncratic differences in perception, and their relation to brain structure, is still unresolved.

# CHAPTER SUMMARY

A number of factors are known to produce significant individual differences in perception.

## AGE

- Performance generally conforms to a U-shaped function, with rapid improvements in the first decade of life, followed by gradual decline after the fifth decade.
- These changes can be attributed to changes in the efficiency of the peripheral sense organs, and in the efficiency of signal transmission within the cortex.

## SEX

- Sex differences are frequently reported in all sensory modalities, with female subjects generally outperforming male subjects except in tasks involving spatial vision.
- Male–female differences are usually small relative to the variability of scores within each sex.
- Physical differences between male and female brains, perhaps as a result of natural selection, could underlie many of the sex differences in performance.

## CULTURE

- A number of studies claim to find differences in perception between subjects from non-industrialised cultures and subjects from industrialised cultures.
- Early studies claimed that non-industrialised subjects found pictures difficult to interpret, and were less prone to visual illusions involving judgements of straight lines and angles.
- Much of the evidence is either weak or subject to alternative interpretations.

## EXPERTISE

- Formal training in music or art produces consistent differences in perception.
- Musicians can make finer discriminations of timbre and auditory streaming than non-musicians.
- Artists show less shape constancy than non-artists, and perform better in tasks involving degraded images.
- Practice at simple visual discriminations typically improves performance by more than 10%, but the effect does not transfer well between different tasks or between different retinal locations.

- Several brain-imaging studies have found physical differences between experts and non-experts, indicating that plasticity in the cortex may be responsible for differences in performance.

## IDIOSYNCRONY

- Marked individual differences in performance have been reported for a number of sensory tasks, with the correspondingly large variation in underlying neural structures. The origin of these differences is still unclear.

# TUTORIALS

## METHODOLOGY IN INFANT VISION

As we saw in the tutorial section of Chapter 1, a number of different techniques have been developed over the past 150 years for studying adult perception. These techniques cannot be employed in developmental studies because of the limitations of infants as experimental subjects. Young infants cannot understand instructions, and cannot tell the experimenter what they are perceiving. They have a limited behavioural repertoire, an inability to concentrate on a given task, and tend to fall asleep frequently.

Experimental psychologists have risen to the challenges posed by research on infant perception, and have developed a range of special techniques that exploit the behaviour of infants, particularly their inquisitiveness and inability to concentrate (see Atkinson, 2000). Standard psychophysical techniques measure an adult's ability to discriminate between two stimuli, and can be used to study sensory thresholds. Developmental techniques also measure discriminability.

### Preferential attention

In this technique the experimenter presents the infant with two stimuli, and measures the relative amount of time the infant devotes to each. In early research the experimenter watched the infant's face and measured how long the child attended to each stimulus. In contemporary studies the experimenter bases measurements on videos of the infant, or on eye fixations, to ensure objectivity. If the infant spends an equal amount of time attending to each stimulus, he or she may be unable to distinguish between them. If he or she attends more to one of the two stimuli, then the experimenter infers that the infant can discriminate between them and, for some reason, prefers one over the other. Fantz (1961) used this technique to show that infants have a spontaneous preference for more complex spatial patterns over simpler patterns. For example, when 2- to 3-month-old subjects were shown a spatially uniform disk and a bull's-eye pattern, they spent over twice as long inspecting the bull's-eye. When shown a bull's-eye and a cartoon face, they looked towards the face for twice the time that they looked at the bull's-eye pattern.

## Habituation

Infants generally become less attentive as they become more familiar with a stimulus, even an interesting one. If the stimulus is presented repeatedly, the infant will spend less and less time attending to it. This effect is called habituation. If the stimulus is changed the infant is likely to show renewed interest in the novel stimulus (dishabituation), provided that he or she can distinguish between the habituated stimulus and the novel stimulus. The change in looking time following a stimulus change provides a measure of stimulus discriminability. This technique can be used to measure the smallest change in stimulation necessary for the infant to detect the change, namely their discrimination threshold.

## Physiological measures

Some techniques do not rely on overt behaviour at all, but instead take physiological measurements that indicate awareness of the stimulus. When an infant habituates, his or her heart rate decreases. An unexpected, and detectable, change in stimulation causes an increase in heart rate. Variation in heart rate thus offers a physiological measure of habituation.

Another commonly used technique involves recording event related potentials (ERPs) from 50 or 60 electrodes fixed to a skull cap. Fluctuations in sensory stimulation ("events") produces minute but measurable fluctuations in electrical potential in the brain. Specialised equipment can detect these fluctuations with millisecond accuracy. The timing, size, and location of ERP activity recorded on the scalp can be used to draw inferences about the time-course of processing in the brain and the location of the source of the activity.

## SENSORY INTEGRATION

The aim of this chapter was to discuss an aspect of perception that is often disregarded in mainstream research, namely individual differences. Another aspect of perception that has been largely neglected until relatively recently is sensory integration. The interaction of several sensory modalities to determine flavour was mentioned in Chapter 2, and synaesthesia was discussed in the tutorial section of the previous chapter. But generally, researchers restrict themselves to work on a particular sensory modality. They conduct research on that modality using stimuli that necessarily exclude all other modalities as far as possible. Subjects in visual experiments usually work in silence, while psychoacoustic experiments often take place in near-darkness. However, natural objects and events are usually multisensory. For example, during a face-to-face conversation with another human, or an encounter with an animal, both vocalisations and visual information (facial expression, lip movement, body attitude) are important. When a car driver presses the throttle pedal and the vehicle accelerates, there is an audible change in engine note, a visible change in the movement seen through the windscreen, and vestibular signals providing a sensation of bodily acceleration. It would be surprising if the sensory systems did not exploit the correlation between different modalities. Recent research has begun to reveal the extent to which signals from multiple sensory systems interact.

## Detection

In a simple laboratory reaction-time experiment, the subject is required to make a response (typically a button press) as soon as he or she detects the onset of a stimulus. Reactions are usually quite rapid, in the order of 200–300 milliseconds, using either visual or auditory stimuli. However, when the stimulus is multisensory, such as a visual event and a simultaneous sound, reaction times are speeded up dramatically, by over 30% (Diederich & Colonius, 2004). Such facilitation may reflect interactions between signals in different sensory systems during the early stages of processing.

## Identification

There is strong evidence that information provided by one sense can influence the perception of stimuli impinging on a different sense. In the classic "cocktail party" problem, we have to understand what someone is saying against a very noisy background. In this situation, visual cues from lip movements, facial expressions, and gestures have a significant impact on comprehension. The improvement in comprehension with visual cues is equivalent to an improvement in signal-to-noise ratio of 15–20 dB (Spence, 2002).

In the McGurk effect (McGurk & MacDonald, 1976), the speech sound actually heard by a listener is altered by observation of the speaker's lip movements. Similar effects have been reported using other sensory combinations. For example, perturbing the sound made as the hands are rubbed together can alter the perception of skin texture (Jousmaki & Hari, 1998).

## Localisation

The apparent location of a sensory event in one modality can be influenced by information in other modalities. Ventriloquism is a long-established form of entertainment that relies on the audience localising speech sounds at the moving lips of the ventriloquist's dummy. We experience this effect regularly when watching television, since the audio speaker is always located at the side or even at the rear of the television, yet we perceive the sounds to emanate from within the visual scene. The illusion is actually due to biases introduced during multisensory interactions. Experimental evidence shows that the apparent location of a sound really is influenced by visual events: a flash of light influences the apparent location of a simultaneous sound (Radeau, 1994). Botvinick and Cohen (1998) describe a dramatic effect involving mis-localisation of tactile stimulation. The experimental subject places an arm underneath a table, and a false arm equipped with a rubber glove is placed in view on the table directly above. The experimenter then strokes the subject's arm while simultaneously showing a brush stroking the false arm. Subjects report that the stroking sensation appears to be localised on the false arm—the arm appears to be their own arm despite obvious indications to the contrary.

## Attention

There are important cross-modal interactions in the spatial allocation of attention. An event in one sensory modality can attract attention to a stimulus presented at the same location but in a different sensory modality. For example, when an abrupt sound attracts visual attention to the location of the sound, it enhances the speed and accuracy of judgements about visual stimuli presented at the same location. On the other hand, when multisensory attention has been attracted to a given location, the ability to respond to stimuli presented in other locations is impaired. In other words, multisensory attention is spatially localised. One implication for driving is that if a car driver's attention is occupied by, for instance, a conversation on a mobile phone (perceptually localised to one side of the head), his or her ability simultaneously to attend to visual events at a different location, namely through the windscreen, is likely to be impaired (Spence & Read, 2003).

# References

Adelson, E., & Bergen, J. (1985). Spatiotemporal energy models for the detection of motion. *Journal of the Optical Society of America, A2*, 284–299.

Adelson, E., & Movshon, A. (1982). Phenomenal coherence of moving visual patterns. *Nature, 300*, 523–525.

Aggleton, J. (1992). *The Amygdala*. New York: Wiley-Liss.

Albright, T. D. (1992). Form-cue invariant motion processing in primate visual cortex. *Science, 255*, 1141–1143.

Allport, G. W., & Pettigrew, T. F. (1957). Cultural influence on the perception of movement: The trapezoidal illusion among Zulus. *Journal of Abnormal and Social Psychology, 55*, 104–113.

Andersen, R. A., & Bradley, D. C. (1998). Perception of three-dimensional structure from motion. *Trends in Cognitive Sciences, 2*, 222–228.

Andrews, T. J., Halpern, S. D., & Purves, D. (1997). Correlated size variations in human visual cortex, lateral geniculate nucleus, and optic tract. *Journal of Neuroscience, 17*, 2859–2868.

Annis R. C., & Frost, B. (1973). Human visual ecology and orientation anisotropies in acuity. *Science, 182*, 729–731.

Anstis, S. M. (1974). A chart demonstrating variations in acuity with retinal position. *Vision Research, 14*, 589–592.

Atema, J. (1977). Functional separation of smell and taste in fish and crustacea. In J. Le Magnen & P. MacLeod (Eds.), *Olfaction and Taste VI* (pp. 165–174). London: Information Retrieval.

Atkinson, J. (2000). *The Developing Visual Brain*. Oxford: Oxford University Press.

Badcock, D., & Shor, C. (1985). Depth-increment detection function for individual spatial channels. *Journal of the Optical Society of America, A2,* 1211–1215.

Baker, C. L., & Braddick, O. J. (1985). Temporal properties of the short-range process in apparent motion. *Perception, 14*, 181–192.

Baker, M. A. (1987). Sensory functioning. In M. A. Baker (Ed.), *Sex Differences in Human Performance* (pp. 5–36). Chichester: Wiley.

Ballard, D., Hayhoe, M., Pook, P., & Rao, R. (1997). Deictic codes for the embodiment of cognition. *Behavioral and Brain Sciences, 20*, 723–767.

Banks, M. S., & Bennett, P. J. (1988). Optical and photoreceptor immaturities limit the spatial and chromatic vision of human neonates. *Journal of the Optical Society of America, A5*, 2059–2079.

Barlow, H. B. (1953). Summation and inhibition in the frog's retina. *Journal of Physiology, 119*, 69–88.

Barlow, H. B. (1972). Single units and sensation: A neuron doctrine for perceptual psychology? *Perception, 1*, 371–394.

Barlow, H. B. (1979). Reconstructing the visual image in space and time. *Nature, 279*, 189–190.

Barlow, H. B., & Hill, R. M. (1963). Selective sensitivity to direction of motion in ganglion cells of the rabbit's retina. *Science, 139*, 412–414.

Baron-Cohen, S., Burt, L., Smith-Laittan, F., Harrison, J., & Bolton, P. (1996). Synaesthesia: prevalence and familiality. *Perception, 25*, 1073–1079.

Baron-Cohen, S., Harrison, J., Goldstein, L. H., & Wyke, M. (1993). Coloured speech perception: Is synaesthesia what happens when modularity breaks down? *Perception, 22*, 419–426.

Bartoshuk, L. M., & Beauchamp, G. K. (1994). Chemical senses. *Annual Review of Psychology, 45*, 419–449.

Beard, B., Levi, D. M., & Reich, L. N. (1995). Perceptual learning in parafoveal vision. *Vision Research, 35*, 1679–1690.

Beauvois, M. W., & Meddis, R. (1997). Time decay of auditory stream biasing. *Perception and Psychophysics, 59*, 81–86.

Beintema, J. A., & Lappe, M. (2002). Perception of biological motion without local image motion. *Proceedings of the National Academy of Sciences USA, 99*, 5661–5663.

Benson, D. F., & Greenberg, J. P. (1969). Visual form agnosia. *Archives of Neurology, 20*, 82–89.

Berglund, B., & Engen, T. (1993). A comparison of self-adaptation and cross-adaptation to odorants presented singly and in mixtures. *Perception, 22*, 103–111.

Bex, P. J., & Baker, C. L. (1999). Motion perception over long interstimulus intervals. *Perception and Psychophysics, 61*, 1066–1074.

Biederman, I. (1987). Recognition-by-components: A theory of human image understanding. *Psychological Review, 94*, 115–147.

Biederman, I., & Cooper, E. E. (1991). Priming contour-deleted images: Evidence for intermediate representations in visual object priming. *Cognitive Psychology, 23*, 3930–4019.

Biederman, I., & Gerhardstein, P. C. (1993). Recognising depth-rotated objects: Evidence for three-dimensional viewpoint invariance. *Journal of Experimental Psychology: Human Perception and Performance, 19*, 1162–1182.

Blake, R. (1993). Cats perceive biological motion. *Psychological Science, 4*, 54–57.

Blakemore, C. B., & Campbell, F. W. (1969). On the existence of neurones in the human visual system selectively sensitive to the size and orientation of retinal images. *Journal of Physiology, 203*, 237–260.

Blakemore, C., & Cooper, G. (1970). Development of the brain depends on the visual environment. *Nature, 228*, 477–478.

Blakemore, C., & Sutton, P. (1969). Size adaptation: A new after-effect. *Science, 166*, 245–247.

Bolton, C. F., Winkelmann, R. K., & Dyck, P. J. (1966). Quantitative study of Meissner's corpuscles in man. *Neurology, 16*, 1–9.

Boring, E. (1942). *Sensation and Perception in the History of Experimental Psychology*. New York: Appleton-Century-Crofts.

Boring, E. (1950). *A History of Experimental Psychology*. Englewood Cliffs, NJ: Prentice Hall.

Bosking, W. H., Zhang, Y., Schofield, B., & Fitzpatrick, D. (1997). Orientation selectivity and the arrangement of horizontal connections in tree shrew striate cortex. *Journal of Neuroscience, 17*, 2112–2127.

Botvinick, M., & Cohen, J. (1998). Rubber hands "feel" touch that eyes see. *Nature, 391*, 756.

Bowns, L. (2001). IOC, vector sum, and squaring: Three different motion effects or one? *Vision Research, 41*, 965–972.

Bracewell, R. N. (1978). *The Fourier Transform and its Applications*. London: McGraw-Hill.

Bracewell, R. N. (1989). The Fourier transform. *Scientific American, 260*(6), 62–69.

Braddick, O. J. (1974). A short-range process in apparent motion. *Vision Research, 14*, 519–527.

Braddick, O. J. (1980). Low-level and high-level processes in apparent motion. *Philosophical Transactions of the Royal Society of London, B209*, 137–151.

Braitenberg, V., & Schuz, A. (1991). *Anatomy of the Cortex*. Berlin: Springer-Verlag.

Bregman, A. S. (1990). *Auditory Scene Analysis: The Perceptual Organisation of Sound*. Cambridge, MA: MIT Press.

Bridgeman, B., & Delgado, D. (1984). Sensory effects of eye press are due to efference. *Perception and Psychophysics, 36*, 482–484.

Brindley, G. S. (1960). *Physiology of the Retina and Visual Pathway*. London: Edward Arnold.

Bruce, V., Green, P. R., & Georgeson, M. A. (2003). *Visual Perception*. Hove, UK: Psychology Press.

Bruce, V., & Humphreys, G. W. (1994). Recognising objects and faces. *Visual Cognition, 1*, 141–180.

Buckley, D., & Frisby, J. P. (1993). Interaction of stereo, texture and outline cues in the shape perception of three-dimensional ridges. *Vision Research, 33*, 919–933.

Bulthoff, H. H., & Edelman, S. (1992). Psychophysical support for a two-dimensional view interpolation theory of object recognition. *Proceedings of the National Academy of Sciences, 89*, 60–64.

Bulthoff, H. H., & Mallot, H. A. (1988). Integration of depth modules: Stereo and shading. *Journal of the Optical Society of America, A5*, 1749–1758.

Burr, D. C., & Morgan, M. J. (1997). Motion deblurring in human vision. *Proceedings of the Royal Society of London, B264*, 431–436.

Burr, D. C., Morgan, M. J., & Morrone, M. C. (1999). Saccadic suppression precedes visual motion analysis. *Current Biology, 9*, 1207–1209.

Burr, D. C., Ross, J., & Morrone, M. C. (1986a). Seeing objects in motion. *Proceedings of the Royal Society of London, B227*, 249–265.

Burr, D. C., Ross, J., & Morrone, M. C. (1986b). Smooth and sampled motion. *Vision Research, 26*, 643–652.

Burt, P., & Julesz, B. (1980). Modifications of the classical notion of Panum's fusional area. *Perception, 9*, 671–682.

Burt, P., & Sperling, G. (1981). Time, distance, and feature trade-offs in visual apparent motion. *Psychological Review, 88*, 171–195.

Cain, W. (1982) Odor identification by males and females: Predictions versus performance. *Chemical Senses, 7*, 129–142.

Cain, D. P., & Bindra, D. (1972). Responses of amygdala single units to odors in the rat. *Experimental Neurology, 35*, 98–110.

Cain, W., & Johnson, F. (1978). Lability of odor pleasantness: Influence of mere exposure. *Perception, 7*, 459–465.

Campbell, F. W. (1957). The depth of field of the human eye. *Optica Acta, 4*, 157–164.

Campbell, F. W., & Gubisch, R. W. (1966). Optical quality of the human eye. *Journal of Physiology, 186*, 558–578.

Campbell, F. W., & Robson, J. G. (1968). Application of Fourier analysis to the visibility of gratings. *Journal of Physiology, 197*, 551–556.

Carey, D. P. (2001). Do action systems resist visual illusions? *Trends in Cognitive Sciences, 5*, 109–113.

Carlson, N. R. (2004). *Physiology of Behavior*. Boston, MA: Pearson.

Carterette, E., & Kendall, R. (1999). Comparative music perception and cognition. In D. Deutsch (Ed.), *The Psychology of Music* (2nd ed., pp. 725–792). San Diego, CA: Academic Press.

Cavanagh, P. (1992). Attention-based motion perception. *Science, 257*, 1563–1565.

Cavanagh, P., & Mather, G. (1989). Motion: The long and short of it. *Spatial Vision, 4*, 103–129.

Charman, W. (1991). The vertebrate dioptric apparatus. In J. Cronly-Dillon & R. Gregory (Eds.), *Vision and Visual Dysfunction Volume II: Evolution of the Eye and Visual System* (pp. 82–117). Basingstoke: Macmillan.

Chaudhari, N., Landin, A. M., & Roper, S. D. (2000). A metabotropic glutamate receptor variant functions as a taste receptor. *Nature Neuroscience, 3*, 113–119.

Chubb, C., & Sperling, G. (1988). Drift-balanced random stimuli: A general basis for studying non-Fourier motion perception. *Journal of the Optical Society of America, A5*, 1986–2006.

Cohen, M. M. (1973). Elevator illusion: Influences of otolith organ activity and neck proprioception. *Perception and Psychophysics, 14*, 401–406.

Cole, J., & Paillard, J. (1995). Living without touch and peripheral information about body position and movement: Studies with deafferented subjects. In J. Bermundez, A. Marcel, & N. Eilan (Eds.), *The Body and the Self*. London: MIT Press.

Collins, D. W., & Kimura, D. (1997). A large sex difference on a two-dimensional mental rotation task. *Behavioral Neuroscience, 111*, 845–849.

Coren, S. (1989). Cross-cultural studies of visual illusions: The physiological confound. *Behavioral and Brain Sciences, 12*, 76–77.

Croner, L., & Kaplan, E. (1995). Receptive fields of P and M ganglion cells across the primate retina. *Vision Research, 35*, 7–24.

Cross, I. (2001). Music, cognition, culture and evolution. *Annals of the New York Academy of Sciences, 930*, 28–42.

Crummer, G., Walton, J., Wayman, J., Hantz, E., & Frisina, R. (1994). Neural processing of musical timbre by musicians, nonmusicians, and musicians possessing absolute pitch. *Journal of the Acoustical Society of America, 95*, 2720–2727.

Cumming, B. G., Johnston, E. B., & Parker, A. J. (1991). Vertical disparities and perception of three-dimensional shape. *Nature, 349*, 411–413.

Curcio, C. A., Sloan, K. R., Packer, O., Hendrickson, A. E., & Kalina, R. E. (1987). Distribution of cones in human and monkey retina—individual variability and radial symmetry. *Science, 236*, 579–582.

Cutting, J. E. (1978). Generation of synthetic male and female walkers through manipulation of a biomechanical invariant. *Perception, 7*, 393–405.

Cutting, J. E., & Proffitt, D. R. (1981). Gait perception as an example of how we may perceive events. In R. Walk & H. L. Pick (Eds.), *Intersensory Perception and Sensory Integration*. New York: Plenum.

Cynader, M., Berman, N., & Hein, A. (1973). Cats reared in stroboscopic illumination: Effects on receptive fields in visual cortex. *Proceedings of the National Academy of Sciences USA, 70*, 1353–1354.

Dacey, D. M. (2000). Parallel pathways for spectral coding in primate retina. *Annual Review of Neuroscience, 23*, 743–775.

Dacey, D. M., & Packer, O. S. (2003). Colour coding in the primate retina: diverse cell types and cone-specific circuitry. *Current Opinion in Neurobiology, 13*, 421–427.

Darwin, C. J. (1997). Auditory grouping. *Trends in Cognitive Sciences, 1*, 327–333.

De Angelis, G. C., & Newsome, W. T. (1999). Organization of disparity-selective neurons in macaque area MT. *Journal of Neuroscience, 19*, 1398–1415.

de Lange, H. (1958). Research into the dynamic nature of the human fovea-cortex systems with intermittent and modulated light. I. Attenuation characteristics with white and colored light. *Journal of the Optical Society of America, 48,* 777–784.

de Monasterio, F. M., Gouras, P., & Tolhurst, D. J. (1976). Spatial summation, response pattern, and conduction velocity of ganglion cells of the rhesus monkey retina. *Vision Research, 16,* 674–678.

De Valois, R., Albrecht, D., & Thorell, L. (1982). Spatial frequency selectivity of cells in macaque visual cortex. *Vision Research, 22,* 545–559.

Dekaban, A. S., & Sadowsky, D. (1978). Changes in brain weights during the span of human life: Relation of brain weights to body heights and body weights. *Annals of Neurology, 4,* 345–356.

Delcomyn, F. (1998). *Foundations of Neurobiology.* Illinois: Freeman.

Delwiche, J. (2004). The impact of perceptual interactions on perceived flavor. *Food Quality and Preference, 15,* 137–146.

Deregowsky, J. B. (1989). Real space and represented space: Cross-cultural perspectives. *Behavioral and Brain Sciences, 12,* 51–119.

Derrington, A. M., & Lennie, P. (1984). Spatial and temporal contrast sensitivities of neurones in lateral geniculate nucleus of macaque. *Journal of Physiology, 357,* 219–240.

Dichgans, J., & Brandt, T. (1973). Optokinetic motion sickness and pseudo-Coriolis effects induced by moving visual stimuli. *Acta Otolaryngologica, 76,* 339–348.

Dick, M., Ullman, S., & Sagi, D. (1991). Short- and long-range processes in structure-from-motion. *Vision Research, 31,* 2025–2028.

Diederich, A., & Colonius, H. (2004). Modelling the time course of multisensory interaction in manual and saccadic responses. In G. Calvert, C. Spence, & R. Stein (Eds.), *Handbook of Multisensory Processes.* Cambridge, MA: MIT Press.

Dosher, B. A., Landy, M. S., & Sperling, G. (1989). Kinetic depth effect and optic flow. I. 3D shape from Fourier motion. *Vision Research, 29,* 1789–1813.

Doty, R., Green, P., Ram, C., & Yankell, S. (1982). Communication of gender from human breath odor: Relationship to perceived intensity and pleasantness. *Hormones and Behavior, 16,* 13–22.

Doty, R. L., Shaman, P., Applebaum, S. L., Giberson, R., Siksorski, L., & Rosenberg, L. (1984). Smell identification ability: Changes with age. *Science, 226,* 1441–1443.

Dougherty, R. F., Koch, V. M., Brewer, A. A., Fischer, B., Modersitzki, J., & Wandell, B. A. (2003). Visual field representations and locations of visual areas V1/2/3 in human visual cortex. *Journal of Vision, 3,* 586–598.

Duncan, R. O., & Boynton, G. M. (2003). Cortical magnification within human primary visual cortex correlates with acuity thresholds. *Neuron, 38,* 659–671.

Eckman, G., Berglund, B., Berglund, U., & Lindvall, T. (1967). Perceived intensity of odor as a function of time of adaptation. *Scandinavian Journal of Psychology, 8,* 177–186.

Edelman, S. (1995). Representation, similarity, and the chorus of prototypes. *Minds and Machines, 5,* 45–68.

Edelman, S. (1997). Computational theories of object recognition. *Trends in Cognitive Sciences, 1,* 296–304.

Edelman, S., & Duvdevani-Bar, S. (1997). A model of visual recognition and categorization. *Philosophical Transactions of the Royal Society of London, B352,* 1191–1202.

Elbert, T., Pantev, C., Wienbruch, C., Rockstroh, B., & Taub, E. (1995). Increased cortical representation of the fingers of the left hand in string players. *Science, 270,* 305–307.

Emerson, R. C., Bergen, J. R., & Adelson, E. H. (1992). Directionally selective complex cells and the computation of motion energy in the cat visual cortex. *Vision Research, 32,* 203–218.

Engel, A. K., & Singer, W. (2001). Temporal binding and the neural correlates of sensory awareness. *Trends in Cognitive Sciences, 5,* 16–25.

Engen, T. (1982). *The Perception of Odors.* New York: Academic Press.

Engen, T., & Ross, B. (1973). Long-term memory of odors with and without verbal descriptions. *Journal of Experimental Psychology, 100,* 221–227.

Enroth-Cugell, C., & Robson, J. G. (1966). The contrast sensitivity of retinal ganglion cells of the cat. *Journal of Physiology, 187,* 517–552.

Epstein, W. (1966). Perceived depth as a function of relative height under three background conditions. *Journal of Experimental Psychology, 72,* 335–338.

Erickson, R. (1982). The "across-fiber pattern" theory: An organizing principle for molar neural function. *Contributions to Sensory Physiology, 6,* 79–110.

Erickson, R. D., Doetsch, G. S., & Marshall, D. A. (1965). The gustatory neural response function. *Journal of General Physiology, 49,* 247–263.

Evans, E. F., Pratt, S.R., & Cooper, N. P. (1989). Correspondence between behavioural and physiological frequency selectivity in the guinea pig. *British Journal of Audiology, 23*, 151–152.

Fahle, M., & Morgan, M. J. (1996). No transfer of perceptual learning between similar stimuli in the same retinal position. *Current Biology, 6*, 292–297.

Fantz, R. L. (1961). The origins of form perception. *Scientific American, 204*(5), 66–72.

Farah, M. J. (1999). *Visual Agnosia.* Cambridge, MA: MIT Press.

Farrell, J. E. (1984). Visible persistence of moving objects. *Journal of Experimental Psychology: Human Perception and Performance, 10*, 502–511.

Farrell, J. E., Pavel, M., & Sperling, G. (1990). The visible persistence of stimuli in stroboscopic motion. *Vision Research, 30*, 921–936.

Felleman, D. J., & van Essen, D. C. (1991). Distributed hierarchical processing in the primate cerebral cortex. *Cerebral Cortex, 1*, 1–47.

Ferrier, D. (1876). *The Functions of the Brain.* London: Smith Elder & Co.

Field, D. J. (1987). Relations between the statistics of natural images and the response properties of cortical cells. *Journal of the Optical Society of America, A4*, 2379–2394.

Field, D. J., Hayes, A., & Hess, R. F. (1993). Contour integration by the human visual system: Evidence for a local "association field". *Vision Research, 33*, 173–193.

Fisher, S. K., & Ciuffreda, K. J. (1988). Accommodation and apparent distance. *Perception, 17*, 609–621.

Fitzpatrick, D., Itoh, K., & Diamond, I. (1983). The laminar organization of the lateral geniculate body and the striate cortex in the squirrel monkey (saimiri sciureus). *Journal of Neuroscience, 3*, 673–702.

Foster, D. H., & Gilson, S. J. (2002). Recognizing novel three-dimensional objects by summing signals from parts and views. *Proceedings of the Royal Society of London, B269*, 1939–1947.

Foster, D. H., & Nascimento, S. M. C. (1994). Relational colour constancy from invariant cone-excitation ratios. *Proceedings of the Royal Society of London, B257*, 115–121.

Fox, R., & McDaniel, C. (1982). The perception of biological motion by human infants. *Science, 218*, 486–487.

Frisina, D. R., & Frisina, R. D. (1997). Speech recognition in noise and presbycusis: Relations to possible neural mechanisms. *Hearing Research, 106*, 95–104.

Fry, G., Bridgman, C., & Ellerbrock, V. (1949). The effects of atmospheric scattering on binocular depth perception. *American Journal of Optometry, 26*, 9–15.

Garcia, J., & Koelling, R. (1966). Relation of cue to consequence in avoidance learning. *Psychonomic Science, 4*, 123–124.

Gardner, M. B., & Gardner, R. S. (1973). Problem of localization in the median plane: Effect of pinnae cavity occlusion. *Journal of the Acoustical Society of America, 53*, 400–408.

Gegenfurtner, K., & Kiper, D. (2003). Color vision. *Annual Review of Neuroscience, 26*, 181–206.

Geisler, W. S., Perry, J. S., Super, B. J., & Gallogly, D. P. (2001). Edge co-occurrence in natural images predicts contour grouping performance. *Vision Research, 41*, 711–724.

Georgeson, M. A. (1992). Human vision combines oriented filters to compute edges. *Proceedings of the Royal Society of London, B249*, 235–245.

Giaschi, D., Douglas, R., Marlin S., & Cynader, M. (1993). The time course of direction-selective adaptation in simple and complex cells in cat striate cortex. *Journal of Neurophysiology, 70*, 2024–2034.

Gibson, J. J. (1950). *The Perception of the Visual World.* Boston, MA: Houghton Mifflin.

Gibson, J. J., & Radner, M. (1937). Adaptation, after-effect and contrast in the perception of tilted lines. I. Quantitative studies. *Journal of Experimental Psychology, 20*, 453–467.

Gilbert, C. D. (1995). Dynamic properties of adult visual cortex. In M. S. Gazzaniga (Ed.), *The Cognitive Neurosciences.* Cambridge, MA: MIT Press.

Gilbert, C. D., & Wiesel, T. N. (1985). Intrinsic connectivity and receptive field properties in visual cortex. *Vision Research, 25*, 365–374.

Gillam, B., & Borsting, E. (1988). The role of monocular regions in stereoscopic displays. *Perception, 17*, 603–608.

Ginsburg, A. P. (1986). Spatial filtering and visual form perception. In K. Boff, L. Kaufman, & J. Thomas (Eds.), *Handbook of Perception and Human Performance Volume II: Cognitive Processes and Performance.* New York: Wiley.

Girard, P., Salin, P., & Bullier, J. (1991). Visual activity in areas V3a and V3 during reversible inactivation of area V1 in the macaque monkey. *Journal of Neurophysiology, 66*, 1493–1503.

Girard, P., Salin, P., & Bullier, J. (1992). Response selectivity of neurons in area MT of the macaque monkey during reversible inactivation of area V1. *Journal of Neurophysiology, 67*, 1437–1446.

Glennerster, A. (1998). Dmax for stereopsis and motion in random dot displays. *Vision Research, 38*, 925–935.

Glickstein, M. (1985). Ferrier's mistake. *Trends in Neurosciences, 8*, 341–344.

Glickstein, M., & Whitteridge, D. (1987). Tatsuji Inouye and the mapping of the visual fields on the human cerebral cortex. *Trends in Neurosciences, 10*, 350–353.

Goldstein, J. L. (1973). An optimum processor theory for the central formation of the pitch of complex tones. *Journal of the Acoustical Society of America, 54*, 1496–1516.

Goodale, M. A., & Milner, A. D. (1992). Separate visual pathways for perception and action. *Trends in Neurosciences, 15*, 20–25.

Gordon, I. E. (1997). *Theories of Visual Perception.* Chichester, UK: Wiley.

Gray, R., & Regan, D. (1997). Vernier step acuity and bisection acuity for texture-defined form. *Vision Research, 37*, 1713–1723.

Graybiel. A., & Hupp, E. D. (1946). The oculogyral illusion: A form of apparent motion which may be observed following stimulation of the semi-circular canals. *Journal of Aviation Medicine, 17*, 3–27.

Green, D. M., & Swets, J. A. (1966). *Signal Detection Theory and Psychophysics.* Chichester, UK: Wiley.

Gregory, R. L. (1980). Perceptions as hypotheses. *Philosophical Transactions of the Royal Society of London, B290*, 181–197.

Gregory, R .L. (1981). *Mind in Science.* Cambridge: Cambridge University Press.

Gregory, R. L. (1998). *Eye and Brain.* London: Weidenfeld & Nicolson.

Grossman, E. D., & Blake, R. (2002). Brain areas active during visual perception of biological motion. *Neuron, 35*, 1167–1175.

Haber, W. B. (1955). Effects of loss of limb on sensory functions. *The Journal of Psychology, 40*, 115–123.

Hagen, M., & Jones, R. (1978). Cultural effects on pictorial perception: How many words is one picture really worth? In R. Walk & H. Pick (Eds.), *Perception and Experience.* New York: Plenum.

Halpern, D. F. (2000). *Sex Differences in Cognitive Abilities.* Mahwah, NJ: Lawrence Erlbaum Associates, Inc.

Halpern, S. D., Andrews, T. J., & Purves, D. (1999). Interindividual variation in human visual performance. *Journal of Cognitive Neuroscience, 11*, 521–534.

Hammett, S. T., Champion, R. A., Morland, A. B., & Thompson, P. G. (2005). A ratio model of

perceived speed in the human visual system. *Proceedings of the Royal Society of London B*, in press (FirstCite online publication).

Harburn, G., Taylor, C., & Welberry, T. (1975). *Atlas of Optical Transforms.* London: Bell & Hyman.

Harmon, L. D., & Julesz, B. (1973). Masking in visual recognition: effects of two-dimensional filtered noise. *Science, 180*, 1194–1197.

Harris, L. R. (1994). Visual motion caused by self motion. In A. T. Smith & R. J. Snowden (Eds.), *Visual Detection of Motion.* London: Academic Press.

Harris, M. G. (1994). Optic and retinal flow. In A. T. Smith & R. J. Snowden (Eds.), *Visual Detection of Motion.* London: Academic Press.

He, S., Cavanagh, P., & Intriligator, J. (1997). Attentional resolution. *Trends in Cognitive Sciences, 1*, 115–120.

Hecht, E. (2002). *Optics.* Reading, MA: Addison-Wesley.

Helmholtz, H. von (1877). *On the Sensations of Tone as a Physiological Basis for the Theory of Music* (A. J. Ellis Ed.) (1954). New York: Dover.

Helmholtz, H. von (1910). *Treatise on Physiological Optics Vol III* (J. P. C. Southall Ed.) (1962). New York: Dover.

Helmholtz, H. von (1911). *Treatise on Physiological Optics Vol II* (J. P. C. Southall Ed.) (1962). New York: Dover.

Henn, V., Young, L. R., & Finley, C. (1974). Vestibular nucleus units in alert monkeys are also influenced by moving visual fields. *Brain Research, 71*, 144–149.

Hering, E. (1964). *Outlines of a Theory of the Light Sense.* Cambridge, MA: Harvard University Press.

Hess, E. H. (1975). The role of pupil size in communication. *Scientific American, 233*(5), 110–119.

Hess, E. H., & Polt, J. M. (1960). Pupil size as related to interest value of visual stimuli. *Science, 132*, 349–350.

Hildreth, E. C., Ando, H., Anderson, R. A., & Treue, S. (1995). Recovering three-dimensional structure from motion with surface reconstruction. *Vision Research, 35*, 117–137.

Hilgetag, C.-C., O'Neill, M. A., & Young, M. P. (1996). Indeterminate organization of the visual hierarchy. *Science, 271*, 776–777.

Hogben, J. H., & DiLollo, V. (1974). Perceptual integration and perceptual segregation of brief visual stimuli. *Vision Research, 14*, 1059–1069.

Horner, W. G. (1834). On the properties of the Daedaleum, a new instrument of optical illusion.

*London and Edinburgh Philosophical Magazine and Journal of Science, 4,* 36–41.

Howard, I. (1982). *Human Visual Orientation.* New York: Wiley.

Howard, I., & Rogers, B. (1995). *Binocular Vision and Stereopsis.* New York: Oxford University Press.

Hubel, D. (1988). *Eye, Brain, and Vision.* New York: Scientific American Library.

Hubel, D., & Wiesel, T. (1959). Receptive fields of single neurones in the cat's striate cortex. *Journal of Physiology, 148,* 574–591.

Hubel, D., & Wiesel, T. (1962). Receptive fields, binocular interaction and functional architecture in the cat's visual cortex. *Journal of Physiology, 160,* 106–154.

Hubel, D., & Wiesel, T. (1968). Receptive fields and functional architecture of monkey striate cortex. *Journal of Physiology, 195,* 215–243.

Hubel, D., & Wiesel, T. (1974). Uniformity of monkey striate cortex: A parallel relationship between field size, scatter, and magnification factor. *Journal of Comparative Neurology, 158,* 295–306.

Hudson, W. (1960). Pictorial depth perception in sub-cultural groups in Africa. *Journal of Social Psychology, 52,* 183–208.

Hudspeth, A. J., & Konishi, M. (2000). Auditory neuroscience: Development, transduction, and integration. *Proceedings of the National Academy of Sciences USA, 97,* 11690–11691.

Hurlbert, A. (1999). Colour vision: Is colour constancy real? *Current Biology, 9,* R558–R561.

Hurlbert, A. (2003). Colour vision: Primary visual cortex shows its influence. *Current Biology, 13,* R270–R272.

Hurvich, L. M., & Jameson, D. (1957). An opponent-process theory of color vision. *Psychological Review, 64,* 384–390.

Huttenlocher, P., & de Courten, C. (1987). The development of synapses in striate cortex of man. *Human Neurobiology, 6,* 1–9.

Ijspeert, J., Van Den Berg, T., & Spekreijse, H. (1993). An improved mathematical description of the foveal visual point spread function with parameters for age, pupil size, and pigmentation. *Vision Research, 33,* 15–20.

Ittelson, W. (1951). Size as a cue to distance: Static localization. *American Journal of Psychology, 64,* 54–57.

Jacobs, R. A. (2002). What determines visual cue reliability? *Trends in Cognitive Sciences, 6,* 345–350.

Jaeger, W. (1972). Genetics of congenital colour deficiencies. In D. Jameson & L. Hurvich (Eds.), *Handbook of Sensory Physiology Volume VII/4: Visual Psychophysics.* Berlin: Springer-Verlag.

Jahoda, G., & McGurk, H. (1974). Pictorial depth perception in Scottish and Ghanaian children. *International Journal of Psychology, 9,* 255–267.

Jeffress, L. A. (1948). A place theory of sound localization. *Journal of Comparative and Physiological Psychology, 41,* 35–49.

Johansson, G. (1973). Visual perception of biological motion and a model for its analysis. *Perception and Psychophysics, 14,* 201–211.

Johansson, G. (1976). Spatio-temporal differentiation and integration in visual motion perception. *Psychological Research, 38,* 379–393.

Johnson, E. N., Hawken, M., & Shapley, R. (2001). The spatial transformation of colour in the primary visual cortex of the macaque monkey. *Nature Neuroscience, 4,* 409–416.

Johnston, E. B., Cumming, B. G., & Landy, M. S. (1994). Integration of stereo and motion shape cues. *Vision Research, 34,* 2259–2275.

Jones, C. M., Braithwaite, V. A., & Healy, S. D. (2003). The evolution of sex differences in spatial ability. *Behavioral Neuroscience, 117,* 403–411.

Jousmaki, V., & Hari, R. (1998). Parchment skin illusion: Sound-biased touch. *Current Biology, 8,* R190.

Kaas, J. H., & Hackett, T. A. (2000). Subdivisions of auditory cortex and processing streams in primates. *Proceedings of the National Academy of Sciences USA, 97,* 11793–11799.

Kahneman, D., Treisman, A., & Gibbs, B. J. (1992). The reviewing of object files: Object-specific integration of information. *Cognitive Psychology, 24,* 175–219.

Kelly, D. H. (1985). Visual processing of moving stimuli. *Journal of the Optical Society of America, A2,* 216–225.

Kersten, D., Knill, D. C., Mamassian, P., & Bulthoff, I. (1996). Illusory motion from shadows. *Nature, 379,* 31.

Kersten, D., Mamassian, P., & Knill, D. C. (1997). Moving cast shadows induce apparent motion in depth. *Perception, 26,* 171–192.

Kersten, D., & Yuille, A. (2003). Bayesian models of object perception. *Current Opinion in Neurobiology, 13,* 150–158.

Kim, U. K., Jorgenson, E., Coon, H., Leppert, M., Risch, N., & Drayna, D. (2003). Positional cloning of the human quantitative trait locus underlying taste sensitivity to phenylthiocarbamide. *Science, 299,* 1221–1225.

Kim, D. O., Molnar, C. E., & Matthews, J. W. (1980). Cochlear mechanics: Nonlinear behaviour in two-tone responses as reflected in cochlear-nerve-fibre responses and in ear-canal sound pressure. *Journal of the Acoustical Society of America, 67*, 1704–1721.

Kingdom, F., & Moulden, B. P. (1992). A multi-channel approach to brightness coding. *Vision Research, 32*, 1565–1582.

Klatzky, R. L., Lederman, S. J., & Metzger, V. A. (1985). Identifying objects by touch: An expert system. *Perception and Psychophysics, 37*, 299–302.

Knill, D. C. (1998). Discrimination of planar surface slant from texture: Human and ideal observers compared. *Vision Research, 38*, 1683–1711.

Knill, D. C., Kersten, D., & Yuille, A. (1996). Introduction: A Bayesian formulation of visual perception. In D. C. Knill & W. Richards (Eds.), *Perception as Bayesian Inference*. Cambridge: Cambridge University Press.

Knudsen, E. I., & Konishi, M. (1978). A neural map of auditory space in the owl. *Science, 200*, 795–797.

Koenderink, J. J., van Doorn, A. J., & Kappers, A. M. L. (1996). Pictorial surface attitude and local depth comparisons. *Perception and Psychophysics, 58*, 163–173.

Kolers, P. A. (1972). *Aspects of Motion Perception*. Oxford: Pergamon.

Koshland, D. E. (1980). Bacterial chemotaxis in relation to neurobiology. *Annual Review of Neurosciences, 3*, 43–75.

Kozbelt, A. (2001). Artists as experts in visual cognition. *Visual Cognition, 8*, 705–723.

Kozlowski, L. T., & Cutting, J. E. (1977). Recognising the sex of a walker from a dynamic point-light display. *Perception and Psychophysics, 21*, 575–580.

Kraft, J. M., & Brainard, D. H. (1999). Mechanisms of color constancy under nearly natural viewing. *Proceedings of the National Academy of Sciences USA, 96*, 307–312.

Kratskin, I. L. (1995). Functional anatomy, central projections, and neurochemistry of the mammalian olfactory bulb. In: R. L. Doty (Ed.), *Handbook of Olfaction and Gustation*, pp. 103–126. New York: Marcel Dekker.

Krubitzer, L. (1995). The organization of the neocortex in mammals: Are species differences really so different? *Trends in Neurosciences, 18*, 408–417.

Kuffler, S. W. (1953). Discharge patterns and functional organization of mammalian retina. *Journal of Neurophysiology, 16*, 37–68.

Lamme, V. A. F., & Roelfsema, P. R. (2000). The distinct modes of vision offered by feedforward and recurrent processing. *Trends in Neurosciences, 23*, 571–579.

Land, M. F., & Nilsson, D.-E. (2002). *Animal Eyes*. Oxford: Oxford University Press.

Landisman, C. E., & Ts'o, D. (2002). Color processing in macaque striate cortex: Relationships to ocular dominance, cytochrome oxidase, and orientation. *Journal of Neurophysiology, 87*, 3126–3137.

Landy, M. S., Graham, N. (2004). Visual perception of texture. In L. M. Chalupa & J. S. Werner (Eds.), *The Visual Neurosciences* (pp. 1106–1118). Cambridge, MA: MIT Press.

Lashley, K. S., Chow, K.-L., & Semmes, J. (1951). An examination of the electrical field theory of cerebral integration. *Psychological Review, 58*, 123–136.

Laughlin, S. B., & de Ruyter van Steveninck, R. R., & Anderson, J. C. (1998). The metabolic cost of neural information, *Nature Neuroscience, 1*, 36–41.

Ledgeway, T., & Smith, A. T. (1997). Changes in perceived speed following adaptation to first-order and second-order motion. *Vision Research, 37*, 215–224.

Lee, B. B., & Kremers, J., & Yeh, T. (1998). Receptive fields of primate retinal ganglion cells studied with a novel technique. *Visual Neuroscience, 15*, 161–175.

Leibowitz, H. W., & Pick, H. A. (1972). Cross-cultural and educational aspects of the Ponzo perspective illusion. *Perception and Psychophysics, 12*, 430–432.

Lelkens, A. M. M., & Koenderink, J. J. (1984). Illusory motion in visual displays. *Vision Research, 24*, 1083–1090.

Lennie, P. (1998). Single units and visual cortical organisation. *Perception, 27*, 889–935.

Lennie, P. (2000). Color vision: Putting it all together. *Current Biology, 10*, R589–R591.

Lennie, P., Haake, P. W., & Williams, D. R. (1991). The design of chromatically opponent receptive fields. In M. S. Landy & J. A. Movshon (Eds.), *Computational Models of Visual Processing* (pp. 71–82). Cambridge, MA: MIT Press.

Lerdahl, F., & Jackendoff, R. (1983). *A Generative Theory of Tonal Music*. Cambridge, MA: MIT Press

Lettvin, J. Y., Maturana, H. R., McCulloch, W. S., & Pitts, W. H. (1959). What the frog's eye tells the frog's brain. *Proceedings of the Institute of Radio Engineers, 47*, 1940–1959. Reprinted in

McCulloch, W. S. (Ed.) (1965). *Embodiments of Mind*. Cambridge, MA: MIT Press.

Levine, J. (1983). Materialism and qualia: The explanatory gap. *Pacific Philosophical Quarterly, 64*, 354–361.

Levine, J. (1999). Explanatory gap. In R. A. Wilson & F. C. Keil (Eds.), *The MIT Encyclopedia of the Cognitive Sciences*. Cambridge, MA: MIT Press.

Lewis, G. (1926). The conservation of photons. *Nature, 118*, 874–875.

Liberman, A. M., Harris, K. S., Hoffman, H. S., & Griffith, B. C. (1957). The discrimination of speech sounds within and across phoneme boundaries. *Journal of Experimental Psychology, 54*, 358–368.

Linsenmeier, R., Frishman, L., Jakeila, H., & Enroth-Cugell, C. (1982). Receptive field properties of X and Y cells in the cat retina derived from contrast sensitivity measurements. *Vision Research, 22*, 1173–1183.

Lishman, J., & Lee, D. (1973). The autonomy of visual kinaesthesis. *Perception, 2*, 287–294.

Liu, J., & Newsome, W. T. (2003). Functional organization of speed tuned neurons in visual area MT. *Journal of Neurophysiology, 89*, 246–256.

Livingstone, M., & Hubel, D. (1982). Thalamic inputs to cytochrome oxidase-rich regions in monkey visual cortex. *Proceedings of the National Academy of Sciences USA, 79*, 6098–6101.

Locke, S., & Kellar, L. (1973). Categorical perception in a non-linguistic mode. *Cortex, 9*, 353–369.

Logothetis, N., & Sheinburg, D. (1996). Visual object recognition. *Annual Review of Neuroscience, 19*, 577–621.

Lorig, T. (2002). The perception of smell. In D. Roberts (Ed.), *Signals and Perception* (pp. 309–318). Basingstoke: Palgrave Macmillan.

Louis, D. S., Greene, T. L., Jacobson, K. E., Rasmussen, C., Kolowich, P., & Goldstein, S. A. (1984). Evaluation of normal values for stationary and moving two-point discrimination in the hand. *Journal of Hand Surgery, 9*, 553–555.

McBurney, D. (1969). Effects of adaptation on human taste function. In C. Pfaffmann (Ed.), *Olfaction and Taste III*. New York: Rockerfeller University Press.

McGurk, H., & MacDonald, T. (1976). Hearing lips and seeing voices. *Nature, 264*, 746–748.

McLean, J., & Palmer, L. A. (1989). Contribution of linear spatiotemporal receptive field structure to velocity selectivity of simple cells in area 17 of cat. *Vision Research, 29*, 675–679.

Maguire, E. A., Gadian, D. G., Johnsrude, I. S., Good, C. D., Ashburner, J., Frackowiak, R. S., & Frith, C. D. (2000). Navigation-related structural change in the hippocampi of taxi drivers. *Proceedings of the National Academy of Sciences USA, 97*, 4398–4403.

Makous, W. (1998). Optics and photometry. In R. H. S. Carpenter & J. Robson (Eds.), *Vision Research: A Practical Guide to Laboratory Methods*. Oxford: Oxford University Press.

Malnic, B., Hirono, J., Sato, T., & Buck, L. B. (1999). Combinatorial receptor codes for odors. *Cell, 96*, 713–723.

Marr, D. (1976). Early processing of visual information. *Philosophical Transactions of the Royal Society of London, B275*, 483–519.

Marr, D. (1977). Analysis of occluding contour. *Proceedings of the Royal Society of London, B197*, 441–475.

Marr, D. (1980). Visual information processing: The structure and creation of visual representations. *Philosophical Transactions of the Royal Society of London, B290*, 199–218.

Marr, D. (1982). *Vision*. San Francisco, CA: Freeman.

Marr, D., & Hildreth, E. C. (1980). Theory of edge detection. *Proceedings of the Royal Society of London, B207*, 187–217.

Marr, D., & Nishihara, H. K. (1978). Representation and recognition of the spatial organisation of three-dimensional shapes. *Proceedings of the Royal Society of London, B200*, 269–294.

Marr, D., & Poggio, T. (1976). Cooperative computation of stereo disparity. *Science, 194*, 283–287.

Marshall, J., Burbeck, C., Ariely, D., Rolland, J., & Martin, K. (1996). Occlusion edge blur: A cue to relative visual depth. *Journal of the Optical Society of America, A13*, 681–688.

Martin, G. N. (1998). *Human Neuropsychology*. Hemel Hempstead, UK: Prentice Hall.

Masland, R. H. (2001). The fundamental plan of the retina. *Nature Neuroscience, 4*, 877–886.

Mather, G. (1980). The movement after-effect and a distribution shift model of direction coding. *Perception, 9*, 379–392.

Mather, G. (1989). Early motion processes and the Kinetic Depth Effect. *Quarterly Journal of Experimental Psychology, 41*, 183–198.

Mather, G. (1996). Image blur as a pictorial depth cue. *Proceedings of the Royal Society of London, B263*, 169–172.

Mather, G., Radford, K., & West, S. (1992). Low-level visual processing of biological motion. *Proceedings of the Royal Society of London, B249*, 149–155.

Mather, G., & Smith, D. R. R. (2000). Depth cue integration: Stereopsis and image blur. *Vision Research, 40*, 3501–3506.

Mather, G., & Smith, D. R. R. (2002). Blur discrimination and its relation to blur-mediated depth perception. *Perception, 31*, 1211–1219.

Mather, G., & Tunley, H. (1995). Temporal filtering enhances direction discrimination in random dot patterns. *Vision Research, 35*, 2105–2116.

Mather, G., Verstraten, F., & Anstis, S. (Eds.) (1998). *The Motion Aftereffect: A Modern Perspective.* Cambridge, MA: MIT Press.

Mather, G., & West, S. (1993). Evidence for second-order motion detectors. *Vision Research, 33*, 1109–1112.

Matthews, N., Meng, X., Xu, P., & Qian, N. (2003). A physiological theory of depth perception from vertical disparity. *Vision Research, 43*, 85–99.

Mayhew, J. E. W., & Frisby, J. P. (1981). Psychophysical and computational studies towards a theory of human stereopsis. *Artificial Intelligence, 17*, 349–385.

Mayhew, J. E. W., & Longuet-Higgins, H. C. (1982). A computational model of binocular depth perception. *Nature, 297*, 376–379.

Meisami, E., Mikhail, L., Baim, D., & Bhatnagar, K. P. (1998). Human olfactory bulb: Aging of glomeruli and mitral cells and a search for the accessory olfactory bulb. *Annals of the New York Academy of Sciences, 855*, 708–715.

Melzack, R. (1990). Phantom limbs and the concept of a neuromatrix. *Trends in Neurosciences, 13*, 88–92.

Merigan, W. (1996). Basic visual capacities and shape discrimination after lesions of extrastriate area V4 in macaques. *Visual Neuroscience, 13*, 51–60.

Merigan, W. H., & Eskin, T. A. (1986). Spatiotemporal vision of macaques with severe loss of P$_\beta$ retinal ganglion cells. *Vision Research, 26*, 1751–1761.

Merigan, W., Nealey, T., & Maunsell, J. (1993). Visual effects of lesions of cortical area V2 in macaques. *Journal of Neuroscience, 13*, 3180–3191.

Merzenich, M., Nelson, R. J., Stryker, M. P., Cynader, M. S., Schoppmann, A., & Zook, J. M. (1984). Somatosensory cortical map changes following digit amputation in adult monkeys. *Journal of Comparative Neurology, 224*, 591–605.

Michotte, A. (1963). *The Perception of Causality.* London: Methuen.

Mikami, A., Newsome, W. T., & Wurtz, R. H. (1986). Motion selectivity in macaque visual cortex. II. Spatiotemporal range of directional interactions in MT and V1. *Journal of Neurophysiology, 55*, 1328–1339.

Miller, G. (2000). Evolution of human music through sexual selection. In N. Wallin, B. Merker, & S. Brown (Eds.), *The Origins of Music* (pp. 329–360). Cambridge, MA: MIT Press.

Miller, I. J., & Reedy, F. E. (1990). Variations in human taste bud density and taste intensity perception. *Physiology and Behavior, 47*, 1213–1219.

Mollon, J. (1993). George Palmer (1740–1795). In C. Nicholls (Ed.), *The Dictionary of National Biography: Missing Persons* (pp. 509–510). Oxford: Oxford University Press.

Mon-Williams, M., & Tresilian, J. R. (2000). An ordinal role for accommodation in distance perception. *Ergonomics, 43*, 391–404.

Moncrieff, R. (1956). Olfactory adaptation and odour likeness. *Journal of Physiology, 133*, 301–316.

Monnier, P., & Shevell, S. K. (2003). Large shifts in color appearance from patterned chromatic backgrounds. *Nature Neuroscience, 6*, 801–802.

Moore, B. C. J. (1973). Frequency difference limens for short-duration tones. *Journal of the Acoustical Society of America, 54*, 610–619.

Moore, B. C. J. (1997). *An Introduction to the Psychology of Hearing.* San Diego, CA: Academic Press.

Moore, B. C. J., & Glasberg, B. R. (1986). The role of frequency selectivity in the perception of loudness, pitch, and time. In B. C. J. Moore (Ed.), *Frequency Selectivity in Hearing.* London: Academic Press.

Morgan, M. (2003). *The Space Between Our Ears.* London: Weidenfeld & Nicolson.

Morgan, M. J. (1980). Analogue models of motion perception. *Philosophical Transactions of the Royal Society of London, B290*, 117–135.

Morgan, M. J. (1986). Positional acuity without monocular cues. *Perception, 15*, 157–162.

Morgan, M. J. (1992). Spatial filtering precedes motion detection. *Nature, 355*, 344–346.

Morgan, M. J. (1996). Visual illusions. In V. Bruce (Ed.), *Unsolved Mysteries of the Mind.* Hove, UK: Psychology Press.

Morgan, M. J., & Cleary, R. (1992). Ambiguous motion in a two-frame sequence. *Vision Research, 32*, 2195–2198.

Morgan, M. J., & Hotopf, N. (1989). Perceived diagonals in grids and lattices. *Vision Research, 29*, 1005–1015.

Morgan, M. J., & Watt, R. J. (1982). Mechanisms of interpolation in human spatial vision. *Nature, 299*, 553–555.

Morgan, M. J., & Watt, R. J. (1997). The combination of filters in early spatial vision: A retrospective analysis of the MIRAGE model. *Perception, 26*, 1073–1088.

Morrell, C. H., Gordon-Salant, S., Pearson, J. D., Brant, L. J., & Fozard, J. L. (1996). Age- and gender-specific reference ranges for hearing level and longitudinal changes in hearing level. *Journal of the Acoustical Society of America, 100*, 1949–1967.

Morrison, J. H., & Hof, P. R. (1997). Changes in cortical circuits during aging. *Clinical Neuroscience Research, 2*, 294–304.

Morrone, M. C., & Burr, D. C. (1988). Feature detection in human vision: A phase-dependent energy model. *Proceedings of the Royal Society of London, B235*, 221–245.

Morrone, M. C., Burr, D. C., & Ross, J. (1994). Illusory brightness step in the Chevreul illusion. *Vision Research, 34*, 1567–1574.

Moulden, B. (1980). After-effects and the integration of patterns of neural activity within a channel. *Philosophical Transactions of the Royal Society of London, B290*, 39–55.

Moulden, B. (1994). Collator units: Second-stage orientational filters. In G. R. Bock & J. A. Goode (Eds.), *Higher-order Processing in the Visual System. Ciba Foundation Symposium 184* (pp. 170–184). Chichester, UK: Wiley.

Moulden, B., & Kingdom, F. (1987). Effect of the number of grey levels on the detectability of a simple line signal in visual noise. *Spatial Vision, 2*, 61–77.

Mountcastle, V. (1957). Modality and topographic properties of single neurons of cat's somatic sensory cortex. *Journal of Neurophysiology, 20*, 408–434.

Movshon, J. A., & Blakemore, C. B. (1973). Orientation specificity and spatial selectivity in human vision. *Perception, 2*, 53–60.

Mueller, C. G. (1951). Frequency of seeing functions for intensity discrimination at various levels of adapting intensity. *Journal of General Physiology, 34*, 463–474.

Nakayama, K., He, Z. J., & Shimojo, S. (1995). Visual surface representation: A critical link between lower-level and higher-level vision. In S. Kosslyn & D. Osherson (Eds.), *Visual Cognition: An Invitation to Cognitive Science* (Vol. 2, 2nd ed.). Cambridge, MA: MIT Press.

Nakayama, K., Shimojo, S., & Silverman, G. H. (1989). Stereoscopic depth: Its relation to image segmentation, grouping and the recognition of occluded objects. *Perception, 18*, 55–68.

Nathans, J. (1989). The genes for color vision. *Scientific American, 260*(1), 42–49.

Nealey, T. A., & Maunsell, J. H. (1994). Magnocellular and parvocellular contributions to the responses of neurons in macaque striate cortex. *Journal of Neuroscience, 14*, 2069–2079.

Neri, P., Morrone, M. C., & Burr, D. C. (1998). Seeing biological motion. *Nature, 395*, 894–896.

Newell, A., & Simon, H. A. (1972). *Human Problem Solving*. Englewood Cliffs, NJ: Prentice Hall.

Newsome, W. T., Mikami, A., & Wurtz, R. H. (1986). Motion selectivity in macaque visual cortex. III. Psychophysics and physiology of apparent motion. *Journal of Neurophysiology, 55*, 1340–1351.

Newsome, W. T., Wurtz, R., Dursteler, M., & Mikami, A. (1985). Deficits in visual motion processing following ibotenic acid lesions of the middle temporal visual area. *Journal of Neuroscience, 5*, 825–840.

Nishida, S., Ledgeway, T., & Edwards, M. (1997). Dual multiple-scale processing for motion in the human visual system. *Vision Research, 37*, 2685–2698.

Nishida, S., & Sato, T. (1995). Motion aftereffect with flickering test patterns reveals higher stages of motion processing. *Vision Research, 35*, 477–490.

Nothdurft, H. C. (1993). The role of features in preattentive vision: Comparison of orientation, motion and colour cues. *Vision Research, 33*, 1937–1958.

Nowlis, G., & Frank, M. (1977). Qualities in hamster taste: Behavioral and neural evidence. In J. Le Magnen & P. MacLeod (Eds.), *Olfaction and Taste VI* (pp. 241–247). London: Information Retrieval.

Nozza, R. J. (1995). Estimating the contribution of non-sensory factors to infant–adult differences in behavioral thresholds. *Hearing Research, 91*, 72–78.

O'Keefe, L., & Movshon, J. A. (1998). Processing of first- and second-order motion signals by neurons in area Mt of the macaque monkey. *Visual Neuroscience, 15*, 305–317.

Olsho, L. W., Koch, E. G., Carter, E. A., Halpin, C. F., & Spetner, N. B. (1988). Pure-tone sensitivity of human infants. *Journal of the Acoustical Society of America, 84*, 1316–1324.

Ooi, T. L., Wu, B., & He, Z. J. J. (2001). Distance determined by the angular declination below the horizon. *Nature, 414*, 197–200.

O'Shea, R., Blackburn, S. G., & Ono, H. (1994). Contrast as a depth cue. *Vision Research, 34*, 1595–1604.

Osterberg, G. (1935). Topography of the layer of rods and cones in the human retina. *Acta Ophthalmologica, Supplement 6*, 1–103.

Overheim, R. D., & Wagner, D. L. (1982). *Light and Color*. New York: John Wiley & Sons, Inc.

Owsley, C., Sekuler, R., & Siemsen, D. (1983). Contrast sensitivity throughout adulthood. *Vision Research, 23*, 689–699.

Palmer, A. R. (1995). Neural signal processing. In B. C. J. Moore (Ed.), *Hearing*. San Diego, CA: Academic Press.

Palmer, A. R., & Russell, I. J. (1986). Phase-locking in the cochlear nerve of the guinea-pig and its relation to the receptor potential of inner hair cells. *Hearing Research, 24*, 1–15.

Palmer, S. E., Rosch, E., & Chase, P. (1981). Canonical perspective and the perception of objects. In J. Long & A. D. Baddeley (Eds.), *Attention and Performance IX*. Hillsdale, NJ: Lawrence Erlbaum Associates, Inc.

Pantle, A. J., & Sekuler, R. W. (1968). Velocity-sensitive elements in human vision: Initial psychophysical evidence. *Vision Research, 8*, 445–450.

Parsons, R. D. (1970). Magnitude estimates of the oculogyral illusion during and following angular acceleration. *Journal of Experimental Psychology, 84*, 230–238.

Patel, A. (2003). Language, music, syntax and the brain. *Nature Neuroscience, 6*, 674–681.

Paul-Brown, D. (1996). Central auditory processing: Current status of research and implications for clinical practice. *American Journal of Audiology, 5*, 41–54.

Paulesu, E., Harrison, J., Baron-Cohen, S., Watson, J. D., Goldstein, L., Heather, J., Frackowiak, R. S., & Frith, C. D. (1995). The physiology of coloured hearing. A PET activation study of colour-word synaesthesia. *Brain, 118*, 661–676.

Paus, T., Zijdenbos, A., Worsley, K., Collins, D. L., Blumenthal, J., Giedd, J. N., Rapoport, J., & Evans, A. C. (1999). Structural maturation of neural pathways in children and adolescents: In vivo study. *Science, 283*, 1908–1911.

Penfield, W., & Rasmussen, T. (1950). *The Cerebral Cortex of Man: A Clinical Study of Localization of Function*. New York: Macmillan.

Pentland, A. P. (1987). A new sense for depth of field. *IEEE Transactions on Pattern Analysis and Machine Intelligence, 9*, 523–531.

Peretz, I., & Coltheart, M. (2003). Modularity of music processing. *Nature Neuroscience, 6*, 688–691.

Perrett, D., Harries, M., Mistlin, A. J., & Chitty, A. J. (1990). Three stages in the classification of body movements by visual neurons. In H. B. Barlow, C. Blakemore, & M. Weston-Smith, (Eds.), *Images and Understanding* (pp. 94–107). Cambridge: Cambridge University Press.

Perrett, D. I., Rolls, E. T., & Caan, W. (1982). Visual neurones responsive to faces in the monkey temporal cortex. *Experimental Brain Research, 47*, 329–342.

Perry, V., Oehler, R., & Cowey, A. (1984). Retinal ganglion cells that project to the dorsal latergal geniculate nucleus in the macaque monkey. *Neuroscience, 12*, 1101–1123.

Peters, A. (2002). Structural changes that occur during normal aging of primate cerebral hemispheres. *Neuroscience and Behavioral Reviews, 26*, 733–741.

Petersen, S., Baker, J., & Allman, J. (1985). Direction-specific adaptation in area MT of the owl monkey. *Brain Research, 346*, 146–150.

Pettet, M. W., McKee, S. P., & Grzywacz, N. (1998). Constraints on long range interactions mediating contour detection. *Vision Research, 38*, 865–879.

Piantanida, T. (1991). Genetics of inherited colour vision deficiencies. In J. Cronly-Dillon & D. H. Foster (Eds.), *Vision and Visual Dysfunction Volume VII: Inherited and Acquired Colour Vision Deficiencies* (pp. 88–114). Basingstoke: Macmillan.

Pinker, S. (1997). *How the Mind Works*. London: Allen Lane.

Pirenne, H. (1948). *Vision and the Eye*. London: Chapman & Hall.

Pirenne, M. (1962). Dark-adaptation and night vision. In H. Davson (Ed.), *The Eye* (Vol. 2, pp. 93–122). New York: Academic Press.

Plack, C. J., & Carlyon, R. P. (1995). Loudness perception and intensity coding. In B. C. J. Moore (Ed.), *Hearing*. San Diego, CA: Academic Press.

Plant, G. T. (1991). Temporal properties of normal and abnormal spatial vision. In J. Cronly-Dillon & D. Regan (Eds.), *Vision and Visual Dysfunction Volume X: Spatial Vision* (pp. 43–63). Basingstoke: Macmillan.

Plomp, R. (1967). Pitch of complex tones. *Journal of the Acoustical Society of America, 41*, 1526–1533.

Poggio, G. F., & Talbot, W. H. (1981). Mechanisms of static and dynamic stereopsis in foveal cortex of the rhesus monkey. *Journal of Physiology, 315*, 469–492.

Pokorny, J., & Smith, V. C. (1986). Colorimetry and color discrimination. In K. R. Boff, L. Kaufman, & J. P. Thomas (Eds.), *Handbook of Perception and Human Performance Volume I: Sensory Processes and Perception*. New York: Wiley.

Polat, U., & Sagi, D. (1994). The architecture of perceptual spatial interactions. *Vision Research, 34*, 73–78.

Pollack, R. H. (1989). Pictures, maybe; illusions, no. *Behavioral and Brain Sciences, 12*, 92–93.

Pollard, S. B., Mayhew, J. E. W., & Frisby, J. P. (1985). PMF: A stereo correspondence algorithm using a disparity gradient limit. *Perception, 14*, 449–470.

Pons, T. P., Garraghty, P. E., Ommaya, A. K., Kaas, J. H., Taub, E., & Mishkin, M. (1991). Massive cortical reorganization after sensory deafferentation in adult macaques. *Science, 252*, 1857–1860.

Popper, K. (1963). *Conjectures and Refutations: The Growth of Scientific Knowledge*. London: Routledge.

Purves, D., Augustine, G., Fitzpatrick, D., Katz, L., LaMantia, A., McNamara, J., & Williams, S. (Eds.) (2001). *Neuroscience* (2nd ed.). Sunderland, MA: Sinauer.

Pylyshyn, Z. W., & Storm, R. W. (1988). Tracking multiple independent targets: Evidence for a parallel tracking mechanism. *Spatial Vision, 3*, 1–19.

Quinlan, P. T., & Humphreys, G. W. (1993). Perceptual frames of reference and 2-dimensional shape recognition—further examination of internal axes. *Perception, 22*, 1343–1364.

Rabin, M. D. (1988). Experience facilitates olfactory quality discrimination. *Perception and Psychophysics, 44*, 532–540.

Radeau, M. (1994). Auditory-visual interaction and modularity. *Current Psychology of Cognition, 13*, 3–51.

Ramachandran, V. S., & Blakesee, S. (1998). *Phantoms in the Brain: Probing the Mysteries of the Human Mind*. New York: William Morrow.

Ramachandran, V. S., Rao, V. M., & Vidyasagar, T. R. (1973). Apparent movement with subjective contours. *Vision Research, 13*, 1399–1401.

Rasch, R., & Plomp, R. (1999). The perception of musical tones. In D. Deutsch (Ed.), *The Psychology of Music* (2nd ed., pp. 89–112). San Diego, CA: Academic Press.

Rauschecker, J. P., & Tian, B. (2000). Mechanisms and streams for processing of "what" and "where" in auditory cortex. *Proceedings of the National Academy of Sciences USA, 97*, 11800–11806.

Rawson, N. E., Gomez, G., Cowart, B., & Restrepo, D. (1998). The use of olfactory receptor neurons (ORNs) from biopsies to study changes in aging and neurodegenerative diseases. *Annals of the New York Academy of Sciences, 855*, 701–707.

Raymond, J. E. (2000). Attentional modulation of visual motion perception. *Trends in Cognitive Science, 4*, 42–49.

Regan, B., Julliot, C., Simmen, F., Vienot, P., Charles-Dominique, P., & Mollon, J. (2001). Fruits, foliage and the evolution of primate colour vision. *Philosophical Transactions of the Royal Society of London, B356*, 229–283.

Reichardt, W. (1961). Autocorrelation, a principle for the evaluation of sensory information by the central nervous system. In W. Rosenblith (Ed.), *Sensory Communication* (pp. 303–317). New York: MIT Press.

Reid, R. C., & Shapley, R. M. (2002). Space and time maps of cone photoreceptor signals in macaque lateral geniculate nucleus. *Journal of Neuroscience, 22*, 6158–6175.

Rensink, R. A., O'Regan, J. K., & Clark, J. J. (1997). To see or not to see: The need for attention to perceive changes in scenes. *Psychological Science, 8*, 368–373.

Ressler, K., Sullivan, S., & Buck, L. (1994). A molecular dissection of spatial patterning in the olfactory system. *Current Opinion in Neurobiology, 4*, 588–596.

Riesenhuber, M., & Poggio, T. (2000). Models of object recognition. *Nature Neuroscience, 3*, 1199–1204.

Robles, L., Ruggiero, M. A., & Rich, N. C. (1986). Basilar membrane mechanics at the base of the chinchilla cochlea. I. Input–output functions, tuning curves, and response phases. *Journal of the Acoustical Society of America, 80*, 1364–1374.

Robson, J. G. (1966). Spatial and temporal contrast sensitivity functions of the visual system. *Journal of the Optical Society of America, 8*, 1141–1142.

Rock, I. (1983). *The Logic of Perception*. Cambridge, MA: MIT Press.

Rock, I., & Palmer, S. (1990). The legacy of Gestalt Psychology. *Scientific American, 263*(6), 48–61.

Rodieck, R. W. (1965). Quantitative analysis of cat retinal ganglion cell response to visual stimuli. *Vision Research, 5*, 583–601.

Rodieck, R. W. (1998). *The First Steps in Seeing*. Sunderland, MA: Sinauer Associates.

Rogers, B. J., & Bradshaw, M. F. (1993). Vertical disparities, differential perspective and binocular stereopsis. *Nature, 361*, 253–255.

Rogers, B. J., & Graham, M. (1979). Motion parallax as an independent cue for depth perception. *Perception, 8*, 125–134.

Rolls, E. T. (2002). The cortical representation of taste and smell. In: C. Rouby, B. Schaal, D. Dubois, R. Gervais, & A. Holley (Eds.) *Olfaction, Taste, and Cognition*. Cambridge, UK: Cambridge University Press.

Roorda, A., Metha, A., Lennie, P., & Williams, D. R. (2001). Packing arrangement of the three cone classes in the primate retina. *Vision Research, 41*, 1291–1306.

Rosner, B., & Meyer, L. (1982). Melodic processes and the perception of music. In D. Deutsch (Ed.), *The Psychology of Music* (1st ed.). New York: Academic Press.

Ruddock, K. (1991). Psychophysics of inherited colour vision deficiencies. In J. Cronly-Dillon & D. H. Foster (Eds.), *Vision and Visual Dysfunction Volume VII: Inherited and Acquired Colour Vision Deficiencies* (pp. 4–37). Basingstoke: Macmillan.

Sachs, M. B., & Kiang, N. Y. S. (1968). Two-tone inhibition in auditory nerve fibres. *Journal of the Acoustical Society of America, 43*, 1120–1128.

Sacks, O., & Wasserman, R. (1987). The case of the colorblind painter. *The New York Review, Nov*, 25–33.

Sceniak, M., Hawken, M., & Shapley, R. (2001). Visual spatial characterization of Macaque V1 neurons. *Journal of Neurophysiology, 85*, 1873–1887.

Schiffman, S. S. (1983). Taste and smell in disease. *New England Journal of Medicine, 308*, 1275–1279, 1337–1343.

Schiller, P., Sandell, J., & Maunsell, J. (1986). Functions of the ON and OFF channels of the visual system. *Nature, 322*, 824–825.

Schmidt, R. F. (Ed.) (1981). *Fundamentals of Sensory Physiology*. Berlin: Springer-Verlag.

Schmolesky, M. T., Wang, Y., Hanes, D. P., Thompson, K. G., Leutgeb, S., Schall, D., & Leventhal, A. G. (1998). Signal timing across the macaque visual system. *Journal of Neurophysiology, 79*, 3272–3278.

Schnapf, J., & Baylor, D. (1987). How photoreceptor cells respond to light. *Scientific American, 256*(4), 32–39.

Schooneveldt, G. P., & Moore, B. C. J. (1989). Comodulation masking release (CMR) as a function of masker bandwidth, modulator bandwidth and signal duration. *Journal of the Acoustical Society of America, 85*, 273–281.

Schreiber, K., Crawford, J. D., Fetter, M., & Tweed, D. (2001). The motor side of depth vision. *Nature, 410*, 819–822.

Schwartz, S., Maquet, P., & Frith, C. (2002). Neural correlates of perceptual learning: A functional MRI study of visual texture discrimination. *Proceedings of the National Academy of Sciences USA, 99*, 17137–17142.

Scott, S., Young, A., Calder, A., Hellawell, D., Aggleton. J., & Johnson, M. (1997). Impaired recognition of fear and anger following bilateral amygdala lesions. *Nature, 385*, 254–257.

Scott, S. K., Blank, C. C., Rosen, S., & Wise, R. J. S. (2000). Identification of a pathway for intelligible speech in the left temporal lobe. *Brain, 123*, 2400–2406.

Segall, M., Campbell, D., & Herskovits, M. (1963). Cultural differences in the perception of geometrical illusions. *Science, 139*, 769–771.

Seiffert, A. E., & Cavanagh, P. (1998). Position displacement, not velocity, is the cue to motion detection of second-order stimuli. *Vision Research, 38*, 3569–3582.

Sharpe, L. T., & Stockman, A. (1999). Rod pathways: The importance of seeing nothing. *Trends in Neurosciences, 22*, 497–504.

Shepard, R. N., & Metzler, J. (1971). Mental rotation of three-dimensional objects. *Science, 171*, 701–703.

Shepherd, G. (1988). *Neurobiology*. New York: Oxford University Press.

Shepherd, G. M. (1994). Discrimination of molecular signals by the olfactory receptor neuron. *Neuron, 13*, 771–790.

Sherman, P. D. (1981). *Colour Vision in the Nineteenth Century: The Young-Helmholtz-Maxwell Theory*. Bristol: Hilger.

Shimokata, H., & Kuzuya, F. (1995). Two-point discrimination test of the skin as an index of sensory aging. *Gerontology, 41*, 267–272.

Sicard, G., & Holley, A. (1984). Receptor cell responses to odorants: Similarities among odorants. *Brain Research, 292*, 283–296.

Sillito, A., & Jones, H. (2002). Corticothalamic interactions in the transfer of visual information. *Philosophical Transactions of the Royal Society of London, B357*, 1739–1752.

Simoncelli, E., & Heeger, D. (1998). A model of neuronal responses in visual area MT. *Vision Research, 38*, 743–761.

Simons, D. J., & Levin, D. T. (1997). Change blindness. *Trends in Cognitive Science, 1*, 261–267.

Smith, A. T. (1994). Correspondence-based and energy-based detection of second-order motion in human vision. *Journal of the Optical Society of America, A11*, 1940–1948.

Smith, A. T., & Edgar, G. K. (1994). Antagonistic comparison of temporal frequency filter outputs as a basis for speed perception. *Vision Research, 34, 253–265.*

Smith, A. T., & Ledgeway, T. (2001). Motion detection in human vision: A unifying approach based on energy and features. *Proceedings of the Royal Society of London, B268*, 1889–1899.

Smith, C. U. M. (2000). *Biology of Sensory Systems.* Chichester, UK: Wiley.

Snowden, R. J., Treue, S., Erickson, R. G., & Andersen, R. A. (1991). The response of area MT neurons to transparent motion. *Journal of Neuroscience, 11*, 2768–2785.

Spence, C. (2002). Multisensory integration, attention, and perception. In D. Roberts (Ed.), *Signals and Perception* (pp. 345–354). Basingstoke: Palgrave Macmillan.

Spence, C., & Read, L. (2003). Speech shadowing while driving: On the difficulty of splitting attention between eye and ear. *Psychological Science, 14*, 251–256.

Sperling, G., & Lu, Z-L. (1998). A systems analysis of visual motion perception. In T. Watanabe (Ed.), *High-level Motion Processing* (pp. 153–183). Cambridge, MA: MIT Press.

Stanislaw, H., & Todorov, N. (1999). Calculation of signal detection theory measures. *Behavior Research Methods, Instruments and Computers, 31*, 137–149.

Stevens, S. S. (1961). Psychophysics of sensory function. In W. A. Rosenblith (Ed.), *Sensory Communication.* Cambridge, MA: MIT Press.

Stevenson, S. B., & Schor, C. M. (1997). Human stereo matching is not restricted to epipolar lines. *Vision Research, 37*, 2717–2723.

Stockman, A., & Sharpe, L. (2000). The spectral sensitivities of the middle- and long-wavelength-sensitive cones derived from measurements in observers of known genotype. *Vision Research, 40*, 1711–1737.

Stoddart, D. (1990). *The Scented Ape.* Cambridge: Cambridge University Press.

Surridge, A., Osorio, D., & Mundy, N. (2003). Evolution and selection of trichromatic vision in primates. *Trends in Ecology and Evolution, 18*, 198–205.

Tanaka, K. (1993). Neural mechanisms of object recognition. *Science, 262*, 685–688.

Tanaka, K. (1998). Representation of visual motion in the extrastriate visual cortex. In T. Watanabe (Ed.), *High-Level Motion Processing.* Cambridge, MA: MIT Press.

Tanaka, K., & Saito, H. (1989). Analysis of motion of the visual field by direction, expansion/contraction and rotation cells clustered in the dorsal part of the medial superior temporal area of the macaque monkey. *Journal of Neurophysiology, 62*, 626–641.

Tarr, M. J., & Bulthoff, H. H. (1995). Is human object recognition better described by geon structural descriptions or by multiple views? Comment on Biederman and Gerhardstein (1993). *Journal of Experimental Psychology: Human Perception and Performance, 21*, 1494–1505.

Teller, D. (1984). Linking propositions. *Vision Research, 24*, 1233–1246.

Thines, G., Costall, A., & Butterworth, G. (Eds.) (1991). *Michotte's Experimental Phenomenology of Perception.* Hillsdale, NJ: Lawrence Erlbaum Associates, Inc.

Thouless, R. (1931). Individual differences in phenomenal regression. *British Journal of Psychology, 22*, 216–241.

Timney, B. N., & Muir, D. W. (1976). Orientation anisotropy: Incidence and magnitude in Caucasian and Chinese subjects. *Science, 193*, 699–701.

Titchener, E. B. (1902). *An Outline of Psychology.* London: Macmillan.

Todd, J. T., Akerstrom, R. A., Reichel, F. D., & Hayes, W. (1988). Apparent rotation in 3-dimensional space: Effects of temporal, spatial and structural factors. *Perception and Psychophysics, 43*, 179–188.

Tolhurst, D. J. (1973). Separate channels for the analysis of the shape and the movement of a moving visual stimulus. *Journal of Physiology, 231*, 385–402.

Tootell, R. B. H., Hadjikhani, N. K., Mendola, J. D., Marrett, S., & Dale, A. M. (1998). From retinotopy to recognition: fMRI in human visual cortex. *Trends in Cognitive Sciences, 2*, 174–183.

Tootell, R. B. H., Reppas, J. B., Dale, A. M., Look, R. B., Sereno, M. I., Malach, R., Brady, T. J., & Rosen, B. R. (1995). Visual motion aftereffect in human cortical area MT revealed by functional magnetic resonance imaging. *Nature, 375*, 139–141.

Tootell, R. B. H., Silverman, M. S., De Valois, R. L., & Jacobs, G. H. (1983). Functional organization of the second cortical visual area of primates. *Science, 220*, 737–739.

Tootell, R. B. H., Silverman, M., Switckes, E., & De Valois, R. (1982). Deoxyglucose analysis of retinotopic organization in primate striate cortex. *Science, 218*, 902–904.

Treue, S., & Trujillo, M. (1999). Feature-based attention influences motion processing gain in macaque visual cortex. *Nature, 399*, 575–579.

Tse, P., & Cavanagh, P., Nakayama, K. (1998). The role of parsing in high-level motion processing. In T. Watanabe (Ed.), *High-Level Motion Processing* (pp. 249–266). Cambridge, MA: MIT Press.

Turnbull, H. W. (1959). *The Correspondence of Isaac Newton, Volume 1*. Cambridge: Cambridge University Press.

Tyler, C. W., & Clark, M. B. (1990). The autostereogram. In J. O. Merritt & S. S. Fisher (Eds.), *Stereoscopic Displays and Applications. S.P.I.E. Proceedings, 1256*, 182–197.

Ullman, S. (1979). *The Interpretation of Visual Motion*. Cambridge, MA: MIT Press.

Ullman, S. (1984a). Visual routines. *Cognition, 18*, 97–159.

Ullman, S. (1984b). Maximising rigidity: The incremental recovery of 3-D stucture from rigid and nonrigid motion. *Perception, 13*, 255–274.

Ullman, S. (1998). Three-dimensional object recognition based on the combination of views. *Cognition, 67*, 21–44.

Ungerleider, L. G., & Mishkin, M. (1982). Two cortical visual systems. In D. J. Ingle, M. A. Goodale, & R. J. W. Mansfield (Eds.), *Analysis of Visual Behavior* (pp. 549–586). Cambridge, MA: MIT Press.

*United States Naval Flight Surgeon's Manual, Third Edition* (1991). Naval Aerospace Medical Institute. Available online at: <http://www.vnh.org/FSManual/fsm91.html>

Viemeister, N. F. (1983). Auditory intensity discrimination at high frequencies in the presence of noise. *Science, 221*, 1206–1208.

Vignier, A., Clement, G., & Trotter, Y. (2001). Distance perception within near visual space. *Perception, 30*, 115–124.

Vogten, L. L. M. (1974). Pre-tone masking: A new result from a new method. In E. Zwicker &

E. Terhardt (Eds.), *Facts and Models in Hearing*. Berlin: Springer-Verlag.

Voyer, D., Voyer, S., & Bryden, M. P. (1995). Magnitude of sex differences in spatial abilities: A meta-analysis and consideration of critical variables. *Psychological Bulletin, 117*, 250–270.

Wachtler, T., Sejnowski, T. J., & Albright, T. D. (2003). Representation of color stimuli in awake Macaque primary visual cortex. *Neuron, 37*, 681–691.

Wade, N. (1983) *Brewster and Wheatstone on Vision*. London: Academic Press.

Wade, N. (2000). William Charles Wells (1757–1817) and vestibular research before Purkinje and Flourens. *Journal of Vestibular Research, 10*, 127–137.

Wallach, H., & O'Leary, A. (1982). Slope of regard as a distance cue. *Perception and Psychophysics, 31*, 145–148.

Walls, G. (1963). *The Vertebrate Eye and its Adaptive Radiations*. New York: Hafner.

Wandell, B. (1995). *Foundations of Vision*. Sunderland, MA: Sinauer Associates.

Warrant, E. J., & Nilsson, D.-E. (1998). Absorption of white light in photoreceptors. *Vision Research, 38*, 195–207.

Watt, R. J. (1988). *Visual Processing*. Hove, UK: Psychology Press.

Watt, R. J., & Morgan, M. J. (1985). A theory of the primitive spatial code in human vision. *Vision Research, 25*, 1661–1674.

Weale, R. (1991). Effects of senescence. In J. Cronly-Dillon, J. J. Kulikowski, V. Walsh, & I. J. Murray (Eds.), *Vision and Visual Dysfunction Volume V: Limits of Vision*. Basingstoke: Macmillan.

Webb, S. J., Monk, C. S., & Nelson, C. A. (2001). Mechanisms of postnatal neurobiological development: Implications for human development. *Developmental Neuropsychology, 19*, 147–171.

Weinshall, D. (1989). Perception of multiple transparent planes in stereo vision. *Nature, 341*, 737–739.

Weiskrantz, L. (1986). *Blindsight*. Oxford: Clarendon Press.

Weiss, E. M., Kemmler, G., Deisenhammer, E. A., Fleischhacker, W. W., & Delazer, M. (2002). Sex differences in cognitive function. *Personality and Individual Differences, 35*, 863–875.

Werker, J., & Desjardins, R. (1995). Listening to speech in the 1st year of life: Experiential influences on phoneme perception. *Current Directions in Psychological Science, 4*, 76–81.

Westheimer, G. (1975). Visual acuity and hyperacuity. *Investigative Ophthalmology, 14*, 570–572.

Westheimer, G., & McKee, S. (1977). Spatial configurations for visual hyperacuity. *Vision Research, 17*, 941–947.

Wever, E. G. (1949). *Theory of Hearing*. New York: Wiley.

White, J. A., Rubinstein, J. T., & Kay, A. R. (2000). Channel noise in neurons. *Trends in Neurosciences, 23*, 131–137.

Whitfield, I. C., & Evans, E. F. (1965). Responses of auditory cortical neurons to stimuli of changing frequency. *Journal of Neurophysiology, 28*, 655–672.

Wiesel, T. N. (1982). Postnatal development of the visual cortex and the influence of environment. *Nature, 299*, 583–591.

Wilcox, M., & Hess, R. (1995). Dmax for stereopsis depends on size, not spatial frequency content. *Vision Research, 35*, 1061–1069.

Wilson, H. C. (1992). A critical review of menstrual synchrony research. *Psychoneuroendocrinology, 17*, 565–591.

Wilson, H. R., & Kim, J. (1994). Perceived direction in the vector sum direction. *Vision Research, 34*, 1835–1842.

Wilson, H. R., Levi, D., Maffei, L., Rovamo, J., & De Valois, R. (1990). The perception of form: From retina to striate cortex. In L. Spillmann & J. Werner (Eds.), *Visual Perception: The Neurophysiological Foundations*. San Diego, CA: Academic Press.

Wilson, H. R., McFarlane, D., & Phillips, G. (1983). Spatial frequency tuning of orientation selective units estimated by oblique masking. *Vision Research, 23*, 873–882.

Wightman, F. L., & Kistler, D. J. (1992). The dominant role of low-frequency interaural time differences in sound localization. *Journal of the Acoustical Society of America, 91*, 1648–1661.

Wong-Riley, M., & Carroll, E. (1984). Effect of impulse blockage on cytochrome oxidase activity in monkey visual system. *Nature, 307*, 262–264.

Wood, R. W. (1895). The "haunted swing" illusion. *Psychological Review, 2*, 277–278.

Wyszecki, G., & Stiles, W. (1982). *Color Science* (2nd ed.). New York: Wiley.

Xiao, Y., & Felleman, D. J. (2004). Projections from primary visual cortex to cytochrome oxidase thin stripes and interstripes of macaque visual area 2. *Proceedings of the National Academy of Sciences USA, 101*, 7147–7151.

Xiao, Y., Wang, Y., & Felleman, D. J. (2003). A spatially organized representation of colour in macaque cortical area V2. *Nature, 421*, 535–539.

Yantis, S. (Ed.) (2001). *Visual Perception*. Hove, UK: Psychology Press.

Yo, C., & Wilson, H. R. (1992). Perceived direction of moving two-dimensional patterns depends on duration, contrast and eccentricity. *Vision Research, 32*, 135–147.

Yost, W. A. (2000). *Fundamentals of Hearing*. San Diego, CA: Academic Press.

Youdelis, C., & Hendrickson, A. (1986). A qualitative and quantitative analysis of the human fovea during development. *Vision Research, 26*, 847–855.

Zald, D., & Pardo, J. (1997). Emotion, olfaction, and the human amygdala: Amygdala activation during aversive olfactory stimulation. *Proceedings of the National Academy of Sciences USA, 94*, 4119–4124.

Zhang, Z., Deriche, R., Faugeras, O., & Luong, Q.-T. (1995). A robust technique for matching two uncalibrated images through the recovery of the unknown epipolar geometry. *Artificial Intelligence, 78*, 87–119.

Zhou, Y.-X., & Baker, C. L. (1993). A processing stream in mammalian visual cortex neurons for non-Fourier responses. *Science, 261*, 98–101.

Zihl, J., Von Cramon, D., & Mai, N. (1983). Selective disturbance of movement vision after bilateral brain damage. *Brain, 106*, 313–340.

# Author index

# Subject index